MW01253384

A Contemporary History of Women's Sport, Part One

This book is an historical survey of women's sport from 1850–1960. It looks at some of the more recent methodological approaches to writing sports history and raises questions about how the history of women's sport has so far been shaped by academic writers. Questions explored in this text include: What are the fresh perspectives and newly available sources for the historian of women's sport? How do these take forward established debates on women's place in sporting culture? How can our appreciation of fashion, travel, food and medical industries be advanced by looking at women's involvement in sport? How can we use some of the contemporary literature on sport in order to look afresh at women's participation? Jean Williams' original research on these topics and more will be a useful resource for scholars in the fields of history, sports studies, writing and popular culture, globalisation and the sociology of gender.

Jean Williams is a Senior Research Fellow in the International Centre for Sports History and Culture at De Montfort University, Leicester.

Routledge Research in Sports History

A Contemporary History of Women's Sport, Part One

Sporting Women, 1850–1960

Jean Williams

Routledge
Taylor & Francis Group
NEW YORK   LONDON

First published 2014
by Routledge
711 Third Avenue, New York, NY 10017

and by Routledge
2 Park Square, Milton Park, Abingdon, Oxon OX14 4RN

*Routledge is an imprint of the Taylor & Francis Group,
an informa business*

Library of Congress Cataloging-in-Publication Data
Williams, Jean, 1964–
  A contemporary history of women's sport, part one : sporting women,
1850–1960 / Jean Williams.
    pages cm. — (Routledge research in sports history ; 3)
    Includes bibliographical references and index.
  1. Sports for women—History—19th century.   2. Sports for women—
History—20th century.   I. Title.
  GV709.W525 2014
  796.082—dc23
  2013040090

ISBN13: 978-0-415-88601-7 (hbk)
ISBN13: 978-1-315-79515-7 (ebk)

Typeset in Sabon
by IBT Global.

Printed and bound in the United States of America
by IBT Global.

Contents

Figures

Acknowledgments

I could not have written this book without having the good fortune to share an office with Dilwyn Porter from 2005 to 2012. Dil wears his learning lightly and what appeared to be a half-hour chat most days was actually a tutorial in how history might be approached. Any mistakes are therefore my own responsibility. Richard Holt suggested I keep this project separate from a collective biography of Britain's women Olympians and, for the most part, I took the wise advice. Tony Collins funded some relief from teaching to get the project back on track. Neil Carter has been particularly generous with references and leads. International Centre for Sports History and Culture colleagues Jeff Hill, Tony Mason, Matt Tayor, James Panter and Rob Colls have all been encouraging. A special note of thanks should also be extended to the students with whom I have been privileged to work since 2006. Unfortunately, there is not the space to name them all individually but it is important to recognise that they have taught me more than I have been able to help them. I am also indebted for several small blessings bestowed on the project by curators and museum professionals who work so hard to preserve artifacts and communicate different kinds of history.

One of the ironies about writing a book on sport and leisure is that the people with whom I usually spend my free time have compromised on my behalf. They have been tolerant to a degree that astonishes me still: my thanks to Kelly, Stuart and Jess; Natalie, Brandon, Ava and Cameron; James and Sarah; Tom and Mark, Kirsty, Lee and Sophie. I am supported by friends who are stoic and generous enough to listen to me enthuse about Jennie Fletcher's gold medals over a curry: Margaret, Debbie, Tony, Annabelle, Cecile and Grace have all been tolerant in this regard. As ever, Simon has been patient beyond words, accompanied me on numerous journeys and even offered to sacrifice our joint savings so I could bid for Jennie Fletcher's gold medal at auction. The money was insufficient but his support has been beyond compare. Having never had a pet as an adult, a stray cat came to visit while I was working up the manuscript and never left. As a charming and fun writing companion Bubkiss has no equal. I would hope the inspiring women discussed in these pages might feel that I have begun to do their stories justice. Now, time to get back to family, friends and the cat.

Introduction
Women and Sport or Women's Sport?

In 1893 I married and went to live on a small farm at Ohau. We were still in the pioneering stage. The house consisted of four rough rooms, or more correctly two, for the lean-to that made the kitchen and annexe was so primitive a structure as not to be properly called anything but a shelter . . . The water we carried from a creek and thought ourselves lucky that we had a permanent supply so handy. Nevertheless, the first effort we made, after we had settled ourselves, was to make a tennis court. Mad? Well, I suppose it was. But, you see, circumstances had robbed us both of the fun and frivolity of youth, so we were bent on snatching some of it at a time when we should have been addressing ourselves to serious things . . . Every Sunday friends came from Levin to play and we forgot chill penury and gave ourselves up to pleasure.[1]

Sport has most often been used as a collective term for physical contests that varied a great deal in their form, organisation and level of skill. Much depended on the interpretation of the individual and how they viewed their activities. An element of challenge against time, distance, the elements, individuals (including a personal best) or groups could mark sporting endeavour as distinct from a leisure pursuit. However, as the quotation from the autobiography of teacher, farmer and community leader Helen Wilson (1869–1957) suggests, attempts to distinguish between sport, leisure and recreation have been notoriously difficult. An activity enjoyed for its own sake might involve difficulty and inconvenience. Defining leisure as non-work also raises problems because, even when unpaid and taken up as voluntary exercise, interests could often involve considerable time, effort and cost.

Widely known for her public work, writing and advocacy, Wilson was one of millions of women who have integrated sport into their everyday experience, at least for a time. She was to become a leading figure in the Women's Division of the New Zealand Farmers' Union and made an Officer of the Most Excellent Order of the British Empire (OBE) in 1937.[2] Despite its brevity, the excerpt indicates three research questions for this work. While we are aware that women and girls have made a historical contribution to sport, how widespread was this involvement and what forms could it take? When and where did the sporting interests of women and girls have a broader impact on cultural, economic, political and social life? Who were the influential individuals and female networks shaping practices in Britain, at international level and then in global terms? Sometimes sport has been a central and intense element of women's daily experience, while for others it has been a transient or peripheral interest.[3] It is this variety of engagement that *A Contemporary History of Women's Sport* seeks to explore.

Sport can be used to look at aspects of the history of gender and women's lives. However, a perhaps more significant perspective in this book is that we cannot really understand the history of sport itself without looking at the prominent ways in which women have wrought its culture. This went beyond leisure and play. For most people, doing sport involved the immediate and the practical. The material object, be it a running shoe, a ball, a garment to swim in, a scrapbook, a beloved toy, a family board game or a minute book had its own life.[4] Have we looked enough at the artifacts that women have used, as well as the written material that they produced in researching sports history?[5] Given that individual identity is symbolically negotiated and physically constructed, sport can be understood by the power, space, time, resources and rules revealed through critical analysis of what Hunter Davies has called boots, balls and haircuts.[6]

Just as gender history often overlooks sport as essentially frivolous or marginal to the experience of women, sports history had traditionally relegated them to servicing roles of patient partners, sandwich-makers and kit-washers. Deborah Hindley's seminal work on the wives of Australian Rules football players is useful here, as is the growing academic and popular literature in general on this topic.[7] Thankfully, the historiography is gradually becoming more varied but tends to cluster on discussions of what activities were considered to be appropriate for women and girls, and those that were were not encouraged. This kind of research can also be developed by local studies, such as Mike Cockayne's work on Altrincham, and the ailing Bowdon cricket club which was in danger of closing in 1900. A three-day fete at the end of June took £800 in receipts to produce a profit of £559; equivalent to three years' income provided by the annual membership fees.[8] Bearing in mind that there was no women's cricket team, as Cockayne reads events, 'It was the young ladies of Bowden who helped to save the club; performing as a main attraction a bicycle musical ride which, according to the *Altrincham and Bowdon Guardian*, was received with great pleasure by the spectators present.'[9] Spouses and family members who washed kit, made picnics, fund-raised and so on to facilitate male sporting activity are a worthy topic for more research.[10] However, the women and girls who took part in sport supported by their parents, friends, sponsors, partners, coaches, neighbours and children are just as fascinating.

The evidence informing this work does not support the thesis that women's defining relationship with sport was to facilitate the participation of men and boys. Stereotypes of women being bound to the home and defined by their function as mothers, which in turn limited their access to, and enthusiasm for, physically-active recreation are unconvincing. Such a characterisation homogenises female experience to a heterosexual, married and child-bearing role, with a life defined by caring for others. This is evidently unsatisfactory. The separation of public and private world in Victorian life has also been much exaggerated. Perceptions of relative female physical weakness compared with activities that have been defined as 'male, modern and athletic' are also overbroad.[11] As the work of writers like Michael Oriard has shown, the growth of sports markets (even supposedly amateur ones) were intertwined with individual taste, civic and commercial ties, family-based leisure and entertainment.[12]

Just as new activities gave reasons to travel far and near, a range of specialist newspapers, magazines, books and catalogues bought the outside world into the nineteenth-century home. Sometimes this was literally the case, given the fascination with gardening and the natural world. Gardening could be both physically demanding work and sedate leisure. The *New Monthly Magazine and Literary Journal*, published in London and then reprinted in New York, first included a piece on the decline of the traditional Old English Garden in 1822.[13] By 1826 John Loudon (1783–1843) had established *The Gardener's Magazine* as a quarterly edition before it became a regular monthly publication. One of the most successful writers, James Shirley Hibbard (1825–1890), was popular with amateur gardeners, encouraging subscribers of *Floral World* and *Garden Guide* to share their problems and tips: a tradition still very much in evidence today. The presiding influence, with over 400 gardens, was Gertrude Jekyll (1843–1932): publishing her first book in 1899, followed by some 1,000 articles on plant design. Of course, a garden was a luxury most people could not afford. Like other physical work outdoors, gardening was guarded as a male occupation, so many of the female working-class 'practitioner-gardeners' working in the Royal Botanic Gardens established in the British Isles from Kew to Edinburgh remain the subject of ongoing research.[14] The example nevertheless suggests that ideas of private and public space, women's work and leisure require nuance and contextualisation.

A Contemporary History of Women's Sport demonstrates that many women were 'sporting' in their interests across a wide variety of disciplines for significant phases of their lives. No particular activity was inherently more appropriate for men or women unless designated as such, and this could change over time. Leading the classic College 'tiger' Cheer at Princeton in the 1870s was considered an activity only appropriate for manly students with correspondingly deep, sonorous voices.[15] Though the fashionable female 'cheergirl' appeared on postcards from 1900 onwards, mixed teams proliferated when pyramid gymnastics added choreographed stunt moves and routines in the 1920s.[16] By 1926, the redoubtable Bonnie and Donnie Cotteral were contributing *Tumbling, Pyramid Building and Stunts for Girls and Women* to the *Athletics for Women* series, dedicating the text: 'To our Benton, Lafayette and Robinson High School Girls in Memory of The Roly-Poly Tumblers and the Topsy-Turvy Clowns'.[17] During World War Two women transformed cheer-leading into an international sport with its own associations, professional leagues, accredited coaches and national styles, such as the Japanese Ouendan form.[18] Community cheerleading and All-Star scholarships now available in a range of countries include an estimated two million participants world-wide. Sport, dance and other forms of physical movement therefore have overlapping histories.[19]

A number of nationally and internationally successful female athletes came to prominence from the middle of the nineteenth century. By the middle of the twentieth century, watching sport and an interest in active leisure was part of wider social change that affected more women and girls. As both producers and consumers, women altered what sport was and perceptions of what it could be. First though, the introduction highlights some problems of definition before outlining the framework of modern and contemporary sport. What do we mean by leisure, recreation and sport? How has women's involvement been described? What are the implications for a history that seeks to explore the contemporary resonance of these debates?

SOME PROBLEMS IN DEFINING SPORT AND WOMEN'S PARTICIPATION

Problems of definition are an inherent part of examining sport because of the way that the word has changed and multiplied. Although sport often sought to categorise individuals, it often failed to reflect a reality that was more complicated. Men and women were not two distinct populations, so gender was a performance and subject to individual interpretation at any one time. Academic work is now addressing the gendered nature of specific activities for both men and women: notable recent examples are Kasia Boddy's *Boxing: A Cultural History* and Erik Jensen's *Body by Weimar*.[20] As these texts signal, cultural methodologies enable new insights into how women experienced the mundane and quotidian aspects of sport and leisure, as well as the heroic or unusual. While academics discuss men's and women's sport, it does not follow that expressing a particular gender identity was a primary, or even the main, reason why people participated. A person's age, class, ethnicity, economic wealth, sexual orientation, religious belief, taste and status might have also shaped their motivation and may have defined their sporting opportunities. Because sport is a bodily practice, performed over time, and described by a lexicon that could be challenged and changed, meaning was neither fixed at the time nor stable in historical analysis. Part of the reason that sport and leisure remains interesting to study today is that people still disagree over what, when, where and how people should use (or abuse) their bodies in the pursuit of gold medals, health and pleasure.

Nor is this lack of certainty over what 'sport' means a recent development: in the eighteenth century, authors writing for an upper class audience viewed teaching through guided exploration, or what we might call 'learning-through-play', as a vital part of good parenting.[21]

The sports of children, should afford exercise, either to body or mind and should contribute to their improvement, either in health or knowledge. The intelligent mother who walks abroad with her children, knows how to promote both at the same time . . . Many vulgar habits, many erroneous notions, many evil principles, arise from the single circumstance of a lady neglecting to accompany her children when they make their excursion beyond their play-ground and not a few from the omission of observing their sports at home. In short I view a mother as a mistress of the revels among her little people. [22]

Sport also has less innocent etymological roots. As Denis Brailsford has shown 'Definitions of sport are never easy and seldom stable' and in the 1790s sports reportage could include bat-fowling, bell ringing and adultery.[23] The modern sense of sport in the older word 'disport' (meaning a diversion from serious duties; relaxation; recreation; entertainment and amusement) is a reminder that the sensual and sexual have long been implied as part of 'taking ones pleasure'.[24] Prostitutes would 'sport blubber', or bare a breast, to attract potential clients. By the eighteenth century, the term 'sporting girl' became slang for a sexually promiscuous woman; whereas a 'sporting man' (as opposed to a sportsman) was also a mercenary but more inclined to gamble as a regular occupation.[25]

Sexual innuendo featured in popular ballads, for example *The Swimming Lady or a Wanton Discovery* printed in 1701. This lyric was accompanied by a woodcut in which a clothed voyeur observed a naked young woman in the river.[26] Whether we see this as evidence of the erotic fascination of the time or of swimming as a leisure activity, the motif was repeated in subsequent popular rhymes. The roles were reversed in an altogether more sinister way in John Cleland's erotic novel *Memoirs of a Woman of Pleasure* (popularly known as Fanny Hill) where a fifteen year old orphan, Harriet, fainted as she observed the son of the local nobility bathing on a hot day, allowing him to take advantage of her unconscious body when he left the water.[27] Given the description of the swimmer as 'wantoning' with the water, the reader of *Fanny Hill* is invited to question the moral reliability of Harriet in her own undoing and she later becomes a notable prostitute.

While 'sporting women' could lack respectability, this was not necessarily the case. The Amazon, a warrior figure who liked physical challenge, was shorthand for those women who preferred the outdoor life, as the lyrics of this popular song illustrate:

The Amazon[28]

Swains I scorn, who nice and fair, shiver at the morning air;
Rough and hardy, bold and free be the Man that's made for me;
Rough and hardy, bold and free be the Man that's made for me

Slaves to Fashion, Slaves to Dress,
Fops themselves alone caress;
Let them without Rival be,
They are not the Men for me

He whose nervous Arm can dart,
The Jav'lin to the Tiger's heart;
From all sense of Danger free,
He's the Man that's made for me.

While his speed outstrips the wind,
Loosely wave his Locks behind,
From fantastick fopp'ry free,
He's the Man that's made for me.

Nor simpring smile, nor dimpled sleek,
Spoil his manly sunburnt cheek,
By weather let him painted be,
He's the Man that's made for me.

If false he proves my Jav'lin can,
Revenge the Perjury of Man,
And soon another, brave as he,
Shall be found the Man for me.

Sport has long had a moral, as well as political and commercial, economy then.[29] Between 1821 and 1828 the serialised monthly *Life in London*, written by Pierce Egan,, was the most extended parable of how sporting life could lead directly to a woman's ruin.[30] In reprints that ran to many subsequent shilling re-editions, Corinthian Kate pursued pleasure for its own sake, as the partner of urbanite Corinthian Tom, while he guided his country cousin, Jerry, through London. Their walks through the capital provided the reader with vicarious insights into street life, exclusive clubs and high society as French *flaneurs* would later in Paris. Kate rose to live in the fashionable St James area of London and then fell to more modest lodgings, continuing the descent to street prostitution, followed by an undignified death. The narrative trigger for this downward mobility was Kate's infidelity to Tom, after which he took up with a new companion for 'games'.

Since Kate was described up to the point of her disloyalty as a fashionably glamorous 'cyprian' (a woman who sought, and embodied, pleasure) Egan moralised the behaviour of women who put themselves very publicly 'on the market' and tried to find a more affluent sponsor. Parallels with those who entertained, or competed, for money and hence, literally named their price, were obvious. The reader was left in little doubt that Kate's pursuit of commodity consumption, sexual display and a life of leisure caused her eventual destruction; public mobility evidence of a lack of moral reserve.[31] Knowing that travel and adventure writing had become established genres in which women enjoyed considerable success, Egan satirised the double-standard of male and female morality, even while the narrative structure of *Life in London* ultimately condoned those same hypocrisies.

Women's athletic contests struggled with notions of respectability. 'Smock' or 'tea' races, so called because the prize was a petticoat, a valuable weight of leaf tea, or a kettle and were recorded in most parts of the country. Leaving the reader to draw their own conclusion from the comparison offered, Brailsford suggests, 'Like the horses, the human racers were often required to run in heats, and particularly so where the prize was on the generous side or where the competitors were women.'[32] A tea race for old women was recorded in William Penny-Brookes' Much Wenlock Festival in Shropshire from the 1850s. This composite of athletics and country sports had, by 1861, developed into the Shropshire Olympic Games. As emerging civic centres developed their own sports culture both modern forms and folk games could appear on the same billing.[33] This allowed respectability to be a miscellany of what was only considered appropriate in carnival celebrations and behaviour that was condoned during every day life.

We could speculate that later nineteenth-century attitudes to female amateurism in sport reacted to these older tawdry implications of playfulness and athletic pleasure by stipulating that women, and especially girls, should not perform for money, on public display, or in vigorous competition.[34] It certainly prompted me to reclaim the title Sporting Women for this book. Whatever the etymological changes of the word sport, its history defies neat classification. However, the connection between sport, recreation and leisure, however loosely defined, involves a discussion of space, place, resources and time. Training or active use of 'spare' time may involve indirect and non-competitive exercise, such as a lone swim in the sea. This might be a short dip for pleasure, but equally might also entail a serious commitment to the task.[35]

Our current definitions can also be counter-intuitive. Unless the idea is to beat some target or competitor, is a physically active pursuit really sport? According to the British Sports Council *Women and Sport* document issued in 1992, the answer is 'yes'. Their classification includes institutionalised, strictly organised and competitive events as well as those that are freely arranged, aesthetic and for leisure.[36] In more recent times many activities have also become what academics have called sportised. To illustrate what this means, while running on a treadmill this evening at my local gym for my standard time, at my usual pace, I could have selected to watch a TV programme in which men and women undertook to reduce their weight in order to win a prize of $10,000. Most contestants were skilful in adopting effective strategies to aid weight loss, bettering their previous 'record'. It was certainly competitive; the least abstemious contender, as measured in a public and scientific manner, was eliminated. Were the rivals of *The*

Biggest Loser more sporting than I? In the sense that they were competing against one another we could say that *The Biggest Loser* contestants were more sporting in their activities and attitude. If my typical training regime enabled me to run a ten-kilometre race at weekends, then the issue might become more ambiguous. Lots of television shows use the competitive elements of physical contest in their format from *The Cube* where action is limited to a box, to *Total Wipeout* with an elaborate course. Aspects of a sportised lexicon also appear in the competitive eating tasks and other challenges of *I'm A Celebrity Get Me Out of Here*.

This book uses the descriptor 'women's sport' advisedly then, to emphasise various active roles often overlooked in conventional histories. Preferring 'women's sport' to 'women in sport' is a personal taste but it is not a distinction that the text reinforces at length. Sport affected the lives of many women in a number of ways. The diversity of female engagement with physical sports work and active leisure cannot be contained in a single volume.[37] I am all too aware that there is little boxing here, for example, and not enough climbing. The use of 'women's sport' is not intended to homogenise female experience and the examples used here are necessarily selective. Doug Booth's *The Field* is one of many to argue a need to redress the way that female activities are overlooked in most academic depictions of sport.[38] It is rare to pick up a book about sport and look for an indexed reference to 'men' because usually that is what the author assumes the volume is about, although if it is written after 1990 there may be a reference to masculinities. Other than texts which have the word gender in the title, an index containing the word 'women' may contain half a dozen references. If there is none at all, it usually reflects the author's assumption that the female role in sport is largely irrelevant. This is a peculiar approach to gender as if it were possible for men to live their days in a hermetically-sealed male world and had no mothers, sisters, wives, lovers, daughters, female friends, servants or colleagues. Though we might discuss why these histories have become the orthodoxy in the academy, this is another subject entirely. Nor is it the book I am interested in writing.

Allen Guttman has gone so far as to suggest that 'It was not, however, until the middle of the twentieth century that scholars began to publish books and essays that deserve to be considered histories of women's sports.'[39] Academic study in sport grew out of the work of writers specialising in social and economic history and sociology. It often reflected the interests of the authors and moral panics of the time. Consequently association football has been very well treated in a range of disciplines with overmuch work on hooliganism and violence. There has also been generous coverage of horse racing, rugby codes, cricket and, more recently, boxing in the British journals. The treatment of American Football, baseball, basketball and ice hockey is also considerable, often approached with more subtle, and inclusive, treatments of gender, race and ethnicity than the British literature. Part of this is the relative maturity of sports history as a discipline in the United States and Canada with the North American Society for Sports History (NASSH) founded in 1972 whereas the British Society for Sports History (BSSH) convened a decade later. The Australian Society for Sports History was founded shortly after in 1983 having held conferences at the University of New South Wales since 1977. The academic sports history community is now a world-wide network with significant clusters also in South America, Africa, New Zealand, Japan and PR China as well as Europe. Though now with a female Chair, the journal of the British society has often neglected women's sport in both its regular and special editions.[40] Perhaps the absence of a female editor for the British, but not the American and Australian, journals can be read as an indication of the general attitude. There have been lots of talented British female sports historians, after all.[41]

As well as recent work, notable examples of British texts include Sheila Fletcher's *Women First: the female tradition in English physical education 1880–1980 published* in 1984; the 1987 edited collection by J. A. Mangan and Roberta Park *From 'Fair Sex' to Feminism: Sport and the Socialization of Women in the Industrial and Post- Industrial Eras*; Kathleen Mc Crone's *Playing the Game* which appeared in 1988; Jennifer Hargreaves' *Sporting Females* and *Heroines of Sport* released in 1994 and 2000 respectively and Catriona M. Parratt's *Working Class Women's Leisure in England 1750–1914,* which came out in book form in 2002.[42] Focussing mainly on the period from the 1850s and into the twentieth century is an approach with its critics. Allen Guttmann's *Women's Sports: A History* published in 1991, devoted the first eight chapters to the period before the twentieth century.[43] In a later review of the literature Guttmann was critical of Uriel Simri's *A Concise World History of Women's Sports* because it was almost entirely based on the nineteenth and twentieth centuries; the first several millennia of western history compressed to just six pages.[44]

This work will focus on modern sport and its contemporary relevance, however it acknowledges thay the processes of modernising sport in the eighteenth and nineteenth centuries built on a much longer history of active leisure as a contested means of 'social salvation' for those who might spend their time in other ways.[45] Folk games could overlap with newer ideas while bureaucracy and record setting were not unknown in traditional sport.[46] Forces shaping modern sport date back at least to the eighteenth century, with rule-making and standardisation emerging from aristocratic gambling cultures and a desire to establish fair play, or at least the appearance of impartiality.[47] In Britain, largely between 1750 and 1830, a predominantly rural workforce moved to expanding urbanised manufacturing centres. Improved travel and media communications encouraged entrepreneurs to take advantage of growing networks. The question of women's rights as citizens in public and private life consequently became more widely contested.[48] Localised collectives of kinship, trade and belief endured in some areas of Britain, while the move towards a more urbanised population helped to facilitate a transnational network of women's sporting interest. Consumerism, technological advance and wider social processes also varied concerns for health and education. While sport could be a vehicle for challenging stereotypes and discrimination, it also changed women's relationships with their own bodies, and with one another. Facilities provided by the state and by 'penny-entrepreneurs', combined with increased geographical mobility, faster communications technology, fashion and medical innovation. These external forces changed the way that women thought about themselves, while participation in sporting contests could also affect the way that wider society perceived individuals and groups.

MODERN SPORT AND RELATED CULTURAL INDUSTRIES FROM THE MID NINETEENTH CENTURY

Historians have increasingly accepted that how an individual chose to spend their time, when they had the freedom so to do, was as telling as how they fulfilled their obligations in life.[49] Modern leisure could incorporate rural pastimes. Consciously 'invented' traditions, institutions and customs sought to use repetition to imply continuity with the past.[50] During the period between the 1850s and 1890s sport was more widely popularised, codified and standardised (albeit in specific forms and at different speeds) for an ever-growing industrialised audience with some collective spare time and surplus income.[51] Commentators do not agree whether the acceleration of these changes led to evolutionary or revolutionary transformations of sporting culture.[52] However, while those who promoted sport for a moral purpose have had considerable attention in the academic literature, the commercial aspects seem to be comparatively under-written.

If church groups and providers of welfare sometimes saw sport as a means of delivering a message, entrepreneurs understood that the leisure of some people could provide work for others. The Great Exhibition of the Industry of All Nations in 1851 had stimulated public discussion over the relative benefits of Free Trade policies, of which a range of sporting goods were already part of small, but identifiable, markets.[53] The topical and the novel were fashionable, with a Jaques and Son of London croquet set featuring expensive ivory inlay that referenced British links with the Empire. Equipment manufacturers such as Aldred of London could exploit the wealth and status of archery enthusiasts with twenty-five inch *pinus silvestris* arrows, tipped with silver. The Exhibition was the first of many, leaving its own legacy in Kensington of the 'Albertopolis' cultural-quarter in recognition of the Prince Regent's role as patron. Some six million people travelled to The Crystal Palace, a glass showcase for trade and commerce as driving urban life, and London as central to international business.[54] Many British clothing and sports brands began to diversify at about this time; several having started out by manufacturing solutions to the perennial problem of the rain.[55] After trade-marking a shower-proof textile in 1853, the company of John Emery became 'Aqua-scutum', the Latin term for water-shield.[56] Its wrappers and coats became modish for the urban elite but also for field-sports and angling. Burberry was formed in 1856, launching its stylish Gabardine fabric in 1880.[57] Slazenger began to trade as a rainwear business in Manchester in 1881, moved to London, and soon after began to produce smart lawn tennis rackets and balls.[58]

Women consequently had long-standing connections with related-industries (such as education, the media, gambling, food, drink, retail, transport and entertainment) and in the wider commercialisation of sporting-goods such as clothing, games and toys.[59] Betty Berry of the Snipe Inn, Manchester may have been the first woman to compete with the nearby Royal Oak public house by specifically constructing a track on which to hold pedestrian races and drew crowds of 3,000 people in the 1840s.[60] Competing for a 'Landlady's prize' became more common, such as that donated by Mrs McMurtie of the Black Bull Hotel in 1878 for the Allander Bowling Club in Scotland.[61] North American taverns were other working-class venues where women extended credit for drinking and gambling, while also controlling equipment, space and behaviour.[62]

As a range of sports like archery, croquet, equestrianism, golf, mountaineering, pedestrianism, skating, swimming, tennis and yachting illustrate, there were signs of assertive female Victorian physicality in urban parks, suburban lawns, across rolling country hunts, in the Alps and on water. For instance, excursion companies, like Thomas Cook made the Alps open to a mass market from 1863 with extensive transport infrastructure at what had been previously remote locations, leading *Punch* to claim that carpeted ascents, illuminated by night, would soon be available to tourists.[63] *Punch* was exaggerating, but telescopes and other viewing technologies were making previously inaccessible locations into potential sports arenas where ascents could be anticipated, followed while in progress and analysed afterwards. Sport was progressively more watched, reported and narrated. Previously remote locations became part of the compression of space and time wrought by improved commnuncations and technology.

For the majority of people stuck in the city for most of their time, the department store displayed sportswear for the wealthy few. 'Just looking' through large glass windows was free, though. In 1820 Elizabeth Harvey inherited her father's linen shop on the understanding that she went into partnership with Colonel Nichols: the subsequent transformation of a successful department store, Harvey Nichols, saw it move to the current location in Knightsbridge in the 1880s. Harrods had already moved to Brompton Road in 1849. Gamages was established in 1878 as a watch shop.[64] Though based in the unfashionable Holborn area of London, a process of undercutting other stores and piecemeal expansion developed Gamages collections of sporting goods, toys, magic tricks, clothes and furniture into the 'People's Popular Emporium'. Choice became integral to the display of these stores and shopping became a leisure activity in itself for the lucky few. National retail chains expanded: Marshall and Snelgrove had branches in London, Leeds and Scarborough; Bainbridge traded in Newcastle-on-Tyne; Milne & Co. did so in Manchester. Customers were encouraged to stay for as long as possible, suggesting that if you could afford to do what you wanted, that choice might well include shopping or active leisure in fashionable surroundings. Even if a person could not afford a leisured aristocrat's 'sporting lifestyle' they could nevertheless buy a piece of it at various price points.

Commercialisation therefore shaped many sports, with women's activities ranging from high to low culture. So while the argument locates the rise of women's sport in terms of capitalism and new markets, this is not the same as seeing commercialism as a progressive force. Nor was growth unchecked. The end of the American Civil War in 1865 and the conclusion of the Franco Prussian War caused anxiety in Britain. The unification of Germany in 1870–1871 challenged the enormous expansion of the British Empire with a relatively rapid shift in the global economic balance.[65] With the rapid industrialisation of both the United States and German economies and the increasing military threat from France, Russia and Germany, public interest in the Empire was intense by the 1890s. Symbolic unity in the form of public pageants and moments of national unanimity did not necessarily reflect the actuality of daily life.

While we know about some wealthy individual women, we know less about the lower classes who had fewer material resources at their disposal. The spectacle of horse racing as part of the British season, patronised by Royalty but involving the lower orders makes this point nicely. Brailsford has horse races with nine women in Newcastle in 1725 and Ripon in 1734, perhaps suggesting a north-east bias.[66] Struna is more downbeat about the chances of researching nineteenth-century female jockeys in the United States.[67] The digitisation of contemporary publications may help in this regard, as more evidence becomes available in the public domain.[68] However, if we know little about female equestrians, women were much in evidence at the races. The grandest expression of status for the British upper class, the Season, was a complex round of social events based on a sporting and entertainment calendar. Venues ranged from racing at Ascot and Goodwood, to the Eton and Harrow cricket match at Lords; the Henley Regatta and yachting at Cowes. The Royal Enclosure at Ascot remained very exclusive: with no more than a hundred stylish ladies attending on horseback in 1875.[69] This was not strictly work, of course, but highlighted the more subtle privileges of benefaction and display.[70] As fashionable events at which to see and be seen, traditional values vied with modern mores. Those who considered themselves among the elite tried not to rub shoulders with the masses but at the same time displayed their wealth and status. Big events could centre on races and competitions, easily understandable for gambling but also often a collective, some would say communal, experience.

Sports clubs and governing bodies began to partly to define themselves by whether they included women as members or not. The Jockey Club was said to have formed at the 'Star and Garter' in Pall Mall in London, before relocating to Newmarket sometime between 1750 and 1752; The Royal and Ancient Golf Club of St Andrews dated its foundation to 1754; The Toxophilite Society first met in 1780 and had just twenty four members before the Prince of Wales became its patron, granting the use of 'Royal' to its title in 1787.[71] The Marylebone Cricket Club (MCC) had also been founded in 1787. All of these were clubs for aristocrats and gentlemen, neither wholly domestic nor work-based, they constituted a homo-social, 'home from home' for the pleasures of association.[72]

Many clubs and national association took on the title 'amateur' from the middle of the 1860s to the end of the century. Though amateurism could have multiple definitions across sports, by the end of the nineteenth century, a widespread ethos tried to distance sport from work or as primarily a commercialised entertainment.[73] Moral panics over the sports-worker were not particularly new, but did intensify as a result of the formation of national governing bodies such as the Football Association (FA) in 1863, the Rugby Football Union (RFU) in 1871, The Amateur Athletic Association (AAA) in 1880 and the Amateur Rowing Association (ARA) in 1882.[74]

Definitions of amateurism differed widely in the precision with which they specified the correct behaviour of players and under what circumstances an individual could obtain material benefit from their talents. Winning was important under amateur rules, but victory was a test of mettle, to be won in a spirit of effortless grace. Codified laws often protected those who kicked, threw, ran or rowed for pleasure from being beaten by those whose work made them more proficient at these tasks.[75] The Amateur Rowing Association insisted on 'gentlemanly' status, a necessary condition of which was that the participant had not done any kind of craft or manual work. The gradually defined 'amateur' had to be an officer in the fighting or civil service, educated at a university or public school, or a member of the liberal professions.[76] Others went further and outlawed participants who had ever benefitted from material gain by playing or teaching any sport. In the case of the Amateur Swimming Association (ASA) this included those who taught swimming for money as a registered coach under their own scheme.

Some women could be granted access to facilities and others debarred, either by informal practices or rules of eligibility, such as those governing amateur participation introduced after an activity was already popular.[77] The craze for croquet spread from a French version of the game to Britain in the 1850s to the United States in the 1860s. Realising that croquet-set manufacturers produced their own rules, Walter Whitmore Jones sought to compile a definitive edition, published by *The Field* in 1866.[78] He was not alone in trying to adapt croquet to appeal to 'crinoline' and 'curate' participants. Any obvious moment of invention has to be treated with caution, as John Jacques and Son of London, had published at least three sets of its rules by 1865, sold 65,000 sets and moved into other sporting goods.[79] James Buchanan, a Piccadilly archery manufacturer, sold standard sets for between twenty-one and thirty-one shillings, with the ultimate twenty-guinea collection including 'Eight mallets with ivory heads; eight ivory balls; gild hoops and balls beautifully coloured and gilt in a mahogany box with red velvet [sic]'.[80]

Organising a tournament, which he won in 1867, Whitmore Jones changed his name to Jones Whitmore and co-created the All England Croquet Club (AECC) with J. H. Walsh, editor of *The Field*, in 1868 for fifty-five founder members.[81] The first AECC 'Lady Championship of England' was held in 1869 and future winners, like Maud Drummond (1868-unkown), who took the Ladies' Gold Medal in 1896, and the Wimbledon Championship Badge in 1897, became stars. Whitmore Jones had previously sought both fame and fortune through other forms of invention, with limited success. Board games and other pastimes were open to innovation, especially for the growing Christmas market. Moderate sales of 'Frogs and Toads' and 'Squails' had convinced Jones Whitmore of the latent profits in parlour entertainment for adults and children. Jaques changed its business model (based on using animal tusks to make dice, false teeth and piano keys), to becoming a hardwood and paper-based firm making toys and past-times. Indoor games could become outdoor sports and vice versa.[82] For instance, Maud Drummond wrote an instructional booklet for indoor croquet and advice on winter games.[83] Croquet passed into popular culture in other ways. Both Lewis Caroll's *Alice's Adventures in Wonderland* (1865) and Louisa May Alcott's *Little Women* (1869) dramatised a degree of croquet rivalry. These books and other magazine articles showed that, with relatively few rules, the game could be far less genteel than was often assumed, especially if a competitor 'rocketed' an opponents ball out of play.[84] So croquet signified commericliasm, sporting sociability and became a literary motif for both love and conflict.

Lawn tennis benefitted from the craze for croquet and was adapted from royal or real tennis in the early 1870s, though it also had rivalries in its inception.[85] Major Thomas Henry 'Harry' Gem played a form of lawn tennis at his friend's home from 1859 onwards, forming a club soon after, and Welshman Major Walton Clopton Wingfield developed his own version, Sphairistikè, publishing several sets of rules in the 1870s. Wingfield was the more commercially minded of the two, selling over a 1,000 sets of equipment at five guineas, mainly to the aristocracy by 1875. He is also now memorialised more than Harry Gem at the lawn tennis museum, Wimbledon and at the International Tennis Hall of Fame. However, not everyone had a large enough lawn to accommodate a court and clubs formed in the suburbs enabling the upper and middle classes to mix. John Moyer Heathcote, a well-known real tennis player at The Marylebone Cricket Club (MCC) invited Wingfield to help establish national rules. The All England Croquet Club (AECC), which had moved to Worple Road, Wimbledon by

1869, became the All England Croquet and Lawn Tennis Club (AECLTC) in 1877. The first tennis championships for men took place the same year.

The Irish influence on English sport has been relatively neglected but was important for women. The first Irish women's tennis tournament in 1879 was won by May Langrishe (1864–1939), who took home £10 and went on to win again in 1883 and 1886.[86] It was not until 1884 that the Wimbledon Ladies' Singles was inaugurated and, from an entry of thirteen players, Maud Watson (1864–1946) become the champion and retained her title the following year. A growing press for tennis mediated the women as sporting stars and they were frequently photographed, for example in N. L. 'Pa' Jackson's early editions of *The Lawn Tennis Magazine*. Though Wimbledon's popularity fluctuated between the 1880s and the 1890s, some 300 clubs were affiliated to the Lawn Tennis Association and this figure tripled during the Edwardian era.[87] The AECLTC remained as the headquarters of croquet and lawn tennis until 1922. Wimbledon championships remained amateur until opened to professionals in 1968. Today, the All-England Lawn Tennis Club (AELTC) bears little reminder of these origins and is emblazoned with sponsorship logos from luxury brands but remains a private member subscription organisation.

Though golf had much older roots and a Ladies Club had formed in St Andrews, Scotland in 1867, popularity also increased noticeably in the late 1880s and 1890s. Women were often confined to simplified and short 'ladies' courses' as part of mixed clubs. The Ladies Golf Union (LGU) was formed in England in 1893 by twenty clubs, hosting an amateur national championship at Lytham and St Anne's. The inaugural victory belonged toy Lady Margaret Scott (1874–1938). She was to retain the first three LGU championships between 1893–1895, with a consummate ease that secured her reputation as the best woman player of her day.[88] What affluent women thought of playing at the least popular times, often on the less attractive parts of the course, is not widely available in the public domain but the idea of a union does seem to have been the spur to create new clubs like Moreton, a few miles from Hoylake.[89]

An inaugural U.S. women's amateur golf championship was held in 1895 at the Meadow Brook Club in Hempstead, New York and Vassar College students took up the game as early as 1898. Local, regional and country-specific variances make a fuller assessment of women's role in the formation of amateur clubs beyond the scope of this introductory survey but it was a significant impetus to grow international competition. The United States had variants of amateur rules that could be more dogmatic than the British, while a perceived gap between the letter of the law and the spirit in which it was conceived, provided scope for jealousies about who had acted in the proper manner.[90]

The games of children and adults (whether casual or organised) became a public concern when defined as 'professional' during this period. There was an important professional innovation that does seem to have excluded women until after the First World War and that was the idea of league competition.[91] Twelve years after the FA introduced a knockout cup in the 1871–2 season, Blackburn Olympic beat the Old Etonians having specially prepared at Blackpool in advance of the Final, sponsored by a Lancashire manufacturer. The paid football player was legalised in 1885 and in 1888 communications technology and transport infrastructure enabled a league, comprised of six Midlands and six Lancashire teams, to hold regular and predictable games against each other. The overall winner was declared the league champion. The Scottish league was founded in 1890 but professionalism resisted until 1893. Rugby football divided into Union and League in 1895 over the issue of 'broken-time' showing amateurism as a form of class-conscious control.[92] After 1914 women's hockey and cricket leagues began to provide forms of rational recreation and welfare. Although resisted by some administrators as against the spirit of pure amateurism, these hockey and cricket leagues were more concerned with well-being than making money, although finance could help to provide local aid to underprivileged groups.

Amateurism was not a coherent philosophy, though the creation of the International Olympic Committee (IOC) from 1894 onwards helped to spread the ideal more widely. However, cash prize vouchers, trinkets and expenses were awarded to amateurs in the early Olympic Games. While the Federation Internationale de Football (FIFA) began to establish principles for world football in quite a gradual manner in 1904, most national soccer teams relied upon some form of professionalism. As well as dictating how a person might behave within a leisure context then, amateur laws also sought to dictate how a person should dress and how they should present themselves under 'officially'-sanctioned competition.[93] Amateurs were meant to be motivated by love of the sport, though this could be more honoured in the breach than the observance, as the case of W. G. Grace, the cricketer who was the most outrageous 'shamateur' of his time, indicated.[94]

If commercialism pre-dated amateurism, it also ran concurrent with numerous interpretations of the ideal and many people 'turned' professional. Between 1868 and 1903 the development of the 'safety bicycle', pneumatic tyres and mass-market production revolutionised personal transportation, leading to a quest for extreme speeds and distances in women's bicycle racing. Working class bicycle racing attracted paying spectators and developed its own literature, including sections of the sporting press from the 1870s. Velodromes in London and New York supported professional women's races sponsored by bicycle manufacturers, the proprietors of purpose-built tracks, the clothing industry and other related trades.[95] Professional bicycle racing therefore helped develop the technology of ordinary models at a considerable distance from amateur control.[96] Gendered product design allied with model diversification also enabled manufacturers to use existing technologies to explore and expand new sports markets (including bicycle and tricycle models for children and tandem designs for adults). At the same time, Rational dress and 'the woman question' specifically linked transport and leisure to female emancipation.[97] The enthusiasm for bicycles foreshadowed women's interest in mechanised mobility of all kinds by the turn of the century.

Upper middle-class women's relationship with the bicycle might also look to horse-riding etiquette. For example, becoming 'A Bicycling Authority for Women' enabled Mary Sargent Hopkins (1847–1924) to discuss 'Costumes, Wheels and Cycling News' in *The Wheelwoman* magazine from 1896 onwards.[98] What should a woman to wear? Should she be accompanied and, if so, by whom? To where was it appropriate that she should travel, and at what speed? Cycling could be 'society', aspirational and fashionable, appearing alongside horse riding and carriage driving as an example of sporting transport.[99] Equestrian and cycle clothing would later influence costumes for other wheeled transport, including 'motoring' with tweed, wool, fur and leather particularly evident.

Amateurism could therefore inhibit the development of a particular sport for women in the long term. The International Cycling Association (ICA), founded by Henry Sturmey in 1892, sought to establish a common definition for world championship contenders but it was a relatively weak organisation and bans imposed on male riders who were considered professional were ignored by other nations. The more powerful Union Cycliste Internationale (UCI) was founded in 1900 but did not admit Britain until 1903 or inaugurate a women's version of the Tour de France, the Tour Feminine Cycliste, until 1955, based on the assumption that women would not be able to endure races over equivalent distances to male competitors. The first Olympic women's road race took place in 1984, eighty-eight years after the first men's event, and that too remains a shorter course.[100]

Renouncing amateurism to benefit financially from physical work implied both dubious character and questionable moral choice. Ethical judgment, bordering at times on spiritual zeal, invested in the supposedly pure motivations of the amateur performer neglected the fact that earning money from sport was sometimes a necessity. Sportsmen and women therefore often claimed to be champions or, more ambitiously 'world champions' in competitions of their own devising. Like the music halls and theatre, sport traversed low and high culture, enabling both amateur and professional commentators to make links with display, fashion and consumerism.[101]

Though poverty excluded some sections of the population, Victorian entertainment catered for a range of ages, tastes and budgets: both rich and poor children could play simple games of 'cup and ball', ninepins, or rolling hoops made of modest wooden materials, for example.[102] The heads of battledore and shuttlecock rackets could be stretched parchment or cheaper gut versions with the same wooden frames. For the very rich, a symbol of disposable wealth could be to dress and accessorise infants with high-end products from Germany and France.[103] While many cheaper toys and games of the period were also imported from Germany, where mass-market production techniques kept costs low, several influential

British manufacturers began to trade in the 1870s and 1880s. The history of sport very rarely discusses the range of patents and inventions on which entrepreneurial individuals hung their hopes of profit. For every large store, there were a host of casualised hawkers willing to produce cheap goods related to outdoor modern amusements. If sport could provide casual work for some performers, its secondary markets also helped people to earn a living. The expansion of the press in particular helped to make events and people important. As well as writing about Maud Drummond; Margaret Scott; May, Beatrice (1863–1939) and Adela (1861–1948) Langrishe, *The Field* and other publications such as *Ladies Realm* reported on 'the little wonder' Charlotte 'Lottie' Dod (1871–1960).[104] If the beauty of the Langrishe sisters and their elaborate outfits distracted reporters, Dod's tennis spoke for itself. Charlotte was the youngest of four children born to Joseph and Margaret Dod, who were Liverpool cotton merchants, brokers and bankers. Along with siblings Ann (1863–1945), William (1867–1954) and Anthony (1869–1943), Charlotte was part of a sports-mad family who played golf, archery, billiards, bowls, bridge, chess and croquet to national standards as well as being winter sports enthusiasts. 'Lottie' would outperform her siblings to become 'the female sporting equivalent of C. B. Fry' and to win Wimbledon aged fifteen in 1887.[105] Rudyard Kipling, whom William met on his way to a bear hunt in 1898, reportedly said of the unusual spelling of the family surname, 'I suppose what it is good enough for God, is good enough for Dod'. There was something of the divine in Lottie and she soon outgrew the 'little' in the literal and figurative sense. Slightly above average height at just over five-feet-six inches, she was not to lose a match at the All England Club from that year until 1893 (but missed the 1889 tournament while yachting and 1890 due to lack of enthusiasm).

The ulimate 'lady-amateur', Dod retired from tennis at twenty-one because she did not want to be seen as a 'pot-hunter' who hoarded titles. The second chapter looks in more detail at her all-round career, in context of her silver medal for archery in the 1908 London Olympic Games. So it is enough here to indicate that Dod was a Victorian sporting legend and was just one of many women to achieve national fame as an athlete. Four of her five Wimbledon singles titles were against Blanche Bingley Hillyard (1863–1946), who won six times herself. Lottie Dod joined Moreton golf club in 1894 as did another all-rounder Molly Graham (1878–1950), who also came from a family of sports enthusiasts.[106] Molly was to go on to win the LGU championship in 1901 and other competitors like Irishwoman Rhona Adair (1878–1961) and Gibraltar-born May Hezlet (1882–1978) were also considered to be stars. Nor was this fame limited to upper- and middle-class society: when word spread of Lottie Dod's appearance at the British Ladies Golf Championship at Troon in 1904, hundreds of workers left the Clydeside shipyards and children skipped school to see her win the match.

Mabel Stringer (1868–1958) who looked after the year book of the LGU and instigated a rigorous handicap system, has often been credited with being the first British female sports journalist, covering golf more or less full time from 1903 onwards, although she was occasionally required to supplement this income working as a lady's companion.[107] Amazingly, Lottie Dod has not been the subject of an academic biographical treatment and given that she met, worked with, was coached by and played against some of the leading athletes of her day this oversight needs redressing. She climbed and undertook extensive cycling tours between 1895, and 1897 with Elizabeth Main (1860–1934), later to become famous as Lizzy Le Blond, the first President of the Ladies' Alpine Club in 1907 and a noted photographer.[108] Quite why Lizzy and Lottie fell out in 1898 remains unclear, but it was a bitter split and Le Blond effectively wrote the Dod out of her memoirs *Day In, Day Out* published in 1928.[109] As well as all-round amateurs, teams of professional female cricketers and women football players made the press regularly in the 1880s and 1890s.[110] Richard Cashman and Amanda Weaver's *Wicket Women: Cricket and Women in Australia* is unusual in the academic literature on Australian sport which, as the authors wryly remark, devotes more titles to animals than to the subject of women.[111] In 1886–87 Lily and Nellie Gregory, daughters of a cricketing family, captained the Fernleas and the Siroccos respectively in a number of games played for charity at what later became Sydney's Cricket Ground. Their British counterparts, the Old English Lady Cricketers (OELC) appear to have been financially exploited by their promoter in 1890 and the early attempt to perform team competition before playing crowds was short-lived. A proposed tour to Australia was abandoned when the manager absconded with the profits. Since 15,000 had attended the Police Athletic Ground in Liverpool, the ability of women performers to create a paying audience was evident.[112] The challenge remains to examine why there appears to be a discontinuous history. The uneven nature of sporting coverage in the media is not unique to women but it can have its own distinctive patterns.

Beyond the media, street-life also contained examples of women and girls enjoying sport. This seems to have been a transformation embraced by all classes, with working people valuing their brief leisure. Across the world, cities opened civic spaces for the active leisure of working-class women. The skating pond at Central Park was designed in a competition with the winning plan such a success in 1858, that on Christmas Day the following year over 50,000 people were reported as visitors.[113] By 1866 *Ladies Pond* catered for female learners or those who were shy, though part of the popularity of skating was the opportunity for couples to hold hands in public. Parks, halls and clubs became arenas for sociability and physical leisure.[114] Meanwhile, New Woman became a cause for concern and celebration encompassing various 'types'. One was the Bachelor Girl, more evident in North America than in Britain, as an urban-based working female living alone.[115] The phrase embraced considerable numbers of women who were in some way opposed to the existing social order and its use extended to legislative acts, public policy and private relationships, in addition to cultural and popular discourses. Notions of femininity changed, as did conceptions of childhood with a greater emphasis on education (rather than work), play and adolescence. For instance, the New Girl identified a separate culture of 'girlhood' increasingly commodified in the space between childhood and marriage.[116]

Though this has been a broad summary of how modern sport for women developed, general tendencies could be subject to considerable regional, local and personal variation. In Catholic communities Sunday was to be an important day for sport after the foundation of the Gaelic Athletic Association (GAA) in Ireland in 1884.[117] Its express intention of promoting 'Irish' games such as camogie, hurling and Gaelic Football as against British forms of soccer, cricket and rugby combined the support of Catholic church and state. Nationalist and church-based collaboration meant participation was expressed in parish, county and provincial groups. Linda Borish's work on the lives of young Jewish women in the United States at the turn of the twentieth century also explores the effect of theological beliefs upon practical patterns of sporting involvement.[118] Our understanding of the intersections of gender, class, ethnicity and religious belief are therefore becoming more sophisticated. Whatever their particular motivation or world-view, evangelists and moral reformers of all kinds have been active in providing female welfare incorporating physical activity. However, women and girls could choose to mould and resist what was provided, so the outcomes were not always as had been originally intended.

The next section outlines how the concept of a contemporary history allows us to see some nineteenth-century ideas endure and others change. Women's work transformed but, for many, family responsibilities did not change. In spite of attempts to limit female working hours and to provide some protection against the worst kinds of exploitation, it was clear that industrialisation and the rise of the British Empire needed more employees than a male workforce could provide, whatever middle class ideals of the 'little woman at home'.[119] Because domestic work was often unpaid and invisible, the female 'double-day', (employment outside the home, followed by the maintenance of family within its walls) gave little free time for personal amusement. Some sporting activities also leant themselves to profitable exploitation more than others, so it can be instructive to differentiate who volunteered, or traded in, a given discipline at any one time, in relation to how it was generally controlled. There has been a tendency to look at the social practices of sports organisations in a rather top-down way.[120] Newspapers and archival evidence can lead to a history of institutions rather than the people who actually delivered and experienced sport. This might incorporate casual labour; the ad hoc activities of athletic entertainers; public and private sector teachers; welfare volunteers; writers and explorers, so there is a considerable range of activity to consider across classes.

A CONTEMPORARY HISTORY OF WOMEN'S SPORT

While recognising that modern sport was historically defined by changes and continuities pre-dating the eighteenth century, this book charts women's experience of sport and leisure from the middle of the nineteenth century to the present day. Looking at the past can tell us a great deal about the present: what, and if, we can learn from what has happened seems less certain. There are consequently three key ways in which a 'contemporary history' is used herein. Dictionary definitions of 'contemporary' incorporate, firstly, people, events or ideas of roughly the same time in history. Modern, mass-spectatorship events with codified rules were established by the end of the nineteenth century. Sport changed and one of the key ways that it altered was that more women took part in a wider range of activities. This accelerated in the first half of the twentieth century when the scope and scale of that involvement increased, though not in an orderly or regular pattern. Secondly, the term denotes what is fashionable, or modern in style. More women followed sport as enthusiasts and engaged with debates about body culture, costume and dress history. There were egalitarian and elitist aspects of popular culture: activities that were to one person's taste or pocket, were simply not appealing or available to others. Notions of active leisure also linked with women's work, as more female professionals entered sport as the nineteenth century progressed. By the early decades of the twentieth century, a few significant women could become wealthy through their sporting fame. A third meaning of contemporary refers to what is current or still in existence. There is much obvious continuity in the change, not least, the ways in which sport for women in the twenty-first century can still defined by attitudes and customs that appear to be traditional, and may be of long-standing. However, these structures and traditions have been constructed and maintained. Understanding how and why this has happened can tell us about how sport has been shaped by, and continues to form, our understanding of society.

To people like Helen Wilson, leisure was important and how they chose to spend their time when not working tells us a great deal about their lives. We may not know what it was like to set up a remote farm in New Zealand, but we can empathise with a wish to enjoy what little 'spare' time was available. Wherever possible, the research has been based on contemporary material to offer an analysis based on evidence in the public domain at the time. Personal items of memorabilia and family history have also been generously lent and donated. Interviews, memoirs and autobiographical sources have been allied with archival research in the International Olympic Museum, Lausanne; the FIFA collections in Zurich and UEFA documentation in Nyon in Switzerland. Other overseas collections have included the Adidas archive in Herzogenerauch, Germany; the Fashion and Technology Institute, New York and the National Sporting Library, Middleburg Virginia. In addition, I have used material from the

National Football Museum in Preston; the Silverstone motor racing library and archive, Northamptonshire and the Brooklands Museum in Surrey; the hockey and Judo holdings at the University of Bath Library Special Collections; The British Olympic Assocation, London; The Wimbledon Museum and Lawn Tennis Association archive; the Women's Library at London Metropolitan University; The V&A Museum of Childhood, Bethnal Green and the National Trust Museum of Childhood Sudbury in Derbyshire; the Amateur Athletic Association papers held in the Special Collections at the University of Birmingham and the Amateur Swimming Association archive in Loughborough. Several local collections of national importance, such as the fashion gallery at Snibston Museum in Leicestershire and the shoe collection at Northamptonshire Museum also helped with the research.

The work has been a long time in development. That longevity has enabled me to collect a variety of texts, most authored by women, which gives an insight into how they have captured and represented their sporting experience. This might be in written form, oral histories, photographic snapshots, journalism, administrative papers, images, toys, games, clothing or collages of mixed media in scrapbooks. The sheer number of women participating in a range of sports over the period that this book covers is remarkable. It has a broadly chronological tapproach in which significant sporting examples and wider themes emerge. One of these is the balance of women's work with other commitments, in conjunction with their sporting interest.

In the first chapter, for instance, sporting variety is viewed through the emergence of working class swimming, middle class hockey and upper class field sports as a way of approaching some developments from the middle of the nineteenth century onwards. While some leisure could be discrete, sports-work could embrace several roles in a single career as a performer; competitor; licensed and accredited 'specialist'; teacher; coach or volunteer.[121] Female gymnastic and physical education instructors had competing priorities: this could include the paid teaching of private, university and high school pupils; offering free classes to working women (dressmakers, shop assistants, women telephonists, cashiers) and welfare work with poor children.[122] It consequently makes more sense to talk of multiple 'careers' for most of the women in this book. For this reason, there is considerable revision of Claire Langhammer's emphasis on life-cycle as a determining factor in female leisure participation.[123] For some women, sport was a defining part of their life-long identity as player, administrator, advocate, coach, colleague and friend.

This is not an encyclopaedic approach but is intended to provide points of departure for other studies. Some of the women will be familiar to scholars of sport and women's leisure but others have been forgotten except for family or local history collections. Wherever possible, the first time a person is mentioned, the text will give their dates of birth and death in order to help with biographical references. Although this might seem intrusive for readers who already are aware of some personalities, it remains a shocking reality in these days of information overload that even Google and Wikipedia cannot provide basic detail on the lives of Maud Drummond, Bonnie and Donnie Cotteral and others already mentioned in this introduction. Hopefully it will become evident that search engines have not been my only, or main, resort. However, this has been an inexact exercise and for this too the patience of the reader is requested. Where there is not a reference to dates of birth and death, confirmation was not available at the time of going to publication. Such biographical work is time-consuming, tricky and can be imprecise but represents an attempt to better place these women in context of their life and times. For consistency, where possible, the bibliographic references use the Oxford Dictionary of National Biography (ODNB), as it is available in most academic and public libraries. Rather than intended to be definitive, the biographical material should be read as indicative of how much more there is to know. I have avoided referencing well known figures from history in this way, but where important women also pursued sport for imporrtant phases of their lives I have also included their dates of birth and death.

Many women and girls involved in sport spoke through various media in a 'symbiotic' relationship that promoted their involvement but also contested their wider place in public life.[124] Education linked sport and leisure to female emancipation.[125] Women began to write about, and to be written into, the history of sport in small numbers but important ways: this almost always involved a discussion of how to dress whether one was hunting game or playing golf.[126] Contemporary publications such as *The Queen* and *The Graphic* showed women wearing new styles of clothing to cycle, fence, sail, play cricket or football, shoot arrows, climb the Alps and participate in ballooning, gymnastic drills, life saving and field sports.[127] In addition, Stephen Hardy has indicated, 'The particular forms of any sport, in any historical period, are hardly inevitable derivatives of some *zeitgeist*. They are the products of conscious decision-making that cries out for more historical investigation. If rule-makers create a special product—the game form—that may exist as a commodity, it is also true that their product seldom exists in isolation.'[128] This helped to think about why swimming took the particular forms that it did, and how that differed from women's hockey and field sports.

The second chapter continues themes of the commercial, imperial and technological milieus shaping public attitudes to sport, along with campaigns for suffrage and education up to 1914. The modern Olympic movement reflected the times in which it was created more than it resembled ancient Greece. As a relatively small sporting and cultural festival in its early days, selective aspects of tradition became reinvented while other elements were forgotten or lost. Competitions organised by the International Olympic Committee (IOC) between 1896 and 1912 had flexible rules and customs. Women were also part of well-established traditions of witness, consumption and display.[129] Both organised forms of sport and individual leisure dictated who represented Great Britain at these early editions of the Olympic Games. As America and Germany industrialised with increasing efficiency, moral panics about a loss of national vitality and efficiency extended to the National Service League (NSL), set up in 1901 to defend the empire and British independence. Increased public interest in the vigour of the nation led to legislation, like the Public Health Act of 1907, permitting local authorities to spend more money on recreation and games.[130] The twin themes of the chapter are internationalism and a fascination with cultural modernity, shown in Olympic connections with the exhibition movement. Geographical mobility combined with improved communications technology to make international networking easier. A growing sense of transnational activism therefore informed campaigns for sport as a right for women before the First World War.

The third chapter is about the modern, some would say modernist, sport of motor racing. Technological and marketplace innovation increased women's access to motorised transport, and then racing. This remains amongst the most neglected topics in sports history generally. Like other activities, we can see multiple and changing use of space, place, resources and time.[131] Women's participatory roles in motor-sport might encompass advertising, self-promotion, supporting a household and indulging a love of danger. Motor-sport involved an inter-related set of roles for men too, in facilitating male and female races. The role of fathers, partners, siblings, relatives, sponsors and male fans of female sport are areas of masculinity often neglected in favour of much-discussed male worlds. Sporting mothers, sisters, aunts, daughters and co-workers are not to be ignored either. Bringing male contributors more fully into the story of women's sport is therefore intended to prompt more careful discussion of gendered collaboration in how sport has been performed. Women novices became skilled racing drivers through a range of support mechanisms and were vital to the growth of the motor industry. Many motoring couples became public figures. The chapter explores how women also helped to lead circuit design, fund track building and contributed to motor racing's 'society' image.

Chapter 4 argues that sporting internationalism was well developed by the 1920s. The chapter makes connections between women's football and wider Olympic networks, to offer a revisionist view of the Games.[132] Women's football reached new heights of popularity with crowds played for charity during World War I. In response, a ban imposed by the Football Association prevented women from playing on Football League grounds or those of Association-affiliated clubs from December 1921.[133] Led by Alice Joséphine Marie Million (1884–1957), Femina, a French football team had already competed against Dick, Kerr's Ladies of Preston in 1920. Under her married name, Alice Milliat was to become the head of an international movement to include more athletic events for women in the Olympic Games from 1921. Women's football was sufficiently established to be part of this wider activist community that also included track and field athletics, a version of Czechoslovakian handball called hanza and basketball. Politician Elaine Burton (1904–1991, later Baroness Burton of Coventry, was among the first British cohort of female track and field athletes at international competitions staged in Monte Carlo at Easter 1921.[134] A team of seven athletes met with great success, notably sprinter Mary Lines (1893–1978), who worked for Schweppes and sometimes trained at the Lyons works facilities next door. Lines recorded a time for 100 yards of 11.4 seconds and became one of the first women to enter the Olympic record books for track and field athletics[135] The Stade Pershing in Paris hosted the first unofficial international athletics match between France and England on 30 October 1921. Mary Lines was again the star of the proceedings, England winning by 52 points to 38.[136] The following day, the Fédération Sportive Féminine Internationale (FSFI) was founded with Milliat as its head and remained the international governing body for women's athletics until the International Amateur Athletic Federation (IAAF) took over in 1936. Also titled Women's Olympic Games in the Paris (1922) and Gothenburg (1926) editions, Milliat gave into pressure to rename these meetings the Women's World Games when they took place in Prague (1930) and were last held in London (1934). These initiatives were held in conjunction with the IOC version of the Olympics and effectively merged in 1936 at the Berlin Games.

The growth of an international women's sport movement linked with other collectives, such as the Worker's Sport Olympiads, and is explored in the context of how more Olympic sports opened to female athletes in the period. In England the Women's Amateur Athletic Association (WAAA) was founded in 1922. Ethel Edburga Clementina Scott (1907–1984) became the first black woman to represent Britain in an international athletics event in Prague. Although five athletic events were introduced at the 1928 Olympics, the British boycotted this slight programme. Hence, at Olympic games in Los Angeles in 1932, the captain of the women's athletics team, Eileen May Hiscock (1909–1958), was already an experienced competitor due to FSFI events. Hiscock won a bronze medal with colleagues in the 4 x 100 metres relay team Nellie Halstead (1910–1991); Violet Blanche Webb (1915–1999) and Gwen Porter (1902-unknown).

Individuals such as Lily Parr (1905–1978) became sporting prodigies, famous at a young age.[137] Parr played regularly the Dick, Kerr's team of Preston, the elite of women's football at the time, from 1920 until 1951. The FA ban was gradually lifted between 1969–1972, long past the end of Parr's career. We can view gender as a factor that limited the acclaim of track and field athletes or limited the ability of footballers to earn a living as a professional from the sport. But these women were also celebrities and much-feted. In one year, from 1921 to 1922, there is evidence that Lily Parr attended at least sixty civic receptions and met several other well-known entertainers, athletes and politicians, including the President of the United States. Parr benefitted from considerable prestige, or what theorists would call 'cultural capital' and financial security, becoming the first person in her family to buy their own home. Not all of the women were so comfortably off, as the collection of women who comprised Britain's female Olympians indicates, so elite performers can help illuminate different aspects of the history of sport.

The fifth chapter describes how, first, inter-war women's hockey and then motor-sport became internationalised. Hockey was a game developed by British Empire connections to New Zealand, then Australia and South Africa. Reciprocal visits to the United States and Europe strengthened friendly feeling but could also highlight cultural differences.[138] British connections maintained networks that would form the basis of future sport and social tours after the foundation of the International Federation of Women's Hockey Associations (IFWHA) in London during 1927. The chapter looks at friendships that combined sport and sociability along these lines. Hockey tours were amateur affairs, allowing women to use new travel and communications technologies in pursuing sport for its own sake. Tours evidenced practical feminism, in that enthusiasts' ties with Australia, Canada, New Zealand, South Africa and certain sections of upper middle class America could take months of planning, fund raising and communication.

Motor-sport, including aviation and powered boat competitions, also proliferated in the inter-war years.[139] Races and record-breaking feats had considerable contemporary resonance given their links with Royalty, militarism, technological modernity and the impetus to map territory at home and abroad.[140] However, rather than duplicate what has already been said about imperial ties, especially with what are sometimes called the 'white' Dominions, the second section looks at more informal aspects of Empire, typified by the activities of the Honourable Mrs Victor Bruce (1895–1990) and her contemporaries. Mary Bruce drove solo 1,700 miles from John O 'Groats to Monte Carlo in a little over seventy hours to win the Coupe des Dames in 1927.[141] She followed this with a series of record-breaking attempts that saw her, both literally and metaphorically, stick a British flag in foreign soil. The rise of motor-car ownership, and racing to 'improve the breed' of each marque took place amongst contradictory imperial narratives. Manufacturers used sporting examples to signal innovation and versatility as a synonym for the virility of the nation.[142] Women were used to advertise vehicles and helped to promote a sense of technocratic Anglophile superiority, nowhere more so than at Brooklands. Canadian-born Kay Petre (1903–1994) began to drive as a novice amateur in the 1930s as the wife of a British enthusiast, as many other women would at this time. Like others, Petre then took several forms of paid employment driving as part of a works' team, before becoming a journalist, car designer and sales consultant.[143]

The final chapter begins with the 1948 London Games as an important media moment in the post-war rehabilitation of the Olympic movement. A few years later *World Sports: International Sports Magazine*, which was established as the official publication of the British Olympic Association, was prompted by the accession and coronation of a twenty-seven year old female head of state to see the period as a new Elizabethan era 'Of rich inventiveness, achievement and glory-in sport and all things.'[144] The second section explores the contested amateur tradition as it manifested itself across a range of women's sports during the 1940s and 1950s. More women became increasingly visible to the general public in a wider range of sports up until the Rome Olympic Games of 1960.[145] By 1960, professional female experts from a variety of sport, leisure and recreation disciplines were embedded in British cultural life. So, while lots of women took part in sport more for the joy of competition than for the fame, there were increasing numbers who were able to make a lucrative and high profile career of their talents.

For reasons of space, the concluding comments relate more to work that remains to be done than what has gone before. Sport was a notably absent feature of most women's rights journals that emerged out of feminism's so-called second-wave in the 1970s. In practical and symbolic terms, women all too often still remain missing from Halls of Fame and other public sites of sport.[146] This began to change in the 1950s and 1960s as the first generation of modern sporting pioneers, like Lottie Dod, were recognised by important institutions and contemporary publications. Secondly, BBC Sports Personality of the Year, inaugurated in 1954, and other awards became an important national means of mediating female sports stars to the British public. Pre-dated by newspaper competitions with similar titles, the BBC event reinforced national recognition of women's place in sport.

There remains a strong tradition of women coming in third place in the BBC Sports Personality of the Year award (Pat Smythe in 1954; Anita Lonsborough in 1960; Angela Mortimer in 1961; Linda Ludgrove in 1962; Anne Packer in 1964; Marion Coakes in 1965; Sally Gunnell in 1992; Tanni Grey-Thompson in 2000; Beth Tweddle in 2006 and Rebecca Adlington in 2008). There have also been eleven second placings for women: Dorothy Hyman in 1962; Beryl Burton in 1967; Jayne Torvill in 1983; Fatima Whitbread in 1986; Sally Gunnell in 1993 and 1994; Denise Lewis in 1998 and 2000; Ellen MacArthur in 2001 and 2005; Jessica Ennis in 2012. The thirteen female winners so far have been Anita Lonsbrough in 1962; Dorothy Hyman in 1963; Mary Rand in 1964; Ann Jones in 1969; HRH Princess Anne in 1971; Mary Peters in 1972; Virginia Wade in 1977; Jayne Torvill (along with Christopher Dean) in 1984; Fatima Whitbread in 1987; Liz Mc Colgan in 1991; Paula Radcliffe in 2002; Kelly Holmes in 2004 and Zara Phillips in 2006. Statisticians will have noted that 1962 remains the only year to have an all female 'top three'.[147]

In spite of these developments there are numerous remaining questions, to be addressed in the second volume of A Contemporary History of Women's Sport from 1960 to the present. How can we use some of the contemporary sources of sport in order to look afresh at women's experiences? How did changes in the media and the increasing role of tabloid newspapers change the way that sport was reported and broadcast? We have some really valuable work on women's athletics, college and university sports, climbing, swimming and works' provision, but where are the large-scale studies that explore the contribution of career-administrators, lifelong experts and leading coaches across a range of activities since 1945? How then, might we understand a diverse range of female engagement across the multiple aspects of sport and leisure? How has this changed as the twentieth century progressed into the twenty-first?

1 Victorian Sporting Variety, Women's Education and Writing

In these days of physical culture for women as well as for men, there is little need to dwell on the advantages of such exercise as the art of natation gives to the body, while every swimmer knows the glorious sensation of cutting through the briny waves, with the froth and foam curling round the head, and the magnificent feeling of freshness and strength which follows the judicious use of the sea bath. And what more interesting sight than that which can be seen now at so many of our seaside resorts, viz. a bevy of fair damsels, clad in pretty and appropriate costume, disporting themselves in Old Ocean, their rosy limbs flashing as they dash through the waves, their shouts of laughter resounding across the water and telling of blithesome happiness and abounding health.[1]

INTRODUCTION: WOMEN, WORK AND SPORT

While women's sport and leisure has most often been seen as providing recreation and consolation for the few from the middle of the nineteenth century onwards, the examples used in this chapter suggest that the meanings derived from physical activities were multiple and diverse. The argument uses an industrial context to focus on different kinds of work, education, play and writing across a variety of leisure and sport. While there is a broad consensus that the expansion of modern sport and industrialisation were inherently related, Victorian female professional performers, sporting pedagogues, and writers are often overlooked in historical and social surveys. Mass participation can often be illuminated by individual case studies, or what theorists would call micro, rather than macro level, research. This chapter develops three sections along class lines to look in particular at working-class female swimmers, middle-class hockey players and upper-class field sports enthusiasts. Of these, swimming was a popular activity, hockey became more widespread across a growing middle class, while hunting, shooting and fishing had both elite and proletarian forms. Although the chapter is limited to these examples for reasons of space, the evidence suggests that sporting variety and its attendant commodification marked the period as a whole.

As the title of the seminal work by Sheila Rowbotham implied, until the mid 1970s both women's work and leisure were part of a 'hidden history'.[2] Much has since been written about women and industrialisation, but these texts often consider paid and unpaid employment as their main focus, rather than recreation. For instance, Britain's growing number of family historians could refer to a list of 300 or so jobs encompassing 'the range and diversity of women's work spanning the last two centuries—from bumboat women and nail-makers to doctors and civil servants.'[3] Readers would have found no athletes listed, either in a generalist or specific category, perhaps giving the impression that women working in sport-related roles was a twentieth-century innovation. This can also extend to academic surveys such as Deborah Simonton's *Women in European Culture and Society: Gender, Skill and Identity from 1700* in which sport has only five indexed references beginning with Suzanne Lenglen's appearance at Wimbledon in 1919.[4]

These orthodoxies can shape the collection and organisation of historical material on women's work and leisure. In a recently re-launched digitisation project, *History to Herstory: Yorkshire Women's lives online 1100 to the Present*, a quick search for sport will yield no result from 80,000 archival pages.[5] Rather than confirming that that there was nothing happening, the example reminds us that our present focus can sometimes shape the histories that we have. So broad generalisations should be treated with caution: gender could sometimes be perceived as less important in the exploitation of workers than class, religion or ethnicity. As the literature on the transformation of the nation-state between 1870 and 1914 indicates, the mass production of myths and manufactured traditions were themselves shifting social entities.[6] Recent work has begun to look at what work and leisure might have meant in the context of specific industries and transport histories, including the railways and canals.[7]

What was considered civilised and respectable leisure could be dependent on circumstance. Pressure groups, like the Royal Society for the Prevention of Cruelty to Animals, formed in 1824, called for laws against 'inhumane' activities but were more focused on urban concerns, like bull baiting, than rural blood-sports and hunting.[8] The 'threshold of embarrassment' in polite society therefore shifted unevenly.[9] From 1831, the formation of the Lord's Day Observance Society limited Sunday work, including that in the home. Monday often became 'wash day': for those women who had no facilities of their own, the wash-house became both a place of hard physical work, story-telling, smoking and drinking.[10] The laundry grew between 1861 and 1901 to become the third largest employment sector for women and the second largest for those over the age of forty-five.[11] Along with employment in the laundry, textile, retail and clerical work comprised the main training opportunities for working-class women. They provided alternatives to 'going into service', which many dreaded because of the long hours, lack of privacy and poor status. However, the range of street hawkers, home-workers and sweat-shops make assessments of the overall numbers of women who were active in the labour market difficult. We know quite a lot about middle-class women working in the nursing and teaching professions in the nineteenth century but comparably little about working-class women in the cultural industries. This includes sports women, be they involved in earning a living as athletes for relatively short or longer periods of time.

Changes in the labour force affected women's work up to 1914 in three key ways that were significant for sport and leisure. Firstly, women were classified with youths and children as workers in a range of industries while specific jobs became legislated as masculine.[12] Protective laws often infantilised women and, in practical terms, limited their opportunities for work. Occupational cultures around manual, technological and professional labour could become gendered, although individuals and groups challenged such divisions. Secondly, while the income of children and women was often vital to the household budget, public awareness also grew of the numbers facing destitution. Many single women supported themselves and, by the later decades of the nineteenth century, the Married Women's Property Acts had liberalised divorce.[13] The feminisation of poverty and the underpayment of female labour (individually and in occupational groups) tended to give women less access to public and private resources. Thirdly, obvious inequalities led to more collective organisation to ask for rights and freedoms. Men often supported these claims and combined with women in trades unions like the Blackburn Weavers' Association, formed in 1854, and the National Union of Teachers, created in 1870. The Society for Promoting the Employment of Women (SPEW) was founded in 1859 and the Prudential Assurance Company formed by women clerks in 1871. Activists spread ideas in journals and pamphlets. A movement to increase the range of work available and to promote improvement in pay and conditions gradually gained moral legitimacy. However, these three overall trends should be viewed as dynamic and subject to regional, local or individual variation.

Women's work was also affected by the changing concept of childhood. One summary has identified the four broad aspects of modern childhood as a move away from work to schooling (effectively turning children from economic assets into financial liabilities); declining birth-rates, which meant fewer children in families; reductions in infant mortality rates and an increasing willingness of the nation state to intervene in the health, education and protection of individuals.[14] A historian of toys supports the general point that, though the wages of women and children were worse affected in times of slump, only 2% of boys and fewer girls aged between five and nine were at work by 1851.[15] The percentage of children as part of the population increased and many may well also have worked outside school hours, so statistics are difficult to confirm. Hugh Cunningham suggests that, for young adults aged between ten and fourteen, the percentage of those who were considered gainfully employed was 36.6% for boys and 19.9% for girls.[16] There seems to be a consensus that most children had some spare leisure in which to play, though the extent of domestic obligations obviously complicates the picture. The examples in the following chapter explore these transient patterns of life and its more long-lasting circumstances.

Just as no authoritative history of industrial Britain can ignore the place of women and children, the same two groups helped to shape occupational cultures. For many working-class girls childhood could be very short and work, from the age of six or seven, might range from scaring birds in rural areas, to bonnet-making in towns and tobacco spinning in cities. Among the more important studies to reveal conflicting attitudes towards childhood was the First Report on the Children's Employment Commission in 1842. This concerned the hypocrisy in the way that boys, girls and women were represented and the conditions to which they were exposed at work in mines. The Second Report, published early the following year (though also dated 1842) covered trades and other manufacturing industries. Transcripts of interviews show work dominating most people's lives but also give an insight into how free time was spent, such as a typical Saturday night in Wolverhampton.[17]

Following the 1847 Ten Hours Act and subsequent factory reforms, women were increasingly seen as a distinct class from men, as were children. Dame schools, run by women in their own home, and Ragged schools (usually established by charities or philanthropists to offer free education) provided poor children with a very basic education. By the time of the rise in mass-spectator sports, such as soccer and rugby in the late 1870s, the living standards, disposable incomes and educational opportunities of the working classes had generally risen and their working hours had been cut. But it was not until 1901 that children under twelve were prohibited from working in factories and workshops and it is telling that another digitised collection of material which looks at the work of the Waifs and Strays Society, from its foundation 1881 to the end of World War One, contains no reference to the social lives of its 22,500 children.[18]

Sport could be both an expression of popular culture and traditional past times: increasing evidence points to different types of female engagement, some of it a lucrative, if fragile, means of earning a living wage. By the later decades of the nineteenth century, the establishment of central governing bodies, codification of rules, national competitions, paying spectators and international audiences for sport changed dramatically. In an uneasy relationship with emergent governing bodies, sport had established itself as a form of commercialised entertainment in ways that still seem familiar. There were many links with other cultural industries. Well-known female swimmers, educationalists and field sports enthusiasts were part of this phenomenon. Unfortunately, there is not enough space to do justice to the adventurers, balloonists, cyclists, mountaineers, pedestrians, 'stunt-girls' (journalists who created their own record-breaking challenges), croquet, tennis or golf players who could just as easily have been used as examples here. The chapter does draw parallels with the entertainment industry more generally though. When women sports stars moved into the movie industry in the twentieth century, they followed others who had performed in theatres, music halls and circuses in the nineteenth century and before.

The section on swimming and the working-class female 'natationist' explores some of the direct and indirect ways that women earned a living from sport in the period. Local bodies, with gradually emerging national affiliations, were set up to organise competitions. The formation of the Amateur Swimming Association (ASA) is a good example of how the creation of sports associations could change and regulate labour markets. After short-lived attempts to establish the National Swimming Association in the 1830s and the British Swimming Society in 1840s, the Metropolitan Swimming Club Association, founded in 1869, gradually came to use the word 'amateur' in its title and became the sole regulatory body for the sport in England.[19] By the 1870s swimming was popular both with large numbers of participants and sizeable audiences on both sides of the Atlantic: 1,500 girls and women used the free public floating baths at Charles Street, New York in 1872 and 4,000 watched women's races arranged by Kate Bennett at Fort Hamilton in 1874.[20] The English ASA had relatively little control of the sport until the mid 1880s, and consequently, a more relaxed attitude to professionals than some other codes. Similar attempts to form a Scottish national association in 1875 failed due to internal conflicts and insufficient funds in 1881. The range of female aquatic activity facilitated by individual working-class women and those active in trade networks was therefore significant and while this has received recent attention, much research remains to be developed on the subject.

The second section looks at how innovators of women's education promoted sporting provision generally. As part of the re-evaluation of this topic, the achievements of physical educators are first set in the midst of wider discussions about access to tuition for women. This segment specifically covers the expansion of hockey as a 'school sport.' Access to further and higher education was important symbolically and practically as a means of female emancipation.[21] Physical fitness for women was seen as a scientific topic with much surveillance and measurement, in the same way that women who entered higher education were endlessly weighed and measured in order to guard against 'overstrain'. A number of Victorian women have been described as physical education 'pioneers' who created a profession after the establishment of Queen's College in 1848. Some women were undoubtedly inspirational: Frances Mary Buss (1827–1894) had attended Queens College and founded the North London Collegiate School for Ladies in 1850.[22] In 1858 Dorothea Beale (1831–1906) became Principal of the already extant Cheltenham Ladies College.[23] The headmistress who devoted herself to her life's work subsequently became part of British popular culture, as the well-known rhyme indicates:

Miss Buss and Miss Beale,
Cupids darts do not feel,
How different from us,
Miss Beale and Miss Buss.

However, focusing on single women educators, headmistresses or patrons can overlook the enthusiasm of students themselves for sport and leisure. The case study of hockey suggests that particular activities became popular at specific institutions in a complex combination of access to facilities, networking, mentoring by teachers and student interest. Those students owned and interpreted their sport as part of their social networks and we can see how sociability helped to translate activities to the student body as part of collegiate identity.

The chapter concludes by suggesting that the study of British women's writing in relation to sport lags somewhat behind that of North American academia. Susan Bandy and a number of other colleagues have refined this area of research.[24] The publication of the first women's magazines included London-based *The Ladies Mercury* in 1693. The *Female Spectator* followed in 1744, *Bibliothek der Frauenfrage* in Germany 1790, *Godey's Ladies Book* in the United States in 1830 and later *Athletic Monthly*, which included 'opinion' essays on appropriate behaviour. The combined effect of increased literacy, advances in printing technology and industrial expansion saw periodicals aimed at women alongside publications assuming a female readership. This extended to the Negro Press in the United States and several specialist papers for the Jewish community.[25] Many of the same conditions that helped sport to spread, such as an increase in leisure time and relative disposable income, helped to encourage a wider 'reading' public, while educational benefits slowly improved circulation. As part of the 'new leisure world' reading itself underwent transformation in its national and international markets.[26] Women's adventure and travel writing were already established genres; a subject explored from a number of perspectives at a recent conference called *Moving Dangerously, Women and Travel 1850–1950* at Newcastle University.[27] Writing about field sports therefore had both elite and imperial overtones.

WORKING-CLASS FEMALE SWIMMERS

Though this part of the chapter focuses on professional women 'natationists', the cross-class interest in swimming, bathing and life-saving was a major contributor to its mass-market appeal. Founded by doctors in 1744, the Royal Humane Society encouraged the controversial new technique of resuscitation and recovery.[28] A growing population near to inland rivers, lakes and canals alarmed those who feared for public safety. Class-based tensions were evident in such organisations and the altruism of the public could not be assumed: there was an original reward of four guineas for the rescuer and a further one guinea to those (usually publicans) taking in a body to be treated on their premises. This led to a swindle, whereby one con artist would pretend to be in difficulty and would share the profits from a staged rescue with their accomplice afterwards. Gradually, medals and certificates replaced the financial rewards. Thereafter, volunteers set up a network of 'receiving houses' in and around the Westminster area of London before a national network developed.

The *Rules of the Royal Humane Society for the Recovery of the Apparently Drowned* were reproduced several times and an 1820 text replicated them under the motto 'Resuscitation: What Thou Doest, Do Quickly':

1. Convey the body to the nearest house.
2. Strip and dry the body.
3. Put young children between two persons in a warm bed.
4. An adult, lay on a blanket or bed in a warm place [sic].
5. Rub with flannel sprinkled with spirits.
6. To restore breathing introduce the pipe of a pair of bellows into one nostril and with the mouth closed inflate the lungs 'til the breast be a little raised. Repeat 'til life appears.
7. Tobacco smoke is to be thrown gently into the fundament, with a proper instrument so as to defend the mouth of the assistant.[29]

Though life saving was a concern well before the mid nineteenth century therefore, the transformation of the railways and, in particular, cheap 'six-penny-dipper' fares for the lower classes made the seaside accessible for ordinary people.[30] Alongside grand piers, exotic winter gardens and fantastic pleasure palaces, there were opportunities for entrepreneurs with more modest aspirations.

Saving lives at sea made Mary Wheatland (1835–1924), a local celebrity in Bognor after she received both bronze and silver life-saving medals; on one occasion saving six girls in a single incident. Sometimes grateful survivors, or their families, would supplement Wheatland's income with a financial reward, other times the reward would be a joint of beef for her large family. The fashion for bathing at the seaside by those who could not swim created the profession of 'dippers' who would accompany people into the water and pull them out after immersion. Some of these, like Mary Wheatland, also became lifeguards. Known as 'Bognor's Mermaid' Wheatland started work sometime between 1848 and 1850 for bathing machine owner Martha Mills, before being employed by Joseph Ragless. Though she lived at a subsistence level and the number of Mary's children remains unclear because many died in infancy and their names were re-used, she was famous for her rescue of at least thirty people; her feats of swimming endurance and for still diving from Bognor Pier at the age of seventy-one. We know more about Wheatland than the other 'bathing women' around at the time because W. P. Marsh produced portraits in both the carte-de-visite and cabinet formats of her from 1875 onwards, often featuring the rope that she used for rescues.[31] With the introduction of the picture postcard in the early 1900s, Marsh began to issue holiday souvenirs and Wheatland was still working then. Her funeral in 1924 was attended by a cortege of Bognor fishermen in recognition of her dedication to lifesaving and lifelong enthusiasm for swimming.

As several commentators have shown, sport has long had a complex link with finance but not always an explicitly commercial one.[32] State intervention, such as the 1846 and 1847 Bath and Wash-houses Acts reflected widespread anxiety over the health and hygiene of the working classes. Revised again, as a more permissive 1878 Public Baths and Washhouses Act, it encouraged local authorities to build more covered swimming pools.[33] Though many men and women travelled by public transport, like railways, to the sea to bathe, swimmers of all kinds used more local urban and rural facilities. In Britain, between 1880 and 1914 over 600 public baths were constructed.[34] Entrance costs could vary from half a penny for children (equal to about twenty pence now) to two-pence for adults who could afford tuition from the attendant.[35] The ASA yearbooks indicate that most facilities had ladies' sections or times set aside for women, and the same was done for children, though it is relatively rare for the names of female swimming teachers to be listed.

The county of Leicestershire is a good example of how local histories can illuminate these larger changes in public provision. Leicester was not awarded the status of a city until 1919 but already had a reputation for manufacturing, especially clothing, light engineering and agriculture: if the modest size of the town hall square is anything to go by, it had none of the aspirations of 'Cottonopolis' Manchester or of nearer neighbour Birmingham, Britain's second-city. Cossington Street Baths was nevertheless one of ten purpose-built facilities in the town and held 2,000 spectators. Outdoor lidos and indoor pools provided leisure for many and work for a few, with Abbey Park Road measuring 100 yards long by thirty yards wide and Bede House Meadows having the same width but extending to 150 yards in length. Both pools were three yards deep. A Leicester County Amateur Swimming Association & Humane Society formed with over twenty affiliated clubs in 1891: 'To promote a knowledge of swimming and the resuscitation of the apparently drowned as well as to recognise acts of bravery.'[36] A schools' team championship was inaugurated in 1897 and instruction was provided for children at least once a week from 1899 onwards. By 1901, 641 boys and 154 girls had been taught to swim under the half price scheme and a local commentator observed: 'In the penny baths the boys get their lesson for a halfpenny, and even among the poorer classes they apparently do not find much difficulty in raising that amount.'[37]

Aside from localised developments, there were some high profile disasters that drew national and international attention to the fact that most women and girls were not taught to swim: for example in London 1878 on the River Thames when a pleasure cruiser, the *Princess Alice*, sank with the loss of 640 lives and only one woman was able to swim to safety. Some 2,000–3,000 people each year were estimated to have drowned accidentally in rivers, lakes and the sea during this period. In Victorian literature drowning became a standard means of dispatching characters, often with mystical overtones of rebirth, as in George Eliot's 1860 novel,

The Mill on the Floss where brother and sister Tom and Maggie Tul-liver drown clasped together, resolving their estrangement. The work was released under the pen name of Mary Ann Evans and was perhaps the most autobiographical of her work, as her brother Isaac disapproved of her co-habitation with George Lewes from 1853 onwards.[38] *The Mill on the Floss* reflected the author's fascination with collective judgment and moral responsibility. Learning to swim became as much a necessity for the urban population as a sporting pastime and so obliged both individu-als to learn and society to act.

Contemporary accounts about swimming multiplied during this period, with one bibliographical record in 1868 citing nineteen freshly published manuals and other instruction books.[39] Several authors deliberated over whether it should be classified as the 'art' of natation; a sanitary form of leisure; necessary for preserving life; an aspect of female emancipation or as healthy exercise.[40] The popularity of women's rowing and other water-based sports helped to promote swimming, with Routledge's *The Art of Rowing for Beginners* (1863) one of many cheap sixpenny handbooks that advocated healthy action of the whole muscular system both in and on the water.[41] A female doctor argued in 1879 that water-based exercise was a particularly feminine antidote to work:

> Swimming calls into exercise muscles which the usual kind of feminine occupations-such as sewing and the lighter kinds of manual labour leave, for the most part, at rest and spares many of those muscles which are commonly overworked. Thus, for instance, the extensions of the fingers and hands are stiffened, and in constant use in swimming, while the corresponding flexes, the slaves of the needle, are relaxed.[42]

Bathing extended to a whole other range of related activities: cold baths were perceived to be beneficial to the inhabitants of populous cities, who, authors claimed, indulged in idleness and led sedentary lives.

Alongside public facilities, private baths opened. Some closed quite quickly: brewer William Dulley (1851–1902) of Wellingborough, Northamp-ton created an indoor swimming pool using the water warmed as a by-product of beer-making in 1892 and, for a few years, local people swam for a penny.[43] There were also civic attempts to commercialise activities, such as at Ashby de La Zouch, a Leicestershire town that attempted to replicate the Spa success of Bath, Cheltenham and nearby Buxton. Originally sited at the Moira colliery, the Spa was moved four miles to Ashby because the con-junction of rough work and refined leisure was considered to be a question-able business model. One commentator considered the facilities as 'Fit only for a Bedlamite to lay out extensive and expensive accommodations upon that spot for bathers.'[44] Civic boosterism played a large part in the early success of the baths. The novel *Ivanhoe* had been published by Sir Walter Scott in 1820 and had encouraged visitors to the town searching for the site of the Tournament Field and the 'stately ruins' of Ashby Castle. The Spa facilities sought to capitalise on this trend and so were named the Ivanhoe Baths when they were completed in 1822. A colonnaded frontage, 150 feet long, welcomed guests who passed through an entrance with thirty-two fluted Doric columns. Inside they found a swimming pool, separate Ladies' and Gentlemen's baths, card and billiard rooms, private treatment areas and a Pump Room in front of which a fountain of spring water fell into a circular basin.

The price structure encouraged those who were poor, and brave enough to encounter miners, to use the old open bath at Moira for free. Meanwhile, at a safe distance away in Ashby, the Ivanhoe Baths drew in over 10,000 visitors annually and they paid between nine pence and four shillings for saltwater, hot and cold treatment. The construction of Ashby racecourse and a Royal Hotel (run by a widowed Mary Chamberlyne) followed, as did picnic excursions by Thomas Cook after the Burton to Leicester railway line opened in 1849. By the 1870s wider access signalled decline: the Saline Bathing Charity had extended the benefits of the spa to the underprivileged, funded by charitable contributions to cover the cost of five shillings per person. A female ward provided for fourteen unfortunates to board there for three weeks at a time and for outpatient treatment for other disadvantaged women. The Ivanhoe Baths themselves fell into disrepair sometime soon after, perhaps as the result of the popularity of going to the seaside. In spite of an attempt at a re-launch in 1888, the deterioration continued but the grounds continued to be used extensively until World War I. The activities of the ladies' croquet club and the 1908 ascent by balloonist Dolly Shepherd (1887–1983), before her descent by parachute, remains the subject of considerable local history interest.[45] State intervention in public health and education therefore combined with an increase in private facilities, though it is not always clear why provision did, or did not, capture the public imagination.

Bathing was an activity that could be done very cheaply or at great expense. Morality constantly found itself confounded by market forces. The expansion, diversification and nationalisation of the popular music and entertainment industry that shaped sport and leisure after 1870, saw a vogue for competitive and endurance events, in addition to scientific, or synchronised, swimming performances.[46] Theatre and music halls covered both high and low culture, enabling sporting performers to explore links with display, fashion and consumerism.[47] Individual entrepreneurs and performers were significant here. Frederick Beckwith (1821–1898), born in Ramsgate, was unusual in not having a background as a riverman, as several professionals before him had been, and in being a better publicist than he was a swimmer according to one historian.[48] This seems unfair since he did win some championship races from the 1850s onwards but he also exploited the commercial potential of swimming, appearing at the London Aquarium and other local theatres.[49] The South London Palace, for instance, ran benefit performances that also included pedestrians and wrestlers.[50]

Unlike Beckwith, who seems to have had a peripatetic existence for twenty years as a swimming entrepreneur, his contemporary Professor Van Glovne (or Van Gloyne) ran an academy in New York that attracted the growing middle classes.[51] Kate Bennett and her sisters taught middle- to upper-class women to swim there but also earned money through tuition at public baths, by giving displays, open-air ballets, aquatic concerts and through sponsoring competitions attended by a paying public at which the victor would win a gold locket or earrings.[52] Kate, who had lost her father to drowning, was driven both to teach people to become proficient in the water and to generate a viable income for herself in a challenging market.

Revealing parts of the figure as part of sporting spectacle had its own vogue. Other decidedly professional female 'natationists' such as Beckwith's daughter Agnes (1862, date of death unknown) and her half sister Lizzy (1880, date of death unknown), combined female athleticism with entertainment performance, coaching and teaching.[53] Agnes swam five-miles in from London Bridge to Greenwich in The Thames in 1875, at the age of fourteen in a time of one hour nine minutes.[54] Subsequent posters would shave two years off her age and two minutes off the time for this feat and summarise her main achievements as: swimming ten miles from Battersea Bridge to Greenwich; covering fifteen miles from Westminster to Richmond and five miles return 'without resting in any way'; staying thirty hours in the pool at the Royal Aquarium 'the greatest feat ever achieved by either sex' and spending 100 hours in the pool in one week 'taking all her meals in the water.'[55] Activities could therefore be public, appear improvised and inclusive of non-paying spectators if this promoted the fame of the individuals. Agnes Beckwith's unsuccessful attempt to swim the twenty-mile distance from Sandy Hook, New Jersey, to Rockaway Pier, New York, in June of 1883 is one example of this.

In tandem, Agnes exploited private audiences who paid to see a rehearsed and repeated act, for instance appearing in music halls and other venues such as the Royal Aquarium, Westminster.[56] Billed as 'The Greatest Lady swimmer in the world', Agnes and her entourage wore considerably less than most women sea-bathers, to swim 'decoratively' in a glass tank in variety of venues on a national tour that was logistically challenging. Agnes married a theatrical agent, William Taylor in 1882, although she kept the Beckwith name, for public performances. Her show was patronised by the Prince and Princess of Wales, yet the ASA did not approve of her feats of endurance or her *costume du bain*; an elaborate black combination of acrobatic brevity with red decorative swags and ruches.[57] She later performed at Hengler's Cirque in Liverpool in 1887 and with PT Barnum at Madison Square Garden. By 1888 professional swimming feats involving the Beckwith family included Lizzy age eight and Bobby aged four at the same venues as amateur swimming competitions under ASA rules.[58] Frederick Beckwith acted as vice President of the Professional Swimming Association (PSA) from 1881 until its collapse in 1891 so amateur competition could

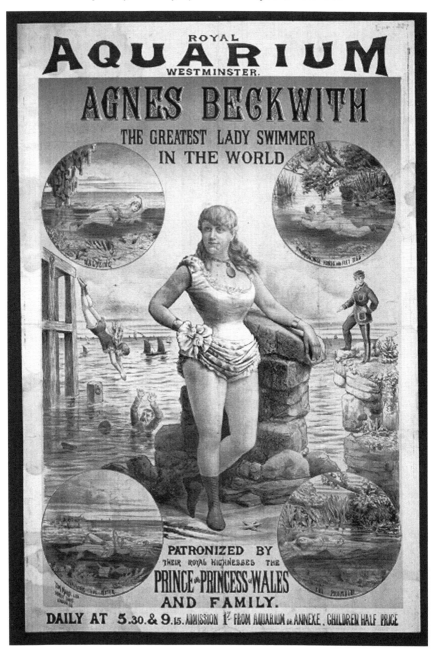

Figure 1.1   Tom Merry, *Agnes Beckwith at Royal Aquarium, Westminster*, lithograph, c. 1885. 'The greatest lady swimmer in the world 1885: Patronised by their Royal Highnesses the Prince and Princess of Wales and family. Daily at 5.30 & 9.15. Admission 1s/–from Aquarium or annexe, children half price' © The British Library Board, London (Evan.339 Royal Aquarium, Westminster).

be concurrent with profitable activities.[59] The ASA always gave national championship races to the swimming baths that offered the highest bid as hosts because of its own poverty. In order to offset the cost of country-wide travel that this entailed, cheap Third Class rail fares were negotiated for amateur competitors.

Lizzy Beckwith developed her song and dance skills into a career in its own right, and the whole Beckwith show became increasingly allied with entertainment rather than sport. Agnes led a troupe of ladies at Bournemouth in 1892 performing a quadrille routine to the enthusiastic applause of many friends and admirers.[60] Though such working-class acumen was excluded by snobbery and social convention from the amateur associations this appears to have happened quite late in the nineteenth century and in a piecemeal way.[61] Shows advertising Agnes continue up to 1909 and 1910 but the place of death and manner of her later years remain unknown. Biographical details for Professor Van Glovne and Kate Bennett are sketchy at best. So there is much still to know about the individual lives and the general scale of the activities of such athlete performers. Recent research also indicates that they did not have this particular sphere of trading to themselves.

Theatre, music halls and multi purpose baths enabled other aquatic performers, such as the four 'Sisters Johnson' (Theresa, Annie, Lizzie and Maude) to perform.[62] It was not unknown for the audience at Blackpool Tower Aquatic and Variety Circus to watch a swimming pantomime or ballet and then get into the water themselves.[63] Audiences might see Annie Luker dive a reported seventy feet from the roof of the London Aquarium in 1894 and she also appeared at Captain Paul Boyton's (1848–1924) Water Show at Earl's Court.[64] Without going into more detail, it is clear that these individual athlete performers would merit more research, as we know relatively little about their basic biographical details or their networks of association. Since much of their expertise was likely to have been passed on by an oral tradition, investigation would be challenging but rewarding. Observers at theses kinds of sporting entertainments were increasingly active participants in the spectacle: new forms of movement and illumination changed the politics of seeing and being seen as part of extensive shifts in 'muscular looking'.[65] Equally, there is much more to know about the experiences of ordinary people who used facilities that were ultimately unsuccessful, such as the Ashby Ivanhoe Baths, and those that showed similar ingenuity, such as Benton's Warm Ocean Swimming Baths in Brooklyn New York, established in 1861.

Two further examples conclude the section on swimming and how it may have provided work in industries related to the wider commercialisation of sport and leisure. First of all, clothing the body to bathe became part of wider mass production and haute couture techniques. Going to the seaside, especially to fashionable resorts, made being seen an opportunity to display wealth, taste, moral values and a good figure. One of the earliest women's swimsuits held by the Fashion Institute of Technology in New York from the late 1850s is a hip-length beige woolen jacket with separate ankle-length bloomers.[66] This is a costume primarily designed to cover the body, with the main embellishment an olive-coloured woven neck detail. By the 1870s a fashionable swimsuit might be cut from wool and silk blended material. The separate pieces comprised a one-piece bloomer and bodice with a detachable matching flared overskirt, complete with iridescent buttons.[67] The measurements of this suit equate to a current US women's size 6 (UK size 10) with the leg-length of the bloomers extending to twenty-nine inches, and a gusset of seventeen inches. More like baggy underwear than outerwear, swimming bloomers were modest and restrained garments under which a corset would also have been worn.

Another ensemble combined knee-length culottes, fastened by buttons to a matching top with sailor collar and an overskirt.[68] These styles and subsequent refinements, with skirts that revealed the bloomers and those that concealed them, indicate that age, wealth and personal choice could vary the interpretation of the short-sleeved sailor-style bloomer before 1900.[69] In shades of red, white and blue; black and dark olive green these designs might feature elaborate detailing, new technologies like hook and eye closings or elastic-effect ruffles and cuffs.[70] These style features and adaptations show variation in bathing costume design for women as the nineteenth century progressed. Even though only high-end pieces have survived, more plebian clothing that has been destroyed or lost to history would further complicate the picture. An authority in 1869 raised the issue of swimming trousers or bloomers:

> Various opinions have been raised respecting the form of dress for the fair sex to use in swimming; my sister Martha introduced various fashions with great applause, but I think the best dress for swimming is a pair of loose trowsers [sic] to extend below the knees, with a loose jacket, the sleeves not to reach so far as the elbows . . . Great heavy flannel dresses that come down to the heels are dangerous.[71]

Sergeant Leahy (champion swimmer of the Red Sea 1849–50) who taught at Eton was more vehement in his analysis and had clearly spent some time experimenting with the buoyancy of female clothing himself:

> Girls ought to learn from seven to thirteen years of age. I have heard people say that there is very little use in teaching girls to swim, as their clothes would prevent their swimming any distance if they fell overboard but I say differently and I offer myself as a test [sic]. Clothe me in a woman's dress and I will engage to swim two hundred or three hundred yards in it.[72]

Just as there were innovations in swimming technique, facilities and display, fashion too changed in subtle and dramatic ways. By the 1880s patented

'Sea-side wear' included the whole family, certainly as far a Leicester-based firm Corah's was concerned. It trademarked St Margaret's-label knitwear and jersey in 1883.[73] Women's underwear combinations and beachwear were shown side by side in the catalogue, making explicit the link between underclothes and outer-wear.[74] Swimsuits were just one sporting example: as well as yachting and football jerseys, golf and cycling hose used trademark Nelson unshrinkable technology.[75] Corah's were internationalist in outlook: they also produced Jantzen swimwear under license from the manufacturer in the United States and exported goods using native-speaking agents in countries on the European mainland.[76]

The final example of toys and seaside games also relates swimming and bathing to the growing industrialisation of sporting goods. The new toy trade press journals included *Fancy Goods and Toy Trades Journal* in 1891; *Games, Toys and Amusements* in 1895 and *Athletic Sports, Games and Toys* in 1895. Previous advertisements in other publications suggest that toys and games, as well as trinkets and souvenirs, progressively became part of a visit to the seaside or to inland stretches of water. Paper dolls, windmills and similar items could be made quite cheaply and sold easily, as Charlie Chaplin outlined in his brief spell as a toy boat hawker: 'With a limited capital of sixpence and at the cost of blistered hands through cutting up cardboard, I was able to turn out three dozen penny boats within a week.'[77] Securing a 600% return provided plenty of impetus to make and sell toys, with an estimated 800 individuals selling cheap versions on the streets of London alone and as many as 15% of the total recorded labour force involved in related trades by 1907.[78]

Christmas was obviously the key time for the industry, but Easter and summer holidays gradually became more crucial with a toyshop in Margate stocking 200 lines in the 1880s. Like boat making, the cheap end of the doll-making market was precarious: 'Individuals were operative, manufacturer, merchant and labourer all rolled into one . . . the stuffing and sewing of bodies and limbs put out to women who by 1850 were earning perhaps 2s 6d per gross.'[79] At the other end of the social scale, the 'Ondine' swimming doll might have accompanied the well-to-do family. The doll's body was made from two pieces of cork with a clockwork mechanism fitted between them and the legs had jointed kneecaps: Ondine could therefore swim in a breast-stroke fashion without getting her straw hat wet.[80]

There were playful aspects of the new sporting goods. For those who could afford to take to the promenade in style, 'horse-tricycles' enabled independent young riders in the 1870s to sit on a toy pony and pedal their way around.[81] Since most rocking-horse manufacturers also sold small-wheeled carriages, it must have seemed a logical combination of materials and technology. Other versions were more elaborate. British toy-making company George and Joseph Lines innovated the 'Galloping Cig' using chains to give a motion meant to replicate greater speed. Galloping Cig was retailed at Gamage's and other new department stores, while mail order deliveries reached customers who could not buy in person. For younger children, the ultimate means of travel was a stroller pushed by a doting parent, or more likely a servant, resembling a carriage and pair: the infant sat in a wicker pushchair and took in the fresh air while holding the reins of two miniature horses. These were sometimes called dog-carts but were items of conspicuous consumption: to make the point further, the toy horses could be customised to resemble bay-hunters or dappled-greys.

Though it is often assumed that toys such as horses had military overtones for Victorian parents or that swings, roundabouts and 'rough play' were limited to boys, memoirs suggest otherwise. Winifred Gynn-Jeffreys (1879–1975) used trays to toboggan down the slopes of Martello Towers at Slaughden, she also played cricket and rounders on the marshes at Aldeburgh and swam on her annual family holiday:

> The beach was full of treasure. Amber, agate, cornelian and jet were all to be found there. But the net result after years of crawling along the shingle produced only two small lumps of amber and a few cornelians [sic]. The remains of the pier were still standing and we would climb the girders, joined by the Vicar's youngest daughter, Connie Thompson. She was more daring than we were and climbed higher. We soon learned to swim thanks to a stern father who would threaten to throw us in the deep water if we cried, and as the pebbled shore was very shelving we were soon out of our depth . . . James Cable, of lifeboat fame, invited us to go out on a lifeboat practice. Dolly and I were allowed to go. The sea became choppy and it was not a very happy experience for some of us.[82]

Even allowing for the effects of memory and nostalgia on these recollections, a sense of freedom and play in the open air prefigured Gwyn-Jeffrey's later interest in hockey and organised games in her teenage years. Admittedly, she was middle class and able to write about her experiences in a way that those who lacked literacy could not. However, we do have some evidence that swimming, 'free-play' and climbing combined with toys and games as an experience of a girls' day out to the beach.

In conclusion, baths that might have been intended as rational hygiene facilities and places where Life Saving skills could be learned, could also provide exercise and social opportunities for people of all classes. Group terms for female swimmers like 'nymphs', 'naiads' 'merry mermaids' or even individual references like a 'swimming Venus' made a fetish of voyeuristic interest in female athletic performers. In much the same way, Victorian painting allowed for female nakedness provided it was draped in cloth in the style of ancient Greece or Rome. The terms were at once classical, mythical and exotic in allusion. Victorian swimming was therefore much more varied in its forms than the rather dualistic narrative that has developed, especially in the more popular books in the historiography of the subject, that normally describe men swimming naked, or wearing very little, and women encumbered by layers of clothing.[83] By the turn of the twentieth century, sport and leisure could mean varying things to a range of people as a cultural phenomenon.[84] Class was not defining: so although there does seem to be some evidence to support the view that the poorer a girl was, the less access she had to leisure and sport, this generalisation has to be carefully considered. Female 'dippers', aquatic performers, 'Professors' and teachers of swimming, clothes manufacturers and toy-makers suggest that necessity could be the proverbial mother of invention, so far as the creation of new opportunities for whatever abilities a person might have. Very few of the women, or men, in this section earned a comfortable living but sport, leisure and play contributed to their income, at least for a time.

The next section of the chapter explores the rise in female educational provision in the second half of the nineteenth century. It also concerns a struggle for independence, citizenship and equality for the growing middle classes. While the 1870 'Forster' Education Act has been seen as a pivotal moment in compulsory elementary education for five to thirteen year olds, implementation was devolved and therefore piecemeal.[85] Nevertheless, as a leisure activity in its own right, more women from a range of classes became aware of an entitlement to read and acquired the habit of so doing. The creation of Working Men's Colleges in 1854 was soon followed by working women's colleges; such as that founded in 1864 by Elizabeth Malleson (née Whitehead, 1828–1916) in Bloomsbury which, in its first year, enrolled 151 students for classes.[86] Suffragists who argued the political case for education in the Women's Social and Political Union (WSPU) and other groups were also influential.[87] Politicians and activists disagreed as to the best course of action. Leading figures in the campaign to enter the medical profession in the 1860s and 1870s held opposing views of the campaign for female education more generally, though often united by a mission to do something for other women.[88] Change in the built environment included the North London Collegiate School opening a purpose-constructed facility in 1879. Changes in location could obscure the sporting traditions of women's education; 'musical gymnastics' and other games had been a part of the North London Collegiate curriculum since 1870.[89]

The following argument deals explicitly with the different philosophical ideals evident in calls for an appropriate education for young women. The growth in school and college sport was one of the unintended consequences of this change in provision and was far from an impersonal process. Fostered by enthusiastic leaders and taken up by students as a topic of discourse and mediation, sports like hockey became one of the ways that the first generation of women students in further and higher education imagined themselves as a wider community.

Figure 1.2   Ralph Rowland 'We Won the Match!.' Postcard Marcus Ward's Series No. 87 Belfast and London: McCaw Stevenson & Orr Ltd., undated, circa 1910. Personal collection of the author.

PIONEERS OF WOMEN'S EDUCATION
AND THE 'HOCKEY-CRAZE'

Before looking specifically at hockey in this section it is worth making the point briefly that the establishment of women's access to higher education was a complex and difficult process. While a full survey of the issue would be impossible here, some of the key personalities are introduced before an explanation of the place of team games in some of the significant institutions. Millicent Garrett Fawcett (1847–1929) hosted one of the earliest meetings to found a woman's higher education college at her home in 1868.[90] Fawcett was well known for her enjoyment of physical exercise. She went to a gymnasium, skated, walked for miles, regularly rode on horseback and rowed. One group in the campaign for women's higher education sought female-appropriate access to universities with a separatist curriculum, taught in discrete institutions. Support came mainly from women governesses who wanted to become teachers and therefore Ladies' Educational Associations sprang up throughout the 1860s. The unlikely figurehead was Anne Jemima Clough (1820–1892), the honourary secretary of the North of England Council for Promoting the Higher Education of Women since 1867. In 1871, with Fawcett's encouragement, Clough acted as Principal of a house for peripatetic university 'extension' lectures for women.[91] This initiative became a limited company based at Newnham Hall, Cambridge in 1875.[92]

Often referred to as a somewhat 'homely' person, Clough was not a sports enthusiast but Newnham developed a games culture.[93] The *College Roll Letter*, which first appeared in 1881, recorded that there was a gymnasium, grass and ash tennis courts with more sports to follow.[94] That same year, women also had access to academic examinations, by which time an expanded Newnham had received royal visits. There were gradually other university women to compete against: Madeline Shaw-Lefevre (835–1914), who became Principal Warden of Somerville Hall, Oxford in 1879, was very much influenced by Clough.[95] According to one of her pupils Lefevre favoured 'The spirit of unobtrusive receptivity and deference to University traditions and prejudices rather than a demand for rights.'[96]

There was an equally strong case being made for female access to male examinations and existing institutions led by Emily Davies (1830–1921) who was a political campaigner in the wider sense of the word. Davies was seemingly indefatigable in her committee work, active in the Langham Place group from 1859 and the Society for Promoting the Employment of Women (SPEW).[97] Briefly editor for both the leading feminist periodicals *The English Women's Journal* and the *Victoria Magazine*, Davies joined the Kensington Society in 1865 with her friends Elizabeth Garrett Anderson (1836–1917) and Barbara Bodichon (1827–1891). Emily Davies co-founded Girton College, Hitchin, in 1869 with Bodichon before it moved to Cambridge as the first residential college for women four years later.[98] Having been a co-founder of Newnham, Millicent Fawcett lent her support to Davies' campaign to open Cambridge degrees to women from 1887 onwards. Emily Davies had strict, sometimes inflexible, opinions of female dress and deportment, at times resenting her co-founder's interference. When a young Jewish woman called Hertha Marks (1854–1923) was not accepted on a Girton scholarship, Bodichon arranged a personal fund for her education as an electrical engineer.[99] However, in 1891 Bodichon donated all of her pictures collection to the college and left another £10,000, helping to secure the financial future of the establishment.

By 1892 Girton and Newnham were debating the merits of their different approaches to women's education on the hockey field, introducing intercollegiate matches before the Cambridge versus Oxford matches began in 1894. Opposing universal female enfranchisement, Davies was last of the original Langham Place group alive to cast her vote when women over thirty were granted suffrage in the December election of 1918. The point of this commentary is that the political intent, and hence the aims and tactics, of the campaigners differed. They were also in direct financial competition for support and Davies' insistence on integration and equivalence was the more contentious position. Moreover, the views of individual women active in these groups changed over time, as the letter collection at the Women's Library indicates.[100] Nevertheless, Davies' uncompromising stance shaped co-educational study, particularly in further and higher education, as a fundamental educational principle.

In spite of the continued disagreement over the aims of educating young women and the means by which this should be done, the last three decades of the nineteenth century effected the most surprising and significant transformation in English education for this generation. Lilian Faithfull (1865–1952) was hockey captain at Somerville College, Oxford, obtaining a first-class degree in English Language and Literature. She then taught as lecturer in English at the Royal Holloway College from 1889–94, before becoming head of King's College Ladies' Department. When she gave up hockey and cycling in later life, Lilian Faithfull took to driving motor-cars and she continued to tour at an advanced age. Her first autobiography, *In the House of My Pilgrimage*, described how her student experience at Somerville College evolved into a career as an academic, manager and pedagogic leader at a time of considerable change:

> Not only was the educational advance extraordinarily rapid, but it met with almost immediate popular recognition and approval. Many of the schools of the past faded away, and some were modernised or converted into High Schools. Surely a more bloodless and complete revolution never took place, and that it was so reflects immense credit on the wisdom and knowledge of the needs of the times possessed by those who conceived and carried out their ideas.[101]

Many of the women were adept at exploiting the letter of the law and educational change. The universities of London and Durham awarded women full degrees but Oxford and Cambridge did not. Faithfull was among the group of over 700 'steamboat ladies' from the Oxford and Cambridge women's colleges who took the ferry to Dublin in order to graduate from their BA and MA degrees from Trinity College between 1904–1907. She claimed an MA by the *ad eundem* privilege in 1905, whereby the three universities of Oxford, Cambridge, and Dublin mutually granted degrees. Thereafter, Oxford and Cambridge universities continued to withhold full membership (and therefore graduation) from women students and the loophole allowing Trinity graduations closed.

Royal Holloway College, built by a wealthy patent medicine manufacturer called Thomas Holloway in memory of his wife, perhaps epitomised the radical and swift change that Faithfull described.[102] Royal Holloway opened in 1886 with twenty-eight students and seven staff having cost £700,000 and dominated the skyline at Egham Hill. The college was largely modelled on the Château de Chambord in France, producing an elaborate building of white marble and red brick with residential accommodation for over 200 boarders set in ninety-five acres of grounds. Boating, hockey, lawn tennis and swimming were mainstays. As with other institutions, the Royal Holloway sporting calendar also incorporated cricket, croquet and cycling, netball and Swedish gymnastics. By 1889 Holloway staff as well as students played hockey in considerable numbers led by Lilian Faithfull.

There had been a number attempts to form national hockey governing bodies for variants of the game but the most influential was founded in 1886 as the Hockey Association by seven London clubs and representatives from Trinity College, Cambridge. By adopting the rules of the male-run Hockey Association in 1893, Holloway women added standardised fixtures with other colleges to their existing ad hoc inter-faculty games.[103] However, this recognition was not reciprocated. By the time Faithfull had moved to become head of Kings College Ladies' Department in 1895, the Hockey Association had rejected an application for women to join their number and refused to nominate a figurehead for a proposed female association. Resolving that the executive would be an all-female board, Faithfull was elected the first President of the All England Women's Hockey Association (AEWHA) and the administration remained this way for almost a hundred years.[104] The men's game flourished amongst those amateurs who considered association football too plebeian in its links and as a British army enthusiasm, with the International Rules Board founded in 1895. Women's hockey took quite different forms, repaying the snobbery of the Hockey Association by retaining the men's association football crest as its badge.

If Holloway was impressive for the architecture, London University was the most significant academic institution, offering women access to degree examinations from 1878 and several female-run colleges became affiliates. Fostering a variety of sports and leisure past times helped to develop a collegiate atmosphere challenged by the particular geography and devolved identity of London University. For instance, philanthropic Unitarian and abolitionist, Elizabeth Jesser Reid (1789–1866) founded 'the Ladies College, 47 Bedford Square' London in 1849 with an initial loan of £1,500 which she had to turn into a gift when the college ran into financial difficulty in 1856. In 1860 Reid gave over the College property to trustees and after her death it moved out of Bloomsbury, becoming a University of London affiliate in 1874.

Drill, lawn tennis, boating, swimming and hockey were notable activities in the developing physical education curriculum, though as a result of the precarious financial situation, the first Bedford gymnasium was not created until 1896. It would seem that students initiated as many activities as the college authorities fostered, given the complex problems of finance and identity Bedford endured before becoming a School of the University in 1900. Gymnastics and drill were considered dull compared with individual games and team sports. Much participation depended on access to resources and facilities. The tennis club involved just twenty-eight of the 200 scholars until better facilities were provided in 1906, whereas the rowing club grew from forty members in 1892 to eighty affiliates by 1901 and 230 enthusiasts of an expanded 400 student population by 1914.[105] Boating was not just popular but highly competitive and incorporated canoe, skiff and sculling races amongst students, alumni and staff. The number of Bedford clubs extended to include fencing (1896); swimming and gymnastics (1897); the Old Students Athletic team (1903); indoor games nights for quoits, shuffleboard and ping-pong (1910); lacrosse and cricket sides (1912) and a netball squad (1914). The union of these initiatives into a central sports executive, with a single subscription fee, marked the dramatic rise of physical activities as fundamental to the institution's core identity when Bedford moved to Regents Park in July 1913.

Rivalry, corporate reputation and an excuse to socialise, often away from public view, were significant factors in developing sport at the women's colleges. However, taking part was not always about other things. Fun, pleasure in physical exercise and enjoyment of the outdoors could be reason enough. Adventure and relatively mild forms of peril were probably the main motivations for the first student trips abroad by bicycle led by Constance Louisa Maynard (1882–1913), the first Mistress of Westfield. An Old Girtonian, Miss Maynard personally enjoyed sport, thought it ideal recreation as an antidote to academic work, as well as being a creator of 'college spirit'. Cycling activities dominated Westfield's calendar. Club-ability also became a fetish. Associated activity included agreeing regulations and subscriptions; arranging training and competitive fixtures; scheduling a calendar of physical and social events; acquiring and maintaining equipment and running committees. Because this is dealt with in more detail later in relation to hockey, the broader point is that sporting activity made a significant contribution to general experience of education for expanding numbers of middle-class women and some girls.

Also to be significant for the rapid expansion of hockey and other team games, the British 'female tradition' of physical education included growing numbers of high schools: notable headmistresses included of Dame Louisa Lumsden (1840–1935) at St Leonards in Fife, Scotland (founded 1877); Penelope Lawrence (1856–1932) creator of Roedean in 1885 and Dame Frances Dove (1847–1942) who led Wycombe Abbey school from 1898.[106] Fletcher argues that these Principals modelled physical education on the style of the Victorian boys' public schools but with an additional focus on gymnastics.[107] Two hours exercise a day in winter and three in summer was standard. Martina Sofia Helena Bergman (1849–1915), more widely known as Madame Bergman-Österberg, contributed a great deal to a 'quite radical' innovation in female education.[108] Bergman-Österberg began twelve years of monopoly with Hampstead Physical Training College opening in 1885, combining team sports with Swedish gymnastics and alternative therapies devised by Per Henrik Ling. Hampstead prepared students from more privileged classes to teach in the new girls' secondary schools. In 1887 Bergman-Österberg transferred the model to Dartford in Kent where she bought a property, Kingsfield, Oakfield Lane in 1895. Until 1897 this remained the only women's college of physical education, with team games like hockey, lacrosse, and cricket popular with students.

The protégés of Madame Bergman-Österberg consequently founded more women's colleges of physical education to support themselves after graduating, starting with Anstey in 1897; Bedford Physical Training College in 1903 and Dunfermline College of Hygiene and Physical Training in 1905, long before Carnegie was established for men in 1933.[109] The Ling association, initially formed against Bergman-Österberg's wishes, had award-bearing powers by 1904. Physiotherapy may owe as much to her interpretations of physical education as sport, since many of the businesses formed by her students were primarily concerned with general health, remedial exercise and hygiene.[110] Whatever the case, the sense of moral purpose and discipline in women's gymnastic teaching after Österberg's death in 1915 was clear. The curriculum of Dartford and similar institutions fitted with a broader 'games for the classes, gym for the masses' philosophy. It reinforced norms of female decorum as much as it changed them, with regimentation and moderation defining the ethos.

Nevertheless, some female-only institutions were clearly entrepreneurial forms of employment and frequently bore the name of their founder. For example, from 1893–95 Rhoda Anstey (1865–1936) attended Madame Bergman Österberg's Hampstead establishment before opening her own 'hygienic home' for ladies.[111] The capital from this entitled her to buy Leasowes in Halesowen, Worcestershire, the former house and gardens of the poet William Shenstone which had fallen into disrepair.[112] The house was essentially a specialist health business, with sixteen acres and a lake. Österberg's stubbornness may also have helped to create secondary markets for her graduates, since Anstey fees were cheaper than at Dartford College.

Tansin Benn cites at least one case of an impoverished pupil who attended Anstey having previously been rejected by Österberg, in spite of representations by the family that she was extraordinarily able.[113] It is perhaps appropriate that this history should have been researched by Tansin Benn, the last appointed lecturer to Anstey College of Physical Education in 1981, and Ida Webb, a student from 1947–1950, who later served as Principal between 1969–1975.

Active in the Women's Social and Political Union, Rhoda Anstey supported the wider enfranchisement of working-class women by hosting meetings at the college. Having helped to form the Ling association and developed its award-bearing rights from 1904 she was later was one of the original members of the Gymnastic Teachers' Suffrage Society, founded in January 1909.[114] Anstey was also a member of the Temperance movement and the Food and Dress Reform League. The relatively late formation of a Ling association is noteworthy, given that many of the women mentioned in this section, from Miss Beal and Miss Buss, Millicent Fawcett and Rhoda Anstey, were part of a network of groups lobbying for change. Further research on the issue would reward us with more insight into the lived practices of these women and the place of sport and leisure in their overall approach to education and health.

The way that hockey developed at King's College (founded in 1829) shows how female education was important to British sport. An international network of athletic interest grew out of pedagogic initiatives to foster collegiate spirit. The University College (founded in 1828) and King's College admitted no women for half a century until Maria Grey, one of the founders of the Girls' Public Day School company in 1872, managed to negotiate a Ladies' Department in Kensington in 1885. Though there was practically no link between the department and London University the appointment of Lilian Faithfull in 1895 raised the academic aspirations of students to London degrees and Oxbridge diplomas. Initiatives to foster communal identity for students from the ages of seventeen to seventy included sport, a college magazine, literary and musical societies.

Those who attended King's were some of the most distinguished women of the time: the Indian poet Sarojini Chattopadhyay (1879–1949, later Naidu), Princess Margaret (1882–1920) and Princess Patricia (1886–1974) of Connaught and Dame Helen Gwynne Vaughan (née Fraser, 1879–1967). Gwynne Vaughan, for example, graduated as a mycologist and was to become a Chief Controller of Queen Mary's Army Auxiliary Corp (QMAAC) in France and then briefly Commandant of the Women's Royal Air Force (WRAF) before a notable academic career.[115] By the time Faithfull left King's in 1907 to become the head of Cheltenham Ladies' College, it was by some way the largest of the London colleges having doubled in size to 500 students (Westfield had a student body of sixty; Royal Holloway numbered 150; Bedford had grown to almost 250 and University College had expanded to over 400 scholars).

King's claimed the first annual college dinner for women and later versions became large sporting 'socials'. Just as the department dropped the title 'ladies' in favour of 'women' because, in Faithfull's view, the former did not pass examinations but the latter did, the All England Women's Hockey Association took its permanent name in September 1896 (having previously been the Ladies' Hockey Association and the All England Ladies' Hockey Association).[116] The eight clubs at the first meeting were: Holloway Hockey Club; Old Newnham; Girton College; Wimbledon House; Weybridge/ Walton (The Croft); Newnham College Cambridge; East Molesey and Somerville, Oxford. Bournemouth, Esher and Wimbledon soon joined, rapidly followed by Blackheath; Leicester, Liverpool and King's College. The Irish Ladies Hockey Union had been formed in 1894 and the first Anglo-Irish game took place in 1896. Ireland took the inaugural victory and England returned the compliment in 1897.

The second fixture was advertised and played in front of a paying audience. Briefly after this, Christobel Lawrence (1869–1952) of Roedean tried to raise a motion of no-confidence in Faithfull's leadership of the organisation.[117] She was defeated and obliged to resign for her disloyalty but defence of the moral tone of women's hockey contributed to the high-amateurism which marked the particular approach of the AEWHA. From 1898 until the first international to be held at Wembley stadium, also against an Irish eleven, in 1951 the AEWHA executive would discourage cup competitions, national championships, and leagues. Internationals were to be friendly occasions. This was to prove naïve, as later chapters will outline, since rivalry stimulated interest in the sport and league competition helped the less fortunate, while polite amateur enthusiasm conspicuously did not.

In the meantime, Faithfull had a particular regard for Kingsian Edith Marie Thompson (1877–1961) and for her ambassadorial skills. [118] Edith was the only daughter of W. F. Thompson and has been previously educated at Norland Place School and Cheltenham Ladies' College. Though she took no examinations at King's she was identified as a natural leader: Faithfull accredited her with 'a magic touch' which ensured success in all she undertook combining sympathy, humour, a grasp of essentials and efficiency. She became Secretary to the appeal for Bedford College, Regents Park while in her twenties, for example. Diplomacy was much needed. The working committee of the AEWHA quickly became a Council; an association wishing to be affiliated was required to have at least ten clubs under its jurisdiction and subscriptions were set at £1. 1s. 0. The official uniform of the All England team was stipulated as a white canvas shirt; Cardinal serge skirt; white canvas cap; white silk tie; a sailor last band in cardinal serge and on both the shirt pocket and cap, the rose of the men's association football badge to be displayed. Where necessary, hat-pins were allowed. A rule also established that young women under sixteen years of age were allowed to play in the national team.

By 1898 regional competitions, including county and 'territorial' matches were inaugurated and an extraordinary meeting agreed that Miss Waldron could write a series of articles to publicise the association's activities. Advertising was frowned upon in poster or newspaper form and a proposed Ladies Field Cup (donated by *The Field* newspaper) was rejected in order to discourage trophy-hunting. By 1899 the AEWHA had a balance sheet of £55.11.6. Such was the success of its expansion as a national association within four years that Appendix 1 summarises the list of seventy-two clubs, their date of election and nominated colours. The list should be read advisedly, since clubs could have two, three or more teams, so the scale of activity went beyond what appears to be a straightforward directory.

The final part of this section looks at the sporting and social networks of the women who played hockey. Beneath the veneer of correctness, there was an intensely competitive and lively social culture, with professional coaches, regular practice and much inconvenience. Enthusiasts included historian Eleanor Constance Lodge (1869–1936); soldier Myrtle Maclagan, (1911–1993); parasitologist Gwendolen Rees (1906–1994) and Romani scholar Dora Yates (1879–1974). Edith Thompson reached this wider audience by founding *The Hockey Field* weekly journal in 1901, at a cost of two-pence, and remained as editor until 1920. Thompson later authored *Hockey as a Game for Women* in 1904 setting out both the practical elements and ideals of the AEWHA. These published works were pre-dated by a collaborative scrapbook called *Hockey Jottings* compiled around 1898 by Thompson and two Kensington friends, the sisters Dorothy (1877–1968) and Winifred Gwyn-Jeffreys.[119] The Gwyn-Jeffreys sisters also collaborated with Thompson on the King's College Magazine. The families may well have been friends before the girls were born as they both had holiday homes in Aldeburgh, Suffolk and the girls were all educated at Norland Place when very young.

In *Hockey Jottings* we see E. M. Thompson, known later in life as 'The Grand Old Lady of British Hockey' as a young woman enjoying a considerable degree of social and sporting enjoyment with her friends. Initially led by the teachers in 1895 as 'blue-stocking' and 'New Womanish' hockey at King's changed to something of a craze by 1900 led by the students. Hockey dinners included songs, skits, speeches, toasts, poems and the resulting mix is a rich source for historians of visual and material culture. By 1900 at least 50 of the 450 students took part in organised hockey clubs. Social events, gossip and inter-house rivalry probably involved more. The magazines were a means of social networking, involving speculation over form, technique, uniforms and winning 'colours' of various kinds. The grimly humorous satire of a hockey players' lot is recognisable sports-banter, especially 'The Sad Story of Dorothy Dubbs', an illustrated cartoon about a young Kingsian who plays her hockey on public ground at Wormwood Scrubs. This tragi-comedy details how Dorothy becomes infatuated by the game, playing past the point of exhaustion to die on the pitch. There is clearly a generational message here: Dorothy's mother feared that sport would turn her daughter from a 'nice' girl to an overstrained wreck. Appendix 2 has a selection from the cartoon as well as other poems, satires and excerpts from the scrapbook to give an indication of the tone of the writing.

We can see that the writing and illustrations opened the game up to the non-player for comment and opinion. Dorothy Gwyn-Jeffreys became an artist and book illustrator in later life; while less is known about Winifred other than that she died in Cheltenham in 1975 and wrote a self-published book about her childhood called *A Victorian Nursery* (1973). The stories in *Hockey Jottings* characterise team sport as a means of character-building in a changing world. Written juvenilia might be dismissed as a series of in-jokes were not Faithfull and Thompson to become significant public figures in their own right. All the more useful for what Marwick has called 'unwitting testimony', and intended for circulation rather than publication, the scrapbook gives an insight into young women's ability to transfer sporting sociability into their writing for contemporaries.[120] The writers take on a number of voices at various points in the scrapbook, including that of a visiting patrician journalist, shocked as much by the bicycle propped against the wall as the forthright attitude of his interviewee. Mocking social convention was obviously popular as the state of the pages suggests that the book was passed around and shared.

Nor were the Kingsians alone in this. The University of Bath special collections also house a 'Writing Album' by Gwendoline Parr (née Hollington 1878–1956) written between 1899 and 1909. Parr played hockey at school in Ulster and by 1899 was playing for Holywood Ladies' Hockey Club. In 1901 she was selected to play for Ireland and went on to captain the national team. Her scrapbook contains poetry, literary extracts, a small number of photographs, press clippings and telegrams. Both her father, a GP by profession, and her mother had played hockey to a reasonable standard. In later life, Gwendoline Parr wrote a letter to the hockey player and journalist Marjorie Pollard (1899–1982), relaying her mother's experience of the first England versus Ireland internationals:

> My mother hated the English! Some of her stories about the incidents in the Ireland v England matches were quite unrepeatable. When describing anyone, the most insulting thing she could say was how English they were. Needless to say she went and married an Englishman. I remember her telling me that in some international match the ground was so muddy that she told all the Irish team to cut several inches off their skirts, they beat the English and they stuck to these shorter skirts even after.'[121]

To conclude this section, the influence of the All England Women's Hockey Association was amplified by administrators' work in the education, health and publishing industries. This in turn, helped to spread the message about hockey's respectable image as a school-sport suitable for 'old girls' and adult women from 1895 onwards. However, the dissemination of team sport was not just about the British middle classes. Students and headmistresses perceived games to be important means of creating cultures of excellence in Australia, Canada, South Africa and North America into the Edwardian period.[122] Women developed these cultures across the British Empire to elite Adelaide academic institutions such as Unley Park School, formed in 1855 and run by the Thornber sisters; Hardwicke College (1882); St Peter's Collegiate School for Girls (1894) and Tormore House (1898).[123]

Hockey has been used as an example of how ideas like athletic meritocracy might spread along with the work ethic that this implied. Sport began as physical recreation in women's colleges, meant to address the possible sedentary and intellectual overstrain of academic work. As a student enthusiasm however, hockey and other games became another arena of liberation for women who wanted to strive to become proficient in a particular discipline, make their college team and then, perhaps, win national selection. Sport fit the incremental pattern of much education in that a novice had to work collaboratively in order to become an expert and we might see it as a form of strenuous aspiration allied to academic ambition. In this way, ideologies of women's work and health were subject to a new aesthetic of the active female scholar who studied hard and played vigorously. The 'Games Mistress' passed into popular culture in the twentieth century, sometimes as an inspirational figure but also to denote unattractive, ruthless and unsympathetic traits. Perhaps the apotheosis of this has been the evolution of the character Agatha Trunchbull, who first appeared as an ex-Olympian and Headmistress of Crunchem Hall Primary School in *Matilda* (1988) by Roald Dahl.[124] The Trunchbull, played with considerable relish by Pam Ferris, became more demonic in the 1996 film of the same name and the 2010 adaptation *Matilda: The Musical* featured a man, Bertie Carvel, in the role to critical acclaim. The stereotype is far removed from the sophisticated lives of some Victorian pioneers of women's sport such as Lilian Faithfull, Edith Thompson and their colleagues. It would be a fascinating project to chart the trajectory from historical reality to fictional depiction and may reveal more about how perceptions of teachers of physical education have changed into the twenty-first century.

As the chapter has summarised so far, women writing about sport in Victorian Britain included a small number of working-class and middle-class authors. The next section considers forms of travel writing well beyond the pocket of most ordinary women. These literary pieces were elitist and polemic rather than popular, in the sense of being widely-read. However, they were influential due to strong elements of pedagogy, insider perspective and instruction. Specialist papers like *Sporting Life*, which concentrated on horse racing, or the *Athletic News*, which covered more codes, were often written from an insular perspective, with densely-packed columns crowded on a single page.[125] Newspapers have been used in sport history, often to mine factual details, at the expense of other literature. Though comprised of short pieces blending fictive and non-fiction elements, many of the edited collections popular from the 1880s onwards give a different perspective than the press. The concluding section therefore develops the theme of women writing sport as experts and opinion-leaders. Field sports writing allowed women to mediate their experience of the sporting moment; describe corporeal pleasure derived from physical activity and partly define British female character in a broader context of colonialism and imperialism.

CONCLUSION

A Sharp, Brisk Gallop over Turfy Downs: Women Writing Field Sports

As swimming and hockey have indicated, Victorian sport and leisure were synonymous with travel and touring. Swimmers such as Agnes Beckwith often lived at subsistence level and so attempted to use overseas markets for their talents. Hockey had ties with Ireland and would later follow British Empire connections, partly prompted by the interests of Faithfull and Thompson in career opportunities for women overseas. A wider enthusiasm for entertainment, active leisure, education and technological advances helped the diffusion of sport generally. At the same time, the news appeared more quickly in print and sport-related writing grew rapidly in the nineteenth century. Swimming and hockey were part of these processes but field sports were perhaps the most prestigious and literaturised because of their links with aristocracy at home and the British Empire abroad.[126] Given the relative neglect of the nineteenth-century novel, serialised fiction, poetry, drama and non-fiction texts like the *Oxford Dictionary of National Biography* (first printed in 1885) and other reference works in the academic literature on sport, there is considerable scope for further research beyond what is possible in this segment.

The best work on professional sports writing has tended to come from the United States and this includes work on women.[127] Originally born in Scotland, James Gordon Bennett Senior used sport such as horse racing, cricket and prize fighting from 1835 to boost the circulation of his newspaper *The New York Herald* combined with a style of journalism based on interviews, scandal and topicality.[128] Joseph Pulitzer ran a sports department at the campaigning *New York World* focusing on horse racing, yachting, boxing and baseball.[129] Women sports journalists included Irish-born Midy (Maria) Morgan (1828–1892), who worked on *The New York Times* from 1869. Morgan was able to transfer interests in judging stock, horse breeding and racing to become a reporter.

New journalistic styles included famous 'stunt girls' who would nar-
rate their own record-breaking feats. Among the first was Nellie Bly, a
pseudonym for Elizabeth Cochrane Seaman (1864–1922), who worked for
Pulitzer at the *World*, reporting, amongst other things, on prize-fights. On
14 November 1889 Nellie Bly left New York by ship in an attempt to beat
the feat made famous by French author Jules Verne; circling the globe in
less than eighty days.[130] On 25 January 1890 Bly succeeded having taken
seventy-two days, six hours and eleven minutes to travel just under 25,000
miles for a reported cost of $1,500.[131] A contemporary, Elizabeth Bisland
(1861–1929) who worked for John Brisben Walker's *Cosmopolitan* journal, had set off to out-do her in the opposite direction and completed the
feat in seventy-six days.[132] Bly and Bisland's stories were intended to be
entertaining, rather than strictly accurate. Vicarious travel was not limited to reading and the lone woman traveller became replicated in popular
culture. The same year J. A. Grozier copyrighted a 'Game of Round the
World with Nelly Bly [sic]: a novel and fascinating game of Land and Sea'
incorporating stops at Aden, Pekin [sic], Manila and Yokohama.[133] The
collectibles market subsequently diversified. These products unfixed travel
from actual geography and 'turned it into metaphor at the very moment
when its cultural significance began to shift under the twofold pressures of
a burgeoning global tourism industry and overseas national expansion.'[134]

The sense of physical contest to many field sports enthusiasts was also
about appearing to dominate a challenging natural environment. It helped,
of course, if you were armed and your intended prey was not. Henry Somerset, the eighth Duke of Beaufort was influenced by the fashion for gaz-
etteers, dictionary compilation and other reference works to found the
Badminton Library, named after his country estate. The series sought to
bring together the sports and pastimes indulged in by upper-class English
men and women in one succession of volumes. Beaufort expected *The Badminton Library of Sports and Pastimes* to be complete before the end of
the nineteenth century and dedicated the series to the Prince of Wales with
the fond note, 'Often have I seen His Royal Highness knocking over driven
grouse or partridges and high-rocketing pheasants in first-rate workman-
like style [sic].'[135] As an aristocrat by birthright and sportsman by profession, it was the highest compliment that Beaufort could give the future King
Edward VII. The first six editions of the Badminton Library comprised
Hunting (1885); *Fishing: Salmon & Trout* (1885); *Fishing: Pike & Coarse
Fish* (1885); *Racing & Steeple-Chasing* (1886); *Shooting: Field & Covert*
(1886) and *Shooting: Moor & Marsh* (1886). Modern sports followed in
1887, with the release of *Cycling* and *Athletics and Football*. Two further
volumes on *Boating* and *Cricket* appeared in 1888.

An expert wrote each chapter of the edited collections and the Badminton Library therefore represented an attempt at a comprehensive, authoritative view of sport synonymous with an elite perspective. There are whole
volumes that do not mention women, for example *Pike and Other Coarse*

Fish. However, in *Salmon and Trout* Henry Cholmondeley-Pennell, author of *The Modern Practical Angler* who had also been Her Majesty's Inspector of Sea-Fisheries, exhorted women anglers to wear a simple short skirt of Linsey wool; an all-wool Norfolk jacket and boots of porpoise hide. He styled them:

> A modern Dame Juliana, punt-fishing under the dip of a Thames chestnut tree in August, or later in the autumn sending her spinning bait skimming into the foam below Hurley Weir. How much of a pleasure, now lost to most of us, is gained by the man whose wife takes heartily to fishing or hunting or whatever other field sport he is devoted to. In this way she becomes not only his helpmate at home, but his 'chum' and true comrade when on his rambles by flood and field.[136]

These differences in practice were partly due to salmon fishing's unprecedented vogue in the second half of the nineteenth century, whereas coarse angling retained connotations of poaching and customary practices.[137] Prominent sportswomen also wrote articles in the *Badminton* series. Lady Georgiana Curzon (1825–1906) authored a chapter on 'Tandem Driving' and appeared to have an admirable constitution: 'We are often told that a tandem is the most dangerous mode of conveyance ever invented by the human mind. There is some truth I concede especially if the persons concerned are afflicted with that unfortunate complaint, "want of nerve".'[138] The *Badminton Library* defended the rural as an antidote to the spread of urban living and driving in 1889 still referred to carriages rather than motor-cars, although this would change within the next ten years.

The series became more concerned with women as it became further suburbanised when *Golf* and *Tennis* were added to its volumes in 1890, *Skating* in 1892, then *Swimming* in 1893. Lottie Dod contributed a chapter in the book on tennis at the height of her fame.[139] Mrs Lilly Groves edited the volume on *Dance* in 1895 and felt compelled to defend its comparative frivolousness relative to field sports.[140] As the chapter by the Countess of Ancaster (1846–1921) made clear though, hosting dances entailed a considerable degree of competitive hospitality. In spite of Beaufort's original plans, by 1902 *Motors and Motor Driving* articulated the frustrations of urban, suburban and rural travel in the twentieth century. Later, imitation publications, like the contribution by Susan, Countess of Malmesbury (1854–1935), on *Cycling* for The Suffolk Sporting Series in 1908, also showed a sense of compressed space for different modes of transport.

Writing chapters and editing whole books was a relatively expensive and exclusive way of entering the spaces and places of knowledge. Books were an agent in the circulation of sporting information, combining visual expression and a physical platform. As the case of Midy Morgan indicates, sporting expertise could be a highly portable set of skills but the books themselves were relatively cumbersome, involving complex syntactical structures and therefore less widely circulated than newspapers. These texts remain valuable on several levels, not least for what they tell historians about the assumed readership and the implicit values that were used to shape narrative.

As multi-layered sources, there is an intricate interplay of self-expression, heritage and erudition. First, the pleasure of sport is evident. Beatrice Violet, Lady Greville (1842–1932) was unequivocal on the benefits of a life in the great outdoors:

> It is scarcely necessary nowadays to offer an apology for sport, with its entrancing excitement, its infinite variety of joys and interests. Women cheerfully share with men, hardships, toil and endurance, climb mountains, sail on the seas, face wind and rain and the chill gusts of winter, as unconcernedly as they once followed their quiet occupations by their firesides. The feverish life of cities too, with its enervating pleasures, is forgotten and neglected for the witchery of legitimate sport, which need not be slaughter or cruelty. Women who prefer exercise and liberty, who revel in the cool sea breeze, and love to feel the fresh mountain air fanning their cheeks who are afraid neither of a little fatigue nor of a little exertion are the better, the truer, and the healthier, and can remain essentially feminine in their thoughts and manners.[141]

It may seem to be a stretch to link Nellie Bly and Lady Greville, but there is evidence in both women's writing of searching out excitement and enduring the elements. Their journeys had quite different purposes however: for Bly the voyage was a means to provide an interesting narrative to support herself and she married a millionaire several years her senior before retiring from journalism. Greville, like most of the writers in this section, did little obvious work and was not employed in the conventional sense of having to earn a living. Indeed, her considerable leisure was more likely to entail manual labour on behalf of others. However, a large house had to be run and a social calendar maintained. Greville's *Ladies in the Field* combined travelogue with a spiritual sense of nature.

> There are emotions deeply seated in the joy of exercise, when the body is brought into play, and masses move in concert, of which the subject is but half conscious . . . The mystery of rhythm and associated energy and blood-tingling in sympathy is here . . . There are days when your very soul would seem to penetrate the grass, when with the smell of damp earth in your nostrils and the rhythm of blood stirring stride underneath you, your forget everything, yourself included. These days live with you.[142]

Secondly, a focus on the character-building aspects of challenge reflects generational concerns with birthright, legacy and Empire.[143] A sensual evocation of the pleasures of sport could therefore coalesce with a sense of placelessness. While the worship of the humble shires was obviously intended to evoke a sense of the British countryside, foreign travel might be contextualised by a parochial world-view. This can make for uncomfortable reading today. Greville's second chapter of *Ladies in the Field*, 'Riding in Ireland and India', reduces the complexity of the Indian sub continent to a pre-breakfast hunting experience devoid of the 'hairy fences' that could be expected in Britain, followed by a leisurely bath and large morning meal taken on a verandah. The debates over Home Rule for Ireland were ignored entirely. This was perhaps surprising considering that Greville's husband was a Liberal MP for Westmeath from 1865 to 1874, the constituency had two MPs and from 1871 the second was Patrick Smyth of the Home Rule Party. An Englishwoman, whose father was also a career politician, Greville may have considered that sport was an escape from affairs of state. It was not a distraction from birthright however, and in some ways the figure of the intrepid sportswoman kept the virtues of the family line prominently on display.

Other contributors to *Ladies in the Field* included Kathleen Florence May, Duchess of Newcastle (1872–1955); Mildred, Lady Boynton (1855–1915) and Rosie Anstruther-Thomson (1872–1956), the daughter of notable Master of Hounds Colonel John Anstruther-Thomson of Charleton and Carntyne. The book chapters include shooting tigers and deer-stalking; kangaroo-hunting; cycling; punting and riding to hounds. Some of the authors took establishment perspectives with them on their travels and, in writing about their overseas experiences, effectively commodified these memories for a domestic audience; albeit a select one. Several women who wrote about field sports were personally bound up with the practicalities of the British Empire and invested their narratives with the character-building qualities of sport, particularly the exportation of invented British traditions of 'pluck' and fair play. Kate Martelli describes a Maharaja as a 'minor' administrator to her husband who was a political agent and superintendent of the estates of Rewa, Central India. Armed with a 450 double-express rifle on a hunt with her husband and sister, Martelli received the memorable advice 'If you don't kill the tiger he will kill you' and took her shot.[144] The phrase has resonance far beyond the author's immediate situation. In this sense, the aristocratic or upper-middle-class female adventurer embodied processes of international travel and imperialism.

Thirdly, while women such as Martelli might have begun as novices they became experts, in part, through the act of writing. Accounts that emphasised the transcendent effects of vigorous sport also informed readers about the practicalities of mastering particular disciplines. Bearing in mind that Greville had written extensively on how to flirt, likening a girl's attitude to a her intended beau as equivalent to a war-horse scenting a battle, there were many practical hints and tips on how sport should be done.[145] Coaching points included good posture and attitude, with the Duchess of

Newcastle opining: 'Anyone with bad hands can never be a really good rider
. . . Always endeavour—should your horse come down with you, and you
have not parted company—to keep your presence of mind.'[146] There was a
predictable line of advice that 'Deer-stalking is like marriage, it should not
be taken lightly', while Mildred Boynton charmingly encouraged novices
with a shotgun to persevere, 'Even though at present, your efforts are rather
like the old woman's false teeth "they misses as often as they hits".'[147]

Finally, it is worth saying that attitudes to blood and field sports could
change. Lady Florence Dixie (1855–1905) was born in Dumfries, the youngest of the six children of Archibald William Douglas, the eighth marquis
of Queensberry.[148] Having married and had two sons, she set off for South
America in 1878 for six months, writing about her trek in *Across Patago-
nia* (1880). She then became a reporter on the war in South Africa. Known
in these situations to have her gun as ready as her pen, in later life Dixie
became convinced of the cruelty of blood sports, which she denounced
in *Horrors of Sport* (1891) and the *Mercilessness of Sport* (1901). In the
broader sense of how Dixie's class occupied their time, had an affinity for
sport and a vocation to share their expertise, women equestrians and field
sports enthusiasts provide examples of where particular kinds of influence
trickled down from the aristocracy.

The book is just one type of material history considered in this chapter.
The opening quotation was a fragment that is attributed to Mrs Professor Beckwith and may, or may not, have been written by her. As well as
considering women involved in the production of sport itself, the argument has looked at some connections with the other cultural industries and
with multiple representations of sport, leisure and work. In taking as the
key theme sporting variety, the examples show that the social and cultural
impact of modern sport were therefore wide-ranging and connected with
other industries. If swimming and female education had their own considerable literature by the end of the Victorian period, the number of texts
which discuss field sports in the period would seem to be more extensive,
as indicated by the generalist catalogues at the British library and those at
specialist holdings such as the National Sporting Library in Middleburg,
Virginia.[149] Sources include reports of race days; riding manuals (including
the correct attire to wear on different occasions); compendia of important
people and places; travelogues; books on the care of animals, biographies
and fiction. The chapter has scarcely done justice to this literature but it has
begun to analyse some of the ways in which the larger body of work might
be approached.

Along with fine art, toys and clothing the range of field sports shows an
enduring link between the aristocracy and other classes. There are clear
trends that many women who played sport and moved into education, also
sometimes wrote about their experiences. Both Ida Mann (1893–1983) and
Gladys Wauchope (1889–1966) drew analogies in their autobiographical
writing between the quest for medical knowledge and the pursuit of an

elusive quarry. Mann, having escaped life as a Post Office clerk, became an Ophthalmologist; the first woman professor at Oxford University in 1944, and entitled her memoirs *The Chase*.[150] Our perception of Victorian sport and leisure has improved through critical engagement with material history and culture. Connections with the British Empire have had a very brief treatment here and it is a topic to which the argument will return in subsequent chapters. The examples have sought to address the question of how women shaped prevailing conceptions of sport across classes, as well as examining how new markets for female work and leisure transformed.

By the end of the nineteenth century, the gendered body was at the centre of representations of sport. Greville summed up the situation: 'Women too have rushed in where mothers fear to tread. Little girls on ponies may be seen holding their own nobly out hunting, while Hyde Park, during the season, is filled with fair, fresh-looking girls in straw hats, covert coats and shirts, driving away the cobwebs of dissipation and the deleterious effects of hot rooms by a mild canter in the early morning.'[151] Women and girls on horseback were symbolically important as participants in a fashionable and expensive leisure activity, but also displaying an entitlement to resources alongside urban promenades, balls and assemblies, music-making and other genteel pursuits. Educational, economic, and political fluxes brought women more fully into public life as citizens and this shaped sport through the rise of the women entrepreneurs pedagogues, administrators and writers. The case studies briefly considered here were indications of a much larger set of conversations and processes, including British migration to the dominions and post-colonial countries. Diverse possibilities for female empowerment were engendered by sport in the nineteenth century. It is to the topic of individual women's physical assertiveness and how networks of female sporting authority developed in the twentieth century that the next chapter now turns.

2   The Olympic Games, Popular Imperialism and the "Woman Question"

Athletic girls have a great pull over their sisters. If you are skilled and well drilled in discipline and sportsmanship, you are bound to benefit in the strife of the world. You are the better able to face disappointments and sorrows. For what do these strenuous games mean? Exercise in the open air, and exercise of a thorough and engrossing character, carried out with cheerful and stimulating surroundings, with scientific methods, rational aims and absorbing chances. Surely that is the foundation of health culture.[1]

As the previous chapter has indicated, a transnational network of women's sporting interest expanded in the second half of the nineteenth century. New kinds of education and social health provision were often the result of self-conscious innovation but could have unintended consequences on leisure and sporting competition. By 1900, 'Women were emerging as a political and social force—they were getting jobs, travelling, motoring, cycling, joining clubs for their hobbies and becoming avid readers of magazines.'[2] Popular entertainment, voluntarism, and the amateur ethos behind many codified sports shaped activities in uneven ways. Victorian booms in croquet, cycling, golf, mountaineering, skating, tennis and field sports had involved a range of female consumers from the expanding middle and upper classes. Swimming involved the lower orders too.[3] Much biographical and life-writing material remains to be developed for female athletes during this period more generally. For instance, Mark Ryan's biography of the 1902 Wimbledon women's singles winner Muriel Robb (1878–1907), who came from Jesmond, Newcastle Upon Tyne reminds us that elite Edwardian women's tennis was by no means just a London-based or Southern phenomenon.[4]

Cosmopolitan perspectives informed individual physical disciplines and women's team sports. For example, what appears to have been the first home international women's association football match took place on the 9 May 1881 when a team calling themselves England played a side named Scotland at Easter Road, Edinburgh.[5] Scotland won 3–0 thanks to goals from Lily St Clair, Louise Cole, and the combined play of Georgina Wright and Isa Stevenson. Although the teams played seven matches that have been identified, some of which may have used rugby rules, information remains patchy and it seems that some players moved from one squad to the other. Edinburgh versus Grimsby scheduled a match in 1887, leading the English port to claim the first women's football club side, though working women in Sunderland also played. A London-based team, the British Ladies Football Club (BLFC), was founded in 1895 with Secretary Nettie Honeyball, although genealogical searches have been unable to ascertain whether she used a pseudonym or shortened given name.[6] The BLFC also played in Scotland and the north-east. Although Lady Florence Dixie agreed to act as President and promoted the club in newspaper interviews, the experiment lasted for less than two seasons, as did the Original English Lady Cricketers professional touring team formed the same year.[7] However, female sports associations with international ties could endure, as the case of hockey and gymnastics has already shown. The White Heather Club, formed in 1887 by eight noblewomen, in Nun Appleton, Yorkshire had fifty members three years later. Most club members were from the highest ranks of society and only two of the original founders lacked a title. The Club was to enjoy a celebration lunch to mark the fortieth anniversary of its founding in 1927.[8]

Broader concerns about Britain's place in the world impacted upon female sport and leisure. The reverses in South Africa, combined with militarisation in Europe and Asia mitigated any sense of domestic self-satisfaction.[9] As America and Germany industrialised with increasing efficiency, moral panics about a loss of national vitality extended to the National Service League (NSL), set up in 1901 to defend the empire and British independence. Public interest in the vigour of the nation also led to legislation, like the Public Health Act of 1907, permitting local authorities to spend more money on recreation and games.[10] Nationalism enhanced civilian militarism, evidenced in an unlikely way through the enthusiasm of a dozen young women who went along to a large Scout Rally at the Crystal Palace on 4 September 1909. The Girl Guide movement had antecedents; such as the use by Charlotte Mason (1842–1923) of excerpts from *Aids to Scouting* (1899) by Robert Baden-Powell in her school teaching and Parent's National Education Union (PNEU) work.[11] Baden-Powell's reputation rested on his heroism in South Africa, especially at the defence of Mafeking, and by the time of the Crystal Palace rally, some 6,000 girls had already registered as 'Boy Scouts'. These foundations aided a rapid expansion of the Guides for at least as many women as girls, although the process of incorporation into the Scout movement was a gradual one. For instance, by 1910 the Nottingham branch of the Girl Guides had 450 members; of these 300 were considered seniors; 80 registered as juniors and 70 enlisted as intermediates (under fourteen years of age).[12]

The perception that previous empires had declined, at home and abroad, due to moral decay underpinned the Girl Guides' ethos to build 'character' through voluntary or civic service. Offering a means of individual fulfillment and social improvement, the publication of *How Girls Can Help Build Up the Empire: A Handbook for Girl Guides* in 1912 made the imperialist tone of the movement explicit.[13] Guide patrols may have had flowers or birds as symbols (rather than lions or leopards as the Scouts had) but it was equally significant that young women were passing badges in life-saving, trekking, gymnastics and so on, wearing an adaptation of military uniform. Girl Guides were encouraged to know about their own country and the wider British Empire.[14] This interest was to reflect the much larger patterns that would take place in other welfare initiatives before World War One. Whether it was to camp in the countryside or travel further afield, personal mobility improved across classes, as did the use of mass communications: increasing numbers of 'ordinary' women and girls wanted to go 'on tour'. There were considerable ambiguities in the value of the Girl Guides for young women but among the messages broadcast by the movement were calls for international harmony and reconciliation.

This chapter focuses on the interplay of nationalistic discourse and friendly international competition in the early versions of the Olympic Games organised by the International Olympic Committee (IOC) after it was founded in 1894 until the outbreak of the First World War. The modern Olympic movement revised the ancient Greek Games to suit the tastes of anglophile French aristocrat, Pierre de Coubertin.[15] His ideas for a modern version of the Olympic Games developed out of a concern for nationwide fitness in France and an internationalist outlook, whereby co-operation though sporting contests could replace military aggression.[16] First held in Athens in 1896, resistance to historical re-enactment of chariot racing and the like indicates that Coubertin and his colleagues aspired to modern sports or current versions of much older activities. The Olympics Games moved, just as people went to it in order to compete, look-on and officiate. What began as a relatively small festival nevertheless set a pattern that was copied by later tournament organisers in other sports. The travelling sporting mega-event would evolve during the twentieth century.[17]

Early Olympic sporting spectacle owed much to the popularity of Exhibition technologies. There is evidence that the commercial aspects of these exhibitions concerned amateur administrators who wished to keep sport somehow pure from profitable motives.[18] There is debate about whether two women did, or did not, compete in the marathon at about the same time as the 1896 Athens competitions. From the inclusion of female athletes in the Paris edition in 1900, the Games highlighted some existing transnational aspects of women's sport and made them more visible. Paradoxically, we know relatively little about famous sportswomen, such the first British female Olympic champion, now recognised as a gold medalist, Charlotte Cooper Sterry (1870–1966), who took two tennis titles in Paris. She won a money prize as medals were not given to participants at this time. Later Olympians, Lottie Dod and Dorothea Lambert Chambers (1878–1960) also held Wimbledon championships several times over before they took their Olympic titles (in archery and tennis respectively). All of them wrote briefly about their philosophy of tennis at what, then, was the highest level: Dod in *Tennis* (1890), part of the Badminton Library series, Sterry and, more extensively, Chambers in *Lawn Tennis for Ladies* (1910).[19]

The established networks for women's tennis, golf, yachting, balloon flight, equestrianism and croquet help to understand why certain activities could be incorporated into the Olympic schedule well before other sports.

Another factor was the Paris Exposition, which was held at the same time as the Games. Defined by a Palace of Optics and an illuminated Celestial Globe, the Exposition celebrated both technological and cultural modernity.[20] Live pigeon shooting might seem a gory anachronism now, but the example suggests the suburbanisation of field sports and a cross-class interest in gadgetry; guns included. Also peripheral to the trade show, in St Louis 'anthropological' displays made curiosities out of groups of indigenous people and the women's programme was limited to six American female archery competitors.[21]

In May 1905 the British Olympic Association (BOA) was formed by representatives of national governing bodies from the following sports: archery, Association football, track and field athletics, cycling, fencing, rowing, Rugby football, skating, swimming and life-saving. The BOA was initially led by the politician and sportsman William Henry Grenfell, Lord Desborough.[22] The principle of moving the Olympic festival to host cities every four years unlocked it from a specific place. The Greek Olympic Committee made an unsuccessful gesture to 'reclaim' the Games as permanent hosts in the Inter Calated Games of 1906 and athletes registered as representatives of their national associations from then onwards.[23] Desborough was President of the Olympic Games held in London in 1908 and, along with his wife Ettie (1867–1952), turned a sporting event into a society occasion with many lavish entertainments.[24] The associated Franco-British Exhibition of 1908 was an elaborate kaleidoscope of influences, and the stadium, although purpose built, was a more basic structure.[25] Several 'firsts' were established in 1908, including the introduction of winter events, like skating; the adoption of an Olympic Charter and the Marathon distance became changed from forty kilometres to 26 miles 385 yards (42 km 195 m) to suit the whims of the Royal family.[26]

There were approximations of 1,971 male competitors in London, compared with a minumum of forty-four registered female athletes.[27] Women took part in five sports in 1908: archery, ice-skating, motor-boat racing, lawn tennis and yachting. This was supplemented by diving and gymnastics demonstrations. Having narrowly missed inclusion, women's swimming first entered the Olympic schedule in 1912 and remained from then on.[28] Even though women made up only a small percentage of the athletes in London, a prominent narrative around the Olympic Games included the political radicalism of the suffragettes and threatened disruption as a result. Bombs, hoaxes and arson were 'classic acts of terrorism' used in a bid to be part of the governance of the country but sport could also showcase the discipline and camaraderie of feminist principles.[29] A growing sense of transnational activism began to call for sport as a right for women into the Edwardian period and beyond. By the time the Olympic Games would return to London in 1948, there would be something like 390 female and 3,714 male competitors.

Alongside competitions in literature, music, painting, sculpture and town planning, Roche has called the effect of social democracy and feminism on the wider Olympic movement, its ideology, rules and rituals 'alternative internationalism'.[30] Barney has suggested that the Stockholm Games of 1912: 'Signalled the arrival of the Olympic Games as the world's premier international sporting event' due to control of the programme by officials of the international sports federations, rather than by individual organising committees.[31] By way of illustration, the Amateur Swimming Association (ASA) consistently declared that it had insufficient funds to help British entrants to Olympic Games but it had international connections by 1907. On 19 July 1908 the Fédération Internationale de Natation (FINA) was formed and the ASA welcomed Olympic and other regular international amateur competition, in large part because it increased the prestige of British swimmers.[32] While British men had competed in aquatic events with considerable success since the first Athens Games, women were to benefit from increased international co-operation when they also began to contest Olympic medals in 1912. Thereafter, athletes' bodies became more visible and the mediation of those bodies increased with the popularity of the Olympic Games.[33]

This atmosphere of technological innovation at the Paris, London and Stockholm Games was part of a wider shift in which the gaze of the spectator became an active part in constructing the event.[34] Audiences could accessorise their role as onlookers and this opened up the sporting goods, toys, games and trinkets market. The increasingly revealed athletic body also led to changes in the markets for sports clothing and uniforms.[35] Just as telescopes enabled climbs in the Alps to be seen from afar by observers, and so sportised a new arena, the Olympics staged quadrennial sporting spectacle. There remains no national museum of sport in England, or a unified public collection of British Olympic artifacts at the time of writing. Though 'legacy' became a somewhat catch-all term in the context of the third London Games in 2012, the occasion did provide an impetus on behalf of academics, museums, libraries and archives to think about the local history and material culture left by previous Games. Re-evaluation of the history of our Olympic sporting heroes has been a considerable reward for the loss of clarity in what legacy might actually mean and how it can be measured. Therefore, after a brief overview of the early female Olympians, the chapter analyses some prominent popular discourses surrounding their participation.

FROM CHATTIE STERRY TO JENNIE FLETCHER: EARLY BRITISH WOMEN OLYMPIANS

A large body of writing has illustrated how the anglophile revivalist of the Olympic Games in modern times, Pierre De Coubertin, was influenced by the success of the British public schools as training grounds in a brand of upper-middle-class masculinity.[36] Team sports in particular were thought to be character building.[37] The founder of the IOC was not an enthusiast of women's sport, however the gradual rise in the number and variety of female athletes indicates that his control of the Olympic Games themselves were somewhat precarious. It is not a story that needs re-telling here. Research that is primarily concerned to detail the prejudice of Coubertin and the IOC can expend considerable energy for small gain. For example, Anita De Frantz has used IOC minutes to argue for a so-far unacknowledged place for Countess Bertha Von Suttner (1843–1914), briefly secretary to Alfred Nobel, as one of fifty leading citizens to attend the first International Olympic Congress at the Sorbonne in 1894.[38] Ana Maria Miragaya has used Bertha Von Suttner's biography to argue that 2,000 people were present but only men spoke at the Congress.[39] The reference to a Von Suttner, according to Miragaya, was to Bertha's deceased father-in-law, not she herself.

The question of inclusion however, is still significant because the IOC did not elect women officials until the final third of the twentieth century. French swimmer and journalist, Monique Berlioux (1925) was to become uniquely powerful beginning in 1969, and would eventually become Director of the International Olympic Committee until she was required to resign in 1985 due to disagreements with the incumbent President, Juan Antonio Samaranch.[40] However, the lack of women in some governing bodies of world-sport did not prevent rising numbers of women from competing in Olympic events (however broadly they might be defined). Olympic appearances could also be part of well-established sporting careers and, of that longer involvement, not necessarily the most significant aspect.

The exact number of Olympic participants remains a subject over which there is some equivocation. In Paris for example, the Exhibition also took place from 14 May to 28 October. Not only did this time-span give scope for a considerable range of activities, it would appear that some competitors did not know whether they were taking part in the World Fair or Olympic Games events. The media called the festival as a whole 'International Games', 'World Championships' and the 'Grand Prix of the Paris Exposition'.[41] The consensus view is that women participated in two sports (tennis and golf), and some acknowledgement is usually made of either croquet or yachting but rarely both. At least five countries were represented in female events: Bohemia, France, Great Britain, Switzerland and US but mixed competition and participants who held dual nationality involved a more complex set of identities. It is difficult to be definitive. Many of the participants, including some women who could be regarded as Olympians, are still not acknowledged as having taken part by the IOC today.

Whatever these difficulties of quantifying who did what, the exhibition movement was to have direct benefits for women's sport between 1900 and 1908 in spite of De Coubertin's antipathy to female athletes.[42] Coubertin recognised the value of the exhibition but by 1899 had withdrawn from active involvement in the schedule for Paris. For both men and women, the programme of Olympic sports took some considerable time to regularise, as the examples of cricket, curling, lacrosse, motor (car, bike and boat) racing, polo, rugby, tug of war and velocipede competitions indicate.[43] Whole sports and particular disciplines have sometimes been in, and then out of, the schedule. The inclusion of women on the United States team in 1900 led to debates about how this affected definitions of amateurism across the major sports bodies. It is fairly clear that all the women in 1900 were amateurs, mostly of the middle class. However this was to change quickly and by 1912 the working-class female amateur swimmer was part of Britain's medal hopes.

Tedder and Daniels suggest that the first female gold-medallist in Paris was American-Swiss yachtswoman Hélène de Pourtalès (1868–1945) who sailed the *Lérina* with her husband to victory on 22 May 1900; competed again on 23 June and finished second in a race two days later.[44] An Italian equestrian, born in Russia, Elvira Guerra (1855–1937) rode her horse *Libertin* in the Hacks and Hunter class but this was later discounted from Olympic competition.[45] Balloonist, Madame Maison, who sailed with her husband to fourth place in an endurance race, was similarly almost lost to the record and we have few details about French croquet players Filleaul Brohy, Marie Ohnier and Madamoiselle Desprès.[46] Croquet competitions included women-only and open disciplines and Mallon has argued that Madame Brohy and Mademoiselle Ohnier may now be considered the first two women Olympians.[47]

Out of an entry of six female tennis players, British Wimbledon star, Charlotte 'Chattie' Cooper won against Frenchwoman Hélèn Prevost (perhaps Yvonne Hélèn, 1880-unknown) in the singles final, held in July. . Curiously, both Marion Jones (1879–1965, later Farqhar) of the US and Hedwig Rosenbaum (also known as Hedwiga Rosenbaumová, 1880–1927) of Bohemia are credited on the current IOC website as being bronze medalists for the women's singles.[48] Cooper also won the mixed doubles title with Reginald Doherty, making her a double-gold medalist, but this is not listed on the official IOC site.[49] Biographical details on Prevost have been difficult to track, but she also appears to have won the silver medal in the mixed doubles with a Scottish-born player of Irish descent, Harold Mahoney; Rosenbaum and Jones were both credited bronze medalists with British partners Archibald Warden and Laurence Doherty respectively. Golfer Margaret Abbott (1876–1955) was one of four Americans competing against six French women. Abbott would now be considered the first female US gold medalist, with her compatriots Pauline 'Polly' Whittier (1876–1946) and Daria Pratt (later Karageorgevich, 1859–1938) winning silver and bronze respectively, although Whittier represented the Golf Club de Saint-Moritz.[50] Charlotte Cooper was given a cash voucher for the singles and doubles win in Paris, not a medal. However, her singles achievments have retrospectively become recognised as equivalent to a gold medal.

Pourtalès narrowly beat Cooper to become the first woman to win an Olympic championship, Daniels and Tedder suggest, the former in an open category rarely acknowledged in 'official' histories.[51] Bill Mallon does not recognise Pourtalès as a competitor but acknowledges that she may have co-owned the vessel and dismisses ballooning on the grounds that, like motor-sport, it was power-assisted performance.[52] This appears questionable and seems not to read the evidence in its context at the time but he is by no means alone in these interpretations. Some IOC members accept that at least twenty-two women took part in 1900, including six tennis players, one yachts-woman, three croquet players, ten golfers, one balloonist and one equestrian.[53] Other participants may well come to light, especially a second female sailor, though the IOC database lists just the seven individual medallists for tennis and golf.[54] In 1904 all of the six female contestants at the St Louis Exposition were United States archers, who competed across three disciplines (the team, the double Columbia and the double National rounds).[55] Matilda Scott Howell (1859–1938) became a triple winner. A 'non-Olympic' women's shooting competition was won by Mabel Taylor of the US.

At the 1908 London Games, archers William and Lottie Dod won a gold and a silver respectively, to become the first brother and sister medallists.[56] Lottie had beaten ninety-nine competitors to take the Royal Toxophilite Society Ladies' Day Gold Medal in 1906, in spite of having only recently joined Welford Park Archers after moving to Newbury. Women's archery competitions often had a larger field than men's and in this the Olympics was an exception with twenty-seven in the male competition and twenty-five in the female.[57] Dod was ahead on the first day in blustery conditions, only to falter on the second and final day of competition, losing the gold medal to Sybil 'Queenie' Newall (1854–1929) of Cheltenham Archers, with Beatrice Hill-Lowe (1868–1951) of Archers of the Teme coming third.[58] This was a record-making result, aside from the achievement of the Dod siblings. At fifty-three years and 275 days, Newall was still the oldest woman to win an Olympic gold medal at the end of the twentieth century. Born in County Louth, and from a well-known family, Hill-Lowe became Ireland's first female Olympic medallist.

Dod may have previously taken up archery at the home of Alice Blanche Legh (1856–1948) when both families lived in Cheshire. Canadian-born Alice Legh was to return to England with her family to Grange-over-Sands, north Lancashire in 1862 and her parents helped re-establish the fashionable status of archery.[59] Though it was not a sport at which she naturally excelled like tennis, Lottie Dod was a close friend of the family before she moved south. After her first victory in 1881 Alice Legh lost the national title to her mother for four consecutive years, she then retained it for seven years from 1886 to 1892 and held it for another successive eight-year period between 1902 and 1909. Overall, Alice would hold twenty-three archery championship titles between 1881 and 1922; a record that remains unbeaten.

Although she won cash awards, equipment and significant amounts of jewellery, Legh considered herself to be an amateur because she paid to enter contests. Tennis players and golfers similarly collected valuable trophies, cups and trinkets. As an 'authority', Legh contributed an article on 'Ladies' Archery' in the text on the sport for the Badminton series, edited by C. J. Longman and H. Walrond.[60] However, Legh did not compete at the 1908 Games, preferring to defend her national title a week later. It would also appear that she chose stand aside for her protégé Queenie Newall.[61] Legh beat Newall by over 150 points to win the 1908 national competition. Newall repaid the compliment by retaining the title for two seasons in 1911 and 1912. Although the war interrupted her athletic career, Newall was still competing in 1928, the year before her death. Dod was therefore the third best woman archer of her time, even by quite generous estimates.

In addition to the twenty-five women archers, Sylvia Marshall Gorham accompanied her husband aboard *Quicksilver* in the motor-boat racing; Frances Rivett-Carnac (née Greenstock 1875–1962) was on board *Heroine* in the 7-metre sailing class and the Duchess of Westminster, Constance Edwina Grosvenor (formerly Lewes, 1876–1970), sailed as owner on her yacht *Sorais*, but is cited in many texts as an additional crew member rather than as an Olympic competitor.[62] In the indoor tennis, Britain's Gwendoline Eastlake-Smith (1883–1941) won the gold and Angela Greene (sometimes called Alice, 1879–1956) the silver medal, while Märtha Adlerstrahle (1868–1956) took bronze for Sweden. Eastlake-Smith celebrated victory by marrying another tennis player, Dr Wharram Henry Lamplough, two days later and competed in 'married-doubles' competitions thereafter.[63] The women's singles was an all-British medal board won by Dorothea Lambert Chambers, over Penelope Boothby (1881–1970) and Ruth Winch (1870–1952).

The women's skating individual competition gold medal went to Florence 'Madge' Syers (1881–1917), who had come out of retirement to compete, and Dorothy Greenhough-Smith (1882–1965) took third place.[64] Else Rendschmidt (1886–1969) won the silver medal for Germany. London-born Syers had entered the World Figure Skating Championships in 1902, forcing the International Skating Union to accept women, as there were no rules to prevent them from competing. She easily won the first women's world championships when they were introduced. Madge supplemented her 1908 Olympic victory with a bronze in the pairs with her husband Edgar. This was a fitting testament to his support, as he had encouraged his wife to more aestheticism in her skating and ambitious, physically demanding routines to become world champion at the time of her Olympic victories. A heart condition forced Madge to cease competition soon after and she died, at age thirty-five, in 1917.

Different aspects of female amateurism can be read in the lives of Lottie Dod, Charlotte Cooper and Dorothea Lambert Chambers, Madge Syers and the other women detailed above. For instance, Edgar Syers was a gentleman of independent means whom Madge had married aged eighteen, and Lottie Dod's father had made sufficient money that his children did not need to work. A young Lottie dominated the Wimbledon Ladies' Singles tournament from 1887 to 1893 and she was still one of Britain's finest sporting icons in 1908 but likely to give up a sport after she felt that she had mastered it, mainly to avoid being seen as a 'pot-hunter'. Therefore, due to space, the argument focuses mainly on the tennis players. As contemporaries, what the examples illustrate is how differently sport manifested itself as part of an individual life-course, although a rigorous approach to specialised training, match play, nutrition and 'concentration' were common factors. Though they were very different personalities, sport remained a lifelong interest, so long as good health allowed.

Although she was famous by 1908, Dod rejected a higher public profile in favour of her own passions for activities that, once mastered, held little further appeal. After the Wimbledon wins, she retired from tennis rather abruptly at the age of twenty-one.[65] Thereafter, she passed the St Moritz Ladies' Skating Test in 1896 then became the second woman to pass the more rigorous men's examination the next year. Dod subsequently climbed extensively and competed on the Cresta Run; cycled on international tours; went on to play hockey for England from 1899 to 1900 and won the Ladies' Golf Union (LGU) Championship in 1904, before then winning the Olympic silver medal.[66] Subsequent invitations to the US produced disappointing performances. The only woman to hold both the Wimbledon and LGU title, Dod's interest in archery marked the beginning of the end of her success in elite competitive sport marred by long spells of sciatica. She had nevertheless been at the top of one sport or another for over twenty years. A long retirement from elite sporting competition mainly revolved around club-level tennis at Roehampton and singing.[67]

Given her other talents, for music in particular, Dod's sporting career seems like a compendium of pastimes pursued by the ultimate lady amateur, able to follow a love of diverse sport and leisure interests largely because she had independent means.[68] Amateurs of Dod's class were often fiercely competitive, but concealed this beneath a gracious veneer. They were also more interested in their own enjoyment than in entertaining spectators. Behind the polite façade, it is clear that many hours were spent honing various sporting talents; for example, Dod was coached by Harold Topham to pass the men's St Moritz skating test, training for at least two hours a day over two months in the winter of 1886–1887. Tennis seemed to come more naturally than golf, whereas in archery Dod was frequently ahead on the first day's play, only to lose either stamina or concentration on the second. Lottie often competed against her brothers and, on occasion, was the only woman in tennis singles or doubles matches with some of the leading male athletes of the day. In 1888, for instance, she played a singles exhibition match with Ernest Renshaw and was partnered by her brother Tony in a friendly tie against the holders of the 1893 Wimbledon men's doubles championships, the Baddeley brothers.

Lottie Dod's extensive administration and voluntary enthusiasm for advancing the cause of women's sport is also often overlooked: expertise gained in one area could easily be transferred to another. A keen member of the All England Women's Hockey Association from 1897, she rapidly rose to become captain of the Spital club team; the Cheshire county side and was appointed President of the Northern Association. Sciatica curtailed her active enthusiasm but her administrative activities continued. In 1901 her mother died and the family took almost a year's break from sport as part of the process of mourning.[69] Otherwise, we can see Lottie Dod, along with her siblings, embracing aspects of sporting popular culture relatively early in the evolution of national and international networks. Though sister Annie and brother Tony both married and had children, Lottie and William remained single, living in one another's company until his death in 1954. A reticence with interviewers hardened into a determination not to talk about her sporting feats in her later years. She was distinguished during her lifetime, though not perhaps to the extent that we would expect now, and died listening to Wimbledon on the radio in June 1960.

Britain's first Olympic champion, Charlotte Cooper was also a well-known figure and her career also seems to epitomise middle-class suburban sport in the late Victorian and Edwardian eras.[70] Charlotte Cooper's five singles successes at Wimbledon (1895, 1896, 1898, 1901 and 1908) put her amongst the all-time greats in the sport. She was twenty-four when she first won and is said to have to cycled to Wimbledon with her racket clipped to a bracket on the front fork of her bike. She was a defeated finalist in 1897, 1899, 1900, 1902 and 1904. Her final win in 1908 at thirty-seven years and 282 days makes her the women's singles most senior champion.[71] Having chosen not to take part in the London 1908 competition, Sterry beat the gold medalist Dorothea Lambert Chambers in the third round that year at Wimbledon. She also beat the Olympic silver medal holder Dora Boothby in the quarter-finals in 1908. Since Wimbledon was followed by the Olympic Games and she had been obliged to enter a knockout stage in the draw for the Olympics, she may not have bothered to enter. Given her Wimbledon victory less than a month earlier, she would have stood a good chance of winning again.

In 1901 Charlotte married solicitor Alfred Sterry, six years her junior, who would become a future President of the International Lawn Tennis Federation in 1913. They had a son, Rex (1903), who was to later serve for many years as Vice Chair of the All England Lawn Tennis Club and a daughter, Gwen (1905), who would become an international tennis player. Sterry therefore became the second woman to win the ladies' singles titles at Wimbledon after becoming a mother. Six-times Wimbledon winner Blanche Bingley Hillyard (1863–1946) had become the first in 1897 and Dorothea Lambert Chambers would follow, after the birth of her first son, by winning the title easily in 1910 and retaining it in 1911. Deaf from the age of twenty-six, Chattie Sterry's sustained enthusiasm for top-level competition contradicts the view that women participated in early Olympic Games tournaments as a distracting amusement. A singles, ladies and mixed doubles title-holder several times over, she continued to compete at Wimbledon Ladies' Finals until 1919.

In contrast to the reserve of Dod, Sterry was also pretty candid about what winning meant:

> Of course it goes without saying that my most memorable and exciting matches will all be those in which I have excelled or been the most distinguished person at the immediate moment . . . Winning my first championship of Ealing Lawn Tennis Club at the age of fourteen was an important moment in my life. How well I remember, bedecked by my proud mother in my best clothes, running off to the Club on the Saturday afternoon to play in the final without a vestige of nerve (would that I had none now) and winning. That was the first really important match in my life.[72]

Like Sterry, Dorothea Douglass first won Wimbledon as a single woman in 1903–1904, and 1906.[73] The first victory in 1903 was an especially good year because she also won the mixed doubles and a badminton singles championship, which was her other main specialism. Douglass was also based at the Ealing Common tennis club, taking a handicap singles first prize at the age of eleven. More local history research could reveal why specifically Ealing and Middlesex generally was such a centre for female tennis talent at this time: six of the first ten Wimbledon female singles champions were born there or lived nearby. After her marriage in 1907 to a local merchant, Dorothea competed as Mrs Lambert Chambers and went on to a longer string of Wimbledon victories than Lottie Dod, Blanche Bingley Hilliard or Charlotte Cooper Sterry. First competing in 1900 Dorothea Lambert Chambers took the Wimbledon title seven times (1903–1904, 1906, 1910–1911, 1913–1914) and appeared in eleven finals.[74]

Lambert Chambers competed at a time when Wimbledon was becoming more significant as an international tournament. She was a beaten finalist in 1905 to May Sutton (1886–1975) of the United States, who became the first champion from overseas. Born in Plymouth, Sutton's family had been based at Acton before emigrating to California. Sutton returned to repeat her singles success over Lambert Chambers in 1907, the year when Norman Brookes of Australia also became the men's singles champion. Dora Boothby won the women's Wimbledon singles competition in 1909 when Lambert Chambers was expecting her first child and Ethel Larcombe (née Tomson 1879–1965) took the title in 1912 when her second was due.[75] This partly explains why Lambert Chambers did not appear in the 1912 Stockholm Games. There was also, perhaps, more strength in depth in Edwardian women's tennis than has been so far acknowledged. Larcombe had already won five All England badminton championships between 1900 and 1906 and was to return to Wimbledon both before World War I and after, retiring aged forty-two.[76] Like other middle-class amateurs she maintained a range of interests, from playing the piano to bridge and golf, plus a devotion to animals. Her husband, Dudley became secretary and manager of the All England Lawn Tennis Club from 1925 until 1939.

Dorothea Lambert Chambers attributed her improvement as a player due, in part, to practising against the best male players of her time. Unlike Larcombe, who seems to have played overseas only once, Lambert Chambers first visited France in 1905 to play in Cannes, an experience she evidently enjoyed, declaring: 'Touring abroad is both an education and a delight.'[77] She also competed at Dinan, Monte Carlo, Nice, Homburg and Baden Baden. The motor-cars waiting outside Wimbledon in photographs from *Lawn Tennis for Ladies* also suggest changes in the way that spectators there began to enjoy a day out. It can only be speculated that Lambert Chambers would have won more at Wimbledon (and possibly the Olympic Games) if the war had not intervened. In 1919, when the Wimbledon championship resumed, she met twenty-year-old Suzanne Lenglen (1899–1938) of France in the final.[78] Lenglen won the first set 10–8 and Chambers the second 6–4. In the final set the lead alternated. At 6–5 and 40–15 up, it looked like Lambert Chambers had two match points, but Lenglen went on to take the set 9–7.[79] The following year the pair met again with the same outcome and from then on the older woman competed only in the doubles. She did however go on to captain a team to the United States and to compete at the highest level until nearly fifty years of age. Meanwhile Suzanne Lenglen capitalised on the theme of youth by publishing *Lawn Tennis for Girls* in 1920, dominating Wimbledon until mid decade and then turning professional.

The 1919 women's singles match has been read as a story of the new overcoming the old, in age, style and approach, mainly based on the press reports. However, as David Gilbert has suggested in his work on women's tennis during the period, this requires considerable revision.[80] In Dorothea Lambert Chambers' own writing, we can see a different narrative and one that appears to be very current. She judges her results as less important than her overall performance:

> To my mind, the great point to remember when you are practising is not that the match must be won, but that all your weak strokes must be improved. Tackle these doggedly in practice . . . How can your game improve or move forward if you make no effort to strengthen what is feeble? Practice then conscientiously and with infinite patience; never mind who beats you. Take each weak stroke in turn, and determine to master it, and I think you will find that you will be amply rewarded for all your painstaking work by a vast improvement and keener enjoyment in your game.[81]

To conclude this section on early Olympic competition and early female participation, there were strong elements of specialised preparation, constant training and psychological focus in the middle-class amateur traditions of women's sport. The strength in depth of women's tennis and golf preceded Olympic competition but limited participation to a relatively affluent few. As a result of this class base, there was more coaching, advice on match preparation and popular history written by women in this period than a recent PhD has suggested.[82] Even the advice to eat fruit, especially bananas, before an afternoon match does not look out of place today. The issue of clothing needs to be read with nuance too. Lottie Dod, in the late 1880s and early 1890s wore shorter skirts and a fetching cricket cap in which to compete at Wimbledon and this was condoned because of her age. May Sutton is known to have worn relatively shorter skirts than Lambert Chambers who, even so, regarded freedom of movement as important to good play. Chattie Cooper served overhead and played an attacking game. Lambert Chambers only changed to an overhead serve after the war, but was a keen reader of her opponent's weakness and a consumate tactician. As anyone who has played club-level tennis would attest, these skills conserve a considerable amount of energy. The application of training, focus and concentration would be extended by the specialist preparation of female working-class amateurs as more British women represented their country in Olympian competition.

By the time of the Stockholm Olympic Games in 1912 women took part in three sports; tennis and the newly inaugurated swimming and diving contests (although the sailing events were mixed, I have yet to find a female competitor).[83] Of the expanded programme for fifty-four female athletes, the aquatic competitions involved forty swimmers and divers from eight countries. Working-class swimmers therefore became more evident in British female Olympic amateur tradition than tennis players, in part, because of their larger numbers. Some were also world class. Irene Steer (1889–1947) of Cardiff Ladies Premier Swimming Club; Isabelle 'Belle' Moore (1894–1975) of Glasgow; Annie Speirs of Derby (1889–1926) and Jennie Fletcher (1890–1968) of Leicester were the gold-winning team in the 4 x 100m freestyle relay event.[84] Steer therefore became Wales' first female Olympic title holder and Moore remains Scotland's only woman swimming gold medallist.[85] Fletcher was also took third place to become Britain's first individual female swimming medallist in the 100m freestyle relay, behind two Australians, Sarah 'Fanny' Durack (1889–1956) and Mina Wylie (1891–1984).[86]

The Australians were swimming a variant of the crawl stroke. This was significantly faster than Fletcher's 'racing' style because the English Amateur Swimming Association thought the crawl both exhausting and inelegant. Jennie fought hard against Grete Rosenborg (1896–1979) of Germany for the bronze medal, while Annie Speirs came in fifth.[87] Win Hayes is therefore not quite correct in saying that Lucy Morton

Figure 2.1   From left to right: Isabella 'Belle' Moore, Jennie Fletcher, Annie Speirs and Irene Steer of the gold-medal winning British 4 X 100 metre Freestyle Relay team at the Stockholm Olympic Games, 1912. The clothed chaperone is thought to be Clara Jarvis, but a Mrs Holmes is also referred to in the official report. The cloaks that women over fourteen were required to wear by ASA rules when not swimming are evident in the bottom right of the picture. Fletcher also won an individual bronze in the freestyle 100 metres. © British Swimming, Loughborough: The British Olympic Association, London.

(1898–1980) became the first British female swimming gold medallist in 1924.[88] After the relay race, Jennie is said to have had her most memorable moment of the Games when King Gustav of Sweden placed the classic laurel wreath on her head, put the gold around her neck and said, 'Well done England.'

Though it was not as glamorous as tennis, British amateur swimmers had access to some of the finest coaches of their day including Walter Brickett (1865–1933) and the professional swimmer Joey Nuttall (1869–1942).[89] They also used the latest technology available to them in the form of silk racing swimsuits adapted from male costumes and John Jarvis (1872–1933), an Olympian in 1900, 1906 and 1908, appears to have been influential in this.[90] The silk racing suits (and woollen diving costumes) remained the standard style for over twenty years, including the Olympic Games of 1924 in Paris:

> At meeting where both sexes are admitted, and in all ASA Championships, competitors must wear costume in accordance with the following regulations.

a) The colous shall be black or dark blue.
b) Trimmings may be used ad lib.
c) The shoulder straps shall not be less than two inches wide.
d) It shall be buttoned at the shoulder, and the armhole cut no lower than three inches from the armpit. Note: For Ladies a shaped arm, at least three inches long shall be inserted.
e) In the front the costume shall reach not lower than two inches below the pit of the neck. Note: For ladies the costume shall be cut straight round the neck.
f) At the back it shall be cut straight from the top of the shoulder to top of shoulder.
g) In the leg portion the costume shall extend to within three inches of the knee, and shall be cut in a straight line round the circumference of each leg.
h) Drawers must be worn underneath the costume. They must be of triangular pattern, with a minimum width of 2/1/2 inches at the fork; they must meet on each hip, and be of not less width than 3 inches on each side when fastened.
i) On leaving the dressing room, lady competitors over 14 years of age must wear a long coat or bath gown before entering and also immediately after leaving the water.[91]

While our attention might be drawn to the gendered aspects of this uniform, the majority of the regulations remained the same for women and men.

Clothing alone indicates that amateur swimmers were trained and competed under different circumstances than the tennis champions so far discussed. However, there were more fundamental distinguishing features in their sporting lives. Belle Moore was the eighth of nine children and often walked two to three miles to the pool to train. Two years after the Olympics, she emigrated to Maryland, in the US, upon marrying George Cameron and taught swimming until a week before her death. Irene Steer began to compete as a breast-stroke specialist, but changed to freestyle and trained in Roath Park Lake. After being Welsh champion from 1907, she retired from competition in 1913 after marrying a director and Chairman of Cardiff City, William Nicolson.[92] Jennie Fletcher worked six days a week for twelve hour shifts in a hosiery factory during her Olympic training.[93] She was required by Amateur Swimming Association (ASA) rules to retire from competitive swimming in 1913 upon taking employment as a baths attendant and teacher.

An amateur is one who has never competed for a money prize, declared wager, or staked bet; who has never taught, pursued or assisted in the practice of swimming, or any other athletic exercise, as a means of pecuniary gain; and who has not, knowingly, or without protest, taken part in any competitions with anyone who is not an amateur.[94]

ENGLISH BATHS AND BATHING PLACES—*Continued.* 244

LANCASHIRE—*continued.*

Town.	No. of Swg Cl.	Bath, Sea, or River Accommodation	For Public or Private use.	Owned by private people or pub. body	Dimensions: L'th. ft.	Dimensions: W'th. ft.	Depth: Dp. ft.	Depth: Sh w. ft.	Depth: in.	Where situated street or locality	Price per ticket to: Ordinary bather.	Price per ticket to: Swim'ng Clubs.	Price per ticket to: School children.	If also used by ladies.	Name of Professional Teacher.	Special features, remarks or criticisms.
Stretford ..	1	Bath	Public	Public	66	30	6	3		Dorset Street	4d & 2d	Half-price	1d	Yes	J.Steward-son & Mrs. Steward-son	Bath thrown open free on Saturday morning to school children and free tuition given
Old Trafford		Bath	Public	Public	70	30	6	3		Northumber-land St.	Not fixed			No		
		Bath	Public	Public	60	27	6	3						Yes		
		Bath	Private	Private	48	19½	5½	3	3	Deaf School						
Swinton ...	1	Bath	Public	Public	75	30	6½	3	6	Swinton hall rd	3d	2d & 1d Boys	Free with Teacher	Yes	None	
Tyldesley ...	1	Bath	Public	Public	66	24	6	3	6	Union Street	2d	1d	1d	Yes		
Ulverston ...	1	Sea	Public	Public						Sea Front						
Walton-in-le-Dale		River	Private	Private			15	1		River Ribble				No		By permission
Warrington	1	Bath	Public	Public	75	45	7	3		Leigh Street	6d			No	None	
Widnes ...		Bath	Public	Public	45	25½	6	3		Waterloo Rd.	6d			No	None	
Wigan ...	3	Bath	Public	Public	68	26	6	3	6	Millgate	6d		2d	Yes	None	
		Bath	Public	Public	58	22	6	3	6	Millgate	3d	2d	1d		None	
		Bath	Public	Public	21	21	4	2	6	Millgate	3d		1d	Yes	None	
Woolton ...	1	Bath	Public	Public	60	30	6 6	3	6		4d & 2d					
LEICESTER.																
Hinckley ..		Bath	Public	Public	75	24	6	3		Station Road	3d		1d	Yes	None	
Leicester ...		Bath	Public	Public	75	30	6½	3		Bath Lane	3d	2d	1d	Yes	Several	Second Class Bath, Admission 1d
	30	Bath	Public	Public	100	45	6½	3		Knighton L'ne	3d	2d	1d			
		Bath	Public	Public	90	33½	6½	3		Vestry Street	4d	3d	1d	Yes		Second Class Bath, Admission 2d
		Bath	Public	Public	100	45	6½	3		Cossington St.	4d	2d	1d	Yes		
		Bath	Public	Public	100	45	6½	3		W.H'mb'rs'ne	4d	2d	1d	Yes	Several	
		River	Public	Public	300	90	9	4		Abbey Pk. Rd.		2d		No	None	
		River	Public	Public	450	90	9	3		Bede House Meadows		2d		No	None	
Loughboro'	1	Bath	Public	Public	75	27	6	3	6					Yes	None	
		Bath	Public	Public	80	30	6	3	6	Queen's Park	3d	3d		Yes		
Market Harboro'	1	Bath	Public	Public	75	27	7	3	6					Yes	None	
Melton Mowbray	1	River	Public					3	6	Swan's Nest				No	None	
Oadby	1	Bath	Public	Public	51	27	6	3	6	Main Road				Yes	None	
LINCOLN.																
Anderley ...		Sea								Beach						
Boston ...	1	Bath	Public	Public	79	54	5 10	2	8		7/6 season	5/- season	One bath free		None	Ladies Bath separate
Cleethorpes	1	Sea, open Bath	Public	G.C. Rly. Co.	84	20	6	2	9	Sea	6d	7/6 Club season				
Gainsboro'	2	Bath	Public	Public	75	20	6	3	6	Lea Road	1d & 2d		1d & 2d	Yes		
Grantham ...		Bath	Public	Corp.	180	67½	6	2	2	LittleGowerby	1/-	1d & 2d		Yes		Ladies 10 to 12 daily and 2 free days
Grimsby ...	7	Bath	Public	Private	50	30	5½			Orwell Street	10/6	7/6 season				
		Bath	Public	School Board	57	25	5	2	9	Higher Grade School	3d		Free			Public 3 days week
Gt. Grimsby		Bath	Public	Private							10/-	season			H. Calew	
Lincoln ...	2	River & Pool	Public	Public	440 yds	20 yds	6ft			River Witham & Brayford		2/6		No		
Skegness ...		Bath	Public	Private							6d				Stimson	
Spalding ...		River	Private	Private						River						
Stamford ...	1	River	Public	Public						River		2/-seas'n	1/-seas'n	No		

Figure 2.2 Swimming facilities in Leicestershire taken from the 1902 Amateur Swimming Association Yearbook. When Jennie Fletcher was growing up there were a variety of indoor and outdoor swimming baths, with a varied pricing structure and some access to tuition. © British Swimming, Loughborough (ASA Yearbook 1902).

Though it cost her amateur status, this job was probably more attractive than other forms of manual labour. After emigrating to Canada in 1917 to help with the health of her husband, who had been gassed during World War One, and bringing up a family of six children, Fletcher taught swimming until she was in her sixties. She was buried with the words 'The greatest lady swimmer' on her headstone and inducted to the International Swimming Hall of Fame in Florida in 1971.

Since this story has been covered more extensively elsewhere, it is enough to conclude here that the number of competitors and type of person representing Britain in the Olympic Games before the First World War diversified. Britain's Isabella Mary White (1894–1972) won a bronze medal in the 10 metre platform dive competition and her memorabilia is held at the British Swimming offices in Loughborough.[95] White was considered rather too fast, judged as 'back-swanked' and somewhat inelegant compared to the Scandinavians who took first and second place. Of all the Stockholm female aquatic competitors, London-born White maintained an Olympic record, though she was unable to claim a medal in either the 1920 Antwerp; the 1924 Paris or the 1928 Amsterdam Games. She did however, take a gold in the 1927 European Championships: a long-standing career that also requires further analysis.

The remaining fourteen female competitors in 1912 were tennis players. The indoor medals went to Britain's Edith Hannam (1878–1951) and Mabel Parton (1881–1962) who took gold and bronze medals respectively, split by silver medalist Thora Castenschiold (1882–1979) of Denmark. The outdoor singles had no British women in the top three for the first time: leaving Marguerite Broquedis (1893–1983) of France, Dora Köring (1880–1945) of Germany and Anne Margarethe Bjurstedt (later better known as a nationalised American, 'Molla' Mallory, 1884–1959) of Norway to take the honours. Hannam also won a mixed doubles gold medal with Charles Dixon. All tennis events were to disappear from the schedule from 1924 for forty years, reappearing in 1984 as an under twenty-one demonstration event and then as a full medal sport in Seoul in 1988 in the newly-professional era. It could be argued that, in the intervening time, female swimming and diving became the most significant focus in the women's programme, until the first track and field athletic competitions in 1928. However, the first British female athletics gold medals would have to wait until 1964.

Stockholm would be the last Olympic Games before the first World War. How then, might we consider the wider narratives affecting perceptions of, and shaped by, early female competitors? The British women Olympians covered in this segment of the chapter demonstrated what could be called practical feminism. This remains a major area for more research. The majority of women's and girls' involvement in sport relied, and continues to depend upon, the efforts of an extraordinary number of volunteers and enthusiasts. At a very basic level, we still don't know why some of the first women Olympians chose to take up an activity or for how long their enthusiasm was sustained.

Little is understood about other all-rounders active in the late nineteenth and early twentieth century who almost made the Olympic team, like aristocrat May 'Toupie' Lowther (1875–1944) who fenced; practiced Ju-Jitsu; played tennis and golf; cycled and 'motored'.[96] She would reach national prominence when women of the Hackett-Lowther Unit would serve on the front line in France in World War I and Lowther was also well known by

SWIMMING
COSTUMES.

Buy direct from the Manufacturer,

A. SILLS,

260, Loughborough Rd., LEICESTER.

Sole Maker by appointment and competition to the Amateur Swimming Association and all the leading Swimming Clubs and Societies.

PRICE LIST.

	Single.		½ Doz.		1 Doz.	
	s.	d.	s.	d.	s.	d.
Gent's Swimming Costumes, perfect fit, can't be beaten	1	6	6	6	12	0
Ditto, super quality, highly recommended	2	0	9	6	18	0
Ditto, trimmed round arms and neck	2	6	12	6	24	0
Ditto, pure Milanese silk ...	10	6	—		—	
Ladies' Swimming Costumes	2	6	12	6	24	0
Ladies' do. do. cashmere trimmings... ...	3	0	16	0	30	0

A.S.A. {bracketing the list above} — *Postage Paid.* {bracketing the right columns}

	s.	d.	s.	d.	s.	d.	s.	d.
Gents' Bathing Drawers— per doz.	3	6	4	6	5	6	6	6
Jarvis Racing Slip ,,	5	6	6	6	—		—	

The lightest and most comfortable drawers ever produced—entirely different from the ordinary article. Worn in all the championships.

Polo Caps 3s. 6d. per set numbered.
Goal Keepers and Referees' Flags 1s. per set.

Terms—Nett Cash with Order.

◆◆◆

☞ **Unsolicited Testimonial (A.S.A.)**

DEAR SIR,

"Yours are the only Costumes I have ever seen which are strictly in accordance with the A.S.A. Laws, and at the same time are so light and well cut as to satisfy our fastest swimmers. I have pleasure in enclosing you order for four dozens for the use of the English representatives in International Matches.

(Signed) GEO. PRAGNELL.

Figure 2.3   A. Sills advertisement for 'Regulation' ASA costumes including silk race-suits from the ASA yearbook of 1902. John Jarvis from Leicester made his name as a double gold medallist in the Paris Games of 1900 as a distance swimmer. Midlands underwear technologies were increasingly used in sporting outerwear. The Milanese silk suits would cost the equivalent of £45 each today. © British Swimming, Loughborough (ASA Yearbook 1902).

her sporting contemporaries.[97] Considered a masculine woman, Lowther later claiming that she was the inspiration for the character of Stephen in Radclyffe Hall's *The Well of Loneliness*.[98] Women's fencing would be introduced in 1924 and would become especially important for British women after World War Two, with Dame Mary Glen Haig (born 1918) being a notable competitor.

Helen Preece (1897-unknown) was also born too early to compete in the Modern Pentathlon, having previously won the Madison Square Horse Show Gold Cup, worth $1000, at the age of fourteen.[99] Labelled a Neo-Amazon, Preece was just fifteen years of age when she applied to compete in the Olympics, having been tutored by her father and friends in shooting, cross-country running, fencing and swimming. Her application was politely declined after being passed around from the IOC to the Swedish organising committee. After this, little is known about her life. Given that the Modern Pentathlon was an enthusiasm of Coubertin's, expressly to find the best all-round Olympic athlete, with distinctly militaristic overtones (rapid-fire pistol shooting; épée fencing; a 300 metre swimming race; a cross-country steeplechase equestrian event and a 4,000 metre cross-country run) his lack of support for her application was not much of a surprise.

The Olympic Games between 1900 and 1912 have therefore to be placed in context of both increased international media communications and more urgent calls for female suffrage and 'declinist' narratives in Britain. The bitter spat between the British and the Americans at the London Games in 1908 was a symptom of larger anxieties. Stockholm was a model of efficiency. Specially reduced Press rates arranged by the Post Office enabled 777 telegrams containing 87,434 words to be transmitted from Britain to Sweden from February 1912 to February 1913.[100] In the reverse direction there were 1710 telegrams containing 158,447 words. All but 103 of the UK-bound telegrams were transmitted in June and July. Pathé-Frères had commenced production in Sweden that year, ensuring world-wide distribution of the Olympic Games in moving images as well as still photography and text. Such was the extent of photographic evidence in the Official Report, that it has now been subdivided into two very large documents online.[101] Britain came fourth in the athletics and third overall behind the US and Sweden, with the 1916 Olympics due for Berlin. This caused some newspapers to charge that Britain had 'lost' the Games, and with it considerable international sporting prestige.

CONCLUSION

Danish 'Lady Gymnasts' delighted onlookers in the London Games of 1908 by wearing calf-length culottes, revealing their ankles as part of their graceful routines.[102] If the commercial, imperial and technological milieu shaped public attitudes to sport, campaigns for suffrage and education, were also being fiercely contested. Anne Lykke Poulson has argued that the public visibility of the gymnastics club movement in Denmark from 1880 was significant in the process of women attaining political citizenship in 1915.[103] In Britain, the link between female physical culture and 'The Woman Question' remains unclear and there is a much-needed book waiting to be written on the subject.[104] The differences between the suffragists of the Women's Social and Political Union and the later suffragettes, who used direct action for women's rights, were not necessarily defining.[105] For instance, it is generally taken that the suffragettes used sporting events and locations as the site of protests, including digging up golf courses. The intersection of sport and politics was more complicated in Britain, particularly around the time of the 1908 London and 1912 Stockholm Olympics.

In 1906 the Liberal party won a large majority and it seemed for a time that the government would give women the vote. When this did not happen more militant action became routine. Edith Margaret Garrud (1872–1971) and her husband William had both trained as teachers of physical education. Edith appears to have been taught Ju-Jitsu by Edward William Barton-Wright from approximately 1899.[106] Kodokan Judo was a relatively unknown form of self-protection gaining popularity with the Japanese police, while the Japan Society's Ju-Jitsu demonstration in 1892 had received little media interest in Britain. Barton-Wright's anglicised amalgamation of the two, Bartitsu, appealed to patriotic instincts to defence of both a personal and public nature.

The Anglo-Japanese alliance, signed in 1902, was followed by a resurgence of nineteenth century interest in *japonisme* (the influence of Japanese art on the West). Organiser of the Women's Freedom League (WFL) athletes' club, Edith Garrud, demonstrated self-defence holds and restraining techniques, on one occasion throwing a thirteen stone policeman. She was four feet, eleven inches tall. Garrud also led the WFL athletes at the Coronation procession in June 1910. Her gymnasium at Argyle Place was used as a refuge by at least half a dozen women who smashed windows in co-ordinated protests on more than one occasion. Ju-Jitsu classes were used as their alibi to evade prosecution.[107] This developed to more aggressive forms of self-defence when Edith Garrud trained the bodyguards of Mrs Pankhurst to use Indian Clubs and wrote a drama called *Ju-Jitsu as a Husband-Tamer: a Suffragette Play with a Moral* in 1911.[108]

Amid this general atmosphere, William Garrud's book *The Complete Ju-Jitsuan* had become the standard work on the subject by 1914.[109] Minimally aggressive self-defence therefore became somewhat fashionable in the wider context of preserving British interests in Asia following the Russo-Japanese war of 1904–1905.[110] This also extended to domestic popular culture. Anglophile mixed martial arts were enough of a vogue for Arthur Conan Doyle to revive Sherlock Holmes, who had been presumed dead since 1893 having fallen into the Swiss Reichenback Falls along with his criminal nemesis Professor Moriarty in *The Adventure of the Final Problem*.[111] Holmes was resurrected in a supposedly overlooked episode before his death *The Hound of the Baskervilles*, published in 1902. More explicitly, *The Adventure of the Empty House* serialised in *The Strand* in 1903, attributed his survival to a Japanese wrestling technique utilising the opponent's weight and aggression. Holmes' use of self-defence had caused the aggressor Moriarty to overbalance alone into the Falls.

So it is interesting to examine the gender politics of the early Olympic Games at the same time as the suffragettes used sport as both a peaceful means of demonstrating their activities, as well as for networking and radical action. On 17 February 1909 Australian-born professional actress Muriel Matters (1877–1969) flew in an airship over the British Houses of Parliament, dropping a hundred-weight of flyers urging 'votes for women.'[112] Having reportedly been radicalised at fourteen by reading the Henrik Ibsen play *A Doll's House* (published in 1879), Matters was later appointed Women's Freedom League organiser for south Wales, and increasingly became involved in labour politics.[113] In June 1913 Derby Emily Wilding Davison (1872–1913) threw herself under the King's horse, Anmer, as it rounded Tattenham Corner. The *Daily Sketch* headline on the day thought that her actions were not the most remarkable aspect of the race, calling it: 'History's Most Wonderful Derby: First Horse Disqualified: A 100 to 1 Chance Wins: Suffragette Nearly Killed By the King's Colt.'[114] Wilding died shortly after and became a suffragette martyr. Others thought her actions irrational, fearing what a less sophisticated woman might do with her vote. It is likely that the campaign would have become more violent had war not been declared in August 1914. Sport and physical activity could be symbolic of emancipation both at a personal and political level and the campaign for suffrage was a significant, but not isolated, example of wider freedoms.

As well as domestic politics, the Olympics were tied up with concerns for British influence overseas. Arthur Conan Doyle had already written a pamphlet *The War in South Africa: its Causes and its Conduct* in 1902 and covered the 1908 Olympic marathon for the *Daily Mail*, owned by Lord Northcliffe.[115] Northcliffe, who had raised nearly £12,000 by public subscription through the *Daily Mail* to financially assist the London Olympic Games in 1908, looked to raise more in the light of what he viewed as a dismal national failure in 1912. By 1913, he had persuaded the celebrated author to become a member of an Olympic financial committee who had to ask for public funds for amateur sport during the Balkan War.[116] While Conan Doyle was on holiday, the committee asked not for £10,000, as he had suggested, but £100,000, leading to accusations of professionalism. By September 1913 the fund stood at just £9,500 and Conan Doyle was challenging the critics that Britain should not stand down from the Games when it had been 'defeated' in 1912. Moreover, he argued, the chief nations had already announced their intention to compete in 1916.

An assessment by longstanding Secretary to the BOA between 1948 and 1974, Kenneth Sandilands 'Sandy' Duncan, suggested that the 300-strong British team cost £13 per head, for a total spend of £4,000 in 1912, including administrators and competitors.[117] This would equate today to a minimum cost of £1,000 per participant using the retail price index.[118] Given the relatively meager conditions in which Olympics took part, and that most of the British athletes provided their own sports uniforms, this was still a considerable outlay. When Olympic competition began again in Belgium in 1920, Duncan estimated that sending the 224 British athletes alone cost £6,400; effectively doubling the amount spent per head. As many of the men were housed in old army bases near Antwerp, this seems a liberal calculation. Even with a generous budget for the administrators and trainers, Conan Doyle's 1913 fund of £9,500 would have more than covered the cost.

In view of these anxieties about popular imperialism, the military strength of European neighbours and concerns about Britain's role in Africa, America and Asia, it is likely that the assessment of Stockholm would have been considerably worse without the medals of the women tennis players, swimmers and divers. With the return of the 1920 Olympics in Antwerp, Suzanne Lenglen again dominated the women's singles for the gold medal. She gave up only four games, three of them in the final against Dorothy Holman (1883–1968) of Britain who also won a silver medal in the ladies' doubles with Winifred Beamish (1883–1972). Lenglen won another gold in the mixed doubles with Max Décugis and a bronze in the women's doubles partnered by Élisabeth d'Ayen (1898–1969). However, Kathleen 'Kitty' McKane (later Godfree, 1896–1992) and Winifred McNair (1877–1954) took gold in the women's doubles; with McKane also partnering one of Britain's finest sportsmen of the day, Maxwell Woosnam, to the silver medal in the mixed competition.[119] However, large festival events like Olympic competition only took place every four years. Relatively new sports and activities began to metaphorically colonise various spans of air, land and sea in record-breaking attempts with more regular frequency. The next chapter considers motor-sport, as representing the cultural modernity of the age, as well as public concerns about domestic and imperial defence.

In a chapter that has primarily been concerned with amateur competition, it is worth saying briefly that ideological and pragmatic feminism could be expressed in professional sport. Annette Kellermann (1887–1975) was the most significant of the sportswomen whose careers ran concurrent with the early Olympic Games able to capitalise on their talents outside amateur structures and codes. After originally being born in Australia to an Australian father and a French mother, a young Annette was afraid of the water and swam to overcome childhood disability. She advocated swimming as a sport for women but also for physical therapy. Though claiming that her mother conducted the Australian Musical Conservatory, Kellermann and her father were often driven by poverty to self-promotion. The grueling nature of distance competition features in her 1918 autobiographical work *How to Swim*.[120]

Kellermann collaborated with newspapers like the Sydney *Bulletin* and the Melbourne *Punch* and dived into a huge tank of live fish at the Melbourne Theatre. She later moved to London, completing fifteen miles in the Thames and being sponsored eight pounds per week by the *Daily Mirror* to attempt to cross the English Channel in 1905. She made it 'three-fourths' of the way across three times in the same year and earned up to £130 each time. The feat attracted endorsements like that of Cadbury's chocolate, and wider fame in Europe with *L'Auto* sponsoring swims in the Seine, followed by races in the Danube. In the United States she promoted a female one-piece swimsuit, adapted from a gymnasium costume. There were reports that Jennie Fletcher was offered a contract to perform with Kellermann in 1907 which the British woman declined. Her place in Olympic history might have been won at the cost of financial gain if this was the case, but it is difficult to substantiate. There was evidently more amateur-professional contact than has been previously acknowledged. While official or 'regulation' suits restricted stylistic innovation, the relative financial weakness of ASA finances allowed 'penny entrepreneurs' and small-scale manufacturers to capitalise on niche markets at the same time as mass production techniques improved.

Also noteworthy, innovators like Kellermann created markets for their talents in ways that built on the success of earlier pioneers like Agnes Beckwith and Kate Bennett, Ethel Golding and so on but used new technologies to reach wider audiences. Claiming that Universal Studios begrudged the $35,000 that it cost to make her first feature film in 1914 *Neptune's Daughter*, Kellermann was vindicated by public interest when the movie returned $1,000,000 at the box office. The next feature made in 1916, *A Daughter of the Gods*, reportedly cost $1,000,000 to make and location scenes were filmed in Jamaica. Famous for the cost and for the tasteful nudity *A Daughter of the Gods* is as much an object of interest to historians of silent film as those of sport. Annette Kellermann's later career combined being an aquatic vaudeville artiste, a movie star and she became, for a time, the highest paid female athlete in the world supported by her American-born husband-manager, James Sullivan. That forms of middle-class amateurism such as has been shown by Lottie Dod, Charlotte Sterry and Dorothea Lambert Chambers co-existed with Kellermann's arch professionalism demonstrates the range of female sporting activity at this time. Neither individuals nor conservative institutions like Wimbledon or the IOC were immune to outside influence.

One aspect of sports history that needs more work is clothing and fashion generally. While Kellermann is often attributed a 'moment of invention' with regard to the one-piece swimming suit for women, we know that by 1902 women were wearing an adaptation of the male 'regulation' swimming costume in Amateur Swimming Association competitions. What has been the British sporting aesthetic spread through costume and design history? How has this been influenced by English, Irish, Scottish and Welsh variation, by ethnic tradition and regional tastes? Though sports history is meant to have embraced a visual and cultural 'turn' of recent years, looking at sporting dress and costume in conjunction with colleagues who are textile historians has questioned my previous reliance on documentary evidence. As outlined in a paper at the British Society for Sports History Conference in Glasgow in 2009, the materiality of sport extends not just to public space, place and time but to personal budgets, style and taste; 'kit' or sports clothing makes this point nicely.[121] Working with archivists and collections specialists such as Phillip French at Leicester City Museums; Philip Warren at Leicester County Museums; Rebecca Shawcross at Northampton Museums (which has a national shoe collection) and Jennifer Farley at the Fashion and Technology Institute, New York has been instructive in terms of beginning to look at the objects and items of clothing themselves.

The material, textile, technology and construction of a garment show considerable nuance during this period. However, only a serious digression to this chapter could do justice to the topic. Cross-referencing individuals items of clothing with catalogues, labels, promotional documentation and so on is absolutely necessary but, as a range of researchers from a variety of disciplines are now finding, the very every-day qualities of the objects used by individuals for sport hold important clues as to a person's lived experience. While a tennis dress from 1903 suggested that the owner wore a corset underneath, blood on the lining of the torso suggests that she also played strenuously enough to have been injured by her undergarments while wearing it.[122] It was not really surprising that Lottie Dod's dress for tennis as a young single woman was quite different than that of Lambert Chambers as a married mother of two. Lambert Chambers, who preferred to wear no hat, jewelry or bracelets and as few hairpins as possible, chose the following costume:

> A plain gored skirt [which] should clear your ankles and have plenty of fullness around the hem . . . A plain shirt without frills or furbelows, a collar, tie and waistband. The taste of the wearer dictates the fabric: serge, flannel and cotton are the most popular. White washes well and does not fade. Personally I prefer white shoes and stockings to be one colour but others choose coloured shoes such as brown or black. If you do not have steel-toed tennis shoes then put men's thick shooting socks over your tennis shoes for grip.[123]

The many varieties of swimming costume, golf-wear, gym suit, tennis and skating dress worn between the 1870s and 1914 show adaptation for the age, physical build, taste and budget of the owner. A wealthy US skater could glide around in an imported French suit of midnight blue silk, trimmed with brown fur or a more staid brown wool dress with a gored design incorporating a kick pleat at the rear, presumably to enable more vigorous action for more speed.[124] A very functional baggy croquet outfit with a sailor collar from 1915 also perhaps suggests that some sports costumes were designed to mask the figure while at play, rather than enhance it.[125] The point of this brief survey is that the view of Edwardian women's clothing as inhibiting serious sporting competition requires much more thought and analysis than it has so far received.

The example of how Kellermann moved out of theatres via the English Channel and into Hollywood legend, is indicative of a general enthusiasm for new products and activities including more body-conscious leisure. As well as appearing in subsequent films like *Venus of the South Seas* (1924) Kellermann also wrote, endorsed and supplied free copies of *The Body Beautiful*, via mail order. This was a trial diet and exercise routine taking 'just fifteen minutes a day'. Satisfied customers could then purchase the regime in full. Billed in *Neptune's Daughter* as 'The Perfect Woman, with measurements that almost surpass belief', it perhaps helped the sale of *Body Beautiful* that it was illustrated with many photographs of the author. Capitalising on an existing market for self-improvement products and promoting herself as a model ideal, Kellermann prolonged an active athletic career into commercial endorsements. She returned to Australia in later life and a biographical film *Million Dollar Mermaid* starring Esther Williams was made in 1952. In 1960 a star was nominated in Kellermann's honour on the Hollywood Walk of Fame. The fashion for record-breaking in which many women Olympians and professional athletes like Kellermann participated was part of a wider zeitgeist. Having used class as a way of helping to understand how sporting careers could be developed through personal contacts and welfare policies, it is worth reflecting that the circumstance into which an individual was born could be changed. Kellermann was able to enjoy a long and comfortable retirement back in Australia after her Hollywood career was over.

Figure 2.4 Jennie Fletcher's gold medal compared with a fivepence piece photographed by the author with the permission of Graham Budd auctions 24 July 2012.

Finally, it is worth saying that amateurism, or 'sport for sport's sake' continued to inspire many British women Olympians up until the 1980s, whatever their class, and this remains under-researched. Furthermore, the club, which had helped in the pre-war success of the middle and working-class women referred to in this chapter, also rose during the inter-war period to foster more sports participation for the masses. This included works' sport and those that catered for specific ethnic groups, as well as those that were locally or regionally based. What were the related social activities of these groups and what kind of good fellowship did they enjoy in addition to their competitive activities? We know that Jennie Fletcher and her sisters were nationally-reknown for their water-polo skills, as well as their swimming and diving ability. As the many photographs of Lottie Dod's family at play and Jennie Fletcher's scrapbook at the International Swimming Hall of Fame in Florida indicate, heterosexual socialising and friendship in sport has been virtually ignored by sports historians. We also know far too little about significant women leaders, coaches, administrators and entrepreneurs. Given the range of activities between 1900 and 1912 presented in this chapter, more local history studies are an obvious place to start to rectify this. The next chapter picks up the same three themes of sociability, cultural modernity and internationalism in relation to motor-sport. While political and practical feminism link the examples, there were also increasingly global aspects of sporting tourism.

3 An Age of Speed

INTRODUCTION

In 1898 the wedding of the Honourable Eleanor Georgina Rolls (1872–1961) and Sir John Courtown Edward Shelley was announced.[1] Held at Ennismore Gardens Church, Kensington on 23 April, the bride was:

> Sister of the Honourable C. S. Rolls who was well known throughout the autocar world as an enthusiastic follower of the latest form of recreative locomotion [sic]. Therefore it is not surprising to hear that Mr Rolls drove friends to the church in an elegant motor Victoria, and also in the procession afterwards back to the residence of his family at Rutland Gate, where a reception attended by some four or five hundred guests was held. So far as we know this is the first time (though it certainly will not be the last) in which an autocar has been used by people of independent position in connection with a wedding of any note.[2]

Eleanor Rolls was not the first woman to ride to her wedding in a car rather than a carriage but, as the daughter of the wealthy Conservative MP for Monmouthshire, John Allan Rolls, First Baron of Llangattock, she was a society bride and therefore the first 'of any note' so far as *The Times* was concerned.[3]

In April 1897, Irma L'Hollier had married Albert Day in the relatively unfashionable location of St Augustin's Roman Catholic Church, Solihull. Irma's father was an importer of foreign-made vehicles and the groom was an assistant manager at the Anglo-French Motor Carriage Company, specialists in Roger-Benz cars. Though it has been difficult to find more biographical information about the couple, the Birmingham marriage was celebrated in *The AutoCar* for using at least three vehicles for 'the diversion of the company' at the reception. *AutoCar* wished the pioneering couple: 'As much happiness in their married life as there was novelty in their wedding, which will stand as the first British motor-car marriage on record.'[4] Perhaps *The Times* meant to put the petrol-heads, Mr and Mrs Albert Day, from Britain's second city in their place. Such nuances of status and taste are a general theme of this chapter. Certainly Charles Stewart Rolls was regarded as an all-round sportsman; a pioneering balloonist and aviator before using a loan from his father to establish one of Britain's first car showrooms, importing cars from overseas before his collaboration with engineer Frederick Henry Royce.[5] While Rolls was a better salesman than a technician, Royce was able to adapt European car design to produce a British marque, first sold to the public in late 1904.[6]

The chapter focuses in particular on how 'motoring' became a sport in Britain with signficant female pioneers. Nationalistic discourses promoted by the media and manufacturing industries combined with elite patronage in the emergence of the British motor industry. The perception of mechanised transport as problematic in a number of ways created tensions in how motor-sport was produced and consumed. Nevertheless, some women became defined in the public imagination as aviators, 'scorchers' or 'motorinas' in the early twentieth century. There was considerable continuity between forms of mechanised transport. The term 'scorchers' admired motorists speeding in excess of the legal limit, while 'motorinas' was a more lyrical and gendered phrase, presumably with balletic origins, for those who appeared to glide. Racing drivers like Dorothy Levitt (1882/3–1922) quickly became famous. Many disappeared from public life just as suddenly. Other developments could be more abiding, although British ambivalence to racing motor-cars on roads led directly to the establishment of Brooklands in 1906 as the world's first purpose-built circuit. The privately-owned track tapped into elite patronage of the British 'season', initially using the lexicon and routines of horse racing. Though most of the women who competed there did so in the inter-war years, there are several notable early examples of women taking part in motor-sport rivalries to be the first, the fastest and the most able to endure. The concluding remarks link motor-sport with other cultural industries, evident in the material culture referenced throughout this chapter.

Often perceived as a creation of the twentieth century, there were important continuities with older forms of leisure and commercial activity in the way that motor-sport was shaped, performed and perceived. If ballooning had previously provided aerial expertise, leisure pursuits on horses, cycles, skates, skis and yachts provided experiences of travelling at speed. Many career drivers continued to combine these older interests with the new as part of a transnational lifestyle. Thomas Pitt Cholmondeley epitomised the cosmopolitan background of motor racing before World War One as he had Norwegian ancestry, was born in New Zealand and made his name in Britain, mainly by racing German cars.[7] Motor-sport could also be ostentatiously social. The Automobile Club de France (ACF) had formed in 1895 as a prestigious luxury men's club of friends including Albert de Dion and its first President, Dutch-born Baron Etienne van Zuylen van Nijevelt. It set the tone for the way much of international motor-sport is still conducted today. The ACF began to organise competitions, sometimes in conjunction with other national organisations such as the Spanish Automobile Club, Automóvil Club Español (ACE). Some would become iconic events such as the Le Mans 24 Hours and the French Grand Prix.[8] Today the club maintains facilities of 10,000 square meters at the Place de la Concorde in which members can eat, exercise, lounge and read in considerable comfort.

From equally privileged beginnings, the Self-Propelled Traffic Association became the Automobile Club of Great Britain and Ireland in 1897, founded by Frederick Richard Simms.[9] Simms hailed from an old Warwickshire family but was born and educated in Germany, buying the rights to sell Daimler engines across the British Empire at the age of twenty-six. In 1907, the Automobile Club was awarded a Royal title and it became better known by the acronym, the RAC. The Edwardian RAC was also very much a gentleman's club with an exclusive membership policy, permitting women to enter the Whitehall Court Offices only between 3pm and 6 pm.[10] For men, it provided a degree of social interaction for those who had been born into money and those who had made a great deal of their own. For example, Ralph Slazenger joined at a time in his life when his London business success with sporting India-rubber goods marked a break from his religious and regional heritage in the Jewish community of Manchester.[11] Already the main supplier of balls to the Wimbledon lawn tennis championships, Slazenger's RAC membership coincided with the floatation of his company on the stock exchange and a rise in company profits to nearly £50,000 per annum. Originally Ralph Slazenger Moss of Manchester, he had renounced Judaism, shortened his name and embraced the corporate life of the City of London; including memberships of numerous livery companies and guilds. Slazenger became Sheriff of London in 1909 and enjoyed networking; public entertainment; conspicuous philanthropy and leading local welfare campaigns.[12] By 1911 the RAC had moved to specially built offices in Pall Mall and in 1913 purchased a country club at Woodcote Park, Epsom. It continues to operate as a private members' organisation from these two venues today.[13]

In spite of these establishment connections, motor racing was slightly suspect in the popular imagination. It therefore passed into culture in ways that ridiculed the enthusiast as much as it admired him or her. First, it was an individualistic sport of the eccentric aristocrat, like Rolls, or the arriviste, such as Slazenger. There were not many muscular Christians who raced cars. Motoring was rich, showy and did not fit with agendas of social reform. Worse still, motor-sport combined heroic modernity with technological fascination and therefore seemed not to have roots in regional folk games or local leisure forms. In spite of requiring a robust constitution, some questioned whether motoring could become a sport at all. Amid anxieties about physical degeneracy, it could appear that the machine, rather than the driver, was doing the work.

Most significant of all, motor-sport was an activity at which people on the European mainland excelled. Unlike the road circuits of France, Italy,

Germany and Spain, where pedestrians and animals came second to the car, motor racing on British highways remained illegal. From November 1896 the Locomotives on Highways Act began to raise the maximum speed from 4 to 12 mph with a further increase to 20 mph in 1903. Several associations, like the British Motor League, sought to defend the interests of the 'ordinary' motorist from general disdain, aggressive legislation and prohibitive cost. Many had limited success. The Automobile Association (AA) was formed in 1905 with the express intention of beating speed traps. By 1919 The British Motor League was asked by a Miss Helen Ward to consider broadening its representation by admitting women onto the committee and to lower subscriptions for light car users, especially Ford owners.[14]

Motor-sport was also morally questionable because it could be fatal, for spectators and participants. Charles Rolls epitomised 'goggles and dust' racing, serving on the Automobile Club committee from 1897 until 1908.[15] In 1900 Rolls won a 1,000 miles reliability trial promoted by *The Daily Mail*. Three years later he established a world land speed record of 93 mph in Dublin. Having set a record for a non-stop flight across the Channel and back in less than two hours, Rolls died in 1910 in an air crash. Shortly after leaving the board of Rolls-Royce to pursue his interest in motor-sport full time, he gained the dubious distinction of becoming the first British man to be killed by 'the science of aviation.' His lack of fear was a commendable upper-class trait. Dying because of an enthusiasm, however, appeared foolhardy.

Using vehicles for sport combined links with engineering production, industrial design, manufacture, retail and distribution. Greater precision and refinement signaled the purpose of motor-sport, as well as its image: vehicle manufacturers and drivers innovated ever faster and more efficient gains in speed and comfort. Nationalistic interests combined with commercial innovation. Manufacturers of fuel wanted to promote a dependence on their products for everyday travel, either in public or private vehicles. This linked with a number of other cultural industries through advertising, sponsorship and new ways of representing cars at speed, including cinematography.[16] Having a small photograph of a particular product, gave way to having advertisements in which the image was the most prominent feature and a sign of premium quality. The more high status an object or person, the greater the chance that they would be photographed and that the image would be large. This was not a British-led change, but it moved from motor-sport to other forms of professional and amateur physical activity.[17] The visual language of sport therefore altered immeasurably.

Transference of technology across different forms of sport and commercial products appeared in the French magazine *La Vie Au Grande Air* (Life in the Great Outdoors). The language of 'science', or in some cases pseudo-science, featured prominently in advertisements of products relating to motor-sport; horse racing; boxing and running. A narrative of improvement was consistent throughout the diverse examples: new four and six cylinder

Hotchkiss cars; enhanced 'Motosacoche' one and two cylinder motorised bicycles; ultra economic Campéador petrol; better quality Lumière photographic paper; refined E. Krauss scientific lenses; more accurate A. Beaujon maps and Dupont wheelchairs with added accessibility.[18] At least some *La Vie Au Grande Air* advertisers assumed a female readership because beauty and thyroid treatments expressly targeted 'Madame'. In addition, Elliman's Universal Embrocation professed to treat most ailments known to humans, plus quite a few of those that also affected horses. The famous kites of Aug. C. Gomès enabled the user to stay in one place and travel visually regardless of whether their motivation to do so was for sport, publicity, meteorology, aerial photography or military purposes. For those who were actually ill, or could afford travel for health reasons, the thermal baths at Vernet les Bains in the Pyrenees or the Grand Hotel in St Moritz in the Alps looked inviting, as did the Palace Hotel near Lake Lucerne in Switzerland. These publications were visually very different than previous sporting magazines packed with text, like the *Athletic News*, with the added benefit that relatively little reading was required.

If technology and science looked to take human beings beyond the limits of what had previously been thought possible, what were to be the consequences? A book initially written for children by Kenneth Grahame called *Wind in the Reeds* (better known as the more poetic *Wind in the Willows*), first published by Methuen in 1908 was very much of its time in reflecting public anxiety about the effect of speed on the upper classes.[19] With an anthropomorphised Mr. Toad, of Toad Hall, who becomes obsessed by speed, it became a favourite with adults, including A. A. Milne who adapted it for the stage. In the plot, Toad was distracted from Toad Hall by his motoring adventures whereupon weasels invaded the family home to plunder its historic treasures. Unlike 'improving books' written for children, designed to teach good behaviour and manners (and therefore not to be read for pleasure), *Wind in the Willows* allowed the reader to be ambivalent about the main protagonist. Toad's character was a mixture of bad manners; he was by turns brash, dishonest, greedy, spontaneous and, above all, addicted to speed. However, the weasels were eventually ousted and the book's closure placed Toad in the tradition of the loveable rogue. He was to be followed by many more motor-sport enthusiasts in British popular culture whose conduct represented an abdication of responsibility for their own safety and an affront to polite behaviour.[20]

As a fashionable aristocratic performance, motoring was aspirational but tapped into wider concerns about rural England. Pamela Horn describes the situation: 'During the years immediately before and after the First World War about six to eight million acres, or 25 per cent of the land of England, was sold by the nobility and gentry. In Wales and Scotland the proportion was nearer 33 per cent.'[21] A factor in the British mistrust of motor-sport was the threat that travelling for pleasure posed to remaining in a work-based community for life, with the social order that this implied. Manufacturers

seemed to be sensitive to these concerns: Raleigh, which produced motorcycles before 1908 and again between 1919 and 1933, had advertisements in
which their machines, complete with female pillion passenger, were able to
take to the air and leap, horse-like, over obstacles like five-bar gates.[22] Such
transcendent imagery had both nostalgic and progressive aspects. The Triumph Girl also used her motorcycle to travel to the countryside.[23] In spite of
the persistence of columns like 'The Doctor's Car' in *The Motor*, which told
bucolic anecdotes about chasing little pigs down country roads while the
eponymous medic listened to the hum of the tractor and observed the falling
leaves, motoring suggested creeping urbanisation.[24] More of the population
were moving than ever before into large towns and conurbations to work
and, if they were lucky, to move slightly out again to live in suburbia.

In spite of these reservations, there were also new opportunities. Regional
variation within Britain saw the spread of distinct kinds of motor-sport at
specific locations. Selwyn Edge, promoter of the Napier car brand, had
won the third Gordon Bennett race (sponsored by the owner of the *New
York Herald*) for the British Automobile Club in 1902.[25] Having been born
in Australia and educated at Belvedere House College, Edge had made his
name as a cyclist and in manufacturing. His RAC and industry connections
magnified the importance of the British victory and moreover, the winner
could host the competition the following year. The win marked the first
time that the Gordon Bennett Cup would be held outside of France. The
1903 race took place in Ireland because of speed restrictions on the British
mainland and Edge was to finish last in a Napier. The occasion invented
a tradition of 'racing green' as a British colour, though the actual shade
could vary. The Isle of Man had hosted the trials for the Irish event before
its own Touring Trophy (TT) began for motorcars in 1904 and motorcycles
in 1907. By 1905 Shelsley Walsh, between Worcester and Kidderminster,
titled itself 'England's International Speed Hill Climb.'[26] Manufacturers
recognised the commercial value of tests of reliability and speed offered by
a range of competitions. Races advertised the successes of both maker and
brand, thereby improving sales. It was a formula that had worked well with
cycling previously but with the added danger of increased speed and more
spectacular crashes.

These different forms of civic boosterism could have uneven and contested receptions.[27] As Simon Vaukins has shown, the TT races gradually
became more important to the political economy of Manx self-identity and
in external constructions of the island.[28] By 1939 a quarter of a million
people lined the thirty-seven and a half-mile road course, which contained
over 200 hazards, including the ascent and descent of Snaefell.[29] The deaths
on the road course of the Isle of Man supposedly gave birth to the phrase
'Dicing with Death' which became abbreviated in the United States to 'dicing' as part of racing vocabulary. Whatever the accuracy of this attribution,
the newspapers had originally doubted whether the TT circuit could be
covered at a mile a minute by a motorcycle. By 1939 the lap record was 90

mph, today riders compete, and some survive crashes, at speeds of over 170 mph.[30] On the island, particular locations, such as the Mannin Beg began to have reputations of their own as particularly challenging or dangerous. This drew artists and photographers to those sites, further reinforcing their mythic status.[31]

While it is possible to generalise that British enthusiasts sought to promote a sense of national vigour at home and abroad through motor-sport, the question of regional variation makes this more complicated. If teasing out 'British' identity from 'English' 'Irish', 'Manx', 'Anglo-Irish' or other descriptors is sometimes difficult then, there are ways in which it is useful. British education, engineering expertise and social cachet exerted 'pull' factors to attract a transnational class of individual, often with a title or independent means. Attending prestigious private schools, followed by a spell at Cambridge or Oxford university could be an important means of networking. Aviators, drivers and mariners then sought to colonise air, land and sea in measured spans to break records of their own devising, as a form of international sporting movement. A British flag was sometimes literally stuck in the ground to mark the achievement. Where this was not possible, a metaphorical flag had to do and the media were particularly important in this respect.

There were also 'push' factors stemming from perceptions that British motoring had to catch-up against nations perceived as larger, wealthier, technologically stronger or more forceful. Several manufacturers, like Rolls Royce, targeted the much smaller internal market before thinking about export. Importing foreign car brands as luxury items was considered unpatriotic and set a bad example to the lower orders but the domestic manufacturing base was small, nor was it a government priority. The United States, with its large and complex domestic consumer industries, provided unwelcome points of comparison. Indy Car racing, particularly at Indianapolis, developed as a specifically American form, quite different from the European emphasis on Grand Prix competitions.[32] German, and French military strength could be interpreted in the British press through the ability of their firms to produce motor vehicles. By 1919, the democratising effects of vehicle-ownership were being defended against allegations of Bolshevism.[33]

The previous chapter used examples from a range of Olympic sports where comparable processes of nationalistic discourse were at work. The general atmosphere of British motoring helped to create a public awareness of some pioneering women, remarkable for their individualism. Aviators, scorchers and motorinas were scrutinised for their achievements, appearances, clothing and lifestyles. Motorised transport provided conspicuous leisure but also the means to break records at the limits of the technology of the time. Though the 'motoring pastoral' has been written about as a mainly male phenomenon, there were plenty of 'motor-maids' who were not content to take the pillion seat and distinguished themselves on land, sea and air.[34] It is difficult to draw clear definitions of amateur and professional activity therefore. The relationships between leisure, work and earnings (including prizes and endorsement fees) were often extremely blurred.

AVIATORS, SCORCHERS AND MOTORINAS: DOROTHY LEVITT AND EARLY WOMEN MOTORISTS

There are currently few academic articles on motor racing as a sporting activity. Adrian Smith's paper 'Sport, Speed and the Technological Imperative' located the inter-war period as of particular historic importance.[35] However, women were also an important part of the early history and feature in a considerable literature, fashion, art and collectibles market. Most people, for example, will be aware of Bertha Benz (1849–1944), who drove 180 kilometres between the cities of Mannheim to Pforzheim in August 1888.[36] The name Mercédès famously came from the daughter of Emil Jellinek, the commercial partner of Karl Benz; Gottlieb Daimler and the 'King of constructors' Wilhelm Maybach. A duo of French aristocratic women made motoring fashionable. Hélène de Rothschild, Baroness van Zuylen (1863–1947) first competed in the 1898 Paris to Amsterdam race under the pseudonym Snail (her husband, Etienne, competed as Escargot). Her compatriot, Anne de Mortemart, Duchess d'Uzès (1847–1933), was also famous for her hunting skills and has been credited with being the first European woman to pass a driving test on 23 April 1898.[37] She also appears to be the first to be caught speeding in her 2-cylinder Delahaye at over 12 km per hour on 9 June in the Bois de Bologne the same year.

The many and varied fashion statements of Camille du Gast (1868–1942) perhaps deserve a paper in their own right. Barbara Burman only briefly references Du Gast in her article on aviators and racing drivers but gives a well-illustrated argument of the move towards image as part of celebrity status in the years between 1900 and 1939.[38] Particularly useful is Burman's argument that the clothing strategies of women who raced and flew in the Edwardian period were creative and often independent of the prevailing fashion system. If the costumes of the Olympic swimmers mentioned in the previous chapter were examples of revelation of the active female body, the racing motorists often accentuated their skill through costume choices. Audacity and bravery were symbolised by clothing associated with the military, hunting or work-wear; comprising items made of leather, fur and flannel. Feminine concessions included veils, generously cut garments and decorative detail.

Du Gast was famous for sometimes wearing full dress uniform and an admiral's hat but was also a daring racer, the 'Amazon with green eyes' who finished thirty-third out of 122 participants in the 1901 Paris to Berlin race.[39] In 1903 the ACF and the ACE organised a Paris to Madrid event, known after as the 'race of death' because fewer than half of the 300 cars finished and there were at least eight casualties, with rumours of many more injured. Du Gast dropped from eighth place to finish to forty-fifth, after stopping to help an overturned De Dietrich and administering first aid to its injured driver. Her patient survived to race again. By 1904 she was invited to become a member of the ACF.

After a ban on women in the 1904 Berlin to Paris Gordon Bennett Cup, supposedly due to their more nervous disposition, Du Gast, also known as 'the Valkyrie of the motor-car', then piloted a Darracq motor-boat (wearing a violet costume and a captain's hat) in an open-sea race from Angiers to Toulon where all of the vessels found misfortune. Rescued by the destroyer Kléber, she was declared the winner two months later.[40] The outfits were but one enthusiasm; other interests and achievements were extensive. A celebrity with a degree of notoriety, Du Gast wrote many of her activities up in journals of the day arguing that sport was vital to the feminist cause. Her husband Jules Crespin was the manager and majority shareholder of the large Dufayels department store when they married in 1890 but he died young in 1896, leaving her one of the wealthiest widows of Belle Époque Paris. Also accomplished in fencing, winter and field sports, Du Gast used her maiden name to avoid accusations that motor races, balloon ascents (followed by parachute descents) and travel writing were designed chiefly as publicity stunts for the Dufayels shops. Du Gast's life outside sport seems to have been equally fantastic. Three scandalous court cases in 1902 saw her accused of posing naked in a portrait but for a Venetian mask. Du Gast was innocent, but lost the legal argument. She then foiled an assassination attempt by her only daughter who was eager to inherit in 1910. Her subsequent work for women's rights; child welfare and animal charities led to the Rue Crespin du Gast being named in her honour in Paris.

However, the British were undoubtedly motor enthusiasts well before World War One. There are estimates of approximately 1,500 cars in Britain by 1906 but cannibalisation of old machinery, considerable variation in design and recycling of material make the number of vehicles difficult to confirm. William Plowden estimates that both car and motorbike ownership stood at ten times that amount by 1914.[41] Against the general background of wealthy elitism, drivers outnumbered vehicles and so, whatever the precise numbers, we can see a broadening of the driving population before the First World War. This provided a small pool of experienced female drivers for ambulance, motorcycle, mail and taxi work, in addition to maintenance expertise, during hostilities.[42] Knowledge and practice provided by these 'war duties' helped to further expand the number of women motorists again in the ensuing peace.

A small minority of female motorists and aviators were able to earn money from their activities, even if this could be a brief and precarious form of employment. American journalist and theatre critic Harriet Quimby (1875–1912) obtained a US pilot's licence in 1911 and a year later became the first woman to fly the English Channel.[43] Known for wearing trousers and knickerbockers while she flew, Quimby also earned money writing 'scenarios', or early screen plays for silent films. She was killed with her passenger after both were thrown from the aircraft into the sea while taking part at a show in Boston in 1912. Other female aviators against whom she raced included the Belgian Hélène Dutrieu (1877–1961) and the Americans Matilde Moisant (1878–1964) and Blanche Stuart Scott (1889–1970).[44] While Dutrieu had multiple careers in motor racing, stunt work and flying, Matilde Moisant was a friend of Harriet Quimby who gave up aviation after surviving her own minor accident in 1912. Blanche Stuart Scott, having driven cars from the age of thirteen, went on to a media career before collecting items for museums and archives in order to memorialise the efforts of early motorists and aviators such as herself. There is obviously a wealth of material to be scrutinised here by academic studies of their lives and careers: not least how far their activities can best be understood as work, sport, voluntarism or leisure.

Some British women also became self-supporting from their motor industry expertise: Hilda Hewlett (née Herbert, 1864–1943) was chiefly known as the artistically-trained wife of the successful romantic novelist Maurice, and mother of two children (Cecco born in 1890 and Pia, 1895). [45] Hilda obtained her British pilot's licence at the age of forty-seven in 1911 and taught her son, a naval officer, to fly. Both had distinguished careers. Hilda Hewlett also drove and ran a successful flying school at Brooklands between 1910 and 1912 before moving into aircraft manufacturing.[46] She separated amicably from her husband in 1915 over his lack of enthusiasm for her career. When he died in 1923, Hilda settled to be near Pia's family in New Zealand, becoming the first President of the Tauranga Aero and Gliding Club. Other enthusiasts were less famous lady amateurs and we know little more about Kitty Loftus and Vera Butler than that they were proud owners of French driving certificates and drove a 5hp Renault Voiturette [sic] across the Alps in 1901.[47] Miss Hampson of Southport appeared equally briefly in *The Autocar* during 1903 having driven 22,000 miles and, the same year, Miss Neville was reported to prefer driving without the need for an accompanying mechanic.[48]

The diversity of vehicles and craft is astonishing. There was much less homogeneity of design because the automotive industry was in its infancy. Product design from this period can look anachronistic today but extended to toys, games and the manufacture of motoring accessories: Whittingham and Wilkin announced in 1899 that they were experimenting with a solid glass brake block for rubber tyres, for instance.[49] Presumably this had only been tested inside in dry conditions. Some design could be gendered: the 'step through' style of women's bicycle design, which assumed the rider would be wearing a skirt or dress, was to be replicated in some early twentieth-century motorcycle designs. The lack of stability at speed caused so many accidents, that modesty eventually gave way to practicality. Devices patented for motorbike pillion passengers included the Tan-Sad footrest, to enable a woman to sit side-saddle in her best outfit, though goodness knows at what speed.[50] Such inventions were speculative in catering for new markets and some products were quickly obsolete. Assuming women did not want to wear goggles, British *Vogue* presented the personal windscreen that projected from the face by about six inches on a frame that slipped over the head and rested on the shoulders.[51] The device came with its own yellow leather carrying case. It would be interesting to know how many were sold.

Photography and the growth of the media industries were also synonymous with motor-sport. We have some wonderful still and moving images because speed was so topical.[52] By 1902 Alfred Harmsworth had endorsed his enthusiasm by editing *Motors and Motor Driving* for the Badminton Library. It contained an engraving with the caption 'Her Majesty the Queen in Her Electric Car at Sandringham.'[53] A 'motor stable' was established at Buckingham Palace for more vehicles and the car became used as part of routine business, though the ceremonial aspects of royal life were left to horsepower. Women of the upper and middle classes relished the new freedoms and opportunities that motor-sport offered. Alfred Harmsworth was ennobled as Viscount Northcliffe in 1905, and through many newspaper titles ensured that the majority of readers who could not afford a car, could read about the lucky few who were able to drive.

By 1908 Northcliffe had bought *The Times*, and, as the previous chapter has briefly discussed, lent his support to sporting occasions such as the Olympic Games.[54] He had already re-launched the *Daily Mirror* in 1904, from being a paper written by women for women, to a publication that was led by established journalists but also using press photography more extensively.[55] Other titles like *The Daily Mail, Daily Express, Daily Chronicle* and *Daily Herald* (founded in 1912 by trade unionists and socialists) followed suit. Press agencies such as Topical, Fox Photos and World Wide increased as a result of the need for a constant supply of images. Harmsworth was as keen to make news as report events. He realised the potential of breaking records, encouraging the construction of the Brooklands circuit for this purpose in early 1906. The same year, *The Daily Mail* offered a prize of £1,000 for the first cross-Channel flight, a sum won in 1909 by Louis Blériot. Accompanying the aviator to a celebratory lunch at the Savoy and cheered on by large crowds, Northcliffe then put up a prize ten times the amount for the first London to Manchester flight.

Seeing representations of things became just as much part of a sports enthusiast's experience as reading about events. Cars themselves became objects of desire. In addition to the daily newspapers, there were many British specialist publications such as *The Car, The Motor, The Light Car and Cycle-Car, The Motorcycle* and *Motorcycling* relying on photographs and other images for substantive amounts of their content.[56] Luxury publications developed this trend with aesthetic influences. The first performance of the Ballet Russe in Paris in 1909 had helped to make oriental references and fur intensely fashionable in publications like *Vogue*. Men and women motorists wearing the latest fur stoles, muffs and toque hats were much in evidence in both its British and American editions.[57] Lord John Douglas-Scott Montagu edited *The Car Illustrated* weekly and the monthly *The Car* magazines. Montagu's visual imagination led to the first winged mascot in a draped robe design to adorn a Rolls Royce, based on the figure of his secretary and mistress Eleanor Vasco Thornton (1880–1915).[58] Later adapted to the more famous *The Spirit of Ecstasy* for all Rolls Royce cars, the early sculpture, called *The Whisperer,* hinted at the secrecy of the relationship as the figure held her forefinger to her lips.

Covers of *The Car* often had a classic portrait head and shoulders photograph: in November 1911 Mrs Maurice Hewlett was celebrated as 'The First Englishwoman to Gain an Aviator's Certificate.'[59] It could have been a painting. The clothing of Hilda Hewlett when attired for flying was not designed to be captured on canvas but snapshots nevertheless provide valuable evidence for historians. For occasions when a camera was not practical or aesthetically satisfactory, drawing could convey speed. Historic motoring artwork has considerable contemporary worth: a Brooks auction catalogue listing *The MG Girl* from 1932 in watercolour and charcoal by Frederick Gordon Crosby had an expected value of £7,000 to 10,000 in 1990 and its value has since risen.[60] F. Gordon Crosby was prolific and diverse in his subjects and styles. He remains one of the most collectible of the fine artists of early motor racing, in spite of some snobbishness by non-enthusiasts that his work is better understood as illustration.

So there was a strong motoring presence in luxury publications, as much concerning what people wore, as which model of car they drove. Chapter 4 of Harmsworth's *Motors* was co-authored by the society journalist, Mary, Lady Jeune (1849–1931) and Baron Etienne Zuylen de Nyvelt. It concluded:

> In the case of motor driving or riding there are two things only to be considered: how a woman can keep herself warm in winter and not be suffocated by the dust in summer without making herself very unattractive. Dress must be regulated to a great extent by the speed at which she travels and it is quite possible to wear a smart hat and pretty clothes if the pace is a comparatively slow one, such as is usual in the Park or in the streets of London. This chapter, however, has to deal with the more serious side of the questions, how a woman should dress who goes on long journeys in every kind of weather, and at a high rate of speed. The best material for excluding the cold is leather, kid or chamois leather: the latter may be recommended for lining the coat, and kid for the outside covering.[61]

Born Susan Marie Elizabeth Stewart-Mackenzie of an impoverished family and a widow at an early age, Mary became the wife of barrister Francis Henry Jeune in 1881 and later Lady St Helier. A society hostess connected with the leading personalities of the day, also a prolific journalist and member of the Primrose League, Mary Jeune preferred a blue Glengarry cap in which to drive over which she tied a large gauze veil. Indeed, by 1906 the large picture hat, tied under the chin with a veil of gauze, chiffon or net, became a fashion for pedestrians who could not afford to own a vehicle and therefore risked being teased by small children in the street who would shout 'Where's your car?'[62]

Such ignominy aside, as the twentieth century progressed more women could fulfill the ambition to journey for sport and to use powered vehicles in competitive activities, in spite of restrictions of both a practical and ideological nature.[63] Goggles would later be worn by more women as pragmatic responses to seeing clearly at greater speed. Items held in the collections at the Fashion Institute of Technology, New York evidence this evolution of female motor clothing with both male and female references, combining both sensible and expensively decorous elements. Duster coats, previously used for walking and horse riding, can be seen to evolve into exquisitely tailored garments with piping and appliqué detail worn to motor, beneath which layers of warming underclothes often included chamois leather worn next to the skin.[64] With the combination of comfort and ostentation, these were costumes in which to see and be seen. However, women motor-sport enthusiasts were not all born to greatness. A brief biographical overview of the career of Dorothy Levitt, the most famous female driver of the age, can illustrate some research challenges that remain until we know about a greater variety of personalities. The Kodak Girl had been used to suggest that 'even women' could master camera equipment, with the slogan 'You press the button, we do the rest' in 1888. At subsequent world expositions, the style of the Kodak Girl's clothes changed, along with the model of camera, in what proved to be a clever way of selling paraphernalia of all kinds to new consumers as the latest gadget. Vehicle manufacturers translated the technique, amongst them Selwyn Edge of Napier cars, probably inspired by France's Camille Du Gast. Dorothy Levitt had previously been employed as a typist at the Napier works and then became a personal assistant to Selwyn Edge.

Born to a wealthy Jewish family in Hackney, probably under the name of Elizabeth Dorothy Levi, no evidence has yet revealed when her father Jacob came to England or if he was born in London. He had anglicised his name to become John Levit, (spelled with a single t) in the 1901 census.[65] Her mother, Julia Raphael has also been difficult to trace via the census, though the maternal line had a range of business interests from jewellery to hotels based in the city. An elder sister, Lilly (1878–1879), died in infancy and a younger sister Elsie Ruby (1892–1963) married Mark Lewis in 1917.[66] The family appear to have been affluent. Details of Dorothy's school days and how she came to work for Edge remain hazy. However, it was clear that Levitt promoted herself just as much as the products that she endorsed: her book *The Woman and The Car* combined political comment, travelogue and practical advice.[67]

The problematic nature of the evidence precludes judgements as to how far Levitt was ambivalent about her Jewish descent but she had a tendency to present herself as from a landed family, citing a West Country heritage, unsubstantiated so far. Continuing the theme, Levitt claimed to be a good horsewoman and shot before taking up driving. She also wrote that she had been sent to France by Napier to learn about car engines, before giving many aristocratic women driving lessons, including royalty. A more prosaic version of events contended that she was given driving lessons by a grudging Leslie Callingham, then a young Napier company salesman, who would later race Bentleys at Brooklands and Le Mans.[68] A well-known 'scorcher', Dorothy was fined for speeding in 1903 and, with a female friend, successfully sued a General Post Office van for damages in a collision the same year.

Whatever the case of how she acquired her driving skills, Levitt won her class in the 1903 Southport Speed Trial in Selwyn Edge's Gladiator car, then sealed her reputation in a 1,000-mile time trial.[69] Equally significant the same year, Levitt, along with Edge and Campbell Muir, won the first Harmsworth Trophy in Ireland. The prize was another innovation by the newspaper magnate in the form of a motor boat race between nations (rather than individuals or manufacturers). The winning crew set a water speed record of the time at almost 20 mph, although it is unclear who was driving at what stages of the victory.

Edge had a number of interests in other motor companies and De Dion offered Dorothy a series of publicity appearances, which she used to prove the seriousness of her intent as a driver. She completed the Hereford 1,000 mile trial in one of two De Dions supplied by the company and revealed an aptitude for self-promotion. First, Levitt insisted that her pet Pomeranian dog, Dodo, would accompany her throughout and secondly, she wore an elaborate costume comprising a duster coat, large picture hat and veil. In spite of the other drivers' resentment at being upstaged in such a manner, Dorothy became popular with her colleagues, the public and car manufacturers. Levitt's charm also impressed journalist, driver and historian S. C. H. 'Sammy' Davis:

> Masculine annoyance was expressed by the appearance one morning of every single car with a toy dog firmly strapped to its bonnet and the uglier the dog the more pleased its owner. But Dorothy had a sense of humour and at the concert given to competitors one evening—to which she as a woman was *not* invited—proceedings were interrupted by the entry of a menial solemnly bearing a gift bag of dog biscuits suitably inscribed by Dorothy for each of the men competitors. Woman had taken game and set [sic]. By unanimous decision she was invited to the remainder of that concert.[70]

Best known as sports editor of *The Autocar*, Davis' account of Levitt's career is the most witty and compelling of many that exist. He knew her personally and was himself integral to racing subculture at the time, driving for Daimler, Aston Martin and Bentley in addition to winning a 24 Hours Le Mans race in 1927. His descriptions could, however, include a degree of exoticism: 'A tall girl with a strong though feminine face, made more attractive by long eyes reminding one of the East.'[71] Between 1903 and 1909 Levitt raced in France, Germany and Scotland. In spite of more extensive work in showrooms and general sales, even Edge could not persuade the Brooklands authorities to let her race in 1907 and it seems that she took to appearing on the European mainland to counter the snub. Newport-born Maud Manville (previously Wallis, 1872–1909), wife of the chairman of Daimler, seems to have been Levitt's greatest rival. Manville had competed in the Brighton Speed Trials in 1905 to take a class win. At the same meeting, Levitt has beaten Camille Du Gast in another race. Manville then drove a works-prepared car round the challenging six-day Herkomer Trial in Germany to considerable acclaim in both 1905 and 1906. Dorothy completed the same event in a Napier without penalties in 1907 to come in fourteenth out of over 170 competitors. Effectively Levitt became both a dedicated driver and a publicist for Napier but maintained that she drove as an amateur.

Appearing on the cover of *The Woman and The Car* in lavish fur coat, gloves and a veil, Levitt was also shown in photographs inside the book priming a carburetor and doing other basic maintenance tasks. Often credited with using a small hand-held mirror to obtain a view behind the car, and thereby 'inventing' the rear view mirror before it was commercially available in 1914, Levitt was also rumoured to carry a Colt revolver for personal protection.[72] The win over Du Gast at Brighton was proclaimed as a 'women's world speed record' of 79 miles per hour and rewarded with the *Autocar* Challenge Trophy. Having prevented Levitt from racing a French-made Mors in the Isle of Man for fear it would promote a foreign brand, Edge provided a larger Napier car to help raise the women's record to 91 mph the following year at Blackpool. Promoted in advertisements as 'The Fastest Girl on Earth' and 'Champion Lady Motorist of the World' Levitt also trained for her pilot's licence in 1909 although there is no evidence that she passed.

Dorothy Levitt was booked to talk about her early aviation experience in March 1910 at the Criterion Restaurant to the Aero Club of the United Kingdom but little is known about her after this until her rather sad end, when she was found dead in bed on 17 May 1922. A subsequent inquest recorded a verdict of misadventure, attributing the cause to morphine poisoning, complicated by heart disease and measles.[73] Having died at 50 Upper Baker Street, London, as a spinster of independent means, this raises several questions as to why Dorothy had not moved, with the rest of her family, to Bristol. A rather cryptic note asked to be buried in a field by the sea and her will left around £200 to her sister Elsie, plus a diamond necklace and ring in lieu of a loan.[74] Where were Dorothy Levitt's items of memorabilia and other trinkets from a well-publicised career subsequently distributed? How did she spend the last twelve years of her life? Was she obliged to withdraw from public life due to ill health or circumstance or did she choose to become a more private citizen?

Levitt's book and regular articles for the *London Daily Graphic* lack reliable autobiographical details but present a version of her life to the reading public. Levitt enjoyed living the life of an independent woman about town in a flat with Dodo, two housekeepers and many friends but this cannot be confirmed through the 1911 census. This could be due to her support of the suffragette boycott, though recent work has suggested that this campaign was not as widespread as has been previously considered, extending to maybe a few thousand women.[75] However, as a self-reliant woman Levitt was perhaps precisely one of the few who would back such a protest. While she was a successful works team driver and received international recognition for her driving abilities it would be interesting to see how many other contemporaries she had. How did her family view her lifestyle and achievements? What did the wider Jewish community think of her anglicised and progressive public persona? Different Jewish communities in Britain have used various athletic enterprises as part of processes of integration and acculturation, but little research has considered motorsport.[76] Like the involvement of Slazenger in the RAC, Dorothy Levitt's career suggests the need to look more at how car ownership and racing figure in the transmigration and identity of the Jewish population in Britain before World War One.

In presenting this rather provisional career of a female 'motorina' many questions of identity and biography therefore remain. The mutual promotion helped both the profile of Edge and Levitt to the extent that some writers have implied a personal as well as a business relationship. This would be difficult to substantiate but perhaps family history will eventually help with this line of enquiry. Dorothy remained single, while Edge married twice. After selling his promotional company S. F. Edge (1907) Ltd. to Napiers in 1912, on condition that he stayed out of the motor trade for seven years, Edge concentrated upon his agricultural interests in Sussex. There he bred pedigree pigs and applied the same technocratic enthusiasm to agriculture that he had to racing cars. Before that though, he was to set a twenty-four hour record at Brooklands in 1907, cementing the reputation of the circuit with the British public as a place where motor-sport could be world-leading. The venue had a public image of understated British refinement but underneath the gloss was an improvised nonconformity. As this section on some of the notable women figures has demonstrated, the recently created traditions of British motor-sport positively embraced eccentricity and the audacity of hope. Whether motor-sport was viewed as self-indulgent or heroically patriotic, Brooklands would provide a focal point for British racing for the following thirty years.

BROOKLANDS: 'THE RIGHT CROWD AND NO OVERCROWDING'

Brooklands in Weybridge, Surrey opened in 1907 and is often called the 'birthplace of British motor-sport.'[77] Husband and wife, Hugh (1848–1926) and Ethel (1864–1956) Locke King provided the land for the circuit close to Brooklands House, which had been built in 1862 by Hugh's father.[78] As the only surviving son, Hugh had inherited 4, 600 acres of land on his father's death in 1885 mainly in Surrey, Sussex and Devon.[79] Having married in 1884, Hugh and Ethel dabbled in development according to their enthusiasms, most notably the Mena House Hotel in Cairo, residential estates at Portmere Park Weybridge and the New Zealand golf club near Byfleet. The Locke Kings had a large 70 horse power Itala car which Ethel often drove. Hugh was less intrepid, saying 'You can't have very big accident in very small car.'[80] The construction of a motor racing track at Brooklands was their largest and most ambitious project, costing an estimated £100,000, plus additional family funds when it became clear that the initial outlay would not be sufficient. The original estimate had been £22,000.

In many ways, Brooklands was a monument to nationalism in the British motor and air industries, of which racing was as much consequence as a purpose. When work began Weybridge was a village with a population of under 6,000. The narrative that accompanied pictures of the construction in the *Illustrated Sporting and Dramatic News*, *Daily Chronicle*, *Daily Graphic*, *Country Gentleman* and *The Daily Mail* frequently referenced great Victorian engineers and their feats. The River Wey was diverted, bridges and railway viaducts commissioned, but crucially, the surface was built of gravel and Portland concrete, not the new, and prohibitively expensive, 'Taafalt' asphalt. Bumps in the race-track would cost many of Brookland's drivers broken noses and lost teeth when encountered at high speed because helmets were often soft and open-faced in design.

Practicalities aside, the venue quickly became known as 'Motoring Ascot' or, more clumsily, the 'Epsom of Automobilism' because of its part in the cosmopolitan lifestyles of the Locke Kings and their friends. The proletarian holiday venue Skegness, in Lincolnshire, would later try to gentrify its image by claiming to be 'Brooklands by the Sea' after hosting races on the sands in the 1920s, featuring well-known drivers from the track, including Ivy Cummings (1900–1971).[81] Ethel Locke King was therefore partly responsible for the funding of one of Britain's most iconic sporting sites and helped to set the tone in which competitions took place at an internationally important sports facility. Her influence need not be overstated: there were only two official women's races before World War One, in spite of constant lobbying by female drivers. However, more evidence of women taking part in mixed events has gradually emerged. Racing aside, it was clear that without her intervention the track would not have been finished and, subsequently, women were very much part of the social scene.

The Locke Kings had not been very successful hoteliers in terms of attending to profits and they embarked on the construction in a rough and ready manner, forming the Brooklands Automobile Racing Club (BARC) in December 1906 before the track was completed.[82] In the first attempt to institutionalise motor-sport in Britain, women could be admitted provided two members of the club committee approved their application. Brooklands was notionally open to all but racing was to be administered by the club who initially had their HQ at Carlton House, Regent Street SW1. The committee was comprised mainly of Lords, Dukes and the odd Prince. It was only twenty miles from the RAC in Piccadilly and had close links with its members, among them Selwyn Edge.[83] There remain a wealth of photographs of Brooklands in construction, deserving more critical attention from historians. Harnessing technology that was evolving, and therefore unpredictable, made national virility synonymous with science, modernity, and individualist pioneering spirit. Just as the metaphor of the body as machine became more widely used, mechanised sports came to stand for national fitness, for progress and a leading place in technocratic development.

The social exclusivity of the BARC, summed up by the motto 'The Right Crowd and No Overcrowding', expressed a particular form of male and female upper-class glamour with a much wider resonance, regardless of who later went to see the racing. As Roger Munting has summarised the attraction of motor-sport to a wider public: 'One did not have to be of the people to be admired by the people.'[84] At the other end of the social scale, more than 1,000 men were involved in the build, mainly of Irish descent. Conditions were difficult and some slept rough on Weybridge Common. The construction took just over a year from being publicly discussed to completion and was hailed as a triumph of British civil engineering. The workforce, sometimes estimated closer to 2,000 men and their families, were an important part of the Brooklands mystique, harking back to the great railway building schemes of the Victorians. What such references disguised was the fact that the track was essentially a rich couple's indulgence and by definition, the cars would travel for miles without actually going anywhere. Wonderful visual contrasts of this class and work-leisure divide remain in photographs of the track when it was finished. Gangs of men, ropes tied around their waist to stop them falling down the steep banking, used brooms to sweep the racing surface by hand, meanwhile spectators in swimsuits had picnics in punts on the River Wey from which to observe the action.[85]

By January 1907 Hugh had a nervous breakdown and was close to bankruptcy, having mortgaged other property to fund Brooklands. Ethel took over and persuaded her family, particularly her brother Francis Gore-Brown KC, an authority on company law, and friends like Ernest de Rodakowski, that more money would be required to save disgrace.[86] A railway engineer designed the banked curves to allow speeds of up to 90 mph but by the 1930s the lap record was in excess of 130 mph. The track had a total length of three and a quarter miles, of which two miles were level and it was 100 feet wide. The Byfleet bank was twenty-one feet and ten inches high. Members' bank was twenty-eight feet and eight inches high. There was seating for 5,000 people in stands and space for 30,000 spectators in total. In reward for such perseverance, Ethel inaugurated the circuit driving the Itala with Hugh as passenger at a lunch on 17 June 1907.[87] Hugh was recovered enough to give a short speech of thanks. The procession was nevertheless provoked by having a woman driver at the front and turned into an impromptu race, with the first three cars reaching speed of over 90 mph. This was followed by an air contest and six car events.[88] Drivers wore coloured smocks 'numbering of the cars not being tolerated' and the Jockey Club starter was used to begin competition. The idea of Grand Prix, literally big prizes, was taken seriously: for entry fees from fifteen to fifty sovereigns, prize money in the first six races ranged from 250 sovereigns to 1,400 sovereigns. A cup race was also valued at 200 sovereigns.[89] By September 1907 concessions were made to spectators in the form of discs with the number of the car on each vehicle.

Therefore, Brooklands was not conceived or built as a stadium in the conventional sense of being a commercially-funded built environment, primarily intended for the performance of sport in front of paying spectators.[90] The circuit was a privately-owned testing site for competitors of motorsport and aviation, to which a paying public were admitted initially for the relatively prohibitive sum of a sovereign, later reduced to a shilling. It was a vast site and spectators could not have seen the cars all the way around, so the latest technology was used to keep a tally of the racing. Race engineers who prepared the vehicles epitomised a do-it-yourself spirit. Unlike horse racing, the cars' owners then got the pleasure of actually driving. Whereas wealthy race horse owners used a paid jockey in silks to risk life and limb, both the considerable financial costs and the physical perils of motor racing were borne by the owner-driver; often enthusiastically so. In that sense, it was a unique spectacle. Just over a year after the opening of Brooklands, William Burke became the first fatality at the track after being thrown out during an accident when riding as a passenger in a Mercedes to gain some experience of the motor industry.[91] More shocking because Burke was just twenty-two years old, at the inquest the Coroner blamed the death on a 'degenerate taste' for motor-sport and the *Daily Graphic* led an inquiry. Racing, however, continued.

Brooklands' significance was magnified because it was better known second-hand than attended in person. On 29 June 1907 Selwyn Edge established a 24-hours solo record by travelling at an average speed of 65 mph to complete over 1,500 miles with a few brief rests in between. He had beaten two other co-driven Napiers, also in British racing green, and smashed a distance record by over 500 miles, which had been set two years before at Indianapolis. With his onboard mechanic and large backup team ignored, the combination of individual pluck and efficient workmanship defined this achievement as a historic record for rugged British individualism. Edge was not above augmenting the effect, brushing his achievement off as a 'holiday.' The constant noise annoyed the Locke King's neighbours so much that no more twenty-four hour attempts were allowed, unless completed by two twelve hour stints, known as a 'Double 12'.

Edge would return to Brooklands in 1922 for a simultaneous attempt on the car and motor-cycle world Double 12 hour record with Preston-born Gwenda Janson (née Glubb, 1884–1990).[92] On this occasion Edge averaged just under 75 mph and broke thirty records for the combined twenty four hour run in a 5.7 litre Spyker. Gwenda Jansen on a 250cc Trump-JAP motorcycle established the first Double 12 on two wheels at just under forty five miles an hour, sustained, it was said, by tea and cigarettes.[93] Gwenda was to go on to become a Brooklands stalwart and opened an engineering factory on the Weybridge site during World War Two, as will be discussed in later chapters.

Women were not allowed to race in the first official Brooklands race meeting 6 July 1907 because, the BARC declared, there were no women jockeys. However, not all conventions developed from horse racing and several kinds of machine could be rivals in the same event. George Eyston remembered early Brookland's competitions: 'Motor cycles competed at BARC car meetings and we were given a coloured sash to wear round the waist as an identification instead of numbers.'[94] In 1908 the ruling banning women was relaxed and a Ladies' Bracelet handicap involved seven contestants who had paid an entry fee of three sovereigns. The second placed driver won a brooch. Muriel Thompson (1875–1939) drove an Austin nicknamed 'Pobble' to win, ahead of Ethel Locke King in her Itala called 'Bambo,' with Christabel Ellis (1888–1954) third in an Arrol-Johnston.[95] Percy F. Spence captured a celebratory image of the occasion for the *Illustrated London News*.[96] Thompson was distinguishable by a purple scarf, Locke King wore one in white and Ellis sported a pale blue sash.[97] Mrs Ada Billing, Lady Muriel Gore-Browne, Miss N. Ridge-Jones and Mrs J. Roland-Hewitt also entered the race, although it has been difficult to get more biographical information on these participants. Hats and coloured scarves aside, the women all wore goggles and adopted a racing position, leaning back at about forty-five degrees with a rope tied around their skirts to prevent any wardrobe malfunction. Christabel Ellis again faced Muriel Thompson in a private match on the 3 August 1908 over three miles and was beaten into second place.[98]

If, in 1908, the women sat more on the cars than in them, racing shells were gradually refined and by 1912 *The Autocar* found Muriel Thompson had gained 'considerable fame' in her modified Austin as a Brooklands favourite.[99] By 1912 the RAC had allowed women as 'associates' into its Gala day.[100] In addition, several car clubs held races at the track, allowing wives and daughters of members to compete. The Essex Motor Club had a short car race in which Miss Goldie 'started off splendidly, but her car, which was fully equipped for touring, had hardly sufficient start to enable her to hold her lead' and she tied for third place in her Delage with Mr Cummings.[101]

The broad point is that there was enough of an interest in women competing at Brooklands before World War I to make the revival of competition in the inter-war period even more enthusiastically received. Ivy Cummings was reportedly eleven or twelve when, left for a short while in a stationary car at Brooklands by her father, she managed to put it in gear and complete a lap before a puncture obliged her to enter the paddock.[102] Though this is not a version of events substantiated by documentary sources, Ivy Cummings did go on to have an outstanding racing career in Britain and France. She was to race with her mother as a passenger in the first post-war Brooklands meeting on 11 April 1920. From that year onwards, there were more female and mixed races, provided women drivers could persuade someone to lend them a car or could afford to buy their own. The rules on whether they had to have a male mechanic at Brooklands fluctuated from year to year, as they did for male drivers. In addition to racing until 1926, Cummings worked in her father's business after the First World War and ran one of at least three women-friendly repair and second hand garages in South London.[103] There may well have been more: Maxwell cars were sold by Marian G. Paige who advertised pointedly: 'Votes for Women! If I cannot get the vote, I can get the goods you want, which is of more interest to you . . . The Only Lady Motor Dealer (11 years practical experience) 199 Piccadilly London [sic].'[104] Business in Light Cars was evidently good because she was trading in Baby Peugeots; Calcotts; Morris-Oxfords; Perrys; Singers and Swifts in subsequent promotions.[105]

In conclusion, because of the qualitative and quantitative changes to racing and its social cachet wrought by Brooklands, Cronin and Holt may have underestimated the contribution of the British to international motor-sport.[106] Enthusiasts' histories demonstrate the assortment of manufacturing brands and models.[107] While 'oval' racing on temporary surfaces had taken place before, the establishment of other purpose-built sites quickly followed, such as the Indianapolis Motor Speedway.[108] However, even before completion, the Brooklands circuit was widely fashionable and its events much reported. The 'Brookland's Nut' passed into popular culture denoting a motorist determined to take a corner on two wheels in a car, rather than four, and who wore a cap with the peak pointing to the back of his head 'at all times and in all places' to indicate his enthusiasm for speed.[109]

Brooklands also became the largest aviation production centre in the country with some 4,300 aircraft built after Vickers aeronautical production moved into the Itala car works, along with other aviation companies from 1915 onwards. The Royal Flying Corps established its headquarters at Weybridge and it was a major public and private training base for pilots. The racing track reopened in 1920, now more popular with spectators, as well as increased royal patronage. Proprietorship of the venue passed to

Ethel with Hugh's death in January 1926, increasing her influence. More women drivers raced at the track in a wider range of events between then and 1939, when it again became an important centre for manufacturing. The racing circuit at Brooklands fell into disrepair during World War II. A museum and archive housed in the remaining buildings chart this history.[110] Another form of legacy remained, as the Weybridge site is currently an industrial park for companies that have interests in aviation, technology, transport, premium brands and leisure.[111]

Because of what appears to be a discontinuous history, and augmented by a somewhat nostalgic atmosphere at the museum, Brooklands can sometimes be overlooked in what little academic work there has been of key motor-sport events.[112] Since motor-sport has often been ignored generally, the 'hot' forms of nationalist expression evident in track construction at Brooklands, along with relatively more banal expressions of identity in its subsequent club rituals, have been much neglected.[113] Hugh Locke King would not receive any public honour for being a benefactor to British motor-sport, in spite of the financial and personal cost he bore. His wife ran a Red Cross hospital on the estate at Brooklands House from 1915 until 1919 and it is likely that she was honoured with a prestigious Dame Commander of the Most Excellent Order of the British Empire (DBE) for this work, rather than her enthusiasm for racing. As to the cars themselves, the first decades of the twentieth century articulated a decidedly nationalistic jealousy in machine-development rivalries. Consequently, time and distance trials often involved literally testing engines developed by manufacturers from different countries to the point of failure. When road racing became too hazardous, circuit-building innovations in Europe, across the Atlantic and into the Southern Hemisphere continued. From a narrative of catching up, the metropolitan and elitist links of Brooklands allowed a world-leading aspect of innovation to be added to the discourse of British motor-sport.

The continuing significance of Italian, French and German motor-sport manufacturers, drivers and sponsors also adds nuance to generalisations about the British diffusion of sport. Speedway in the inter-war period has been described as synonymous with Antipodian popularisation in sporting spectacle but this neglects early British motorcycle riders, of whom some of the more well known were women.[114] Brooklands has been but one way of understanding the national context in England, let alone Britain. It does however reflect contemporary campaigns supported by the wealthy benefactors, like the Locke King,s and media entrepreneurs, such as Northcliffe, responding to domestic politics and external challenges by developing British car manufacturing and competition expertise.

The development of motor-sport was to have unexpected benefits for the British war-effort during World War I and there is much research that remains to be done on this topic.[115] Muriel Thompson joined the Women's Transport Service, adapting her Cadillac to be an ambulance and served on the Western Front between 1915 and 1918; she was awarded the Military Medal, the Croix de Guerre and the Order of Leopold II for bravery under fire while supplying troops at the Front Line with clothes and food. A plaque at Ypres commemorates Thompson and other the First Aid Nursing Yeomanry (FANY) members who served there. The Military Medal recognised that driving skills enabling nurses to pick up wounded soldiers while under fire before treating their injuries.[116] Christabel Ellis was appointed a commandant of the Women's Legion, another voluntary organisation and, from 1916, began the collection of experienced women drivers to work for the Army Service Corps (ASC). Gwenda Janson came from a military family and learned to drive a car at Cheltenham Ladies' College, having been taught maintenance skills by her brother, who would become the noted Arabist Sir John Bagot Glubb.[117] After volunteering for the Scottish Women's Hospitals Organisation, Gwenda drove ambulances in Russia and Romaina where she was awarded both the Cross of St George and St Stanislaus.[118] Since many of the women used their skills again in World War II, there is evidently a whole research agenda relating to an aptitude for motoring for work and leisure. Women's sport and war remains another under-written topic.

Ethel Locke King took a controlling interest in Brooklands in 1927 after the death of Hugh. It is also significant perhaps, that the British Racing Drivers' Club (BRDC) was not formed until 1928 and the first British Grand Prix had already been held at Brooklands in 1926. The BARC may well have been more progressive than the chauvinist BRDC who only allowed 'foreigners' and women to have associate status. Today, women (though not foreign nationals) are still classified as BRDC honourary members. We could debate the extent to which Brooklands popularised motoring amongst the general public in spite of its social exclusivity. The example also indicates that individuals, especially eccentric enthusiasts, could have considerable influence, just as much as larger changes in society and culture. In the building of the Brooklands motor circuit, on what had originally been farm-land, we could see elements of a threat to the countryside and unconventional upper-class patronage of sport which *Wind in the Willows* set out to pastiche. However, the Locke King's saw their enterprise as providing leadership for the British motor industry that the government of the day were unable, or unwilling, to provide.

CONCLUSION

There were contradictory processes expressed between the aristocracy and the bourgeoisie through car ownership in the late Victorian and Edwardian period. Hereditary privileges had become increasingly subject to market forces, evidenced by the sale of land and country houses. Industrial principles were exemplified by the increasing production of motor vehicles and related products. At the same time, the aristocracy still defined aesthetic refinement as a combination of wealth, beauty and fame; even if the latter involved a degree of notoriety. When a royal motor stable was established and the likes of Eleanor Rolls used a car at her wedding at the end of the nineteenth century, it signalled a self-conscious modernity in terms of commodity culture. The car became a visually striking manifestation of privilege that members of emergent groups (professionals; doctors; politicians; entertainers; city financiers; the manufacturing classes) could buy to be seen about town or borrow to race.

George Eyston, who lost his father when he was seventeen years of age, just as the First World War broke out, ended his late autobiography *Safety Last* with two telling sentences: 'Racing events like the Targa Floria and Mille Miglia have for me considerable glamour. In consequence I shall always remember being at Sienna when Stirling Moss averaged nearly 100 mph on [sic] his Mercedes Benz in the Mille Miglia, something hardly possible to understand.'[119] He had dedicated an earlier 1933 autobiography *Flat Out* to romantic adventurers and fighting pioneers.[120] Racing signalled an imaginative way to disguise the regularity, plainness and uniformity of mass-market design. Motor vehicle ownership in this period marked social and economic superiority as a relative kind of exclusivity, rather than an absolute one. Like the example of the motorcycle advertisements referenced in the introductory comments of this chapter, the transformative possibilities included those that amused, excited and perhaps frightened consumers a little. As objects of desire with a high degree of public visibility the aeroplane, car, motorcycle and three-wheeled light car became synonymous with upper-class living. As members of the social elite, the number of early women motorists was relatively small but they were to have considerable symbolic significance.

Enthusiastic female motorists and aviators took to the physically and technically demanding aspects of newer forms of sport. Some of the narratives drew on longer traditions, as sport had a long pre-history involving travel. Frenchwoman Jeanne Hervaux (1885-?) was a successful hill-climber and reportedly performed an exhibition 'loop-the loop' at the Crystal Palace in a car but became better known as a pilot in a Blériot from 1909. A short-lived attempt to open a flying school for women seems to have been her last known activity and she has been lost to the record from then on. As the case of Dorothy Levitt has shown, women who were celebrated as famous for short periods could also disappear quite quickly thereafter. There are a lot of local and enthusiast histories taking place that may well uncover more detail.

However, Tony Kushner's work on Jewish memory and locality in Hampshire might also provide useful lines of enquiry on the establishment of Jewish communities in London and the provinces.[121] On the one hand, Levitt's claim that she was from the 'West Country' may have been a deliberately vague attempt to gentrify and anglicise her heritage. On the other, census material shows that Dorothy's parents had moved to Bristol by the time of her death, as had her sister. Whether the Levi or Raphael families had originally landed in a south-west port, before moving to London and then relocated back nearer to the sea remains unclear. Kushner has no indexed reference to Bristol, but his work shows how push and pull factors affected broader patterns of Jewish migration from British port cities, to London and out again. In this sense, Levitt's claim to have West Country roots may not have been as ambivalent about her Jewish heritage as it first appeared. It could celebrate links with an established Jewish community, such as Kushner details in Portsmouth. Either way, further biographical work might provide important clues. One author has defended her 'creative reconstruction' of some events of the life of another famous racing driver, Hellé Nice (1900– 1984), due to a lack of sources and as the result of writing about a woman who continued to reinvent herself throughout her life. [122] The mythology created as a result of lack of evidence about the lives of some women drivers is itself a range of material for academic historians to analyse.

After looking at some important personalities the chapter has also centred on themes of place, rites and ceremonies. Brooklands invented a tradition of glamour to draw in the upper classes and those who would imitate their behaviour to the circuit. The central components of motor-sport were:

> The superb injection of fantasy into public rituals and consumption practices, and [glamour] arose from the opportunities that these supplied for possible or imaginary transformations of the self. It was the market and industrial production on the one hand, and equality and the erosion of structured deference on the other. [123]

Women socialites and drivers were integral to the reputation of motor racing: Ethel Locke King helped to create a theatre in which wealth, beauty and notoriety were performed. The daughters of car salesmen could mix with aristocrats who bought vehicles. While motor-sport was not universally admired because of the danger, cost and fear of physical degeneracy, it had some cachet. Compared with the effortless grace much valued by upper-class aristocracy, motor-ownership had associations of new money, social climbing and earnest enthusiasm all of which were slightly vulgar, as was conspicuous consumption.

For the most part, historians of sport have made extensive use of newspapers, second only to institutional archival evidence in terms of the hierarchy of sources. [124] The use of the press as a public relations vehicle for modern sport meant that copy produced by elite administrators was often gratefully received as 'insider' and 'official' versions of events and, as such, privileged. [125] Comparably little attention has been paid to changes in the media industries inflected by motor-sport and the enthusiasm for mechanised travel by individuals, such as Alfred Harmsworth. The diffusion of sport was subject to fluxes across different kinds of media. Therefore the centrality of automobiles, motorcycling and aviation to French magazines such as *La Vie Au Grande Air* suggests that a self-conscious modernity lay at the heart of the urge to tour. A female competitor or a man with fine skin tone is marked as an X in the European Circuit Air Race of 1911.[126] Advertisements also promoted other leisure pursuits such as women of dubious sobriety extolling the benefits of Dubonnet enhanced by Quinquina.[127] Cosmopolitan tastes manifest themselves, in how motor sport developed but just as imporantly in the many social activities scheduled in the Brookland's club house.[128]

Like the early Olympic Games, motor-sport derived many of its defining narratives from the enthusiastic patronage of aristocrats and related commercial links. The corporate, mercantile core of amateur activities was often masked behind a disinterested, and therefore disingenuous, public face. Were those whose private incomes enabled them to compete in motor-sport for large prizes the professionals, or those who were paid to race for a team and therefore supported British manufacturers in the wider market? If the clothing, food and transport industries were to benefit from Olympic travel, the extent of media and automotive industry sponsorship in motor-sport can hardly be overstated. The range of activities therefore provides an important counterpoint to arguments about how heavily governing bodies were able to regulate the relationship between sport and business generally in this period.

While it is often argued that the ethos of amateurism implied an antipathy to commercialisation, the relationship between the amateur and professional driver was unclear. Every visible surface of the vehicle and driver became a medium for advertising (either by means of subtle endorsement or outright branding). Buying and selling cars gave the narrative around the sport a thoroughly commercial lexicon and it was no coincidence that much of this was shared with horse racing, a sport that appeared to unite aristocrats and commoners. Dual themes of elitism (the few who actually owned cars) and egalitarianism (the many who might aspire to own a vehicle, could watch at races or read about those who attended) connected classes. The sheer variety of vehicle catered to this sense of hierarchy involving price, size of engine, personal comfort and privacy.

The narrative about national physical fitness therefore had many layers. While there were undoubtedly arguments about women being mother to the race, and therefore better off at home, there were also heroic accounts of women who could conquer new technologies, the elements and their own temperaments. Most upper-class women had, after all, fulfilled the majority of their obligations to the nation when they had produced an heir. Other healthy children were a luxury. Some of the women referred to in this chapter were unmarried, or childless, had difficult relationships with their offspring or sent their children away at a relatively early age to board at school. The actual nursing and raising of upper-class children could be left to a succession of nannies, sometimes the same women who had provided identical services for the family for generations. This left a considerable amount of time for conspicuous leisure. The idea of having spare time and sporting interests was part of a fashionable lifestyle in luxury magazines, away from what actually happened at tracks like Brooklands. The upper classes were seen to embrace motoring modernity but they also led where the growing middle classes would eventually aspire to follow. As the examples of the volunteers who used their skills for war-work in this chapter suggests, when asked to demonstrate their bravery in more serious circumstances than racing cars, several of the Brooklands women responded. When peace was declared and racing resumed, between 1920 and 1939 there would be the highest concentration of internationally-famous women racing drivers at the circuit than there had been before, or would be at any single venue since.

4 Football Interconnections and Olympic Parallels

What will happen in the next few years? It is almost certain that within five years some girl will run the 100 yards in 10 and a half seconds and be able to jump well over five feet [sic]. It must be admitted that none of the girl swimmers have been able to reach the great speed shown by Johnny Weismuller, but the point is they have made a remarkable series of advances in the last year which shows imposing possibilities later on.[1]

Dress regulations were so strict that it was a bit of a shock for a woman's knee-cap to be seen as she ran.[2]

This chapter explores a series of interconnections and parallel developments in international women's sport after World War I had emphasised the need for female physical fitness, courage, stamina and technological skill. Female labour was to be vital for Britain's industry and infrastructure during the war but women workers were not so respected in peace. Half a million women who had paid their insurance contributions as munitions operatives from 1917 onwards were asked to give up those jobs by 1921, facing neither retraining nor entitlements after being forced into uninsured trades.[3]

The evidence of how this affected sport and leisure remains fragmentary though, unless a specific occupational culture, sports club or company kept records.[4] Consequently, the academic analysis of the effect of war on women's work and education has not been matched by anything like the same discussion of leisure and sport.[5] There does seem to be a general consensus that after a relatively brief peak between 1917 and 1919, when women comprised perhaps half of the British labour force, the female proportion of workers outside the home remained somewhere between 25% and 30% from 1911 and 1931.[6] With casual labour and piece-work inside the home, the number of women who were economically active exceeded this, while regional variation and relative economic prosperity in particular industries also affected individual life-chances.

The British empire's death toll was given as 900,000 with two million more wounded: many men and women were still in uniform in photographs of 1919 and 1920.[7] If there was uncertainty brought on by new challenges of post-war reconstruction, there were also opportunities. Highly visible aspects of women's political and social progress in Britain included the 1918 Representation of the People Act, which gave the vote to women over the age of thirty who held property, were eligible to vote in local elections (or were married to householders) and those with a university degree.[8] The Eligibility of Women Act allowed individuals to stand as MPs and, in 1919, the Sex Discrimination (Removal) Act was intended to dismantle barriers to the professions, though legislation alone could not alter work-practices, admission to education or access to leisure.[9]

On 1 December 1919 Lady Nancy Astor the first woman MP, was elected member for Plymouth in a by-election and took the oath sponsored by the incumbent Prime Minister, David Lloyd George, and former premier Arthur Balfour.[10] While Nancy Astor was considered by leading feminists of the day to be more of a socialite than politically aware, thousands of women wrote to her with their concerns. The society hostess and charity patron, Katharine Stewart-Murray, The Duchess of Atholl became the first woman MP in Scotland but was traditionalist to the extent of arguing against the need to extend women's suffrage, let alone supporting reform to raise the school leaving age.[11] Similarly, Gwendolen Guiness, Lady Iveagh led the Conservative Party's women's advisory committee from 1925 to 1933, accruing one million female members, though most of her campaigns were not motivated by the plight of the common woman.[12]

Politicians like Margaret Bondfield worked more practically to improve the conditions of shop assistants and she became elected President of the Trades Union Congress in 1923. The following year was to see the first brief Labour government led by Ramsay MacDonald. The Equal Franchise Bill of 1928 gave the vote to a further one and a half million women between the ages of twenty-one and twenty-five. Ellen Wilkinson had sponsored 'the flapper vote' and also won the right to eat in the Strangers' Dining Room of the House of Commons; in respect of which her male colleagues donated a gift of a gas stove.[13] By 1929 Bondfield had become the first woman Cabinet minister. If the 'woman question' remained very much part of post war rebuilding so was sport, and female access to physical competition in a variety of disciplines became politicised to an unprecedented degree. One of the pioneers was the future MP Elaine Burton (1904–1991), later Baroness Burton of Coventry, who wore shorts and spiked running shoes to win a Northern Counties Ladies' 100 yards championship in 1919.[14] Elaine's upper-class father was a hurdles finalist at the 1908 Olympic Games and he inspired her lifelong enthusiasm for sports. However, she did not share her father's politics, considering that he had squandered a private inheritance and sometimes challenging young men to race against Elaine in return for wagers of small change.

This chapter outlines developments in the inter-war period by looking at transnational currents across sports codes, from football to track and field athletics. This is an enormous topic to consider and the founding of national and international federations in women's sport during the 1920s could be a book in its own right. Evidence so far points to uneven developments, often shaped by chance. The analysis concerns changes in British women's football and the foundation in France of an international federation for women's sport. As the previous chapters have shown, processes that were to have world-wide effects often began from specific geographic, social and cultural locations.

Women's football grew rapidly between 1917 and 1922 in Britain largely as a result of the changing nature of female work.[15] The structures of women's athletics grew mainly in educational settings but there were also several talented working-class athletes. In 1921 a women's section was formed at London's Kensington Athletic Club with Sophie Eliott-Lynn (1896–1939) and Vera Palmer (1901–1998) both important enthusiasts before breaking away in 1923 to found Middlesex Ladies' Athletic Club.[16] Where women worked or studied together, they often played together.[17] This included war-work, often done alongside men, and particularly dangerous munitions manufacturing, nursing or communications work: Elliot Lynn rode a Harley Davidson as a despatch rider for the War Office and served in France in the Women's Army Auxiliary Corps (WAAC) before returning to her agricultural and zoological studies in peacetime.[18]

Well-known examples of nineteenth century company paternalism had already benefitted female recreation and sporting provision, such as provided by Quakers Joseph Rowntree and George Cadbury.[19] War-time industrial welfare schemes also sought to monitor women's leisure as well as their work. The manufacturing and service sectors gave some women the camaraderie, contacts and time to initiate their own activities. On occasion, this might spread beyond the company itself. In particular, the first short section explores the contacts of one of the most well-known British football teams, Dick, Kerr's Ladies from Preston Lancashire, who were formed in 1917 and continued to play until 1965. This works' team fostered networks in order to facilitate competition and raise funds for charity, more after World War I had concluded than during the conflict. Due to the confines of space, the discussion focuses on their style of sports tour, moving gradually out of a localised network to make transnational connections. This might be seen as marked increased female sporting mobility but there were also some examples of migration (either in the long or short term) and a lot of 'curiosity tourism'. Large crowds were drawn to watch women's football and international sporting tournaments. Individual female athletes ranged far and wide in search of competition and collegial active leisure. Going 'on tour' implied a wide range of activities beyond sport itself.

The second longer section of the chapter links the activities of the British football players and Alice Joséphine Marie Million (1884–1957), a young rower from Nantes in France.[20] Married and widowed relatively soon after, Alice Milliat worked as a translator and became President of the Femina women's sports club in 1915, three years after its formation by Pierre Payssé.[21] In France, the exclusion of women from male sports federations had led to a rise in the number of sports clubs dedicated to their interests, such as En Avant. Académia, founded in 1915, supported a range of physical activities including natural movement dance inspired by Isadora Duncan (1877–1927); bicycling; football and rugby (or barette). A French national track and field athletics meeting in 1917 showcased some of the leading all-round sportswomen like javelin and shot-put enthusiast Violette Gourard Morris (1895–1944).[22] 'La Morris', as she became celebrated, was an imposing athlete who also boxed; swam; played football and drove cars professionally. Alice Milliat became President of the Fédération des Sociétés Féminines Sportives de France (FSFSF) in 1919, and thereby inaugurated a national coalition of female sports clubs.[23]

Milliat first visited Preston in 1920 as a non-playing administrator with the Paris-based Femina women's football team and was much impressed by the local hospitality and public support for the Dick, Kerr Ladies in Preston. In her subsequent career as an administrator and activist, she devoted considerable energy to promoting women's sports. With the expansion of the programme of the Olympic Games now overseen by the international federations of sport, rather than local organising committees, Milliat targetted athletics as fundamental to the inclusion of more women in a greater range of disciplines. There were also important differences, as women's football was an unregulated form of female leisure and, perhaps, casual work. Team games nevertheless featured strongly in Milliat's vision for more democratic sport. The International Amateur Athletics Federation (IAAF) had been created in August 1913 with Swedish administrator Sigfried Edström elected as its President. As Carly Adams has shown, the IAAF worked closely with the IOC because of the central role of athletics in the programme of sports; this enhanced Edström's relationship with de Coubertin and therefore his ability to gain significant positions in international sport.[24] In 1920, Edström was co-opted as a member of the IOC, and one year later he joined the executive board.

While women's swimming, diving, skating, tennis and a mixed yachting event would feature at the Antwerp Olympic Games in 1920, female track and field athletics were not admitted. As a direct response to the International Olympic Committee's refusal to Milliat's request, the FSFSF broadened its remit. In her brief survey of the issues, Hargreaves has characterised Milliat's relations with the IAAF and the IOC as: 'A process incorporating pockets of resistance, ambiguities and struggles.'[25] In 1921, female representatives from France, Great Britain, Italy, Norway, Sweden and Switzerland took part in the first international athletics meeting inaugurated by Milliat, staged in Monte Carlo. By October 1921, the Fédération Sportive Féminine Internationale (FSFI) had begun to campaign on a worldwide scale for the advancement of women's sport, specifically targeting the inclusion of athletics in the Olympic programme.[26] In 1922 the first Women's Olympic Games was staged as a separatist event with 101 competitors taking part in front of crowds of 20,000 spectators. At the seventh IOC Olympiad, held in Antwerp, there had been approximately eighty female participants.

Although this was an emerging transnationalism, football and athletics nevertheless provide unmistakable connectivity between different kinds of sport and therefore diverse women from a range of backgrounds. Lynne Robinson sub-titled her thesis on the social history of women's athletics in Britain between 1921 and 1960 *Tripping Daintily Into The Arena*, but basic biographical details manifest a greater range of gender identities than this gentrified title implies.[27] The expansion of the media in the inter war period was undoubtedly a factor. In 1922 the British Broadcasting Company (BBC) had been formed to send out short 'sponsored' programmes to the 8,000 people who had paid fifteen shillings for a radio constructors' licence.[28] There were various 'internationalist' mega-events to report, such as the first Worker's Olympics, held in Prague in 1921 and Soviet Games from 1924 with an explicitly socialist interpretation.[29] Sporting supernationalism continued to grow, with bourgeoise commercial tournaments like the first football World Cup hosted by Uruguay in 1930 and those that combined politics and trade, such as the Empire Games, staged the same year in Hamilton. Though these may have had their roots in developments before the First World War, each sought to challenge, adapt and reinterpret modern tournament design. So resistance to women's increased participation has to be seen in context of IOC authoritarianism in response to what a self-appointed elite perceived as a series of Olympic-related political conflicts and crises. Athletics tended towards an institutionalised, standardised bureaucracy and Milliat's attempts to have women's world records from the Women's Olympic Games recognised by the IAAF were part of an overall strategy of integration.

A heightened awareness of what was happening internationally in women's sport was therefore manifest in contemporary texts.[30] Though space precludes any in-depth treatment of the issue here, sport itself became more politicised due to its adoption by the worker sport movement, which had already established a socialist tradition by the 1920s, including the British Red Star netball team.[31] While Milliat and the leaders of the FSFI were steeped in an amateur bourgeois ethos, the resistance to women's participation from the Football Association in England and the International Olympic Committee politicised an unprecedented degree of growth in the democratisation of sport. These interconnections are worth scrutiny because decisions made in 1921 and 1928 would shape the public image of the female football player and athletics competitor until at least the 1960s. We could argue that we still contend with some of the issues raised today. However, the analysis is intended to stimulate more debate and research rather than provide a definitive account. But the chapter does ask questions with much contemporary resonance, not least, why do we have gendered labour markets in sports like football? Which athletes can, and should, be recognised as Olympians?

Biographical study of Milliat's life, like that of all-rounders like Gourard Morris and star football players like Lily Parr (1905–1978) remains underdeveloped. However the chapter is only partly concerned with reconstructing the lives of individuals who should be more well-known. There is a much larger web of interconnections implied by these personal ties that are, as yet, imperfectly understood. The parallel developments of the IOC-organised Olympic programme from Antwerp in 1920 to Berlin in 1936 cannot be understood without considering the influence of Milliat's Women's World Games. The section therefore concludes with a focus on the life of one 'Olympian' who remains unacknowledged by the IOC; the American flag bearer in the 1922 Paris Women's Olympic Games, Lucille Ellerbe Godbold (1900–1981).[32] One of seven children from a family of educators, 'Miss Ludy' taught at Columbia College in South Carolina for fifty-eight years. A 'Ludy Bowl' touch-football game was inaugurated at Colombia in her honour in 1955 and a $1.1 million sports facility was named after her in 1974. In 1968 Ludy became the first woman admitted to the South Carolina Athletic Hall of Fame. In many respects, Godbold's life and career were exemplars of Olympism, as she was dedicated to inspiring many young women to take up sport and physical activity (reportedly saying that she taught everything but golf and dance).[33] By looking at the different lives of Milliat, Parr, Morris, Godbold and others, in comparison with the IOC-recognised women Olympians from this period, the chapter argues that we need more work on the complex and contingent associations outlined here in the inter-war period.

THE DICK, KERR LADIES FOOTBALL TEAM AND FEMALE SPORTING TOURS

Popular historian Patrick Brennan has used the term *Munitionettes* football to describe women playing matches in front of crowds of up 55,000 in aid of charity between 1917 and 1921.[34] This is something of a misnomer in two senses. Firstly, once the Eastern front had collapsed, the demand for munitions decreased and demobilisation began before the Armistice in November 1918. The most famous team, Dick, Kerr Ladies had began to play seriously in October 1917 based at the Strand Road tram building and light railway works, originally founded by W. B. Dick and John Kerr of Kilmarnock. The team would play more in peacetime than during hostilities, therefore. Regional pride had, of course, been developing for a much longer period with a music hall song commemorating Preston North End as first champions of the Football League and of the FA Challenge Cup in 1889.[35]

Secondly, there were other work-based women's teams such as Horrockses' Ladies, of the mill owned by the family known as the Cotton Kings of Preston, and Atalanta, an affiliation of professional women, such as teachers and nurses.[36] Brennan has also shown that the Lancashire United Transport Company based in Atherton had a team as early as 1915 and the women of the Preston Army Pay Corps had already played at Deepdale, the home of Preston North End Football Club in 1916, before Dick, Kerr Ladies.[37] Other kinds of industrial welfare and generalist enthusiasm should therefore be acknowledged in this period. Lyons tearooms had several women's football teams too, for instance.[38] Like other intended forms of 'rational recreation', football could be used for the players' varied motivations and adapted to suit a variety of purposes. Football seems to have been chosen by the players, rather than the management, as a preferred sport and leisure activity.

This said, minute books of Preston North End, held at the National Football Museum, indicate that those acting on behalf of the women used the existing connection with the Dick, Kerr men's football team in approaching 'Proud Preston' for the use of its ground.[39] Dick, Kerr's male munitions workers used Deepdale for a match on 27 December 1915, after which they were entertained to tea at a cost of 2 shillings 6 d per head.[40] Further applications were made for men's munitions games and Preston North End were also later to play against a team representing Dick, Kerr's men on 13 April 1918.[41] The women's played first against male colleagues during tea breaks but the format developed into women's matches for charitable purposes, a pattern which lasted until the team disbanded in 1965. Deepdale ground was granted by the Preston committee on 30 October 1917 for a game against T. Coulthard and Co. Ltd munitions workers to be played Christmas Day. The board also offered their support in the forms of advertisements on Preston North End posters, to be jointly paid for by the club and Dick, Kerr's women.[42] The experiment had obviously been financially popular as the game raised £488 7 shillings for the Moor Park Hospital in the process. As the *Lancashire Daily Post* saw Dick, Kerr's 4–0 victory: 'Quite a number of their shots at goal would not have disgraced a regular professional except in direction, and even professionals have been known on occasion to be a trifle wide of the target. Their forward work, indeed was often surprisingly good.'[43] This was a match report rather than a novelty, even as a first game.

In the initial four-game season, Dick, Kerr Ladies Football Club the remaining home fixtures took place against local rivals Lancaster (1–1 draw); Barrow (2–0 win) and Bolton (5–1 win). A ten-game second season for 1918–1919 followed and manager Alfred Frankland first wrote to other clubs via the newspapers to set up a Lancashire women's league. He seems to have abandoned the idea by the end of 1919. That Dick, Kerr's Ladies' had national broadsheet recognition is shown by the illustrated report: 'Ladies at Football England v France by a Special Correspondent' *The Times* 7 May 1920. A similar tie the next year at Longton Park, Stoke with a crowd of 15,000 was titled 'England v France' so there was also popular media coverage because *The Daily Mirror* had two photographs of striker Lily Parr on page eight. The first caption accompanied an action shot of Parr 'Beating the French goalkeeper for the fifth time' and the second showed team-mates 'Chairing Miss L Parr after the match. She scored all five goals'.[44]

There remained active support from the Preston North End Board until August 1920. While 80% of the gate receipts were given over to Dick, Kerr's after expenses, there were also arrangements for practice matches at £12.00 for a Saturday fixture, £3.00 per week for training mid-week nights and £20 for Christmas Day fixtures.[45] Disappointingly, the financial records between 1915 and 1921 have been lost. It is now difficult to know whether use of other large Football League grounds such as Goodison Park, Old Trafford and Stamford Bridge from late 1920 and into 1921 was an ongoing attempt to win a larger audience or motivated by necessity as Deepdale became increasingly less available.

Unlike Galvin and Bushell's findings, there were local women's leagues around at the time and so the sports tours were not necessarily a response to a shortage of opposition.[46] In the 1920–1921 season a Bradford Ladies' League had two divisions, for example. In descending order from the top of the table, the first division teams were: College Ladies; Old Hansonians; Bradford; Odsal; Undercliffe; Grange; Tartan; Shipley; Frizinghall and Saltaire. The second division clubs were: Sion; Bowling; Cawthorns; Tetley Street; Phone Exchange; St Aidens; YWCA; Westgate; C. M. & M. Ladies and Eastbrook. [47] There was evidently more than one cup or knockout competition as in the week of the reference, YWCA were due to meet Tetley Street in the Second Round Hospital Tournament (replay) to be refereed by Mr Millar.[48] Not all of the above were work-based teams and some reflected other affiliations or geographical locations. It is unclear whether any or all of the matches were played for charity or whether players were awarded expenses. Most teams in the Bradford league had played nine or ten games, as opposed to almost sixty contested by Dick, Kerr's in 1920–1921. There were also photographs of Lister's Ladies, Manningham and YWCA teams playing cricket in the summer and it would be good to know how many women played in both these and the hockey teams to which the article refers. A typical match was reported in *The Lancashire Daily Post* on 14 March 1921 with gate receipts of £210 followed by tea and a complimentary performance at the Hippodrome.

Helen Jones has suggested that industrial welfare schemes included sport and leisure to attract the best workers but there is no evidence that women's football was popularised by such a singular cause at this time.[49] More convincingly, Peter Burke's work on women's workplace Australian Rules football between 1915 and 1918 indicated that a mix of company welfare, a reduced schedule for male matches, patriotic employers and improved public relations boosted female participation.[50] Not all Dick, Kerr's players worked at the factory and yet the degree of civic recognition they enjoyed as representatives of the firm was considerable. Transfers to play for the Preston-based team widened from Lancastrians but biographical detail on the team members remains sparse. By now too, the rivalry had broadened to include Manchester, home of the British Westinghouse works team Heywood Ladies and, by March 1919, Newcastle United Ladies who played at St James Park in front of crowds of 35,000. Their striker, Winnie McKenna, already had 130 goals to her name for Vaughan Ladies. The playing personnel was certainly drawn from out-side the immediate area, with Frenchwoman Louise Ourry (1905–1984) and, later, Scottish players Nancy 'The Cannonball' Thomson (1906–2010) mov-ing to Preston and working while they played. Some of the players did not work for Dick, Kerr or live in Preston at all. So what began as a works team quickly became less representative of the company than it was competitive: a process outlined in Chuck Korr's classic study of company paternalism giving way to professionalism in the case of West Ham United.[51]

In 1920 and 1921 the crowds grew, although we cannot be sure how much motivation to attend by paying spectators was down to altruism or enjoyment. The coal disputes of 1921 and 1926 saw more sides develop in response to localised deprivation: teams included the Soup Canteen Ladies; Blaydon Ladies' FC and the Marley Hill Spankers.[52] International inter-est, which had been sporadic, also became more sustained. Jules Rimet, President of the French football association (and soon to become Presi-dent of FIFA) assisted with the first England versus France match held in Paris in October 1920: the game was refereed by a Monsieur Wallon.[53] Women's matches in France and in England seemed to be gathering status and support.[54] In early March 1921 *The Lancashire Daily Post* announced an international 9–0 win against a Scotland side at Celtic Park. Many of the England team were Dick, Kerr players and the Preston team had played again in an 8–1 win the previous Saturday at Coventry City in front of 27,000 with gate receipts £1,622. The players reportedly travelled around on 'two special saloon cars put on without cost by the railway company' from Coventry to Leeds and then to a match in Hull.[55]

Dick, Kerr's won the game by four goals to nil and acquired a famous new admirer:

> A crowd of 21,000 paid £1,160 towards the Hull Unemployed Fund at a ladies' football match on the Hull N. U. ground . . . There was remarkable enthusiasm both in the city and on the ground, the teams being given a splendid reception. Georges Carpentier, the famous French boxer, who kicked off, created some amusement by kissing the rival captains before the game started . . . At the Hull City Hall the same evening Carpentier presented the winning side with the Yorkshire Ladies' Premier Charity Cup. The French boxer obtained all the auto-graphs of the Preston Ladies team.[56]

An article in *The Football Favourite* reported ambitious plans for more widespread visits:

> Can Girls Play Football? Of Course!
>
> To-day another very fine fixture is due to be played on the Elland Road ground, Leeds. The rival teams are Dick, Kerr's versus Yorkshire and

Lancashire ladies. Lucky Leeds! You are in for a real treat! I must mention that Dick, Kerr's have been invited to visit Canada. Indeed, letters have been received from all parts of the Empire imploring the famous Preston lassies to 'come over'. The matter of a world tour is under consideration but the state of the clubs finances will probably be a deciding factor . . . A Ladies' Football Association is already an established fact. It flourishes under the title the Yorkshire Ladies' Football and Baseball FA. Moreover this association is offering a Ladies' Football Challenge Cup competition between all teams in England.[57]

The magazine, aimed at the youth market, had first featured Dick, Kerr's on its cover on the 4 September 1920 and included illustrations of women players in the magazine in most editions in 1921. An ongoing fictionalised serial based on their dominance changed from 'Meg Foster' to become 'Captain Meg! The Pride of Blake's Crusaders' and then, from 16 April 1921, 'Football Island: A Splendid New Story of Meg Foster' which may have been influenced by the idea of Dick, Kerr's proposed world tour. The magazine carried advertisements for skirt patterns and other items of girls' clothing indicating an assumed female readership. In June 1921 local and national newspapers reported on: 'Dick, Kerr's Most Successful Season. The team having won 58 out of 59 games, the other being drawn in Paris, with a total of 393 goals for, 16 against.'[58] The report described the Crewe Cottage Hospital Cup and the Ex-service Men's Cup as: 'A handsome massive silver trophy given by Mr Hogge, MP for East Edinburgh worth about £100 . . . Some £46,000 has been raised for charity so far.' The concluding game of the 1920–1921 football season a week later at the Crewe Alexandra ground, Gresty Road, saw an 8–0 win over a Welsh XI before Dick, Kerr's departed for a short tour of the Isle of Man. *The Isle of Man Daily Times* announced

> The visit of the famous Dick, Kerr International Ladies' Team has aroused widespread interest in the Island. They have been instrumental in raising vast sums of money for charitable objects in England . . . Amongst the defeated teams are teams representing the France, Scotland, Ireland and Wales also teams representing the Rest of the United Kingdom . . . It is pleasing to note that Manx charitable objects will benefit to some extent.[59]

The column is next to one of the few newspaper advertisements for a women's game, announcing: 'Room has been made for ten thousand spectators' at the racecourse at Ramsay who were expected to pay 'A Popular Price of One Shilling'. Bad weather beset the tour but games were played at Port Erin on the 10 August and concluded at Douglas three days later, where Dick, Kerr's won 4–0 at the Belle Vue ground.[60]

Without wishing to cover all of the games in detail, as a result of the general success of women's games in attracting paying spectators, the FA 'banned' women's teams from playing football on League and Association-affiliated grounds from 5 December 1921. The FA ruled that too much money had been absorbed in expenses and the game was 'unsuitable' for women. Following the ban, some medical opinion held that football was too vigorous a game and affected women 'internally', contrary to the evidence from 1917 that no serious injury had been sustained, except a report that Florrie Redford (1900–1986) had once been bitten on the ankle by a dog while playing.[61] Exhibition games sought to question the ban, for example, Lyon's Ladies 'performed' for thirty members of the press at Sudbury on 13 December 1921. Alfred Frankland then invited twenty plus doctors to watch a Dick, Kerr game on Boxing Day 1921 where the suitability of the sport was deemed by one reporter as no more taxing than a day's heavy washing or work.

> One of Dick, Kerr's best players is a nurse at the Whittingham Lunatic Asylum. Recently she was on duty all night in charge of refractory patients. When she came off duty she cycled seven miles in the wet to Preston, travelled by train to the Midlands, played a fine game in the afternoon before a record crowd and was back on duty at Whittingham late the same night.[62]

Nomad writing in the *Yorkshire Sports* suggested that, 'If the lady players want to defeat the injunction of the FA all they need do is to popularise the game to such an extent in their own particular circles until they attain the power to snap their fingers at the present policy of the FA.'[63] After the ban, the celebrity of Dick, Kerr's took on a degree of notoriety, subsequent schedules became both more widespread and less frequent than the 1920\1 season. The Dick, Kerr factory became English Electric in 1926 and distanced themselves from Frankland and the women's team. Due to Frankland's contacts, several players like Lily Parr retrained as nurses to work at Whittingham hospital, a mental health facility.[64] A fixture list developed outside of any formal league or association in order to be 'the undefeated British Champions' and then 'World's Champions'. Although officially called Preston from 1926, the Dick, Kerr's name remains the one by which the team is best remembered today, effectively outlasting the company.

Other well-known teams such as Bath; Hey's Brewery, Bradford; Chorley; Darwen; Lyons and St Helen's did not join the English Ladies Football Association either though a reported sixty clubs did express an interest. Since its President was Len Bridgett, director of Stoke United Ladies FC, the team largely comprised of his female relatives and managed by his brother Arthur, this is not so surprising. Stoke, also known as Bridgett's United, got a bye in the inaugural English Ladies Football Association Challenge Cup of 1922, so joining would have meant that Frankland had to co-operate with a midlands initiative led by a rival team who were looking to defeat Dick, Kerr Ladies. The Bridgett's United manager and trainer,

Arthur Bridgett had played for England and Sunderland as a left winger and returned to work in male professional football in 1923 after which the Stoke women's team disbanded. The English Ladies Football Association, led by Len, also dissolved soon after.

For equally petty political reasons, the attempt to form a national association of women's football clubs in France in 1919 also faltered. Team sport, rather than physical culture, has often been called a 'peculiar business' because it relied on competitive cooperation rather than outright monopoly. The 'sporting tours' arranged by Alfred Frankland meant that Dick, Kerr Ladies Football Club could play more matches (and make more money for charity and expenses) than amateur leagues would allow. Lily Parr was to captain the 1922 Dick, Kerr Ladies tour to the United States. By the early 1920s women were playing soccer in the United States as part of intramural programmes and the sports had become sufficiently established to produce books like Frost and Cubberley's *Field Hockey and Soccer for Women* and the Smith book of Soccer in 1924.[65] Yet college Principals did not want their 'nice' girls to play against working-class factory operatives, nurses or shop workers. This meant that the Dick, Kerr Ladies played against male professional and semi professional teams in the US. On their return to Britain in 1923 the impetus to form a coherent, nationwide response to the FA ban had been lost. The FA ban remained and was enforced periodically until informally rescinded following the intervention of FIFA in the late 1960s and formally withdrawn when the first FA international England women's team was formed in 1972.

The Dick, Kerr example is therefore a rare and early case of selling women's team sport to a paying public. The format used charitable fund-raising as its rationale but the benevolent causes varied to a considerable degree. Football raised money for charity but also paid expenses, enabling some performers like 'star' player Lily Parr to become the first person in her family to own their own homes.[66] Whether this was because of the relatively steady income she reputedly earned from 'broken time' payments of ten shillings a game, or this in combination with her work as a nurse, is now difficult to say. Regardless of distinctions of the activities of Dick, Kerr's as semi professional or casually profitable, from very local beginnings in a factory in Preston in 1917, we can see a web of contacts develop across the United Kingdom, into Europe and the United States, bringing friendship, civic esteem and a moderately comfortable lifestyle for some physically gifted working women.

There remains for an academic collective biography of the players to be written, in order to really understand who played for the Dick, Kerr's Ladies team. The model here would be M. Ann Hall's pioneering book on the Edmonton Commercial Graduates basketball team, who also had extensive contacts with the FSFI, and played to men's rules between 1915 and 1940.[67] Lily Parr enjoyed widespread acclaim in the United States and Europe during the inter war years, and became the first woman admitted to the inaugural Hall of Fame at the English National Football Museum in 2002.[68] A long-time leading member of team, very little is known about her playing career over three decades, let alone her private life. Yet Parr achieved celebrity (a word used to describe her at the time) early in her career. Fame, in this case, meant civic, media and public recognition; sharing a sporting stage with some of the key entertainers of the time, for example, Harry Weldon's Team of Lady Internationals' competed in aid of unemployed ex-servicemen, Liverpool hospitals and the Variety Artistes Benevolent Funds.[69] A reported crowd of 25,000 in Liverpool produced £1,500 in declared gate receipts but more people saw this in the cinema on screen. With the high point of a President of the United States between 1921 and 1923, Warren Harding, 'kicking off' one of their matches in Washington in 1922, Lily Parr and her colleagues were received by a range of municipal and political dignitaries. Large audiences of mainly male football fans paid to watch her play. Thanks to the work of local historians like Gail Newsham, Patrick Brennan and Barbara Jacobs the team's exploits are remembered today but not really defined: we only partly comprehend their place in international women's sport more widely.[70]

While women's association football has a history going back at least to the 1880s in England, between 1917 and 1922 it became a popular phenomenon without leading to the establishment of a governing body. This is unusual compared with other team sports like hockey but not especially so. Women's rugby union had its own heroines going back to the 1880s but had less widespread support than football: Maria Eley (1900–1906) played full-back for Cardiff Ladies when they lost 6–0 against Newport on 16 December 1917, went on to have eight children and lived to the age of 106.[71] Still calling bingo and very much part of community life at this advanced age, Eley attributed her longevity to abstinence of both tobacco and alcohol, combined with a love of rugby. New cross-code research is proving that we have to look at the enthusiasms of individual women as well as the international spread of female interest to better understand how increasing numbers became involved and, where possible, sustained their sporting careers.[72]

However, though there seems strong evidence for 150 women's teams by the early 1920s, the lack of an association led to specific types of sporting tour. The working-class male organisers and female players were mainly drawn from a competitive industrial social context and created networks that suited small-scale entrepreneurialism. There were also an opportunities for like-minded individuals to take holidays and trips together, as well as receiving civic welcomes for their sporting prowess. These celebrations comprised dinners of several courses; a show; a singsong on the bus and an overnight stay. Lily Parr is as often photographed in scrapbook snapshots of her football career in a posh frock having a good time, cigarette and drink in hand, as she is in her football kit. She scored an estimated 1,000 goals, so perhaps we can guess what an exciting social schedule football provided for a nurse who supported herself life-long.

Dick, Kerr's and other women's football teams who popularised their sport for commercial purposes (whether or not profits were given to charity or absorbed in 'expenses') were faced with defining a market for their product in a leisure economy with established companies, monopolies and ways of doing business. Individual players and teams were able to enjoy travel within Britain and beyond as an aspect of their sporting experience, in spite of the FA ban.[73] The regulation of the League sector as a male professional occupation and of the Association game generally as a masculine pursuit severely curtailed developments without quashing them entirely.

These conflicts illustrate some of the practical and political difficulties concerning activism in sport for women's rights. Coalitions with other sports were one element of this. As with soccer, charity events held during World War I had incorporated several sprint meetings in their programmes and the Women's Amateur Athletic Association (WAAA) was founded in 1922 in direct response to a refusal by the Amateur Athletic Association (AAA) to facilitate female competition. The Scottish WAAA was later founded in 1930 and the Welsh WAAA in 1952. Although the loss of the early minutes means that most historians have to rely on secondary sources to look at the history of domestic development, we can deduce that the IOC resistance to female track and field had a wider resonance, benefitting women administrators and participants in the short term because they controlled their own events and organisations.[74] There were interconnections between football and athletics in the attempt to form a Women's Olympic Games that the next segment of the chapter will now explore.

ALICE MILLIAT AND THE WOMEN'S OLYMPIC GAMES

What makes the connection between women's football in Britain and Alice Milliat particularly significant was that she was to lead proposals for a Women's Olympic movement from 1921 onwards. Whether we understand this as a separatist initiative or primarily designed to integrate with the International Olympic Committee version of the Games, this has been a neglected area of research largely because sources are dispersed. Some correspondence resides in the IOC archive in Lausanne. More documents are held by the National Sporting Museum, Paris and others are housed in the WAAA files, in the Harold Abraham collections at Birmingham University. However, this has meant that Milliat's contribution to women's athletics and sport more generally has been underestimated. There was also much cross-code participation. Many athletic war meetings were held under the auspices of the AAA and it was only in peacetime that amateur male administrators became increasingly frosty about female participation.[75] The daughter of a miner, Alice Woods (1899–1991) from St Helens, had already won an 80 yards sprint at Blackpool in 1918 under AAA rules, in just under eleven seconds. Alice's older brother John (better known as

Jack, played football on a semi professional basis for Stalybridge Celtic and then Halifax Town. Against her mother's wishes, Alice began to play for the Dick, Kerr's team in 1919, becoming a key member of the team but continuing to live at home in St Helens.

Alice Milliat achieved the inclusion of some women's track and field athletic events in the International Olympic Committee version of the games between 1928 and 1936 after a considerable degree of agitation. Before the outbreak of the Second World War, she had also hosted several international conferences on women's sport and staged four major tournaments. Milliat had planned for a fifth event to be held in Austria during 1938, which was abandoned because of the German Anschluss. The integration of women's athletics was achieved in the face of considerable, sustained opposition at the highest levels of the IOC. The diplomatic relations between Milliat, the International Amateur Athletic Federation and the IOC around this period can seem labyrinthine. Yet these debates show tactical alliance and the willingness to use dispute to win concessions in advancing the cause of women's sport.

It would be perfectly possible to view the relations between Milliat, the IAAF and the IOC from the point of view of the propaganda material each group developed as a way of influencing public opinion. There was as much a circulation of ideas as a movement of bodies to compete in athletics. There has been a consensus view that cold war politics after 1945 made women's athletics more important, as it undoubtedly did Olympic sport generally.[76] However, this reading of external forces shaping perceptions of women athletes can be revised somewhat if we consider the agency of Milliat and her supporters during the 1920s and 1930s. Female Olympians contributed to overall national medal tallies and therefore the involvement of women was already politicised in a number of ways. The concessions won by Milliat did not satisfy her or the wider community that she represented, but FSFI vision for women's sport provided an alternative to the limited IOC programme. The FSFI Women's Olympiads and the IOC Olympic Games provided an ambitious international stage on which to contest female national virility. In turn, this became part of Olympic national coaching cultures and therefore symbolic of the private and state-owned physical regimes of participating countries.

The first separatist Women's Olympic Games took place in Paris, France in 1922, followed by Gothenberg, Sweden in 1926; Prague, Czechoslovakia in 1930 and London, England in 1934.[77] Milliat settled for the title 'women's world games' from the 1926 competition onwards. The patrimony of the Olympic project has meant, for instance, that London 2012 was the first Olympic and Paralympic Games with roughly the same numbers of male and female athletes, with a hugely expanded cohort of 10,500 competitors. Having attended the first Olympic women's boxing competition in London, the incumbent IOC President Count Jacques Rogge made a case for the slow growth of women's sports in the schedule over the next ten years. In this at least, he was a force for conservatism in the model of his predecessors.[78]

As treasurer, general secretary and then President of the Fédération des Sociétés Féminines Sportives de France (FSFSF) Alice Milliat initiated national track and field competitions at Asnières in 1920 (also including basketball; football and gymnastics demonstrations). The international Monte Carlo meeting followed in 1921. Violette Morris, who had first played football for Femina in 1917, won the javelin and shot put. Morris had boxed; swam; ran and played water polo for the Libellules (Strange Dragonflies) team in Paris; before going on to race cycles and Benjamin cycle-cars (three-wheeled vehicles), becoming something of a household name.[79] Finishing fourth in the Bol D' Or motor race in 1922, Morris won the Paris-Pyrenees-Paris rally for her class the same year, also contesting the 1923 Paris-Nice event and the 1927 Bol D' Or.

The week-long programme in Monte Carlo proved widespread interest on behalf of women entrants and paying spectators.[80] The star of the seven-woman English squad was captain Mary Lines (1893–1978), a relatively unknown worker for Schweppes (a carbonated drinks manufacturer in Drury Lane) who trained at the Lyons company track nearby.[81] The Lyons company directors supported many sports and leisure pursuits for their workers and subsequently gave The Perpetual Cup to a women's athletics meeting from 1924. This featured in the company magazine *Lyons Mail* with Vera Searle (née Palmer) the winner for the first three years. In Monte Carolo, Mary Lines benefitted from access to the Lyons training ground, as she set world record to win both the 60 metres and 250 metres races. She also won the long jump; contributed to victories in both sprint relays and finished second in the 800 metres.[82] Between 1921 and 1924, in her short athletics career, Lines set a total of thirty-three world records or best performances in track and field events.[83] This included the first IOC-recognised female 100-metre record of 12.8 seconds in 1922 in which Nora Callebout also figured prominently.[84] Monte Carlo also prompted an international congress to develop women's advocacy for more sports events. American, Austrian, British Czechoslovakian, French, Spanish representatives attended the inaugural meetings in Paris on October 31 1921 where the Fédération Sportive Féminine Internationale (FSFI) was formed. The Dick, Kerr Ladies precedent of using major sports stadia for women's football matches appears to have influenced the choice of the Stade Pershing in October 1921 for a France versus England athletics international. Most of the English team were drawn from Regent Street and Woolwich Polytechnics, however Mary Lines dominated again to lead an England victory by fifty-two points to thirty-eight.

In August 1922 the Stade Pershing in Paris hosted the first Women's Olympic Games and thirty-eight countries sent representatives to the second parallel congress.[85] British athletes also dominated in 1922 (with 50 points); the United States came second (31); France took third place

(29); followed by Czechoslovakia (12) and Switzerland (6).[86] In spite of the strength in depth of Czechoslovakian worker's sport, only Marie Mejzlikova won an event; but she took the 60-metre sprint in seven and three-quarter seconds and would later become a world record holder over 100 metres. Unfortunately, she remains one of the leading figures of women's athletics about which little is now known. Quite how points were calculated also remains unclear and there were occasionally tied events: Britain's Hilda Hatt (1903–1975) and Nancy Voorhees (1904–1979) of the United States came equal-first in the high jump, though subsequently the record was awarded to the American woman for fewer failed attempts.[87]

Hurdles became Hilda Hatt's main event in WAAA championships, inaugurated at the Oxo Grounds, Bromley Kent during August 1923.[88] Vera Palmer's father, Albert, was an assistant secretary of Chelsea Football Club and one of the unsuccessful petitioners for an Association Football Freemasonry lodge in 1920. The family contacts led to women's inter club athletic matches being hosted at Stamford Bridge in June and July 1925 in front of large crowds and sponsored by *The Daily Mirror*. Here, Phyllis Green (1908–1999) would become the first woman to record over five feet in the high jump. Green won both the high and long jump competitions at the WAAA championships in 1926, the first double of its kind, not repeated until 1955. By now married, Vera Searle (née Palmer) took a silver medal in the 250-metre race at the 1926 Women's World Games, while the outstanding female sprinter of her generation Eileen Edwards (1908–1988) took the gold. Searle became better known as a long-serving administrator until the WAAA did eventually merge with the men's AAA in 1991.[89]

Business houses had often hosted athletics for women before WAAA competitions (including Dunlop, Lillywhite, Lyons, the Post Office, the Police and Selfridges), as did universities like Manchester in 1921 and Birmingham from 1922. So sporting connections were well established before the WAAA affiliated to the FSFI. The attitude of the IOC was not always in tune with wider social changes and it was clear that pseudo-scientific narratives about the harm of over-exertion to women's health had more of a basis in ideology than in evidence.[90] The Minutes of the WAAA for the five years between 1922–1927 having been lost, the following summary is based on a report compiled by the founding members housed in the Birmingham University Special Collections.[91] The formation of the WAAA provided a focus for an increase in school, university, club and industry track and field competition. Competitors like Sophie Eliott Lynn promoted women's athletics and an active lifestyle generally, as did prolific author and influential coach Captain F. A. M. (Frederick Annesley Michael) Webster.[92]

A number of athletic clubs to which women were affiliated directly referenced the Olympic Games, such as the London Olympiades Athletic Club (LOAC) at Regent Street Polytechnic. Olympique of Paris was another multi-sport club to use a similar title, and for whom Violette Morris quickly became a celebrated football captain. As well as participating at the Women's Olympic Games, Olympiades also travelled to Brussels setting several records at the Stade Du Parc, Duden. What was it like to compete at this time? In a 1972 interview, Vera Searle described competition as confined to women over eighteen years of age; dressed in modest long shorts, vests and spikes and entailing a travel schedule based around the need to work. It was not for the faint-hearted:

> The WAAA rule governing running kit read: 'Women shall wear loose tunics of optional length with elbow-length sleeves. The knickers shall be dark and close-fitting and shall not be more than four inches from the ground when kneeling.' Without bras or tracksuits, it was a custom to wear running kit for international matches though tunics were not to be tucked in. For the World Women's Games in 1926 the Women's AAA had a uniform of a white blazer carrying the red rose badge and white pleated skirts, just below the knee [sic]. The FSFI called a special meeting to rule that all nations would parade in their competition uniform. Internationals were confined largely to Paris and Brussels but we went to Gothenburg in 1926 by sea and everyone was sick! The schedule was, leave London on Saturday morning; arrive in Paris for dinner; compete Sunday morning; leave the Banquet in time for midnight express for the coast and be back in the office Monday morning.[93]

However, financial weakness meant that the FSFI had to curtail its activities, underlined during the third congress on 31 July 1924 when the situation was so acute that an annual meeting had to be deferred to a bi-annual assembly. By 1926 the IAAF had agreed to take control of the women's programme at the 1928 Olympic Games but rather then the ten events agreed with Milliat, offered only five.

Henri de Baillet-Latour had objected to the unauthorised use of the term 'Olympic' for the women's games soon after he became IOC President in the autumn of 1925, as he also did when the student games began to use the title. The British women read the inclusion of five events in 1928 as a de facto attempt by the IAAF and the IOC to dissolve the FSFI and withdrew a team in protest. This remains the only gender-based boycott in Olympic history, although some nations still continue not to send female athletes to the Games. The stand-off eventually led Milliat to comply with a delegation from the IAAF, conforming to the technical rules and general conduct outlined by them. Financial difficulties in maintaining an international network of the scope of the FSFI would later dictate further assimilation. Further concessions followed, such as renouncing team games and cycling in order to maintain some control of track and field athletics.

The 1926 Gothenburg Games would be privately funded and have eighty-one participants, almost one fifth less than in 1922. Competing against international rivals was not the only burden that athletes faced:

We took ourselves very seriously in the early twenties. For one thing the whole of the medical profession was against women participating in athletics, they said we were leaving our womanhood on the track to the detriment of the future generation and it was possible that none of us would have children [sic]. Further, the athletes were constantly being referred to by the Press as the 'pioneers of athletics for the women's movement' and we tried to conduct themselves as such.[94]

In the 1928 Amsterdam Olympic Games the five women's track and field events were the 100 metres; high jump; 800 metres; discus and the 4 x 100 metres relay. Milliat had repeatedly asked for more disciplines.[95] In spite of a world record time by first place athlete Linda Radke of Germany in 2:16.8 and personal bests for second placed Kinuye Hitomi of Japan and third placed Inga Gentzel, Sweden, the 800 metres was not contested again by women in the Olympic Games until 1960.[96] Allegations that competitors were distressed and fell onto the tracks were much exaggerated.[97] Since this was the first time Germany had joined Olympic competition since World War I, Radke's success marked an international resurgence for their female athletes, although it has been difficult to obtain more information on her sporting career, as it has been for Gentzel. As we become more familiar with the lives and careers of more female athletes, we will be able to assess transnational influences more effectively.

Kinuye Hitomi (sometimes spelled Kinue or Kinuyé, 1907–1931), based in Osaka, was a particularly significant and under-researched athlete who competed at Women's World Games in 1926 and 1930.[98] As well as holding women's sprint, middle distance and hurdle records for Japan, she was also a good discus thrower. Hitomi traded world records in the long and triple jump with Britain's Muriel Cornell (1906–1996); registering 5 metres 98 centimetres in 1928, for instance.[99] As Wray Vamplew has noted, Cornell was deprived of an opportunity to compete because triple jump was not included on the Olympic programme until 1948, but she managed the British women's team in 1936 after injury ended her career and became a WAAA stalwart.[100]

In spite of her untimely death at the age of twenty-four, after returning from competing in Europe, Kinuye Hitomi appears to be the personification of the 'sporting girls' that appeared in Japanese girls' magazines in the 1920s and 1930s. As the work of Miho Koishihara has shown, in contrast to 'yamato nadeshiko' a compliant, highly feminine traditional ideal, the sports girl dared to play tennis, be photographed in a swimming costume or to run with their legs exposed.[101] As well as fictional protagonists of short stories, role models who had achieved international recognition were featured in *Shoulo kurabu* (Girls' Club), one of the most popular magazines with a circulation approaching half a million copies. In addition to other popular Olympians, like multiple swimming medallist Hideko Maehata (1914–1995), non-fiction stories covered the attendance of Japanese athletes at the Olympic and World Women's Games. Kinuye Hitomi featured at least twice in such picture stories, first in 1928 declaring her ambition to set a world record in the 800 metres and second, in October 1931 as 'The Benefactress of Athletics'.[102]

Middle distance events, including the half-mile and cross-country distances, continued to develop under WAAA auspices, with athletes like Gladys 'Sally' Lunn (1908–1988) competing.[103] A postwoman in Birmingham, Lunn started running with Birchfield Harriers and her first international successes came in 1930 at the Women's World Games, when she won the 800 metres race. At the WAAA championships in 1932 she broke the world 880 yards record in a time of two minutes, eighteen seconds. At the White City World Games she set a world 1000 metres record, completing the distance in almost three minutes flat and registered a mile time of five minutes, seventeen seconds in 1937. Clearly, if there had been a women's 800 metres race at the 1932 Los Angeles or the 1936 Berlin Olympic Games, Sally Lunn would have been a strong medal contender. Barbara Keys has suggested that these were the two most important international sporting events of the decade but we can see significant aspects of cultural internationalism outside of, and away from, these mega events.[104] There were multiple layers of globalisation therefore, involving some contradictory constructions of what women's sport represented.

In conclusion, thanks to the work of historians like Duval, Lovesey, Robinson and Watman we are beginning to understand the significance of Florence Birchenough (1894–1973) captain of the British team at the 1926 Women's World Games and her colleagues. Much remains to be known about Mary Lines, Vera Searle and more famous athletes like Sophie Elliot Lynn. It would seem that Ethel Edburga Clementina Scott (1907–1984), a member of the 4 × 100 metres relay team, which came second in Prague, might be the first woman of Caribbean descent to represent Britain in athletics.[105] Her father was a merchant seaman born in Jamaica and she later worked as a medical secretary. Other competitors and administrators have yet to find their place in history.

This kind of collective biography is however vital for understanding that sport and gender could be a difficult and contentious subject during this period. Mary Weston (1905–1978) was the daughter of a leading stoker on HMS Vivid, and his wife, Susan Ann, née Snow. Weston took Florence Birchenough's WAAA title in the shot in 1925 and 1928, before achieving victories in the shot, discus, and javelin at the WAAA championships in 1929. Owing to a medical condition, Weston's gender was incorrectly identified as female at birth, and she was brought up as a girl. Following corrective surgery, Weston's birth was re-registered in 1936 as male. Mark Edward Louis Weston worked as a physiotherapist; married and had three children.

Future IOC President and leader of the United States Olympic Committee, Avery Brundage later claimed to have received a letter from a 'concerned citizen' who had met a female athlete with a deep voice and large feet. Brundage used this as evidence in support of his opinion that women competitors should have gender tests to protect those who were 'truly' female.[106] Whether the letter existed or the athlete concerned was Weston or the Czech runner Zdenka Koubkova (1913-?) who changed sex in 1934, the tone of Brundage's letter to Baillet-Latour was crude in the extreme. It nevertheless set much of the tone for future IOC narratives on gender testing. The view that competitors with inter sex attributes and transitioned athletes might have advantages over female rivals remained an unpleasantly persistent myth.

Born in Poland, Stanislawa Walasiewiczówna (1911–1980) (also known as Stefania Walasiewicz and Stella Walsh after her family moved to America when she was three months old) was also an FSFI record holder. In the 1930 Women's World Games she won three sprint distances (60, 100 and 200 metres) representing the Pologne club, a nationalist organisation in Poland and overseas.[107] As well as being an Olympic gold medal winner in 1932, Walsh was listed in the 1934 Women's World Games programme as holding world records over the same three distances, so she could have expected to win more gold medals in 1936. However, having accused American rival Helen Stephens (1918 -1994) of being a man, Walsh came second to her in the 100 metres. She eventually took US citizenship in 1947 and had a short-lived marriage to boxer Neil Olsen, working on community athletics before her untimely death in 1980. Unspecified male characteristics were identified at the autopsy and she was officially regarded as intersex, although Walsh's records stand, as do her medals. Dora Ratjen (1918–2008) of Germany also had a condition that led to her being raised as a woman, before being identified as a man in 1938 and living the rest of his life as Heinrich. Ratjen returned his gold medal for the 1938 European Athletics Championship, having set a world record in the high jump. As the examples indicate, there was conflicting medical evidence that male characteristics, however defined, actually constituted a competitive advantage. Nevertheless, these moral panics were translated into medicalised narratives around 'protecting' sport for women.[108]

Questions of sexuality could also lead to discrimination. Violette Morris visited Britain as captain of the Olympique of Paris football team in 1922 to raise money for the reconstruction of Rheims, playing four losing matches against Dick, Kerr at Cardiff, Preston, Liverpool and Hyde and another against Hey's Brewery in Bradford.[109] 'La Morris' claimed to have had both breasts removed to better perform as a driver and athlete and though she married book-seller, Cyprien Gourard, her public persona became increasingly radicalised. Friendships with the Parisienne elite like Josephine Baker and other women led to a considerable degree of discrimination. Dressing in male clothes, smoking and, on occasion, fighting on the football pitch, Morris was distanced by Milliat from 'respectable' FSFI competition in the late 1920s and failed in a much publicised court case to have her competitor's licence restored in 1929. Disappointed at missing out on the discus competition in the 1928 Olympic Games, Morris had opened an accessory shop in Paris before being saved from bankruptcy in the 1929 financial crisis by a racing contract with BNC cyclecars. A former German racing rival and journalist, Gertrude Hannecker increasingly flattered Morris in her role as a recruiting agent for the Nazi intelligence service the Sicherheitsdienst des Reichsführers (SS or SD). The bitterness over Milliat's treatment of Morris' sexuality seems to have made her susceptible to these compliments: a paradox given the regime's attitude to homosexuality.

By 1933 Alice Milliat was ill and struggling to coordinate the sporting success for which she had largely been responsible at international level. She had dropped football from the activities of the FSFI, though Liselott Diem has found evidence of a request for soccer by an English Women's Sport Federation.[110] A proposed triathlon competition was probably not as we would know the sport today, but was deemed a less interesting multi-sport competition by 1934 than a pentathlon of athletic events. From 1930 Germany's nineteen athletes led the medal tally from England for the first time, as they did again in London in 1934, so there is much to be done about the role of the FSFI competitions in developing national athletics cultures in a range of countries, not just in Britain. The sole Canadian entry in 1930 had been the six players of the University of British Columbia basketball team, unlike 1924 when the Edmonton Grads had toured Europe.[111] Unsurprisingly, in the 1930 Hazena (handball) competition, Czechoslovakia took the title.

The WAAA London organising committee for the Women's World Championships in 1934 were led by John Beresford, Baron Decies. Other patrons included the great and the good from British sport including Lord Aberdare; Lord Desborough; Lord Hawke and those from London society such as Gordon Selfridge.[112] Eileen Hiscock (1909–1958), who had captained of the British women's athletic team in Los Angeles and was the current English 100 metre record holder, spoke the oath at the opening ceremony: 'We take part in the true spirit of sportsmanship . . . for the honour of women's athletics and for the glory of sport.' Lord Desborough released a dove. The programme notes featured Gladys Lunn as the 800 metres title holder. There were ambitious proposals that visiting teams would have free accommodation and full board in London in 1934 so the practical and social arrangements deserve more attention from researchers. The events were the 60 metres; 80 metres hurdles; 100 metres; 200 metres; 800 metres; 4x100 metres relay; pentathlon; high jump; discus; javelin; shot put; basketball and Hazena. Countries competing included America, Austria, Belgium, Canada, Czechoslovakia, England, France, Germany, Holland, Hungary, Italy, Japan, Latvia, Palestine, Poland, Rhodesia, South Africa, Sweden and Yugoslavia.

Women who took part in FSFI events travelled in Britain and Europe to represent their club, experiencing cosmopolitan influences and freedoms impossible for those who did not have these opportunities. Important decision-making roles were also to have long legacies, not otherwise available because of the IOC patrimony. In relation to the points made about networks, parallels and interconnections in this chapter, it is important to remember that the Olympic programme for women became generally more diverse between 1920 and 1936. Swimming and diving continued to be staple British women's medal events in official Olympic competition when tennis disappeared from the programme in 1924. Fencing was introduced in 1924 (only the foil discipline though); gymnastics became a full medal event in 1928; figure skating moved from being held on the Summer Games programme in 1920 to the first Winter Games in 1924. Yachting remained a mixed event with Dorothy Wright (1889–1960), from West Ham taking part as the only woman and winning a gold medal aboard *Ancora* in 1920, a vessel jointly owned by her husband and father.[113] MH Roney appeared in the eight-metre class in 1928 and Beryl Preston (1901–1979) also competed on the water in 1936.

A demonstration of women's speed skating took place in 1936 (to become a full medal sport in 1960) and the same year Helen Blane (1913–1990), Amy Birnie Duthie (1905–1994), Jeanette Kessler (1908–1972) and Evelyne Pinching (1915–1988) represented Britain in the alpine skiing events. The first woman to carry the flag for Britain at an Olympic opening ceremony was skater Mollie Phillips (1907–1994) at the 1932 Lake Placid Winter Games. Heather Guinness (1910–1942) was to win silver in the foil in Los Angeles losing to Ellen Preis (1912–2007) of Austria. The Welsh swimmer Elizabeth Davies (1912–2001) won a bronze behind Eleanor Holm (1913–2004) of America and Philomena Mealing (1912–2002) of Australia in the individual 100-metre backstroke competition. With colleagues Margaret Cooper (1909–2002); Edna Hughes (1916–1990) and Helen Varcoe (1907–1995), Davies led the British team to the 4 x 100 metre bronze medal behind the United States and the Netherlands.[114]

So, although this chapter has looked at the controversies surrounding football, which would not appear on the Olympic programme until 1996 in Atlanta, and the problematic inclusion of some track and field athletics disciplines, this wider context shows women changing the Games in both physical, visual and symbolic ways. Because the Olympics has a single medal tally of gold, silver and bronze per country women became important to the ways in which nations imagined themselves at such competitive tournaments, either by their inclusion or exclusion.[115]

At the Olympic Games in Los Angeles in 1932, the captain of the British women's track and field team, Eileen Hiscock, along with Nellie Halstead (1910–1991); Gwen Porter (1902-unknown) and Violet Webb (1915–1999) became Britain's first athletics medallists, taking a bronze in the 4 × 100 metres relay. Four years later Hiscock led the relay team of Audrey Brown (1913–2005); Barbara Burke (1917–1998) and Violet Olney (1911–1999) to a silver medal at the Berlin Olympics in a dramatic race.[116] The only other British female medal in 1936 was the silver won by Dorothy Odam (1920) for the high jump.

Figure 4.1 Sammelwerk 'Olympia 1932: Ellen Preis (Austria); Heather Seymour-Guinness (England) and Erna Bogan (Hungary) on the podium to receive their foil medals' (Berlin: Sammelwerk circa 1932); personal collection of the author. This and similar images show how international standing in women's sport could be conveyed in visual form, whatever language of the collector. These cards were as popular in Germany as in the UK, and collectors could find small vouchers to build up their portfolio of images in a range of everyday goods from margarine to cigarettes and coffee.

Just as the FSFI had encouraged teams of no more than twelve for the athletics programme of the 1930 and 1934 women's games, the British continued to send this number to IOC Olympic Games in 1932 and 1936. As this section has tried to demonstrate, the IOC version of the Games was part of, but did not define, the sporting career of many of these women. Nellie Halstead ran the anchor leg of the relay in 1932 and was a versatile athlete; her colleague Violet Webb disproved that sport was harmful to athletes' offspring in the most inspiring way when her daughter Janet Simpson (1944–2010) also won a bronze medal as a member of the 4 × 100 metre relay team at the 1964 Olympics. However, the otherwise indefatigable Milliat seems to have become increasingly weary by the time of the ninth and final FSFI congress in Berlin in 1936. Her writing campaign to promote women's sport circulated ideas and polemics in favour of women's physical education to a degree that it has scarcely been possible to convey here. Calls for Olympic women's hockey, an equestrian event 'for Amazones' and gymnastics were all registered by the mid 1930s.[117] In addition, we have yet to set the increase in the number of women's sport associations that grew in the 1920s in context of her influence.

There is also much biographical work that remains on groups and individuals: Violette Gourard Morris joined the subsequent Ligue Football Féminine de Football Association as a player for the Dunlop Sport team in 1933 and took part in at least 200 matches during her career.[118] However the degree of discrimination that Morris experienced in Paris appeared to make her more interested and successful in motor-sport. She also became increasingly right-wing and violent. Morris attended the 1936 Berlin Games like some other 'celebrity athletes' as a guest of Hitler and was awarded a special medal of honour. After becoming a collaborator with the German occupying forces, Morris was assassinated by the British intelligence services on 26 April 1944 and is more often remembered as an interrogator and spy than sportswoman.[119] We know that she played in at least one match against Dick, Kerr's when Lily Parr would have been about seventeen years old in 1922. What did Lily and Violette make of each other? What can sporting tours tell us about the cosmopolitan influences that British women like Lily, who lived in Preston all her adult life, experienced as part of their enthusiasm and skill?

The gradual and contested process of FSFI assimilation between 1920 and 1936 reflects this policy tension. However, Milliat's actions were also successful to the extent of stimulating broader coverage in the contemporary media over two questions with much continued relevance: why should women take up sports? For whom and for what purpose are versions of the Olympic Games intended? If, by 1926, the records set under FSFI competition were ratified by the IAAF, why are the women who took part still not always officially recognised as Olympians? We might expect that such a mature organisation would be able to retrospectively address this aspect of its own history.

Although Milliat is often attributed as a feminist icon in the international development of women's sport and supported female suffrage, she was not as radical as Morris or other activists in Britain and the United States. It would not be until after World War II that French women obtained the vote and the female Olympic star of the period was Micheline Ostermeyer (1922–2001) who won two gold medals in the discuss and shot put, plus a bronze in the high jump at the 1948 London Olympic Games.[120] As a full time concert pianist, Ostermeyer reflected a strong French female amateur tradition to which Milliat dedicated herself and which provided a focal point for international women's competition, not just in athletics. After the Second World War and the death of Henri de Baillet-Latour, Sigfried Edström became President of the IOC and remained so until 1952, although Olympic activities were much curtailed between 1939 and 1946. Avery Brundage succeeded his good friend to become the fifth President of the IOC and remained in office until 1972.[121] He also sought to limit women's programmes, both to feminine 'appropriate' sports and in protecting the overall schedule from 'gigantism'. Only gradually and with little good grace has gender equality featured as an Olympic priority since he left the IOC.

While the IOC and IAAF did not want to regulate, let alone develop women's sport, by the early 1920s it could ill afford to be seen *not* to control this aspect of international competition. If governing bodies were ambivalent, *The Cincinnati Enquirer* was not and showed a full compliment of the women about to sail to represent America as front page, headline news on 20 August 1922. Maybelle Gilliland; Elizabeth Stine; team captain Floreida Batson; Janet Snow and Camille Sable knelt in the front row of the photograph (although spellings vary across newspaper reports and biographical details remain scant).[122] Standing behind were Lucille Godbold; Frances Meade; Nancy Voorhees; Suzanne Backer; Louise Voorhees; Anne Harwick and Esther Greenwood. Maybelle Gilliland and Elizabeth Stine both came from Leonia NJ high school; Floreida Batson held the high and low hurdles records and was an alumna of Rosemary Hall, while Camille Sable also specialised in hurdles as the Newark NJ public school representative.[123] Nancy Voorhees of the Ethel Walker School New York; Florida State College student, Anne Harwick, and Janet Snow of Rye, New Jersey also featured in action shots, as did Katherine Agar from Oaksmere who might have been the thirteenth competitor to make the six-day crossing on the *Aquitania*. The IOC file contains newspaper clippings and other press cuttings, difficult to attribute, that show a thirteen-athlete team, accompanied by male coaches and Godbold leading the early stages of the 1,000 metre race before finishing fourth to a world record breaking time of 3.12 seconds by France's Mademoiselle Breard.

If hyperbole from Estill can be forgiven on Godbold's return, the reported 1,500 people who turned out to see her victory parade for bringing the laurel wreath to the small South Carolina town, suggests that an Olympic title could mean quite a lot in 1922. As Mark Dyreson has noted, this was especially the case after the success of the US female swimmers and divers in the Antwerp Olympic Games in 1920.[124] Ludy claimed to have won ten of the US total of 31 points and was therefore perceived, locally at least, as the star athlete of the team that came second in the event.[125] Having accepted the position as head of the Columbia College athletic department immediately after, Godbold did not so much join an institution as become one. By 1976 a Columbia College staff newsletter claimed she held a 1922 gold medal for the shot put, achieved with a world record distance; a bronze medal for the 1,000 metres and a silver for the javelin.[126] We might equivocate over the accuracy of these achievements, but Godbold's lifelong dedication to teaching physical education is apparent. Both her mother and sister also taught at Columbia, and her popularity extended beyond sport to a hit cameo in the annual faculty follies as her alter ego 'Flaming Mame'.

A marker on Highway 321 still proclaims that Godbold was an Olympic gold medallist from Estill who subsequently became an outstanding educator to the local community. The example suggests a need to revise our understanding of the place of athletics within IOC events to include the Women's World Games. Godbold's life story also suggests a need to nuance discourse around the female physical education in North American colleges at this time. The Women's Division of the National Amateur Athletic Federation of America (NAAF) established a National Convention of the American Physical Education Association in Springfield, Massachusetts in 1923.[127] Under the advisement of Lou Henry Hoover, the wife of Herbert Hoover and later First Lady when he became President in 1929, subscribing educators agreed that intercollegiate competition was a vulgarisation of the more noble collaborative impulse in sport. What the Women's Division of the NAAF called, 'the spirit of play for its own sake' had to be protected by women for girl athletes.[128]

This was an alternative to the chauvinism and veiled professionalism of American Football and other male college sport which had rapidly expanded after the Great War. Activities like the service programme initiated by Walter Camp had introduced thousands of young men to games.[129] As Oriard has shown, the 'preparedness crisis' of the First World War was an important context for the renewed emphasis on rugged sports, at the same time the economy was booming and leisure time was expanding. The marketing of a new consumption ethic helped the United States sporting explosion of the 1920s and 1930s.

In contrast 'Play Days' brought together teams comprised of female students from different institutions who were encouraged to enjoy taking part rather than wanting to win. Interscholastic competition was frowned upon in Alabama, Kansas, Oregon and Texas; basketball for girls was abolished at Lexington High School in Kentucky and the State Teachers College, Indiana in favour of play days while in Georgia radio announcements appealed for 'safe, sound and wholesome' athletics.[130] The idea of a 'girl in every game and a game for every girl' led to 'sports days' with intra college teams or, even more polite competitions between colleges challenging one another and posting the results by telegraph.[131] Travel, gate receipts and spectators were discouraged; medical surveillance was much encouraged.[132] Even so, it is evident that top North American female athletes like Godbold and her colleagues in 1922 sought more competitive international rivalries and relished their experience of challenge. As an educator Godbold encouraged exactly the kind of sporting enjoyment for its own sake that the Women's Division of the NAAF advocated, so the two philosophies were not mutually exclusive. There are further interconnections that need unpicking here.

CONCLUSION: THE MULTIPLE CAREERS OF INTER-WAR SPORTSWOMEN

This chapter began by looking at how some women's experience of work changed their access to leisure. In turn, this saw sport become a form of labour in itself for some female competitors, entrepreneurs, volunteer administrators and educationalists. Sometimes this was a short lived or casual form of employment, and it could be an unstable way to earn money for individuals and local communities. For other important figures, being an all-rounder or able to work on parallel careers provided more options. For a few women stars, sport was their life-long passion and vocation, whether they were paid to perform; benefitted from 'shamateur' arrangements or it actually cost them money to play. There was not space to do justice to the inter-war multi-taskers, like of golfer Joyce Wethered (1901–1998) Lady Heathcoat-Amory, who was British Ladies Amateur champion in 1922, 1924, 1925 and 1929; a Curtis Cup captain from 1932 and first President of the English Ladies' Golf Association in 1951. In 1933 she became golf adviser at Fortnum and Mason's.[133] On 5 March 1934 the Royal and Ancient ruled that Wethered was not eligible to participate in amateur competitions if her role involved receiving any 'consideration' from the King's grocer. Touring the United States and Canada in 1935, from May until September, to promote the John Wannamaker Company, it was reputed that the tour earned her in excess of £4,000, having received a guarantee of $300 per match. Wethered played at least fifty-two matches. After her marriage, she also became a Royal Horticultural Society gold medal winner, and was to be reinstated as an amateur by the Royal and Ancient in 1954 when Lady Heathcoat-Amory. Perhaps the title helped. Her great rival of the 1920s 'Cecil' Leitch (1891–1977) had an even more diverse professional portfolio also excelling in journalism; selling antiques; as director of the Cinema House group introducing the first foreign films to Britain; a noted committee-woman and founder of The Women Golfers' Museum in 1938.[134]

The decades of the 1920s and 1930s saw a growth both in women's sports associations and international federations in general. The chapter began by looking at some of the worlwide currents that influenced the growth of women's sport, often beginning from specific local cultures of work and leisure. The global sports star could be so described during this period because the transport and communications infrastructure existed to make events easily reported and broadcast to a wide audience. When internationally famous French sportsman Georges Carpenter kicked off a women's football match in Hull, after losing his heavyweight title to American Jack Dempsey in New York in the first million dollar fight a year earlier, we can begin to see the global in the local.[135] The friendly rivalry between Mary Lines, Kinuye Hitomi, Muriel Cornell and other athletes at FSFI events allowed difference to be displayed and contested. This was not simply about gender but included other forms of identity including ethnicity, sexuality, class and age. Not all the examples from the chapter have been about the few elite women of the leisure class like Wethered and Leitch.

Mobility of both a national kind within England, then Britain and abroad shaped the public image of Dick, Kerr's Ladies' football club. In this way, the munitions workers and nurses who comprised the majority of the team were imagined to have a right to leisure outside the home because of their public-spirited work. What made their success so contentious was the highly visible expansion of their supporter base with its altruistic, charitable, ethos. Following the ban in 1921, the team's management did not so much seem to lose its way as modify its ambition. Continuing to play 'on tour' and claiming to be the effective 'world champions' became a defining identity that coincided with the Football League expanding its activities and the BBC being created. Increasingly, the media was used to make sporting events moments of 'national communion'.[136] Sport could appear to unite the country and some women were part of these iconic moments.[137] Among them were Cecil Leitch and Joyce Wethered whose duels were front-page news, especially the 1925 British Open at Troon where thousands watched and tens of thousands more read about the result, arousing an enthusiasm unmatched by any golfing successor of the period. The more makeshift rituals of Dick, Kerr games after the 1921 ban were dwarfed in comparison; played out on public playing fields where collecting large contained crowds and charging entrance was nigh on impossible. The differentiation in the performance of male, mainstream football at important times and prestigious places contrasted vividly with the symbolic space allocated to women's football and this shapes perceptions of the relative worth of the gendered nature of professionalism today.

Dick, Kerr's failed to agree to the principles of association, in favour of a robust self-determination. Was this parochialism or evidence of small-scale entrepreneurialism? As a relative newcomer, women's football shows that some sports adopted alternative means of developing networks. Enthusiasts were not necessarily motivated by sporting amateurism and not all commercial ventures were grand in their ambitions. What this preliminary survey has shown is that more work is needed to appreciate the extent to which the players and their management supported the international role taken up by Milliat in order to develop women's sport. Scrapbooks of the sporting and social round experienced by the players suggest that transnational friendships could last for decades and increased mobility could potentially lead to life-changing migration, so there is much still to explore.

However, the Olympic Games and other established tournaments involving women could be important for amateurs to develop lucrative professional careers. International governing bodies differed in approach: the International Lawn Tennis Federation (ILTF) had been formed in 1912, though it took a while for the United States Lawn Tennis Association (USLTA) to join.[138] Suzanne Lenglen's 1919 victory at Wimbledon was followed by a win the 1920 Olympic singles gold medal in Antwerp, supplemented by a mixed double gold and a women's doubles bronze.[139] Lenglen's subsequent rivalry with Californian Helen Wills (1905–1998) made tennis fashionable beyond the upper middle classes as a leaner silhouette promoted new versions of femininity.

Lenglen wore a bandeau and a Jean Patou sleeveless costume, with a pleated shorter skirt combined with a monogrammed sleeveless cardigan; Wills favoured the eye-shade. By the end of the 1920s it was acceptable to play bare-headed. Lenglen took the Wimbledon singles title in 1919–1923 and 1925.[140] Due to illness Lenglen was forced to withdraw from Wimbledon in 1924, leaving Britain's Kitty McKane to beat the eighteen year old Wills for the title. It also meant that Lenglen was unable to give the athletes' oath at the 1924 Paris Games, let alone compete.[141] Wills therefore took the distinction of two Olympic medals in Paris (singles and doubles) in what would be the last time that tennis would be included on the IOC schedule until 1988.

Compared with pre-war British dominance at Wimbledon, international rivalries in women's tennis seemed clear evidence of a growing transnationalism, regardless of whether it was in or out of the Olympic programme. If there were European influences, there was also a clear Californian image developed by Helen Wills (known as Wills Moody after her marriage in 1929) who won the Wimbledon singles in 1927–1930, 1932 and 1933, 1935 and 1938. As Mrs Kathleen Godfree, the British woman went on to win the singles in 1926 and won the mixed doubles with her husband. Wills was known as 'Poker Faced Helen' but her record of eight Wimbledon titles in the 1920s and 1930s stood for nearly fifty years. As one of the first internationally famous sportswomen, in 1929 Wills Moody appeared on the cover of *Time* and sat for Diego Rivera who was sculpting the fresco 'California' for the San Francisco Stock Exchange, though it later had to be adapted so as not to resemble a living person.[142] If further evidence were needed of her part in the Californication of sports-culture, in 1932 she entered work in the Olympic Arts Competition and Exhibition after publishing her book *Tennis* in 1928, illustrated with etchings and self-portraits.[143] An autobiography *Fifteen Thirty* and a whodunit *Death Serves an Ace* followed in 1937 and 1939 respectively.[144]

In her later appearances as an amateur, Lenglen's costumes featured in American Vogue from 1926, becoming ever more elaborate with scarves, bangles, belted cardigans, an overcoat with fur trimmings and increasingly diaphanous dress fabrics.[145] Helen Wills favoured the sun-visor over a groomed bob haircut from 1927. Her white stockings had seams and her fur-trimmed overcoat was black at the most famous clash between the American and the Frenchwoman in 1926 at the Carlton. Lenglen won on style as well as points; inspiring devotee Teddy Tinling to move into tenniswear and then on to wedding dresses.[146] Sportswear became the province of haute couture housess like Chanel and Patou but also available to a wider audience.

Sportswear continued to be increasingly freeing when actually used for competition and Englishness could have its own fashionable elements: Betty Nutthall (1911–1983) caused something of a stir by winning the US women's singles and doubles championships in 1930 'Without stockings, in a white dress with red band round her hips.'[147] Though she was never to win Wimbledon and her career high in 1929 was world's fourth ranked woman, Nutthall became the first non-American to win a women's singles title at the U.S. Championships since 1892 and the last British female player to do so until Virginia Wade in 1968. Nutthall took the surname Shoesmith upon marriage and became a resident of New York: she was perhaps more famous in the US and France than in Britain.

Tennis had been characteristically waiting for an English Wimbledon for some time and it uncharacteristically got it in 1934 when Dorothy Round (1908–1982) and Fred Perry regained the singles titles from two Americans.[148] Dorothy Round triumphed at Wimbledon again in 1937, by which time Perry had won his three victories and become professional. Tennis was linked by commerce and enthusiasm to mass games. Table tennis, for instance, was initially a game played in the home, before becoming patented under the commercial name Ping Pong, until formalising itself in 1927 to the English Table Tennis Association and hosting an annual Open competition. By 1938–9 there were 230 leagues, 5,000 clubs and 80,000 registered players.[149] Fred Perry had won the table tennis world championship in 1929, the year before he first competed at Wimbledon. Table tennis gave a grounding in strategy, skill and discipline for some women who moved between the two forms.

The exclusive class bias of the lawn tennis club could be less daunting if skills earned in a parlour game could be translated onto the court. Biographical details are sparse on table tennis heroine Doris 'Dolly' Gubbins, a leading player for Wales, who won the inaugural English Open title in the 1926 season but lost in the World Championships held the same year in

London, to Maria Mednyanszky of Hungary.[150] Mednyanszky held the title until 1931. In looking at the frameworks of internationalism and national-ism, it may be that elite spectator sport has been emphasised at the cost of participant culture. How was Dolly Gubbins imagined as a symbol of Welsh nationalism, for example, particularly in beating the English at a tournament like the 1926 championships? How would Scotland's Helen Elliott similarly be viewed when she came to prominence in the 1950s by winning two World mixed doubles with Viktor Barna, a Hungarian Jew who took British citizenship in 1952?

In spite of fluctuations in the world economy and in the fortunes of wom-en's sport, inter-war fashion and sporting goods proliferated as well as the number of tournaments themselves. This is a research agenda in itself. Cos-mopolitanism enabled increasingly young individuals to style themselves in sports-wear and skating was an ideal blend of the aesthetic and athletic. The fashion and fitness industries used well-known women and men to sell prod-ucts, not just sporting goods. Norway's Sonja Henie (1912–1969) was perhaps the most astute self-publicist of her generation.[151] From 1927 to 1939 Henie dominated figure skating winning ten consecutive world titles and individual gold medals at three Olympic Games in St. Moritz, Switzerland (1928), Lake Placid (1932), and at Garmisch-Partenkirchen in Bavaria (1936). Britain's young star, Cecilia Colledge (1920–2008) came a very close second to Henie in 1936. Turning professional that year, Henie became for a time one of the highest paid actresses in Hollywood movies with the successful release of *One in A Million*. In response, Avery Brundage took the position that ama-teur Olympic athletes could no longer appear in motion pictures and those who wrote articles about figure-skating risked their eligibility.[152] However, high-profile athletes were not just beneficiaries of social conditions of the time but also created their own markets. Professionalism allowed those, like Sonja Henie to form and own their public image, promote touring shows like her Hollywood Ice Revue and use endorsements to generate income away from the control of amateur administrators.

Ceclia Colledge remains the youngest-ever female Olympian after appearing at the 1932 Games at eleven years and eighty-two days became a dominant amateur, although she had a close enough relationship with her coach that he initially lived with the family. Her great rival, and British col-league in 1932, Megan Taylor (1920–1993) was just thirty-four days older. Turning professional in 1946, Colledge moved to the United States and taught skating from 1951 until 1995. She and Taylor appeared in several reviews like Ice Capades and this linked sport, performance and glamour.

Half skirts, bifurcated culottes, trouserskirts and knickerbockers were commended by *Vogue* for their practical nature, especially for fishing, ski-ing and skating. The development of Lastex in the 1930s enabled greater freedom and practicality. Jersey fabrics, washable silks and crepe de chine gave lightness, pliability and elegance in summer; gabardine warmth and ventilation in winter. The golf jumper became a female staple. Colour,

Figure 4.2   Gladys Carson's Identity Card for the 1924 Paris Olympics, where she took a bronze medal in the individual 200 metre breast-stroke. © By permission of David Hewitt, son of Gladys Carson, personal collection.

not all commercial ventures were grand in their ambitions. What this pre-liminary survey has shown is that more work is needed to appreciate the extent to which the players and their management supported the interna-tional role taken up by Milliat in order to develop women's sport. Scrap-books of the sporting and social round experienced by the players suggest that transnational friendships could last for decades and increased mobil-ity could potentially lead to life-changing migration, so there is much still to explore.

However, the Olympic Games and other established tournaments involv-ing women could be important for amateurs to develop lucrative professional careers. International governing bodies differed in approach: the Interna-tional Lawn Tennis Federation (ILTF) had been formed in 1912, though it took a while for the United States Lawn Tennis Association (USLTA) to join.[138] Suzanne Lenglen's 1919 victory at Wimbledon was followed by a win the 1920 Olympic singles gold medal in Antwerp, supplemented by a mixed double gold and a women's doubles bronze.[139] Lenglen's subsequent rivalry with Californian Helen Wills (1905–1998) made tennis fashionable beyond the upper middle classes as a leaner silhouette promoted new ver-sions of femininity.

Lenglen wore a bandeau and a Jean Patou sleeveless costume, with a pleated shorter skirt combined with a monogrammed sleeveless cardigan; Wills favoured the eye-shade. By the end of the 1920s it was acceptable to play bare-headed. Lenglen took the Wimbledon singles title in 1919–1923 and 1925.[140] Due to illness Lenglen was forced to withdraw from Wimble-don in 1924, leaving Britain's Kitty McKane to beat the eighteen year old Wills for the title. It also meant that Lenglen was unable to give the ath-letes' oath at the 1924 Paris Games, let alone compete.[141] Wills therefore took the distinction of two Olympic medals in Paris (singles and doubles) in what would be the last time that tennis would be included on the IOC schedule until 1988.

Compared with pre-war British dominance at Wimbledon, international rivalries in women's tennis seemed clear evidence of a growing transnation-alism, regardless of whether it was in or out of the Olympic programme. If there were European influences, there was also a clear Californian image developed by Helen Wills (known as Wills Moody after her marriage in 1929) who won the Wimbledon singles in 1927–1930, 1932 and 1933, 1935 and 1938. As Mrs Kathleen Godfree, the British woman went on to win the singles in 1926 and won the mixed doubles with her husband. Wills was known as 'Poker Faced Helen' but her record of eight Wimbledon titles in the 1920s and 1930s stood for nearly fifty years. As one of the first interna-tionally famous sportswomen, in 1929 Wills Moody appeared on the cover of *Time* and sat for Diego Rivera who was sculpting the fresco 'California' for the San Francisco Stock Exchange, though it later had to be adapted so as not to resemble a living person.[142] If further evidence were needed of her part in the Californication of sports-culture, in 1932 she entered work in the Olympic Arts Competition and Exhibition after publishing her book *Tennis* in 1928, illustrated with etchings and self-portraits.[143] An autobiography *Fifteen Thirty* and a whodunit *Death Serves an Ace* followed in 1937 and 1939 respectively.[144]

In her later appearances as an amateur, Lenglen's costumes featured in American Vogue from 1926, becoming ever more elaborate with scarves, bangles, belted cardigans, an overcoat with fur trimmings and increasingly diaphanous dress fabrics.[145] Helen Wills favoured the sun-visor over a groomed bob haircut from 1927. Her white stockings had seams and her fur-trimmed overcoat was black at the most famous clash between the American and the Frenchwoman in 1926 at the Carlton. Lenglen won on style as well as points; inspiring devotee Teddy Tinling to move into tenniswear and then on to wedding dresses.[146] Sportswear became the province of haute couture housess like Chanel and Patou but also available to a wider audience.

Sportswear continued to be increasingly freeing when actually used for competition and Englishness could have its own fashionable elements: Betty Nutthall (1911–1983) caused something of a stir by winning the US women's singles and doubles championships in 1930 'Without stockings, in a white dress with red band round her hips.'[147] Though she was never to win Wimbledon and her career high in 1929 was world's fourth ranked woman, Nutthall became the first non-American to win a women's singles title at the U.S. Championships since 1892 and the last British female player to do so until Virginia Wade in 1968. Nutthall took the surname Shoesmith upon marriage and became a resident of New York: she was perhaps more famous in the US and France than in Britain.

Tennis had been characteristically waiting for an English Wimbledon for some time and it uncharacteristically got it in 1934 when Dorothy Round (1908–1982) and Fred Perry regained the singles titles from two Americans.[148] Dorothy Round triumphed at Wimbledon again in 1937, by which time Perry had won his three victories and become professional. Tennis was linked by commerce and enthusiasm to mass games. Table tennis, for instance, was initially a game played in the home, before becoming patented under the commercial name Ping Pong, until formalising itself in 1927 to the English Table Tennis Association and hosting an annual Open competition. By 1938–9 there were 230 leagues, 5,000 clubs and 80,000 registered players.[149] Fred Perry had won the table tennis world championship in 1929, the year before he first competed at Wimbledon. Table tennis gave a grounding in strategy, skill and discipline for some women who moved between the two forms.

The exclusive class bias of the lawn tennis club could be less daunting if skills earned in a parlour game could be translated onto the court. Biographical details are sparse on table tennis heroine Doris 'Dolly' Gubbins, a leading player for Wales, who won the inaugural English Open title in the 1926 season but lost in the World Championships held the same year in

AEHWA trips to South Africa (1925) and Australia (1927), in addition to receiving touring parties from overseas, believing that the comradeship of sport was important in promoting good relations between nations.

In 1918 Thompson had helped to found the Ex-Service Women's Association, which provided free passages to the dominions for women who had served in the war.[13] Subsequently, the difficult position of educated single women in Britain caused Thompson to work with schoolgirls, teachers, nurses and secretarial workers to help them visit, and possibly migrate, to countries within the Empire where there was also a demographic surplus of men. From 1921 she was a member of the executive of the Six Point Group, a feminist organisation which campaigned for formal equality between the genders, and of the Women's Sanitary and Health Visitors' Association. From the late 1920s, under the auspices of the Society for the Overseas Settlement of British Women (SOSBW), Thompson supervised regular tours of British schoolgirls to the Dominions to give an insight into the opportunities for professional careers. In 1937 Thompson succeeded Gladys Pott (1867–1961) to become the second chair of the SOSBW, which had become absorbed into a department of state.[14] A tireless committee-woman, she was also a member of the National Playing Fields Association and spoke of the importance of open spaces for less-advantaged children. In 1930 she was a member of a commission appointed by *The Lancet* to investigate ways of making nursing a more attractive career for women. From 1921 to 1927, and again from 1929 to 1931, Thompson was a member of Aldeburgh town council.

Thompson's contemporary Hilda Mary Light (1890–1969) had also worked as a nurse between 1916 and 1919 for the Voluntary Aid Detachment (VAD) stationed in Abbeville and Wimereux, France.[15] An outstanding hockey player, in 1924 Hilda Light achieved the first distinction of captaining her club, county, territory and country simultaneously.[16] She retired as a player in 1925, but then served as President of the Association from 1931 to 1947. Light had already become the secretary of the Booksellers' Association of Great Britain and Ireland, a position which she held from 1929 to 1946. When Light took over, AEWHA regulated 1,400 clubs, spread over forty-three county associations and four further allied 'Dominion Associations' with a total of 60,000 afiliated players.[17] By 1939 there were over 2,100 clubs in forty-six county associations; five Territorial Associations who co-ordinated regional competitions and a further 200 clubs based in northern Leagues.

With some satisfaction, Light and Thompson could look back on the expansion of AEWHA from ten clubs in 1895 to world-wide authority by 1939. Other affiliates included: the National Association of Girls' and Mixed Clubs; the All-Australia Women's Hockey Association; the All-Ceylon Women's Hockey Association; the All-South Africa and Rhodesia Women's Hockey Association; the British Guiana Women's Hockey Association; the New Zealand Women's Hockey Association; the Shanghai

Ladies' Hockey Association and the Alexandria Sporting Club.[18] Nor was this influence limited to hockey: Heron Maxwell had moved on to preside over the Women's Cricket Association (WCA) from 1926 until the Second World War along the same international lines but fewer clubs and players.[19] In 1937, the WCA had a membership high point of 208 adult clubs, 94 affiliated schools and a triangle of Test matches against Australia and New Zealand.[20] While many of the same processes and people were at work, hockey was more of a mass participation sport.

Hamilton, Heron Maxwell, Light, Thompson and their contemporaries began to internationalise hockey by co-founding the International Federation of Women's Hockey Associations (IFWHA), in London during 1927.[21] Travel was so integral to the way that they subsequently expanded the network that Hamilton was obliged to cut short a hockey tour in 1952 due to illness, and she died from cancer just over two years later. Thompson crossed Canada and returned by tramp steamer in the year before her death in 1961. Light was taken fatally ill while in London to draft a common set of rules for women's and men's hockey in 1969. These are some of the more well-known personalities but the section also refers to other cases of lifelong enthusiasts and volunteers. Many remain unknown. In these days of search-engines and wiki-encyclopedias, it perhaps says something about the status of women's sport that no information exists in the public domain without further geneological research of census material and local newspapers. Hamilton, Thompson and Light were of national importance beyond their sporting interests as this introductory summary indicates. Much more primary research remains to be done to contextualise their contribution to sport, national life and international co-operation.

Hockey tours were amateur affairs, allowing women to use new travel and communications technologies to pursue sport in new territories. Networks were partially underpinned by links established by the British dominions and other post-colonial bonds.[22] Tours enabled a kind of practical feminism, in that enthusiasts' ties with Australia, Canada, New Zealand, South Africa and sections of upper-middle-class America and Europe privileged a common past in their contemporary exchanges. Individuals who facilitated tours had agendas to provide women with new opportunities of a personal and professional kind. Conservative politics could meld with progressive action and vice versa. At this time, women's hockey was a sport of anglophile affiliation, even if this took indigenous forms that made, say, an Australian player's experience very different from that of her colleague in the United States. We have only to look at *The Eagle*, the publication of the United States Field Hockey Association (USFHA), to see that national identity could be expressed in many ways by friendly tours, such as the September 1939 visit to British Guiana.[23] Supranational networks were promoted in hockey from the middle of the 1920s in an effort to democratise the sport at home and abroad, to a certain degree. The calendar of events allowed the interplay of national and international representation in ways that were as much about taking part, as winning. So long, of course, as England was victorious. When Marie Hamilton and Edith Thompson toasted each other in Sydney, their friendship tells us about international sporting friendship. It also gives an insight into the economic, political and cultural developments in women's lives during this period in time.

If hockey followed selected patterns of the British Empire, the important exceptions were Canada and India (the latter first sent a women's team to the international conference in Folkestone in 1953). The same imperial narratives infused motor-racing, aviation and power-boating.[24] Motorised competitions nevertheless had considerable contemporary resonance given their links with militarism, technological modernity and the impetus to map territory at home and abroad.[25] While the biggest news story of 1919 was the scuttling of the German fleet at Scapa Flow, the next largest was the first trans-atlantic flight of Captain Alcock and Lieutenant Arthur Whitten Brown from Newfoundland to Clifden in Ireland in just over sixteen hours.[26] They were both knighted and awarded £10,000 prize money by Lord Northcliffe's *Daily Mail* although the excitement was marred by the death of Alcock soon after in an air crash in France. The first meeting held at Brooklands after World War I took place the next year on 11 April 1920. Using transport for leisure, sport, publicity or propaganda remained risky in the inter-war period. The R101 airship crashed on its inaugural voyage from Cardington Airfield to India in 1930 killing Lord Christopher Thomson, the minister for Air, and forty-seven other people, when it came down in France after being airborne for only six hours.[27] The failure of a £2.5 million government scheme demonstrated that the cost of safe commercial passenger transport would perhaps better be left to the private sector, especially at a time of high, widespread unemployment. Although the R100, the twin model built by the private firm Vickers, had reached Canada in seventy-nine hours the same year, airships became gradually less fashionable as the variety of motorised transport continued to grow.

Rather than duplicate the same themes as hockey's imperial ties, especially with what were sometimes called the 'white' Dominions, the second section focuses on more informal aspects of Empire. These were typified by the activities of the Honourable Mrs Victor Bruce (1895–1990), born in Chelmsford, Essex as Mildred Mary Petre of Coptfold Hall.[28] The marriage of her parents, Mary reported in her autobiography, was an unhappy one with an overly anxious, dramatic mother (an American actress, known for her Shakespearean roles) and a lugubrious father.[29] Little wonder then, that Mary showed an early fascination for getting out of the house, often travelling at speed. She claimed to be the first woman ever arrested for speeding in a motorbike at between 55 and 60 mph in 1911 with her collie dog, Laddie, in the sidecar. Mary Petre also claimed to be the first woman to crash, a few months under the age of sixteen, while travelling along country lanes.

Automobiles at least gave more stability and Mary married the Honourable Victor Austin Bruce in 1926. Victor was a member of the AC works team and had become the first Englishman to win the Monte Carlo Rally in 1926. Mary drove solo 1,700 miles from John O'Groats to Monte Carlo to win the Coupe des Dames in 1927, with her husband, the motoring editor of the *Daily Sketch* and an engineer as her three passengers.[30] It took seventy hours and twenty minutes non-stop, finishing to a lavish welcome outside the Casino. Under the sponsorship of Selwyn Edge and the AC factory, the Bruce's continued a further 8,000 miles on a distance trial for the RAC and AA from Monte Carlo to Tunis, then to Tangier and eventually returned to England through Italy and Spain. This was immediately followed by a 1,000 miles time-trial at Montlhéry near Paris in which husband and wife shared the driving. The string of achievements, mediated by the key figures in the British press, made the couple 'motoring celebrities.' In respect of the records and publicity, Selwyn Edge gave Mary the car as a gift.

After the distance trial, Mary Bruce took the works AC 250 miles north of the Arctic Circle, reaching within forty miles of the Arctic Ocean, by travelling though Finnish Lapland and Greenland, in order plant a Union Jack flag in the middle of a forest to mark the accomplishment. While this provided a practical demonstration that the car could endure such a journey, the serialised travelogue for the newspapers characterised Bruce and her compatriots as benign explorers. Although very few people would ever see the flag, given its isolated position, the symbolic value of claiming a record for Britain was enormous. The Victorian stereotype of the British inventor-entrepreneur was reinvented in motor-sport, as was pioneering friendly invasion. As the section shows, this extended to light aviation and motorised boating. The casual manner of Mary Bruce's preparation made record-breaking travel appear to be less exceptional. She effectively domesticated the light plane as the 'aerial motor-car' and the motor-boat in a similar way as a natural extension of her interests. However, by writing about her feats, Mary Bruce both magnified the public response to these lonely enterprises and capitalised on her expertise.

International sporting rivalries also became more important, in part because of the way that political, cultural and economic ideologies used competition between nations for propaganda.[31] If the previous chapters have suggested that the workers' sport movement and the rise of the Left was significant in the inter-war period, equally important were the politics of the Right. Martin Pugh has characterised Anglo-Irish motorist Fay Taylour (1904–1983), as typifying the 'fast' women who were attracted to the British Union of Fascists after it was formed by Oswald Moseley (1896–1980) in 1932.[32] However, political figures of the inter-war years could move from socialism to fascism, prompted in part to do so by the extreme circumstances caused by economic collapse and mass, long-term, unemployment.[33] Taylour's life was controversial in many ways; her affair with Moseley led to imprisonment in Holloway and then internment on the Isle of Wight when Britain entered the Second World War. Before then, she was perhaps best known as a speedway rider, competing against male and other female rivals, such as Yorkshire's Eva Asquith (1906–1980), at Crystal Palace and Wembley in 1928.

Taylour toured Australia and New Zealand in 1929 before returning to win the Cinders trophy for the fastest lap in an international contest at Wembley.[34] Speedway was a fragile way of earning a living. She was obliged to return to Australia and New Zealand later that year, because women's speedway riders were banned from competition in Britian on 15 May 1930 after a 'women's meeting' at Wembley. Also racing in Europe and the United States, Taylor was amongst the most prominent personalities in inter-war motor-sport, winning a 500 miles race in a Talbot at Brooklands, averaging 98.37 mph in 1930.[35] Racing frequently at the circuit for the next four years (and regularly in the top three finishers) her Brooklands career was brought to an abrupt end when she came second to Doreen Evans (1916–1982) in the 1934 Mountain Handicap while driving the Penn-Hughes 2.6 Alfa Romeo.[36] Taylour ignored all chequered flags and continued to lap the circuit after the race was over for quite some time. Her progress was only halted when a particularly incensed marshall stood in her path, after which she was fined and excluded from the circuit. Taylour appeared unpeturbed and won the Leinster Trophy Road Race driving an Adler the same year. In May 1935 she won the women's race at the Donington circuit in a Frazer Nash. Following the war Taylous was released back to her native Ireland, although she eventually settled in Dorset and wrote an unfinished autobiography. Continuing to compete in midget car racing in the United States and Formula Cooper in Britain until 1959, the Moseley affair was never renounced and undoubtedly affected her popularity, though a young Stirling Moss was happy to ask her advice.[37] A skilled motor bike, light car and Brooklands competitor, much remains to be known about her racing career, life and politics.

The language of motor-sport was inflected by horse racing and imperial narratives: 'improving the breed' of each marque took place in a wider context of national discourse. The rise of motor-car ownership multiplied the range of products and materials, often using sporting examples to signal innovation and versatility.[38] By far the largest festival linking industry and leisure was the British Empire Exhibition which opened at Wembley 23 April 1924 (St. George's Day). In attendance were 250,000 people, 11 Cabinet Ministers and 50 members of British and foreign royalty attended. As an attraction in itself, Wembley attempted to sum up 'The Whole Empire in Little!' for one and sixpence.[39] The £12,000,000 exhibition closed down in October the following year having been seen by 28,000,000 people at a loss of £2,000,000.[40] Various sporting tournaments borrowed narratives of patriotic discourse in 'friendly' imperial competition during the inter-war period, such as the British Empire Games at the White City Stadium, London, in 1934 which incorporated seventeen nations.

The first Industrial Design Competition was also launched by the Royal Society of Arts in 1924, to bring together the work of young designers and the needs of manufacturers.[41] Firms and individuals funded the inaugural prizes, enabling over a £1,000 of grants and travelling scholarships to be awarded. The Royal Society hosted annual exhibitions of this competition, with each designer-manufacturer partnership showcasing their collaboration in identical shop windows and the remaining photographs in the archives are a rich source for historians of sport-related goods.[42] Exhibitons of leather; rubber; wood; fabric; metalwork; glass and other materials used sporting examples in succesive evolutions of design. This showcased Britain design and manufacturing expertise as the centre of a much wider 'Empire shop' for commodity exchange.[43] By 1936 the distinction 'Royal Designer for Industry' became established as the highest honour for a creative engineer to be obtained in the United Kingdom. The Empire Exhibition of 1938 held in Glasgow, once called the 'Empire's second city', also reinforced these political, economic and cultural ties.

Colonial celebrations placed Britain as central to world culture, while new travel technologies could enable sportsmen and women to explore its margins.[44] The section of the chapter on Brooklands therefore explores motor-sport as an example of informal Empire, though underpinned by formal links in trade, diplomacy and communications.[45] There were obvious examples of this such as the British Empire Trophy Race from 1934 but a wider sense of entitlement was perhaps more significant, encapsulated by the Empire Marketing Board motto 'Highways of Empire' between 1926 and 1939.[46] As a link between the changing industrial balance of world power and sport, motor racing reflected domestic anxieties and international ambition. Nowhere was attitude more important than at Brooklands. The three photographs of Doreen Evans (1916–1982) in the National Portrait Gallery evidence this sense of privilege.[47] Known as a part of a 'motoring-family', Evans' parents and her two brothers were already part of the Brooklands set when she began to race there at seventeen.

If the British Racing Driver's Club (BRDC) began life in 1927 wanting to belittle female participation by downgrading women to the status of honourary members of its organisation, manufacturers wanted high-profile female drivers to promote their goods. It would have been equally possible to write about the popularity of rallying, motor touring and flying as activities in themselves in order to illustrate the resulting tensions. Though it has been difficult to locate more biographical information on the following women drivers, a report of the 1934 Scottish Rally celebrated the success of Dorothy Champney (1909–1958) driving a Riley, Jackie Astbury in a Singer; Marjorie Smith steering an Alvis and Cynthia Labouchere negotiating a Singer Nine expertly through the Devil's Elbow section of the course; also notable was Maude Flewitt's striking yellow Austin with an innovative rubber washable roof.[48] Of the fifty-nine class-one starters, twenty were women; as were twelve of the sixty-five class-two competitors. The Singer and Triumph motor-club teams were entirely female; Dorothy Champney took the most prestigious Ladies' Prize to lead the mixed Riley team to overall victory; Jessie Sleigh, Annie Ross and Marjorie Smith also lined up alongside male colleagues.[49] The author of the piece concluded, 'The driving of the women was beyond all praise. They always knew what to do, were never flurried and made very few mistakes. Their average efficiency was very much higher than that of the men.'[50]

However, due to the constraints of space, the focus is on how women helped to promote a sense of technocratic Anglophile superiority at Brooklands. Evidence from the Silverstone and Brookland's archive, in addition to the autobiographies of many racing drivers, suggests that there was a contemporary perception of continuity between racing and record breaking.[51] Power unit technology of the day prioritised endurance and reliability as necessary precursors to greater speed, especially over long distances.[52] As significant investors in motor-sport, vehicle manufacturers were important non-governmental sponsors of women drivers. In terms of cultural transfer, motorists like Kay Petre (1903–1994) and the Honourable Mildred Mary Bruce became icons for men and women, before working in the motor and aeronautical industries respectively. They began to drive as novice amateurs, as many other women would at this time, before taking paid employment; in Petre's case shaping aspects of car design and sales, including the Mini, after she retired from competitive racing.[53] Mary Bruce went further, having aspired to become a millionaire as a child, she bought and sold air companies; pioneering aspects of freight and passenger transport in Britain, Europe and the United States.[54] Brooklands was therefore a locus of this technocratic, class-based sporting endeavour.

'WE'VE GONE ALMOST COMPLETELY ENGLISH': THE ESTABLISHMENT OF THE INTERNATIONAL FEDERATION OF WOMEN'S HOCKEY ASSOCIATIONS[55]

The All England Women's Hockey Association (AEWHA) tours developed close connections between sections of middle-class women throughout the world. Although there were discussions to establish an English national AEWHA base in the 1920s and 1930s, several key members were teachers, and hockey gradually became institutionalised as a 'school-sport' in private and state institutions rather than one specific place. Disseminating an enthusiasm for the sport amongst younger participants became more of a priority, so that an AEWHA education sub-committee was formed and this produced the Hockey Film in 1928.[56] The promotional feature cost £197 1 shilling and 6 pence to make, of which the AEWHA funded just £31 and the majority came from donations totalling £157 16 shillings 6 pence. An additional £8 5 shillings was raised by combined ticket sales from a screening in Wimbledon and a related exhibition at Wardour Street, London.

The AEWHA may have begun as a London-based association but in the interwar period hockey became a nation-wide enthusiasm: Garnet Valentine Spooner (better known as 'G.V.') was a notable player for various Yorkshire clubs between 1911–1930, before settling in Barnsley.[57] Northern league competition also became the most pressing domestic problem for the AEWHA executive. Leagues had hierarchical structures which intensified club rivries, both features were considered undesireable by the AEWHA since its ethos actively discouraged 'pot-hunting' and an undue emphasis on winning. Taking the view that the game needed no championship, trophy, or league table to make it more worthy, the AEWHA had tolerated an Oldham league with thrty six teams in four divisions since 1913.

When Hilda Light took over as AEWHA President, the number of league-affilated clubs had expanded to at least 121. More players were probably involved but unaffiliated, for instance, an appeal for sticks came from the Women's Section of the Sheffield Social Centres where 4,500 women under 30 were unemployed and hockey, handicrafts and care skills were thought to be an antidote.[58] So the AEWHA had to risk not having complete control over women's hockey in England or accept that leagues had already become an established feature of the domestic game. Because industrial centres, especially Lancashire and Cheshire, had already expanded the clubs for under-privileged players in the north, the AEWHA had to accept that its own contradictory position had prevented it from helping the less well-off and leagues were grudgingly accepted. By 1939 the Insurance Offices Women's Hockey Association; the Railway Athletic Association (Women's Hockey Section); the Civil Service and the United Banks Women's Hockey Association strengthened the sense of welfarism, while several works' clubs also increased the diversity of employed women affiliated to the association. There were also some very large clubs, such as Meridian in Nottingham, which regularly fielded between four and five teams.[59] Edgbaston had around sixty members in 1937, so were able to run three Saturday and two Wednesday teams. Wallington ran four weekend and two midweek elevens for its ninety members, who enjoyed exclusive use of two grounds.

In 1935 Hilda Light also ensured that hockey was a constituent of the Women's Team Games Board, formed to encourage adult female participation in physical exercise. During the period of Light's leadership the schools' affiliation fee to the AEWHA was reduced which increased the number of participating institutions from 358 in 1930 to 715 in 1939. Hockey was therefore very establishment in its leadership but increasingly democratic in its player profile. The AEWHA had representation on the National Playing Fields Association councils, at both local and national level; the Central Council for Recreation and Physical Training; the British Sports and Games Association and the National Fitness Council. These connections would see former England international, Marjorie Pollard (1899–1982), appointed as the first national organiser of the Women's Team Games Board, while also working as a teacher and journalist.[60] Pollard helped to establish the

Women's Cricket Association (WCA) in 1926; Light and Thompson were active in the formation of the All England Netball Association (AEWNA) the same year and hockey also maintained close links with lacrosse (a Southern Counties Lacrosse Association had been active before the First World War).[61] Pollard would edit *Hockey Field* for thirty-four years and co-ordinated *Women's Cricket* for nineteen years, eventually writing for *The Guardian*. Although cricket developed distinct rivalries in the form of triangular tournaments between England, Australia and New Zealand from 1934 onwards, the discussion concentrates on hockey because of its fundamental influence on other sports and public life.[62] For example, for most British girls school team games would come to mean hockey and net-ball. If a young woman's parents were affluent, she might also have the good fortune to play lacrosse.

There were minor elements of public entertainment and commercialism for altruistic purposes, including charitable fund-raising, but hockey was mainly played for the enjoyment and edification of the players. There were, if anything, more 'hockey-families' in this period than there had been before, helped by the fact that it was a sport that could be enjoyed by both men and women for decades. There is a history of mixed sport waiting to be written and hockey would feature strongly in such a project.[63]

Though personal details remain hazy, Christina Goodman (married name Dony), donated eight scrapbooks, compiled between 1928 and 1948, plus her mother's notes to the archive at Bath University.[64] Goodman played centre for Edgbaston Ladies Hockey Club between 1929–1950. Her three sisters, Mary (Mrs Blakemore); Barbara and Geraldine (Mrs Wynn) also played for the club. Goodman played for Warwickshire between 1929 and 1949 and for the Midlands between 1933 and 1948 (excluding the war years). Christina was an international reserve in 1935; part of the national team that toured the USA in 1936 and competed at regional level in England in 1937, before playing regularly again in the national squad in the 1946–7 season. Her mother, Florence Mayne (1880–1949), had been a founder member of the Dales Ladies Hockey Club in Birmingham in 1898, which later became Edgbaston Ladies. Florence Mayne was captain of Warwickshire, played for the Midlands region between 1902–06 and was an international reserve in 1906. She married Harold Goodman of Birmingham 1907. Christine claimed that at one county match at Kala-mazoo ground, Birmingham all four Goodman women played together in a county side against Worcestershire and though it has not been possible to substantiate this yet, it seems possible. The expansion of the AEWHA activities in the inter-war period increased the media profiles for individual players and women's hockey as a whole, becoming something of an anglo-centric mission for 'high' amateurism. The male-led Fédération Interna-tionale de Hockey (FIH) was formed in 1924 as a direct response to the exclusion of the sport from the programme for the Paris Olympic Games. Many European nations admitted women's hockey as part of the activities of an umbrella national association, so FIH grew over the same period as the AEWHA but not to the same degree. The visit by a Dutch team from Haarlem seems to have been among the first 'international' competitions but similar fixtures often involved British women living abroad.[65]

Light continued to defend the association's policy of women-only governance as fundamental to the, 'Truly amateur spirit in which our games are played.'[66] AEWHA members gained organisational experience from running an international sport and took this into other fields of voluntary activity. Equally, the association benefitted from the public profile of women like Thompson, Pollard and Light. The English association was also the dominant international side until at least 1939 and could be condescending. Several applications were made by the United States Field Hockey Association to affiliate directly but these were politely declined. As the slogan from the Spalding advertisement that opened this section indicated, the image of the 'formidable' English woman could be glamorised to sell sporting goods and clothing.[67] Contemporary historians of women's sport were also at pains to point out national differences between the robust 'English' model of how hockey was played and the style of the more refined 'average American girl.'[68] There were particularly fierce debates in magazines like *The Sportswoman* about whether the competitive spirit in which hockey internationals were played contravened the collaborative ethos esteemed by North American female educators.[69] Such 'high' amateurism was therefore international but had nationalised inflections.

The tours were opportunities to travel by land and sea, to socialise and experience new cultures. The wonderful diaries and scrapbooks kept by many players and now held at the AEWHA archives, manifest how these journeys could change perspective. We know the extensive and elaborate menus from which the players chose their food; to what 'casual' deck games and welcome concerts they were invited on board ship; how they sought to counter travel sickness and what they thought of the countries that they visited. Preparatory advice to novice sea travellers, who were going to cross the Equator for the first time in their lives, cautioned:

> First and foremost, Luggage [sic]: don't stint yourself in the way of underclothes. Laundry: good clothes are spoilt and *wasted* on board on sticky and briny seats [sic]. Coiffure: can be a nightmare unless you go properly armed and equipped for Bobbing and Shingling during the tour. Footgear [sic]: at least two pairs of plimsolls or good tennis shoes will reap their own rewards. For Mal-de-Mer: Ginger Ale and Tiger nuts are an excellent preventative.[70]

In 1914 the first major AEWHA overseas tour had been to New Zealand where, of twenty-six games played, the visitors had won twenty-two, drew one and lost just three. England scored a total of 183 goals compared to 36 registered by the host clubs.[71] Importantly, tours could raise money: the overall profit on this occasion running to £30 and 17 shillings.[72] Given that the Association had ended 1913 with just £10 on the balance sheet, in the inter-war period, the tendency to tour became more frequent and widespread. England's overseas tour record from 1921 to 1931 was as follows:

1921	USA	played 15	won 15	(259 goals to 10)
1922	Denmark	played 3	won 3	(24 goals to 2)
1925	South Africa	played 14	won 14	(78 goals to 6)
1926	Germany	played 4	won 4	(49 goals nil)
1927	Australia	played 19	won 19	(228 goals to 9)
1928	USA	won 15	won 15	(229 goals to 3)
1930	South Africa	played 16	won 14 drawn 1 lost 1	(75 goals to 18)

Players like Joyce Whitehead (1900–1978) took part in these overseas tours before an international federation was created. We have her notes and photographs of the 1925 South Africa visit spanning May to September. A typical day on board ship as a third-class passenger would begin with a breakfast of several courses, followed by boat drill and correspondence; a break at eleven o'clock for beef tea; games of quoits; lunch; further deck games and evening concerts or themed fancy dress dances, one of which Whitehead attended as 'The Old Woman Who Lived in a Shoe'.[73] Arriving at Cape Town, Whitehead and her colleagues visited a snake farm at Port Elizabeth; picnicked at Queenstown; witnessed 'native' huts at King Williamstown; stopped at a whaling station at Pietermaritzburg; were invited to swim in a shark-proof pool at Durban; travelled briefly through Mafeking, Bechuanaland, Kandahar Island and on to Livingstone and Victoria Falls. The tour party stopped for a few days in Johannesburg and at Hartbeesspoort Dam. On the return voyage, the ship might call at Tenerife or another Mediterranean location. Whitehead was also a keen cricketer, swimmer, and tennis player, so these details are a preliminary indication of her more extensive travel schedule related to sport.

Empire tournaments and Home Countries internationals would provide vital links in the formation of the International Federation of Women's Hockey Associations (IFWHA) in 1927 by representatives from Australia, Denmark, England, Ireland, Scotland, South Africa, the USA and Wales.[74] The federation aimed to safeguard the interests of women's hockey worldwide; to promote friendly communication between women players and to work towards uniformity in the rules across affiliated nations. The federation established a series of triennial conferences, presumably to differentiate their activities from any connections with an Olympic-cycle, but the reasons are not really clear. The inaugural conference hosted in Geneva, Switzerland during 1930, typically included exhibition matches to lessen the competitive atmosphere and emphasise the spirit of co-operation. In the meantime, the Empire Tournament in South Africa included Australia, England and Scotland. The Australian tour to England in October 1930, captained by Tory Wicks, demonstrated hockey's high profile. Australian players wearing gold and green tunics were presented to George V and Queen Mary. As reproduced from the original programme notes, the Australian squad, was comprised of the following individuals: [75]

Goal	1. E. Tazewell (South Australia) Vice Capt.
Backs	2. Tory Wicks (New South Wales) Captain
	3. Connie Charlesworth (Tasmania)
	4. Jean Wright (Western Australia)
Halves	5. Alison Ramsay (Victoria)
	6. Merle Taylor (Victoria)
	7. Alice Forster (Victoria)
	8. Carlie Hansen (Queensland)
Forwards	9. Phyllis Buckland (Queensland)
	10. Barbara Thomas (New South Wales)
	11. Rita Flynn (New South Wales)
	12. Mrs Macrea (New South Wales)
	13. Mable Cashmore (South Australia)
	14. Jean McKay (South Australia)
	15. Molly Bloore (Victoria)

Winnifred Brown (1899–1984) winner of the King's Cup air race in 1930, kept goal for England and signed autographs or souvenir programmes (which cost three pence), during the interval. The queue was substantial and the interval extended. Brown had beaten eighty-seven other competitors over a 753 miles course to win the Kings Cup; was photographed receiving her cup from Sir Philip Sassoon and became something of a national treasure.[76] Also an accomplished sailor, Brown later joined Saunders Roe, the flying boat constructors, in Beaumaris as Chief Coxwain and worked with the RAF during the Second World War.[77]

By the second IFWHA meeting in Copenhagen from the 6–10 September 1933, the number of teams taking part had expanded but not all represented nations, they were: Denmark; England; Holland; Ireland; 'Overseas etceteras'; Scotland; Magdeburg; USA; 'Danish Reserves' and Wales. A number of the England, Scotland and Wales players travelled together via Harwich to Esbjerg on board the S.S. Pankeston. Magdeburg (nickname 'the green-red team') had previously visited England (wearing shorter skirts than the conventional English tunics, combined with knee-high socks and berets) to play against Northmptonshire in 1931. Their players were listed by surname as Wagner in goal; Dschenfzig and Dulon as Backs; Weyergang, Woelfel and Weyergang as Halves with Rasmus, Fresdorf, Freytag, Fayber and Hoff as Forwards.[78] Subsequent conferences, held around the world, were accompanied by increasingly competitive international tournaments.

Tours to post-colonial nations also sharpened rivalry. The 1928 tour to the United States showed the sporting dominance of the English: the highest score being a 30–0 win in Chicago and lowest a 6–0 victory against the North East team at Rye, New York. American hospitality won many more moral victories, however. At Chicago and New York the English team stayed in impressive hotels; at Rye they were entertained at the Westchester Biltmore Club, one of the more luxurious country clubs in USA. The open attitude and cordiality appeared to overwhelm the English who reported with grudging enthusiasm that: 'They were all scrupulous in fulfilling every engagement that had been made for them, sometimes no light task when meals from breakfast onwards had been arranged in different houses . . . The touring team was privileged to attend the USFHA General Meeting and also to see their Hockey Film which cost £500 & was a gift to the association [sic].'[79] Sadly, the minutes do not record what Light, Thompson and the others thought of the American film, which had cost more than twice their own efforts.

The United States also sent a visiting team to England in October 1933 captained by Miss Anne Townsend, (who worked as a book reviewer for a newspaper in Philadelphia).[80] Ten of the fifteen players on the 1933 tour came from the same city and were at pains to point out that most were not of private means but worked as secretaries and teachers. Oustanding American rival talents were identified by AEWHA officials as Barbara Black, Betty Cadbury, Virginia Vanderbeck, Susanne Ridgeway-Cross, Helen Howe and Betty Richey, though it has been difficult to find more details about these women. The visitors were said to be much taken by British female sporting dress reform, which Townsend summarised as: 'We are interested in how quickly you take off your clothes and how much.'

Given that this period of dress history is often described in terms of sporting influence being led by European designers like Elsa Schiaparelli, Coco Chanel and Jean Patou or American influences, most notably the 'play-clothes' of Claire McCardell, the dissemination of an 'English-look', or perhaps a 'British-style' remains to be researched.[81] Gym tunics with a dropped waist, sashes and stockings gave way to the hockey shirt, shorter skirts (frequently pleated, gored or divided) and knee-high socks. Goalkeepers were permitted to wear trousers by 1939.[82] Two piece suits with matching shirts and skirts were becoming more widespread for games generally, as was the one-piece 'shorts-dress' and tailored 'smart' sports clothes. The one or two piece ensemble, complete with matching blazer for formal occasions, would form the 'uniform' of hockey for years to come. Until the twenty-first century skirts would be preferred to shorts for both national hockey and cricket teams, in spite of player complaints on the issue of dress.

The English team tour to America in 1936 coincided with the third Triennial Conference of the IFWHA. The squad left Southampton on the 30 September; landed in New York on the 5 October; then travelled to Baltimore and Washington (staying three days in each case); continued to Virgina Sweet Briar and Williamsburg between the 11–17 October; spent three days in Moorestown, New Jersey and then stayed in New York for two weeks. The return voyage took six days from New York to Southampton to disembark on 10 November. Cruising itself had become more popular and the women provide an example of consumers for the industry, which grew from approximately 70,000 passengers in 1931 to 550,000 by 1937.[83] Teams were an obvious market, guaranteeing multiple ticket sales in spite of the slump occasioned when Britain came off the Gold Standard in 1931, making the cost of holidays abroad more expensive. Touring involved a considerable time commitment, and the English also hosted the South African team in 1936; another logistical challenge.

As Joyce Whitehead's photographs show, tours were not always innocent diversions from world politics. The 1936 Easter tour to Germany by a team called the Wagtails saw them compete against a backdrop of Nazi flags at Munchen Gladbach and Berlin, before travelling by rail to Cologne. The information is patchy and it is not always possible to date games precisely or relate snapshots to a particular place. However, there was some useful information about the German team and nationally strong hockey clubs: 'Goalkeeper: Miss Richter (ASC Leipzig); Backs: Mrs Kobe (Red and White Club), Miss Hargus (Lubeck), Miss Klare Voss (Berlin) and Miss Annelis Von Lautz (Harvestehude HC); Forwards: Miss Gensert (S. C. Frankfurt), Miss Oldenburg (Berlin), sisters Inge and Marga Trede (Uhlenhorster Klippern Club, Hamburg); Helga Keller lead the attack with Miss Mauritz, both of the Red and White Club.'[84] A snippet from the German programme, written in English, informed readers:

> Women's hockey in Germany belongs to the young sports which have recently grown up [sic]. Thirty-five or forty years ago, men and women played it together and for us it is like a fairy tale if we compare the costumes of those days with those of today. There are already a thousand German girls and women playing it with great enthusiasm and new players are constantly being enrolled because they find that this sport keeps them young, supple, healthy and cheerful [sic]. Next Sunday will be a landmark in the history of hockey for women. England's international eleven, brilliantly proven after dozens of matches to be the most respected and feared opponents in the world, will meet Germany's hockey players in the first international match on the Berlin hockey club's field at Dahlem (Underground Station Oskar Helene Heim). We know what the English ladies are capable of. They are the best players in the world and if one watches their play one forgets that they are women, so perfect and masterly is their style [sic].[85]

By way of concluding this section, there are a number of ways of developing the work on hockey, its connections within the British Empire and beyond. First, we could look at other sports and not just netball, cricket or lacrosse. Other women's sports also developed competitions with Australia, South

Africa, New Zealand and other British dominions. A minority activity, like croquet inaugurated the MacRobertson Shield in 1925, donated by the eponymous Australian confectionary magnate.[86] This was first contested by Australia and an English team led by the legendary Miss Dorothy Dyne Steele (1884–1965). Known by all as 'D. D.', Steele refused to travel to the return match in Australia in 1927 unless her expenses were paid in full: a clear case of where amateur rules were relaxed to help the best players to compete.[87] D. D. went on to manage croquet tours to Australia and New Zealand before turning to hunting once arthritis ended her active playing career. It is now quite clear that she did not need her expenses to be paid. It was generally supposed that D. D. lived together with her sister Evelyn (1890–1974), who was also an able croquet player, because they were impoverished. This assumption persisted until Evelyn left £120,000 in her estate on her death in 1974.[88] Perhaps shamateurism (involving covert forms of payment of various kinds) was more of an element in these sporting tours than we are currently aware.

Secondly, the financial aspects of hockey tours have been difficult to ascertain but would reward further analysis. Taking the preparations for the 1934 WCA cricket tour as a parallel, players were advised that they should pay their own expenses to and from Australia, but were then the guests of the hosting national association from the moment they landed on foreign soil. Each tourist was advised to budget £100 unless the trip was extended to New Zealand, in which case it would cost an extra £5.[89] Of course, this raises the possibility that those who could afford to go on a particular trip represented their country instead, perhaps, of the most able players. Cricket tours could make a nice profit: after the 1937 visit of Australia to England, the Women's Cricket Association reported with approval that: 'The balance of £1,229 13 shillings 1d is very satisfactory indeed.'[90] Given that the remainder of the accounts covered £280 for the year, the scale and importance of tours to cricket was evident.

Hockey seems to have been less of a draw for crowds, mainly because it was not always played at grounds like Old Trafford or the Oval, as cricket was. Hospitality and fund-raising activities could include share-cards where, for a donation of 6d, participants wrote their name on a grid comprised of famous cricketers or football teams and the person whose name corresponded with that selected by a prize draw would win a shilling. Whatever the specifics of funding the tours, by 1946 the AEWHA had a £420 operating surplus on an annual turnover of £1,490.[91] The tours, films, books and media work, plus the sale of equipment, had shown enterprising ways of funding and expanding this most amateur of sports. Nor has there been enough space here to adequately reflect how sports good retailers (Lillywhites and Spaldings); shoe manufacturers and clothing suppliers; hotels; travel companies and other local businesses capitalised on this market.

Finally, though the information here has been mainly presented from an English point of view, further research can identify the networking conventions of the other constituent IFWHA nations. For example, Appendix Five lists the Scottish and Irish players in a 1935 international contested between the two countries. Scotland had beaten England for the first time in March 1933 by two goals to one at Merton Abbey, so a new competitiveness reflected the overall improvement in international standards. Appendix Six gives an indication of some Welsh and English national representatives in the same year. Appendix Seven details the South African international players who toured England in 1936. This very provisional collection of biographical sketches exemplifies regional, educational, work and leisure patterns to be further explored. What multiple personal and professional roles did hockey administrators juggle? How were individual's world-views changed or confirmed by such transnational experience? Can we map this kind of tourism to compare it with other patterns of mobility, temporary migration and emigration that affected women's lives during this period? In moving, now, to look at the example of motor racing, the chapter explores cases of where a quite different range of sporting activity became more female-led between the mid 1920s and the late 1930s. To travel at speed, in style became a prominent activity in its own right and the impetus to have women role models came from the commercial sector, rather than an amateur tradition.

HIGHWAYS OF EMPIRE: WOMEN RACERS AT BROOKLANDS

The previous section of this chapter looked at the development of international women's hockey competitions as bound up with imperial, and postcolonial, networks. Some of the same processes were at work in motorised competition by land, sea and air but in ways that may appear to be less obvious. Firstly, motor-sport and record breaking made the individual and the nation synonymous. National virility and entrepreneurialism were, for example, personified by Charles Lindbergh, a US air-mail pilot, otherwise known as the 'lucky fool' because of his previously unsuccessful air record attempts.[92] Completing the New York to Paris route in 1927 in a thirty-three hour flight, he won world acclaim. As 'Lindy' the pilot became a national hero and stayed over at the White House for a few days. The first American woman across the Atlantic in 1928, Amelia Earhart (1897–1937), had no less publicity.[93] Four years later she was to do the same flight solo.[94] Earhart was lost piloting a £20,000 Lockheed Electra, known as a 'flying laboratory' on a round the world attempt.[95] Having negotiated South America, Africa, India and Batavia she had intended to land at the Howland Island Air-Base in the mid Pacific. In spite of intensive searches, her body was never recovered.

British aviator Amy Johnson (1903–41) was second only to Edith Cavell, and ahead of Joan of Arc, as the 'must-see' personality so far as schoolgirl visitors to Madam Tussaud's were concerned in 1932.[96] According to myth 'Johnnie' gave up being a typist in a London office in 1930 to fly 9,000 lone miles from England to Port Darwin, Australia with only 100 hours experience.[97] Compared with the lengthy and expensive development of the R101 airship, it seemed like the country needed more plucky amateurs rather than bureaucratic government intervention. However, Johnson was part of a new technocracy, having previously graduated from Sheffield University and trained at technical school of the De Havilland (DH) aircraft company.[98] In 1927 she received the first licensed engineer's certificate awarded by the Air Ministry to a woman.[99] She was to marry Jim Mollison in an unorthodox ceremony where she wore black in 1932 but, due to his drinking and infidelities, they were divorced by 1934.[100]

Briefly unsuccessful as a racing driver and girl about town, Johnson was more influential as the President and one of the co-founders of the Women's Engineering Society (WES). She received several other international honours.[101] Johnson was lost in active service for the select Air Transport Auxiliary (ATA) over the Thames Estuary in 1941.[102] In addition to many newsreels, a 1941 feature film called *They Flew Alone* featured two of Britain's most popular actors, Anna Neagle and Robert Newton based on the Johnson and Mollison story. The mythology around 'lost' women pilots who put national interests above their own safety can be long-lasting. My Dad, who was sixteen years old and an Air Cadet desperate to join the growing service in 1941, has still not got a good word to say about Mollison due to his rakish treatment of his 'wonderful Amy'.

Secondly, while Aerhart and Johnson are perhaps the best-known female aviators there were other notable deaths, provoking complex responses to national pride and hope in motorised exploration.[103] Controversies surrounded car, boat and aviation record-breaking attempts; with many people wondering what was the point of combining technology, wealth and bravery in this way for little obvious practical gain. Youth could add to the sense of folly: the fate of the Hon. Elsie Mackay (1893–1928) remains a mystery to this day.[104] Mackay had previously worked as an actress under the name Poppy Wyndham and then designed boat interiors for her father, who was a shipping magnate. She was photographed in full flying gear, apart from some fashionable Mary Jane shoes, before set off from RAF Cranwell on an Atlantic flight attempt.[105] Neither her body, that of her co-pilot or nor the single-engined Stinson Detroiter aeroplane, named *The Endeavour*, were found. However, if the pioneer survived, there were fortunes and reputations to be made. Janet Aitken Kidd (1908–1988), daughter of Max Aitken, Lord Beaverbrook, also recalled in her autobiography how flying could be a perilous experience.[106] She was however, to survive and have a long career as a society beauty, often photographed by leading portraitists.

Thirdly, the routes chosen by aspiring record breakers were often those considered most valuable for potential passenger and freight services, so

FLYING - MR. & MRS. J. A. MOLLISON

Figure 5.1   Ardarth Tobacco Co Ltd 'Mr and Mrs J A Mollison' London: Ardarth Tobacco Co Ltd no 152, circa 1936. Personal collection of the author. As one of many photocard or cigarette card series, this shows how Amy Johnson and other sportswomen were mediated to a wider audience as part of everyday activities.

were not always as whimsical as Mackay and Kidd's enthusiasms. Replacing the attempts by airships to offer a passenger service, *Canopus* became the first of the Empire Flying Boats, resplendent with a luxurious smoking saloon. It departed from Southampton for Durban in July 1937, completing a distance of 8,000 miles in six and a half days, bettering previous schedules by forty-eight hours.[107] Attempts to span land, sea and air could be narrated before, during and after the fact by the newspapers, thereby enabling the media to partially define endeavours in public consciousness. If a woman was involved, a larger public relations story was almost guaranteed. Beryl Markham (1902–1986) left Abingdon, Berkshire on 4 September 1936 and became the first person to fly solo across the Atlantic from east to west, in spite of a forced landing in Nova Scotia rather than New York, as she had planned. Born in Leicester, Markham grew up in Kenya, lived for a while in the United States and also had a successful career as a race-horse trainer, as her 1942 autobiography *West with the Night* outlined.[108] Overcoming the head-winds across the Atlantic suggested that a passenger service was theoretically possible. This was beneficial for commercial reasons as well as for national prestige.

The fourth component that made motorised speed and exploration significant was that from 1926 the rivalry between Kaye Don, Malcolm Campbell and Sir Henry O'Neil de Hane Segrave appeared to make the British world-leaders.[109] 'De Hane' became the first British national to win a Grand Prix in 1923 before also holding the land and sea records simultaneously shortly before his death.[110] Seagrave and his mechanic Halliwell hit an object in the water at Lake Windermere after traveling at over 100 mph in their vessel *Miss England II* having broken the world record.[111] As Major Seagrave, he had competed with Malcolm Campbell for the world land speed record in *Golden Arrow*.[112] Campbell was to break the land speed record in *Blue Bird* at 245mph mph in 1931.[113] One of the more under-estimated of these men and driver of the *Thunderbolt*, Captain George Eyston (holder of the Military Cross and an OBE), was to be a keen supporter of women in motor-sport.[114] With Cecil Kimber of the MG sportscar company, Eyston developed a team of six female drivers in three Midget cars for the Le Mans 24 Hours race in 1935.[115] They became variously known as 'George's Young Ladies'; 'The Dancing Daughters', after a radio play of the same name and 'The Kimbergarten'. All three cars completed the race, (finishing in twenty-forth, twenty-fifth and twenty-sixth place respectively) achieving maximum publicity for MG but production problems the following year meant that the racing team was abandoned.[116] However, this kind of industry support was by no means unusual.

After World War I, perhaps the first and most prominent woman to epitomise the intersection of industrial contacts, imperial record-breaking and racing was Violet Cordery (1903–1983) who competed in the 1920 South Harting Hill Climb driving a Silver Hawk, one of the newly popular

1,500cc 'light cars'. She also took part in two British Motor Cycle Racing Club handicaps driving an Eric-Campbell the same year at Brooklands.[117] Both the Eric-Campbell and the Silver Hawk were early attempts at manufacturing motor-cars by her brother-in-law, Albert Noel Campbell Macklin. [118] After Campbell Macklin's association with Eric-Campbell ended, a maximum of twelve Silver Hawks were produced at his country house Fairmile in Cobham, Surrey using 1,498cc Coventry Simplex engines, said to have a guaranteed speed of 70 mph.[119] Cordery won the Ladies race at the Junior Car Club May meeting at Brooklands in 1921 at a speed of 49.7 mph (though sources disagree whether this was using an Eric Campbell or Silver Hawk but given the date, most likely the latter).

Violet Cordery was, however, best known for the records she set behind the wheel of a range of Invictas: an evolution from the Silver Hawk designed by Noel Macklin to offer motorists 'effortless performance'.[120] Backed by his neighbours, of the Tate & Lyle sugar dynasty, Macklin designed the Invicta with enormous torque (pulling power) that demanded little or no gear-changing.[121] Such was the flexibility of the engine, owners were expected to use just first and top gear. It made sense therefore, to have a young woman driver to demonstrate the ease and robustness of the marque. Occasionally assisted by her sister, Evelyn, Violet spent the 1920s and early 1930s promoting Invictas via a range of record-breaking attempts. This included success at Brooklands such as winning the West Kent MC Half Mile Sprint in 1925 driving a 2.7-litre model (when William Boddy says she was 23 years of age); the Middlesex Car Club Ladies' Race in June 1928 and the Essex MC meeting in September the same year.[122] Motor-sport combined expensive engineering contests using innovative technology with the rather romantic figure of the lone driver or pilot. Individuals were often recognised at the expense of team efforts.

Distiller and politician Sir Thomas Dewar first presented a trophy in his name to the Royal Automobile Club in 1904.[123] Awarded by the RAC's Technical Committee for the most meritorious performance by an automobile manufacturer in certified trials, The Dewar Trophy was awarded nineteen times during the years 1906 to 1929, there being some years when it was considered that no performance merited the trophy. Having led a team of six drivers around Italy's Monza circuit for 10,000 miles at an average speed of 56.47 mph, Cordery continued to the 15,000 miles record at an average speed of 55.76 mph in 1926.[124] Violet then became the first female beneficiary of the Dewar Trophy later that year and given the name 'The Long Distance Lady' after she piloted round Paris' Montlhéry track for 5,000 miles at an average 70.7 mph in a record attempt supervised by the Royal Automobile Club.[125] Cordery led a team of male drivers (Moy/ Mills/ Garland/ Byng) driving an Invicta to break world and class records from 4,000 to 5,000 miles. It is noticeable that only Cordery was awarded the trophy for an Invicta team effort, reinventing pioneering myths about how the land, sea and air could be colonised by the British, albeit for a limited time. Because it so obviously appeared to involve an enthusiasm for risk and danger, motorsport also often expressed personal rivalries on an epic scale and narratives blended heroic, sacrificial, fatalist and triumphal elements.

In 1927, accompanied by a mechanic, a nurse, and a Royal Automobile Club observer, Cordery drove around the world, such as she was able to do.[126] The team covered 10, 266 miles in five months, travelling at an average speed of 24.6 mph through Europe, Africa, India, Australia, the United States and Canada. This received considerable media and press attention with Pathé newsreels showing her departure, arrival and some particularly shaky footage of her progress through India, for example.[127] In 1928, the Cordery sisters combined forces for yet another record-breaking attempt at Brooklands. Over the course of twenty-one days, Violet and Evelyn covered 30,000 miles in 30,000 minutes at an average speed of 61.57 mph.[128] This earned Violet a second Dewar Trophy in 1929. Rallying also proved the Invicta's build quality. By 1930, Violet had driven a 4.5-litre tourer from London to Monte Carlo; completed a return journey between London to John O' Groats and another run from London to Edinburgh, and back.[129] Later Invicta sports models were also exhibited at Olympia from 1930 onwards, notable for their more sinuous lines. On 7 September 1931 *The Western Australian* reminded its readers of Cordery's visit to the Southern Hemisphere and announced that, at the age of 28, she had become engaged to John Stuart Hindmarsh.[130] The paper reported that Violet had decided to give up motor racing and take up aviation instead: her future husband being accomplished in both. John Hindmarsh had been to school at Sherborne, Dorset before going to Military College Sandhurst for Officer Training and subsequently gained a commission in the Royal Army Tank Corps, posted to 2nd Battalion at Cranwell in 1928.[131] In 1930 John was seconded to the Royal Air Force and learned to fly. He was a noted Talbot and Lagonda driver in the 1930s. Violet and John had two daughters; Susanne (1932) and Sally, the latter born shortly after John's win in the Le Mans 24 Hours race in 1935. Preferring aviation, John Hindmarsh resigned his commission with the army and formally joined the RAF to secure a post as a pilot with the Hawker group in 1935. He was killed at Brooklands, test-flying a Hurricane in September 1938. Having withdrawn from racing soon after, Violet lived quietly into old age before dying at her home 13 Broom Hall, Oxshott, Surrey on 30 December 1983, leaving an estate of £25,000. Their daughter, Susanne, married the prominent racing driver, Roy Salvadori (1922–2012), an Essex-born Grand Prix competitor of Italian descent.

Even if the record-breakers did not go anywhere, other than repeatedly round a track, feats were of considerable symbolic importance in pioneering cutting-edge techniques. The aspirational, bourgeois leadership of motoring and aviation looked back to Britain's role in the industrial revolution and forwards to increasing efficiency, technocracy and specialisation in sport. A spirit of impulse and play was nevertheless preserved through the charade of considering this an amateur enterprise, even while petrol, tyre and vehicle manufacturers often sponsored individuals and teams. Women were a market that car manufacturers could ill-afford to ignore. Henry Ford's 'Tin Lizzie' was not a car that appealed, in spite of overall sales passing fifteen million in 1927: a British-made Morris two-seater could be bought for just over two pounds less. Morris later used the same American marketing techniques like hire purchase, local dealerships and aggressive promotions that Ford had pioneered.[132] The continuity between road models and racing marques can be evidenced by the example of Wolseley Motors Ltd, one of the oldest English manufacturers, which produced the Sports Ten in 1921 with a lighter aluminium body. One of these expensive examples was driven by a Mrs Knox at Brooklands, reaching speeds of over seventy mph.[133] Having a woman driver was almost bound to offer publicity and this in turn created leisure opportunities for a few female racers that also could become work.

In Britain's growing car-culture, women were an important demographic for domestic manufacturers, particularly for the smaller 'light cars'. For instance, Ruth (1894–1981) and Bill (1897–1979) Urquhart Dykes won the 12-Hour Record at Brooklands at an average speed of 81.38 miles in 1928 as one of many husband and wife driving teams.[134] She was Irish, the daughter of Dr and Mrs Hegarty of Clonbur, and he was Scottish, the son of Major William Alston Dykes.[135] They married in 1921 and broke several track records, hill climbed and rallied from then until 1929. The 1928 12-Hour Record was a considerable achievement considering both drove for the Alvis works team and their combined enthusiasm meant that their Alvis 12/50 had already clocked over 100, 000 miles before the attempt.

Amid this general atmosphere of record-setting; mapping; mercantile and nationalistic competitiveness, the attitude of the Brooklands Automobile Racing Club (BARC) also changed. By 1931 the Racing, Aviation, Election and House and Wine Sub-Committees were busy throughout the season (the first meeting on eleven occasions) but the Safety Sub-Committee's work was deemed to be complete and it was accordingly dissolved.[136] There had been 'only' two fatalities that year. Three-lap ladies' races continued from 1920 followed by mixed events, first offered by clubs who used the circuit and then major BARC competitions. Those who were more active often had access to their own vehicle, were loaned machines by manufacturers, or perhaps sponsored by a works team.

May Cunliffe (1906–1975) first drove a supercharged 3-litre Bentley in the hill climb at Shelsley Walsh in 1926 with considerable success, then on the sands at Southport in 1927.[137] Cunliffe often competed against the leading male racers of the day including Malcolm Campbell. She then bought a 1924 Sunbeam, known for previously shedding a tyre at Brooklands, killing the driver and injuring his mechanic. In 1928 the Sunbeam overturned at 100 mph while racing at Southport, breaking May's arm, cutting her face and killing her father who was passenger: the photograph of the accident and the story went around the world.[138] Cunliffe's mother sold the car on to

Kaye Don who went on to race it on sand and at Brooklands. Having survived, Don set up a motorcycle dealership in retirement. Apparently undeterred, Cunliffe became Mrs Millington before retiring from motor-sport to take up aviation, also driving service vehicles for the US army during the Second World War and a Kleft Racer 500 in the 1950s.

For one of Cunliffe's contemporaries, Mary Bruce, participating in hill climbs, racing on sand, track-days and rallying could also be complimentary challenges. If the single most common word used to describe the hockey administrators previously referred to in this chapter was 'indefatigable', Mary Bruce, amongst others, seemed to want to prove that women drivers were inexhaustible. While she drove a lot at Brooklands, particularly in 1928, and was certainly part of its social and cultural milieu, Mary Bruce became a personality. The books were just as much part of her entrepreneurialism as the feats. The first of these was called *Nine Thousand Miles in Eight Weeks—Being an Account of an Epic Journey by Motor-Car through Eleven Countries and Two Continents*.[139] Much given to self-promotion, Mary Bruce was thankfully to become keen on more succinct titles.[140] She also fictionalised her accomplishments in a humorous style in *Penelope*, serialised short stories that appeared in *Sketch*, later collected in a book *The Peregrinations of Penelope* (1930).

At the Montlhéry track outside Paris in 1928, Victor and Mary Bruce were determinedly nationalistic in seeking to outdo the American Chrysler team who had set a 10,000 miles record by averaging at 60 mph. Driving for six hour shifts, Victor and Mary Bruce broke seventeen world records, including 15,000 miles in nine days at an average of sixty eight mph.[141] It had taken 13,000 laps. After further races at Brooklands in 1928, Mary's solo 24 hours run at Montlhéry in a 4 ½ litre Bentley set further records of 2,164 miles at an average of nearly ninety mph on 7 June 1929. Astute to every opportunity, a perhaps apocryphal story followed that Mary had taken an officially-sanctioned short comfort break, during which she drank what she assumed to be water from a can. It turned out to be petrol and shortly after British Petroleum (BP) were able to endorse the fact that their fuel had kept both the Bentley and the driver going.[142] She therefore obtained the fuel gratis and added another sponsor to her portfolio.

The diversity of Mary Bruce's activities can be assessed by the solo return journey across the English Channel and back in 1 hour 47 minutes piloting a motor boat named *Mosquito*. Then she 'Beat the Berengaria' for a distance record over 24 hours by driving 694 nautical miles solo in October 1929. Following another Monte Carlo rally in 1930, boredom set in. After finding that she had a spare half hour between appointments, Bruce bought an Blackburn aeroplane for £550 from a shop in Burlington Gardens, which came with the charming guarantee: 'Bluebird: Honeymoon model, ready to go anywhere'. She then learned to fly and clocked just forty hours of flight time before a solo around the world trip followed, though sections of the trip had to be completed by boat.

Bruce met Miss Bouko, one of Japan's pioneer aviators, on the way, landed in the United States and came home to a reception led by Amy Johnson and Winifred Spooner (1900–1933) in 1931. Versatile in the extreme, Bruce did not just excel in motor-sport. She came second to Colonel Llewellyn at her first Royal International Horse Show at Olympia and won the 1939 Open Jumping class at the Royal Horse Show at Windsor. Victor and she were to divorce in 1941 but Mary retained her title, becoming thereafter known in motoring circles as 'The First' Honourable Mrs Victor Bruce, when Victor remarried, and devoting herself to their son, Tony.

Mary Bruce also fulfilled her childhood ambition of becoming a sterling millionaire with aeronautical contracts during the war and property development after. It seems an unbelieveable range of activities. Air to air re-fuelling in an endurance flight using Marconi mobile radio technology was another experiment, as was joining a flying circus called the British Hospital Air Pageants, with Pauline Gower (later Fahie, 1910–1947) and Dorothy Spicer (later Pearse, 1908–1946) among her colleagues.[143] This was one of several air circuses operating around the country, which, like traditional circuses would travel from town to town to cater for an 'air mad' public. Each pilot charged fifteen shillings for a five minute tourist flight. What did the people who took part in these early passenger flights make of their experience? How did they view the pilots? Did they pre-date longer trips for leisure for most of the participants?

Other entrepreneurial activity included forming 'Air Dispatch' (also known as the Dawn Express) at Croydon to carry newspapers across to Paris by breakfast. Similarly, when Bruce inaugurated a service called 'The Tube of the Air' linking Heston, Hanworth, Gatwick and other airports, with passengers buyng their tickets from the pilot, it was an important form of short-haul flight taking much the same circular route as the current M25. Mary Bruce also claimed to have employed the first female air steward in 1937, 'a very attractive blonde' called Daphne Vickers.[144] Whatever the historical accuracy of some of these claims, Bruce cast herslef in the mould of British entrepreneur-pioneer-inventor and appears to have been accepted as such by the public.

Many women had short, interrupted or multiple careers at Brooklands.[145] The driver and aviator born Eileen May Fountain, but better known as Jill Scott (1902–1974), was a prime example of how personal circumstance could affect a public persona. Jill left her first husband William Berkeley ('W. B'. or 'Bummer', as he was popularly known) for Ernest Mortimer (E. M.) Thomas in 1930 and effectively had two phases of popularity at Brooklands.[146] In the first between 1928 and 1932 Jill Scott became the first woman elected to the BRDC in 1928 (although this was quickly changed to 'honourary' status) by winning a prestigious BARC 120 mph badge. Her attitude often described as 'swashbuckling', Jill Scott also learned to fly in 1927 and ran an Avro aircraft for a number of years before returning to race at Brooklands as Mrs E. M. Thomas in a Grand Prix Bugatti.[147]

A striking woman who wore a cherry red helmet, overalls and shoes while racing, it was said that Ernest was so devoted to his wife that he took his own life within three months of her death in 1974. Jill Scott had a daughter with Bummer, called Sheila, who seems to have been packed off to boarding school at a young age, from where she went to Cheltenham Ladies College and then Cambridge.[148] Acting as a distant mother to Sheila from there on, Jill and Ernest left everything in their estate to their son, Peter, who pre deceased them both. A charity shop therefore became the beneficiary of a Brooklands 120 mph badge and other memorabilia (including an engraved stopwatch from Delage and photograph albums) when the Scott's daughter was obliged to clear the effects of her equally neglectful father following his death. Complicated marriage and family arrangements were by no means unusual and challenge attempts to provide a collective biography of the women racers. They also shade our understanding of private lives and public reputations.

If anyone could match Mary Bruce's versatility and Jill Scott's capacity for controversy it was Gwenda Glubb, who was born at Burnaby Villas, Fulwood, Lancashire on 1 June 1894.[149] She the only daughter of Frances Letitia, née Bagot and Frederic Manley Glubb, a major general in the Royal Engineers and later knighted. The army officer and Arabist (who became known as Glubb Pasha) Sir John Bagot MC, Distinguished Service Order (DSO), OBE was her younger brother.[150] Combining Cornish and Irish descent, Gwenda was educated at Cheltenham Ladies College, before joining the Scottish Women's Hospitals Organisation as a volunteer to the Eastern front during World War I. Having been decorated for her bravery in driving ambulances in Russia and the Balkans, she returned home and, taught motor driving in Hyde Park for the Women's Legion.

Gwenda's enthusiasm for driving was said to perplex her mother, whom she met in adulthood occasionally for tea. This cannot have been helped when Gwenda was cited in newspaper reports in 1919 for sleeping with her Camp Commander, Sam Janson. The story came out because of the Violet Douglas-Pennant inquiry.[151] Doulgas-Pennant had been dismissed as the head of the Women's Royal Air Force in 1918 having reported sexual immorality in the service generally, and specifically at Hurst Park Camp between the Commander and a young airwoman. However, no proof was found, Douglas-Pennant was discredited and the press reported Gwenda's engagement to Sam Janson as a romantic outcome of the proceedings. A short-lived marriage followed in 1920 no doubt helped by the fact that her husband was a Director of Spyker auto company, and Gwenda had racing ambitions. Janson began divorce proceedings in 1922 citing Robert Neil Stewart as co-respondent. Gwenda married Stewart, who had contacts at Trump motorcycles, in 1924. Gwenda raced Ner-a-Car in 1,000-mile trials from 1921 and rode a 249cc Trump-JAP to establish the Double-12 record on two wheels at Brooklands in 1922. She also co-rode a Rudge, established a speed record for three wheel vehicles in a Morgan at Montléry of 118 mph and survived a bad accident when the back wheel of a Terot-JAP collapsed, crashing at over 100 mph. By 1937 she had married the mechanic who prepared her car, Wallace Douglas Hawkes (1893–1974).

Like Mary Bruce, Gwenda Stewart/ Hawkes preferred to hold absolute records, rather than the unofficial women's titles.[152] These attempts mostly happened away from the public eye, including new outright lap records of 145.94 and then 149 mph at Montlhéry in 1934, but they made her legendary. Thinking that it would draw publicity, the Brooklands promoters decided to rival her against 'The Darling of the Brooklands Crowd' Kay Petre at the circuit in 1935. The resulting 135.95 lap by Hawkes was an offical record for class E cars (up to 2,000 c.c.) and was only marginally beaten by the same size vehicle at Brooklands once, by well-known racing motorist Freddie Dixon two months after the Stewart-Petre race.[153] It must have given Gwenda some satisfaction that contrived women's lap records were abandoned after this race but of the achievement itself, she was understated:

> Personally I find Montlhéry the easier proposition but probably that is because I know the Autodrome better than Brooklands. Familiarity is everything. I'd turned Brooklands at over 130 only about half a dozen times in my life, when the existing Women's Lap Record was set up, whereas Montlhéry is home from home to me. The snag at Brooklands as everyone knows, is the unbanked and completely blind curve made by the Vickers factory. A front-wheeled car like the Derby is delightfully tractable, but one mustn't attempt to point it somewhere it doesn't want to go. The Big Bump [sic] over the Wey Viaduct is another potential snare for a light machine. First time round at really high speed I took the Derby over the Bump and, although I lifted my foot for the whoopsy-daisy, just as it tells you in the primers, the whole transmission was smashed on landing. Subsequently, I have always steered a course below the Bump.[154]

In respect of the achievement, Gwenda Stewart and Kay Petre earned two of a total of seventeen prestigious Brooklands 130 mph badges issued before the circuit fell into disrepair in 1939. There were too many other Gwenda Stewart/Hawkes records to list here on two, three and four wheels, but suffice to say that she and Kay Petre had already both been elected to honourary membership of the BDRC in 1931 and 1934 respectively. Gwenda Stewart also drove a large American Dusenberg in 1936 at Brooklands sharing the drive with its owner, Jack Duller, and competed in other races like the Le Mans 24 Hours.

In the remaining years before and during the war, Gwenda and Douglas Hawkes ran the Brooklands Engineering Company at the circuit, where she worked a lathe, as well as overseeing the men. She also served in the London Auxiliary Ambulance Service. After 1945, the Hawkes' retired to sail the Mediterranean aboard their yacht Elpis, escaping the publicity of being a motoring couple.[155] They eventually settled in Poros and Gwenda moved to mainland Greece after Douglas died of lung disease. She also survied her brother who died in 1986 and suffered only slightly from arthiritis in fingers until her death in 1990 aged 95. Unlike Mary Bruce, there are wonderful stories of her nomadic life difficult to confirm because she refused to discuss them, though it is clear that she preferred living and racing in France to Britain. Sammy Davis reported that she went to Alsaka in 1922 because it was 'more interesting' to dogsled than drive a car.[156] In 1929, she left in an open motor-boat with Stewart and Hawke to cross the North Sea and declined to elaborate on their adventures. Given their long collaboration and the fact that she was at some point married to both men, we can only speculate about their personal and professional relationships.

Quite aside from the sporting aspects of motor racing, the number of people who met and married their spouse at Brooklands requires a book in itself. It would not be a dull volume. Elsie 'Bill' Wisdom (1904–1972) was born in Tooting Graveney, London the third of seven children and the only daughter of Bejamin John Gleed, master watchmaker and shopkeeper, and his wife Emma Amelia nee Avenell.[157] Nicknamed 'Bill', as a child she rode as 'ballast' on the back of her brothers' motorcycles before being old enough to drive the machines for herself. It was thought that four wheels would be more 'safe' and her first car was a G. W. K. named after the manufacturers Grice, Wood and Keiller, a make that was soon obsolete. In a 1931 *The Auto Motor Journal* interview Wisdom characterised herself as 'An ethusiastic motorist' from the age of sixteen, first on two wheels, then four.[158] Early in 1925 she married Charles Thomas Swain from whom she obtained a divorce in 1929. She continued to race and, according to Sammy Davis, was competing in a supercharged Lea-Francis, particularly excelling at hill climbs, when she met the amateur racing driver and journalist Thomas Henry 'Tommy' Wisdom, whom she married on 14 March 1930. He was motoring editor of the *Daily Herald*, *Sporting Life*, and *Sunday People* for more than thirty years and a founder of the Guild of Motoring Writers.

Bill had her first drive at the Brooklands circuit as an unwelcome wedding present when Tommy announced that he had entered her for the Ladies March Handicap. It became racing legend that she did not speak to him for some time because of his 'unilateral' decision to enter her for the event. She nevertheless lapped at over 95mph and the resulting win established her as an extremely popular international personality, said to be the only driver still on terms with a pit crew after a Monte Carlo rally.[159] Becoming an authority as a writer as well, she sometimes outdid her husband on a hill climbs at Shelsey Walsh in the same car. Her first notable achievement in a mixed race at Brooklands came in the 1931 Junior Car Club's 'double-twelve-hour' or 'Double-12' race. This was a high profile event; effectively a twenty four hour race held over two days, as continuous competitions into the night had been banned at Brooklands, due to the noise and inconvenience to nearby Weybridge residents. In 1931 Bill entered in a Frazer Nash with Don Aldington and, though the car retired early on, it signalled more ambitions to enter major events. She also began to differentiate herself from Jill Scott and her other female contemporaries by wearing a black hemet and overalls. It perhaps helped her reputation that Brooklands was changing in the early 1930s and a Brooklands Automobile Racing Club (BARC) prejudice against women entering its pretigious events could be circumvented by entering club competitions hosted at the circuit to gain valuable experience of larger races. Even so, John Cobb was required to verify that she was able to handle a Leyland purchased with a view to tackling the Ladies' speed record.[160]

Bill went on to gain a Brooklands 120 mph badge after she took Jill Scott's record in autumn 1932 to win the BARC ladies handicap and register a speed of 121.47 mph.[161] She followed this with a more prestigious triumph in 1932 in the Junior Car Club (JCC) 1,000 mile race, competing with the Australian Joan Richmond (1905–1999), in a works team Riley. Richmond had previously tried horse racing and turned to cars when female jockeys were not accepted.[162] After coming fifth in the 1931 Australian Grand Prix, Richmond and two other Rileys had left Melbourne to compete in the Monte Carlo Rally for that year, crossing India and the Apennines before completing the race. This drew her to the attention of Victor Riley who offered her a drive alongside Bill Wisdom.[163] The JCC classic was a celebrated success over several classes of car and some of the most famous male drivers of the day, using a handicap system, so an outright win gained considerable media coverage. By 1933 Elsie Wisdom had cemented her place at Brooklands by coming third to two male drivers in the JCC International Trophy over 250 miles. Just seven of the twenty eight starters completed the race. The following year she drove a Talbot in a Ladies' Handicap at the circuit to come third behind Doreen Evans and Fay Taylour.

In 1933 Wisdom's international reputation was also established as a member of the Aston Martin works team (of three cars) at the Le Mans 24 Hours race. She co-drove with founder of the Aston Martin Owner's Club, Mortimer Morris-Goodall, while colleagues Sammy Davis and A. C. Bertelli, Pat Driscoll and Clifton Penn-Hughes raced the other two vehicles.[164] Though her car did not complete the race due to losing a cap for a crank bearing, it was clear that Wisdom drove on merit. Nor was she the only female Aston Martin works driver: Doreen Evans came from a motoring family who ran the Bellevue Garage in Wandsworth, a leading MG agency. Evans would later retire from motor-sport in 1936 to take up aviation after moving to America to marry her Aston Martin team-mate Alan Phipps. As can be seen from the lack of biographical information above, as many men as women racing drivers await their historian from this period.

There are many stories of the women drivers of the day experiencing considerable discomfort while trying to maintain a calm public face. Elsie

Wisdom's injury sustained in an attempt on the Ladies' Record using the outer circuit of Brooklands during 1934 became something of a racing legend.[165] She borrowed Freddie Dixon's Riley and the car's owner only grudgingly lent the vehicle for three laps in the morning and three in the afternoon. A loud bang followed by repeated severe pains to her right arm bought Wisdom's first run to a premature end. A rear tyre tread had come loose, acting as a high-speed flail until the car was stationery. When a new tyre had been fitted, she took the record in the afternoon session at 126.73 mph.

In 1935 Bill Wisdom partnered Kay Petre in a works Riley at the Le Mans Prix d'Endurance race, in the same race that George Eyston led the MG 'Dancing Daughter's' team driven by Barbara Skinner, Eileen Ellison, Colleen Eaton, Joan Richmond, Doreen Evans and Margaret Allen. Though the Riley had to retire, the occasion marked an unusually high number of women drivers in the event, including France's Anne Itier (1890–1980). France's Odette Siko had already been in the first female team to complete the race with Marguerite Mareuse driving a Bugatti in 1930, and came fourth overall in 1932, setting a record for women drivers that remains today. Another Le Mans start for Bill Wisdom followed in 1938 in an MG Midget PB with Arthur Dobson, but ended prematurely with clutch and radiator trouble. Bill had first driven a Fiat 508S in the Irish Tourist Trophy in 1935 and in 1938 she favoured an MG PB, partnered with Dorothy Stanley Turner. They finish 23rd overall and Wisdom also won an international motor boat race for the Atlantis trophy the same year.

Although she and Tommy moved increasingly into rally driving after World War II, there were some notable earlier successes, such as their win in the 1936 International Alpine Trial in a Jaguar SS100. Always impeccably dressed, Tommy Wisdom was an RAF Wing Commander during the Second World War, favouring a trademark look of a Homburg hat, monocle and cigarette when not in uniform. In 1949 he was part of a team which broke the world speed record on the Bonneville Salt Flats. The same year, Elsie co-drove a Morris Minor in the Monte Carlo Rally, with Betty Haig (1906–1987) and Barbara Marshall (no dates).[166] Tommy remained supportive of Bill's career until they were both hospitalised in the 1951 Alpine Rally and she drove less competitively afterwards. Another serious fire in 1953 at Le Mans left Tommy badly burned but he continued to compete, taking part in the last of his twenty-five Mont Carlo rallies in 1969. The Wisdom's love of rallying and racing therefore overlapped with the motoring career of their daughter, Ann (1933) who was photographed aged three watching her mother tune a Leyland at Brooklands.[167] She later became a noted rally driver after she passed her driving test in 1956 and, known informally as 'Wiz', achieved a notable victory in the 1960 Liège-Rome-Liège rally in an Austin Healey 3000 with Pat Moss Carlsson (1934–2008).[168]

Many women were involved in engineering, styling, driving and flying as forms of work and entrepreneurship.[169] Like opportunities in new technologies today, much of this activity was ad hoc. This section on the Brooklands women concludes with perhaps the most famous and influential: Kay Petre (née Defries) was encouraged learn to drive by her parents. Born in Toronto 10 May 1903, her father was a well-known barrister and the family travelled extensively as his firm had clients in England and Ireland. Kay Defries attended a boarding school in Nova Scotia, then studied in Eastbourne, England. On holiday back in Toronto, aged 16, she was taught to drive by a naval cadet, an experience which she described some years later:

> A favourite remark many people make to women drivers, which seems to them to explain why a few of the weaker sex enjoy handling cars, is 'But you must be a born driver and love speed.' Perhaps it does apply to some of them, but during my six years of racing all the women who achieved success in cars did so only after hard work and long practice. Many of them undoubtedly had a *flair* for driving, but I was not so gifted. In fact I was anything but a born driver. My earliest driving in Canada was punctuated with frequent visits to a garage boasting a sign that said, 'Fenders straightened while you wait.' The family saloon and I spent many hours on their premises . . . [170]

Defries then moved with her mother to a pension on the Left Bank of Paris where she attended art classes at the Academie de la Grande Chaumiere, off Boulevard Montearnasse. She met her future husband Henry Petre (1884–1962) while ice skating and they married in 1928. Henry Petre was a confirmed bachelor nicknamed 'Peter the Monk' and a Brooklands pilot (who flew amongst other things a Deperdussin monoplane, one of the more sporting aircraft of the day) so it caused some surprise that they married so quickly.[171] Shortly after Kay began racing a Wolsley Hornet Henry bought her for her birthday (supposedly to save the gear box in his Invicta) and became identified by her diminutive stature, photogenic appearance and tailored pale blue silk or leather 'Sidcot' overalls. The visual contrast between her five foot, eight stone frame and the large Bugattis and ERAs that she sometimes drove, merited endless photographs.[172]

In 1934 Kay Petre became one of Brooklands 120 mph badge-holders driving a borrowed 10½-litre Delage in a friendly rivalry against Bill Wisdom and was elected a BRDC honorary member.[173] This section has already summarised a number of her successes, but other triumphs also included driving Donald Healey's big Invicta at the Brighton Speed Trials; buying Thomas Fotheringham's 2 litre unsupercharged Bugatti for £150 to race at Lewes Speed trials, Shelsley Walsh, and Brooklands; guiding a Delage occasionally around the circuit and making famous her white Riley with accessorised matching overalls. By 1937 Kay Petre had become an Austin team works driver with Bert Hadley and Charles Goodacre racing at Le Mans, Crystal Palace, Donington, Brooklands and Shelsley Walsh. Her career seems to have been a mixture of hard work, spartan conditions and 'banter', as she later recalled:

> Lord Ausin did not believe in lavish living for his team. Wherever we went, we went as a team; drivers, mechanics and Capt. Bill Sewell, the team manager. We stayed in the same hotel and all worked together. Bert and Charlie worked on their own cars, both being in the Experimental Shop at Austin's. Because my mechanical skill was almost zero, I had the lowly job of washing the cars after practice . . . Once Charlie Goodacre and I went to London Zoo and had our photograph taken with one of the Chimpanzees sitting in the middle with his arms around our necks. We sent this photo, in postcard from, to Bert Hadley, marking it 'The Austin Team'. It went up on the notice board in the Experiemental Shop. Bert did not think it funny.[174]

Kay Petre was internationally famous. German aviator Elly Beinhorn (1907–2007) gave an account of flying her husband, the racing driver Bernd Rosemeyer (1909–1938), to South Africa so that he could participate in the Grand Prix at East London on the Eastern Cape on the 1 January 1937.[175] No stranger to driving 6 litre Auto-Unions herself, Beinhorn recorded the anticipation of Rosemeyer and his entourage to meet Petre. Although Kay Petre was forced to retire from the race itself and Rosemeyer was disappointed to come fifth, in the Cape Town Grand Prix two weeks later, he won, setting a new lap record and his new English friend came sixth in her Riley. The acquaintance was to be renewed when Rosemeyer travelled to Donington in England for the last race of the season on 2 October, and won for the Auto Union works team.[176]

However the dinner date between Petre and Rosemeyer in order to celebrate his victory failed to materialise because of the crash that effectively ended her career.[177] During the Friday practice session at Brooklands that weekend, Petre was lapping fast on the inside of the circuit in an Austin Seven and Reg Parnell was overtaking her on outside track. In torrential rain his MG Magnette caught the lip of the turn at the Byfleet banking and span his car down by ninety degrees to collide 'T-bone' style with the Austin which turned over several times, tearing off every filler cap and flinging Petre out of the vehicle.

Usually described as 'Reg Parnell's MG accident' since his racing licence was revoked, the incident put Petre in a coma and was photographed just before impact, becoming an iconic moment in sport.[178] It seemed that she would not survive as she lay in Weybridge hospital gravely ill. Rosemeyer was distraught to find her in a coma and left the flowers from his winner's wreath at her bedside.[179] Of his visit, the racing manager of Mecedez Benz, Alfred Neubauer wrote somewhat ominously: 'He was not to know that this would be the last time that he would ever see her—or that Donington was to be his last victory.'[180] On 28 January 1938 Rosemeyer was killed attempting to regain his 'Flying Kilometre' and 'Fying Mile' record times in Frankfurt and Petre remained in hospital for four months, requiring physical therapy and plastic surgery before her release. Reg Parnell resumed his racing career at Brooklands in March 1939 and the first person to congratulate him on his placings at this meeting was Kay Petre.[181] The consensus seemed to be that the accident had been no more than a 'racing incident.'

Kay subsequently recovered, acted as Patron to a number of automobile associations, such as the Harrow Car Club, and later became Motoring Correspondent of the *Daily Graphic*. She also acted also as the paper's food correspondent during the war and attended Lord Woolton's regular conferences.[182] In later interviews Petre said that she regarded her journalism as her most serious career: one of her scoops was the prediction of Stirling Moss as a future star in 1948 when he was only 17.[183] As someone who was quite short she also joked that she had invented a special seat: 'the Petre Patent Pew for Petite Persons', and this ability to design was formalised by an appointment as colour and style consultant in 1950 to the British Motor Corporation at Longbridge. Petre also appeared in advertisments for Austin. She continued to drive the cars at vintage races; for instance, wearing her characteristic pale blue at Oulton Park in 1961 to match the livery of a side valved 750cc.[184] One of her projects was the interior and colour range of the original Mini but she was forced to retire in 1965 due to failing memory, perhaps not helped by her earlier accident. After Henry's death in 1962, she returned to Canada but found it too cold and returned to live in a London nursing home where she also enjoyed investment and Bridge.[185]

In conclusion, the last full racing season at Brooklands was in 1938 and the ending of Petre's main career seems a good way to sum up the end of an era. It has been possible to trace the careers of something like eighty women who raced at Brooklands at least once, in addition to the aviation activity at the site. Compared with perhaps 1,000 men who competed there, this is a minority, but, as this brief attempt at a collective biogaphy has shown, there are a range of personalities to research. Kay Petre moved from novice to keen amateur and on to multiple professional careers in the automotive industry and its related media arm.

This trajectory could be seen through her control of her own image. In early photographs it is clear that she did not want to wear goggles and there are shots where she is shown to have been injured by a flying stone on the forehead. Perhaps mindful of her eyesight, goggles later became a sign of occupational honour when driving, and, pushed up on the head after a race, a sign of professionalism. Along with cigarettes and tissues Petre was reported to keep a make up kit under her car seat and clearly wanted to be feminine but also to drive fast. Her overalls also became increasingly close cut to reveal her bust and waist from the original coverall double breasted design that she wore at the start of her career. The photographs are valuable sources to see how Petre became increasingly practised in presentational techniques from the fashion and film industries and very much part of the construction of her own glamorous image. Ready almost at a moment to be photographed, she was nonetheless serious about her racing.

Motor-sport is central to understanding sport history because of the more general points it makes about how the creative and manufacturing industries could develop in tandem. We generally tell a story of sport developing in urban centres to which people have moved in search of work. In contrast to the swathe of pastoral green of a football or cricket pitch in an urban environment, city-to-city races and the construction of asphalt circuits took industrialisation further into the countryside. It also complicates our understanding of individual pursuits and team sports. While traditional sports could be seen as escaping from work, the relentless quest for improvement in endurance and speed reflected mechanised manufacturing. Motor-sport could therefore provide some women with highly conspicuous leisure; others with an opportunity for dangerous work; a few the chance to enter related trades and a handful to write about their experiences. What began as ostentatious leisure at Brooklands, bringing men and women together to enjoy one another's company, became women's work with a much wider commercial, and military, resonance.

The Games [sic] that we have been playing have given us experience that may be invaluable in the days to come. Some of our girl trials drivers will surely be equally expert at handling an ambulance [sic]. Here's a first-class outlet for their enthusiasm, and, from what I hear, their services would be very welcome to the authorities concerned.[186]

CONCLUSION

As an internationalised team game, hockey was indicative of how particular sports cultures shaped networks in ways that overlapped with women's work. Though it was mainly a way for women to socialise with other women, the tours did have mixed and family elements. As has been suggested, whether we look at food, clothing, accommodation, leisure, mass tourism or transnational communication, international tours by visiting national teams were often associated with much more than hockey or any other sport. Even in America, field hockey was heavily shaped by English culture and ideology. There were varying inflections of Englishness because of the variety of women involved and this no doubt changed as the 'grand old ladies' like Thompson and Light were succeeded by women like Pollard. The 1920s and 1930s were a fascinating period during which the older pioneers of women's education and physical activity, like Constance Maynard (1866–1935) took advantage of new technologies and opportunities.[187]

However, it is the scrapbooks of the less well-known hockey players that show how sport was experienced by increasing numbers of women and girls. Hockey scrapbooks that have survived are a rich but tantalising source until more genealogical research is completed; the relatively unknown F. I. Bryan visited Australia just once between 28 May and 23 July 1927; while the more well-known Margaret Peggy Lodge toured widely between 1929 and 1950, after first playing for Gloucestershire in 1928 and for the West in 1932, becoming an international reserve the same year.[188] Lodge toured the United States in 1937 and 1947, New Zealand in 1938 and the Netherlands in 1950.[189] Audrey Cattrell, who played for Kent and the East of England, travelled to South Africa in 1930 and America in 1936.[190] The trips obviously meant a lot to Phyllis Carlbach in 1935 and 1936, as she took photographs of what the inside of a third-class stateroom looked like, collected the wonderful illustrated menus and kept every one of the issues of the *RMS Queen Mary* 'North Atlantic Edition' of the *Ocean Times* published on board Cunard White Star Liners for the duration of the voyage.[191]

The pattern continued after the Second World War, for example Barbara West was a member of Kingston and Hove Ladies Hockey Club between 1935–56, captaining the team from 1937.[192] She also played for Sussex and the South Reserves. West played regularly for the South after the Second World War, before refereeing at county, territorial and international matches from 1952 onwards. Coaches, referees and administrators could enjoy travel as well as players: a huge area of future work to develop. By this time the game was being dominated by all-round hockey and cricket players, like Mary Russell Vick (known better as MRV, 1922–2012), and played at Wembley in front of Queen Elizabeth.[193] The improved international profile of the game during the inter-war years and its wider social reverberations no doubt help this growing respect. By 1950 the executive council of IFWHA showed much less of an English bias comprising C. Bange (France); D. Burrell (Australia); M. Couqueque (Holland); E. Dietrich (SA); N. Drysdale (Scotland) M. Ewing (New Zealand); E Heilbuta (Denmark); N. Huet (Ireland); A. D. Jones (Wales) D .Lasbrey (SA); E. Shellenberger (USA) and Hilda Light (England).[194] By the early 1970s there were twenty-two countries, mainly in Europe, with women's sections in the FIH and thirty-six associations affiliated to the IFWHA. Hockey was therefore a relatively rare case in English sport of being predominantly female in administration, style and culture. Hilda Light summarised this as 'Contest without conflict, rivarly without rancour and struggle without strife.'[195]

It is a cause of personal regret that Agatha Christie did not do for the Brooklands circuit what she did for the Orient Express or Nile cruises; such a shrewd observer of class, gender and xenophobia would surely have dissected the atmosphere better than socialite Barbara Cartland who has a reading room in the iconic clubhouse named in her honour.[196] Given the egos, the range of personalities, and other entertainments on offer, it is highly unlikely that much reading took place there. A hoax race staged by

Cartland in 1931 rehearsed its conclusion six times for the cameras so that it would look more exciting and undermined some of the real risks faced by women drivers. Cartland having decided before the off that Princess Imeretinsky would win, due to the seniority of her title.[197] However, from this very society atmosphere, the 'Brookland's Crowd' saw the world as its plaything, to dissect in whatever vehicle appealed to the individual by way of a personal challenge. By crossing a span and claiming it for Britain, the actions of motor-sport enthusiasts became a synecdoche for the imperial project of the nation at a time when that was under increasing threat.

Jean and Thelma Archer; Yvonne Arnaud; Dorothy Bean; Leonie Bentley; Florence Blenkiron; The Hon Mrs Joan Chetwynd; Violet Cordery; Marjorie Cottle; May Cunliffe; Ivy Cummings; Rita Don; 'Auntie' Durrant (who served in the club bar); Jessie Ennis; Lady Diana Finch-Halton; Mamie Frazer-Nash; Vera Godfrey; Margaret Jennings (née Allan); Audrey Latham (wife of Tim Birkin); Margaret Longaby; M. J. Machononochie; 'Paddy' Naismith; Ivy Pickett; Winifred Pink; Irene Schwedler; Lady Doris Seagrave; Tilly Shilling; Barbara Skinner; Dorothy Stanley-Turner; Violet Worsley and Teresa Wallach were just some of those who raced at Brooklands in the 1920s and 1930s.[198] As Sammy Davis' has pointed out in *Atalanta*, there were many, many more.[199] Some specialised in motorcycle racing, others cars and several competed using both these and three-wheeled 'light cars'.

Dorothy Conyers Nelson Champney who won the Scottish rally in 1934 mentioned in the introduction, was born at Scarborough in 1909, the daughter of Frederick D'Arcy Champney, a gentleman of independent means. She established a motoring career before marrying (William) Victor Riley, MD of the Riley Motor Co family in 1934. Dorothy continued her driving career after the couple had a son and daughter and continued to have an association with the motor industry until both died in 1958. Brooklands had many 'racing couples' and even where there was undoubted antipathy to female drivers from the likes of John Cobb and BRDC administrators, the active encouragement of men was vital for women's participation. The examples of hockey and motor racing suggest that we need to refine our understanding of sports teams and other kinds of collaboration. Mixed sport requires consideration across classes and codes because masculinity has not always been policed so carefully as has been suggested by writers who focus on football; cricket and rugby. Appendix 8 summarises an outline of activity pursued at the circuit by some of the most well-known women racing drivers but this is a partial and provisional assessment, open to further refinement.

The stereotype of the steel-nerved pioneer determined to capture records in the national interest combined ideas of home defence and a destiny extending beyond established borders. This included women who came to Britain in order to fulfil their ambitions as well as those who travelled to Empire countries as part of their careers. Like Jean Batten (1909–1982),

Figure 5.2   Ardarth Tobacco Co Ltd 'Jean Batten' London: Ardarth Tobacco Co Ltd, circa 1936. Personal collection of the author. Having been made a Commander of the British Empire (CBE) in 1936, Jean Batten became a widely mediated star. The daughter of a New Zealand dentist, Batten would later be called 'The Garbo of the Skies' because she resented the amount of acclaim that followed her record-breaking successes.

the daughter of a dental surgeon in New Zealand, the fascination with motor-sport in Britain provided Richmond with acclaim, personal and professional opportunities.[200] Batten gained her private and commercial licenses in London in 1932 before setting records to Australia and Brazil.[201] In 1936 she was created Commander of the British Empire (CBE), awarded the Cross of Chevalier of the French Legion of Honour and, for the second successive year, the Royal Aero Club's Britannia Trophy. When Batten landed her Percival Gull monoplane at Croydon in October 1937 having, for the second time, broken the Australia to England flight record, she was a well-established enough heroine to appear on cigarette cards, on newsreels and in the international press.[202] In 1938, she was the first woman to be awarded the medal of the Fédération Aéronautique Internationale.

Nor were the British alone in viewing motor-sport as indicative of national vitality at home and overseas.[203] As Simon Martin has indicated, although not a Fascist creation, the Coppa della Mille Miglia race held over 1,000 miles was supported by the regime and exploited by it for propaganda.[204] As member number one of the Italian Automobile Club, Mussolini used motor racing to enhance the standing of Italy overseas, and brands such as Fiat, Alfa Romeo, Ferrari and Maserati benefitted from his enthusiasm.[205] Amidst a more general militarisation of sport in Germany from 1934 onwards, Hitler followed suit with Auto Unions and Mercedes.[206] Betty Haig became the winner of the 1936 Olympic Rally, driving a works team Singer. Centred on Berlin and timed to coincide with the Games, Haig's example was the only car recorded to have won an Olympic medal. German aviator Elly Beinhorn-Rosemeyer also sought to capitalise on the publicity of the Games by flying a Taifun, a German sports aircraft, across three continents from Damascus (Asia); to Cairo (Africa) to Berlin within twenty-four hours on 3 August 1936.[207]

In comparison, though it remained a racing marquee, the liquidisation of Bentley in 1931 was indicative of the wider economic slump, allowing it to be acquired by Rolls Royce. This meant that cheaper models of cars such as Alvis, Riley, Lea-Francis, Austin and MG Midget became raced more often. Less ostentatious races also became part of the international calendar, like the Ulster TT, the Belgian and Irish Grand Prix, which boosted civic pride and local tourism.[208] Nevertheless, British resolution in the face of other imperial projects and technological advances required moral strength as well as expertise. Increasingly, an elite group of women racers came to be admired for these qualities.

Mixed sport is virtually a neglected topic in the academic literature, but the social etiquette of the sports club had many forms. Using sport to socialise with other women and with men was hardly novel and Brooklands was one of many newly-visible spaces and places of modernity, The first person into the Lansbury Lido on 16 June 1930 was twenty-one year old Kathleen Murphy of Pinner who had arrived at the gate at 5 a.m.[209] For such enthusiasm, she was given a medal by Alfred Rowley, secretary of the Serpentine

Swimming Club. The occasion marked the opening of pubic mixed bathing in Hyde Park on the Serpentine, the project of George Lansbury, the First Commissioner of Works. Kathleen was by no means alone. A vogue for mixed bathing and for wearing sports and leisure wear in order to show off male and female 'figures' became evident, in spite of widespread poverty following the economic dislocation of the depression. So there were working-class examples that could have been used as case studies in this chapter. Swimming, lifestyle sports like mountaineering, walking and cycling would have made similar points about male and female collaboration in sporting enjoyment and, in some cases, work.This also extended to 'traditional' pursuits with militaristic overtones. For example, Marjorie Foster (1893–1974) made 280 points out of a possible 300 in 1930 to beat 861 men and 4 women to win the heavily militaristic Sovereign's Prize at Bisley.[210] Having served with the Women's Legion of Motor Drivers during World War I, it was perhaps fitting that the residents of Frimley bough her a motor-car as a token of pride, in addition to the letter she received from George V, £250 in prize money and the gold medal.[211] With her partner Blanche Badcock (1893–1957), Foster ran a poultry farm before again using her driving, shooting and nursing skills during World War II receiving an MBE in recognition.

The influence of Gunji Koizumi (1885–1965), on the judo careers of women like Sarah Mayer (circa 1900–1937) and Enid Russell Smith (1903–1989) was another reminder that influences came from the East as well as the West.[212] The first non-Japanese woman to be awarded a black belt in 1935, Mayer trained in Japan from February 1934 and wrote seven letters to Koizumi about her training, her experience of Japanese culture and Judo experts that she met and with whom she had worked.[213] Her interest appeared to have been relatively short-lived before she returned to the stage as a writer and performer but little is known of her life. Russell Smith was a member of the Kensington Budok-wai Judo club and inter-war Europe's leading female exponent, though she worked professionally as a senior civil servant in the Ministry of Health.[214] A certain 'self-made' and ascetic quality of training the body in martial arts, boxing or the more moderate 'keep fit' exercises of appealed across classes.

There were other women entrepreneurs who combined their sporting interests with earning a living. These different forms of employment could also blend voluntary, amateur, professional and paid work. Irish equestrian and socialite Joan Grubb (1889–1968) has been credited as the first woman to ride astride at the Olympia London International Horse Show before the First World War but this appears to have been more widespread than is generally claimed.[215] Marjory Avis Bullows, (later Lady Wright 1890–1980) an accomplished horsewoman and master of the Tedworth hounds, also rode astride. Bullows achieved the first clear round at Olympia in 1924 on her pony If Not, a chestnut gelding supposed to have graduated from pulling a milk float and who would go on to win over £3, 000 in prize money.[216] Whatever the pony's background, Bullows with the help of her husband, created a middle-class 'riding school.' Using cab horses between shifts as school hacks for pupils, and sharing the fees fifty-fifty with the taxi owner in Moseley, Birmingham, she was then able to buy her own stables at Metchely.

Introducing 'working pupils', Bullows was able to establish careers in equine and stable management for women. As Lady Wright, after her 1928, marriage to the judge, Sir Robert (1869–1964), the innovation began to extend equestrian expertise beyond the military and those of independent means. This, in turn may have been influenced by war-work when Russley Park in Wiltshire, Bradfield and Holyport near Maidenhead all used women supervisors to oversee either the training of horses for active service, or to manage their recuperation when injured, psychologically or physically, during conflict.[217]

Commodification and commercialisation extended to amateur and professional sport from the inter-war period onwards. Auto illustrations by Ransom for the Die Dame company, who published a motoring number every year to coincide with the Berlin motor show, costumed women in designs that incorporated spark plugs, batteries, petrol and rubber.[218] This wider mediation extended to advertisements for Wolf motorcycles from 1932, for example, showing a young woman with bobbed hair wearing a one-piece bathing suit and plimsolls astride a machine on the beach, while a male admirer looked on.[219] In 1931 the factory had been expanded and a trade stand was taken at Olympia. The 'Cub' model, with a 98 c.c. engine, sold for only £15 and 15 shillings. The 'Wolf Silver Super Sport' was powered by a 196 c.c. engine and sold for £34. Originally a bicycle manufacturing company, Wolf reverted to cycle production during and after the Second World War. Raleigh motorcycles were later to diversify their product range from cycles to motorcycles then typewriters as a way of capitalising on their light engineering methods. Products were often advertised side-by-side.

As the advertisement of the little girl in a 'Brooklands' model toy car at the British Industries Fair in 1931 indicated, speed could be aspirational and fashionable.[220] It could also be lucrative as the Lines Brother's Limited stand of Tri-ang 'strong' vehicle replicas was the single largest display at the exhibition.[221] This commercial interest in the female and family market extended to vehicles, clothing, toys, equipment and the sale of sporting goods more generally:

Said the Sporting Goods Journal last year: 'Sporting goods dealers have suddenly become awakened to the fact that there is more profit in playing for the trade of the ladies than in catering exclusively for men.' The growing participation of women in sport during recent years is as striking as the change from bloomers of 1900 to the shorts of 1935. It may or may not be an exaggeration to say that women play many games today to be seen in costume; but the point is that they play.[222]

This extended to commodities that would not necessarily help with sporting performance, on the track or elsewhere. In the 1930s a woman in ski clothes, resting on the slopes advised readers that: 'Smoking a Camel certainly makes all the difference'.[223] Similarly, not everyone who wore sports clothing in the 1920s and 1930s intended to do anything strenuous. Tennis shoes became something of a fashionable item for men and women after Adidas first mass-produced versions in 1931. The launch of rubber and canvas shoes Keds (male) and Kedettes (female) featured straplines emphasising indpendence and fun such as 'Enjoy things together!'[224] An extended a process of celebrity endorsement begun with the launch of the Converse All Star in 1917, re-branded in 1923 as the Chuck Taylor All Star when the basketball player endorsed them as his preferred shoe. By 1935 Converse had released the Jack Purcell after the renowned badminton and tennis champion, with a rubber 'smile' in the toe and it became popular as streetwear in Hollywood. Gradually by the 1930s female cheerleaders and athletes adopted the Kedettes and other canvas rubber soled shoes for sport and for leisure wear. Articles and advertisements featured sports goods and clothing, exemplified by The Burberry Model in the brands' Motor Gown or Golf Costume (with 'Pivot' sleeve) as conspicuous, exclusive consumption.[225]

This chapter has highlighted some potential new areas of research but was not able to develop the way that sport and other industries intersected in any great detail: the expansion of models, games and replicas is but one area of research deserving more analysis. We might look at the popularity for touring-based board games, like *Fliver* or *The New Game of Motor Tour*. Replica vehicles also domesticated speed and developed a sense of entitlement to travel.[226] Lines often joked that their toy models were the cheapest cars in the world. In the fiercely competitive collectibles market surrounding motor-sport, especially for classic cars, the link between a reputation and an endorsed product also continues to have considerable value beyond the merely historic.

The difficulty of proving the provenance of a particular vehicle continues to emphasise the mythical status surrounding racing motorists like Violet Cordery and John Hindmarsh. For example, a 1933 Lagonda 2 Litre normally aspirated tourer was advertised for sale in 2011, with the registration APH 889, of which Violet Hindmarsh was said to have been the first keeper but no surviving ledgers exist to prove the connection.[227] The Lagonda did not meet its reserve price on this occasion and other models made the same year vary in value from £30,000 to £155,000. Such racing associations will continue affect the value of cars for generations to come quite beyond the legacy of track and technology history of Cordery and her contemporaries.

The next chapter begins by looking at how the 1948 Olympic Games help us to understand the strenghts and weaknesses of British sport after the debilitating effects of war. The narratives around the need for modernisation link sport with other aspects of national life that were to prove generally beneficial for women's access to a greater range of activities, but more importantly, also for more young women and girls.

6 Women, Sport and Culture
From the 1948 London Olympic Games to Rome 1960

And now I curl up like the terrified Orpheus who was torn to pieces by excited women. I cannot see anything in women's athletics, except women at their worst. The masculine ones dominate and the only kick I get out of these displays is when someone wholly feminine puts it across her flat-chested, bass-voiced opponents and makes the Olympic grade by sheer grace and agility. Even the accomplishment is trivial. Cannot the 'muscle molls' as Paul Gallico terms them, go elsewhere for their records? After all we have to draw the line somewhere and Helen Stephens or Stella Walsh would be a doughty opponent on the wing at Twickenham. But would this be a 'good thing'? We are getting perilously near the 'bearded women' sensation in a circus by including women in an Olympiad. This is only personal fastidiousness. It is not another case against the Olympic Games. I would sooner have Baby Shows and Beauty competitions added than let the institution lapse [sic].[1]

One of the many voices that debated Britain's plans to host the first Olympic Games after World War II belonged to Bevil Gordon D'Urban Rudd. Like many epigrams, the excerpt above reveals as much about the teller, as the tale of women's sport. Rudd was a South African athlete of 'Randlord' heritage; an heir of gold and diamond dynasties who collectively controlled the most valuable mines in the world from the 1880s to the First World War. His father had been a director of De Beers.[2] After excelling at St Andrew's College, Grahamstown, Bevil Rudd became a Rhodes Scholar at Trinity College, Oxford before serving in the British army during World War I. He had therefore come from new money rather than an old family.

Rudd had taken a gold medal in the 400m individual race at the 1920 Antwerp Olympics for South Africa; a silver medal in the 4 x 400m relay and a bronze medal in the 800m event behind Britain's Albert Hill and Philip Noel-Baker.[3] Coached by Sam Mussabini, Albert Hill had completed a historic double at the relatively advanced age of thirty-one years in 1920 by also winning a gold in the 1500 metres (and a silver in the team 3000-metres event).[4] A railway worker, in 1921 Hill also won the Amateur Athletics Association (AAA) Championships mile race within a second of the world record, before beginning a precarious career as a professional coach.[5] In contrast, Noel-Baker would become a career politician, dine with Virginia Woolf and win the Nobel Peace Prize in 1959.[6] In light of these social contrasts, Rudd's antipathy to women can be read as part of his larger nostalgia for a mythical Golden Age of sport as a gentlemanly amateur pursuit.

However, his was not the only perspective. A few years later *World Sports: International Sports Magazine*, which was established as the official publication of the British Olympic Association (BOA), was prompted by the accession of a twenty-five year old female head of state to see the period as a new Elizabethan era. The coronation ceremony of Queen Elizabeth II sixteen months later was celebrated by *World Sports* as heralding a period of: 'Rich inventiveness, achievement and glory—in sport and all things.'[7] This chapter explores the contested amateur tradition as it manifested itself across a range of women's sports during the 1940s and 1950s. More women amateurs became increasingly visible to the general public in a wider range of sports in the approach to the Rome Olympic Games of 1960.[8] Using Olympic Games as a way of demarking the period of time covered by the chapter is therefore indicative rather than binding. What appeared to be a new era of female competition also highlighted significant continuities, including increased specialisation; shamateurism and varied kinds of sport-related work. By 1960, professional female experts from a variety of sports, leisure and recreational disciplines were also embedded in British cultural life. Many became global stars. While lots of women took part in sport more for the joy of competition than for the fame, there were increasing numbers who were to enjoy high public profiles.

Janie Hampton, Bob Phillips and Martin Polley have written extensively on the wider British contribution to Olympic history and legacy.[9] Technological innovation was to be important in 1948, including photo finishes and BBC outside broadcasts. A sense of time, space and place changed as simultaneous multi-media records of events became increasingly the norm. Radio, television and film presented the Olympics as one of the first big post-war opportunities for sporting communion. However, this was not necessarily a national moment, as most of the half a million TV viewers lived within eighty miles of London.[10] For the British Press and radio, Olympic competition was a small sign that the war was over and things were slowly improving, though David Kynaston has questioned the degree to which Olympic ideals were embraced, given the everyday priorities of post-war reconstruction.[11] Although less than 5% of the adult population had a television set in their homes (it has been estimated at about 70, 000 in total) Olympic outside broadcasts provided one of the milestones of post-war TV transmission, following the Victory Parade in 1946 and the Royal Wedding of Princess Elizabeth and Prince Phillip in 1947. This was a particular 'media moment' in British sport where a competitor might see their first television set shortly before appearing on the screen, as Dorothy Tyler (née Odam, 1920), a high jump competitor, reported that she had done.[12]

There seemed to be as much continuity as change even so: for Robert Edelman London 1948 was, 'The last of the pre-war Games' before Cold War rivalries changed the intensity of nationalism from Helsinki 1952

onwards.[13] London 1948 was the last Olympic Games where the literature, art, sculpture, architecture, etchings and musical compositions were
awarded medals, and we are beginning to understand more about their
role in design history and culture.[14] Other commentators would argue
that the Olympics had already been radically politicised at the 1936 Berlin edition, which were so overlaid with propaganda and symbolism that
they might be considered a postmodern event; any sporting values lost
under Nazi misinformation.[15] In addition, Peter Beck has argued that
Cold War narratives were already present in 1948.[16] Moreover, he suggests the forthcoming cricket test series, in which the Australians were to
visit Britain, was of greater importance than the Games, at least so far as
The Times was concerned.

The Olympics were, by comparison a 'foreign' tournament on home soil,
revealing anxieties about Britain's place in the world. From 1930 onwards
the British Empire Games had shown how ambiguous Britain's imperial
sovereignty could be when expressed in sporting terms. The shift towards
Commonwealth and post-colonial relations following the 1947 partition of
India and Pakistan radically changed perceptions of black and South Asian
communities in Britain.[17] On 22 June 1948 HMS Windrush arrived carrying just under 500 people from Jamaica, the first large group of West Indian
immigrants to Britain. The changes affected British sport but also showed
that 'national' identity could combine a fusion, and perhaps a confusion, of
elements. C. L. R. James and others contemporary writers dissected these
complexities in ways that still reward further study.[18]

Arthur Wint, a Jamaican-born sprinter who had dominated British running since 1946, was one of the outstanding personalities at the 1948 Olympic Games.[19] Having joined the British Commonwealth Air Training Plan,
he served as an active combat pilot. In 1947 Wint had resigned his commission to study medicine at St Barts, London before becoming Jamaica's
first Olympic gold medalist by winning the 400 metres in 1948 and a silver
in the 800 metres. He also took a gold with the 4 x 400 metres relay team
for Jamaica in 1952, winning another individual silver medal in the 800
metres.[20] In 1954, Wint was made a Member of the British Empire (MBE)
before serving as Jamaica's High Commissioner to Britain and ambassador
to Sweden and Denmark from 1974 to 1978.

While often-referred to as the 'austerity games' therefore, grandiose
and elaborate settings part of what Britain wanted to present to the world,
with a very English flavour to events at Henley, Torbay and at venues in
and around London. Nor did post-war Britain open its arms to the rest
of the world without reserve. The number of nations was limited to sixty;
enemy nations like Germany and Japan were excluded. The Soviet Union
was not a member of the IOC but sent a delegation of ten representatives
to the congress held in London.[21] Diplomacy meant that nations like Israel
stayed away. In other cases poverty meant that teams could be small, if they
travelled at all: athletes from Ceylon, Panama and Turkey reached the last

six of their events for the first time. Unsurprisingly, the United States had the most conspicuous medal success, with Britain coming a lowly twelfth, leading the honourary Secretary of the British Amateur Athletic Board and manager of the British team, Jack Crump, to argue that something larger than sport had been at stake.[22]

For women's sport, the London 1948 Olympics looked selectively backwards and forwards: absent from the Games was Mrs Winifred Pritchard, who had won four races in the Royal Yacht Association trials but was prevented by IOC rules from representing her country as late as May 1948.[23] In spite of women previously competing on water, she was informed that mixed sailing events would be 'introduced' in 1952. Beryl Preston (1901) had been the most recent female competitor at the 1936 Berlin Games but Britain would not have a female yachting representative again until 1960 when Jean Mitchell (1901) took part in the Star class. Although a female kayaking discipline was introduced in 1948, canoeing or any event over 500 metres was considered too strenuous for women. Britain nevertheless had several notable female competitors with Joyce Richards; Shirley Ascot (1930); Patricia Moody (1914) and Marian Tucker (1937) representing their country between 1948 and 1964.[24] Of the five sports open to women in 1948 track and field athletics, gymnastics, fencing and kayaking were minority interests and only swimming a genuinely popular recreational activity. The disciplines available to female athletes within those sports were also limited and somewhat arbitrary. In spite of the dramaturgical effects of pomp, ritual and spectacle at the second London Olympics, it could be said that the wider cultural practices (or how most people did sport), were not to be reflected in the programme of events.

The values expressed by successive Olympic Games had long been invented, contradictory and multifaceted rather than rational or coherent.[25] Whether understood as a media-created event or sporting festival, the Games were exceptional by their very nature as a quadrennial tournament. They were also but one option from a much wider set of choices on offer to the British public. The *Radio Times* ran a feature for those asking 'What else is on besides the Olympics?' and the answer included Edward Percy's thriller *The Shop at Sly Corner*; a Murdoch and Horne 'Light Programme'; Promenade Concerts; Gluck's opera *Orpheus and Eurydice* in addition to reports from the House of Lords and a travelogue on Sydney, Australia.[26] As the advertisements in the *Picture Post* souvenir edition indicate, the Olympics were used to promote products that had tangential sporting connotations at best, such as large colour endorsements for Drene shampoo; Berketex clothes; Fortune chocolates by Caley of Norwich; Crosbie's VIP table sauce and Gibbs' S.R. toothpaste.[27] Women featured prominently throughout the *Picture Post* as athletes; part of the choir; dignitaries; spectators; volunteers and so on. Female models also featured in promotions for Royal Enfield bicycles; Mackesons's Stout; Victory V lozenges and National Savings, in addition to features on health, the home and beauty.

Clearly, sport and the Olympics were not the only game in town in 1948.[28] However, authors who write about Olympic competition generally focus on other sporting developments only to the extent that they directly contextualise the Games. The schedule of events in London was not really representative of wider British sport and leisure for girls and women in the 1940s and 1950s. This is an obvious argument but one that has had little academic attention. Part of the post-war boom in active leisure and spectator sport took place because there were legions of hobbyists for every elite performer. Girls and women were part of this general trend. One survey of 4,238 young female adults between 11–18 years of age conducted in 1951 showed a response of 96% to the question 'Are you interested in sport?' with 3.2% answering that they were not and 0.8% replying in the 'Don't Know' category.[29]

The chapter therefore begins with an assessment of Britain's female Olympians at the London 1948 Games before a second section looking at some other sports and the wider involvement of women and girls. High profile cases aside, we know much less about those women who would never win a gold medal but who enjoyed sport and physical recreation, either for brief intervals or long periods of time. There is considerable revision required here. The role of motherhood in limiting female involvement outside the home has a more-well established literature than examples of where women juggled multiple responsibilities.[30] While the vast international sporting festivals that form the Olympic canon are part of this chapter therefore, it also looks at some women and girls who made the winners' rostrum in other competitions, and those who only just managed to get to the field of play.[31]

This approach was prompted the wide-ranging coverage of women's sport in three contemporary texts, in addition to the magazine *World Sports*. James Rivers edited two volumes, *The Sports Book* released in 1946 and *The Sports Book 2* published in 1948. Rivers' collections contained articles written by informed enthusiasts, journalists or insiders and were designed to give an overview of post-war British sport in the approach to London 1948. As such, they showed how narratives for the educated generalist could incorporate discussion of women's sport. Carolyn Dingle's *Sports For Girls*, published by the *News Chronicle* in 1951 provided an alternative perspective. Some Olympians, high profile administrators and prominent journalists wrote short, often polemic, pieces. The sports editor of, the *News Chronicle*, William John Hicks, conducted a survey of young women aged eleven to eighteen years of age, largely as a result of a changing his mind about the value of female sporting spectacle. Though a problematic source, this survey provided a starting point for discussions, not just about how young women participated in a range of activities, but also how they perceived British sporting culture and international developments.

The official publication of the British Olympic Association, *World Sports* actually had a varied range of activities in its pages from archery and table tennis to motor racing and rugby. There was a regular feature on women's sport, written for an extended period by former national squash champion between 1932 and 1934 and tennis player, Susan Noel (1921–1991). Swimming journalist Pat Besford (1919–1988) also contributed regularly but there were also many generalist pieces where women featured in the magazines.[32] The range of advertisements and the *Buttericks* sports fashion pattern service indicated an assumed female readership. In addition, coverage by male journalists often highlighted women athletes. These and other contemporary texts, in addition to archival evidence, indicated that women helped to shape varied sporting and recreation cultures, from touring the continent by cycle or becoming professional snooker players to journalism and writing forms of sports history.[33] There was a plethora of material that had to be left out and it was quite clear that there could be a book on the period between 1948 and 1960 alone. However, all too often the academic literature on the lives of girls and women in this period has ignored active recreation in assessments of female work and leisure.[34]

THE LONDON OLYMPIAD 1948: APPROXIMATELY 4,100 ATHLETES OF WHOM APPROXIMATELY 400 WERE WOMEN

The 1936 Berlin Olympics had been superbly organised but fatally linked in the public mind with Nazism. Helsinki would have hosted the games in 1940 if war had not broken out in Europe. But the British Olympic Committee, led by Lord Aberdare, continued to press the claims of London. In early January of 1942 the IOC lost its President, when Count Henry de Baillet-Latour died and Vice-President Sigfrid Edström took over as figurehead. In spite of the fragile idea of sport uniting nations during a world war, Edström had been able to send twenty-seven circulars to help keep the IOC active, helped by way of Sweden's neutrality and his role as Chair of ASEA, an electrical firm with good communication facilities.[35] In June 1944 the IOC celebrated the fiftieth anniversary of the Olympic Movement and Edström, at the age of seventy-four, proposed Avery Brundage as his Vice President to act in his stead. Since the headquarters of the IOC had also been in neutral Switzerland, there was a relatively easy resumption of activities in 1946 when thirteen new members were elected to the executive committee.

Britain was hardly in a fit state to host such an international event as an Olympic Games. Post-war reconstruction had barely begun. British governments had been ambivalent about the value of international sport and British sport objected to state interference. But if the Games were to go ahead in 1948, government help would be essential. In January 1946 Lord Burghley of the British Olympic Committee met the Foreign Secretary, Ernest Bevin and Philip Noel-Baker, who was briefly Minister of State.[36] Bevin was not a sports fan but Baker was, having been President of the Cambridge

University athletic club from 1910–1912 and a co-founder of the Achilles Athletics Club, for Oxbridge graduates. While Noel-Baker became the minister in charge of the Olympics therefore, Bevin was a pragmatist and an internationalist, agreeing that tourists might bring much-needed foreign currency (especially US dollars). Cabinet support followed, as did some financial backing.

There were plenty of sceptics, especially during the bad winter of 1947 as mid-week sports events were cancelled to save industrial production and rationing remained in place. London was short of accommodation, building materials, food, fuel and transport. Many of the women competitors were housed at Southlands College in Wimbledon, and for some training took place at the Butlins Holiday Camp, Clacton on Sea. In the main, the drivers for the Olympic transport fleet between venues came from the Women's Royal Voluntary Service (WRVS). In addition to the service personnel, hundreds of students and other people, young and old, volunteered to help, either living in wartime RAF camps or remaining at home.[37]

Popular ambivalence centred on whether an Olympic Games was the correct way to spend money in harsh times; not least in the £4,000 of hospitality lavished on dignitaries by amateur administrators.[38] In stark contrast to the conditions endured by ordinary spectators and competitors, the social round for the well-appointed took in the Royal Institute of British Architects, Portland Place; a reception on the Terrace at the House of Commons, followed by dinner at the Dorchester for 150 guests; travel by Rolls Royce to dine at the Empire Stadium; meeting the Mayor at Mansion House and other social functions too numerous even for the official report to mention.[39] Many of those who insisted on sport as an amateur endeavour had useful food and drink industry connections, such as Ian St John Lawston Johnstone, Lord Luke of Pavenham of the Bovril meat extract dynasty who became a British member of the IOC in 1951.[40] Products like Bovril, which had become staples of a wartime diet, featured prominently in Olympic promotions for health and fitness in the 1950s and 1960s. Today this would be called 'ambient' marketing or product placement and is but one reminder that amateur sports could have highly commercialised elements. In the words of one writer on the subject, the story of the 1948 Olympics was about: 'How London Rescued The Games.'[41] The overwhelming priority for the IOC at the end of the Second World War was to restore the image of Olympism. Where better to do this than in the home of sport, which had provided the original model of amateur competition? Even so, narratives of the British rescuing the Games from Nazi ideals tend to ignore the continuities of propaganda, symbolism and patriarchy. They also downplay wider tensions in British society as it changed after 1945. Snobbery remained rife. Although the owner of Wembley stadium, Arthur Elvin, was made an honorary freeman of the borough of Wembley in 1945, appointed MBE in the same year, and knighted in 1946, he was not asked to serve on the London 1948 organising committee nor did he receive an honour afterwards.[42] This was all the more surprising given that his company Wembley Stadium Ltd provided the stadium and the Empire Pool next door rent-free, also offering the organising committee a £62,500 interest-free loan, plus the expert services of its permanent staff.[43]

The whole thing cost three-quarters of a million pounds and returned a small profit after tax of approximately 20,000. It therefore became an occasion when the Olympic Games, with a small government subsidy (for accommodation upgrades, competitor travel and food) made a respectable surplus. There were other forms of prejudice. Although additional waves of European Jewish migrants had received asylum in Britain in the 1930s onwards, anti-alien attitudes would mean that they were not to become citizens until the 1950s.[44] Suspicion also affected those who were already established in sport. Though Arthur Gold would later be knighted for his contribution to athletics administration, he claimed that anti-semitism was partly responsible for his relatively late election to a county committee when in his thirties and he remained a minor figure in 1948, before becoming more important in the 1960s.[45]

The British tried to choreograph the ideal of the gentlemanly amateur, embodied in the running grace of John Mark who carried the Olympic torch at the opening ceremony.[46] Six foot and blonde, the twenty-two year old medical student, a former president of the Cambridge University Athletic Club, appeared to personify a rather Aryan interpretation of Youth and Vitality.[47] The reality of sporting excellence could look somewhat different: Britain's fastest miler in 1936 and 1937, Sydney Wooderson was rather skinny, with bony knees, thinning hair, glasses and was coached, somewhat controversially, by Albert Hill.[48] 'The Mighty Atom' had been a fireman and then seen active service as an army engineer in the war before returning to form in 1945.[49] Even George VI and Queen Mary were said to sympathise with the way that 'poor Sydney' was neglected for the sake of rather more glamorous John Mark.

The Americans, who had been Britain's bitterest rivals in 1908, were now her closest friends and allies. The victories of black male athletes from the United States were much in evidence: for instance, the *Picture Post* souvenir edition had 100-metres gold medalist Harrison 'Bones' Dillard dominating the cover image. Another male star of the 1948 Olympic Games was Czechoslovakian Emil Zátopek, Born one of six children in a working-class family, Zátopek trained in his army boots and ran with an expression that reflected his extreme exertion to win the 10,000 metres race. Amateurism denoting conspicuous leisure, entitlement and wealth was comparatively dissolute compared with this kind of preparation. Zátopek then finished second behind Gaston Reiff from Belgium in the 5,000 metres.[50] Reputed to carry his fiancée, javelin thrower Dana Ingrová (1922), on his back when training in the forest, Zátopek knocked twelve seconds off the 10,000 metres Olympic record. He would go on to excel even more and win three gold medals in 1952 (adding the marathon distance) and his now-wife, Dana Ingrová-Zatopekova, also taking the gold for the javelin.[51]

The outstanding female athlete of the London 1948 Games was equally challenging to notions of gentlemanly amateurism. Though limited by rules of the time to four events, Francina 'Fanny' Elsje Blankers-Koen (1918–2004) won gold in the 80 metres hurdles, 100 metres, 200 metres and 4 x 100 relay for the Netherlands.[52] As she held world records in both the long and high jump, she would probably have won those too, if she had been allowed to compete in six events. The British Press had not predicted her dominance and most papers were not kind: the *Picture Post* reminded readers that 'Mrs F. E. Blankers Koen does the 100 metres in 11.9 seconds. At home in Holland she is the mother of two children' while 'Miss D. G. Manley, the typist from Woodford Green [finished] three tenths of a second behind the winner.'[53] Shirley Strickland (later De La Hunty, 1925–2004) of Australia took third place.

Unlike Blankers-Koen, who had competed in the 1936 Berlin Games, Dorothy Manley (1927) was twenty-one, worked full time in the city for the Suez Canal Company and London was her first international sprint event. Similarly, Britain's Audrey Williamson (1926–2010) was twenty-two years old, when she came second to Blankers-Koen in the 200 metres with Audrey 'Mickey' Patterson (1927–1996) of the United States taking the bronze.[54] It took judges forty-five minutes to award the bronze to Patterson, ahead of Shirley Strickland, and the New Orleans resident therefore became the first African-American woman to win an Olympic medal on 29 July 1948.[55]

Journalists, led by Jack Crump, had said that Blankers-Koen, a thirty-year-old mother of two, was too old for Olympic victory against the young British women. This narrative characterised a victory of domestic youth over foreign experience, conveniently ignoring the fact that thirty was not *that* old. Jan Blankers, who coached his wife, used the criticism as part of his motivational talks when her energy sapped. Fanny would eventually compete eleven times in heats and finals to win every race that she entered over two weeks in 1948. She won the 80 metres hurdles in a photo finish from nineteen year-old Oxford ballet dancer Maureen Gardner (1928–1974) who had taken up sprinting a few years earlier to recover from illness.[56] Shirley Strickland-De La Hunty of Australia again took the third place. Soon after the Olympics, Gardner married her coach Geoff Dyson who would become Chief National Coach and help to change the nature of specialist British preparation for major events.[57] Maureen Dyson took the national WAAA titles in 1950 and 1951 before retiring from competition, but remained an prominent advocate for ballet, sport and physical fitness for women.

In a chapter called 'We Are Winning!' Gardener claimed her greatest victory had not been coming second to Blankers-Koen and sharing a world record time at the Olympic Games. This experience has been exceeded by

winning back her national British 80 metres hurdles title from Jean Des-
forges (1929) in 1950 after the birth of her first son, Timothy.[58] Just as her
husband promoted the work of the English Schools Athletic Association,
Maureen Dyson became an important figurehead for adults and children;
she won 17% of the vote to be named the favourite sportswoman in the
Sport for Girls poll ahead of Gussy Moran (16%); Diane and Rosalind
Rowe (7.7%); Fanny Blankers Koen (5%); Barbara Ann Scott (4%) and
Louise Brough (2.7%) in 1951.[59] This compared favourably with votes for
the favourite sportsman poll headed by Denis Compton (18%); Len Hutton (10.5%); Reg Harris (10.2%) and Don Bradman (5.5 %), though the
low overall number of votes for these individuals perhaps suggests that the
readers were more involved in sports than willing spectators.

When it became apparent that Blankers-Koen was in the early stages
of pregnancy with her third child when she had won her 1948 medals,
the cliché of the advantage of youth had to be revised.[60] So did other ideas
of physical excellence: Xenia Stad-de-Jong (1922–2012) was the starting
member of the Dutch 4x100 metres relay team with whom Blankers-Koen
won her fourth gold medal in 1948. Stad-de-Jong was nick-named 'Tom
Thumb' because of her small stature.[61] Given that Blankers-Koen again
beat Gardner in European competition in 1951, dire warnings of athletics
harming frail female physiques were shown to be superstition masked as
science. This did not prevent such narratives from being influential. A historical analysis of women's Olympic participation written by a self-declared
'supporter' of female exercise, Dr Frederick Messerli, suggested the need
for experts like himself to supervise their activities.[62] One of the unpleasant
legacies of Olympic regulation since this period has remained the medicalised surveillance of femininity for elite athletic performers.[63] Even so, more
women competed in a wider range of Olympic events as the twentieth century progressed, many encouraged by their families and local community,
coaches and volunteers. Some, like Maureen Gardner, could capitalise on
their amateur medals to endorse sports-wear and related products.[64]

More international female athletes became familiar to the British public,
although women numbered only approximately 10% of the overall number
of competitors at the London Olympics. The opening ceremony saw most
female national team members combine coloured blazers with some form
of traditional dress, although New Look styles; pleated skirts and embel-
lishments added fashion touches. The United States team were agreed as
the most glamorous in their white high-heeled shoes and insouciance in
front of the cameras. For headgear, panama hats and straw boaters had
fewer military connotations than the beret, which was worn by the British,
Argentines and Americans.[65] Pong Sik Pak, a discus competitor would be
the only woman in the Korean team.[66] Alice Coachman (1923) took the
gold in the high jump to become the first African-American woman to win
an event outright. She received a motorcade reception on her return home
in Albany, Georgia but, owing to racial segregation laws, was not allowed

to address the crowd.[67] Noemi Simonetto De Portela (1926–2011) would win a silver medal in the long jump for Argentina, after a successful career in South American championships since 1941. What did these women make of their reception in Britain?

In a foreword to a book on the history of women's athletics written seven years later, Blankers-Koen ignored the unkind headlines and described her public reception as a blend of assimilation and anglophile fandom:

> It will probably not come as a surprise to anyone that, since the Olympic Games of 1948, I have become used to giving my autograph to every type of person, even in strange places where I thought no one could know me. That is the reason when,in 1951, I was not at all surprised by a lady walking up to my table and inquiring if I were Mrs Fanny Blankers-Koen . . . The lady had, she said, been very angry with me in 1948 owing to my prevention of three English girls from receiving gold medals. This scared me somewhat, but the lady continued to say that she had reconsidered her opinion immediately after the Games. She came to the conclusion that 'Fanny belonged to us'. With these words she took away my apprehensive feelings and hit the nail on the head [sic].[68]

It would require more analysis to see how widespread this warmth was. Although Britain was therefore not quite at ease with its own identity, it enjoyed its role as host, even where sporting success on home soil could be scarce. Amid anxieties about the changes to British society and the cost (in financial and symbolic terms) of the war, British women Olympians repre-sented part of the wider imagined community of Great Britain: this could combine national, regional and local identities.

Britain's Dorothy Tyler was a married mother of two and aged twenty-eight in 1948. She had also competed at the Berlin Olmpics in 1936, as one of twelve women in the athletics team for Great Britain and won the silver medal behind Hungary's Ibolya Csák (1915–2006) in the high jump and ahead of Germany's Elfriede Kaun (1914–2008), though all three recording a height of 1.60 metres.[69] Having worked as a physical training instructor and then as a driver in the air force during the war, she was posted to dif-ferent stations and at one time served with the Dam Busters. Tyler married and had two sons, David (born in 1946) and Barry (born 1947). There was a much-reproduced photograph at the time of the Games of Dorothy Tyler holding a washing up bowl and 'training' by leaping over a line of nappies, while David played in the garden.[70] The boys were left with their grandmother while Dorothy competed in the London Olympics against her domestic rival, a Physical Education teacher at Wembley School, Bertha Crowther (1921–2012) and eighteen others. Using a self-taught scissor kick, Odam came second to Coachman and finished ahead of France's Micheline Ostermeyer, who had already taken two gold medals in the discus and the shot put.[71] Twenty five year old Ostermeyer might have been named female athlete of the Games, with Australian Shirley Strickland also a storng contender, were it not for Blankers-Koen's dominance.[72]

There were nine athletics events in 1948 for women and new competitive standards set, with one world record and six new Olympic records. However, the British did not feature on the podium for any of the three throwing disciplines (javelin, discus and shot-put) or for the long jump. Nor did they feature in the 4 x 100 relay medals after coming fourth behind teams from the Netherlands, Australia and Canada. The team comprised Dorothy Manley (later Parlett); Maureen Gardner; Muriel Pletts (1931) who also took part in the 100 metres heats, and Margaret Walker (later Prince, 1925) who competed in the 200 metres preliminaries.[73] One thing that the concentration on medalists has ignored was the larger cohort of women who became Olympians and had the experience of representing their country in 1948. For example, contemporary reports were more generous than current estimates in considering top six finishers to be 'winners.'[74]

Appreciating the full female team in 1948 could risk becoming list-like, but for the few winners there were many more who took part: the following includes some of those who participated, along with their date of birth because the collective biography of our Olympians still has to be developed much further: Joan Upton (1922) competed in the 80 metres hurdles; Doris Batter (1929) and Winifred Jordan (1920) took part in the 100 metres heats; Sylvia Cheeseman (1929) ran in the 200 metres; Margaret Birtwhistle (1925) threw the shot put and discus; Gladys Clarke (1923) and Marian Long (1920) cast the javelin; Bertha Crowther (1921) disputed the high jump and the 80 metres hurdles; Margaret Erskine (1925), Lorna Lee (1931) and Joan Shepherd (1924) challenged for the long jump; Dora Gardner (1912) braved the high jump; Bevis Reid (1919) and Elspeth Whyte (1926) contested the shot put and the discus.[75]

In order to keep the focus on the 1948 Olympics for now, the wider culture of British women's athletics has been included in the next section, especially competition under Women's Amateur Athletic Association control, harriers clubs and race walking. An overlooked aspect of the tiny elite who won places, and then a few medals at Olympics was that this did not accurately reflect the strength in depth of cross country or track and field athletics. With a background in both, even Jack Crump could see that female hopefuls suffered from neglect by the sporting establishment, although Lilleshall Hall had been designated by the Central Council of Physical Recreation as a national home for sporting education.[76] It would be an interesting aspect of further study to look at how much the London Olympics of 1948 changed perceptions of women's sport. Although there was help and assistance from both male and female coaches, teachers, administrators and journalists much of it was piecemeal and unfocussed. As such, many girls and women would continue to improvise training regimes themselves. These included Mary Bignall (1940, later Rand, Toomey and Reese) who won the first Olympic Gold

Medal in track and field with a new world record in the long jump at the 1964 Tokyo Olympics.[77]

The lack of resource and political will in Britain's preparation for female amateur athletes meant that domestic neglect, as much as cold war politics, shaped women's access to funding, expertise and competition. A lack of expectation and ambition for Britain's female athletes provided a contrast to those countries, like the United States, Netherlands, Soviet Union and East Germany who saw that winning women's Olympic medals was a relatively easy way of boosting the international prestige of a particular national team. This was not just evident at the Olympic Games: several commentators have indicated that Empire Games held after 1945 began to show the difficult nature of Britain's relationship with the emerging Commonwealth countries. This vague and fractured sense of connection in the 1950s has been characterised by one Canadian writer as 'Liquid imperialism.'[78]

Swimming and diving had many of the same problems as athletic training but also had pockets of coaching excellence. Competitive sports like athletics and swimming were considered to have the potential to overstrain the average child or adolescent in Britain's schools, with more consideration given to regulation and regimentation than free play.[79] Max Ritter, the long-term secretary of the international swimming federation (Fédération Internationale de Natation or FINA) had seen what he thought was progress: 'We have come through an amphibious war, and our amphibious sport has advanced accordingly.'[80] A German who migrated to the United States in 1910, Ritter became President of FINA and co-ordinated membership growth from the eight original national associations at the London Games of 1908 to more than ninety countries at the Tokyo Olympics in 1964. First as a demonstration event in 1952, then as a full medal discipline in 1956, synchronised swimming would be included on the schedule as a female-only event.

The regulation of amateurism was rigid, but US college athletes, intensive training regimes (such as produced Japanese dominance in the 1932 and 1936 Olympic Games) and state-sponsored programmes tended toward increased specialisation and intensive training. In consequence, British female competitors had to be extremely talented and have the good fortune to live near to good facilities with coaching expertise, while also showing considerable dedication. Technical innovation in strokes also saw the butterfly used in men's breast-stroke events, although the Amateur Swimming Association (ASA) in England continued to frown on this practice in domestic competition.[81] By 1953 what the ASA referred to as the dolphin/butterfly stroke was being taught as a distinct variation and would become a discipline in its own right in Olympic competition from 1956.[82]

The return of ASA competition produced two female nineteen-year old 'discoveries' when the national swimming championships resumed in 1946; Nancy Riach (1927–1947) of the Motherwell Amateur Swimming and Water Polo Club in North Lanarkshire, Scotland and Margaret

Wellington (1926, later Restrick) of Beckenham Ladies' Swimming Club, in South London. The rivalry between Scottish industrialism and English metropolitanism was evident in the representation of the two swimmers: Nancy Riach was born in Motherwell, which was the locus of Scottish steel production, and hence known as Steelopolis; while Margaret Wellington worked in London's financial district.

Nancy Riach was a native of Motherwell but was slightly better-off than many of her team mates, as her father rose to the rank of police inspector and her mother was a teacher. Her parents were also part of the Orange order and voted Conservative, whereas the superintendent of the corporation baths, David Crabb was a member of the Communist Party who believed in potential, persuading the Motherwell and Wishaw council to keep the facility open in wartime, as part of his wider belief in working class self-help and improvement.[83] Crabb, unlike most English amateur coaches, trained children as young as eight years old for competition. Having broken into the sport as a twelve year old, Riach had shown ability in crawl, backstroke and breast-stroke before breaking the British 100 yard freestyle record of sixty-one seconds, then one and one-fifth of a second outside the women's world record. Although her religious beliefs prevented Sunday competition, Riach was a star draw at Motherwell club 'swimming circus' galas, often accompanied by pipe and drum music.[84] She also modelled swimwear and a sports journalist with the Glasgow *Sunday Mail*, promoted her as an ideal of Scottish womanhood. She received fan mail from servicemen abroad during the war and it was clearly important that she could beat the English.

By 1946 Riach was to hold over twenty-eight swimming records and was described as the finest swimmer in the British Empire because of her dominance in all strokes.[85] With a supposed slogan: 'The bigger the test, the faster I go' Riach already held a gold medal from the World Youth Games in 1947 and seemed to be the main female British Olympic hope for the London 1948 Olympics.[86] The claim that she swam not for herself but for Scotland became an ominous obligation when Riach fell ill at the 1947 European Swimming Championships in Monte Carlo. She decided to compete against doctor's orders having contracted polio. [87] According to Graham Walker, the swimmer was just one victim of the epidemic then sweeping Britain with 662 cases notified in England and Wales, and over 150 cases in the week before her trip.[88] Having already won a bronze medal in the 4x100 metres freestyle relay, with Catherine Gibson (1931), Lilian Preece (1928) and Margaret Wellington, Riach died at twenty years old. Pathé newsreels covered the large somber crowds at the funeral.[89] Due to infighting, an appeal launched to raise £20,000 did not establish a permanent memorial in Riach's memory. Nor does she appear in Huntington-Whiteley and Holt's *Book of British Sporting Heroes*, maybe because she did not reach a wider audience and a more extensive following. She was, however, recognised in the Scottish Swimming Hall of Fame and the

Scottish Amateur Swimming Association raised a fund which, beginning in 1949, provided a Nancy Riach memorial medal for the person judged to have done the most in each year to promote the sport.

In contrast, Margaret Wellington, more slightly built than Nancy Riach, appeared to benefit from the suburban sophistication of Beckenham, Kent. Wellington declared that she had little natural talent and her weekly visits with the Alexandra Junior School to the local pool were enough to make most coaches weep: 'If there is one thing I have proved in my life as a sportswoman, it is that a national swimming champion can be fashioned out of the most hopeless-looking material.'[90] In this brief autobiographical account of her career, Wellington wrote that she did not take swimming seriously enough to increase her training visits from one to seven days a week until she was fifteen and a half. This had a dramatic effect, as she would finish second in the national 100 yards freestyle final in 1946. She then came a close third to Riach and Gibson at the 1947 national finals and reached Pathé's attention as the 'Mermaid in the City', because she worked at a bank and trained nearby.[91]

Wellington was part of the team that finished fourth in the 4x100 metres freestyle event at the 1948 Summer Olympics with colleagues Cathie Gibson, Patricia Neilsen (1930) and Lilian Preece.[92] We can only speculate whether Riach, rather than Neilsen, might have helped the team to make bronze. Wellington married her coach, Basil Restorick, in 1951 and wrote of the opportunities for travel provided by swimming.[93] These included travelling to the Empire Games in New Zealand in 1950 by boat. A return air trip for the Christchurch Centenary Celebration Games in 1951 took in Rome, Cairo, Karachi, Calcutta, Singapore, Darwin, Fiji, Hawaii, San Francisco, Hollywood and New York. Including five weeks in New Zealand, this trip took two months, enabling Wellington to meet Test cricketers including Denis Compton, in addition to film stars Jane Powell and Dorothy Lamour. Although a relatively minor figure in Britain's Olympic tradition, Wellington's brief moment of fame shows that amateurism could clearly have its benefits. The only other female swimmer on the trip was national backstroke champion in 1938, Helen Yate (1921), who had been able to continue to train during the war in her home-town of Plymouth due to a Women's Royal Navy Service posting there. Yate also benefitted from being de-mobbed to concentrate on her athletic career but, ultimately, finished out of the Olympic medals in 1948 to Denmark's Karen Harup (1924–2009), Suzanne Zimmerman (1925) of the United States and Australia's Judith Davies (1928).[94]

Cathie Gibson (1931, later Brown), another Motherwell-born swimmer, won the lone medal for British swimming in 1948 by taking the bronze in the 400 metres freestyle event. David Crabb's coaching relationship with Nancy Riach may well have staled for a number of reasons before 1947, including that her family moved seven miles away to Airdrie, so that Gibson became his main focus.[95] Therefore intra-regional rivalries and personal politics also fused with any sense of national Scottish identity and wider sense of Britishness. Gibson's father and brothers had close connections with the local pool and she worked as a clerk, often attending competitions alone as the family could not justify the cost of their support in person. Gibson had been almost as famous as Riach: she placed second in both the 400 metres freestyle and 100 metres backstroke and won a bronze in the 100 m freestyle relay at the European championships in Monte Carlo.[96]

However, the loss of Riach placed an additional burden of expectation on Gibson, whose family could not afford to accompany her to London. Travelling alone, she qualified as the fastest loser in the 400 metres freestyle final, rather than in her more favoured backstroke event.[97] Gibson was within half a second of the Olympic record for her bronze medal so its was an overall improvement, perhaps combined with a lack of international race experience. Even so, she did considerably better than her older rival Lorna Frampton (1920), who could not maintain a comeback after twelve years of war and finished out of the medals.

Writing in *The Sports Book* of 1946 W. J. Howcroft had identified Bristol; Carlisle; Leeds; London (particularly the Penguin Club); Merseyside (especially the Garston Club), Newport and Stafford as among the more important centres for youth swimming development, in addition to a return of Oxbridge and college competition. All of this was overshadowed by coaching developments under Crabb's control.[98] Amongst the other possible freestyle individual medalists were Motherwell's Margaret Girvan (1932–1979) and Bromley's Patricia Neilsen, who were considered to be just the right age for swimming competition at fourteen and sixteen years of age respectively. Unlike Neilsen, Girvan would have to wait to become an Olympian until 1956. Although Howcroft dismissed trainee teacher Vera Ellery (1926) as an erratic competitor, she would make the team in London, whereas Pamela Ballantyne, the All-India champion, would not. Phyllis Linton (1929) of Wales would travel widely with her swimming in both Olympic and British Empire Games in the early 1950s without becoming a medalist, having begun the sport to overcome chronic asthma.

Howcroft's predictions for the breast-stroke contenders included Northampton's Elizabeth Church (1930), Glasgow's Helen Orr Gordon (1934, also known as Eleanor Gordon, later Mackay) and Brighton's Jean Caplin (1930) in spite of the latter's recent bout of pneumonia. Howcroft was quite right in these three cases but could not have forseen that Gordon would also take part in the 1952 Olympics to win the sole individual medal in the 200 metres breast-stroke. Thanks to a recent auction of her sporting memorabilia, we can see the change in racing swimwear technology as the standard issue costume changed from the silk suits worn in 1948, to designs made of nylon by 1952.[99] While Gordon competed again in 1956, the outstanding British swimmers in Melbourne were Judy Grinham (1939) and Margaret Edwards (1939) who took gold and bronze in the 100 metres backstroke respectively, with the silver claimed by Carine

Cone of the United States.[100] Gordon's navy blue wool blazer made by Bourne and Hollingworth, luggage labels, memorabilia and programmes were sold as a combined lot for £2500 in 2012 and her experiences are one of several possibly lost to record as a result of having no national museum of sport in Britain.[101]

A lack of racing expertise was perhaps understandable after twelve years of war and the 1939 national backstroke champion, Vivan Basset-Lowke of Northampton was past her best in 1946. Doris Storey (1919) of Leeds was another established competitor in the 1936 Olympic, British Empire and European competition but had spent the war working in a Yorkshire weaving mill and did not return to form. Her younger sister, Thelma, did not quite make the transition to senior competition; nor did Rosina Daymond of Newport, Maureen Jones of Bristol or Pamela Ballantyne, a protégé of Highgate diver Jonny Johnston in Bombay before re-locating to Britain at sixteen.[102] Of course, these things happen, but it would be interesting to know why they did not fulfill their potential. However competitive women's swimming gradually became more diverse with some butterfly, open water and longer events, with Vera Ellery holding a British half-mile freestyle record. The gaps in the biographical record are evident from this summary and more localised study is undoubtedly a way forward in rectifying this.

By 1948 Howcroft seemed more optimistic with the English, Scottish and Welsh Amateur Swimming Associatons operating Olympic schemes however, he thought women's diving had little about which to be encouraged Edna Childs (1922) and Peggy Winterton had appeared to be affected by nerves in Monte Carlo due to 'our sea-bound insularity.'[103] However, Winterton's short-sightedness might also have been a factor since it was reportedly so bad that she was unable to see the water from the high dive board. By experimenting with contact lenses she hoped to become as good as Betty Slade (1921), who had held European titles and had competed in the Berlin Olympic Games. Unfortunately, Winterton would not overcome this disability and Edna Childs competed with Denise Newman of the Mermaid Swimming Club, though her pre-war performances were better than her post-war record.[104] Lettice Bisbrown (1919); Kay Cuthbert (1925); Esme Harris and Maire Hider competed the team.[105] The 1952 women's diving team comprised Dorothy Drew (1934); Valerie Lloyd Chandos (1933); Phyllis Long (1936) who also competed in 1956 and 1960; Diana Spencer (1934) and Charmain Welsh (1937) who also took part in 1956. Probably due to cost, this was the extent of the female diving team in the Melbourne Games. If swimming was a genuinely popular activity from which clubs could draw promising youngsters, the remaining Olympic sports like canoeing, fencing and gymnastics depended on smaller cohorts of participants. As the introduction, has indicated, Britain was represented for the first time without much distinction in the women's kayaking. The foil also had an unbroken tradition of British female representation since the discipline was introduced in the Paris Games of 1924. Unlike canoeing, this included some world-class talent.

The woman who would go on to be the most significant of the British female fencers would not win a medal at the London Games of 1948. Mary Glen Haig (née James, 1918) contested the foil at four Olympic Games from 1948 to 1960. Her colleagues in London were another newcomer, Gytte Minton, and experienced competitor Elizabeth Arbuthnot (1916) who had also competed in 1936. However, Britain's leading foilist of this generation was slightly too young for London 1948, reflecting the different age profile of fencing in comparison with athletics and swimming. Gillian Sheen (1928) had first taken up the sport at North Forland School in Kent and won the schoolgirls title in 1945.[106] She took the Junior Championships in 1947 and, on leaving school, went to University College Hospital, London to train as a dental surgeon. This meant that she occasionally missed important competitions to take exams.

Gillian Sheen won her first senior national title until 1949, took the British Universities title for five consecutive years and won a gold medal at the World Universities Championships in 1951. In the 1952 Olympics she was eliminated in the second round (the gold went to Irene Camber of Italy). However, in 1956 Sheen took the gold medal for Great Britain, also competing in 1960 alongside Glen Haig when a team foil event was added to the schedule.[107] Britain's three female Olympic fencing silver medals (Gladys Davis in 1924; Muriel Freeman in 1928 and Judy Guiness in 1932) had therefore eventually been complemented by a gold. Sheen continued to compete until 1963 before marrying and moving to New York where, as Mrs Donaldson, she set up a dental practice with her husband.

Aileen Harding (1933), a pupil at the Lady Margaret High School in Cardiff, informed readers of *Sport For Girls* that it was possible to begin to master fencing at the relatively advanced age of thirty.[108] However, Harding would be a junior champion who did not made the transition to Olympic competition. She won the Schoolgirls' Foil Championship in 1949 and would be one of seventeen women to represent Wales at the 1954 British Empire Games in Vancouver.[109] Harding took the bronze medal behind Mary Glen Haig and Gillian Sheen but so far there is no evidence of her consideration for Olympic selection. Her article was illustrated with two photographs: the first, of the Women's Royal Navy Service (WRNS) inter-services team of 1950 (comprising Benita Allen of Guildford; Elsie Bone of Sunderland; Jane Williams of Godalming and Prudence Grundy of Hastings). The second showed Glyn Reynolds coaching a group including Shirley Seaborne at Cardiff University.[110] The archives of services and the armed forces sport, plus university collections would therefore seem to be a good place to begin to develop this line of research.

Mary Glen Haig was the most important of the women fencers because she became the third female member of the International Olympic Committee in 1982–1983. The process of her nomination and election was supported by the personal recommendation of HRH Prince Phillip.[111] Glen Haig had been influenced to take up fencing by her father who competed in the 1908 London Games. A senior administrator at Kings College Hospital, she won two gold medals at the British Empire Games in 1950 and 1954. On Glen Haig's retirement from Olympic competition new talents such as Jeanette Bailey (1931); Judith Bain (1944); Jeanette Bewley-Cathie (1940, later Wardell-Yerburgh); Eva Davies; Julia Davis (1941); Susan Green (1950); Shirley Netherway (1937); Thoresa Offredy (1930); Mary Stafford and Mary Watts-Tobin (1939) represented Britain in the 1960s and early 1970s.[112] Though the social mix of these athletes was not very diverse, the access of women to further and higher education can be read in the number able to take up such a specialised activity.[113]

Glen Haig was asked to become Chair of the Central Council of Physical Recreation during the 1970s, with support from important administrators within English sport, including Sir Denis Follows, Secretary of the Football Association. Follows was a cautious moderniser of women's sport and helped to overturn the FA's ban on women's football in 1970, which earned him an honourary lifetime Presidency of the Women's Football Association.[114] Very much part of England's sporting establishment then, Glen Haig was appointed a Member of the Order of the British Empire (MBE) in 1971; promoted to Commander (CBE) in the 1977 and made Dame Commander (DBE) in the 1993 New Year Honours. Having been awarded honourary membership of the IOC since 2008, Glen Haig is currently suffering from ill health and therefore had an ambassadorial, rather than an active, role in the 2012 London Olympic Games.

Finally then, to the women gymnasts: Team competitions had been held in 1928, 1936 and 1948. Holland and Germany has taken the previous gold medals and on this occasion Czechoslovakia, Hungary and the United States team filled the podium. The Czech victory was particularly poignant as one of their team had died while in London. The eight-woman British team in 1948 came ninth: they were Joan Airey, Cissie Davies (1932); P. Evans; Dorothy Hey; Irene Hurst (1930); Mary Hirst (1918); Audrey Rennard; and Dorothy Smith.[115] The official report does not mention Clarice Bell (1911, previously Hanson) but she may have been a reserve. A pigtailed seventeen-year-old Italian performer, L. Micheli, came third overall and charmed the British officials in the process so it is worth correcting a perception that gymnastics became infantilised as a direct result of Cold War politics in the 1970s.[116]

Also judged a success were demonstration events of men's lacrosse and a demonstration of Swedish gymnastics by 200 female and 200 male performers affiliated to the Svenska Gymnastikforbundet of Stockholm.[117] The latter was particularly significant, for in 1949 15,000 gymnasts participated in the second Lingiad (an international festival to celebrate the teaching of Per Henrick Ling) at the Olympic Stadium in Stockholm involving some 600 Britains.[118] There were overlaps with general body cultures and 'fitness' regimes away from sport. In 1952 an individual Women's Artistic Gymnastic competition was added to the Olympic schedule, comprising floor exercises; vault; uneven bars; balance beam; as well as an overall personal medal and a team competition. At the 1952 Helsinki Games, the Soviet Union women's gymnastics team won the first of its eight consecutive gold medals. The inaugural edition was dominated by the Soviet Union, Hungary and Czechoslovakia.

Women from a range of countries achieved many successes in the final round of Olympic medals in the Arts competition in 1948.[119] Further analysis of this last edition before the idea of a cultural Olympiad took hold, and particularly the wider effects on design history, require our consideration but this is not the place for that discussion.[120] In drawing this section of the London Olympic Games of 1948 to a close, it perhaps suited war-weary Britain to be told by the President of the International Olympic Committee, Siegried Edström that the aesthetic gloss of London had worked:

> Wembley Stadium itself, where day after day huge crowds assembled, has surpassed in magnificence and convenience any previous home of the Games. All the other Olympic venues, too were splendidly organised both from the spectators' and competitors' point of view. Torquay I found much nicer than Nice; Henley recaptured the atmosphere of the old, old days; while at Aldershot and Sandhurst competitions went on in the friendliest manner.'[121]

MORE FOR THE JOY THAN THE FAME? POST-WAR PROFESSIONAL AND AMATEUR SPORTS

The 1951 survey already referred to in this chapter in *Sport For Girls* coincided with a year of national reflection and celebration, culminating in the Festival of Britain. The Festival had, for the most part, taken part in fine weather. This also helped to produce large audiences for the visiting Australian women's cricket team at Old Trafford in Manchester, Trent Bridge in Nottingham and The Oval, London the same year. When the young women between eleven and eighteen years were asked by the questionnaires issued by the editors of *Sport For Girls* which sports they preferred to watch, cricket was the clear favourite in the top ten with 75% expressing an interest, followed by soccer (54%); ice hockey (47%); rugby (45%); speedway (35%); lawn tennis (28%); swimming (28%); horse racing or jumping (12%); hockey (11%) and netball (9%).[122]

Many young women were fans of the top male cricket players, so it seems respondents had access to newspapers or live sport. It is hard to say if the tour by the Australian women (only the second to England after a gap of fourteen years) had further popularised the game.[123] Particularly intriguing here, was the degree if interest in 'new' sports like ice hockey and speedway but traditional team games like soccer, rugby and cricket indicate that we may have to think about female fans inside and outside the ground during this period. The findings were in marked contrast to the top eleven participant sports for young women in the same investigation. This read: rounders (92.5%); netball (86%); swimming (78%); lawn tennis (77.5%); hockey (75%); cycling (73.5%); table tennis (66%); athletics (46%); ice and roller skating (39%); cricket (38%) and badminton (14%). Football had a dismal 0.5% participation rate amongst girls in spite of the continuation of teams like Dick, Kerr's Ladies until the mid 1960s. However, this may have reflected that it was an adult worker's sport rather than a school-based game so the findings have to be read in conjunction with other information.

The questionnaire was completed by thirteen schools located in Birmingham; Camarthanshire; Devonshire; Derbyshire; two institutions in Glamorganshire; Liverpool; London; Manchester; Northamptonshire; Northumberland; Nottinghamshire and Yorkshire. Without giving too much significance to the findings therefore, sport appears to have compared favourably with other hobbies such as reading (50%); dancing (36%); collecting, including stamps (35%); needlework (23%); music (19.6%); hiking (18%); arts and crafts (9%); theatre and radio (6%) and gardening (3.7%). Cricket was declared to be the 'favourite' sport for young women because of the combination of spectator interest and participation, but this was the interpretation of the compiler rather than a wider consensus. It raises the intriguing question how far a girls' taste for sport might be moulded by her family and the role played by individuals in engaging her interest. Perhaps many fathers thought cricket an appropriate game with which to bond with their daughter, or should researches be looking in the direction of mothers, brothers, aunts and uncles?

That schools should be the focus of the questionnaire, rather than community clubs, reflected a new emphasis on provision for the young in British life after the Second World War. There remains considerable debate as to how radically this changed after 1945 or whether this represented any kind of politics of consensus.[124] The wider concern with social inclusion came to the fore during World War II, articulated by the 1942 Beveridge Report which sought dispose of the five main obstacles to reconstruction: want, disease, ignorance squalor and idleness.[125] A Labour government was elected in 1945 with a large majority under Clement Atlee and pledged to craft the 'welfare state'; combining collective social rights with individual freedom and responsibilities. Rather than a moment of 'creation' on 5 July 1948, the welfare state comprised a whole series of legislative changes to social security (Family Allowance Act, 1945; National Insurance Act, 1946 and the National Assistance Act in 1948); health (the creation of a National Health Service, 1944 and the National Health Service Act in 1946); housing (New Towns Act, 1946 and the Town And Country Planning Act in 1948) education and welfare (the Butler Education Act, 1944 and the Children Act in 1948).[126] Between 1945 and 1951 one-fifth of the economy came under public ownership by Labour governments: nationalisation took place across the railways; gas; electricity; coal and steel industries, in addition to the Bank of England.[127]

These reforms generally benefitted women to a lesser extent than men, given traditional elements within the Labour administration and the emphasis on full employment rather than equal pay.[128] Class could be important and exclusive policies in educational establishments left the proportion of female university students at about 25% until the 1960s. Welfare-related policies were to be subsequently contested, as both taxation and labour market issues had limited attention. As work using the Mass Observation archives at the University of Sussex, Brighton have also shown, the large-scale transition from war to peace could have very personal interpretations.[129] Conscious attempts to enact wide-scale change could produce a degree of unpopularity: although it won 48.8% of all votes cast in the 1951 election (a higher proportion than the victorious Conservative party), Labour would not hold a secure Commons majority again until 1966.[130] The Suez crisis in 1956 undermined confidence in international relations while expectations of a more comfortable and secure life were not always fulfilled.[131]

Nevertheless, compared with 1939, when 88% of the population left education at the age of fourteen, the Education Act of 1944 established free secondary education for all, and more people were educated for longer periods of their lives than ever before.[132] Comprehensive education had its critics and class continued to shape privilege in grammar schools and university entrance, but a chance for every child became a wider societal aspiration.[133] Meritocracy was by no means a uniformly agreed upon principle or a fact in many lives, but it was an increasingly discussed idea.

It is this broader set of debates, heavily inflected by post-war conservatism and the self-conscious modernisation shown by the welfare state, that this section of the chapter explores. Given the challenge of space, coverage is indicative: there were smaller and more localised discussions within each sport, which future studies will unpick. Concerns about amateur and professional status, funding, youth development, national identity and entertaining the whole family were evident in most activities, however. We therefore see a range of views and a more diverse interpretation of sport and leisure than are normally discussed in texts that focus solely on Olympic events in this period.

The Olympic Games were therefore subject to much wider discourses about what sport should achieve and who should be involved. This included discussions about the role of the state, the responsibility of individuals and of national groups dedicated to recreational and elite fitness. Maureen Dyson's chapter argued: 'This is an age in which physical fitness is essential in keeping pace with the fast moving life of 1951 and it is just as essential for the woman to keep herself attuned to the pace of life as the man.'[134] Vocational articles demonstrated that elite career and sport-related jobs were increasingly possible: *Sport For Girls* pieces included those written by tennis professional Gussy Moran (1923–2012); politician Elaine Burton (1904–1991); hotel proprietor and snooker professional Thelma Carpenter; farmer and equestrian Elizabeth Harland; journalists and broadcasters

Audrey Russell, Marjorie Pollard, Sylvia Gray and Winifred Munday; landscape gardener Marjorie Mc Quade and teachers Margaret Boyd, Ursula Gunnery and Ursula Bryan. Though sports are presented in alphabetical order in the second section of this chapter therefore, this is not intended as an encyclopedic view of women's sport in 1940s and 1950s Britain. Nor is it comprehensive in the sense of concentrating solely on the most important examples. Some niche interests and minority activities are included to show a range of sports and recreation that developed away from high-profile Olympic tournaments.

BOWLS

Contemporary texts suggested that the tension between development for the many and the few was keenly debated across a range of sports. The Secretary of the English Bowling Association (EBA) reported that there were thirty-one county associations with 1,691 clubs, and eighteen minor associations affiliated to the organisation in November 1945.[135] The national championships for 1946 attracted 28,424 competitors. Since these figures only relate to the EBA, other unaffiliated clubs would have been active and it has been difficult to assess the number of women players, as the archivist at Bowls England was unable to give any registration figures for this period.[136] Some bowls enthusiasts had links with other sports, such as the Orpington club, founded in 1929 as an adjunct of the local tennis and hockey premises. Others clubs had women's sections and some were also women-only organisations.

Given the extent of this activity, Herbert Collings, a prominent journalist of the sport, chided the International Bowling Board (IBB) for their reticence in recognising female competitors.

> Women players have come into bowls and having been given the freedom of the green by both private and public green clubs, they have come to stay [sic]. In some clubs they play side by side with the men; in others they play on rinks reserved for them. But, although women players have their own national associations, international matches and national championships, they are not recognised by the International Bowling Board or the men's national associations [sic]. Their open tournaments are not licensed by the IBB. Mixed tournaments, triples and rinks are prohibited by that body. A woman tennis player may play with her husband in mixed doubles in the Centre Court at Wimbledon but a woman bowls player must not partner her husband in a mixed pairs game at Hastings & St. Leonards or any open tournament.[137]

In 1930 bowls had made its debut at the Commonwealth Games, in Hamilton, Canada but women were not included in the schedule. Collings considered that an ongoing exclusion from IBB activity was inappropriate to post-war reconstruction as it was 'The governing body of bowls for men throughout the every English-speaking country in the world' but had no control over women's associations or women players.[138] The paradox was a tension in the regulation and development of sport that several international federations and governing bodies would share in the remainder of the twentieth century. However, away from the gendered structural cultures of world-governing bodies, more localised voluntarism and amateur enthusiasm could provide networking opportunities for women.

Age, class and family commitments were not as defining in limiting sporting involvement as they have been held to be.[139] One of the consistent narratives in Sport For Girls was that there should be more provision for younger and older women rather than just young adult female participants. Flat and crown green versions of bowls had shown considerable development, especially for older competitors after Ethel Tiggs ('Tiggie'), along with Clara Johns, instigated the English Women's Bowling Association in 1931.

> Grandmothers in their sixties and seventies are still winning honours in the most severe of national and county tests. A few streamlined and comparatively young women made their appearance in 1947, but the experienced 'veterans' more than held their own against the newcomers. The right temperament for match play at bowls cannot be developed in one season . . . Mrs E. S. Tigg of Kingston Canbury B.C. is the outstanding woman player of the moment, capable of giving any single-handed champion a good game. [140]

The age and social profile of Britain's sporting women can therefore partly be assessed via a range of activities not often considered in sport history. Friends and neighbours would have aware of the quotidian interests of women like Tiggie, who blended an enthusiasm for bowls with her other daily activities.[141] This did not mean that enthusiasts were not important or elite performers.

Although biographical detail remains sparse, Ethel Tigg helped to found the Waddon Residents club in 1922 and oversaw the launch of the Surrey County Women's Bowls Association in 1931 with the Countess of Rosebery (Dame Eva Primrose, 1892–1987) as its patron.[142] This was a key step in the creation of the English Women's Bowling Association in 1931. Ethel Tigg then took both the inaugural Surrey county and national singles titles in 1932.[143] A well-known bowling personality, Tiggie went on to have an international career between 1932 and 1936, before returning to England duty between 1947 and 1948.[144] She maintained an active administrative career as Secretary of the Oxsted and Limpsfield Ladies Bowling Club between 1921–1932; the honourary competition Secretary for Waddon Residents Bowling Club from 1933–1945 and Secretary for the English Women's Bowls Association (EWBA) from 1931 until 1945. Although it was titled an

English association, plenty of clubs from Ireland, Scotland and Wales were affiliated in the 461 listed in the yearbook for 1951, in addition to mixed clubs involving female members not necessarily included.[145]

The Collings excerpt also ties in with lines of more general enquiry already raised in previous chapters. Few historians of sport have examined the sporting and social enthusiasms of married or cohabiting couples.[146] As previous chapters have indicated, our understanding of domestic relations and the use of shared space will remain arguably incomplete without knowing how individuals spent their leisure time both in, and away from, home.[147] Like bowling, the Archery International, inaugurated in 1930, had teams of ten men and ten women, so friendly international competition helped to provide a focus for national interest. This spanned a wide range of ages. The junior national champion in 1948 was Ann Penelope Marston (1938), while the leading adult competitor was Mrs Petronella De Wharton Burr, twice Archery International winner and the wife of the headmaster of Belmont Preparatory School, near Brighton.[148] Although archery often had far fewer club members than other sports, famous couples included Ingo and Erna Simon, of Jewish descent and both world champions. The Simon's spent many years researching the history of archery and donated their collection to Manchester Museum in 1946.[149] The broad principle of looking at sporting companionship applies across a range of activity whether people lived alone, co-habited or were married for at least some of their lives. Why did the Simon's excel at archery? What did Ethel Tigg's husband think of his wife's bowls career? What were the domestic arrangements that facilitated this sporting enthusiasm?

CRICKET

The regional breakdown of the *Sports For Girls* survey of participation in various activities identified that cricket was more popular in Derbyshire (75%); Northampton (61%); Yorkshire (53%); Manchester (45%); Glamorganshire (44%) and Nottingham (44%) than Liverpool and Birmingham (both 36%); Devon (31%); Camarthanshire (20%) or Northumberland (17%).[150] It was not listed as an activity for the London school used, so this was perhaps dependent on the facilities and enthusiasm of particular institutions. Marjorie Pollard claimed that the WCA had 120 women's clubs and over 100 girls' schools as affiliates by 1951, with an active youth policy in spite of the limited number of pitches available.[151] Given the continuity between school and adult cricket, it may not be surprising to find that many amateurs worked in education, but others came from the factory or shop floor; offices and administration.

The honourary secretary of the Midland Counties Women's Cricket Association during this period, Eileen White, had been born in 1912, the middle child of Nottingham couple Grace and Percy White.[152] Eileen had an elder sister, Marjorie (born in 1910) and younger brother, Kenneth (born in 1918). Educated at Mundella Grammar School in Nottingham, Eileen played cricket and hockey at school from ten years of age. The family have photos of her in the Mundella Cricket side at about the age of fourteen in 1926 and she later captained the school team. In this she was fortunate, in more ways than one. Only 13% of girls went to the two city-based Grammar schools, Mundella and Manning, while High Pavement served the county. Of these, Mundella had the strongest tradition for cricket. The game was already popular in the family as two of Eileen's uncles, Herman W. Dexter and John Dexter, played semi-professionally. Another uncle, Walter Dexter, was an umpire.

On leaving school, Eileen began to work as an auditor for Boots in Nottingham, helping to start the Notts County Women's Cricket Association in 1933 and remaining on the committee for three decades. She also held a membership of Trent Bridge. White played for the Boots works' side (which had been established in 1918) as first bat, captain and secretary from 1933 until 1945. Then she founded a more informal team based on friendships called the Nottingham Casuals Cricket Club and remained as captain and secretary until a serious accident ended her active career in 1954.[153] Eileen then turned to golf. Before that, she seems to have been a consistently very good, if not a great, player.

From 1933 to 1952, Eileen White was opening bat for the Nottingham county side; from 1936 to 1954 she was opener for the Midland's region and her career high was scoring seventy-nine runs against the Australian Touring team in 1951, after being coached by Bill Voce.[154] Eileen was part of local, regional and national rivalries as she played against teams including: Player's Cigarette Factory; Lyons Tea-House; the biscuit and confectionary manufacturer Peak Freans; Nottingham University; Chesterfield University College; Civil Service headquarters; British Drug Houses; Mansfield Shoe manufacturers and a collective named simply, Nottingham. A member of the Women's Cricket Association executive; umpire; chief liaison officer with overseas touring teams and lead-organiser of some Test matches, Eileen White was an active force for cricket in the region, at national and international level. Nor was cricket her only enthusiasm; she performed and made costumes for the Nottingham Theatre Club; the People's Theatre; West Bridgford Operatic Society and the City Opera Players.

Eileen White's varied interests offer an interesting perspective as to how regional differences could affect women's work and leisure. While there seems to be a broad consensus that women comprised about one-third of the workforce outside the home in the 1950s, Nottingham had a proportion of female labour 10% higher than the average figure for England and Wales (although figures generally tend to underestimate casual work).[155] The city's reputation as 'Queen of the Midlands', in part reflected the greater visibility of women in the workforce but also the number and variety of public houses, dance halls, cinemas and entertainments. White's scrapbooks represent continuity between her business, sporting and social contacts. It is highly unlikely that those with whom she worked did not know about her social interests and vice versa since the WCA often listed professional addresses as well as personal details.[156]

White's lifetime collection of pictures, postcards, dinner invitations and small written notes self-consciously memorialise events, places and people. Menu cards, badges, programmes and personalised clothing enrich our understanding of women's experiences of sport and sociability immeasurably as aspects of material history. Although a peripheral player for England therefore, and not mentioned in a book written to mark fifty years of women's Test cricket, Eileen's personal collection testifies to how sport shaped the life experience of like-minded women. In turn, the sources show how Eileen's patient dedication to cricket as a player, administrator and enthusiast helped to define the forms that it took.[157]

The 1951 England and Australia Test match series perhaps attracted more popular comment than usual because, in men's cricket, the South African team were to visit the same year and the rivalry was not so intense.[158] It helped that in Festival of Britain year, Australia's women cricketers were defending their Test victory of 1948–1949. With one win each and a draw, the series was as much a victory for diplomacy and was followed by a Test against New Zeeland in 1954. Helped by increasing prosperity, women's Test cricket became contested with more frequently: England travelled to Australia and New Zealand in 1957–1958 and 1968–1969; Australia returned to England in 1963; New Zealand revisited in 1966. Having hosted the Australians in a game versus the Midlands, Eileen White was the overall lead co-ordinator of the 1954 visit by New Zealand and oversaw the second Test match, played at the County Ground, Worcester.[159]

There were clearly defined protocols for receiving guests, entertaining dignitaries and providing related teas or social functions for many of the tours. Each had a meticulously ordered separate file in Eileen's collection. As well as these international developments, high profile Tests helped the overall interest in women's cricket so that by 1953 there were estimated to be 9,000 female players across 330 clubs. These included colleges and schools; affiliates from the army, navy and air force teams; clubs from both the Republic and Northern Ireland; Australia; Holland; New Zealand and South Africa.[160]

Neville Cardus felt in 1951 that the Australian women came from a wider social background than the English: Mollie Dive held a BSc from Sydney University and worked as a research officer in the Commonwealth Scientific Organisation; Ruth Dow was a fifth-year medical student; the opening bat, Mary Allit was a farmer and horse trainer; wicket keeper, Gladys Philips a machinist; Betty Wilson, a clerk and Amy Hudson a factory supervisor.[161] With developing biographical work on more of the players involved, we could begin to debate if he was correct in this perception. Muriel Lowe (1914–1966), who played for Boots and England in 1937, ran a travel agency and by 1944 Eileen White had re-trained as a psychiatric social worker, for example. A protégé of White's at the Casuals was Enid Bakewell (1941), who became a physical education teacher and was reportedly the first woman to score over 1,000 runs and taking more than 100 wickets in an international Test, during the England Women's tour of Australia and New Zealand in 1968–1969.[162]

As Martin Polley has pointed out, women's cricket was the first in a series of female sports to set up a world cup competition in 1973 (two years before the men's competition was created), with women's football and rugby union following suit in 1991.[163] At the 1993 Cricket Women's World Cup Australia teams from the following nations contested the honours: Denmark; England; Holland; Ireland; India; New Zealand and the West Indies.[164] These matches were hosted at prestigious grounds, which included the John Player Sports Ground in Nottingham; Charterhouse College; Eton College, the Bank of England Sports Ground at Roehampton and Wellington College, Berkshire. Still very interested in the game when she died in 2008 at age 96, Eileen White would have seen the dramatic changes from the establishment of the Women's Cricket Association to the expanded World Cup competition. While these tournaments (like the expansion of the Olympic Games) created more spaces for the expression of national identity, there were many other aspects of identity, patronage and commercial opportunities that remain to be disclosed.

CYCLING

Eileen Sheridan (1924), the outstanding woman cyclist of her generation was five feet (1.5 metres) tall and just over seven stone (46 kilos). Born in Coventry, Eileen began as a tourer in 1944 with her local club and had her first child, Clive, in 1947. Although unimaginative journalists continued to call her 'The Housewife Cyclist' throughout her career, Sheridan quickly returned to racing form to take the leading amateur titles (including distances of 25, 50 and 100 miles) in both 1949 and 1950.[165] This culminated in receiving the Bidlake Trophy for the finest performances by a man or woman in 1950 by way of celebrating the increased standard of women's cycling generally. Then, in an effort to take all the twenty available national records from 25 to 1,000 miles governed by the Women's Road Records Association (WRRA), Sheridan contacted Hercules cycles of Birmingham to invite them to custom-build to her specification and sponsor her activities. Claiming that no amateur could fund such a schedule, Sheridan aimed to beat the sixteen records held by Marguerite Wilson (1918) whose professional career as a cyclist was interrupted by the war. Also known as 'The Blonde Bombshell', Wilson had won the annual Bidlake Memorial Prize in 1939 for completing the Land's End to John O'Groats distance in 2 days 22 hours and 52 minutes and 1,000 miles in 3 days 11 hours and 44 minutes.

After the war she worked as an air-steward for BOAC. Sheridan's first professional ride in 1952, from London to Portsmouth and back, beat Wilson's record by nearly three minutes, a pattern that continued.

Professional cycling under Women's Road Records Association rules was an odd form of professionalism, however. Strict rules against advance publicity were intended to prevent crowds gathering at key points during a record attempt, including at the finish. When the *Daily Mirror* announced an attempt on the Lands End to London record attempt in advance, Sheridan was disqualified, although she beat the existing time by 23 minutes. After taking twenty-one titles, Sheridan retired to have her second child and in 1956 published her autobiography *Wonder Wheels*, which she dedicated to her father 'Who always encouraged me to believe that anything was possible.'[166] The Land's End to John O'Groats record of two days and eleven hours became her most popularly celebrated feat.[167] Her influence on young club cyclists, like Eileen Newman (1930) of the Central Wheelers Cycling Club and Valerie Tomlinson, a staff member of the Cyclists' Touring Club was evidenced in *Sport For Girls*.[168]

This combination of record breaking and touring could also advertise parts of the British Isles as tourist venues for those keen to travel and either unwilling or unable to do so by motor transport. Racing cycles, touring with friends and using the latest gadgets to compete were all evident in press coverage of female leisure on the Isle of Man, for example, for those who could not afford the £40 or so to make it over to the mainland of Europe.[169] After developing skills as a glass engraver following her retirement from competition, Sheridan would continue to be involved in cycling in Coventry, the Midlands and internationally although she has been ignored by histories of sport in the city.[170] Her duties included acting as chaperone to Jo Bowers (1935) and Beryl Burton (1937) to the 1962 world pursuit championships in Milan.[171] Several of Sheridan's records lasted for a decade or more in spite of the creative nature of the support systems used to facilitate the longer distances, which included a glorified caravan/ toilet arrangement on a low-loader lorry. Although many people regard Beryl Burton as the greatest female British cyclist never to have appeared at an Olympic Games, a handful of Sheridan's records remain unbeaten today. Burton and Sheridan were by no means alone.

EQUESTRIANISM

Like many of the sports covered here, post-war equestrianism covered a multitude of activities. In some sense there were continuities with motorsport, since access to the best resources available could dictate the success of an individual woman's career. Put simply, women have had the most success in equestrian sport when they owned their own horses, had access to training facilities and could afford (as an amateur or professional) to enter events under their own control. As such, combined training competitions such as Eventing (dressage, a test of speed and endurance over fences and show jumping) and individual specialisation, such as dressage or show-jumping provide more evidence of wide female participation than racing, on the flat or over hurdles.

World War II saw the mechanisation of cavalry battalions, which weakened the military links with the Olympic versions of dressage, show-jumping and eventing which had been reserved until that point for officers. In British post-war civilian life, more people used cycles or motor transport for and so the horse increasingly became linked with leisure, rather than work. The International Olympic Committee and Fédération Équestre Internationale (FEI, founded in 1921) gradually admitted women to the three disciplines at the Games, beginning with dressage in 1952, show-jumping in 1956 and three-day eventing (combining dressage, jumping and cross-country) in 1964. At the equestrian events held during the Berlin Games in 1936 only twenty-nine riders from eleven countries had competed; while the 1948 London Games had forty-six entrants; subsequent to the 1952 Helsinki Olympics, the top twenty-five competitors in each discipline competed for the final rounds. Pat Smythe (1928–1996) would not appear at the 1948 Olympic Game but was obliged to lend her horse to the male British team to help their efforts, though it was not used. By 1947 her performance at the first International Horse Show at the White City meant selection to the British team, an international career that continued until 1963.[172] Following her win at the 1949 Grand Prix in Brussels she was named leading show-jumper of the year and her dominance in national championships continued between 1952 and 1962.

Smythe was not alone. Ireland's Iris Kellet (1926–2011) won the Dublin Grand Prix in 1948. The following year she won the Princess Elizabeth Cup at the White City, London, on her horse Rusty and came second the following year.[173] Such rivalry meant that horse-riding developed a notable female following as a post-war sport open to those outside of the military. Smythe and Kellet also helped to popularise equestrian television spectacle involving physical courage and elegance.[174] In spite of its upper class associations, the rules of show jumping were relatively easy to understand and time limits made the events exciting. Much of the popularity was based on a David and Goliath motif, such as the Horse of the Year duel in 1950 between the relatively diminutive Smythe and Finality tying for equal first place with the statuesque Harry Llewellyn and his horse Foxhunter.[175] As Sportswoman of the Year in 1952 (with Len Hutton as sportsman) Smythe ranked in Britain's sporting elite at a young age. Madame Tussads made a waxwork; she guest appeared on BBC Radio 4 programme *The Archers* and then *Desert Island Discs*.

However, fame did not bring a steady rise to financial security. The early death of Smythe's father and then her mother in a road accident in 1953 left Pat to manage and finance her show-jumping career single-handedly. She endorsed the carbonated drink Lucozade and Harry Hall clothing, and in co-operation with the British Equestrian Fund, won prize money and amassed other valuable items such as Rolex watches.[176] The IOC president Avery Brundage, was troubled by her writing, but so long as it was suspended for the duration of Olympic competition, did not disqualify her. Although she seemed to be a sporting icon for a more meritocratic Britain, Smythe was also astute in shaping her own public image as a hardworking woman who had earned her opportunities, and overcame personal tragedy by sheer determination.[177] To grieve for her mother for example, she took a short skiing trip before returning to the Cotswolds to redouble her efforts to manage the survival of the family farm.

Women were invited to compete for show-jumping medals for the first time in the Olympic Games in 1956 and Smythe, as part of the British team, won bronze. She had already been made an OBE the same year and was a published author with the first of several autobiographies called *Jump For Joy* (1954), also writing for the *Daily Express*. At the 1960 Rome Olympic Games two of the British show jumping squad were women, though only three representatives were allowed to ride in the team competition. Dawn Wofford (née Palethorpe, 1936) came twentieth overall in the individual competition and Pat Smythe came eleventh on Flanagan. With three refusals, the British team was disqualified before Smythe had a chance to compete. Dawn Palethorpe followed Pat Smythe's lead by moving into writing, publishing *My Horses and I* in 1956, as well as encouraging young riders as an executive of the Pony Club.[178]

The 1950s and early 1960s were, then, important times for a swift change in the image of horse riding. In 1947 the Pony Club had 1,700 members, by 1962 this had grown to over 30,000; and, after a peak of 43,000 registrations in 1982 it current membership stands at approximately 32,000 young people.[179] The Riding for the Disabled Association (RDA incorporating Carriage Driving) was established in 1965 to provide exercise, therapy and fun. Originally the Advisory Council on Riding for the Disabled, its membership grew quickly to become one of the most successful of sporting charities, with current estimates of 18,000 volunteers facilitating 430,000 rides and drives for 28,000 participants.[180] There were also wider changes. With eleven books on the market and two more to be published in 1961, Smythe could afford to buy Sudgrove in the Cotswolds with 150 acres and a pig farm. She married Sam Koechlin, father of three small children, in September 1963 and had two daughters, Monica and Lucy. This was hardly a retirement to the domestic sphere though. Joining the World Wildlife Fund in 1961, Pat Smythe used her fame to draw attention to the need for conservation of animals and natural resources.

Horse-racing has already been covered by Caroline Ramsden, Joyce Kay and Roger Munting, so it has less space here, though there are estimates of women making up almost a third of the crowd at some major events.[181] While Florence Nagle (1894–1988) had trained her first winner in 1920, Jockey Club attitudes meant that licenses were held by a husband or male employee, usually the head stable lad, until 1966.[182] Helen Johnstone Houghton (1910–2011) became the first woman trainer to win an English Classic when Gilles de Retz won the 2,000 Guineas at 50–1 in 1956. However, her husband had been killed while out hunting in 1956 and so the win was recorded in the name of Helen's then assistant, Charles Jerdein, who eventually ended up as an art dealer 'Selling old masters to old mistresses' in New York.[183] It was clearly nonsense that Nagle needed protecting from a male racing environment and she took the Jockey Club to court. They conceded the case before the action was heard, recognising that it was out of touch.[184] Thirty years after her application was refused by the Jockey Club with the words 'Women are not persons within the meaning of the Rules (of Racing)', Norah Wilmot (1887–1988) became the first to train a winning horse under their rules in August 1966.[185] Between the granting of licenses and 1973 seventeen women became recognised trainers and had collectively trained over 300 winners.

Attitudes to female jockeys were less enlightened than those towards trainers. Women could be preferred by trainers as stable staff and work riders since they were perceived to have a more gentle and encouraging riding style than male jockeys. So far as racing though, in July 1966 the National Hunt Committee announced that they would allow women to ride against men in designated events over hurdles. Judy Goodhew (1942) had already competed under her husband's license and applied in 1971 to ride under The Jockey Club Rules (after it had amalgamated the National Hunt Committee) but was refused.[186]

The Lady Jockey Association was formed in response with Meriel Tufnell (1948) in the Chair and, after an eighteen-month campaign, the Jockey Club again conceded the point.[187] Found to have had dislocated hips at birth, Tufnell had persisted in a range of equestrian sports since childhood. She rode Scorched Earth in a field of twenty-one runners to win the Goya Ladies' Race at Kempton in May 1972, with a first prize of £949.[188] A further ten races followed that year. Outside of racing and training, Tufnell took up golf and clay pigeon shooting, including at Bisley. Her own childhood disabilities led her to become patron of SPARKS (Sports Aiding Medical Research for Kids), where golf and shooting days became important fund raising events. However, with only one or two professional jockeys today compared with about 146 registered as amateurs, the legacy of Tufnell and her contemporaries is difficult to judge.[189] Women trainers were not always supportive of female riders in big races and, as events like the Grand National receive increasing criticism from the general public for cruelty, there is a residual risk shared by women who pursue sports with high injury rates.

GOLF

Women golfers were also competing internationally from the 1940s onwards. This was most conspicuous in the United States and particularly against sporting legend Mildred Ella Didrickson-Zaharias (1911–1956).[190] Babe Zaharias rose to fame at the 1932 Olympic Games, taking a gold in the 80 metres hurdles and javelin and a silver in the high jump before moving into golf in 1934, often finding the amateur/ professional rules to her disadvantage. After winning the 1946 US Women's title and the 1947 British Ladies championship as an amateur, she then dominated the Ladies Professional Golf Association of which she was a founding member.[191] The 1947 victory marked the first occasion that a player from the United States had taken the British title and Zaharias played to the gallery with trick shots and highland flings. With at least eighty-five major titles to her name, Babe was still the leading US women's golfer when she died. However, her athleticism, changing appearance, child-less marriage to professional wrestler George Zaharias and capacity for self-promotion made her one of those sporting figures who continue to mean a range of things to different people.

Individual stars like Zaharias aside, there is a critical mass of biographical work still to do on women's golf. Jean Hetherington won the first postwar British women's title in 1946 from Philomena Garvey (1926-2009) of Ireland, while Jaqueline Gordon was runner up to Zaharias in 1947. Other Scottish notables were Jean Donald; Belle Mc Corkindale; Moira Patterson and Jessie Valentine. Catherine MacCann and Valerie Reddan of Ireland also made the finals of British Ladies Amateur Golf Championship, winning in 1951 and coming runner up in 1949 respectively. Significant English players included Farnham's Molly Wallis, Birkdale's Frances Stephens, Ferndown's Maureen Ruttle, Yorkshire's Peggie Burton and Manchester's Peggy Edwards.[192] In spite of the chauvenistic tone of the following excerpt, there was a general consensus of the need to rationalise the women's game.

> Lastly, one great and overdue reform concerns the handicapping system. Women golfers, under the Ladies' Golf Union, has a handicapping scheme so complex that it is incomprehensible to the masculine mind, but it has one virtue at least—the grip which it holds on all members of the L. G. U. clubs. Their handicaps may undergo frequent changes, but they always reflect current form, and if sufficient cards are not returned within a stated period, the handicap lapses altogether. Despite the standard scratch score system of the English Golf Union, it is still possible for men golfers to retaining high handicaps for reasons of avarice, or to keep low ones at the dictates of vanity.[193]

The first Curtis Cup Match, had been contesed by female amateurs of the United States Golf Association and the Ladies Golf Union in 1932 at the Wentworth Club in England. With a biennial format won by the United States between 1932 and 1950, the Great Britain and Ireladn team had won for the first time on home soil at Muirfiled in Scotland in 1952. In

preparation to defend the title at Merion Gold Club, Ardmore Pennyslva-
nia in 1954, the LGU had nominated three players, Jeanne Bisgood, Jessie
Valentine and Philomena Garvey to co-ordinate preparations as the respec-
tive champions of England, Scotland and Ireland. It was not to be. Lady
Katherine Cairns had been the first captain of a Great Britain and Ireland
team to take the trophy in 1952, a feat that would be repeated in 1956,
under the captaincy of Zara Bolton, and again in 1958 led by Ireland's
Daisy Ferguson.

Angela Ward (1937) of Margate took up golf on holiday with her parents
before eventually becoming part of the winning British Curtis Cup team.[194]
Another member of the 1956 team, Veronica Anstey (1925) of Edgbaston,
took up golf as a seventeen-year-old to recuperate from typhoid. She went
on to win the Australian Championship, the New Zealand Championship
and the Victoria State Championship in 1955.[195] In 1960 she married fellow
golfer John Charles Beharrell who was a lifelong player, administrator, collector and committeeman, eventually becoming a director of the Royal and
Ancient Golf Club of St Andrews Trust and director of the R&A Foundation. As a couple they would actively encourage junior and adult golf, particularly in the Midlands and have national, and international influence.
Australia and New Zealand also boasted some world-class players who
often showcased their talents in the Tasman Cup including Pat Borthwick,
Judith Percy, Joan Fletcher and Jean Horwell.[196]

While the history of the Ladies Golf Course at St Andrews Scotland
dated from 1867 and the Royal North Devon Women's Golf Club at West-
ward Ho! from 1868, the overall pattern of female participation after 1945
warns against interpreting sport as a story of steady progress. The Second World War was particularly disastrous for ordinary women golfers,
because some courses were lost to agriculture. When clubs resumed more
competitive activities committees would often institute formal or informal
rules limiting female access, either to the main greens or the eighteen-hole
course. A recent study of Fulwell in London, formed in 1904, shows exactly
these processes. A rapid expansion of members between 1920 and 1939
had seen consistent numbers of around 300 female golfers. By 1947 the
number of registered female members had fallen to eighty-four.[197]

Peter Wynn gives three specific reasons for this, other than general post-
war reconstruction. First was a loss of the short course to agricultural use,
negotiations for the renewal of the lease taking until 1958 to restore the
facility. Secondly, the fact that Fulwell now had only one course led to new
rules reducing the available female memberships to 125 (compared with
250 full memberships for men). Thirdly, a rigorous formal vetting process
and informal 'sponsorship' could regulate who was invited to join, and perhaps more importantly, who was not. Wynn's analysis therefore balances
the mixed motives of those who wanted to join such a club (including those
who just wanted a game of golf) against the structural mechanisms for limiting access. The overall numbers of women belonging to golf clubs did not
rise dramatically until the years between 1979 (88, 419 women registered)

to 1998 (136,583 female affiliated players).[198] Changes in affluence, social behaviour and ideas of equity clearly moved slowly in the selective world of the club house.

LAWN TENNIS AND RACKET SPORTS

The Table Tennis finals for the English Championship at Wembley in 1946 attracted 10,000 spectators.[199] There was a great deal of overlap with lawn tennis. Fred Perry's father had famously suggested his son made the transition to the outdoor game after winning the Table Tennis World Championship in 1929 because it would be more lucrative.[200] Other racket sports, like badminton and squash, were generally perceived to be less exclusive than lawn tennis, although table tennis was perhaps the most democratic of the four main racket sports. Just as Perry had suffered from his professional attitude whilst playing as an amateur, especially at Wimbledon, table tennis relied upon indoor stadiums, music and exhibition halls large enough to accommodate the crowds in what some called a 'stage game' rather than a sport. A degree of moral judgment still prevailed over those who chose to exploit their athletic talents for money.

> Since Perry turned to professionalism after winning the championship at Wimbledon in 1936, his third successive year, an Englishman has never achieved success on that arena [sic]. Indeed, Perry is the only Englishman to have won at the New Wimbledon. Our women fared slightly better. But even they failed lamentably in the Wightman Cup match against the U.S. both at Wimbledon and in the U.S. In the singles, Miss Dorothy Round (now Mrs. Little) succeeded in 1934 and 1937 at Wimbledon. Yet in both those years Mrs Helen Wills Moody did not play, the next best player was an Englishwoman. So we can preen ourselves that if we did not possess the best woman player in the world we certainly did have the next best. As an example, Miss Kay Stammers (now Mrs Menzies) reached the final at Wimbledon in 1939, the last Wimbledon before the war when she was easily beaten by Miss Alice Marble, who that day played superlative lawn tennis, the best women's tennis I have ever watched, in my opinion, even better than Mlle. Lenglen or Mrs Moody at their zenith [sic].[201]

During World War II, the Lawn Tennis Association (LTA) reduced its activity to a small executive committee to look after financial affairs. Red Cross and other charity matches were therefore organised by individuals. The Junior Lawn Tennis Club of Great Britain was formed outside the auspices of the LTA in 1940 for male and female players under the age of eighteen, later becoming absorbed by the governing body during peacetime.[202] By 1951 the Ministry of Education and the Central Council for Physical Recreation had pledged £1,800 per year for a national coaching scheme, which by 1952 had held fifty-two courses, and been attended by almost 1,200 trainees.[203]

A similar sum was provided by the LTA for coaching schemes, meaning that general participation increased and over two million people were estimated to play the game, some informally on parks and public facilities.

In view of the increased international competitiveness of women's tennis, Stanley Doust's assessment of the Wightman Cup match against the United States at Wimbledon in 1948 can be read as a defence of British amateurism.

> To prove that the gap between the U.S. women players and our own is narrowing I dare to prophesy that the U.S. will not win a 'blood-less' match as they did in 1946 but, in the words of the boxing world, 'they will know that have been in a fight' . . . Mrs Kay Menzies has announced her intention of retiring from the game . . . It is to be hoped that Kay will be the non-playing captain of the British team. Her match experience will be a great asset to our young players—much better than the advice of the best professional coach in the world because the professional, who knows all about stroke production, is quite ignorant about tactics and strategy.[204]

This defensiveness masked a lack of coaching culture at the elite female amateur level in Britain: between the resumption of the Wimbledon in 1946 and 1955, the ladies singles competition final match would be an American contest. The LTA had no clear system for what we would call talent identification today. While Kay Menzies (née Stammers, 1914–2005) had won Wimbledon in 1939, designed her own outfits and was much pho-tographed in the press, she moved to South Africa in 1949 and there was no clear successor. Angela Barrett (later Mortimer, 1932) reached the last eight of Wimbledon six times between 1953 and 1960 and she, along with Jean Quertier (1927); Jean Walker Smith (1925–2010); Anne Haydon Jones (1938); and Joy Gannon (1928, later Mottram) provided most of the British highlights of women's tennis.[205]

Anne Haydon's father had been a table tennis player and she took part in five World Championships in the 1950s as well as becoming ranked in the top three British female lawn tennis players.[206] She would go on to win a Wimbledon doubles title in 1968 and the singles final in the 1969.[207] Gannon became as well-known for her Teddy Tingling dresses as her ten-nis, while the real rising star of British tennis was Christine Truman (1941) but the crowd favourite did not win a Wimbledon singles title.[208] Another promising young player who did not make the elite of women's tennis was Gem Hoahing (1921) who was born in Hong Kong but represented Brit-ain.[209] After taking a junior title in Middlesex at the age of 14 by winning all her matches 6–0 6–0, she appeared at the Wimbledon Championships between 1937 and 1961; including defeating Gussie Moran (1923–2012) in 1949 before the latter turned professional.[210]

Perry remained a trenchant critic of the LTA after his move to the United States, particularly in its unwillingness to develop promising young players. As 'Gorgeous Gussie' Moran made clear, she had little choice but to become professional if she were to take on relatively small jobs like posing for endorsements or writing for newspapers.[211] Moran accepted an offer of $50,000 in 1950 from Bobby Riggs for joining his professional tour. Professional women's tennis was of a much higher standard than amateur play, as Moran was to find out when she continually lost to the other woman on the Riggs tour, the 1946 Wimbledon singles champion Pauline Betz (later Addie, 1919–2011). Revealed as a very good, but not great, player, Moran was reportedly horrified when Riggs told Betz to 'Go easy on Gussie' for the sake of closer matches to please the crowds.[212]

Others were at pains to point out that amateurism meant that many aspiring young women and girls were often left to devise their own training schemes and regimes.

> Walking from my hotel to the lawn tennis courts I saw two girls, one eleven and the other twelve, knocking the ball over the net under the critical eye of their mother. I watched for some time and then walked over to where the mother was sitting and asked what was the idea of making her children repeat the same stroke over and over again. She smilingly replied 'Have you heard of Suzanne Lenglen? Well she learned accuracy because her father used to place five-franc pieces on the court for Suzanne to aim at. That is what I am doing now. Go and look at the court.' This I did and found there were pennies distributed on various parts of the court. They were made to aim at one penny till it was hit before passing on to another. And the child that hit a penny kept it as a prize. Well, here were two youngsters (and their tireless mother helping) willing to go through the drudgery and monotony of learning to be accurate like Suzanne.[213]

Just as Perry suffered discrimination on the grounds of class, ethnicity was also a factor in British tennis. Angela Buxton (1934) was not allowed to join the Cumberland Club in London because of her Jewish background although she was able to affiliate to Queen's.[214] Travelling to the United States to try to develop her career, Buxton and her mother were also prevented from using the Los Angeles Tennis Club and instead practiced on public courts. Buxton progressed to the elite nevertheless and would lose in the 1956 singles final at Wimbledon to American Shirley Irvin (1927). This would be her most successful year, as she won the ladies' doubles trophy with African American Althea Gibson (1927–2003), after the pair had also taken the French doubles title.[215] While the online Wimbledon Lawn Tennis Museum display acknowledges that Gibson changed the history of the competition by becoming the first AfricanAmerican to win a singles title at the championships, Buxton's contribution remains unmentioned.[216] This would tend to support her claim in a 2004 interview that, having applied in the 1950s she still remained on the waiting list at the All England Lawn

Figure 6.1   R&J Hill 'Celebrities of Sport Series of 50: Number 4 Jean Nicholl' London R&J Hill, circa 1936. Personal collection of the author. Jean Nicholl was being hailed as a sixteen-year-old lawn tennis prodigy at the time that this cigarette card was issued. Lauded too, as a first-class swimmer and golfer, Nicholl's likeness has been subject to some budget-level production values, but she would nevertheless have been sufficiently recognizable to the general public.

Tennis Club over fifty years later. An injury forced Buxton's retirement at the age of twenty-two although she maintained a continuing interest in sports development.

After growing up in Harlem, Althea Gibson became a proficient young paddleball player (a form of racket sport) but it would take a letter of complaint from respected tennis champion Alice Marble (1913–1990) for the US Lawn Tennis Association to allow her to compete at the highest level by participating at Forest Hills, New York in 1950.[217] Gibson would take both the US and Wimbledon titles again in 1958, with Britain's Angela Mortimer (1932) losing in the London final.[218] Gibson turned professional soon after, diversifying in films and singing as well as appearing in the Ladies Professional Golf Association (LPGA) tour from 1964.[219] Discrimination in hotels and clubs also marred her golf career although she played in 171 golf tournaments between 1963 and 1977.[220] Along with many honours, the Althea Gibson foundation memorialises her many and varied achievements.[221] In spite of elitism and discrimination, Wimbledon women champions continued to become more diverse. In 1959 Brazilian Maria Bueno (1939) would take the first of her three Wimbledon wins. It was not until 1961 that Angela Barrett would win the first all-British women's singles final against Christine Truman since 1914.[222]

English Table Tennis Association (ETTA) expanded rapidly from nineteen leagues in 1927 to 230 in 1939, involving 5,000 clubs and 80,000 registered players.[223] At the same time, there was a view that table tennis belonged more in the world of theatre than that of sport. Various catalogues indicate that table tennis became more widespread as a result of the domestication of many sporting hobbies. Miniaturised versions of sport were for sale as toys, parlour games and other body culture interests that people could pursue at home.[224] The trivialisation of the sport was helped by the mix of amateurs and professionals, adding to the idea that a person was entitled to capitalise on their athletic ability, as entertainers did. The third article in a series asking 'What's wrong with British sport?' in *Lilliput* (subtitled a 'man's magazine') argued that 'the line between amateurism and professionalism is so blurred as to be meaningless . . . in these days of 'power sport' a player who aspires to world class must train and compete the year round with and against players of equal caliber.'[225] Amateur and professional distinction was already considered out of date in many quarters. The English Table Tennis Association (ETTA) recognised players, rather than amateurs or professional, and appeared to foreshadow a time when Wimbledon would become an open championship.

> A player is not allowed to accept money for competing in tournaments, but if he wishes to capitalise his skill in any other way (coaching, exhibitions, sponsoring equipment), he must receive permission from the ETTA both in principle and for each contract. Each decision is reached on the basis that the player's first duty is to the game: for

example, he would not be allowed to sponsor unsuitable equipment, or to engage in a contract which would prevent his playing in a tournament. The result is that there is no underhand dealing, the best players can devote the necessary time to the game, and they stay in the game to the benefit of playing standards throughout the sport. It is significant too, that table tennis is one of the few sports in which we consistently hold our own.[226]

English world champions included Vera Dace-Thomas (1921) who also played lawn tennis to a high standard, as did Jean Nicholl (1920, later Bostock) and Margaret Osborne (1921). Perhaps the most famous British players though, were twins Rosalind and Diane Rowe (1933), right- and left-handed players respectively, and able to develop their profile beyond the sport after taking the world championship doubles at the age of seventeen in 1950.[227] Introduced to the sport by their father at home in Greenford Middlesex at the age of fourteen, both women continued to work as secretarial administrators but also wrote extensively and made public appearances. The twins were coached by the leading personality of the time, Victor Barna, a Hungarian Jew who took British citizenship and worked for the Dunlop company, promoting their products. Table tennis had quite different patterns of international rivalry from lawn tennis with the Swaything Cup for men and the Marcel Corbillion cup for women. It was one of several sports in Britain to benefit from the effects of inward migration prompted by the Second World War as many Europeans, especially those from Czechoslovakia, Poland and Hungary, boosted popularity in the UK.[228] India and Japan were also internationally successful but the most famous woman player, Romanian Angelica Rozeanu (1921–2006) was also of Jewish descent and eventually settled in Israel.

Other racket sports also overlapped with lawn and table tennis: a national women's squash competition had been contested since 1922 and by the 1950s the Wolfe-Noel Cup was contested by Great Britain and United States teams. The leading British player was Janet Morgan (1921–1990, later Shardlow) who wrote *Squash Rackets for Women* in 1953 and her closest challenger Sheila Speight (later Mackintoish); followed by 'Welsh stylist' Rachel Byrne.[229] The most significant American rivals were Eleanora Sears; twins Betty and Peggy Howe; Jane Austin; Charlotte Prizer; 'Bobbie' Banks and 'Nanny' Stockton.[230] Badminton also held its forty-seventh All England Championships at the Empire Pool Wembley in 1957, with Britain's Heather Ward (1938) then a hopeful to beat the dominant American player of her generation Judy Devlin (1935).[231] After taking the doubles title with American Margaret Varner (1927, later Bloss) at the 1958 Championships, Ward beat Devlin to the singles final a year later. *World Sports* had many advertisements for rackets, bats, endorsed balls and shuttlecocks, whitening and related products so both direct sporting goods and products using similar technologies added to the public impact of racket sports..

The move to 'open' the elite competitions of world tennis to the professionals in the 1960s, were part of a longer series of changing attitudes to making money from sport. However, the amateur ideal was, and in some ways still remains, enduring. The idea that players owed sport something was important. The invented tradition of Althea Gibson's foundation bearing her name has often been replicated since this period, by an individual or sometimes a group, often with the justification of giving something back to sport. This has been a paradoxical process whereby putting money, expertise and time into sport for future generations therefore relies on the ability of individuals to leverage considerable sums of money on their name as a brand. The twin principles of not participating in sport primarily for money, and of having a duty to others rather than oneself could have contradictory elements therefore. The amateur ideal has been particularly enduring in female sport ever since. While individual women have negotiated particular roles as sports professionals, the reinvention of service to sport, rather than earning a living from it, has served as a conservative force against more fundamental change. We have far fewer women sports professional than men. There remain far fewer administrators, high-profile bureaucrats and influencers than female participants and this requires further analysis in its own right.

MOTOR RACING

Whole ways of doing motor-sport were devastated by the war effort. For example Brooklands, the dedicated high speed track, had the banking flattened, was then built upon and sold to airplane manufacturers shortly after the Armistice. Crystal Palace had a small road circuit but the post-war reconstruction of the estate did not include provision for motor-sport. Donnington Park, near Derby, was in need of considerable repair before resuming racing for car enthusiasts and has arguably remained more appealing to motor cyclists (and to some extent cyclists) since. While Indianapolis in the United Sates, Montlhéry in France, Monza in Italy and Arvus in Germany also required post-war repair, they had been better preserved than British tracks. The attraction for motor racing fans during the 1940s and early 1950s of road circuits such as the Isle of Man Tourist Trophy, and hill climbs such as Shelsey Walsh near Worcester can be seen in this context.

By 1947 the entrepreneurs who had taken speedway from the Ilford Motor Club's first meeting in Epping Forest in 1928 to a league competition attracting four million spectators, had a problem with riders and mechanics.

A first-class mechanic such as Harry Richards of Wembley receives about £12 a week with a small bonus for teams wins, for a working week of some 72 hours during the season [sic]! To offset this he gets a salary in the winter, for good mechanics are even scarcer than riders. They are in such short supply that Mr. Johnny Hoskins who controls

Bradford, Newcastle and Glasgow intends trying out girls who serviced vehicles and aircraft in the WAAF. Whether members of the fair sex will have sufficient concentration to adjust a red hot engine in a race against the clock—a rider is allowed 2 mins. to get his machine ready should it break down before a race starts—remains to be seen. But I am banking on women doing the job.[232]

Sheila Hart was already a co-director at Sheffield Speedway, having been an assistant to E.O. Spence at Belle Vue. The writer argued that women's leagues were a way forward for the sport:

> To succeed in a real way every sport must cater for women. Not only as spectators—we have our women lawn tennis stars, golfers, cricketers, footballers and even billiard players. So let women take an active part in speedway racing . . . Women have played a noble part in the war and thousands have proved themselves first-class motorcyclists in the military and civil-defence services. So why should we not give them a chance on the speedway? Form a women's league . . . in 1947 there should be material for half a dozen teams.[233]

The league did not materialise and experiments were short-lived. The eventual predominance of the British Racing Driver's Club and its base at Silverstone, meant that Grand Prix, and motor racing became almost a male preserve. However there were important exceptions.

The 1950s were an era of great women rally drivers and female equestrians with several personalities moving between the two sports. Patsy Burt (1928–2001); Sheila van Damm (1922) the daughter of a London theatre impresario; Vivian van Damm (1895–1960); Brenda Dickinson (1934) and Patrica Coundley (1934) all alternated their enthusiasm between horses and cars.[234] Burt owned two Jowett Javelins; an XK 120 coupé and a 2.6 litre Aston Martin, winning her first race in 1954 at Brands Hatch.[235] Van Damm got her break in rallying during 1950, driving a works-prepared Sunbeam Talbot in the *Daily Express* event. Sponsored by her father's infamous Windmill Theatre, and navigated by her sister Nona, Sheila drove with the motto 'Windmill Girl' proudly emblazoned down the side of her car. They were third in the Coupe des Dames, and the Rootes team offered Sheila a works seat for the following season.

Anne Newton (1920–2003, later Hall) from Huddersfield, West Yorkshire, joined Van Damm at Rootes and went on to drive in over 100 major rallies in a career spanning fifteen years, which she combined with bringing up three children.[236] The daughter of a prominent car dealer, Anne Newton first took the wheel at the age of ten, driving up and down the long farm track to the family's home at Stirley Hill. Nancy Mitchell and Pat Faichney won the Alpine Rally Coupe des Alpes for a perfect run and the Coupe des Dames simultaneously in 1956.[237] Valerie Domleo; Rosemary Seers;

Christabel Carlisle; Pauline Mayman and Patricia Ozanne were less well known by the general public.[238]

However, Pat Moss (1934–2008) was undoubtedly Britain's best known and most successful female rally driver, with three outright wins and seven podium finishes in international rallies. Her father Alfred was dentist who had driven in the 1924 Indianapolis 500 race while studying in the US.[239] Pat's mother Aileen enjoyed car rallies and trials in Singer and Marendaz sports cars. Like her brother Stirling, she enjoyed equestrian as well as motoring pursuits. Pat Moss became part of the British show jumping team in 1952, before representing the country in a number of international competitions. In 1953 she was presented to the Queen after winning the Queen Elizabeth Cup at White City. Like equestrian Pat Smythe, she represented one of the 'new Elizabethan' women of the era and was as popular in the media as on the roads.

Having been taught to drive by her brother at the age of eleven, Stirling's manager asked Pat to navigate for him in a night rally 1954, and she soon began racing in her own Morris Minor. She became a Marcus Chambers B. M. C. 'works' member driving an M.G. and insisted on being paid a cash fee. Ann Wisdom (Wiz) became her navigator after obtaining her driving licence in 1956. The combination went on to win the European Ladies Touring Championship in 1958 and 1960 plus 'placing' in several on open events. As a personality, Moss was an integral part of the glamour of the motor racing scene and its many parties in a way that was both very British and cosmopolitan.[240] However, the 1960s were, if anything more successful than the 1950s as she became bored with winning Ladies' prizes and focussed on open competition. On five occasions she was European Ladies' Rally Champion (1958, 1960, 1962, 1964–65); won the Coupe des Dames in the Monte Carlo Rally eight times and scored Mini Cooper's first big victory in the Tulip Rally of 1962.[241]

The way that Pat Moss won the 1960 Liège-Rome-Liège rally with Ann Wisdom in an Austin Healey 3000 became the stuff of legend. In what was described as a motoring equivalent of the *marathon de la route* of the Tour de France, because it was virtually non stop 2,885 miles over four days and two nights, the victory earned the Moss the Driver of the Year award from the Guild of Motoring writers, another first for an all-female crew. However, what became known as 'Pat's Liège' was also the first time an all-British car and crew had won the rally, and the first time that Britain had won the Interland Tropy; la Trophée des Nations; the women's cup; the manufacturers team prize; the club team prize and two class wins simultaneously. In 1992 the first issue of *Historic Race and Rally* magazine spent 10% of the total editorial on the 1960 win, featuring Moss' car, registration number URX 727. This was brand new in 1960, raced only four events, was only ever driven by Pat and Anne Wisdom, after which Moss bought it from the works for £500 in 1970.[242]

Having married Saab's leading driver Erick Carlsson in 1963 and giving birth to her daughter Susie in 1969, Pat Moss's retainer with BMC was only £1000 a year. When offered £5,000 to join Ford, which coincided with

Anne's retirement in 1962 to raise a family, Moss began a less successful period of competition followed by subsequent moves to Saab and Lancia. A stint at Renault Alpine followed, with a tenth place overall in the 1972 Monte Carlo. By now many of her racing friends has retired or were in team management, and by the mid-1970s she was driving for Toyota in the Monte Carlo; finally deciding, in 1974, to retire.

Pat Moss was the most famous but not a lone pioneer in racing rally cars therefore. There is a whole other book to be written on women and motorsport. The range of drivers mentioned here should also caution against those who would single out relatively recent examples as indications of progress. Will Carling suggested Tracy Edwards and the crew of Maiden, the first all-female team to compete in the Whitbread Round the World Yacht Race, had broken new ground by linking with sail-makers, sponsors and other key suppliers. [243] In some senses Carling was correct, but motor racing also had its technical and commercial specialists, covering aspects of promotional responsibility and working as a team sport, although with a prominent personality. Just as Pat Moss had the example of her brother to follow in the 1950s, she also had the precedent set by Dorothy Levitt much earlier.

TRACK AND FIELD ATHLETICS AND
WOMEN'S DISTANCE RUNNING

By 1937, a fifteenth annual Women's Amateur Athletics Association (WAAA) Coronation Championships had been staged at the White City Stadium, Shepherds Bush, for a challenge cup donated by the department store, Selfridges. [244] There was a degree of support from the sporting establishment for women's athletics and some commercial interest in the programme of major events. One year later, the last vestiges of Alice Milliat's Women's World Games effectively became the IAAF European Championships for women's athletics in 1938. The Second World War reduced the overall numbers of athletics clubs dramatically for both men and women. The number of clubs affiliated to the AAA in 1946 was 326 (a drop of 157 from 1939) with smaller numbers for the WAAA. [245] The resumption of WAAA Games had taken place in the build up to the Olympics on 2 August 1947 at Polytechnic Stadium Chiswick: effectively the twentieth running of the championships interrupted by war. Although the 200 metres was a new addition to the Olympic schedule in 1948, Britain had been staging longer events of up to three miles, under the less glamorous auspices of cross-country and road walking disciplines, since at least 1932. [246] These races were tolerated (at a distance) by the International Amateur Athletics Federation as less jarring to the body than track competitions. Another international took place at the White City Stadium in July 1949, followed a month later by a meeting involving France, England and the Netherlands.

A one-mile walk and one-mile relay race were included, in addition to an 800 metres competition and field events.[247]

Club rivalry was intense: The Sidney Parkes Trophy for the club with most points went to Essex Ladies Athletic Club in 1938, 1939 and 1953; Mitcham Ladies Athletic Club in 1946 and 1947; Palatine School, Blackpool in 1948; Chesterfield Harriers and Ladies Athletic Club in 1949; Orpington Ladies Athletic Club in 1950; Birchfield Harriers Ladies Club in 1951 and Spartan Ladies Athletic Club in 1952 and 1954.[248] In 1955 The Alexander Sports Ground, Perry Barr Birmingham hosted a Junior and Intermediate track and Field Championships with Princess Margaret as patron.[249] Competitors could take part in field events like the long jump; discus; javelin; high jump and shot or the track disciplines of 100 metres; 880 yards; 70 yards hurdles; one-mile walk and the 4 x 110 yards relay. Good manners were encouraged by a hiatus in the running events for a five-minute break to watch the progress of the field and throwing events.

The involvement of Harriers clubs was significant for British women's middle and long distance running. The London Olympiades Athletic Club had first held a mile event in 1932 at their Battersea Park Sports.[250] Connie Mason of Middlesex Ladies Athletic Club established a world women's one mile walk record of just under seven minutes, fifty four seconds in 1931 before knocking a further nine seconds off this time the following month at Stamford Bridge.[251] She also held the two-mile record of seventeen minutes fifty seconds. Although the mile run was not recognised by the International Amateur Athletics Federation (IAAF) as a track event, this and longer distances up to three miles could be covered by cross-country running or road walking, leading to competitive opportunities well beyond the immediate control of the international federation and the IOC.[252] Prominent teams like Airedale Harriers; Birchfield Harriers; Birminghm Atalanta; Dudley Ladies Athletic Club; Hallamshire Harriers; Ilford Athletic Club; London Olympiades; Manchester Athletic Club; North Shields Polytechnic Athletic Club; Sheffield United Harriers Athletic Club; Small Heath Harriers and Winton Harriers were involved.[253]

The 1950s have often described as a golden age of British athletics. While the achievements of Roger Bannister in running the first four-minute mile on 6 May 1954 have now been subjected to robust analysis by academics, the achievement also provided an impetus for a women's five-minute attempt.[254] Shortly after, a British record was established by Diane Leather (1933, later Charles) of Birchfield Harriers during the Midlands Women's AAA Championships at Birmingham's Alexander Sports Ground, 29 May 1954 in four minutes fifty-nine second, without a pace-maker.[255] Leather improved this by almost fifteen seconds a year later to register a time of four minutes forty-five seconds at the White City on 21 September 1955. Leather regularly came in the top three against the leading Soviet sprinters over 800 metres in European competition in the 1950s but the inclusion of the distance into the 1960 Olympic schedule in Rome saw her past her best

and she was eliminated in her heats.[256] While perceptions of a golden age
have been revised therefore, Leather was one of many women athletes who
enjoyed a friendly rivalry against international representatives in regular
competitions during the 1950s.[257]

By the time of the twenty-ninth annual Championships in August 1956 at
White City Stadium, the WAAA executive was comprised of the Northern
Counties WAAA (Bury, Lancashire); Midland Counties WAAA (Birmingham); Southern Counties WAAA (Surrey) and the Welsh WAAA (Glamorgan). Harold Abrahams acted as legal adviser to the association, aided by
Sir Arthur Porritt as the honourary medical officer, with Dr Dorothy Marshall (1904–1978) as his assistant. There was also a commercial element
with adverts for Horlicks, Bovril and Lucozade regularly featuring female
athletes, in addition to sporting fashions and other goods. Although most
female competitors suffered financial hardship in this amateur tradition,
'furniture meetings' were also a chance to win household items for those
looking to set up, or improve, a home. Sending an athlete to compete at the
Empire Games in Canada or New Zealand during this period cost around
£200 by sea or £300 by air (slightly less by chartered airline) in addition
to accommodation and subsistence; about £500 in all. For the individual,
there were aspects of shamateurism and benefits to be had from amateur
competition, from civic pride to paid travel and personal privileges. From
the point of view of the officials making the selection, an all-rounder who
could compete in two or three events might be considered better value than
a star who excelled in one discipline.

George Pallet's book *Athletics for Women* was therefore one of many
contemporary texts which reveal an intricate pattern to domestic and international competition.[258] Pallet was attached to the Hermes club and vice
president of Spartan Ladies' Athletic Club. He dedicated his book in particular to Sheila Lerwill (1928) former world high jump record holder 'Who,
during our partnership in quest of a record never flinched from her exacting
training and who taught me as much as I was able to teach her' and other
women athletes.[259] While a three-match thirteen day tour to Bourdeux,
Moscow and Prague might cause Jack Crump concern in the pages of *World
Sports*, Norris NcWhirter was sufficiently smitten by Russian middle distance runner Nina Otkalenko (1928), or 'Ballerina Nina' as he preferred
to call her, to include a relatively rare full page colour photograph with his
article.[260] Like Leather, Otkalenko suffered from the lack of an 800 metres
race in the Olympic schedule and their rivalry would undoubtedly have led
to them becoming more famous had this distance featured.

Without wishing to look at all the different kinds of competition, we can
see a varied range of women's athletics on track, road and across country.
This was eventually to change the Olympic Games, with more disciplines
being added to the programme in the 1960s. Magazines like *World Sports*
became ever more international in scope as development programmes and
coaching schemes in other countries seemed to modernise athletics faster

than in Britain. The role of the coach and the extent of training schemes requires more consideration, as does the function of schools in promoting physical fitness, let alone sport, for girls in this period.[261] The contribution of the education system appears to have been over-exaggerated as part of post-war changes. For many girls it was an uninspiring curriculum and Geoff Dyon's desire to modernise athletics was ultimately frustrated, forcing him to resign his post as the first Chief National Coach and move to Ottawa Canada to take up a post as Director of Training with the Royal Canadian Legion.[262]

For instance, a Nottinghamshire Education Committee Rural Schools PE course in November 1953 comprised a lackluster regime based on repetitious activities: an ash pole, a medicine ball and a bench were the only equipment.[263] Business houses, works teams and private clubs were also important for athletics, while more remains to be understood about harriers clubs and cross-country races. Another point of research would be the extent to which women's athletics featured in discussions of the general health of the country, such as a campaign for a national British Fitness badge scheme launched by World Sports in 1949.

CONCLUSION

This chapter started with a polemic, one of many voices on women and sport in the period. Newspaper columnists were as much concerned with their own profile as reporting accurately, so passionate pieces on gender were often used by writers fully aware that they angered readers more than they illuminated issues. Contradicting oneself in an article was not necessarily bad for business. Paul Gallico has often been credited as being a sports writer who championed misogyny, and with good reason. However, being critical to witty effect was not the same thing as thinking critically and many subsequent British writers like Brian Glanville imitated the same style. Gallico wrote articles dissociating himself from boxing (the sport where he had defined his reputation) as a brutal form, saying that he preferred intelligence and musical skill as more masculine pursuits.[264] While this could be read as an amusing exercise in taking the columnist's opinion beyond a logical conclusion, it hardly tells us much about the sport of pugilism itself. Nor was that necessarily its prime intention. That Gallico could critique aspects of masculinity, as well as femininity, has been little acknowledged. His confusion about gender remains a subtext to the writing, whatever his ostensible subject. The opening quotation in this chapter from Bevil Rudd appears to have been equally unfocussed.

Gender was recognised as one of many ways of performing identity in post-war Britain and applied as much to differing concepts of manliness as femininity. Polemics such as those written by Rudd, Gallico and others should be contextualised by an increased willingness to discuss gender, sexuality and transsexual identity from the middle of the 1940s onwards. The publication of Michael Dillon's *Self: a Study of Ethics and Endocrinology* was published as among the first studies in female to male gender reassignment in 1946.[265] Robert Cowell (1921) added his autobiography to this literature, detailing his transition from male to female identity and living afterwards as Roberta.[266] Cowell's case was more famous than Dillon, as he had been a married racing driver with two children and a World War II Spitfire pilot. Though it is not clear whether the two had a relationship, we can see that meanings attached to biological sex at birth, chosen gender identity and sexuality become more widely discussed in the public domain. This is a potentially rewarding area for further study.

This chapter used the second London Olympic Games as a starting point to examine wider issues affecting of women's sport in the 1940s and 1950s, particularly the fluxes of amateurism and professionalism that shaped participation. This remains a largely under-researched topic for women's sport in a period that has been part of a recent re-appraisal by a range of historians specialising in female experiences.[267] It can be interesting to read Harold Abrahams' predictions for the 1948 London Olympic Games. The twelve-year gap between Berlin and London produced extremely modest expectations:

> Latest reports suggest that there will be representatives from over forty nine different nations, and for the twenty-four men's events and nine events for women we are informed that the totals reached at Berlin in 1936, when the games were last held, will be exceeded. At Berlin there were over 750 male competitors and nearly one hundred women. Quite frankly I think the official estimate that the Berlin figures will be beaten optimistic. We must remember that there is no Germany and no Japan, so far as these Games are concerned, and no Latvia, Estonia and Lithuania. Moreover we would be burying our head in the sand if we imagined that the very serious economic conditions throughout the world will not have a great effect on the number of countries that can afford the luxury of a large team.[268]

Ever the amateur, Abrahams then went on to differentiate between medal 'success' and 'distinction' by which he meant getting a place in the final. Citing the 'Pure mathematics' twenty-two men's athletic disciplines and nine women's events, Abrahams concluded that there would be more losers than winners. Nevertheless, he expected Maureen Gardner to have 'A very fine chance of bringing the first women's Olympic athletic title to Great Britain. In the 80 metres hurdles she has already returned 11.6 seconds. This is very definitely Olympic class.'[269] Dorothy Odam-Tyler, Abrahams reminded readers, had placed second in Berlin in the high jump and as British record holder she was a medal hope, along with Sylvia Cheeseman and Margaret Lucas. These few names were particularly modest given the extent of WAAA activity since 1922 and the variety of participation in Harriers clubs, road walking and other activity away from the track.

In a pained excerpt from his book George Pallet remarked how difficult it was to compile even recent historical evidence of women's athletics:

> Never, I feel, can there have been a more undocumented subject than women's athletics, but this feeling is doubtless borne of the extreme difficulty experienced in obtaining information. In the early days details of even important women's meetings were not published. Research was hindered by the refusal of governing bodies to allow access to their minute books on the grounds that the contents were confidential— such is the lot of the seeker after facts. [270]

In view of this frustration, it is worth bearing in mind that in the 1952 Helsinki Games, only Shirley Cawley (1932) would win an individual athletics medal for Britain, a bronze in the long jump. The 4 x 100 metres relay team (Heather Armitage; Sylvia Cheeseman; Jean Desforges; June Foulds) would also come third behind the United States of American and Germany, (who had been admitted as the Federal Republic of Germany, as the German Democratic Republic was not represented on this occasion). [271]

We know relatively little about how the overseas female athletes were viewed by domestic media or what the British women thought of their travels abroad. Further study of *World Sport* magazine and other popular texts might help here. Fanny Blankers-Koen summarised her experiences:

> My visits to Great Britain have always been the most memorable part of my happiest days as an athlete. I have always been very much at home in the United Kingdom, the greatest hospitality and friendship continually showering on me. I first came to Britain in 1936. From these first days in Blackpool I have repeatedly crossed the Channel with the greatest of pleasure. I do not know how many times I have been in your country, but I can say that my friend Dorothy Tyler Odam and I have seen several generations of English athletes come and go. During the events I was often hard pressed but the result has always been a friendly and sporting contest. I am proud to say that victor and losers have become, and still are, the best of friends. It therefore follows that I was as much at home as I am in my own country. [272]

For Britain, Heather Armitage (1933) and June Foulds-Paul (1934) would compete again in Melbourne in 1956 in the 100 metres, 200 metres and as part of the relay team; Audrey Bennett (1936) in the high jump; Diana Coates (1932) the javelin; Suzanne Farmer in the discus and shot put; Thelma Hopkins (1936) in the high jump and long jump; Sheila Hoskins (1936) in the long jump; Carole Quinton (1936) and Pauline Threapleton-Wainwright (1933) the 80 metres hurdles. [273] A one-off, Dorothy Tyler took part in her fourth Olympic high jump event in 1956 to span twenty years of Olympic Games' competition. Anne Pashley (1935) would complete the 4 x 100 metres relay team in Melbourne with Jean Scrivens (1935) to take the silver medal behind Australia and ahead of the United States but only Thelma Hopkins would win an individual athletics medal, a bronze in the high jump.[274] Athletic activity was not centred on England and Wales, although selection procedures might favour those in WAAA competitions. In Northern Ireland, Anita De Gregory (1949, later Doherty) who was born in the Bahamas, perhaps became the first Afro-Caribbean woman to become an athletics international, by courtesy of her studentship at Ulster College in a Belfast versus Scotland tournament in 1970. De Gregory was to win a 400m in 60.1 seconds.[275] Without wishing to labour the point about diversity, there remains much to explore in this period and dualistic treatments of Eastern and Western European female athletes based on crude stereotypes have not been particularly helpful.[276]

Like a range of other sports and disciplines, Olympic equestrianism became more important and slightly more inclusive. Lis Hartel (1921–2009) from Denmark became the first woman in the equestrian sports to win an Olympic medal when she won silver dressage medals at the 1952 and 1956 Summer Olympics. Affected by polio below her knees and in her arms, she required help to get on and off her horse. A seven times winner of the Danish dressage title, she and her therapist pioneered riding for therapeutic purposes in Europe. Liselott Linsenhoff of Germany took home a team silver and individual bronze in 1956, and team gold in 1968. Winning the individual title in 1972 made her the first woman gold medalist ever in this discipline. She also won an individual gold and team silver in 1972, making a total of five Olympic podiums. Talented Olympic British female riders included Marion Coakes (1947, later Mould) who had such success with Stroller that she won the *Daily Mirror* Sportswoman of the Year award at nineteen in 1965. At the 1968 Olympics she won silver to become the first women to win an individual medal in show-jumping. She was also briefly referenced in a *Monty Python's Flying Circus* sketch.

Ann Moore (1951) on Psalm also won a silver medal in Munich in 1972 but retired in 1974 as the horse, by then thirteen, was passed his best. Wales' Debbie Johnsey (1957) became the youngest competitor in a show jumping contest at Montreal in 1976, narrowly missing out on a medal. She married Gary Plumley, a goalkeeper who played for Newport County and Cardiff City; their daughter Gemma was also an Olympic equestrian hopeful.[277] Caroline Bradley (1969–1983) was never an Olympian because she was not selected for the 1972 Olympics and had been ruled a professional by 1976 for accepting prize money. Though she could not afford to own Tigre, she was the outstanding woman rider of her generation on the borrowed horse and died of heart failure at the age of just thirty-four.[278] Four years later, the rules regarding professionalism were reclassified and equestrianism became an 'open' sport. Nevertheless, the wider participation of girls and women from the 1950s and 1960s onwards continued to reap benefits at the elite level.

The Olympic revival of 1948 did not end with the Summer Games. At the fifth Winter Games in Saint Moritz 1948 twenty-seven women from nine countries took part. Born in India, Jeanette Altwegg (1930) was brought up in Lancashire where her father worked for the Liverpool Cotton Exchange. Jeanette's father became a naturalised British citizen but moved back to Switzerland in 1946 when the Cotton Exchange was nationalised. A promising lawn tennis player, who had made to the junior finals at Wimbledon in 1947, Jeanette skated since the age of six. She was to win bronze for the individual figure skating in St Moritz in 1948 behind Barbara Ann Scott (1928–2012) of Canada and Eva Pawlik (1927–1983) of Austria.

Defending her European title eight days before the Oslo Olympic Games in 1952, Altwegg took the gold medal but refused large sums of money to turn professional and perform in ice shows.[279] She has often been described as the ultimate amateur, but contemporary interviews indicate that the skater was able to prepare for competition by training seven hours a day, five days a week either at Streatham rink or in Switzerand, depending where the family was.[280] After Altwegg retired from skating at the age of twenty-two, she moved to Switzerland to work with war orphans for a year at the Pestalozzi Children's village and was awarded a CBE before marrying Marc Wirz and having four children. In 1983, their daughter Christina became the world curling champion at Moose Jaw, Canada.

Jeanatte Altwegg's amateur career needed extensive specialised practice to win gold medals because of the athletic innovations of the male gold Olympic medalist in 1948 and 1952, Dick Button. With the emphasis on athletically daring jumps and spins, Button and other male competitors transformed men's skating into a recognisably sporting form, whereas for women it remained an aesthetic performance.[281] Button was also well-placed to capitalise on touring professional ice shows after retiring as an amateur to take a Harvard degree in law, before moving into television guest appearances and Olympic commentary from 1960. This had a direct effect on female competitors, especially in mixed pairs competitions, as they gradually improved their fitness and athleticism to incorporate jumps and twists in their own routines. Nevertheless, this was a slow process as Altwegg was to be the lone British female figure-skating gold medalist between Madge Syers in 1908 and Jayne Torvill (1957) in 1984.

Other British skating Olympians in 1948 included Marion Davis (1928), Madie Linzee (1928) Jennifer Nicks (1932–1980) and Winifred Silverthorne (1925). Patricia Devries (1930), Peri Horne (1932), Valda Osbourn (1934) and Barbara Wyatt (1930) comprised the female competitors in 1952.[282] One year later Mollie Phillips (1907–1994), who had been the first woman to carry the team flag at an opening Olympic ceremony in 1932 at Lake Placid, became the first woman referee in an ice dance world championship. A trained lawyer, Phillips would become the first female High Sherriff of

Camarthenshire in 1961, succeeding her father. A magistrate and cattle-breeder, she went on to judge over 50 world, Olympic and European championships in her ling and active life. In 1956, the British members of the Olympic skating team were Erica Batchelor (1933); Joyce Coates (1939); Carolyn Krau (1943); Diane Peach (1940) and Yvonne Sugden (1939). Krau also took part in the 1960 Winter Olympics in Squaw Valley, California with Patricia Pauley (1941). At the Winter Games held at Cortina D' Ampezzo in 1956, cross country skiing also had two new events for women a 10 kilometre and a 3 x 5 kilometre relay.

It remains to unpick what kind of sporting legacy our female Olympians have left, as well as their place in our social and cultural history. As Bolz has shown in her recent work on the monumental exercise of stadium building, the word 'legacy' has itself shifted meaning from establishing a peace movement for youthful sporting co-operation to becoming a term denoting brand-building, participation rates and infrastructure projects.[283] Our ideas of Olympism, physical and mental disability have also changed radically. The International Games for the Deaf and Dumb, or 'Silent Olympics' were first staged in Paris in 1924, involving the British Deaf Amateur Sports Association and fourteen other nations.[284] Towards the end of World War II, Sir Ludwig Guttmann, a German-born Jew who moved to Britain before the Second World War founded the National Spinal Injuries Centre at Stoke Mandeville Hospital in Aylesbury. In Edinburgh The Thistle Foundation created accommodation for disabled ex-servicemen and women by Sir Francis and Lady Tudsbery, with a swimming pool and gymnasium.[285]

On 28 July 1948 fourteen paralysed ex-servicemen and two ex-servicewomen from Stoke Mandeville competed against the Royal Star and Garter Home, Clapham Park in an archery competition on the lawns of the Aylesbury hospital. Though 'clinical sport' was not new, it did become an increasing part of medical discourse as part of physical, emotional and psychological therapy and government funding increased significantly.[286] The number of Stoke Mandeville sports proliferated to netball, bowling, javelin, shot-put and snooker, before an international Games were held against Dutch competitors in 1952. By 1960, 350 men and women from 24 countries would contest the Paralympic Games right after the Olympic closing ceremony in Rome.

The chapter also looked at sport away from the Olympic elite. With more space, it would have been possible to explore the extraordinary autobiographies of women bullfighters Conchita Cintron (1922) and Patricia Mc Cormick (1930) or the careers of mountaineers like Eileen Healey (1921–2010) who filmed the tragic 1959 all-female expedition in the Himalayas.[287] The chapter has argued that there were contradictory and complex processes at work linking personal domestic arrangements, work, leisure and public space in the 1940s and 1950s. This included new forms of older activities. After greyhound racing was introduced from America in 1926, women comprised around 40% of spectators within two years.[288] It has been estimated that there were 230 tracks in Britain by 1935, with big cities having more than one venue (such as Manchester's Belle Vue and White City), in addition to multi-use venues such as Stamford Bridge football ground, the home of Chelsea FC.[289] During World War II women greyhound racing trainers and kennel assistants replaced those called for military duty. Their remarkable success in open and graded races became part of the sub-culture, even when many subsequently lost their jobs once war was over.[290] 'Going to the dogs' nevertheless remained a popular night out for couples in the 1940s and 1950s.

Other pastimes, such as darts, benefited from women's increased involvement in the public house, though inter war photographs of the *News of The World Championships* show maybe one woman for every ten men in the audience, so there are evidently gendered patterns for participation and spectator events.[291] However, relatively unusual activities like greyhound racing, ice hockey and speedway were part of a longer history of presenting sporting spectacle to attract a wider audience. Amateur sports like cricket, hockey, lacrosse, rowing, tennis and volleyball were staging large events to draw in spectators. With thirty rowing clubs affiliated to the Women's Amateur Rowing Association, from business houses and Civil Service teams to University sides, regattas were an important means of raising the profile of Amy Gentry OBE and her colleagues.[292]

Like other cultural industries that required considerable resources for their production, distribution, consumption and reception, sport and the media have been perceived as relatively closed to women until the later decades of the twentieth century. Victoria Bennett has argued that by the time of the 1948 Games, media industry structures were in place that made sports-writing a male preserve.[293] However, the material used in this chapter indicates that this situation was more open than Bennett has suggested. Pat Besford, a freelance swimming correspondent for *The Daily Telegraph* (for many years), *The Daily Mail* and other papers, was one of the most respected sports journalists of the post-war era. She covered ten Olympic Games from London 1948, and reported on swimming, diving, synchronised swimming, water polo and, latterly, archery at world tournaments, European Championships, Commonwealth Games and national events for over forty years. As an administrator, she oversaw the accreditation, communication facilities and other arrangements for British sports journalists and photographers attending the Olympic Games. In addition, Besford acted as President of the swimming commission of the International Sports Writers' Association, was first female Chair of the Sports Writers' Association of Great Britain, and the author of four books.

As the examples across a range of sports and publications have illustrated, women could use their sporting experience as a platform to become a columnist or writer. As Joyce Kay's recent work has shown, it might be challenging to earn a full time living from writing but a range of endorsements could follow for those willing to diversify.[294] Reading was also an important leisure activity in its own right. Magazines like *Picture Post* could have more images on a page than text so were also a means of vicarious engagement for a variety of tastes and consumers. Here, sport could be treated in its broadest sense to mean health, body culture, love of the outdoors, specialist knowledge or a materialistic acquisition of gadgets. Even niche uppper class magazine like *Country Life* included more relaxed leisure-wear fashions, like sweaters, alongside tweed-based costumes and those using new yarns like Rayon.[295] Lower middle class readers of *House Beautiful* who were keen to build or establish their own home might browse advertisements for Gor-Ray slacks or 'Rufflette' curtain tracks in which a female racing driver with a number one on her car signalled efficiency and reliability with the strapline: 'You're on the right track'.[296] British editions of *Vanity Fair* which pitched themselves at 'The Younger, Smarter Woman' advertised fully-fashioned sports knitwear, and beach clothing, in addition to tennis clothing in the new fabric of Terylene, designed by Teddy Tinling.[297]

Sport was therefore part of the development of mass markets more defined by the 1950s but present in earlier periods. It is also worth remarking that from the middle of the twentieth century onwards, mergers and takeovers could share influences across sectors of industry. Clothing makes this point nicely. The Viyella brand began in 1784 on the Nottinghamshire–Derbyshire border, later in 1894 developing a worsted yarn (55% merino wool 45% long staple cotton) suitable for both weaving and knitting of shirts and nightshirts.[298] The company further expanded into hosiery and other garments, so that by the 1980s other brands owned by the Viyella group included British Van Heusen; Ladybird; Allen Solly; Aertex; Peter England and Tootal & Byford. Manufacturing, point of sale advertising and the clothing itself changed across these product ranges. While not appearing to be an obvious starting point for the historian of sport therefore, there is plenty of scope for looking at how active leisure and recreation provided markets for new and existing textile technologies in this and other clothing brands for women, men, girls and boys.

Tourism and travel were also related commercial activities. As one manufacturer of the Epco Minor trolley-jack pointed out, lightweight models could be 'Just the Jack for Jill' if her car broke down and a tyre needed a repair.[299] The increase in female personal mobility is borne out in popular men's magazines as well as the increasing use of motor-savvy women as a sign of modernity in women's magazines. Advertisements of many kinds use cosmopolitanism as a mark of fashionable good taste. At the peak of this was car ownership, so that by 1961 Volkswagen brought out a range in 'Sparkling gay colours in all their most fashionable shades-with a deep lustre that's made to last.'[300] The Birmingham Small Arms (BSA) manufacturer had also already moved into the cheaper motorcycle market with a blonde Monroe-esque woman in pink shorts and toning nail polish, white T-shirt and sandals pointing to a distant horizon from her BSA Bantam 125 because 'The BSA Bantam Goes Everywhere.'[301] In the days before compulsory helmets, she and her companion (on the 150 model) have gone to a fashionable beach resort with azure skies and palm trees. It doesn't look much like Clacton, Skegness or Scarborough. Another blonde wearing shorts in the same shade as the companies yellow logo, also met friends at the beach though she had travelled solo on 'The Scintillating BSA Sunbeam' scooter.[302] As a publicity stunt a BSA Sunbeam Scooter had been ridden from Land's End to John O Groat's and back. Over the 1837 miles it clocked it achieved an average of 35mph and averaged 102 miles to the gallon.

The need for publicity had been occasioned by BSA's interest in the market created by the urban popularity of the Vespa, an Italian scooter brand first made in 1946 by Piaggio. By 1951 it was being manufactured under licence in Bristol and within four years over a million Vespas were on Europe's roads. Fernando Innocenti started the Lambretta company in 1931 and it produced its first scooter in 1947, named after the area in Milan, Lambrate, where the factory was situated. By 1971 four million had been produced worldwide, many of whom were women able to ride the 'step through' design of the Innocenti in even the briefest of miniskirts.[303] Much of the advertising for the Vespa featured young women wearing Capri pants or denim jeans.[304] Examples are extensive across a range of high-, mid- and low-market publications, for example, *John Bull and Illustrated* was available every Wednesday for four and a half pence.[305] The likes of Bevil Rudd would no doubt have been horrified by these developments, but women had moved, metaphorically and literally, from the back seat to the front.

Conclusion

A proud, stately old lady . . . older, even, than Wimbledon itself. We
found her living in a rest home for elderly people in Hampshire. The
name: Charlotte (Lottie) Dod . . . the girl, who, beginning as a 15-year-
old in 1887, won five Wimbledon singles titles; who combined tennis
skill with outstanding proficiency at hockey; archery; skating and
other sports; who won the women's British open golf championship.
The teenage 'Little Wonder' is now an affable 85. Wimbledon's oldest
surviving singles champion: an old lady with time and tranquility in
which to ponder golden memories. As we took this exclusive picture
of her in the quiet of her room, it was like walking away from the roar
of the modern crowd into the hushed hall of history.[1]

In an article to mark the eightieth anniversary of the first Wimbledon
championships, Dr Willy Meisl made the point that, although many of the
sporting rituals first invented in Victorian Britain were still visible, Queen
Elizabeth II would see a fundamentally changed sporting tournament on
her first visit as reigning monarch in 1957. As an Austrian-Jewish sports
journalist who had emigrated to London in 1934, his own career was testament to some of those differences in the media; the extent of government
involvement in sporting international relations and a growing connectivity
of world-wide developments. Although the piece treated Lottie Dod with
all the hushed reverence usually reserved for a museum-piece, it reflected a
core sense of historical significance amid sporting and social change. Wimbledon may have been the last of the tennis Grand Slams to offer equal prize
money to the men and women winners in 2007, but corporate sponsorship
deals with premium brands meant that, by then, profiting from tournaments was only one of several revenue streams on which leading female
players could depend. As the chapters of this book have shown neither
Wimbledon, various football leagues, cricket's County championship nor
the Olympic movement had managed to sequester themselves from outside
influence in spite of a considerable degree of insularity.

Elite athletes, in the twenty-first century, do not play. Their work
involves committing to the serious and prolonged pursuit of excellence in
their own abilities; to surpass the accomplishment of others and to use
whatever means up to, and sometimes beyond, the laws of the time to
define new improvements. One of the challenges of this work has been to
assess the extent to which sports culture has changed. Leafing through a
copy of *Sky Sports* it would be quite possible to argue a post-feminist sporting age where individual merit and personality, rather than definitions of
gender, define participation. *Sky* seems to be something for every taste. A
Co-operative World Netball Series showcased the top six nations (England,

Australia, New Zealand, Jamaica, Samoa and Malawi) in 2009.[2] Having competed in The World Series Renault Championship in 2007, Pippa Mann (1983), became the first British woman to contest the IZOD IndyCar Series.[3] Hyper-muscled female wrestlers in small lycra outfits, wearing full make up and big hair were also featured as part of the World Wrestling Entertainment Incorporated 'Hell in a Cell' format. A few pages away, Paula Radcliffe (1973) was advertised as lead contender for the Women's World Half Marathon Championship and French designer Chloe Ruchon (1983) had created Barbie-Foot, a £10,000 table-football game where all the players were individually styled Barbie dolls. Snooker legend Ronnie O Sullivan was also happy to share his enthusiasm for running with readers of *Sky Sports* magazine, citing Ethiopian middle distance runner Tirunesh Dibaba (1985), the 5,000 and 10,000 metre Olympic gold medalist, as 'a legend of an athlete and a hero of mine.'[4] Are we to understand this mixture of sporting stories as examples of increasing individualism; post-feminist globalisation or are they too complicated to be understood at all?

A closer reading of these examples suggests that we still have gendered labour markets in many of the most prestigious sports at the elite level and this has only recently begin to transform. Beneficiaries have included elite athletes like Paula Radcliffe and Dibaba, who have become millionaires at relatively young ages by running in long distance races. First with a 15,000 metres event at the 1972 Moscow Games, then the introduction of the women's Olympic marathon at the Los Angeles 1984 Games, female endurance events have become increasingly televised spectacles. Not only is endurance running highly technical, medically specialized and mentally challenging, the media has no choice but to represent female physical challenge, and in some cases distress. A wider 'ripple-effect' of increasing numbers of women running alongside men to test themselves against the distance has been one of the biggest changes in world-wide sporting culture, and its attendant commodification, since the 1980s. A visit to any sports shop will attest, the very simple activity of running has become one of the most accessorized sporting performances on the high street. There are also now a higher number of people who have completed a marathon distance, either by walking or running, in an organsied event than at any previous point in history.

This said, the reinvention of the competitive urge as unfeminine can take contemporary forms, as evidenced by the many women-only charity fundraising events such as the 'Race for Life' in aid of cancer charities. Here an inclusive female-only ethos encourages participants to 'Simply walk, jog or run' for 5 kilometres to raise money: in short to exercise because it is a good health strategy, a way of remembering those loved ones who have died from cancer and altruistic. Accompanied by all kinds of pink paraphernalia, the carnival atmosphere indicates that the Race for Life is about collaboration, not competition. However, the rise of women's running over serious distances, such as half and full marathons, as part of mass events and as a profession has been a significant aspect of sporting spectacle in the last sixty years. By the time the first Olympic marathon was run in 1984, over 1,000 'ordinary' women had already competed in the London marathon, first held in 1981. The elite winner for the first two years in that event was Joyce Smith (1937) who, in her mid forties, ran the distance in under two and a half hours on both occasions.[5] The London Marathon and the Great Run Series attest to an expansion of these kinds of activity since the 1980s for club runners and amongst those who wish to raise money for charity. This remains a story for a later piece, made particularly complex by the role of the Avon cosmetic company who sponsored some of the first all-women marathons in the late 1970s. Women's sport, even when reported by conservative media entities like *Sky*, has become defined by a vague advocacy in terms of seeing participation as a blend of liberation; health and self-discipline. This needs to be seen in its proper context. It was not until the 1960s that the state became directly involved in sport with the setting up of the Sports Development Council in 1963. Successive British governments expanded the role of the state but remained ambivalent about direct funding, and in 1972 the Sports Council was granted a royal charter with the slogan 'Sport For All'. The 1970s saw an extensive programme of re-building of British leisure and sports centres; what had been twenty-seven facilities in 1972 and was to become nearly 800 by 1981. The aerobics boom of the 1970s and 1980s also meant a growing body-consciousness. On the one hand, Western obesity became more widespread as lifestyles became sedentary and 'fast-food' outlets increased. On the other, for more women, most of the time, the body was something to be worked on in the increasing numbers of private gyms that sprang up to accommodate fitness as part of an aspirational celebrity-endorsed lifestyle. Jane Fonda (1937) may well have been the most famous, but into the twenty-first century every soap opera actor who wanted to make some money lost a stone (or more) before endorsing his or her own version of a diet and fitness regime.

By the 1970s elite sport had transformed from a volunteer culture dominated by amateur values to professional standards but there was also a concomitant detachment of most female athletes from the goals of women's liberation in Britain. In the United States, the Women's Sports Foundation for example was co-founded by Billie Jean Moffitt King (1943) who had called for a boycott of Grand Slams which discriminated against the earnings of women tennis players. Winning six Wimbledon titles, four US Opens and continuously ranking within the top ten for seventeen years, Bille Jean King's fame went beyond tennis, especially after the famed win in the Battle of the Sexes match against Bobby Riggs in 1973. King ranked number twenty in a list of the most important Americans in *Life* magazine in 1990. Able to benefit from the activism and high profile of King and others who fought for equal prize money, The Women's Sport Foundation enjoys a much higher profile in the United States than the parallel organization in the UK.

It was only in the 1970s that the male football, rugby and cricket governing bodies began to show a grudging interest in the number of female players taking up their sport. Europe sometimes led the way. In 1970 the Deutscher Sportbund decided officially to sponsor women's soccer teams and national tournaments in 1974. The number of German women enrolled in the Fussballverband by 1985 was 441,932 in 3,443 teams. More may have played under gymnastics and tennis federation teams. Women constituted 15% of the national soccer federation but were not fully recognised as players until 1976. This mass participation has slowly developed but Germany now vies for the United States as the foremost women's soccer nation at elite level in the world in the twenty first century. The question of how to translate this to professional female team sport remains an issue with which most sports governing bodies are now concerned.

While there is a broad agreement about a need to improve the place of women in sport, there is no consensus about how that advance should be measured, or by whom. Nostalgia can be recycled by a media perspective that labels women 'pioneers' in various physical activities. This is often not so much an ignorance of the history of women's sport as an assumption that there is no historical dimension beyond recent progress. The personal challenge for each individual also speaks to the wider problematic nature of women's involvement. Referring constantly to sportswomen as innovators effectively operates as a synecdoche that conflates each woman's achievements (or failures) with the wider group. This is a process in need of further analysis.

The introduction to this book set out some of the problems of defining sport and a key finding has been that it is possible to over-state the effect of large trends by overlooking the smaller initiatives of millions of women world-wide. Some of the most famous women athletes are amongst the examples used here, but there are a number of figures who only just register in history, largely because no one has thought to look for them. Most people will not have heard of Phoebe Rolt (1954). Like thousands of men and women each weekend, Rolt is nevertheless a good example of the sports tourist, having adapted the training, traveling and competitive aspects of equestrian events to motor racing. Phoebe's racing budget of £3,284 enabled her to become European Champion for historic single-seaters in 1992, driving a Formula Junior Elva.[6] An average cost of £410 per outing, she took part in eight races across Europe, with an additional £24,000 investment in the car itself, a 1960 Elva type 200 FJ. This has presumably been a cost borne out of enthusiasm. How many more are there like her? More localized study and the compilation of biographical details in future work will hopefully help to answer this, and other, questions.

If sport has grown immeasurably in the period between 1850 and 1960, as people had more time and money to pursue their own interests, the analysis has highlighted the intersection with other cultural industries as providers of female leisure and recreation. By the 1960s many sports and lifestyle

magazines such as *Modern Motoring and Travel* had their own women's
pages, often written by women, in this case, Eleanor Goodman. Priced 1s
6d and published monthly, the magazine included a two page section sub-
titled: 'A Breath of Fresh Air: A Page For The Woman Motorist'. The editorial used the second person to speak directly to women. There was always a
review of a car, in February of 1962 it was 'A blunt little two seater which
was—to say the least—unusual. It was a beetle shaped 9 h.p. Singer Porlock
which first left Coventry in 1931. Anyway, it went.'[7] The accessories page,
featuring grease guns, backrests and thermostats, was modeled entirely by
women. In addition to the accessories and review, there was a photograph
of Goodman, an advertisement for a pure wool three-piece costume by
Holyrood at £13 11s and 6d, recipe advice on the importance of a substantial but varied breakfast, accompanied by humorous observations on
pedestrianism and parking. Reader Wendy Woldrun wrote in a letter that
was published, greeting the return of a woman's page but asking that there
should be more attention to the cars and less fashion.

    Without being gender specific, an interest in widening horizons, and
particularly 'Continental' travel, saw caravanning and traveling by car to
camp abroad also aimed at a family market. Mary Johns' piece 'Nomads in
the Alps' is a travelogue combining the sights of her tour and 'how to' eat
well while abroad, particularly in celebration of the Michelin guide.

> The only fixed thing about our holiday was the air ferry reservation
> from Southend to Calais. With camping equipment stowed in the
> back of the Gazelle, we intended for three care-free weeks to go as we
> pleased. The first night only was spent at a hotel . . . The round trip of
> 2,000 miles cost little more than £100 including air fares. Camp sites
> in France averaged between 3s nd 5s a night, a little more in Switzer-
> land. Shopping is simplicity itself. A reasonable lunch can be obtained
> from big tourist hotels, and the numerous charcuteries display tempt-
> ing dainties for a picnic. With a good map you just go as you please.[8]

If touring and motoring enabled people to go abroad to pursue their interests, there is also another whole literature on the very domestic connections
between gambling and shopping as part of a family day out. Having a game
of cards or a wager, going to the races and later, coupon gambling or playing bingo were a social, often familial and collective activity; albeit one that
could be feminised as 'having bit of a flutter'.[9] Bingo was a prime example
of social gambling, which could be combined with a visit to the sea-side,
or a night out. The rise of mail order firms in the twentieth century such
as Kay and Co., Grattan, Empire Stores and Littlewoods was based on
social shopping networks. This meant that Pools betting on the outcome of
football matches could use existing shopping connections to distribute cou-
pons. Not only did these firms employ large numbers of women directly,
they utilized neighbourhood links to reach families who paid agents for

their completed Pools coupon. It therefore should come as no real surprise that by 1948 a family day out could have gambling *as* leisure:

> From lunch until tea time we dozed in the lounge then walked to the sea front and along to Butlin's Amusement Park, a huge place with every kind of amusement and every kind of gamble designed to make young and old spend money like water . . . W. tried a gamble, taking three tickets for a mechanical device with many actors' names coming up in turn. My ticket had 'Ginger Rogers' on it but she did not bring me any luck, neither had W. or D. any luck with theirs. A woman with a large family won a huge 'Teddy Bear.'[10]

Women's participation in these kinds of collaborative speculative expenditure requiring luck, and judgment, also require more analysis. The use of 'spare' money left over from personal or family budgets allowed some women to access a range of leisure experiences and recreational goods, depending on resources. The debates that ensued reflected moral ambiguity in the midst of a wider leisure market for pleasurable pursuits. In the current deregulated market for gambling, women have been targetted by advertisers of sport-related betting and in gendered activities. The use of online, in-game betting, often using a mobile phone or tablet device, mean that women (and men) can gamble wherever and whenever they choose. Since the connections with the sport and gambling industry have become increasingly inter-twined, as have links with social media, there remains much to understand about these processes.

The examples in this book have evidenced a wider coverage of women in the sporting press than might be expected from the academic literature generally. The use of the BBC Sports Personality ratings from 1954 until the present day is one key marker of how the media has helped to note, memorialise and in some ways institutionalize female sporting performance in Britain. The chapters have also provided many examples of how women have gained national and international honours, either through sport or in related careers. Even within team games and elite institutions, there have been increasing numbers of women, like Wendy Owen (1954), who became part of the first official women's England association football team in September 1972, and making their stories available in the public domain.[11] We might read from this processes of commercialization, openness in sport and so forth but another of the key points has been the use of biography, life writing and autobiography since the 1850s to suggest that this was not a new trend. Writing about a life in sport has been one of the submerged traditions of women's participation only partially recovered by this work.

In 1964 'Plucky little Ann Packer put Britain back on the gold standard in the Olympic Games here in Tokyo today—and with a world 800 metres record time of 2min 1.1 sec at that'.[12] Packer's middle distance career had started, it was reported, as a joke only six weeks before the Olympics when team manager Marea Hartmann (1920–1994) had asked, 'How about having a bash at the 800 metres?' in what the Wilson government would come to call 'Our most successful Olympics for 44 years'.[13] The press attention focused on Packer as fiancée of Robbie Brightwell who had failed to win the 400 metres. She retired from competitive immediately afterwards, at the age of twenty-two, to get married and start a family. Mary Rand was already a married mother of one when she won her long jump gold medal at the same Olympics. Youth culture had helped to make female athletes famous from the 1850s but by the 1960s the media industry and grown and needed more stories, with instantaneous appeal. The *Evening News* in 1968 carried photographs and captions of 'The Girls Who Seek to Strike Gold' in Mexico, anticipating success. Since the televised Games became colour transmissions and digitised recordings new technologies helped to create the female sporting athlete as hero.

Arguably most of the 'Golden Girls' of the 1960s, 1970s and 1980s, like Rand and Packer, were responsible for important British medals but did not go on to develop a role in public life. For many who competed at the Olympics this was especially true. On Saturday 9 October 1982 Christina Boxer crossed the line to take the 1500 metre gold at the Commonwealth Games in Brisbane. It was to be the highlight of her career after becoming the first British woman to break two minutes for the 800 metres in Turin in 1979 and before finishing fourth in the 1500 metres at the Seoul Olympics in 1988. Coming fourth was no underachievement, as Boxer remembered: 'Coming off the last bend I was catching everybody and for a tiny while was in third place about 20 m from the end [sic].'[14]

Boxer went on to have a career as a sports development worker at Malvern College Worcestershire. However, increasingly women athletes like Mary Peters (1939) a gold medalist in the Pentathlon in 1972; Jamaican-born Tessa Sanderson (1956) who won the javelin competition in 1984 and, more recently, middle distance runner Kelly Holmes (1970) have used Olympic success as platforms for post-competition careers. Though not an obvious advocate of women's sport, the high media profile of HRH Princess Anne (1950) who was an Olympic Competitor in 1976; became President of the British Olympic Association and elected to the International Olympic Committee in 1988 has drawn attention to female leadership and administration. Her daughter Zara Tindall (previously Phillips, 1981) became a silver medalist with the equestrian team in 2012.

In the early 1990s, Liz McColgan (1964) and Yvonne Murray (1964) were the two premier female Scottish long-distance athletes. One commentator located the national tensions 'From the editorial perspective of Glasgow, being from small towns like Liz McColgan's Arbroath and Yvonne Murray's Musselburgh in itself constitutes a moral advantage, derived mainly from not being from Glasgow. These towns, whose whereabouts Glaswegians can only guess at, are perceived as pre-modern, and therefore innocent and wholesome.'[15] The small size of the Scotland and international media markets meant that both women left for a time to pursue more specialized training regimes and lucrative markets for their sporting talent.

This was a new aspect of an old tradition of football's 'anglo' players who moved south, often to England. While golf has been perceived as quintessentially Scottish but cosmopolitan, in drawing visitors to the country as well as being disseminated in new markets globally, moving to where the money is can create ambivalence in an individual's reputation. McColgan's sophisticated approach to her training and professional preparation often resulted in lukewarm newspaper coverage of her achievements in the English press; including her 10,000 metre world title triumph at the Tokyo World Championships in 1991. Now a mother of five, her divorce in 2012 was mainly reported in terms of financial difficulty and a loss of lifestyle, rather than as a personal misfortune. How have the markets for sport changed to help women like Mc Colgan and Murray establish post-competition careers? How then, can biographies of other women who became public figures as a result of their sporting abilities help us to deconstruct global forces between the 1960s and the present day? What of the legions of less-famous athletes?

There remains a lot of work to be done on gender in discussing both the globalization of sport and the contribution of sport to processes of globalization. There are generally three aspects of globalization understood to affect sport; an intensification of sporting relations (with the Olympic Games becoming more important as the twentieth century progressed); local identities becoming transformed by world-wide comparisons (such as national medal tables in Olympic competition) and local consciousness of the world (such as moving to markets where sporting talent can enable greater affluence). When Stella Walsh first competed for Poland at the Los Angeles Olympic Games in 1932 and again in Berlin, she understood that the tournament was a vehicle for her sporting talents.[16] However, a rule preventing citizens who had represented one nation from competing for their adopted country kept her out of both the 1948 and the 1952 Olympics (at least in her own mind). The rule-change allowing her to compete for the United States under her American citizenship coincided with her marriage to Harry Olsen but her competitive best was past and she was not selected. There were aspects of gender, class and ethnicity in shaping her career as well as individual choice therefore.

As has been indicated here, the increasingly global nature of national and international sports-scenes have been subject to variation over time, space, place, gender, age, race, ethnicity, physicality and so on. While satellite, media and communications technologies, travel and consumption of sports goods appear to suggest that the world is becoming increasingly smaller, an improved international presence is not the same as a particular sport or personality being globally significant. At the most simple level, it is difficult to think of a female sports product, a particular code or a single discipline that exists in every country of the world. It is even more difficult to think of it being experienced the same way in each country. Running is not the same in Arab-world as it is in the West; swimming does not always connote the same messages in Africa as it does in Australasia. Globalisation can be a somewhat fashionable catch-all and discretion in its use has to include an awareness of its limitations as a grand motif.

The rise of disability sport is another reminder that interpretations can differ across cultures. Paralympians had their champion in Ludwig Guttmann. Eunice Kennedy Shriver (1921–2009) was to be the instigator of a similar movement for learning disability.[17] Eunice was fifth of nine children of the famous political family in the United States and sponsored the first Special Olympics for mentally impaired athletes after being inspired to do something for her elder sister, who was severely disabled and institutionalised at the age of twenty-three. Shriver determined to erase the social stigma of mental disability and, as director of the Joseph P. Kennedy Junior Foundation, had the means and influence to develop the work of the foundation, renamed in her honour by Congress in 2008. The same year, a portrait of Shriver was unveiled at the Smithsonian in which she was depicted as surrounded by four Special Olympic athletes. More than three million people from over 185 countries trained for the 2011 Special Olympics in Athens. While this was the largest sporting gathering for athletes with intellectual disabilities, it does not have the same status under the IOC umbrella that the Paralympics have benefitted from. Differing kinds of disability sport can evidence global diversity therefore, but are not always directly comparable in organization, ethos or practice.

A fascination for speed and modernity has been expressed in the growth in the toys, games and clothing markets during this period as childhood has become ever-more commoditized. A relatively trivial example like roller-skating illustrates that, at different points in time, an activity can be reinvented for new consumers. Originally a music-hall act in the late 1840s, roller-skating had an obvious advantage to entrepreneurs over the ice form because it could be done indoors and therefore year-round. Attempts to open public facilities were often short-lived: a rink in Hale, near Manchester, in 1870 closed within two years. Almost forty years later, a more gentrified Princess Rink on Oakfield Road Altrincham had more success in 1909 with its maple floor, spectator side-seating and refreshment lounge.[18] Competitions were reported in the local newspaper and three skating sessions available each day, in addition to a ninety-minute period set aside in the early evening for beginners. Transitory success also marked a similar venue in Loughborough: the Premier Roller Skating Rink lasted less than a year to be replaced by a café and billiards room.[19]

If these were relatively low-cost cases, available to the live-in servants of the suburban middle classes, there are other examples from North America of women and men roller-skating together in 1885, wearing fashionable costumes in decorous interiors.[20] The range of roller activity in the Sally Fox Collection of women's sport at the Schlesinger Library, Harvard is intriguing. These include photographs of sculptor Abastenia St Leger Eberle with a figure of a girl roller-dancing from 1905 and a telegraph office worker using skates in her work. There is also a poster for a combined ballet-roller show, sponsored by the German Youth Association from US army records in 1948–50, which places this as part of post-war reconstruction processes.[21] First formalised as an association in 1924 the Fédération Internationale de Roller Sports (International Roller Sports Federation, FIRS) now has many sporting versions such as aggressive inline and roller hockey, as well as aesthetic and recreational disciplines. Are we best to understand this collection of diverse historical interpretations of roller-skating as transport, technology, aesthetic self-expression or as sport?

Do we best understand such activities by connection with the past or by recent transformation? So-called lifestyle sports and processes of Californication helped to popularise small-wheel personal transport from fashion statement to sporting activity between the 1950s and 1970s. Roller-disco in particular revived interest from the mid 1970s and, on a recent trip to Stratford Upon Avon, a teenage event was advertised as a Saturday night fixture at the local leisure centre. On a visit to Lausanne a week later, young executives in suits whizzed past me using skateboards and customised 'trick' and 'kick' scooters to get up and down the hilly terrain. It is not uncommon today, if the transport infrastructure is in place, to see people commute to work by roller-blading in some of the world's major cities, alongside people using inline skates for leisure and exercise.

Without wanting to pursue the example further, suffice to say here that the local expression and the international transfer of such activities is interesting, let alone the technical developments and what they tell us about manufacture, advertising and retail. Some historians of sport would dismiss these examples as not directly involving competition but this neglects how people interact playfully with their manmade and natural environment via technology that has, in some forms, been sportised. A wider sense of legacy is also present in our built environment. Having written in the previous chapters about how some sports performers went into music halls, theatres, ice-reviews and films, the humble roller skate can evidence how athletic performance has been influenced, and in some cases created by, the entertainment industry. The neglect of motor-sport generally in the literature makes a similar case for the transport trade. Future work can further dissect these transnational processes, as functions of increasingly worldwide markets, as the twentieth century developed.

So to what extent are theories of globalization useful in talking about women's participation in sport? Cosmopolitan fashions that promoted female sportswear and leisurewear suggest that this may not just be evidenced by examples taken from the media. While British women may have adopted the one-piece swimming costume from the late Victorian period, the two-piece bikini; playsuits; shorts; beach to evening wear combinations and so on, were influenced by 'Continental' fashion, a fascination with Asia and influences from the United States. British women's experiences of wearing these items will have been as different from their American and European counterparts as they were similar. By 2007, along with Steffi Graf (1969), Billy Jean King was one of only two sportswomen to have had a tennis trainer designed with her endorsement by Adidas.[22] The other woman credited with her own shoes, trainers and sandals was hip-hop artist Missy Elliot's (Respect ME) line, representing the cross over from athletic gear to street wear and popular culture via the increasingly corporate approach of rappers, music producers and executives such as Jay-Z and 50 Cent. Like many men, women wear training shoes to signal aspects of lifestyle quite apart from their sporting interests.

Distinguishing transnational commercial markets for goods and products from how people performed sport is not always helpful. If one of the points of this book was to critique the homogeneous classification of 'women's sport', the heterogeneous economic, political and cultural nature of globalization also make this a complex topic. Globalisation can therefore not simply be determined as good or bad; a process of downward cascade or popular engagement; economically driven by centre and consumed by periphery. As is evident from the numerous examples of sporting women in this book, the differing interests of individuals, localized communities and large groups mean that powerful drivers can be embraced or resisted. What also emerges clearly is women initiating, producing and exploiting sporting events that became international in scale. Female activism had been historically formed and mobilized through access to physical activities. Sporting participation was extensive and affected almost every demographic group from young girls to grandmothers. Likewise, female interest in sport has to be read in its widest sense and had a discernable influence on British political, social and cultural life. By the 1960s most kinds of sporting involvement had been breached by women and they had led some significant aspects of its performance and values. Understanding broader sporting traditions necessarily entails an appreciation of the emergence of assertive female physicality and its subsequent re-definition by diverse women.

Appendix 1
Clubs Belonging to the All England Women's Hockey Association (AEWHA) in the 1899–1900 Season and Their Colours

There were a total of seventy-two clubs, including Edinburgh. The date of election to the All England Women's Hockey Association is on the left of the page and the colours are detailed under the club name.

Wherever possible I have kept the definitions of club colours as the original document so inconsistencies in describing items of clothing, such as skirt/skirts or shirt/blouse, reflected the records of the time. I have also kept the original spelling and syntax. While some clubs do stipulate specific shades for particular garments, others used a general colour; Red, White and Blue, for example.

Date of Election:	Name (Colours)
Oct. 1897	Atalanta Hockey Club, Bromley *(Colours-Light Blue Shirt, Dark Blue Tie and Hat-band)*
Jan. 1898	Bath Ladies' Hockey Club, Bath *(Colours-Electric Blue Shirt, White Tie and Waistband, Electric Blue and White Hat-band)*
Sep. 1896	Bayford Ladies' Hockey Club, Hertford *(Colours-Scarlet, Grey and White)*
Apr. 1899	Beckenham Ladies' Hockey Club, Hertford *(Colours-Green Skirt, White Shirt, Green and Pale Blue Striped Tie)*
Nov. 1897	Bedford College Hockey Club, York Place W. *(Colours-Black, Red and White)*
Nov. 1897	Bergman-Österberg Physical Training College Hockey Club, Dartford *(Colours-Navy Tunic, White Jersey, Badge in Blue and Gold)*
Nov. 1899	Bexhill Ladies' Hockey Club, St Leonards-on-Sea *(No colours listed)*
May 1896	Blackheath Ladies' Hockey Club, Blackheath *(Colours-Blue and Red)*
Nov. 1895	Bournemouth Ladies' Hockey Club, Bournemouth *(Colours-White Shirts, Dark Green Skirts, Green, Red and White Ties and Hat-bands)*

Apr. 1899	Brighton Ladies' Hockey Club, Brighton *(Colours-Navy Skirts, Scarlet , White Ties and Belts)*
Apr. 1897	Broxbourne Ladies' Hockey Club, Herts *(Colours-Navy Skirts, White Shirt, Pale Blue, Black and White Striped Tie)*
Apr. 1897	Bushey Ladies' Hockey Club, Herts *(Colours-White, Yellow and Blue)*
Mar. 1899	Caterham Ladies' Hockey Club, Caterham *(Colours-Red, White and Black)*
Jan. 1898	Caversham Savoyards Hockey Club, Queen Anne's School, Oxon *(Colours-Green Skirt, White Jersey, Red and Green Tie; Badge)*
Nov. 1896	Chiswick Ladies' Hockey Club, Gunnersbury W. *(Colours-Black and Yellow; Monogram in Yellow)*
Nov. 1895	Columbine Hockey Club, Gloucester Gardens W. *(Colours-Two Shades of Mauve and Yellow)*
Nov. 1897	Ealing Ladies' Hockey Club, West Kensington *(Colours-Red and Blue)*
Jan. 1897	Eastbourne Ladies' Hockey Club, Eastbourne *(Colours-Myrtle Green Shirts, Myrtle Green and Blue Striped Ties)*
Apr. 1895	East Molesey Ladies' Hockey Club East Molesey *(Colours-Cambridge and Black)*
Sep. 1899	East Southsea Ladies' Hockey Club, Southsea *(Colours-Dark Blue Dresses, Dark Blue and White Ties)*
Nov. 1898	Englefield Green Ladies' Hockey Club, Englefield Green *(Colours-Brown and Pale Blue)*
Sep. 1899	Fleet Ladies' Hockey Club, Hants *(Colours-Grey Shirts, Scarlet Ties, Scarlet and Grey Hat-bands)*
Apr. 1895	Girton College Hockey Club, Cambridge *(Colours-Navy Blue and Crimson)*
Nov. 1896	Grassendale Hockey Club, Hants *(Colours-Scarlet and Blue)*
Apr. 1897	Grasshopper or Mid-Herts Hockey Club *(Colours-White Shirts and Caps, Green, Black and White Ties)*
Sep. 1899	Guildford Ladies' Hockey Club, Guildford *(Colours-Yellow Shirts, Black Skirts and Ties)*
Nov. 1898	Hadley and Barnet Ladies' Hockey Club *(Colours-White Shirts, Dark Ties and Caps, with White Badge)*

Jan. 1897	Hampstead Ladies' Hockey Club, Hampstead *(Colours-Green Skirt, Blouse, Green White and Scarlet Ties)*
Apr. 1898	Harrow Ladies' Hockey Club, Harrow *(Colours-Dark Blue, White and Mauve Shirts)*
Apr. 1899	Hendon Hall Hockey Club, Hendon *(Colours-Dark Green Skirt, Cream Shirt, Scarlet and Green Tie and Belt, Scarlet Tam o' Shanter)*
Apr. 1899	Hendon Ladies' Hockey Club, Hendon *(Colours-Black Skirts, Royal Blue Shirts, Black and Blue Hat-bands)*
Apr. 1898	Hertford Ladies' Hockey Club, Hertford *(Colours-Red Stripes on Cornflower Blue, Red Ties, Dark Blue Skirt)*
Oct. 1897	Hitchin and North Herts Ladies' Hockey Club, Hitchin *(Colours-Starch and White)*
Sep. 1899	Huntingdon Ladies' Hockey Club, Huntingdon *(Colours-Navy Skirt, and White Striped Shirt, Scarlet Tie and Cap)*
Nov. 1898	Ilford Ladies' Hockey Club, Ilford *(Colours-Scarlet and Navy)*
Nov. 1898	Kingston and Hove Ladies' Hockey Club, Sussex *(Colours-Pale Blue and Striped Shirts, Pink, Black and White Ties and Hat-bands)*
Nov. 1896	Lady Margaret Hall Hockey Club, Oxford *(Colours-Light and Dark Blue)*
Dec. 1898	Old Lady Margaret Hall Hockey Club, Peterborough *(Colours-White Shirts, Dark Blue Ties with Mauve, Yellow and White Stripes)*
Nov. 1899	Mayfield Hockey Club, Southgate, *(Colours-Navy Skirt, White Cotton Shirt, Scarlet Tie and Belt)*
Apr. 1895	Newnham College Hockey Club, Cambridge *(Colours-Blue and Gold; Monogram worked in Gold)*
Apr. 1895	Amalgamated Newnham College Hockey Club, Wimbledon *(Colours-White Blouse, Scarlet Cap and Tie)*
Apr. 1897	Oxford Etceteras' Hockey Club, Oxford *(Colours-Black Skirt, White , White, Black and Yellow Striped Ties and Hat-bands)*
Mar. 1899	Ramsgate Ladies' Hockey Club, Ramsgate *(Colours-White and Pale Blue)*
Mar. 1899	Richmond Ladies' Hockey Club, Richmond *(Colours-Grey Blue Skirts, White Shirts, Dark Blue, Light Blue and Yellow Ties and Hat-bands)*

Apr. 1895	Roedean School Hockey Club, Brighton (*Colours-White Stripe on Navy Blue*)
Dec, 1898	Royal Free Hospital Hockey Club, WC (*Colours-Black Skirt, White Shirt, Black and Gold Shoulder Sash*)
Apr. 1895	Royal Holloway College Hockey Club, Egham (*Colours-Green; Badge worked in Green and Pink*)
Apr. 1895	Somerville College Hockey Club, Ramsgate (*Colours-Scarlet and Black*)
Sep. 1899	Southfields Ladies' Hockey Club, Putney SW (*Colours-Blue and White*)
Sep. 1899	South Hants Ladies' Hockey Club, Southampton (*Colours-Dark Skirt, Pink Shirt, Dark Green, Pink and White Tie*)
Apr. 1899	Speedwell Hockey Club, Woking (*Colours-Speedwell Blue Shirts, White Badge*)
Oct. 1897	St Quintin Hockey Club, Kensington Palace Gardens (No colours listed)
Nov. 1898	Surbiton Ladies' Hockey Club, Surbiton (*Colours-Electric Blue*)
Apr. 1895	Sutton High School Hockey Club, Sutton (*Colours-Heliotrope and White*)
Apr. 1899	Sutton High School Hockey Club, Sutton (*Colours-Heliotrope and White*)
Oct. 1897	Sutton Ladies' Hockey Club, Sutton Surrey (*Colours-Green Shirts, Red, Green and White Striped Ties and Hat-bands*)
Nov. 1898	Teddington Ladies' Hockey Club, Teddington (*Colours-Navy Blue, Ties and Hat-bands*)
Sep. 1899	The Barons Hockey Club, Reigate (*Colours-Black Skirt, Cream Shirt, Olive Green and Sky Blue Ties and Hat-bands*)
Apr. 1899	The Foresters' Hockey Club (Sutton), Surrey (*Colours-Foresters' Green Shirts, Buff and Green Ties*)
Jan. 1897	Tonbridge Ladies' Hockey Club, Tonbridge (*Colours-Green, Black and White*)
Oct. 1897	Tunbridge Wells Ladies' Hockey Club, Tunbrdige Wells (*Colours-Grey, White and Cherry*)
Sep. 1898	Waters' (Mrs) Hockey Club, Epping (*Colours-Dark Blue, Light Blue, Cerise and White Ties and Bands*)

Apr. 1895	The Croft Hockey Club, Walton-on-Thames (*Colours-Cerise, Buff and*)
Apr. 1899	Westfield College Hockey Club, Hampstead NW (*Colours-White Shirts, Blue Skirts, Coral and Brown Ties*)
Nov. 1899	West Grove Ladies' Hockey Club, Mill Hill NW (*Colours-Dark Green Skirt, White Shirt, Green and Mauve Tie, Hat-band and Badge*)
Oct. 1897	Wimbledon Ladies' Hockey Club, Wimbledon (*Colours-Red and White*)
Apr. 1897	Winchester Ladies' Hockey Club, Winchester (*Colours-Pale Blue, Black and White*)
Sep. 1899	Winchmore Hill Ladies' Hockey Club, Winchmore Hill N (*Colours-Scarlet Shirt with White Badge, dark Blue and Scarlet ties and Hat-bands*)
Apr. 1899	Windsor Ladies' Hockey Club, Walton-on-Thames (*Colours-Dark Green Skirts and Caps, White Shirts, Orange Sash*)
Nov. 1899	Woodford Ladies' Hockey Club, Woodford Green (No Colours listed)
Nov. 1899	Edinburgh Ladies' Hockey Club, Edinburgh (*Colours-Navy Skirt, Pale Blue Shirt, Scarlet Tie*)

Appendix 2
Dorothy Gwyn Jeffreys; Winifred Gwyn Jeffreys and Edith M. Thomson *Hockey Jottings* (unpublished: Kensington, London circa 1898). All England Women's Hockey Association (AEWHA) File D/1/1 Bath University Archive and Special Collections, Bath

The scrapbook contains poems, stories, hockey player profiles, accounts of matches and water colour illustrations relating to King's College Ladies' Hockey Club. The cover has the words Hockey Jottings and the date 1898. The inside cover has the initials DGJ, EMT, WGJ. Since it is unpublished I have tried to reflect its use of varied typography, images and text by my own comments in italics. The excerpts in this appendix represent approximately half of the material in the scrapbook, chosen for its representative flavour, rather than by any systematic selection.

Hockey Jottings: Dedication 'To Our Readers: The Editors wish it to be clearly understood that this paper is read entirely at the reader's own risk, and that they must absolutely decline to hold themselves responsible for any hurt, injured, or wounded feelings which may result. They will also take this opportunity of stating that they are unable to vouch for, either the truth or justice of any of the statements contained within, or for the correctness of the spelling.' *(Handwritten)*

(First line drawing)

1. People We Hear About *(Typewritten in blue)*

The Hon Sec of the KCHC

It was a dark gloomy day towards the end of December and the metropolis was shrouded in its habitual pall of thick yellow fog. It was with a certain feeling of timidity most unusual in one of my profession that I found myself at the portal of one of those commodious family residences which are so frequently seen in the neighbourhood of Hyde Park. My courage sank still lower when I was ushered directly into the presence of the far-famed secretary of the King's College Hockey Club. To my intense relief however, my professional instinct at once asserted itself, and almost mechanically I began to make mental notes of my surroundings, for I felt that the time for producing the inevitable note book had hardly arrived.

I found myself in a charming boudoir, which contained a somehwat curious assortment of miscellaneous articles, which I at once felt were symbolic of the versatile mind of the owner. In one corner I observed a dainty Premier bicycle rather inadequately concealed beneath a small duster; in another lay a mingled heap of Hockey sticks of every pattern and design, which I afterwards learnt were gifts from numerous admirers. Almost every sport had here its representative-here lay a box of Silvertown golf balls, there lay a tennis racket a pair of skates and a cricket bat, in the further corner stood a throng of geological specimens flanked on either side by drivers, irons, brassies and patterns of every decription, and I noted as a special mark of her skill in all sports, that the ubiquitous 'niblick' had here no place. *(Image of patrician journalist with notebook)*

My confusion having now somewhat subsided, I ventured to turn my attention to my hostess, who had not desisted from her writing on my entrance. She was seated at a large writing table, which was littered with cards of fixtures, challenges and lists of Members, with here and there an essay on some abstruss subject. At her left hand lay relays of Fountain Pens, and whenever the one she was writing with went wrong, which it frequently did, she instantly flung it down and seized another. As I gazed at her noticed that a reflective mood occasionally took possession of her, during which she pensively shook ink from her pen onto the floor, and from the appearance of the carpet beneath her chair, I concluded that this was her ususal practice. At length on my giving a deprecatory cough she flung down her pen and declared herself at my service. I promptly produced my workbook and we set to work. *(Image of woman with bike at desk)*

She informed me that when I entered that she was engaged in the engrossing task of translating Ibsen from the original into Gothic and from Gothic into Middle English Dialect, the latter of which she considered was a language extraordinarily well adapted to the drama. She then told me that she was well used to interviewers and their little ways and at once proceeded to give me brief and concise summary of the leading events of her life. I heard that she had undertaken the duties of Hon. Secretary of that well-known club the KCHC in January 1896 and that since that auspicious date the club had enjoyed a period of prosperity and success. Her extraordinary capacity for the post which she has filled with such conspicuous skill is too well-known to need mention here. Every paper of the day had devoted several leading articles to the chronicling of her many achievements in the worlds of Literature and of Sports, and every Magazine has given to its Public a more or less inflattering reproduction of her well-known features. Miss Sp-rg-on [sic] however, gave me to understand that she had other and wider interests apart from those of sport, and indeed the walls of the room, to which I now turned my attention for the first time bore ample evidence of the fact. *(Two small photographs)*

Along one side extended a capacious book-case, filled with books whose very names are a liberal education. Here I noticed Plato, Dante, Chaucer and Shelley side by side with 'Alice in Wonderland' and the 'Hunting of the Snark'. I had not time for further doscoveries however, as my hostess continued her conversation, and I was unwilling to defraud the public of one syllable. I next learnt that she was then engaged in arousing a love of literature in our youthful aristocracy. Spenser, she told me had already called forth exceptional signs of genius from the scions of several noble houses. She was also, she said, well accustomed to public-lecturing and had on more than one occasion held forth before a large and distinguished audience. That group of poets erroneously termed the 'Lake School' were her speciality, and on Shelley in particular she was generally acknowledged to be the greatest living authority. Space will not permit me to dwell at length upon the various other interests of this accomplished lady, for they would furnish material for several other articles. Perhaps on some future occasion I may venture to place before the public several volumes on this inexhaustible subject, for in that way only can I hope to do it justice. *(Image with red hat band, back of chair)*

As I left the house and went out again into the busy world, I felt that the few bright minutes I had passed had armed me afresh for the battle of life. For Miss Sp-rg-eon [sic] possesses an indescribable charm of manner and a most delightful personality which cannot fail to win all hearts. It was a great shock to me to be aroused from my mediations on this fascinating lady, by the news that my next call was to be on Miss Th-mp-on, [sic] but an interviewer has no choice and so I was obliged to make the best of my way towards Campden Hill. *(Initials EMT with watercolours by DG and photo of Miss Spurgeon by Kate Pragnell, Sloane Street Knightsbridge SW)*

2. Nonsense Rhyme

There was a young girl who would say,
As she shot the first goal of the day
'It just trickled through
I had nothing to do
But I happened to be in that way.' *(Initials EMT)*

3. The Backbone: A Poem

I
The members of the Hockey Club all heard with consternation,
That someone new had joined it, knowing nothing of the play
And it was widely rumoured, t'was a backboneless creation,
(What kind of creature this could be, none knew so none could say.)

Image of a stooped woman

II

With ample stock of rules and books and other hockey knowledge
She thought she wanted nothing to be champion of the game
So she went off to the captain, and enlisted with King's College
But found without a backbone that the game was rather tame.
Image of a stooped woman in a red shirt holding hockey stick

III

To see her try to hit the ball was truly agonising
No strength was in her body and she looked as limp as string
And the way in which she slipped about was really quite surprising
For she always was upon the ground when playing on the wing.

IV

Or, if by some unlucky chance you came into collision
You'd wish you hadn't done it, for she tumbled down and cried
And sad to say she then became on object of derision
And soon was known to all the club as 'droop personified'.

V

So later, quite excusably, it struck her
That she could not play at hockey any more than she could fly
So she thought it might be better to give up the childish tucker
And adopt a linen collar, at least she thought she'd try.
Image of determined–looking player with white collar

VI

So with heroic courage, which we all should try to copy
She bought a linen collar which was eighteen inches round
And she thought with joy and gladness 'I shall never more be sloppy
But the pride of all the members, when I'm on the hockey ground.'

VII

But she found that more was wanted, before her name was noted
And that backbones are essential if you really want to play
So five weeks daily practice by all the club was voted
For they thought to get a backbone, that was the only way.

VIII

When five long weeks were over, she returned in all her glory
She was quite another creature and had got a long backbone
With her nose which once was boneless it was quite another story
For it now was arched and stiffened, more decided in its tone.

Image of upright hockey player

IX
And her hair which once was lanky, now was brushed and combed
 back tidy
And she runs so straight and upright and refrains from tumbling down
So you ought to go and see her, on a Tuesday or a Friday
For she plays so well at hockey, she's the talk of all the town. *Initials WEGJ*

4. The Hockey Dinner 8 November 1897 *image of a half dozen women in evening dress around a piano*

We feel that in treating this subject we are trespassing somewhat on the grounds of our esteemed contemporary the 'King's College Magazine' but we are sure that our readers would be terribly disappointed did we omit to notice this great event. The annual dinner is a very well-known institution and raises the King's College Hockey Club above the level of ordinary clubs. It was started in 1893 and has up to the present time taken place twice. It has been commented on by all the leading papers of the day, notably 'Girls', 'Home Notes' and the 'Gentlewoman'. Back numbers of the two last can be obtained from any newsagent, but 'Girls' unfortunatley ceased to appear shorlty after reproducing a photograph of the 'KC Bicycling Club'. I might just mention by the way that the Bicycling Club is entirely comprised of numbers of the Hockey Club who are at a loose end in the Summer.

We are now speaking of the Second Annual Dinner, which took place on November 8th and was generally voted a most successful entertainment. No men were admitted, so it is unnecessary to make more than a passing mention of the food. It will be sufficient to state that everyone had had enough to eat, in spite of the qualm suffered by some of the Committee on the subject, that though several of the dishes looked decidedly curious, those who were brave enough to attempt them were none the worse; and the display of sweets was simply magnificent. The menus were tastefully decorated with suitable subjects by our Goal-keeper whose artisitc talents have so enriched this Magazine [sic]. Some excitement was caused by the appearance of the Hockey Song, printed slips of which had been thought-fully placed beneath every napkin. The general opinion seemed to be that it was a special hymn, and when the well known strains of 'Tommy Atkins' struck up, some few began to wonder whether they had joined the Salvation Army. The Chief feature of the evening was undoubtedly the speeches and we feel that we may dilate on this subject as much as we like, our contem-porary having for some unknown reason omitted all mention of it.

The toast of the 'College' was replied to with much feeling by Miss M-rl-y, [sic] slight confusion being caused by some of the guests who were already becoming rowdy, not quite grasping the fact that the subject was a serious one. She deserves great credit for having kept herself so well in hand, for not once did she allow the expressions 'alma mater' or 'espirit de corps' to escape her. This may have been merely an extraordinary oversight or-which seems more likely- the result of threats made by several unruly members to hiss loudly if she showed the least inclination to use either of these characteristic phrases [sic].

Miss Ev-l-ne F-th-ll [sic] who sat conning her speech, on receiving the long-expected signal sprang eagerly to her feet; she had seemed very restless since the beginning of dinner and had only been held in her place by the vigorous endeavours of her neighbours. To the intense surprise of everyone however, she did not even know her 'piece', but producing a crumpled fragment of paper proceeded to read a very long and classical address. Her frequent and familiar allusions to Plato, Aristotle and Homer proved her extensive reading, and it was evidently quite impossible for her to bring herself down to the level of her hearers. The applause at the conclusion was, however, tremendous, for it is a well known fact that people prefer that which they do not understand. . . . A small reception of former members of the Club was held later, and after a little music the remainder of the tme was passed in playing strange and weird games, the most noteworthy feature of which was the life-like representation of 'Nansen' by Miss Lupton.

Initials EMT: Fridtjof Nansen (1861–1930) was a Norwegian explorer, scientist, diplomat, humanitarian and Nobel Peace Prize laureate.

5. Nonsense Rhymes

II
We've a wonderful player at Centre
And we are sure that you could not invent a
More capable leader
Or better wing feeder
And from scoring-well none can prevent her.

III
There was a young girl who'd declare
That the team couldn't do up its hair;
That the length of each skirt
Made its trail in the dirt
That its boots were in shocking repair

6. Women who have got on *typewritten in blue*

Miss Ed-th J M-rl-y [sic]

The name of M-rl-y is one that has become celebrated in the literary and legal annals of our country and it is destined to gain additional lustre in the world of hockey in the person of Miss Ed-th M-rl-y who has rapidly come to the front as a professional stick raiser of exceptional talent.

She was quite willing to talk to me in reply to a question as to whether such perfection of her art had been acquired after long training and practice. She said, 'No, two or three years ago it suddenly developed itself, and from that time I have never lost this extraordinary power, which, though it displays itself in many people, had never been known to so nearly attain perfection as in my case.' *(Sketches and small photographs)*

7. The Sad History of Dorothy Dubbs

I
Dorothy Dubbs of Wormwood Scrubbs
Was happy as a girl could be
For her only thought was to do as she ought
So her life from care was free
And her mother cried, with a natural pride
'What a charming girl is she!'

II
Oh! Dorothy Dubbs of Wormwood scrubbs
There's trouble in store for you!
For she heard one day, from a friend to say
That if she had nothing to do,
She might come round to the College Ground
A Hockey match to view.

III
So Dorothy Dubbs of Wormwood Scrubbs
Set off the very next day.
And her mother's reply, to her fond goodbye
Was: 'Don't let them make you play.
Tho' it's up-to-date you know how I hate
Girls who behave in that way.'

IV
Oh! Mrs Dubbs of Wormwood Scrubbs
Your warning was quite in vain!
For the Spirit of Sport your daughter has caught,
And she won't come home again
She has joined six clubs at Wormwood Scrubbs
And has hockey on the Brain [sic]!

V
Poor Dorothy Dubbs of Wormwood Scrubbs
In matches all day she'd play,

and when they were o'er she'd clamour for more,
Tho' half dead with fatigue she'd lay.
Tho' she could not walk, she still would talk
of the goals she'd shot that day.

VI
Poor Dorothy Dubbs of Wormwood scrubbs
Died in the thick of the fight
And to see her tomb in the gathering gloom
Is a melancholy sight;
And they say that her ghost
May be seen at its post
On any moonlit night.

8. Nonsense rhymes

IV
There was once a girl who played 'back'
Whom no one could call 'slack'
For in spite of her fads
And affection for pads
When she once got the ball she *could* whack.

V
There is a young girl who's so tall
She simply could *not* see the ball
So she charges the foe
With her head very low
The result is-blue stars and a fall.

VI
There once were two girls who refused
To let the Pavilion be used
They complained of the look
Of a skirt on a hook
And the piles of odd boots they abused.

9. Bushey V KCHC 2nd XI 27 January 1898
(with apologies to 'I Once Had A Dear Little Doll, dears')

Against Bushey we once played a match, dears,
It wasn't the pleasantest game
For they were so horribly rough, dears
That we all came off wounded, or lame-

And two of our team didn't come, dears
For one of them 'just missed' her train
And the other-I'm sure I don't know, dears
For she never was heard of again-

Well up till half time was called, dears
All went off quite happy and calm
For the goals were one to each side, dears
So we felt we'd no cause for alarm-

But we thought that the others looked cross dears
And we saw that they were getting up steam,
For they were the pick of their club, dears
While we were our second best team-

But once more we each got a goal, dears,
And rhen they got angrier still
And determined if they wouldn't win, dears
At least some of us they would kill-

So up came to one of our team, dears,
A girl with a face stern and red
And she lifted her stick in the air, dears,
And gave her a crack on the head-

Then out poured the blood in a stream, dears,
And they wrapped up her head in a shawl
But she said as she walked from the field, dears,
'Oh, it really is nothing at all.'

Then they took her away to a house, dears,
And did for her all that they could do
But they hadn't got any raw beef, dears,
So they gave her some cold Irish stew-

So luck didn't favour the brave, dears,
And the goals became two to their four
Though the one who had 'just missed' her train, dears,
Had turned up five minutes before-

The moral of this story is quite plain, dears,
Never 'just miss' your train from the town,
And 'wire' if you can't play at all, dears,
Or else you'll be fined half-a crown. *Initials WEGJ*

Appendix 3
Women's Participation in the Modern Olympic Summer Games 1896–2004

The following table summarises the officially recognised numbers for women's participation in the Summer Olympic Games, though there remain disputes over whether some events were Olympic, part of Exhibitions or Women's World Games.

Year	Sports	Events	Countries	Participants
1896	0	0	0	0
1900	6	10	5	22
1904	1	2	1	6
1908	2	3	4	44
1912	2	4	11	55
1920	2	4	13	77
1924	3	11	20	136
1928	4	15	26	290
1932	3	14	18	127
1936	4	15	26	328
1948	5	19	33	385
1952	6	25	51	518
1956	6	26	39	384
1960	6	29	45	610
1964	7	33	53	683
1968	7	39	54	781
1972	8	43	65	1058
1976	11	49	66	1247
1980	12	50	54	1125
1984	14	62	94	1567
1988	17	86	117	2186
1992	19	98	136	2708
1996	21	108	169	3626
2000	25	132	199	4069
2004[1]	26	135	201	4306

Adapted from IOC archive and Steph Daniels and Anita Tedder 'A Proper Spectacle': Women Olympians 1900–1936 Bedford: ZeNaNa Press and International Olympic Committee figures at http://www.olympic.org/ioc accessed 20 January 2013.
[1]This represented 40.74% of 10,568 athletes with 59% of 6,262 male athletes. For women, this was a 2.5% increase on Sydney, 6.7% increase on Atlanta 1996, 11.8% on Barcelona 1992 and 14.6 on Seoul 1988.

Appendix 4
Schedule of International Federation of Women's Hockey Associations (IFWHA) Conferences 1930–1983

The International Federation of Women's Hockey Associations (IFWHA) was formed in 1927 by founding countries Australia, Denmark, England, Ireland, Scotland, South Africa, the United States of America and Wales. It aimed to safeguard the interests of women's hockey world-wide, to promote friendly communication between women players and to work towards uniformity in the rules of the games.

The first triennial conference of the IFWHA was held in Geneva, Switzerland in 1930. No tournament was held on this occasion but exhibition matches were played. Subsequent conferences, held around the world, were accompanied by an international tournament. International tours by visiting national teams were often associated with each conference, in addition to those arranged directly between countries.

First Triennial Conference:	Geneva, Switzerland 4–8 July 1930
Second Triennial Conference:	Copenhagen, Denmark 5–10 September 1933
Third Triennial Conference:	Philadelphia, USA 20 October–1 November 1936
Fourth Triennial Conference:	Cancelled due to outbreak of war 1939
Fourth Triennial Conference:	Johannesburg, South Africa 29 June–12 July 1950
Fifth Triennial Conference:	Folkestone, Kent 28 September–10 October 1953
Sixth Triennial Conference:	Sydney, Australia 20 May–2 June 1956
Seventh Triennial Conference:	Amsterdam, Netherlands 23 Apri–7 May 1959
Eighth Conference:	Towson, Maryland 4–19 September 1963
Ninth Conference:	Leverkusen-Cologne, Germany 11–26 September 1967
Tenth Conference:	Auckland, New Zealand 19 August–2 September 1971
Eleventh Conference:	Edinburgh, Scotland 28 August–11 September 1975
Twelfth Conference:	Vancouver, Canada 16–30 August 1979
Thirteenth and Final Conference:	Kuala Lumpur, Malaysia 8–11 April 1983

Appendix 5
Scotland versus Ireland Programme 23 March 1935 at Glasgow High Schools' Club Ground, Old Anniesland

Player profiles are copied directly from the Programme notes with all spellings, syntactical and grammatical constructions accurate to the original.

Scottish team-playing in Purple and White

1. **Mrs A. Cleland** (Goal) **Captain**. International 1923–24, 1927–35. Plays for East of Scotland and Edinburgh Western. Toured in America and Copenhagen. Educated at Irvine Academy.

2. **J. Bryce** (R. Back) International 1928–30, 33, 35. Reserve 1926–27, 1921–32. Played for North of Scotland 1923–24, 28–31, South 1925–27, Midlands 1932–33. Toured Copenhagen 1933. Plays for Broughty Ferry Club Games. Educated at St. Leonards, and now a member of staff there.

3. **J. R. Caird** (L. Back) International 1932–35. Played for East of Scotland 1928–35, and plays for Edinburgh Western. Educated at St George's Edinburgh and Edinburgh University. Is now Assistant Cataloguer of Manuscripts, National Library of Scotland.

4. **M. J. M. Couper** (R. Half) International 1932–35. Played for East of Scotland 1926, 28–35. Has played for Edinburgh University and Edinburgh Ladies. Was educated at Knox School, Haddington and Edinburgh University. Is now a member of the teaching profession.

5. **I. Hutchison** (C. Half) Vice Captain. International 1930–35. Reserve 1929. Plays for West District and Anglo-Sceptics, Durham County and Cartha Clubs. Educated at Queens Park School, Glasgow, and Glasgow University. Is now a member of the teaching profession.

6. **M. S. Keay** (L. Half) International 1934–35. Played for West District 1931–35. Toured Copenhagen 1933. Plays for Park School Former Pupils' Club, having been educated there. Has post as a Businesss Manager.

7. **A. Forrester** (R. Wing) International 1930, 32–35. Reserve 1929. Plays for the Midlands of Scotland and Madras College F. P. Club. Educated at Broughton and Edinburgh University. Is now a member of the teaching profession.

8. **N. Campbell** (R. Inner) International 1931–35. Plays for East of Scotland and Women Watsonians' Hockey Club. Toured Copenhagen 1933. Educated at George Watson's Ladies' College and Edinburgh University. Is now a Doctor at the Royal Infirmary, Edinburgh.

9. **E. McKerrow** (C. Forward) International 1935. Reserve 1932, 34. Played for South of Scotland 1927–30, 32–35 and for Ediburgh Ladies and Dumfries. Toured S. Africa 1930, USA 1931 and Denmark 1933 and was a member of the British Wanderers Team, Egypt 1934. Educated at St Leonards.

10. **E. W. Herriot** (L. Inner) International 1933–35. Reserve 1932. Played for East of Scotland 1930–34 and for Edinburgh Western. Toured Denmark. Educated at St George's and Edinburgh University. Is now Secretary to the Geological Department of the University of Edinburgh.

11. **M. Kennedy** (L. Wing) International 1935. Reserve 1933–34. Played for West District 1927–34 and for Hutchesons' Girls FP Hockey Club, having been educated there. Is a Masseuse.

Irish Team-playing in Green and White

1. **M. E. Carter** (Goal) International 1933. Played for English Reserves 1930, 1031, 1934 and for Midlands (England) 1929, 1932, 1933, 1935.

2. **F. Daly** (R. Back) International 1931–35. Played for Munster since 1931. Is a B Umpire. Was at Mount Anville School, Co Dublin.

3. **V. Mahoney** (L. Back) International 1932 and 1935. Reserve 1934. Toured Copenhagen and Germany 1933. Played for Leinster Juniors 1929, Seniors 1930–35 and at Midlands Tournament (England) since 1934. Member of Maids of the Mountain's Club, Dublin since 1929. Educated at Convent of Sacred Heart, Mount Anville, Dunorum. Represents Leinster for Tennis.

4. **R. Huet** (R. Half) International 1931, 1934. Played for Leinster 1931, 1932, 33, 34, 35. Toured USA 1933. Educated Bishop's Fort, Waterford.

5. **F. Kearney** (C. Half) International 1934–35. Played for Munster 1933, 1934, 1935. Member of Cork Club.

6. **O. Peatt** (L. Half) **Captain**. International 1929, 32, 34, 35. Played for Ulster 1927–31, West of England since 1926, Herefordshire since 1924, Leominster since 1923. Toured Copenhagen 1933.

7. **J. Harman** (R. Wing) International 1933, 34, 35. Played for Munster 1933, 34, 35. Played for Queenstown (Co. Cork) for ten years and captained for two. Also played for Cheltenham College for three years 1929-31 and captained for one.

8. **K. Kirkwood** (R. Inner) International 1927, 1931, 32, 33. Played for Ulster 1926, 27, 29, 1935 and for Anglo-Irish 1932–33.

9. **R. Mc Sweeney** (C. Forward) International 1927, 1933. Played for Munster 1927, 28, 30, 31, 32, 33, 34, 35. Member of Cork HC.

10. **J. Burns** (L. Inner) International 1935. Played for Munster 1934, 1935. From 1931–1935 member of Old Rochelle Club.

11. **N. Barry** (L. Wing) International 1933, 34, 35. Played for Munster 1933, 34, 35 and Cork club since 1929. Toured in Copenhagen 1933. Was at Farnborough Hill College, Hants.

Appendix 6
Wales versus England Programme 10 March 1935 Merton Abbey, Wimbledon

Player profiles have been copied directly from the Programme notes with all spellings, syntactical and grammatical constructions accurate to the original.

The Welsh Team

Mrs V. Jones (Goal) International 1935 v. Scotland and Ireland. Played for Monmouthshire and S. Wales 1935. Plays for Newport Athletic.

C. Owen (R. Back) International 1933, 34, 35. Played for Liverpool Lancashire, Flintshire, North England, North Wales.

Mrs Phillips (née D. New) (L. Back) International !931, 32, 33, 35. Reserve 1930. Played for Glamorgan since 1927 and South Wales 1931, 32, 33. Educated at Cardiff High School and University College of South Wales and Monmouthsire. Plays for Whitchurch.

B. Morgan (R. Half) International 1931, 32, 33, 34, 35. Reserve 1930. Plays for Dorset, South Wales and Whitchurch. Educated Neath School and Barry Training College. Captained hockey, cricket, tennis. Plays for Neath Ladies Club.

N. Tupholme (C. Half) International 1930. Reserve 1933, 35. Played for North Wales 1928, 29, 30, 31.32, 33, 34, 35. Flintshire1927, 28, 29, 30, 31.32, 33, 34, 35. Captain since 1932. Educated Hillside, Clifton, Bristol. Captain Liverpool Ladies' and Hawarden Bridge Clubs.

N. Roberts (L. Half) International 1932, 32, 34, 35. Played for Lancashire, Anglesey, North Wales. Educated Aigburth Vale, Liverpool and Liverpool University. Is now on the staff as Science mistress at Bangor County School. Plays for Beaumaris club.

G. Roberts (R. Wing) International 1932, 33, 34, 35, North Wales 1932, 34, 35. Educated Wrexham School and St Mary's College Bangor.

D. Williams (R. Inner) International 1927, 28, 29, 30, 31, 32, 33, 34, 35. Played for North Wales 1927–35, Montgomery 1927–30, Denbighshire

1930–33. Educated Howell's School Denbigh and Anstey PTC. Is now on the staff at Anstey. Played Lacrosse for Midlands 1926, 1927, and Wales 1929, 30, 34.

E. Haines (C. Forward) **Captain**. International 1924, 25, 27–35. Has played for North Wales since 1924 and East of England since 1928, Caernarvonshire 1921–24, Essex 1925–35. Educated Caernarvon County School and university College Bangor. Is now on the staff of Barking Abbey School. Plays for Ilford Club, Essex.

F. M. French (L. Inner) International 1934–35. South of England Reserves 1932, 33, 34, 35, South Wales 1934, 35, Sussex 1931, 32, 33, 34, 35, Glamorgan 1934-35. Plays for Cardiff Athletic Club. Educated High School for Girls, Chicester, Sussex (colours for netball, hockey and rounders). Chelsea College of Physical Education (1st XI Hockey, 1st XI lacrosse, 1st VII netball and 1st XI rounders). 'B' Umpire of the AEWHA. On the staff of Girls' County School, Aberdare.

B. Hier (L. Wing) International 1934–35, Leicester 1932–34, Glamorgan 1934–35. Plays for Llanelly Ladies. Educated Pembroke Dock County School and St. George's College, Red Lion Square, London.

The English Team

E. M Arnold (Goal) International 1925, 27, 32, 33, 35. Reserve 1928–31, 34. Toured in Germany 1926. Copenhagen tournament 1933. Played for East 1928–35. A member of Chiswick LHC. 'A' Register Umpire. Educated at Brentwood School, Southport and Dartford PTC. Formerly on the staff at Dartford PTC. Coached Welsh hockey camps 1931–34. Now on the staff at Streatham County Secondary School.

M. M. Knott (R. Back) Captain. International 1923–24, 26, 28–35. Toured in Germany 1926, USA 1928. Captain of Touring Team to South Africa 1930. Has played for Atalanta, Kent and East since 1922. 'B' Register Umpire. Educated at St Clair Tunbridge Wells, and Bedford PTC. Now on the staff of James Allen's Girls' School.

M. E. Collins (L. Back) International 1933–35. Reserve 1928, 30. Has played for Sussex since 1922 and the South since 1929, and plays for Highgate and South Saxons. Educated at Seaford Ladies' College and Dartford PTC. Now on the staff of Carlyle Secondary School for Girls, Chelsea.

P. M. E. Burness (R. Half) International 1926–35. Toured in Germany 1926. Played for South 1926–33, a d West 1933–35, Surrey 1926–33 and Somerset 1933–35. Was a member of Woking Swifts and now plays for Lansdown (sic). 'B' Register Umpire. Educated at St Bernard's school, Bexhill-on-Sea. Now on the staff of Bath High School.

R. E. Maddox (C. Half) International 1931–33, 35. Played for West 1930–35 and Dorset 1928–35. A member of Countryside since 1928. Toured Copenhagen 1933. Educated at Bournemouth High School. Now on the staff of Dorchester School, Parkstone.

R. Blaxland (L. Half) International 1931, 35. Reserve 1929, 32–34. Played for East 1928–35, Kent 1927, 29 and Herts 1929–35. A member of Haslar LHC. Is a 'B' Register Umpire. Educated at the Royal Naval School Twickenham and Dartford PTC. Now on the staff of St Joan of Arc's Convent, Rickmansworth.

Mrs A. M. Pilley (nee Tuckett) (R. Wing) International 1931–32, 25. Reserve 1930, 34. Toured in Denmark and Germany. Has played for West since 1930 and Gloucester since 1927. Has been a member of Weston, St Cross, Bath and Lansdowne Clubs. Educated at Clifton High School and is now practising as a solicitor in Bristol.

B. J. Dickinson (R. Inner) International 1934–35. Played for Midlands 1928, 29, 31–35, Worcestershire 1921–30, Warwickshire 1930–35 and for Edgbaston Club. Is a 'B' Register Umpire. Educated at Halesown Grammar School, Reading University and Birmingham School of Art. Now on the staff of Saltley Secondary School, Birmingham.

J. Ellis (C. Forward) International 1930–35. Played for South since 1930 and Surrey since 1929. A member of Wimbledon. Toured S. Africa in 1930, Copenhagen n 1933 and with the British Wanderers in Egypt 1934. Educated at The Study, Wimbledon and the Abbey Malvern Wells.

H. Redman (L. Insider) Reserve 1935, West 1935–36, Gloucester 1932–35, Bristol University 1931–35. Educated Stroud High School, now studying at Bristol University.

B. R. Eccles (L. Wing) International 1933–34. Reserve 1935. Played for North 1933–35, Lancs since 1932 and Freshfield Club. Educated at St Leonard's School, St Andrew's amd Bedford PTC. Now on the staff at Howell's School, Denbigh.

Appendix 7
South Africa National Women's Hockey Team taken from the England versus South Africa Programme 28 November 1936 Merton Abbey, Wimbledon

Player profiles have been copied directly from the Programme notes with all spellings, syntactical and grammatical constructions as the original.

South Africa

1. **F. Hoch** Educated at Girls' Collegiate, Pietermaritzburg. Graduate of Natal University.

2. **M. Brunton** Eduated at Maritzburg. Played for Hilton Ladies' Hockey Club and for Natal. Played for South Africa at the Empire Tournament. Sister of the international Association Football Captain.

3. **M. Currie** BA of Rhodes University. Now taking a commercial course. Played for Albany for three seasons. Captain of Northern Tranasvaal this year.

4. **E. Veale** Educated at the Girls' High School, Pretoria. While a schoolgirl represented Northern Transvaal and has played ever since with the exception of two years when she was seriously ill. Is the Hon. Treasurer of the All South Africa and Rhodesia Women's Hockey Association. Is now on the clerical staff of Pretoria General Hospital.

5. **I. White-Smith** Educated at St Michael's Bloemfontein and the Training College Cape Town. Represented Orange Free State, Western Province and Natal in the Inter-Provincial Tournaments. Played for South Africa in the Empire Hockey Tournament in 1930.

6. **K. McKay** Educated at Jeppe High School. Plays for Jeppe Old Girls' Hockey Club. Represented the Southern Transvaal as a half back and a back. On the clerical staff of a Johannesburg firm.

7. **J. Austin** Educated at Durban High School. Plays for Durban Ladies' Hockey Club and her province, Natal, as right wing.

8. **M. Hendry**, Captain. Educated at St Andrews Johannesburg, Potchestroom High School and the Training College, Capetown. Played for school, college, the Western Province and Natal. Is now Games Mistress at the Technical College Durban.

9. **E. Hartmann** Educated at Jeppe High School and the Witwatersrand University. Played for Jeppe old Girls' Hockey Club and the Southern Transvaal for many years. Elected captain this year. Has been teaching in Johannesburg. After this tour is over she if going to Denmark for three years to train as a gymnastic and Games mistress.

10. **J. Craddock** Vice-Captain. Educated at St Anne's College, Natal and the Chelsea College of Physical Education, England. Plays for Durban Ladies Hockey Club and Natal. Is the Durban Golf Champion and was the runner up in the South African Ladies' Golf championship two years ago.

11. **E. Bawden** Educated at Epworth High School, Pietrmaritzburg. Plays for Durban Ladies' Hockey Club and Natal. Provincial Hockey Secretary for Natal. She is an accomplished Cellist.

Appendix 8
The Brooklands Racing Careers of Some Prominent Women Drivers Between 1920–1938

This following represents an attempt to chart the careers of some prominent women competitors at Brooklands. The occasional first name has been elusive.

Name	Meetings attended	Events	Years Active
Margaret Allen	17	28	1932–1936
Hon. Joan Chetwynd	13	19	1928–1933
Violet Cordery	8	12	1920–1928
Ivy Cummings	12	13	1920–1928
Ruth Urqhart Dykes	12	18	1926–1929
Eileen Ellison	12	13	1932–1936
Doreen Evans	16	30	1934–1936
G. Hedges	15	28	1931–1937
Gwenda Janson/Stewart/Hawkes	16	20	1920–1937
Henrietta Lister	12	22	1924–1928
P. McOstrich	32	62	1931–1939
Kay Petre	30	48	1932–1938
Joan Richmond	18	23	1932–1937
Jill Scott/Thomas	19	31	1926–1939
Irene Schweidler	16	20	1928–1937
Dorothy Stanley-Turner	15	24	1935–1939
Fay Taylour	12	14	1928–1938
Elsie 'Bill' Wisdom	19	25	1930–1936
Victoria Worsley	16	19	1928–1933

Sources: Brooklands race card records; John Granger 'Women at Brooklands' Letter to John Bullock 28 July 1998 Brooklands Library and Archive, Weybridge Surrey; S. C. H. Davis Atalanta: Women as Racing Drivers (London: Foulis, 1957); James Beckett (ed.) Membership of the BRDC 1928–2008 (Northants: BRDC, 2008).

Notes

NOTES TO THE INTRODUCTION

1. Helen Wilson *My First Eighty Years* (Hamilton: Paul's Book Arcade, 1951) p. 131.
2. Bronwen Jones 'Helen Mary Wilson 1869–1957' *The Dictionary of New Zealand Biography: Te Ara—the Encyclopedia of New Zealand* http://www.teara.govt.nz/en/biographies/3w24/1 accessed 12 December 2012.
3. Jack Williams and Jeff Hills (eds.) *Sport and Identity in the North of England* (Keele: University of Keele Press, 1996) pp. 5–6.
4. Susan Sontag *On Photography* (London: Penguin, 1979) p. 74.
5. Susan Bandy and Anne Darden *Crossing Boundaries: An International Anthology Of Women's Experiences In Sport* (Champaign, Illinois: Human Kinetics, 1999).
6. Hunter Davies *Boots, Balls and Haircuts* (London: Cassell Illustrated, 2003).
7. Deborah Hindley *In the Outer–Not on the Outer: Women and Australian Rules Football* (unpublished PhD thesis, Perth: Murdoch University, 2006); Tina Moore *Bobby Moore: By the Person Who Knew Him Best* (London: HarperSport, 2006); Jessie Paisley 'In Her Own Words' *Liverpool Football Club* http://www.liverpoolfc.tv/news/latest-news/jessie-paisley-in-her-own-words accessed 8 February 2012.
8. Michael Cockayne *The Evolution and Development of Modern Sport in Altrincham and Its Immediate Surrounds circa 1850–1914* (unpublished MA thesis, Leicester: De Montfort University, 2008) p. 26.
9. ibid.
10. Catriona M. Parratt 'From the History of Women in Sport to Women's Sport History: A Research Agenda' in D. Margaret Costa and Sharon R. Guthrie (eds.) *Women and Sport: Interdisciplinary Perspectives* (Champaign, Illinois: Human Kinetics, 1994) pp. 7–9.
11. Nancy Struna '"Good Wives" and "Gardeners", Spinners and "Fearless Riders": Middle and Upper Rank Women in Early American Sporting Culture' in J. A. Mangan and Roberta J. Park (eds.) *From 'Fair Sex' to Feminism: Sport and the Socialization of Women in the Industrial and Post- Industrial Eras* (London: Frank Cass, 1987) p. 244.
12. Michael Oriard *Dreaming of Heroes: American Sports Fiction, 1868–1980* (Chicago: Nelson- Hall, 1982); *Reading Football: How the Popular Press Created an American Spectacle* (Chapel Hill and London: University of North Carolina Press, 1993).
13. Anon. 'An Old English Garden' *The New Monthly Magazine and Literary Journal* 3 1822 (Philadelphia and New York: E. Litterell and R. N. Henry, 1822) pp. 224–26.

14. Deborah Reid 'Scotland: Women Gardeners' Memories Wanted' *Royal Horticultural Society* http://www.rhs.org.uk/News/Scotland accessed 6 March 2012.
15. Anon. 'College Oratory' *Princetonian* 1:13 22 February 1877 p. 4 Princetonian Digital Archives http://theprince.princeton.edu accessed 12 January 2012.
16. Michael Oriard *King Football: Sport and Spectacle in the Golden Age of Radio, Newsreels, Movies & Magazines, The Weekly & The Daily Press* (Chapel Hill and London: University of North Carolina Press, 2001) p. 180.
17. Bonnie and Donnie Cotteral (Department of Physical Education, St Joseph's High School, Missouri) *Tumbling, Pyramid Building and Stunts for Girls and Women* (New York: Barnes and Noble, 1926) Foreword.
18. Varisty, the Universal Cheerleaders Association, was founded in 1974 http://www.varsity.com/about/company; The British Cheerleading Association was formed in 1984 http://www.cheerleading.org.uk; The International Cheer Union was created in 1998 http://cheerunion.org all sites accessed 12 January 2012.
19. Eduardo P. Archetti *Masculinities: Football, Polo and the Tango in Argentina* (London: Berg, 1999).
20. Kasia Boddy *Boxing: A Cultural History* (London: Reaktion Books, 2008); Erik Jensen *Body By Weimar: Athletes, Gender and German Modernity* (New York: Oxford University Press, 2010).
21. Whyte Melville, Kate Coventry Surtee and the Honourable Crasher *The Art of Teaching in Sport: Designed as a Prelude to a Set of Toys for Enabling Ladies to Instil the Rudiments of Spelling, Reading, Grammar, and Arithmetic under the Idea of Amusements* (John Marshall: London, 1770) British Library London Shelfmark 12983.b33.
22. ibid pp. 5–6.
23. Dennis Brailsford *A Taste for Diversions: Sport in Georgian England* (London: The Lutterworth Press, 1999) p. 7.
24. The Oxford English Dictionary 'Sport' Oxford English Dictionary Online http://www.oed.com/viewdictionaryentry/Entry/187478 accessed 1 March 2012.
25. The Oxford English Dictionary 'Sporting Girl or Woman' Oxford English Dictionary Online http://www.oed.com/view/Entry/187490 accessed 1 March 2012.
26. Susie Parr *The Story of Swimming* (Stockport: Dewi Lewis Media, 2011) p. 20.
27. Peter Sabor (ed.) John Cleland *Memoirs of a Woman of Pleasure* (Oxford: Oxford University Press, 1999 originally published in two parts in 1748 and 1749) p. 99.
28. Anon. *Lords and Ladies Who Deal in the (sic) Sport: The Pleasures of 1722* (London: Songs: 1722) unpaginated British Library London Shelfmark 425aa7.
29. Jean Williams 'The Curious Mystery of the "Olimpick Games": Did Shakespeare know Dover . . . and Does it Matter?' in Jeff Hill and Jean Williams (eds.) *Sport and Literature: a special edition of Sport in History* 29: 2 June 2009 pp. 150–171.
30. Pierce Egan *Life in London, or, The Day and Night Scenes of Jerry Hawthorn, esq. and His Elegant Friend Corinthian Tom* (Cambridge: Cambridge University Press, 2011 first published London: Sherwood, Neely and Jones, 1821).
31. Jane Rendell *The Pursuit of Pleasure: Gender, Space & Architecture in Regency London* (London: Continuum, 2002) pp. 138–39.

32. Dennis Brailsford *A Taste for Diversions* pp. 29–30.
33. Peter Radford 'Women's Foot-Races in the 18th and 19th Centuries: A Popular and Widespread Practice' *Canadian Journal of History of Sport and Physical Education* 25:1 May 1994 pp. 50–61.
34. Lincoln Allison *Amateurism in Sport: An Analysis and a Defence* (London: Frank Cass, 2001).
35. Susie Parr *The Story of Swimming* (Stockport: Dewi Lewis Media, 2011) p. 35.
36. Sports Council *Women and Sport: A Consultation Document* (London: Sports Council 1992) p. 2; Sports Council *Women and Sport: Policy and Frameworks for Action* (London: Sports Council, 1993) pp. 1-2.
37. Nancy Struna 'Reframing the Direction of Change in the History of Sport' *International Journal of the History of Sport* 18:4 December 2001 pp. 1–15.
38. Doug Booth *The Field: Truth and Fiction in Sport History* (London and New York: Routledge, 2005).
39. Allen Guttmann 'Historical Vicissitudes' in Annette R. Hofmann and Else Trangbaek (eds.) *International Perspectives on Sporting Women in Past and Present* (Denmark: Institute of Exercise and Social Sciences University of Copenhagen, 2005) p. 12.
40. Carol Osborne and Fiona Skillen (eds.) *Women and Sport a special edition of Sport in History* 2:2 June 2010.
41. Lynne Duval 'The Development of Women's Track and Field in England: The Role of the Athletic Club, 1920s-1950s' *The Sports Historian* 21:1 2001 pp. 1–34; Wray Vamplew and Joyce Kay (eds.) *Encyclopaedia of British Horseracing* (London and NY: Routledge, 2005); Emma Griffin *Blood Sport, Hunting in Britain since 1066* (New Haven and London: Yale University Press, 2007); Vanessa Heggie *A History of British Sports Medicine* (Manchester: Manchester University Press, 2011).
42. Sheila Fletcher *Women First: The Female Tradition in English Physical Education 1880–1980* (London: Frank Cass, 1984); J. A. Mangan and Roberta J. Park (eds.) *From 'Fair Sex' to Feminism: Sport and the Socialization of Women in the Industrial and Post- Industrial Eras* (London: Frank Cass, 1987); Kathleen McCrone *Playing the Game: Sport and the Physical Emancipation of English Women 1870–1914* (Lexington: University Press of Kentucky, 1988; Jennifer Hargreaves *Sporting Females: Critical Issues in the History and Sociology of Women's Sport* (London: Routledge, 1994) and *Heroines of Sport: The Politics of Difference and Identity* (London: Routledge, 2000); Catriona M. Parratt *'More than Mere Amusement': Working Class Women's Leisure in England 1750–1914* (Boston: Northeastern University Press, 2002).
43. Allen Guttmann *Women's Sports: A History* (New York: Columbia University Press, 1991).
44. Uriel Simri *A Concise History of Women's Sports* (Netanya: Wingate Institute, 1983) pp. 1–6.
45. Peter Bailey *Leisure and Class in Victorian England* (London: Routledge, 1978).
46. Arnd Kruger and John Marshall Carter *Ritual and Record: Sports Records and Quantification in Pre Modern Societies* (Westport, Connecticut: Greenwod Press, 1990).
47. Robert Malcolmson *Popular Recreations in English Society 1700–1850* (Cambridge: Cambridge University Press, 1973); Peter Radford *The Celebrated Captain Barclay: Sport, Money and Fame in Regency Britain* (London: Headline, 2001).
48. Mary Wollstonecraft A Vindication of the Rights of Woman 1792 available to download at Project Gutenberg Literary Archive Foundation http://www.gutenberg.org/etext/3420 accessed 14 August 2009.

49. Peter Bailey *Leisure and Class in Victorian England* (Oxon: Routledge, 1978).
50. Eric Hobsbawm and Terence Ranger *The Invention of Tradition* (Cambridge: Cambridge University Press, 1992).
51. Allen Guttmann *From Ritual to Record: The Nature of Modern Sports* (New York: Columbia University Press, 2004, originally published 1978) pp. 15–55.
52. Mike Huggins *The Victorians and Sport* (Hambledon: Continuum, 2004) p. 4.
53. Jeffrey A. Auerbach *The Great Exhibition of 1851: A Nation on Display* (New Haven and London: Yale University Press, 1999).
54. Anon. 'Mary Callinack (Kelynack), eighty-four years of age, walked from Penzance to the Great Exhibition' *London Times* 24 September 1851 p. 5.
55. 'Fashion V Sport' Victoria and Albert Museum, London http://www.vam. ac.uk/microsites/fashion-v-sport accessed 2 November 2011; 'Sporting Life' The Museum at the Fashion Institute of Technology, New York City http:// fitnyc.edu accessed 2 November 2011; 'Sally Fox Collection' Schlesinger Library, Harvard University, Cambridge, Massachusetts http://www.radcliffe. edu/schles accessed 2 November 2011.
56. Aquascutum http://www.aquascutum.com/timeline accessed 1 November 2011.
57. Burberry http://www.burberryplc.com/bbry/corporateprofile/history accessed 1 November 2011.
58. Reginald Brace 'Slazenger's Centenary' in John Barrett and Lance Tinjay (eds.) *Slazenger's World of Tennis 1981: The Official Yearbook of the International Tennis Federation* (London: Slazenger's/ Queen Anne Press, 1981) pp. 280–283.
59. Stephen Hardy 'Entrepreneurs, Organizations and the Sports Marketplace: Subjects in Search of Historians' *Journal of Sport History* 13:1 Spring 1986 pp. 14–34.
60. Peter Swain 'Pedestrianism, the Public House and Gambling in Nineteenth-Century South-East Lancashire' *Sport in History* 32:3 September 2012 p. 395.
61. Tony Collins and Wray Vamplew *Mud, Sweat and Beers: A Cultural History of Sport and Alcohol* (Oxford and New York: Berg, 2002) p. 28.
62. Nancy Struna 'The Recreational Experiences of Early American Women' in D. Margaret Costa and Sharon R Guthrie (eds.) *Women and Sport: Interdisciplinary Perspectives* (Champaign, Illinois: Human Kinetics, 1994) p. 49.
63. Ann C. Colley *Victorians in the Mountains: Sinking the Sublime* (Burlington and Surrey: Ashgate, 2010).
64. Kenneth D. Brown *The British Toy Business: A History Since 1700* (London and Rio Grande: The Hambledon Press, 1996) p. 18.
65. Katharine Moore 'The Pan-Britannic Festival: A Tangible but Forlorn Expression of Imperial Unity' in J. A. Mangan (ed.) *Pleasure, Profit and Proselytism: British Culture and Sport at Home and Abroad 1700–1914* (London: Frank Cass, 1988) pp. 144–145.
66. Dennis Brailsford *A Taste for Diversions* p. 146.
67. Nancy Struna 'The Recreational Experiences of Early American Women' p. 52.
68. The British Library *Nineteenth Century British Library Newspapers Database* http://newspapers.bl.uk/blcs/ accessed 19 June 2009.
69. Gillian Newsum *Women and Horses* (London: The Sportsman's Press, 1988) p. 110.
70. Kathleen McCrone, 'Class, Gender and English Women's Sport 1890–1914' *Journal of Sport History* 18:1 Spring 1991 pp. 159–82.

71. Colonel H. Walrond 'Archery: The Royal Toxophilite Society' *British Olympic Association Yearbook 1914* (London: British Olympic Association 1914) p. 37.
72. John Tosh *A Man's Place: Masculinity and the Middle-Class Home in Victorian England* (New Hampshire and London: Yale University Press, 2007) p. 187.
73. Neil Tranter *Sport, Economy and Society in Britain 1750–1914* (Cambridge: Cambridge University Press, 1998) p. 2.
74. Lincoln Allison *Amateurism in Sport* pp.165–171 see Appendix 1 Chronology of Amateurism in British and Olympic Sport 1863–1995 for an overview of the formation of various sporting associations.
75. Tony Collins *A Social History of English Rugby Union* (London: Routledge, 2009) p. 11.
76. Amateur Athletic Association http://www.aaa-athletics.org/history.htm accessed 11 July 2009.
77. Lincoln Allison *Amateurism in Sport* p. 165.
78. D. M. C. Pritchard *The History of Croquet* (London: Cassell Ltd, 1981) p. 11.
79. Jaques of London 'Traditional Games from Jaques of London' http://www.jaqueslondon.co.uk/ accessed 18 December 2012.
80. David Drazin *Croquet: A Bibliography of Specialist Books and Pamphlets Complete to 1997* (New Castle, Delaware and Winchester: Oak Knoll Press and St Paul's Bibliographies, 1999).
81. Elizabeth Williams 'Walter Whitmore Jones 1831–1872' *Oxford Dictionary of National Biography* Oxford University Press http://www.oxforddnb.com/view/article/100464 accessed 15 May 2012.
82. Ben Schott *Schott's Sporting, Gaming and Idling Miscellany* (London: Bloomsbury, 2004).
83. Maud F. Drummond 'Croquet, with hints and tips for Players' *The Girl's Own Paper* 303: 2 April 1905 p. 35.
84. R. M. Lewis 'American Croquet in the 1860s: Playing the Game and Winning' *Journal of Sport History* 18:3 December 1991 pp. 365–386.
85. Wimbledon Lawn Tennis Museum http://www.wimbledon.org/en_GB/about/museum/museum_history.html accessed 1 October 2009.
86. Mark Ryan 'The Langrishe Sisters and the Early Years of the Irish Championships' *Tennis Forum.com* http://www.tennisforum.com accessed 16 March 2012.
87. Richard Holt *Sport and the British* (Oxford: Clarendon Press, 1991) pp. 125–128.
88. Kathleen E. McCrone 'Lady Margaret Rachel Scott (1874–1938)' *Oxford Dictionary of National Biography* Oxford University Press http://www.oxforddnb.com/view/article/50305 accessed 7 December 2012.
89. Lewine Mair *One Hundred Years of Women's Golf* (Edinburgh: Mainstream Publishing in conjunction with the Ladies Golf Union, 1993).
90. Lynn E. Couturier 'Dissenting Voices: The Discourse of Competition in *The Sportswoman*' *Journal of Sport History* 39:2 Summer 2012 pp. 265–282.
91. Tony Mason *Association Football and English Society 1863–1915* (Brighton: Harvester, 1980).
92. Tony Collins *Rugby's Great Split: Class, Culture and the Origins of Rugby League Football* (London: Cass, 1998; new and expanded edition, Routledge: 2006); Tony Collins *Rugby League in Twentieth Century Britain* (Oxon: Routledge, 2006).
93. Mike Huggins and J. A Mangan (eds.) *Disreputable Pleasures: Less Virtuous Victorians at Play* (London and New York: Frank Cass, 2004); Christopher

Love *A Social History of Swimming in England, 1800–1918* (London: Routledge, 2007).

94. David Kynaston *W.G.'s Birthday Party* (London: Bloomsbury, 2010).
95. A. Horrall *Popular Culture in London, c.1890–1918* (Manchester: Manchester University Press, 2001).
96. Andrew Ritchie *Quest For Speed: A History of Early Bicycle Racing 1868–1903* (San Francisco: Cycle Publishing / Van der Plas Publications, 2011).
97. Anon. 'Rational Dress for Cyclists' *The Pall Mall Gazette* 26 February 1894 p. 12.
98. Mary Sergent Hopkins *The Wheelwoman* July 1896 Andrew Ritchie Website http://andrewritchie.wordpress.com accessed 12 March 2012.
99. Mrs Elizabeth Robins Pennell 'Cycling' in Beatrice Violet, Baroness Greville (ed.) *Ladies in the Field: Sketches of Sport* (London: Ward and Downey Ltd, 1894) p. 264.
100. Shelley Lucas 'Women's Cycle Racing: Enduring Meanings' *Journal of Sport History* 39:2 Summer 2012 pp. 227–242.
101. Stephen Gundle *Glamour: A History* (Oxford: Oxford University Press, 2008) p. 124.
102. Hamley Brothers Ltd *Hamley's Games and Toys Catalogue July 1915* Hamley's File, V & A Museum of Childhood, Bethnal Green London.
103. Kenneth D. Brown *The British Toy Business* p. 41.
104. Jeffrey Pearson *Lottie Dod: Champion of Champions, The Story of an Athlete* (Wirral, Merseyside: Countyvise, 1988) p. 16.
105. James Huntingdon-Whitely and Richard Holt *The Book of British Sporting Heroes* (London: National Portrait Gallery, 1999) p. 88.
106. Diana Up-to-Date 'Sportswoman's Page' *The Illustrated Sporting and Dramatic News* 1 June 1901 p. 53.
107. Mark Pottle 'Mabel Emily Stringer (1868–1958)' *Oxford Dictionary of National Biography* Oxford University Press http://www.oxforddnb.com/view/article/63388 accessed 7 December 2012.
108. Peter H. Hansen 'Elizabeth Alice Frances Le Blond (1860–1934)' *Oxford Dictionary of National Biography* Oxford University Press http://www.oxforddnb.com/view/article/52565 accessed 7 December 2012.
109. Madie Armstrong *Breaking the Shackles of Convention: Elizabeth Le Blond in the Mountains (1880–1920)* unpublished PhD, Leicester: De Montfort University 2014 pp. 10–15.
110. Nancy Joy *Maiden Over* (London: Sporting Handbooks, 1950); Rachel Heyhoe-Flint and Netta Rheinberg *Fair Play: The Story of Women's Cricket* (London: Angus and Robertson, 1976); Gail Newsham *In a League of Their Own! Dick, Kerr Ladies' Football Club* (Chorley, Lancashire: Pride of Place, 1994); Sue Lopez *Women on the Ball* (London: Scarlet, 1997); Alethea Melling "'Ray of the Rovers' The Working Class Heroine in Popular Football Fiction 1915–25" *The International Journal of The History of Sport* 16:1 April 1998; Alethea Melling 'Cultural Differentiation, Shared Aspiration: The Entente Cordirale of International Ladies' Football 1920–45' *The European Sports History Review* 1 April 1998; Barbara Jacobs *The Dick, Kerr's Ladies* (London: Constable and Robinson, 2004); Patrick Brennan *The Munitionettes: A History of Women's Football in North East England during the Great War* (Tyne and Wear: Donmouth Publishing, 2007).
111. Richard Cashman and Amanda Weaver *Wicket Women: Cricket and Women in Australia* (Kensington: New South Wales University Press, 1991) p. 10.
112. Kathleen E. McCrone 'Class, Gender, and English Women's Sport c. 1890–1914' p. 161.

113. Central Park Conservancy http://www.centralparknyc.org/history-of-ice-skating.html accessed 2 December 2011.
114. Kathy Peiss *Cheap Amusements: Working Women and Leisure in Turn of the Century New York* (Philadelphia: Temple University Press, 1986) p. 3.
115. Carolyn Nelson (ed.) *A New Woman Reader: Fiction, Articles, and Drama of the 1890's* (London: Broadview Press, 2000).
116. Sally Mitchell *The New Girls: Girls' Culture in England 1880–1915* (New York: Columbia University Press, 1995).
117. Mike Cronin, Mark Duncan and Paul Rouse *The GAA: A People's History* (Cork: The Collins Press, 2009) p. 14.
118. Linda J. Borish 'Women Sport and the American Jewish Identity in the Late Nineteenth and Early Twentieth Centuries' in Timothy Chandler and Tara Magdalinski (eds.) *With God on Their Side: Sport in the Service of Religion* (London: Routledge, 2002) p. 71.
119. Linda Colley *Britons—Forging the Nation 1707–1837* (London: Pimlico, 2003).
120. Jeffrey Hill *Sport in History: An Introduction* (Basingstoke: Palgrave Macmillan, 2011) pp. 3–7.
121. Lynne Emery 'From Lowell Mills to the Halls of Fame: Industrial League Sport for Women' in D. Margaret Costa and Sharon R. Guthrie (eds.) *Women and Sport: Interdisciplinary Perspectives* (Champaign, Illinois: Human Kinetics, 1994) p. 108.
122. Jennifer Hargreaves *Sporting Females* pp. 78–79.
123. Claire Langhamer *Women's Leisure in England* 1920–1960 (Manchester: Manchester University Press, 2000) pp. 5–6.
124. Tony Mason *Association Football* pp. 194–95.
125. Anon. 'Rational Dress for Cyclists' *The Pall Mall Gazette* 26 February 1894.
126. Beatrice Violet, Baroness Greville (ed.) *Ladies in the Field: Sketches of Sport* (London: Ward and Downey Ltd, 1894).
127. Anon. 'The Ladies Archery Match in the Royal Toxophilite Society's Grounds, Regent's Park' *The Graphic* 9 July 1870, cover.
128. Stephen H. Hardy 'Entrepreneurs, Organizations and the Sports Marketplace' in S. W. Pope (ed.) *The New American Sport History: Recent Approaches and Perspectives* (Urbana and Chicago: University of Illinois Press, 1997) p. 344.
129. Martin Polley *The British Olympics: Britain's Olympic Heritage 1612–2012* (Swindon: Played in Britain, 2011).
130. Jeffrey Hill *Sport, Leisure and Culture in Twentieth Century Britain* (Basingstoke: Palgrave Macmillan, 2002) p. 151.
131. Catriona M. Parratt *'More than Mere Amusement'* p. 45.
132. Jan Graydon '"But it's more than a game, It's an institution": Feminist Perspectives on Sport' *Feminist Review* 13 February 1983 p. 23.
133. Jean Williams *A Game For Rough Girls: A History of Women's Football in England* (London: Routledge, 2003) p. 26; *A Beautiful Game: International Perspectives on Women's Football* (London: Berg 2007) p. 30.
134. Duncan Sutherland '(Frances) Elaine Burton, Baroness Burton of Coventry 1904–1991' *Oxford Dictionary of National Biography* Oxford University Press http://www.oxforddnb.com/view/article/49597 accessed 18 December 2012.
135. Anon. 'Miss Lines' *Daily News* 28 April 1921, Lyons Press Cuttings File ACC/3527/427/1, London Metropolitan Archives. I am grateful to Steve Crewe for this reference.
136. Mel Watman 'Women Athletes between the World Wars 1919–1939' *Oxford Dictionary of National Biography* Oxford University Press http://www.oxforddnb.com/view/article/103699 accessed 18 December 2012.

137. Jean Williams 'Lilian Parr (1905–1978)' *Oxford Dictionary of National Biography* Oxford University Press http://www.oxforddnb.com/view/article/102447 accessed 18 December 2012.
138. Lynn E. Couturier 'Dissenting Voices: The Discourse of Competition in *The Sportswoman'* pp. 267–8.
139. Mike Huggins and Jack Williams *Sport and the English 1918–1939 Between the Wars* (London: Routledge, 2006) pp. 63–64 has only one paragraph on car racing and aviation.
140. Juliet Gardiner *The Thirties: An Intimate History* (London: Harper Press, 2010) pp.52–67.
141. The Hon. Mrs Victor Bruce *Nine Lives Plus, Record Breaking o Land Sea and in the Air: An Autobiographical Account* (London: Pelham Books, 1974) pp. 42–47.
142. Bruce Jones *Grand Prix Yesterday and Today: 100 Years of Motor Racing* (Singapore: Carlton Books, 2006) p. 96.
143. Key Petre 'My Motor Racing' in The Publication Committee (eds.) *The British Racing Drivers' Club Silver Jubilee Book* (London: The British Racing Drivers' Club, 1952) p. 139.
144. Cecil Bear 'Happy and Glorious' *World Sports: The International Sports Magazine* 19: 5 May 1953 (London: Country and Sporting Publications, May 1953) p. 5.
145. David Maraniss *Rome 1960: The Olympics That Changed the World* (New York, London, Toronto, Sydney: Simon & Schuster, 2008) p. xiii.
146. Bruce Kidd 'Missing: Women From Sports Halls of Fame' *CAAWS Action Bulletin* Winter, 1995 http://www.caaws.ca/e/milestones/women_history/missing accessed 3 January 2012.
147. British Broadcasting Corporation BBC Sports Personality of the Year http://www.bbc.co.uk/pressoffice/keyfacts/stories/spoty.shtml accessed 19 December 2012.

NOTES TO CHAPTER 1

1. Mrs Professor Beckwith 'Swimming for Ladies' *The Oracle* 11 October 1890 p. 14. I am grateful to Dilwyn Porter for this reference.
2. Sheila Rowbotham *Hidden From History: Three Hundred Years of Women's Oppression* (London: Pluto, 1973). See also Deborah Simonton *A History of European Women's Work, 1700 to the Present* (London: Routledge, 1998) and Katrina Honeyman *Women, Gender and Industrialization in England 1700–1870* (Basingstoke: Macmillan, 2000).
3. Margaret Ward *Female Occupations: Women's Employment 1850–1950* (Berkshire: Countryside Books, 2008) p. 3.
4. Deborah Simonton *Women in European Culture and Society: Gender, Skill and Identity from 1700* (London and New York: Routledge, 2011) p. 386.
5. Big Lottery Fund; West Yorkshire Archive Service; the University of Huddersfield; The Bronte Society; Hull Local Studies Library and Leeds City Council Libraries *History to Herstory: Yorkshire Women's lives online, 1100 to the Present* http://www.historytoherstory.org.uk/ accessed 5 March 2012.
6. Eric Hobsbawm and Terence Ranger (eds.) *The Invention of Tradition* (Cambridge: Cambridge University Press, 1983); Eric Hobsbawm *Nations and Nationalism since 1780: Programme, Myth, Reality* (Cambridge: Cambridge University Press, 1990); Benedict Anderson *Imagined Communities: Reflections on the Origin and Spread of Nationalism* (London; New York: Verso, 1983, revised edition 2006).

7. Wendy Freer *Women and Children of the Cut* (Derby: The Railway and Canal Historical Society, 1995); Helena Wojtczak *Railway Women: Exploitation, Betrayal and Triumph in the Workplace* (Sussex: Hastings Press, 2005).
8. For a contemporary view of folk and regional games see William Hone (ed.) Joseph Strutt *The Sports and Pastimes of the People of England; Including the Rural and Domestic Recreations, May Games, Mummeries, Shows, Processions, Pageants and Pompous Spectacles from the Earliest Period to the Present Time* (London: Thomas Tegg, 1845).
9. Norbert Elias, Eric Dunning, Johan Goudsblom, Stephen Mennell *The Civilizing Process: Sociogenetic and Psychogenetic Investigations* (Oxford: Blackwell, 2000) p. 414.
10. The Women's Library 'Dirty Linen Exhibition' *The Women's Library: London Metropolitan University* 28 September to 21 December 2009. In 1846, the Goulston Square public washhouse opened, bringing improved washing and laundry facilities to women in the East End of London. The façade now fronts The Women's Library, currently part of London Metropolitan University.
11. Gerry Holloway *Women and Work in Britain since 1840* (London and New York: Routledge, 2005) p. 97.
12. Carol E. Morgan *Women Workers and Gender Identities 1835–1913: The Cotton and Metal Industries in England* (London: Routledge, 2001).
13. Linda Hirshman and Jane Larson *Hard Bargains: The Politics of Sex* (Oxford and New York: Oxford University Press, 1998) p. 165.
14. Peter N. Stearns *Childhood in World History* (London and New York: Routledge, 2011 second edition) pp. 71–83.
15. Kenneth D. Brown *The British Toy Business: A History since 1700* (London and Rio Grande: The Hambledon Press, 1996) p. 40.
16. Hugh Cunningham *The Children of the Poor: Representations of Childhood since the Seventeenth Century* (Oxford: Blackwell, 1991) p. 161.
17. Children's Employment Commission *Appendix to the Report of the Commissioners Trades and Manufactures Part II Reports and Evidence from Sub Commissioners* (London: British Parliamentary Papers, 1842) p. 15.
18. The Children's Society *Hidden Lives Revealed: A Virtual Archive of Children's Lives in Care 1881–1981* http://www.hiddenlives.org.uk accessed 5 March 2012.
19. Ian Keil and Don Wix *In the Swim: The History of the Amateur Swimming Association from 1869 to 1994* (Loughborough: Swimming Times Publications Ltd, 1996) pp. 35–36.
20. Lisa Bier *Fighting the Current: The Rise of American Women's Swimming 1870–1926* (New York: McFarland and Company, 2011) p. 33.
21. Kathleen E. McCrone *Sport and the Physical Emancipation of English Women, 1870–1914* (London: Routledge, 1988).
22. Elizabeth Coutts 'Frances Mary Buss (1827–1894)' *Oxford Dictionary of National Biography* Oxford University Press http://www.oxforddnb.com/view/article/37249 accessed 10 March 2012.
23. Jacqueline Beaumont 'Dorothea Beale (1831–1906)' *Oxford Dictionary of National Biography* Oxford University Press http://www.oxforddnb.com/view/article/30655 accessed 10 March 2012.
24. Susan Bandy 'Shared Femininities and Shared Feminisms: Women's Sporting Magazines of the late 19th and Early 20th Centuries' in Annette R. Hofmann and Else Trangbaek (eds.) *International Perspectives on Sporting Women in Past and Present* (Denmark: Institute of Exercise and Social Sciences University of Copenhagen, 2005) p. 84.
25. Linda D. Williams 'Sportswomen in Black and White: Sports History from an Afro American Perspective' in Pamela J. Creedon *Women Media and Sport: Challenging Gender Values* (London: Sage, 1994) p. 45.

26. Peter Bailey *Leisure and Class in Victorian England* (London: Routledge, 1978) p. 124.
27. Emma Short *Moving Dangerously: A Conference on Women and Travel 1850–1950* Newcastle University, 13–14 April 2012 http://movingdanger-ously.wordpress.com accessed 11 April 2012.
28. Royal Humane Society 'History of the Society' Royal Humane Society' http://www.royalhumanesociety.org.uk accessed 12 March 2012. The archive of the Royal Humane Society was gifted to the London Metropolitan Archives in October 2008.
29. T. Hughes *The Whole Art of Swimming* (London: W. Lewis, 1820) p. 35.
30. John Walton *The English Seaside Resort: A Social History 1750–1914* (Leicester: Leicester University Press, 1983); John Walton *The British Seaside: Holidays and Resorts in the Twentieth Century* (Manchester: Manchester University Press, 2000).
31. David Simkin 'William Pankhurst Marsh' *Sussex Photo History Society* http://www.photohistory-sussex.co.uk/MarshGallery.htm accessed 11 April 2012.
32. Nancy L. Struna *People of Prowess: Sport, Leisure and Labor in Early Anglo-America* (Urbana: University of Illinois Press, 1996); Adrian Harvey *Football: The First Hundred Years, The Untold Story* (London: Routledge, 2005).
33. Claire Parker 'The Rise of Competitive Swimming 1840–1878' *The Sports Historian* 21:2 2001 pp. 54–67; Christopher Love 'Social Class and the Swimming World: Amateurs and Professionals' *International Journal of the History of Sport* 24:5 2007 pp. 603–619.
34. Ian Gordon & Simon Inglis *Great Lengths: The Historic Indoor Swimming Pools of Britain* (London: English Heritage, 2009).
35. Anon. *ASA Handbook 1902 Containing List of English Swimming Clubs, Laws of Swimming and Rules of Water Polo, Past and Present Champions, Programme for the Year* (Nottingham: J. Littlewood, 1903) p. 200; T. M. Yeaden ASA Secretary (ed.) *ASA Handbook 1913 ASA Handbook 1913 Containing a List of English Swimming Clubs; Laws of Swimming and Rules of Water Polo; Past and Present Champions and Programme for the Year* (London: Hanbury, Tomsett & Co., 1913) pp. 262–263. The annual yearbooks were printed early in the following year.
36. Kelly's Directories Ltd *Kelly's Directory of Leicestershire and Rutland 1900* (Leicester: Kelly's Directories Ltd, 1900) p. 528.
37. J. A. Jarvis *The Art of Swimming: With Notes on Polo and Aids to Life Saving* (London: Hutchinson and Co, 1902) pp. 69–72; Peter Bilsborough, 'John Arthur Jarvis (1872–1933)' *Oxford Dictionary of National Biography* www.oxforddnb.com/view/article/65070 accessed 15 October 2011. See also the International Swimming Hall of Fame entry 'John Arthur Jarvis: Honor Swimmer 1968' http://www.ishof.org/honorees/68/68jajarvis accessed 15 October 2011.
38. Rosemary Ashton 'Marian Evans [George Eliot] (1819–1880)' *Oxford Dictionary of National Biography* Oxford University Press http://www.oxforddnb.com/view/article/6794 accessed 12 December 2012.
39. Anon. *Swimming: A Bibliographical List of Works on Swimming* (London: John Russell Smith, 1868).
40. James A. Bennett *The Art of Swimming for Beginners: Exemplified by Diagrams From Which Both Sexes may Learn to Swim and Float on Water* (London: H. Lea, 1858); S. R. Powers *Why Do Women Not Swim? Voices From Many Waters: Ladies' National Association for the Diffusion of Sanitary Knowledge* (London: Groombridge and Sons, 1859); George Forrest

Routledge's Sixpenny Handbooks: A Handbook of Swimming and Skating (London: Routledge, Warne and Routledge, 1860); Henry Gurr *The Champion Handbooks: Swimming* (London: Darton and Hodge, 1866); Charles Steed (several years champion swimmer of England and Victoria) *Manual Swimming* (London: Lockwood and Co, 1867); 'Seargeant' Leahy [sic], with Preface by Mrs Oliphant *The Art of Swimming in the Eton Style* (London: Macmillan & Company, 1875); Captain Matthew Webb *Swimmers' Companion* (London: R March and Company, circa 1877)..

41. Anon. 'Rowing Exercise for Ladies' *Routledge's The Art of Rowing for Beginners* (London: Henry Lea, 1863) p. 36.
42. Mrs Hoggan MD *Swimming and Its Relation to the Health of Women: Read Before the Women's Union Swimming Club at 36 Great Queen Street WC 21 April 1879* (London: The Women's Printing Society Ltd, 1879) p. 2.
43. The Wellingborough Museum at William Dulley's Baths run by the Winifred Wharton Trust http://www.wellingboroughmuseum.co.uk accessed 29 February 2012.
44. Kenneth Hillier *Ashby De La Zouch: The Spa Town* (Ashby: C. J. Lewis, 1983) p. 20.
45. Ashby De La Zouch Museums http://www.ashbydelazouchmuseum.org.uk accessed 6 April 2012.
46. Dave Russell *Popular Music in England 1840–1914: A Social History* (Manchester and New York: Manchester University Press, 1987, revised edition 1997) pp. 4–12.
47. Stephen Gundle *Glamour: A History* (Oxford: Oxford University Press, 2008) p. 124.
48. Clare Parker 'The Rise of Competitive Swimming 1840–1878' pp. 54–67.
49. Dave Day, 'Frederick Edward Beckwith, (1821–1898)' *Oxford Dictionary of National Biography* Oxford University Press http://www.oxforddnb.com/view/article/102444 accessed 12 December 2012.
50. John Graham 'Champion Wrestler' *South London Palace London, Lambeth* (London: A. Carter, Printer, 226, Southwark Bridge Road, undated) Shelfmark Evan.766 The British Library, London.
51. Lisa Bier *Fighting the Current*: p. 15.
52. Lisa Bier *Fighting the Current* p. 16–17.
53. David Day '"A Modern Naiad": Nineteenth Century Female Professional Natationists' *Women's History Network Women and Leisure Conference* University of Staffordshire 8 November 2008.
54. Anon. 'Miss Agnes Beckwith' *The Pall Mall Gazette* 2 September 1875 p. 4.
55. Anon. 'Prof. Beckwith's Amphibious Family' no place, publisher or date given shelfmark Evan.814 The British Library, London.
56. Dave Day 'London Swimming Professors: Victorian Craftsmen and Aquatic Entrepreneurs' in Neil Carter (ed.) *Sport in History: Special Edition Coaching Cultures* 30:1 2010 pp. 32–54.
57. Royal Aquarium Westminster *Agnes Beckwith, the greatest lady swimmer in the world Patronized by their Royal Highnesses the Prince and Princess of Wales and family. Daily at 5.30 & 9.15. Admission 1s/- from Aquarium or annexe, children half price* c 1885, shelfmark Evan.339 The British Library, London.
58. Hastings Swimming Baths 'The Beckwith's Farewell' *Hastings Swimming Baths* 3 September 1888, shelfmark Evan.1667 The British Library, London.
59. Tony Mason *Sport in Britain* (London: Faber and Faber, 1988) p. 25.
60. Unknown author 'The Baths, Bournemouth, August 1892' *The Era* 27 August 1892 p. 13.

61. Dave Day *Coaching Practices and Coaching Lives in Nineteenth and Early Twentieth Century England* (unpublished PhD thesis De Montfort University Leicester, 2008).

62. Keith Myerscough 'Nymphs, Naiads and Natation' *Seventh Annual Conference of Sports History Ireland,* Hunt Museum Limerick 10 September 2011.

63. Keith Myerscough *Blackpool's Triplets: Health, Pleasure and Recreation 1875–1904* (unpublished MA Sport History and Culture thesis De Montfort University Leicester, 2009) p. 45.

64. Anon. 'The Diving Belle' *The Pall Mall Gazette* 17 March 1894, p. 6.

65. Lynda Nead *The Haunted Gallery: Painting, Photography and Film c1900* (New Haven and London: Yale University Press, 2007) pp. 34–35.

66. Two-piece swimsuit set, no maker c.1850s object number P90.16.1 The Museum at the Fashion Institute of Technology New York.

67. Two-piece swimsuit set, no maker c.1870s object number P90.43.2 The Museum at the Fashion Institute of Technology New York. This item has short bell sleeves and a left shoulder tab treatment with three white buttons.

68. Three-piece swimsuit set, no maker c1884 object number P84.8.4 The Museum at the Fashion Institute of Technology New York..

69. Atlantic *The Milbury Bathing Dress* c1900 object number P90.24.3; H. M. Bull *Swimwear Set* c. 1900 object number P93.29.1 The Museum at the Fashion Institute of Technology New York.

70. Mrs H. Adams Traphagen *School Swimsuit* no maker c. 1895 object number P92.5.12 has some glass or gelatine detailing to the buttons; two-piece swimsuit set, no maker c1895 object number P84.36.1 is the most elaborately tucked, braided and trimmed of all the late nineteenth century pieces held at The Museum at the Fashion Institute of Technology New York.

71. Paulin Huggett Pearce *The Warriors' Swimming Book and Ladies' Guide: Including the Poem on Waterloo; Queen Victoria's Reign; Death and Funeral of the Duke of Wellington etc in Two Parts* (London: T. H. Roberts, 1869) pp. 15–16.

72. 'Seargeant' Leahy [sic] *The Art of Swimming in the Eton Style* p. 52.

73. C. W. Webb *An Historical Record of Nathaniel Corah & Sons Ltd. Manufacturers of Hosiery, Underwear and Outerwear* (St. Margaret's Works Leicester: N. Corah & Sons Ltd, 1948).

74. Corah's of Leicester *Corah's of Leicester Advertising Catalogue 1912* Corah's of Leicester 1815–1965 File, University of Leicester, Special Collections.

75. Leicester Chamber of Commerce *City of Leicester Year Book 1921* Corah's of Leicester 1815–1965 File, University of Leicester, Special Collections.

76. Corah's of Leicester, Jantzen labels and license plans circa 1912, Leicester County Museum Store, Barrow Upon Soar.

77. Charles Chaplin (with David Robinson) *My Autobiography* (London: Penguin Modern Classics 1966, first published by Bodely Head 1964) pp. 63–64.

78. Kenneth D. Brown *The British Toy Business* p. 77.

79. Kenneth D. Brown *The British Toy Business* pp. 32–33.

80. Betty Cadbury Collection 'Ondine Swimming Doll c1880' *Sudbury Hall National Trust Museum of Childhood* Sudbury, Derbyshire.

81. V&A Museum of Childhood, Bethnal Green 'Pedal tricycle horses' http://www.vam.ac.uk/moc/collections/toys/toy_horses accessed 5 March 2012.

82. Winifred Gwyn-Jeffreys *A Victorian Nursery* (Cheltenham: Hayman and Son Ltd, 1970) pp. 27–28.

83. Sarah Kennedy *The Swimsuit: A Fashion History From 1920s Biarritz and The Birth of The Bikini to Sportswear Styles and Catwalk Trends* (London: Carlton Books, 2007).

84. J.A Mangan (ed.) *Pleasure, Profit and Proselytism: British Culture and Sport at Home and Abroad 1700–1914* (London: Frank Cass, 1988).
85. J. S. Maclure *Educational Documents: England and Wales: 1816 to the Present Day* (London: Methuen, 1979); Michael Sanderson *Education and Economic Decline in Britain 1870 to the 1990s* (Cambridge: Cambridge University Press, 1998).
86. June Purvis and Margaret Hales *Achievement and Inequality in Education* (London: Routledge and Kegan Paul, 1983); Thomas Kelly *A History of Adult Education in Great Britain from the Middle Ages to the Twentieth Century* (Liverpool: Liverpool University Press, 1992) p. 171.
87. Elizabeth Crawford *The Women's Suffrage Movement: A Reference Guide 1866–1928* (London and New York: Routledge, 2001) p. 240.
88. Carol Dyhouse *Students: A Gendered History* (London: Routledge, 2006) p. 63–64.
89. English Heritage 'Musical Gymnastics at North London Collegiate School' *Visible in Stone: Women's History Through Buildings 1850–1950* http://www.english-heritage.org.uk/discover/people-and-places/womens-history/visible-in-stone accessed 12 March 2012.
90. Janet Howarth 'Dame Millicent Garrett Fawcett (1847–1929)' *Oxford Dictionary of National Biography* Oxford University Press http://www.oxforddnb.com/view/article/33096 accessed 13 December 2012.
91. Gillian Sutherland 'Anne Jemima Clough (1820–1892)' *Oxford Dictionary of National Biography* Oxford University Press http://www.oxforddnb.com/view/article/5710 accessed 7 March 2012.
92. Gillian Sutherland *Faith, Duty and Power of Mind: The Cloughs and Their Circle, 1829–1960* (Cambridge, Cambridge University Press, 2006).
93. Kathleen E. McCrone 'The "Lady Blue": Sport at the Oxbridge Women's Colleges from their foundation to 1914' *British Journal of Sports History* 3 September 1986 pp. 191–215.
94. Anne Thomson, College Archivist Newnham College Cambridge, personal communication 8 March 2012.
95. Enid Huws Jones 'Madeleine Septimia Shaw-Lefevre (1835–1914)' *Oxford Dictionary of National Biography* Oxford University Press. http://www.oxforddnb.com/view/article/48463 accessed 12 December 2012.
96. Lilian M. Faithfull *In the House of My Pilgrimage* (London: Chatto & Windus, 1924) p. 53.
97. Cambridge University Press 'Emily Davies' *Orlando: Women's Writing in the British Isles From the Beginnings to the Present* Cambridge University Press http://orlando.cambridge.org accessed 7 March 2012; Papers of Sarah Emily Davies (1830–1921: Records 1847–1919) at http://www-lib.girton.cam.ac.uk/archive/davies.htm accessed 12 March 2012.
98. Daphne Bennett *Emily Davies and the Liberation of Women* (London: André Deutsch, 1990); Ann B. Murphy and Deirdre Raftery (eds.) *Emily Davies: Collected Letters 1861–1875* (Charlottesville: University of Virginia Press, 2003).
99. Pam Hirsch 'Barbara Leigh Smith Bodichon (1827–1891)' *Oxford Dictionary of National Biography* Oxford University Press http://www.oxforddnb.com/view/article/2755 accessed 12 December 2012.
100. Various authors *Autograph Letter Collection: Female Education 1850–1951* Originals in Box AL 6 (ALC1784–1858) London Metropolitan University: The Women's Library.
101. Lilian M. Faithfull *In the House of My Pilgrimage* pp. 79–81.
102. T. A. B. Corley 'Thomas Holloway (1800–1883)' *Oxford Dictionary of National Biography* Oxford University Press http://www.oxforddnb.com/view/article/13577 accessed 12 December 2012.

103. All England Women's Hockey Association 'Minutes of Meetings of the Women's Hockey Association 10 April 1895, Brighton' *File A/1/1 Softback Notebook* pp. 1–2 Hockey England archives, Special Collections, University of Bath, hereafter Hockey archives, Bath.

104. Marjorie Pollard *Fifty Years of Women's Hockey: The All England Women's Hockey Association* (Letchworth: St. Christopher Press, 1945) p. 4.

105. Kathleen E. McCrone 'Emancipation or Recreation? The Development of Women's Sport at the University of London' *The International Journal of the History of Sport* 7:2 1990 pp. 207.

106. Elizabeth J. Morse 'Dame Louisa Innes Lumsden (1840–1935)' *Oxford Dictionary of National Biography* Oxford University Press http://www.oxforddnb.com/view/article/48571 accessed 10 March 2012.

107. Sheila Fletcher *Women First: The Female Tradition in English Physical Education 1880–1980* (London: Frank Cass, 1984).

108. Jennifer Hargreaves *Sporting Females* (London: Routledge, 1994) p. 57.

109. Richard Holt *Sport and the British: A Modern History* (Clarendon Press: Oxford 1989) pp. 57–59.

110. Sheila Fletcher 'Martina Sofia Helena Bergman Österberg (1849–1915)' *Oxford Dictionary of National Biography* Oxford University Press http://www.oxforddnb.com/view/article/47656 accessed 13 December 2012.

111. Tansin Benn and Ida Webb 'Rhoda Anstey (1865—1936)' *Connecting Histories Project and Birmingham Stories*: The School of Education at Birmingham University http://www.connectinghistories.org.uk/ accessed 10 August 2009.

112. Paul Baines 'William Shenstone (1714–1763)'*Oxford Dictionary of National Biography* Oxford University Press http://www.oxforddnb.com/view/article/25321 accessed 29 December 2012.

113. Tansin Benn and Ida Webb 'Rhoda Anstey (1865–1936)' p. 4.

114. Steve Bailey and Wray Vamplew *100 Years of Physical Education* (London: Physical Education Association Centenary Publication, 1999) pp. 58–60.

115. Mary R. S. Creese 'Dame Helen Charlotte Isabella Gwynne-Vaughan (1879–1967)' *Oxford Dictionary of National Biography* Oxford University Press http://www.oxforddnb.com/view/article/33623 accessed 29 December 2012.

116. All England Women's Hockey Association 'Minutes of Meeting of the Women's Hockey Association 10 April 1895, Brighton' *File A/1/1 Softback Notebook* pp. 1–2 Hockey archives, Bath.

117. All England Women's Hockey Association 'Letter from AEWHA Secretary to the President 12 January 1897, 13 Kensington Square London' *File A/1/1 Softback Notebook* p. 23 Hockey archives, Bath.

118. Jean Williams 'Edith Marie Thompson (1877–1961)' *Oxford Dictionary of National Biography* Oxford University Press http://www.oxforddnb.com/view/article/103423 accessed 13 December 2012.

119. Dorothy Gwyn Jeffreys, Winifred Gwyn Jeffreys and E.M. Thompson *Hockey Jottings* (unpublished, c.1898) Hockey archives, Bath; Kathleen Mc Crone 'Emancipation or Recreation?' p. 229.

120. Arthur Marwick 'The Fundamentals of History: What is History?' *Institute of Historical Research: Focus* http://www.history.ac.uk/ihr/Focus/Whatishistory/marwick1.html accessed 13 March 2012.

121. Gwendoline Parr 'Letter to Marjorie Pollard 14 January 1970, 10 Salisbury Avenue Harpenden Herts' *File D/1/ 2 Writing Album* Hockey archives, Bath.

122. André Odendaal 'South Africa's Black Victorians: Sport and Society in South Africa in the Nieneteenth Century' in J.A Mangan (ed.) *Pleasure, Profit and Proselytism: British Culture and Sport at Home and Abroad 1700–1914*

(London: Frank Cass, 1988) p. 198; Louie Traikovski 'The Importance of Sport to Students and Headmistresses at Four Private Melbourne Schools from 1900 to 1914' *Australian Society for Sports History Bulletin* 28 June 1998 pp. 2–5.

123. John A. Daly 'A New Britannia in the Antipodes: Sport Class and Community in Colonial South Australia' in J.A Mangan (ed.) *Pleasure, Profit and Proselytism: British Culture and Sport at Home and Abroad 1700–1914* (London: Frank Cass, 1988) p. 166.

124. Roald Dahl *Matilda* (London: Puffin, 2007 originally published by Jonathan Cape 1988) p. 76.

125. Jeffrey Hill *Sport in History: An Introduction* (Basingstoke: Palgrave Macmillan, 2011) p. 93.

126. Steve Redhead *Post-Fandom and the Millennial Blues* (London and New York: Routledge, 1997) p. 20.

127. Pamela J. Creedon 'Women in Toyland: A Look in American Newspaper Sports Journalism' in Pamela J. Creedon (ed.) *Women Sport and Media: Challenging Gender Values* (London: Sage, 1994) pp. 69.

128. James L. Crouthamel *Bennett's New York Herald and the Rise of the Popular Press* (Syracuse, New York: Syracuse University Press, 1989) pp. 19–20.

129. Nancy Whitelaw *Joseph Pulitzer and The New York World: Makers of the Media* (Greensboro, North Carolina: Morgan Reynolds, 2000) p. 30.

130. Jules Verne *Around the World in Eighty Days* (Philadelphia: Porter & Coates, 1873 originally published in France in 1872).

131. Nellie Bly *Nellie Bly's Book: Around the World in Seventy-Two Days* (New York City: Pictorial Weeklies Company, 1890).

132. Elizabeth Bisland *A Flying Trip Around the World in Seven Stages* (New York: Harper Brothers, 1891).

133. J. A. Grozier *Round the World With Nelly (sic) Bly: A Novel and Fascinating Game with Plenty of Excitement on Land and Sea* (New York: McLoughlin Bros. 1890) object number: 2000.44 The Liman Collection, New York Historical Society.

134. Edlie Wong 'Around the World and Across the Board: Nellie Bly and the Geography of Games' *American Studies Department Symposium* (New Brunswick, NJ: Rutgers University, 4 February 2005) p. 3 available at www.lateledipenelope.it/public/EdlieWongSymposiumPaperSp05.pdf accessed 12 December 2012.

135. His Grace The Duke of Beaufort, K.G. (ed.) *Driving* (London: Longman, Greens and Company, 1889) p. ii.

136. Henry Cholmondeley-Pennell (ed.) *Fishing: Salmon and Trout* (London: Longmans, Green and Company, 1885) pp. 112–113.

137. Tim Shakesheff 'Anglers, Poachers and The Commercial Interest: Conflict On The River Wye, 1861–1915' *Sport and Leisure History Seminar* 10 May 2010 Senate House, Institute of Historical Research, London.

138. Lady Georgiana Curzon 'Tandem Driving' in His Grace The Duke of Beaufort K.G. (ed.) *Driving* p. 147.

139. Lottie Dod 'Tennis for Ladies' in J.M. Heathcote *Tennis, Lawn Tennis, Rackets and Fives The Badminton Library* (London: Longmans and Co., 1891) pp, 300–307

140. Mrs Lilly Groves FRGS (ed. illustrated by Percy Macquoid) *Dance* (London: Longmans, Green and Company, 1895).

141. Beatrice Violet, Lady Greville (ed.) *Ladies in the Field: Sketches of Sport* (London: Ward and Downey Ltd, 1894) preface.

142. Beatrice Violet, Lady Greville (ed.) 'Hunting in the Shires' *Ladies in the Field* pp. 31–53. See also Beatrice Violet, Lady Greville *The Gentlewoman's Book of Sports* (London: Henry, 1892).

143. Wray Vamplew *The Turf* (London: Penguin, 1976); Mike Huggins, *Flat Racing and British Society* (London and New York: Routledge, 2001); Wray Vamplew and Joyce Kay (eds.) *Encyclopedia of British Horseracing* (London and New York: Routledge, 2005); Emma Griffin, *Blood Sport, Hunting in Britain since 1066* (New Haven and London: Yale University Press, 2007).

144. Mrs C. Martelli 'Tigers I have Shot' in Beatrice Violet, Lady Greville (ed.) *Ladies in the Field* p. 156.

145. Beatrice Violet, Lady Greville *The Gentlewoman in Society* (London: Henry, 1892).

146. 'K' The Duchess of Newcastle 'Horses and Their Riders' in Beatrice Violet, Lady Greville (ed.) *Ladies in the Field* p. 66.

147. Mildred Boynton 'Covert Shooting' in Beatrice Violet, Lady Greville (ed.) *Ladies in the Field* p. 200.

148. Dorothy Middleton 'Lady Florence Caroline Dixie [née Douglas] (1855–1905)' *Oxford Dictionary of National Biography* Oxford University Press www.oxforddnb.com/view/article/32836 accessed 22 May 2012.

149. Henry Thomas Alken *Going to Epsom Races: A Ludicrous Amusement Consisting of Modern Costume, Characters, Dandies, Equipages and Horsemanship* (London: S & H Fuller, 1819); John Allen *Principles of Modern Riding for Ladies, in which all Late Improvements are Applied to Practice on the Promenade & the Road* (London: Tegg, 1825); Professor Furbor *The Lady's Equestrian Companion; or, the Golden Key to Equitation* (London: Saunders and Otley, 1847); Mervyn Richardson *Horsemanship, or, The Art of Riding and Managing a Horse :Adapted for the Guidance of Ladies and Gentlemen, on the Road and in the Field* (London: Longman, Brown, Green, and Longman, 1853); J. Stirling Clarke *The Ladies' Equestrian Guide; or The Habit and The Horse: A Treatise on Female Equitation* (London: Day & Son, 1857); Edith Somerville *Through Connemara in a Governess Cart* (London: W. H. Allen & Co. Ltd, 1893).

150. Ida Mann *'The Chase': First Part of her Draft Autobiography [1974]* Catalogue of papers of Ida Mann (1921–2007) Bodleian Library, University of Oxford http://www.bodleian.ox.ac.uk/bodley/library accessed 11 January 2012.

151. Beatrice Violet, Lady Greville *Ladies in the Field* p. 4.

NOTES TO CHAPTER 2

1. Mrs Lambert Chambers *Lawn Tennis for Ladies* (London: Methuen & Co. Ltd, 1910) p. 5.

2. Brian Braithwaite *Women's Magazines: The First 300 years* (London: P. Owen, 1995) p. 10.

3. Christopher Love *A Social History of Swimming in England, 1800–1918* (London: Routledge, 2007) pp. 180–185.

4. Mark Ryan 'Muriel Robb (1878–1907): A Little-Known Wimbledon Singles Champion' *Tennis Forum* http://www.tennisforum.com accessed 24 April 2012.

5. Anon. 'Ladies International Match: Scotland Versus England' *The Glasgow Herald* 9 May 1881 http://www.donmouth.co.uk/womens_football/1881. html accessed 22 May 2012.

6. Patrick Brennan 'Nettie Honeyball' http://www.donmouth.co.uk/womens_football/nettie_honeyball.html accessed 12 December 2012.

7. David Allen and Sons *The Original English Lady Cricketers* circa 1895 object number TN.2008.297 MCC Museum Lord's, London.

8. White Heather Club *Menu Card for the 40th Anniversary Dinner of the White Heather Club 1927* object number TN.2008.411 MCC Museum Lord's, London.

9. G. R. Searle *The Quest For National Efficiency 1899–1914* (Oxford: Basil Blackwell, 1971); Rowena Hammal 'How Long Before the Sunset? British attitudes to war 1871–1914' *History Review* 2010 http://www.historytoday.com accessed 21 April 2012.

10. Jeffrey Hill *Sport, Leisure and Culture in Twentieth Century Britain* (Basingstoke: Palgrave Macmillan, 2002) p. 151.

11. Barbara Caine 'Charlotte Maria Shaw Mason (1842–1923)'*Oxford Dictionary of National Biography* Oxford University Press http://www.oxforddnb.com/view/article/37743 accessed 4 January 2013.

12. Rowena Edlin-White *A Hundred Years Ago: The Beginnings of Girl Guiding in Nottinghamshire* (Nottingham: Smallprint, 2009) pp. 5–6.

13. Allen Warren 'Robert Stephenson Smyth Baden-Powell, first Baron Baden-Powell (1857–1941)' *Oxford Dictionary of National Biography* Oxford University Press http://www.oxforddnb.com/view/article/30520 accessed 4 January 2013.

14. Allen Warren 'Olave St Clair Baden-Powell, Lady Baden-Powell (1889–1977)' *Oxford Dictionary of National Biography* Oxford University Press http://www.oxforddnb.com/view/article/30779 accessed 4 January 2013.

15. John J. MacAloon *This Great Symbol: Pierre de Coubertin and the Origins of the Modern Olympic Games* (Chicago: University of Chicago Press, 1981); John J. MacAloon *Brides of Victory: Nationalism and Gender in Olympic Ritual* (London: Berg, 1997).

16. Martin Polley *The British Olympics: Britain's Olympic Heritage 1612–2012* (Swindon: Played in Britain, 2011) p. 10.

17. British Olympic Association *Chasing Gold: Centenary of the British Olympic Association* (London: Getty Images, 2005) p. 12–15.

18. British Olympic Association 'Minutes of British Olympic Council Meeting 20 December 1906, Bath Club' *British Olympic Association Minute Book 1900–1910* unpaginated, British Olympic Association Archives, Wandsworth London. Hereafter BOA archives, London.

19. Miss L. Dod 'Lawn Tennis for Ladies' in J. M. Heathcote (eds.) *Tennis, Lawn Tennis, Badminton, Fives: The Badminton Library of Sports and Pastimes* (London: Longmans, Green and Company, 1891).

20. Lynda Nead *The Haunted Gallery: Painting, Photography and Film c1900* (New Haven and London: Yale University Press, 2007) pp. 34–35.

21. Alan Tomlinson 'Olympic Survivals: The Olympic Games as a Global Phenomenon' in Lincoln Allison (ed.) *The Global Politics of Sport: The Role of Global Institutions in Sport* (Oxon: Routledge, 2005) pp. 46–62.

22. Ian F. W. Beckett 'William Henry Grenfell, Baron Desborough (1855–1945)' *Oxford Dictionary of National Biography* Oxford University Press http://www.oxforddnb.com/view/article/33566 accessed 4 January 2013.

23. Lord Desborough of Taplow *Letter to De Coubertin 14 May 1906* Correspondence of the National Olympic Committee of Great Britain 1892–1927 file: International Olympic Committee Museum and Archive, Lausanne. Hereafter IOC archive, Lausanne.

24. Jane Ridley and Clayre Percy 'Ethel Anne Priscilla Grenfell, Lady Desborough (1867–1952)' *Oxford Dictionary of National Biography* Oxford University Press http://www.oxforddnb.com/view/article/40733 accessed 4 January 2013.

25. Rebecca Jenkins *The First London Olympics 1908* (London: Piaktus, 2008) p. xv.

26. British Olympic Association *Yearbook 1914: Containing Information with Regard to The International Olympic Committee, the British Olympic Council and Record of the International Olympic Games* (Publications of the NOC of Great Britain 1914 file: IOC Archive, Lausanne) pp. 58–59. Hereafter *BOA Yearbook 1914*.

27. Bill Mallon & Ian Buchanan *The 1908 Olympic Games: Results for All Competitors in All Events, with Commentary* (McFarland, 2000).

28. British Olympic Council 'Council Meeting: Minutes 21 October 1907 108 Victoria Street' *British Olympic Association Minute Book 1900–1910* unpaginated, BOA archives, London. Both the Danish and Norwegian Olympic Committees supported this request.

29. Joyce Kay 'It Wasn't Just Emily Davison! Sport, Suffrage and Society in Edwardian Britain' *International Journal of the History of Sport* 25:10 2008 pp. 1338–1354.

30. Maurice Roche *Mega-Events and Modernity: Olympics and Expos in the Growth of Global Culture* (London: Routledge, 2000) p. 101.

31. Robert K. Barney 'The Olympic Games in Modern Times: An Overview' in Gerald P. Schaus and Stephen R. Wenn (eds) *Onward to the Olympics: Historical Perspectives on The Olympic Games* (Waterloo, Ontario: Wilfred Laurier University Press, 2007) p. 221.

32. The Sporting Life *Olympic Games of London 1908: A Complete Record with Photographs of Winners of the Olympic Games held at the Stadium, Shepherd's Bush London July 13–25* (London: The Sporting Life, 1908) pp. 124–145 BOA archive, London.

33. Patricia Campbell Warner *When the Girls Came Out to Play* (Amherst and Boston: University of Massachusetts Press, 2006) p. 90.

34. Erik Bergvall (translated by Edward Adams-Ray) *The Fifth Olympiad: The Official Report of The Olympic Games of Stockholm 1912* (Stockholm: Wahlström & Widstrand, 1912) pp. 66–72; available at LA 84 Foundation http://www.la84foundation.org accessed 23 June 2011. Hereafter *Official Report Stockholm 1912*.

35. A. W. Gamage Ltd 'The Sports House of the West' *Golf, Programme and Regulations: Olympic Games of London 1908* (London: British Olympic Council, 1908) p. 11 BOA archive, London.

36. Pierre De Coubertin *Olympic Memoirs* (Lausanne: International Olympic Committee, 1997).

37. Tony Collins *A Social History of English Rugby Union* (Oxon: Routledge, 2009) p. 11.

38. Anita De Frantz 'Women's participation in the Olympic Games: Lessons and Challenges For the Future' in International Olympic Committee *Final Report of the International Olympic Committee's 2nd IOC Conference on Women and Sport: New perspectives for the XXI century* (Paris: International Olympic Committee, 2000) pp. 21–35.

39. Ana Maria Maragaya *The Process of Inclusion of Women in the Olympic Games* unpublished PhD thesis Rio De Janeiro: Universidade Gama Filho, 2006 p. 159.

40. Joanna Davenport 'Monique Berlioux: Her Association with Three IOC Presidents' *Citius, Altius, Fortius* (became *Journal of Olympic History* in 1997) 4:3 1996 pp. 10–18.

41. M. D. Mérillon (ed.) 'Concours D' Exercises Physiques Et De Sports' *Expostition Universelle Internationale de 1900 À Paris: Concours Internationaux D'Exercises Physiques et de Sports* (Paris: Ministére Du Commerce, De L'Industrie Des Postes et Des Télégraphes, 1901) Part One pp. 41–47.

42. Pierre De Coubertin *Olympic Memoirs* (International Olympic Committee, 1997) p. 125.
43. Bill Mallon *The 1900 Olympic Games: Results for All Competitors in All Events, with Commentary* (Jefferson, North Carolina: McFarland and Company, 1998) pp. 10–17.
44. Stephanie Daniels and Anita Tedder *'A Proper Spectacle': Women Olympians 1900–1936* (Bedford: Zee Na Na Press, 2000) p. 10.
45. M. D. Mérillon (ed.) 'Sport Hippique' *Expostition Universelle Internationale de 1900 À Paris: Concours Internationaux D'Exercises Physiques et de Sports* (Paris: Ministére Du Commerce, De L'Industrie Des Postes et Des Télégraphes, 1901) Part Two pp. 283–289.
46. Stephanie Daniels and Anita Tedder *A Proper Spectacle'* pp. 3–5; Bill Mallon *The 1900 Olympic Games* p. 13.
47. Bill Mallon 'The First Two Women Olympians' *Citius, Altius, Fortius* (became *Journal of Olympic History* in 1997) 3:3 1995 p. 38.
48. International Olympic Committee *Olympic.Org: Official Website of the Olympic Movement* http://www.olympic.org/medallists accessed 23 April 2012.
49. M. D. Mérillon (ed.) 'Concours D' Exercises Physiques Et De Sports: Lawn Tennis' *Expostition Universelle Internationale de 1900 À Paris: Concours Internationaux D'Exercises Physiques et de Sports* (Paris: Ministére Du Commerce, De L'Industrie Des Postes et Des Télégraphes, 1901) Part One pp. 70–71.
50. M. D. Mérillon (ed.) 'Concours D' Exercises Physiques Et De Sports: Concours de Jeu de Golf' *Expostition Universelle Internationale de 1900 À Paris: Concours Internationaux D'Exercises Physiques et de Sports* (Paris: Ministére Du Commerce, De L'Industrie Des Postes et Des Télégraphes, 1901) Part One pp. 77–78.
51. Stephanie Daniels and Anita Tedder *'A Proper Spectacle'* p. 5.
52. Bill Mallon *The 1900 Olympic Games* p. 13.
53. Anita De Frantz 'Women's participation in the Olympic Games' p. 28.
54. International Olympic Committee *Olympic.Org: Official Website of the Olympic Movement* http://www.olympic.org/medallists accessed 23 April 2012.
55. Bill Mallon *The 1904 Olympic Games: Results for All Competitors in All Events, with commentary* (Jefferson, North Carolina: McFarland & Co. 1999) pp. 47–48.
56. Jeremy Malies 'Charlotte [Lottie] Dod (1871–1960)' *Oxford Dictionary of National Biography* Oxford University Press http://www.oxforddnb.com/view/article/37363 accessed 7 January 2013.
57. British Olympic Council *Olympic Games of 1908: Programme, Rules and Conditions of Competition for Swimming, Diving and Water Polo* (London: British Olympic Council, 1909) p. 4 BOA archive, London.
58. James Bancroft 'Sybil Fenton 'Queenie' Newall 1854–1929' *Oxford Dictionary of National Biography* Oxford University Press www.oxforddnb.com accessed 24 April 2012.
59. Hugh D. Hewitt Soar 'Alice Blanche Legh (1856–1948)' *Oxford Dictionary of National Biography* Oxford University Press www.oxforddnb.com accessed 24 May 2012.
60. Miss Alice Legh 'Ladies' Archery' in C. J. Longman and H. Walrond (eds.) *Archery: The Badminton Library of Sports and Pastimes* (London: Longmans, Green and Company, 1894 pp. 380–392).
61. James Bancroft 'Sybil Fenton 'Queenie' Newall 1854–1929'.

62. Bill Mallon and Ian Buchanan *The 1908 Olympic Games: Results for All Competitors in All Events, with commentary* (Jefferson, North Carolina: McFarland and Company, 2000).
63. Rebecca Jenkins *The First London Olympics 1908* p. 65.
64. Judith Wilson 'Florence Madeline 'Madge' Syers [née Cave] 1881–1917' *Oxford Dictionary of National Biography* Oxford University Press www.oxforddnb.com accessed 24 April 2012.
65. Jeffrey Pearson *Lottie Dod: Champion of Champions, The Story of an Athlete* (Wirral, Meryseside: Countyvise, 1988) p. 16.
66. James Huntingdon-Whitely and Richard Holt *The Book of British Sporting Heroes* (London: National Portrait Gallery, 1999) p. 88
67. Jeffrey Pearson *Lottie Dod: Champion of Champions* p. 18.
68. Jeremy Malies 'Charlotte 'Lottie' Dod (1871–1960)' *Oxford Dictionary of National Biography* Oxford University Press http://www.oxforddnb.com/view/article/37363 accessed 7 January 2013.
69. Jeffrey Pearson *Lottie Dod: Champion of Champions* pp. 53–55.
70. John Barrett and Alan Little *Wimbledon: Ladies' Singles Champions 1884–2004* (London: Wimbledon Lawn Tennis Museum, 2005) p. 10.
71. J. G. Smyth 'Charlotte Renaigle Sterry (née Cooper) 1870–1966' *Oxford Dictionary of National Biography* Oxford University Press www.oxforddnb.com accessed 30 October 2011.
72. Mrs Sterry 'My Most Memorable Match' in Mrs Lambert Chambers *Lawn Tennis for Ladies* pp. 113.
73. Mark Pottle 'Dorothea Katharine Lambert Chambers [née Douglass] (1878–1960)' *Oxford Dictionary of National Biography* Oxford University Press http://www.oxforddnb.com/view/article/32353 accessed 23 April 2012.
74. John Barrett and Alan Little *Wimbledon: Ladies' Singles Champions 1884–2004* p. 12.
75. Wimbledon Lawn Tennis Museum *Roll of Honour* http://aeltc2011.wimbledon.com/players/rolls-of-honour/ladies-singles accessed 14 June 2011.
76. Mark Ryan 'Ethel Warneford Larcombe [née Thomson] (1879–1965)' *Oxford Dictionary of National Biography* Oxford University Press http://www.oxforddnb.com accessed 15 May 2012.
77. Mrs Lambert Chambers *Lawn Tennis for Ladies* p. 25.
78. Alan Little *Suzanne Lenglen: Tennis Idol of the Twenties* (London: Wimbledon Lawn Tennis Museum, 2005).
79. Mark Pottle 'Dorothea Katharine Lambert Chambers [née Douglass] (1878–1960)'.
80. David Gilbert 'The Vicar's Daughter and The Goddess of Tennis: Cultural Geographies of Sporting Femininity and Bodily Practice in Edwardian Suburbia' *Cultural Geographies* 18:2 2011 pp. 187–207.
81. Mrs Lambert Chambers *Lawn Tennis for Ladies* p. 4.
82. Janine Van Someren *Women's Sporting Lives: A Biographical Study of Elite Amateur Tennis Players at Wimbledon* unpublished PhD thesis, University of Southampton, December 2012 pp. 16–17.
83. Erik Bergvall (translated Edward Adams-Ray) *The Fifth Olympiad: The Official Report of The Olympic Games of Stockholm 1912)* pp. 66–72.
84. Jean Williams, 'Jane 'Jennie' Fletcher (1890–1968)' *Oxford Dictionary of National Biography* Oxford University Press http://www.oxforddnb.com/view/article/102443 accessed 8 January 2013.
85. Sport Scotland 'Isabella 'Belle' Mary Moore (1894–1975)' *Scottish Sports Hall of Fame* Sport Scotland http://www.sportscotland.org.uk/sshf/Isabella_Mary_Moore accessed 8 December 2012.

86. Jean Williams 'Aquadynamics and the Athletocracy: Jennie Fletcher and the British Women's 4 x 100 metre Freestyle Relay Team at the 1912 Stockholm Olympic Games' in John Hughson (ed.) *Costume* 46:2 Summer 2012 pp. 145–164.

87. Erik Bergvall (translated Edward Adams-Ray) 'Plate 36 Winners in the Fifth Olympiad Fanny Durack 100 m Free style [sic] Ladies and Great Britain's team in 400m Team Race for Ladies' [sic] *The Fifth Olympiad: The Official Report of The Olympic Games of Stockholm 1912)* p. 851.

88. Win Hayes 'Lucy Morton (1898–1980)' *Oxford Dictionary of National Biography* http://www.oxforddnb.com accessed 14 July 2011.

89. Dave Day 'Walter Septimus Brickett (1865–1933)' *Oxford Dictionary of National Biography* Oxford University Press http://www.oxforddnb.com/ view/article/102445 accessed 8 January 2013.

90. Peter Bilsborough, 'Jarvis, John Arthur (1872–1933)' *Oxford Dictionary of National Biography* www.oxforddnb.com/view/article/65070 accessed 15 October 2011; International Swimming Hall of Fame 'John Arthur Jarvis: Honor Swimmer, 1968' http://www.ishof.org/honorees/68/68jajarvis accessed 15 October 2011.

91. Anon. *ASA Handbook 1902 Containing List of English Swimming Clubs, Laws of Swimming and Rules of Water Polo, Past and Present Champions, Programme for the Year* (Gainborough: J. Littlewood, 1903) British Swimming archive, Loughborough.

92. Jo Manning 'First champ "would be thrilled"' *BBC News* 11 August 2008 http://news.bbc.co.uk/1/hi/wales/7554196.stm accessed 8 December 2012.

93. Jean Williams 'The Most Important Photograph in the History of Women's Olympic Participation: Jennie Fletcher and the British 4×100 Freestyle relay team at the Stockholm 1912 Games' in Martin Polley (ed.) *Sport in History, Special Issue: Britain, Britons and the Olympic Games* 32:2 pp. 204–230.

94. British Olympic Council *Olympic Games of 1908: Programme, Rules and Conditions of Competition for Swimming, Diving and Water Polo* (London: British Olympic Council, 1909) p. 4 BOA archive, London.

95. International Olympic Committee 'Searchable Database of Olympic Medallists' http://www.olympic.org/medallists accessed 16 December 2011.

96. Diana Souhami *The Trial of Radclyffe Hall* (New York: Doubleday, 1999) pp. 172–173.

97. Miss Toupie Lowther 'Ladies' Play' in Reginald Frank and Hugh Lawrence Doherty *Lawn Tennis* (New York: The Baker and Taylor Company, 1903) pp. 132–141.

98. Radclyffe Hall *The Well of Loneliness* (London: Jonathan Cape, 1928); Judith Halberstam *Female Masculinity* (Durham, North Carolina: Duke University Press, 1998) pp. 184–185.

99. Anon. 'Neo-Amazonian' *Louisville Herald* 7 July 1912 unpaginated National Olympic Committee: British Olympic Association Press File IOC archive, Lausanne.

100. General Post Office 'Transmission of press telegrams between the United Kingdom and Sweden, Denmark and Norway: transmission of telegrams respecting the Olympic Games, Stockholm 11 April 1913' record T 1/11533, The National Archives, Kew http://www.nationalarchives.gov.uk accessed 16 May 2012.

101. Erik Bergvall *The Fifth Olympiad: The Official Report of The Olympic Games of Stockholm 1912* p. 10.

102. British Olympic Council *Official Report of the Olympic Games London 1908* p. 12.

103. Anne Lykke Poulson 'Women's Gymnastics and citizenship in Denmark in the Early Twentieth Century' *Women's History Magazine* 59 2008 (Oxford: Women's History Network. 2008) pp. 26–35.
104. Joyce Kay '"No Time for Recreations till the Vote is Won?" Suffrage Activists and Leisure in Edwardian Britain' *Women's History Review* 16:4 2007 pp. 535–553.
105. Millicent Garrett, Dame Fawcett *Women's Suffrage: A Short History of a Great Movement* (London and Edinburgh, T. C. and E. C. Jack, c 1912). See also primary sources available at National Union of Women's Suffrage Societies collections http://www.nationalarchives.gov.uk accessed 10 December 2011.
106. Emelyne Godfrey 'Edward William Barton Wright (1860–1951)' *Oxford Dictionary of National Biography* Oxford University Press www.oxfordnb.com accessed 15 May 2012.
107. Edith Garrud 'The World We Live In: Self Defence' *Votes for Women* 4 March 1910 p. 355.
108. Edith Garrud 'Ju-Jitsu as a Husband-Tamer: A Suffragette Play with a Moral' *Health and Strength* 8 April 1911.
109. Elizabeth Crawford *The Women's Suffrage Movement: A Reference Guide, 1866–1928* (London and New York: Routledge, 2001) p. 240.
110. Rupert Richard Arrowsmith *Modernism and the Museum: Asian, African, and Pacific Art and the London Avant-Garde* (Oxford: Oxford University Press, 2011).
111. Owen Dudley Edwards 'Sir Arthur Ignatius Conan Doyle (1859–1930)' *Oxford Dictionary of National Biography* Oxford University Press http://www.oxforddnb.com/view/article/32887 accessed 9 January 2013.
112. Muriel Matters 'Scrapbook for 1909: Muriel Matters' BBC Archive National Programme 9 February 1939 http://www.bbc.co.uk/archive/suffragettes/8315.shtml accessed 16 May 2012.
113. David Doughan 'Muriel Lilah Matters-Porter (1877–1969)' *Oxford Dictionary of National Biography* Oxford University Press http://www.oxforddnb.com/view/article/63878 accessed 9 January 2013.
114. 'History's Most Wonderful Derby' *Daily Sketch* 5 June 1913 Headline. See also 'Time to Remember: The 1913 Derby' BBC Archive unknown programme 16 June 1939 http://www.bbc.co.uk/archive/suffragettes/8317.shtml accessed 16 May 2012.
115. D. George Boyce 'Alfred Charles William Harmsworth, Viscount Northcliffe (1865–1922)' *Oxford Dictionary of National Biography* Oxford University Press http://www.oxforddnb.com/view/article/33717 accessed 9 January 2013.
116. Peter Lovesey 'Conan Doyle and The Olympics' *Journal of Olympic History* 10 December 2001 pp. 6–9.
117. K. S. Duncan 'British Olympic Association spend per Games 1896–1968 6 March 1972' *Correspondance File 1964–1978* unpaginated BOA archive London.
118. Measuring Worth Calculator http://www.measuringworth.com accessed 24 April 2012.
119. International Olympic Committee 'Olympic Games Medals, Results, Sports, Athletes: Antwerp 1920' International Olympic Committee http://www.olympic.org/content/results-and-medalists/gamesandsportsummary/ accessed 10 April 2012.
120. Annette Kellermann *How to Swim* (London: George H. Doran Company, 1918) British Library, London.
121. Dilwyn Porter and Jean Williams 'Kit: Selling Sports Clothing in Britain, c.1870–1950' *BSSH Conference* 18 July 2009 University of Stirling.

122. Two-piece tennis dress, no manufacturer c1903 object number P84.26.4 The Museum at the Fashion Institute of Technology, New York.
123. Mrs Lambert Chambers *Lawn Tennis for Ladies* pp.65–67.
124. Champot skating suit 24 Rue Royale Paris c1915 object number P84.3.1; skating dress, no manufacturer c1912 object number P84.29.8 The Museum at the Fashion Institute of Technology, New York.
125. Croquet outfit, no manufacturer c1915 object number P92.15.1 The Museum at the Fashion Institute of Technology, New York.

NOTES TO CHAPTER 3

1. Charles Mosley (ed.) *Burke's Peerage, Baronetage & Knightage Volume 1* (Wilmington: Burke's Peerage Genealogical Books Ltd, 2003) p. 1079.
2. Anon. 'Court Circular' *The Times* 25 April 1898 p. 10.
3. Obituary 'Sir John Shelley-Rolls' *The Times* 21 February 1951 p. 6.
4. Anon. 'An Autocar Wedding: The First Event of the Kind in England' *The Autocar* 1 May 1897 p. 285. My thanks to Tony Beadle for this reference.
5. David J. Jeremy 'Sir (Frederick) Henry Royce, baronet (1863–1933)' *Oxford Dictionary of National Biography* Oxford University Press http://www.oxforddnb.com/view/article/35860 accessed 18 May 2012.
6. London Stereoscopic & Photographic Company *Honourable Charles Stewart Rolls:* London: London Stereoscopic & Photographic Company circa 1900, National Portrait Gallery, photographic collection item NPG x129586; Sir (John) Benjamin Stone *Luncheon Party to French and English Aviators: House of Commons* Sir (John) Benjamin Stone, 15 September 1909 National Portrait Gallery, photographic collection item NPG x32600 http://www.npg.org.uk accessed 20 June 2012.
7. T. P. Cholmonedley Tapper *Amateur Racing Driver* (London: G. T. Foulis & Co. Ltd, 1953) p. 11.
8. Georges Fraichard (translated by Louis Klemantaski) *The Le Mans Story* (London: The Bodley Head, 1954) p. 15.
9. Richard A. Storey 'Frederick Richard Simms (1863–1944)' *Oxford Dictionary of National Biography* Oxford University Press http://www.oxforddnb.com/view/article/40814 accessed 11 January 2013.
10. Piers Breedon *The Motoring Century: The Story of the Royal Automobile Club* (London: Bloomsbury Publishing, 1997) p. 44.
11. J. R. Lowerson 'Ralph Slazenger (1845–1910)' *Oxford Dictionary of National Biography* Oxford University Press http://www.oxforddnb.com/view/article/39048 accessed 28 June 2012.
12. Reginald Brace 'Slazenger's Centenary' in John Barrett and Lance Tinjay (eds.) *Slazenger's World of Tennis 1981: The Official Yearbook of the International Tennis Federation* (London: Queen Anne Press/ Slazengers, 1981) pp. 281–282.
13. Sarah Walmsley (ed.) *Pell Mell and Woodcote: The Magazine of the Royal Automobile Club* 134 April 2011 (London: Royal Automobile Club, 2011).
14. Anon. 'The British Motor League' *The Motor* 21 January 1919 p. 578.
15. David J. Jeremy 'Charles Stewart Rolls (1877–1910)' Oxford Dictionary of National Biography Oxford University Press http://www.oxforddnb.com/view/article/35817 accessed 18 May 2012.
16. E. S. Tompkins *Speed Camera: The Amateur Photography of Motor Racing* (London: G. T. Foulis & Co. Ltd, 1946).
17. Claude Rouxel and Laurent Friry *Gotha de L'Automobile Francaise* (Paris: Editions ETAI, 2010).

318   *Notes*

18. Pierre Lafitte & Company *La Vie Au Grande Air* No. 665 17 June (Paris: Pierre Lafitte & Company, 1911) pp. ii–iv.
19. Peter Hunt 'Kenneth Grahame (1859–1932)' *Oxford Dictionary of National Biography* Oxford University Press http://www.oxforddnb.com/view/article/33511 accessed 18 May 2012.
20. Basil Dean *No Limit* (London: Associated Talking Pictures, 1935). The film involves George Formby as a chimney sweep George Shuttleworth who tunes his own motorcycle, having stolen money from his grandfather to enter the TT races as an amateur. He wins the race, a professional contract with Rainbow motorcycles and befriends Florence Desmond. The film is still shown at the races.
21. Pamela Horn *Women in the 1920s* (Stroud: Amberley, 2010 first published 1995) p. 53.
22. Leo Cheney for Raleigh *Raleigh, The Gold Motorcycle: Takes Everything in Its Stride* (Nottingham: Raleigh Industries, 1924).
23. Triumph *The Triumph Girl: Motor Cycle Series B* (Gloucester: Robert Opie Collection, Museum of Advertising and Packaging, undated).
24. Anon. 'The Doctor's Car' *The Motor* 21 January 1919 p. 578.
25. David Thoms 'Selwyn Francis Edge (1868–1940)' *Oxford Dictionary of National Biography* Oxford University Press http://www.oxforddnb.com/view/article/32970 accessed 29 June 2012.
26. C. A. N. May *Shelsley Walsh: England's International Speed Hill-Climb* (London: G. T. Foulis & Co. Ltd, 1946).
27. S. C. H. Davis *A Racing Motorist: His Adventures at the Wheel in Peace and War* (London: Iliffe and Sons Ltd, 1949).
28. Simon Vaukins *The Isle of Man Tourist Trophy Motorcycle Races 1907 to the 1960s: Politics, Economics and National Identity* (unpublished PhD thesis, University of Lancaster, 2008).
29. Laurence H. Cade 'T. T. Racing' in James Rivers (ed.) *The Sports Book* (London: Macdonald and Co., 1946) p. 220.
30. Richard De Aragues *TT3D: Closer to the Edge* (London: Entertainment One, 2011).
31. Bryan De Grineau 'The Mannin Beg . . . An Artists Impressions' *The Light Car* 8 June 1934 p. 61.
32. Jean Williams 'Making the Pilgrimage to the Yard of Brick: The Indianapolis 500' in Jeffrey Hill, Kevin Moore and Jason Wood (eds.) *Sport, History and Heritage: An Investigation into the Public Representation of Sport* (Rochester, New York and Woodbridge, Suffolk: Boydell and Brewer, 2012) pp. 247–263.
33. Anon. 'The British Motor League' *The Motor* 21 January 1919 pp. 578.
34. David Matless *Landscape and Englishness* (London, 1988) p. 63; Wren Sidhe 'H. V. Morton's Pilgrimages to Englishness' *Literature and History* 12:1 Spring 2003 pp. 57–71.
35. Adrian Smith 'Sport, Speed and the Technological Imperative: Dealing With the Declinists' *Historians on Sport Symposium* De Montfort University, Leicester 30 October 2007.
36. Jean-François Bouzanquet *Fast Ladies: Female Racing Drivers 1888–1970* (Dorchester: Veloce, 2009) p. 11.
37. Jean-François Bouzanquet *Fast Ladies* p. 12.
38. Barbara Burman 'Racing Bodies: Dress and Pioneer Women Aviators and Racing Drivers' *Women's History Review* 9:2 2000 pp. 299–326.
39. S. C. H. Davis *Atalanta: Women as Racing Drivers* (London: G. T. Foulis & Co. Ltd, 1957) p. 17.
40. Jean-François Bouzanquet *Fast Ladies* p. 14.

41. William Plowden *The Motor Car and Politics 1896–1970* (London: The Bodley Head, 1971) p. 14.
42. Julie Wosk *Women and the Machine: Representations from the Spinning Wheel to the Electronic Age* (Baltimore, Maryland: Johns Hopkins University Press, 2001) pp. 141–142.
43. Anon. 'Miss Quimby Dies in Airship Fall' *The New York Times* 2 July 2 1912 p. 1.
44. Blanche Stuart Scott Collection, accession number XXXX-0062 *National Air And Space Archives and Museum, Smithsonian Institution* Washington, DC.
45. Royal Aeronautical Society 'From Pioneers to Presidents: Celebrating a Century of Flight' *Royal Aeronautical Society Women in Aviation and Aerospace Confer*ence Hamilton Place, London 14 October 2011.
46. M. H. Goodall *Flying Start: Flying Schools and Clubs at Brooklands, 1910–1939* (Weybridge: Brooklands Museum Trust, 1995) p. 16.
47. Shirley Carpenter 'The Lady Autocarist Prepares for the Hazards of a Motor Drive [sic]' *The Autocar* 9 December 1955 pp. 970–971.
48. ibid.
49. Anon. 'Carriage Builders Messrs. Thomas Whittingham and Wilkin, London [sic]' *The Autocar* 15 April 1899 p. 5.
50. Tan-Sad *Tan-Sad: Pillion Riding Comfort and Safety Motor Cycle Series A* (Gloucester: Robert Opie Collection, Museum of Advertising and Packaging, undated).
51. Charlie Lee Potter *Sportswear in Vogue since 1910* (New York: Abbeville Press, 1984) p. 11.
52. British Pathé 'Emancipation of Women 1890–1930' http://www.british-pathe.com film identity: 2261.01; ITN Source 'USA, Water Sports: Speedboat towing girl on raft, 1916' http://www.itnsource.com clip reference: BGT407050077 accessed 29 June 2012.
53. Alfred C. Harmsworth *Motors and Motor Driving* (London and Bombay: Longmans, Green and Company, 1902).
54. D. George Boyce 'Alfred Charles William Harmsworth, Viscount Northcliffe (1865–1922)' *Oxford Dictionary of National Biography* Oxford University Press http://www.oxforddnb.com/view/article/33717 accessed 22 June 2012.
55. Roger Hargreaves and Bill Deedes *Daily Encounters: Photographs From Fleet Street* (London: National Portrait Gallery, 2007) pp.40–41.
56. Rosie Whorlow '"The Latest Scare": British Leisure Magazines and the Cause of the Feminine Motorcycle Rider' *Women and Leisure 1890–1939: Women's History Network Conference Midlands Region* University of Staffordshire 8 November 2008.
57. Charlie Lee Potter *Sportswear in Vogue since 1910* pp. 10–13.
58. Beaulieu Motor Museum *Flying Lady Centennial Exhibition 5 May-30 October 2011* http://www.beaulieu.co.uk/news/flying-lady accessed 5 January 2012.
59. Lord Montagu (ed.) 'Mrs Maurice Helwett, the First Englishwoman to Gain an Aviator's Certificate' *The Car: A Journal of Travel by Land, Sea and Air (Illustrated)* 497 29 November 1911 (London: Countryside Publishing, 1911) cover image.
60. Brooks auctions 'Frederick Gordon Crosby *The MG Girl* advertisement, watercolour and charcoal-cover artwork for *The Autocar* 29 April 1932' *Brooks Auctions Motor Sport Catalogue 1990* (London: Brooks, 1990) p. 34.
61. Lady Jeune and Baron Zuylen de Nyvelt 'Dress for Motoring' in Alfred C. Harmsworth *Motors and Motor Driving* p. 66.

62. Shirley Carpenter 'The Lady Autocarist' p. 971.
63. Sean O'Connell *The Car and British Society: Class, Gender and Motoring 1896–1939* (Manchester: Manchester University Press, 1998).
64. No maker, duster coat in brown linen circa 1878 item P.80.8.1; no maker, duster coat in tan linen circa 1880s item P85.5.1; G. J. Oberist, duster coat in tan unbleached linen circa 1900 item P 69.168.218; Bergdorf Goodman, duster coat in tan linen with black braid trim circa 1906 item P84.21.23; no maker, duster coat in beige Dupion silk circa 1916 item P85.159.7; Gift of *Connoisseur* magazine and the Palm Beach Cloth Company duster coat in cream linen-wool blend with mother of pearl buttons circa 1916 item P84.29.3 The Museum at the Fashion Institute of Technology, New York.
65. John Levit 'Islington: Highbury household schedule number: 233 piece: 196 folio: 22' *1901 England Census*: 'Islington: Highbury p. 36 http://ancestry.co.uk accessed 29 June 2012.
66. Ann Kramer personal communication 29 June 2012; Ann Kramer 'Dorothy Elizabeth Levitt (1882–1922)' *Oxford Dictionary of National Biography* http://www.oxforddnb.com/view/article/92721 accessed 25 Setpember 2013.
67. Dorothy Levitt *The Woman and the Car: A Chatty Little Handbook for All Women Who Motor Or Who Want To Motor* (London: Hugh Evelyn, 1909).
68. John Bullock *Fast Women: The Drivers Who Changed the Face of Motor Racing* (London: Robson Books, 2002) pp. 15–17.
69. S. C. H. Davis 'Dorothy Levitt' *Atalanta: Women as Racing Drivers* (London: Foulis, 1957) pp. 31–45.
70. S. C. H. Davis 'Dorothy Levitt' *Atalanta* p. 34.
71. S. C. H. Davis 'Dorothy Levitt' *Atalanta* p. 32.
72. Ann Kramer *Sussex Women: A Sussex Guide* (Alfriston, Sussex: Snake River Press, 2007) pp. 61–64.
73. Edgar Claxton 'Register of Death: Dorothy Elizabeth Levi, 22 May 1922 reference number DYD 047027 *General Register Office, Crown Copyright* (North Marylebone, London, 22 May 1922). I am grateful to Mark Curthoys for providing this reference.
74. Ann Kramer personal communication 29 June 2012.
75. Elizabeth Crawford and Jill Liddington 'If Women Do Not Count, Neither Shall They Be Counted': Suffrage, Citizenship and the Battle for the 1911 Census' *History Workshop Journal* http://hwj.oxfordjournals.org/hwj.dbq064 accessed 29 June 2012.
76. David Dee '"Nothing Specifically Jewish in Athletics?": Sport, Physical Recreation and the Jewish Youth Movement in London 1895–1914' *The London Journal* 34:2 2010 pp. 81–100.
77. William Boddy *The History of Brooklands Motor Course: Complied from the Official Records of the Brooklands Automobile Racing Club* (London: Grenville Publishing, 1957) p. 5.
78. Colin Parry 'Dame Ethel Locke King [née Gore-Browne] (1864–1956)' *Oxford Dictionary of National Biography* Oxford University Press http://www.oxforddnb.com/view/article/52021 and John Pulford 'Hugh Fortescue Locke King (1848–1926)' *Oxford Dictionary of National Biography* Oxford University Press http://www.oxforddnb.com/view/article/66280 accessed 20 June 2012.
79. G. C. Boas, rev. H. C. G. Matthew 'Peter John Locke King (1811–1885) *Oxford Dictionary of National Biography* Oxford University Press http://www.oxforddnb.com/view/article/64231 accessed 20 June 2012.

80. William Boddy *The History of Brooklands Motor Course* p. 15.
81. British Pathé 'Brooklands by the Sea: Skegness, Lincolnshire 1925' http:// www.britishpathe.com film identity: 406.07 accessed 29 June 2012.
82. William Boddy *The Story of Brooklands: The World's First Motor Course: Complied from the Official Records of the Brooklands Automobile Racing Club* Volume 2 (London: Grenville Publishing, 1959) pp. 290–292.
83. David Thoms 'Selwyn Francis Edge'.
84. Roger Munting 'Dick Seaman-Was He a Hero or a Villain?' *Bulletin of the British Society of Sports History* December 2010 p. 23.
85. John Tennant *Motor Racing: The Golden Age* (London: Cassell Illustrated, 2004) pp. 110–111 and pp. 366–367.
86. Brooklands Automobile Racing Club 'Item: Inaugural Race Meeting' *BARC Minute Book June 1907* Brooklands Museum and Archive, Weybridge, Surrey p. 7. Hereafter Brooklands Museum.
87. William Boddy *The Story of Brooklands* Volume 2 p. 293.
88. Brooklands Automobile Racing Club 'Item: Races and Aviation Meeting' *BARC Minute Book June 1907* Brooklands Museum p. 3.
89. Brooklands Automobile Racing Club 'Item: Prize funds and Race Protocols' *Minute Book June 1907* Brooklands Museum p. 5.
90. Neils Kayser Nielsen 'The Stadium in the City—a Modern Story' in John Bale and Olaf Moen (eds.) The *Stadium and the City* (Keele University Press: Keele, 1995) pp. 15–34.
91. William Boddy *The Story of Brooklands* p. 293.
92. Anon. 'Double '"Double 12": When a 250cc Motorcycle and a 5.7 litre Car Shared Brooklands for a Unique Record' *Brooklands Society Gazette* 8: 1 1983 pp. 22–23.
93. Jean Williams 'Gwenda Glubb, Janson, Stewart, Hawkes (1894–1990)' *Oxford Dictionary of National Biography* Oxford University Press http:// www.oxforddnb.com/view/article/92722 accessed 25 Septemeber 2013.
94. George Eyston *Safety Last* (Spalding: Vincent Publishing, 1975) p. 18.
95. Lynette Beardwood 'Muriel Annie Thompson (1875–1939)' *Oxford Dictionary of National Biography* Oxford University Press http://www.oxforddnb.com/view/article/68164 accessed 12 January 2013.
96. Percy F. Spence 'Women Even in Motor Racing' *Brooklands Society Gazette* 13:1 1988 p. 37.
97. Brooklands Automobile Racing Club 'Item: Fifth Race: Result 4 July 1908' *BARC Minute Book July 1908* Brooklands Museum.
98. Brooklands Automobile Racing Club 'Item: Third Race: Result 3 August 1908 *BARC Minute Book* Brooklands Museum.
99. Brooklands Automobile Racing Club 'On the Track' *The Autocar* 3 August 1912 p. 194.
100. Anon 'On the Track: The RAC and Associates Gala Day' *The Autocar* 3 August 1912 p. 196.
101. Anon. 'New and Notes: Gala Meeting of the Essex Motor Club' *The Motor* 20 August 1912 p. 102.
102. John Bullock *Fast Women* p. 33.
103. Georgine Clarsen *Eat My Dust: Early Women Motorists* (Baltimore, Maryland: Johns Hopkins University Press, 2008) pp. 40–41.
104. Marian G. Paige 'Maxwell: Votes for Women' *The Motor* 27 July 1915 p. 56.
105. Marian G. Paige '£20, 000 to be invested in Light Cars' *The Light Car* 6 December 1916 p. 10.
106. Mike Cronin and Richard Holt 'The Globalisation of Sport' *History Today* 53: 7 July 2003 pp. 26–33.

107. Gregor Grant *British Sports Cars* (London: G. T. Foulis & Co. Ltd, 1947).
108. Floyd Clymer *Indianapolis 500 mile Race History* (Los Angeles: Floyd Clymer Publishing, 1946).
109. Anon. 'The Brookland's Nut' *Car* 4 October 1911 p. 235.
110. Brooklands Museum *Welcome to Brooklands: Birthplace of British Motorsport and Aviation* http://www.brooklandsmuseum.com accessed 20 June 2012.
111. Kevin Moore *Museums and Popular Culture: Contemporary Issues in Museum Culture* (Leicester: Leicester University Press, 1996).
112. Peter O'Kane 'A History of the "Triple Crown" of Motor Racing: The Indianapolis 500, the Le Mans 10 Hours and the Monaco Grand Prix' *International Journal of the History of Sport* 28: 2 2011 pp. 281–299.
113. Michael Billig *Banal Nationalism* (London: Sage, 1995) pp. 43–44.
114. Jack Williams '"A Wild Orgy of Speed": Responses to Speedway in Britain before the Second World War' *The Sports Historian* 19:1 May 1999 pp. 1–15.
115. Tony Mason and Eliza Riedi *Sport and the Military: The British Armed Forces 1880–1960* (Cambridge, Cambridge University Press, 2010).
116. Alice Mc Dermott 'In Florence Nightingale's Footsteps: A Biography of Mary O'Connell Bianconi with Particular Reference to her Nursing Career' (Waterford: Waterford Institute of Technology) http://www.wit.ie/MaryOConnellBianconiBiographyfull.pdf accessed 29 June 2012 p. 15.
117. James Lunt 'Sir John Bagot Glubb (1897–1986)' *Oxford Dictionary of National Biography* Oxford University Press http://www.oxforddnb.com/view/article/40128 accessed 12 January 2013.
118. S. C. H. Davis 'Gwenda Hawkes' *Atalanta* pp. 77–79.
119. George Eyston *Safety Last* p. 156–157.
120. George Eyston *Flat Out* (Spalding: Vincent Publishing Company, 1976; first published in 1933) pp. 22–23.
121. Tony Kushner *Anglo-Jewry since 1066: Place Locality and Memory* (Manchester: Manchester University Press, 2009) pp. 44–45.
122. Miranda Seymour *The Bugatti Queen: In Search of a Motor Racing Legend* (London: Simon and Schuster, 2004) p. xvii.
123. Stephen Gundle *Glamour: A History* (Oxford: Oxford University Press, 2008) p. 19.
124. Tony Mason 'All the Winners and the Half Times . . . ' *The Sports Historian* 13:2 May 1993 pp. 3–4; Douglas Booth *The Field: Truth And Fiction in Sport History* (London and New York: Routledge, 2005) pp. 89–90.
125. John Osbourne '"To Keep the Life of the Nation on the Old Lines": The *Athletic News* and the First World War' *Journal of Sport History* 14:2 Summer, 1987 pp.138–139.
126. Marcel Viollette 'Le Circuit Européen' *La Vie Au Grande Air* No 665 17 June (Paris: Pierre Lafitte & Company, 1911) p. 390. See also the photograph of Madamoiselle Max Stross Lavaggi, the tennis player p. 402.
127. Pierre Lafitte & Company *La Vie Au Grande Air* 649:25 February (Paris: Pierre Lafitte & Company, 1911) pp. ii; 118 and 128.
128. Ian Boutle 'Speed Lies in the Lap of the English': Motor Records, Masculinity and the Nation, 1907–1914 *Twentieth Century British History* published online January 28 2012 http://www.oxfordjournals.org/content/early/2012/01/28/tcbh.hwr068.full.pdf accessed 31 January 2012.

NOTES TO CHAPTER 4

1. Anon. 'Look Out for the Girl Athletes' *Collier's: The National Weekly* 21 February 1925 *Femmes et Sport: Correspondance Concernant Les Fédérations Féminines 1925–1938 DGI 204963* International Olympic Committee

Archive and Museum, Lausanne. Hereafter, Women and Sport file IOC archive, Lausanne.

2. Vera Searle 'Early Days of the WAAA' *Women's AAA Golden Jubilee Championships Progrmme, Sponsored by Birds Eye Foods, Crystal Palace 1972* (London: WAAA, 1972) pp. 26–27 Women's Amateur Athletics Association files, Box 1, Harold Abrahams Collection, Birmingham University Special Collections. Hereafter, WAAA files, Birmingham University. At the time of my visit in February 2010, the three boxes of WAAA material had not been indexed.

3. Anon. 'Workless Women' *The Lancashire Daily Post* 9 February 1921 p. 5.

4. Catriona Parratt '"The Making of the Healthy and the Happy Home": Education, Recreation, and the Production of Working-Class Womanhood at the Rowntree Cocoa Works, York, c.1889–1914' in Jack Williams and Jeff Hill (eds.) *Sport and Identity in the North of England* (Keele: University of Keele Press, 1996) pp. 53—83.

5. Gail Braybon *Women Workers in the First World War* (London: Croom Helm, 1981); Gail Braybon and Penny Summerfield *Out of the Cage: Women's Experiences in Two World Wars* (London: Pandora, 1987); Martin Pugh *Women and The Women's Movement in Britain 1914–1999* (London: Macmillan, 2000).

6. Pamela Horn 'Appendix 1: Working Women' *Women in the 1920s* (Stroud: Amberley, 2010) pp. 212–213.

7. The Daily Express *These Tremendous Years 1919–1938: A History in Photographs of Life and Events, Big and Little, in Britain and The World since The War* (London: Daily Express Publications, 1938) p. 15.

8. Gerry Holloway *Women and Work in Britain since 1840* (London: Routledge, 2005) pp. 147–148.

9. Carol Dyhouse *Students: A Gendered History* (London: Routledge, 2006) pp. 9–11.

10. Martin Pugh 'Nancy Witcher Astor, Viscountess Astor (1879–1964)' *Oxford Dictionary of National Biography* Oxford University Press http://www.oxforddnb.com/view/article/30489 accessed 11 July 2012.

11. Duncan Sutherland 'Katharine Marjory Stewart-Murray, Duchess of Atholl (1874–1960)' *Oxford Dictionary of National Biography* Oxford University Press http://www.oxforddnb.com/view/article/36301 accessed 11 July 2012.

12. Martin Pugh 'Gwendolen Florence Mary Guiness, Countess of Iveagh (1881–1966)' *Oxford Dictionary of National Biography* Oxford University Press http://www.oxforddnb.com/view/article/33602 accessed 11 July 2012.

13. The Daily Express *These Tremendous Years* pp.28–33.

14. Duncan Sutherland 'Frances Elaine Burton, Baroness Burton of Coventry (1904–1991)' *Oxford Dictionary of National Biography* Oxford University Press http://www.oxforddnb.com/view/article/49597 accessed 10 August 2012.

15. Alethea Melling '"Ray of the Rovers:" The Working Class Heroine in Popular Football Fiction 1915–25' *The International Journal of The History of Sport* 15:1 April 1998 pp. 97–122; Alethea Melling 'Cultural Differentiation, Shared Aspiration: The Entente Cordiale of International Ladies' Football 1920–45' *The European Sports History Review* 1 1999 pp. 27–53.

16. Mel Watman 'Women Athletes between the World Wars (1919–1939)' *Oxford Dictionary of National Biography* Oxford University Press http://www.oxforddnb.com/view/article/103699 accessed 10 August 2012.

17. Patricia Vertinsky *The Eternally Wounded Woman: Women, Doctors and Exercise in the Late Nineteenth Century* (Manchester and New York: Manchester University Press, 1990) p. 132.

18. Mark Pottle 'Sophie Catherine Theresa Mary Heath, Lady Heath (1896–1939)' *Oxford Dictionary of National Biography* Oxford University Press http://www.oxforddnb.com/view/article/67141 accessed 10 August 2012.

19. Catriona M. Parratt *More Than Mere Amusement: Working Class Women's Leisure 1750–1914* (Boston, Massachusetts: Northeastern University Press, 2001) pp. 188–189.
20. André Drevon *Alice Milliat: La Pasionaria du Sport Feminine* (Paris: Vuibert, 2005) p. 5.
21. Ghislane Quintillan 'Alice Milliat and the Women's Games' *Olympic Review* 36:31 2000 pp. 27–28 (Lausanne: International Olympic Committee, 2000) http://www.la84foundation.org/OlympicInformationCenter/OlympicReview/2000 accessed 12 August 2012.
22. Wendy Michallat 'Droit au But: Violette Morris and Women's Football in "Les Années Folles"' *French Studies Bulletin* 26:1 2005 pp. 13–17.
23. Mary H. Leigh and Thérèse M. Bonin 'The Pioneering Role of Madame Alice Milliat and the FSFI in Establishing International Track and Field Competition for Women' *Journal of Sport History* 4:1 1977 pp. 72–83.
24. Carly Adams 'Fighting for Acceptance: Sigfrid Edström and Avery Brundage: Their Efforts to Shape and Control Women's Participation in the Olympic Games' in Kevin B. Wamsley, Robert K. Barney and Scott G. Martyn (eds.) *Global Nexus Engaged: Sixth International Symposium for Olympic Research 2002* (International Centre for Olympic Studies: University of Western Ontario Canada, 2002) pp. 143–148.
25. Jennifer Hargreaves 'Women and the Olympic Phenomenon' in Alan Tomlinson and Gary Whannel (eds.) *Five Ring Circus: Money, Power and Politics at the Olympic Games* (London: Pluto Press, 1984) p. 59.
26. Thierry Terret 'From Alice Milliat to Marie-Thérèse Eyquem: Revisiting Women's Sport in France (1920s–1960s)' *The International Journal of the History of Sport* 27:7 2010 pp. 1154–1172.
27. Lynne Robinson *Tripping Daintily Into the Arena: A Social History of English Women's Athletics 1921–1960* (unpublished PhD thesis, Warwick University Warwickshire, 1997).
28. The Daily Express *These Tremendous Years* p. 48.
29. Maurice Roche *Mega-Events and Modernity: Olympics and Expos in the Growth of Global Culture* (London and New York: Routledge, 2000) p. 101.
30. Florence A. Somers *Principles of Women's Athletics* (New York: A. S. Barnes and Company, 1930).
31. Stephen Jones 'Sport, Politics and The Labour Movement: The British Workers' Sports Federation, 1923–1935' *The International Journal of the History of Sport* 2:2 1985 pp. 154–178; Stephen Jones 'The British Workers' Sports Federation: 1923–1935' in Arnd Krüger and James Riordan (eds.) *The Story of Worker Sport* (Champaign, Illinois: Human Kinetics, 1996) p. 109.
32. John C. Pritchett *Library Director of Columbia College Letter to Olympic Museum and Enclosures 17 September 1996* Femmes et Sport: Publications diverses (journaux et magazines entiers) 1952–1981 file reference DGI 204964 IOC archive, Lausanne.
33. Linda M. Gallagher '1st Female Olympic Medallist is SC Native' *The State* unpaginated c. 1922 Femmes et Sport: Publications diverses (journaux et magazines entiers) 1952–1981 file reference DGI 204964 IOC archive, Lausanne.
34. Patrick Brennan *The Munitionettes: A History of Women's Football in North East England during the Great War* (Tyne and Wear: Donmouth Publishing, 2007).
35. Matthew Taylor *The Leaguers: The Making of Professional Football in England, 1900–1939* (Liverpool: Liverpool University Press, 2005).

36. Margaret Burscough *The Horrockses: Cotton Kings of Preston* (Preston: Carnegie Publishing, 2004).
37. Patrick Brennan 'The Dick, Kerr Ladies' FC' *Women's Football* http://www. donmouth.co.uk/womens_football/dick_kerr.html accessed 6 October 20.
38. Steve Crewe 'With Comradeship and Good Temper': A Cross-Sector Analysis of Company Welfare (unpublished PhD thesis, De Montfort University Leicester, 2014).
39. Preston North End Board 'Resolved: Dick, Kerr's Munitions Team' *Preston North End Board Minute Books* 14 December 1915 p. 3 The National Football Museum, Preston.
40. Preston North End Board 'Resolved: Dick, Kerr's Munitions Team' *Preston North End Board Minute Books* 3 March 1916 p. 5 The National Football Museum, Preston.
41. Preston North End Board 'Resolved: PNE Game against Dick, Kerr's' *Preston North End Board Minute Books* 14 December 1918 p. 28 The National Football Museum, Preston.
42. Preston North End Board 'Resolved: Coulthard Foundry Game against Dick, Kerr's Ladies' *Preston North End Board Minute Books* 14 October 1917 p. 3 The National Football Museum, Preston.
43. Anon. 'Ladies at football' *Lancashire Daily Post* 27 December 1917.
44. Anon. 'Women's "International" Dick, Kerr's, The Women's "Soccer" Side, Defeated the French Women's Team 5–1 (Exclusive)' *The Daily Mirror* 18 May 1921 p. 8. I am grateful to Neil Carter for all references to *The Daily Mirror*.
45. Preston North End Board 'Resolved: Agree to let Dick, Kerr's and Co Ladies Football Club and deputation rent our ground for this season 1918 and 19, £12 for Saturday match Dick, Kerr agreeing to take the ground for at least ten matches [sic]' *Preston North End Board Minute Books* 5 February 1918 p. 25; Preston North End Board 'Resolved: That we regret we cannot allow the proposed charity match to be played by Dick, Kerr's Ladies' *Preston North End Board Minute Books* 24 August 1920 p. 35 National Football Museum, Preston.
46. Robert Galvin and Mark Bushell *Football's Greatest Heroes: The National Football Museum Hall of Fame* (London: Robson Books 2005) p. 11 'At the time there were no organised women's leagues.'
47. Nomad 'My Notebook' *Yorkshire Sports* 8 January 1921 p. 5; Nomad 'My Notebook' *Yorkshire Sports* 11 June 1921 pp. 2–3.
48. Anon. 'New Rivals to Dick, Kerr's Eleven' *The Daily Mirror* 23 March 1921 cover.
49. Helen Jones 'Employer's Welfare Schemes and Industrial Relations in Inter War Britain' *Business History* 25: 1 1983 pp. 61–75.
50. Peter Burke *A Social History of Workplace Australian Football 1860–1939* (unpublished PhD Royal Melbourne Institute of Technology University Melbourne, 2008) pp. 142–160.
51. Charles P. Korr *West Ham United: The Making of a Football Club* (Urbana: University of Illinois Press, 1986).
52. Patrick Brennan 'Soup Kitchen Soccer: Women's football in North-East England during the 1921 and 1926 Coal Disputes' *Women's Football* http://www.donmouth.co.uk/ accessed 2 January 2012.
53. Paul Dietschy Histoire du Football (Paris: Librairie Académique Perrin, 2010) p. 503.
54. Laurence Prudhomme-Poncet Histoire du Football Feminine au XXème Siècle: Espaces et Temps du Sport (Paris: LíHarmattann, 2003) p. 10.

55. Anon. 'Dick, Kerr's Still Winning' *The Lancashire Daily Post* 2 March 1921 p. 4.
56. Anon. 'Dick, Kerr's Ladies' Success' *The Lancashire Daily Post* 21 March 1921 p. 5.
57. Anon. 'Can Girls Play Football? Of Course They Can' *The Football Favourite* 1:32 9 April 1921 (London: Amalgamated Press, 1921) pp. 9–12.
58. Anon 'Dick, Kerr's Most Successful Season' *The Lancashire Daily Post* 6 June 1921 p. 5; Anon.'Women Footballers' Fine Record' *The Daily* Mirror 7 June 1921 p. 3.
59. Anon 'Lady Footballers' Tour' *The Isle of Man Daily Times* 8 August 1921 p. 8.
60. Anon. 'Lady Footballers' *The Isle of Man Daily Times* 15 August 1921 p. 8; Anon. 'Another Win for Dick, Kerr's' *The Lancashire Daily Post* 15 August 1921 p. 15.
61. Anon. 'Health Giving Kicks–Girl Footballer Who Scored 368 Goals Saw Doctor Only Once' *The Daily Mirror* 9 December 1921 p. 7.
62. Anon 'Ladies Football-Banned by the Football Association' *The Lancashire Daily Post* 6 December 1921 p. 5.
63. Nomad 'My Notebook' *Yorkshire Sports* 10 December 1921 p. 2.
64. Jean Williams *A Beautiful Game: International Perspective on Women and Football* (London: Berg 2007) p. 124.
65. H. Frost and H. Cubberley *Field Hockey and Soccer for Women* (New York: Charles Scribner and Sons, 1923); M. Knighton 'Development of Soccer for Girls' *The American Physical Education Review* 34 1929 pp. 372.
66. Jean Williams 'Lilian Parr (1905–1978)' *Oxford Dictionary of National Biography* Oxford University Press http://www.oxforddnb.com/view/article/102447 accessed 11 July 2012.
67. M. Ann Hall *The Grads Are Playing Tonight: The Story of the Edmonton Commercial Graduates Basketball Club* (Edmonton: The University of Alberta Press, 2011).
68. Jean Williams, 'Lilian Parr (1905–1978)' accessed 2 Aug 2012.
69. British Pathe *Playing Adam's Game* (circa 1917) film number 1078.11; *Women Footballers* 26 April 1920 film number 210.03; *Soccer by Searchlight* 20 December 1920 film number 224.36; *Fun and Football for Charity* 17 February 1921 film number 228.35 http://www.britishpathe.com accessed 11 July 2012. See also ITN Source *Ladies' Football Match: Carpentier kicks off* 17 December 1921 film number BP25052283412 http://www.itnsource.com accessed 3 August 2012.
70. David J. Williamson *Belles of the Ball: A History of Women's Football* (Devon: R&D Associates, 1991); Sue Lopez *Women on the Ball: A Guide to Women's Football* (London: Scarlet Press, 1997); Gail Newsham *In a League of Their Own! The Dick, Kerr Ladies' Football Club* (London: Scarlet, 1998); Barbara Jacobs *The Dick, Kerr's Ladies* (London: Constable and Robinson 2004); Patrick Brennan *The Munitionettes*.
71. Anon. 'Rugby is the secret of 106-year-olds longevity!' *Penarth Times* 23 January 2006 http://www.penarthtimes.co.uk/archive accessed 14 August 2012.
72. Rob Hess and Nikki Wedgewood (eds.) *Women, Football and History* (Hawthorn, Victoria: Maribyrnong Press, 2011).
73. John Bale, Mette K. Christensen and Gertrude Pfister (eds.) *Writing Lives in Sport: Biographies, Life-Histories and Methods* (Langelandsgade: Aarhus, 2004).
74. Lynne Duval 'The Development of Women's Track and Field in England: The Role of the Athletic Club 1920s-1950s' *The Sports Historian* 21:1 May 2001 pp. 1–34.

75. Harold Abrahams *Fifty Years of the Amateur Athletic Association Championships* (London: Carborundum, 1961).
76. Rob Beamish 'Totalitarian Regimes and Cold War Sport' in Stephen Wagg and David L. Andrews (eds.) *East Plays West: Sport and the Cold War* (London and New York: Routledge, 2006) pp. 11–26.
77. Alice Milliat *Letter to Count Baillet Latour President of IOC, 23 Rue du Trône Brusselles 25 January 1935* unpaginated Women and Sport File' IOC archives, Lausanne.
78. Peter Tatchell *Unequal Olympics: An Open Letter to Jacques Rogge 27 July 2012* Peter Tatchell Homepage http://www.petertatchell.net/sport/Unequal-Olympics-An-Open-Letter-to-Jacques-Rogge.htm accessed 2 August 2012.
79. Jean François Bouzanquet *Fast Ladies: Female Racing Drivers 1888–1970* (Dorchester: Veloce, 2010) pp. 22–25.
80. Laurence Prudhomme-Poncet *Histoire Du Football Féminin* pp. 53–54.
81. J. Lyons & Company online archive http://www.kzwp.com/lyons/index.htm accessed 10 August 2012.
82. Mel Watman 'Women Athletes between the World Wars 1919–1939: Mary Lines [married name Smith] (1893–1978)' *Oxford Dictionary of National Biography* Oxford University Press http://www.oxforddnb.com/view/article/103699 accessed 15 August 2012.
83. Fédération Sportive Féminine Internationale *Jeux Féminins Mondiaux Londres 1934* (Paris: 3 Rue De Varenne, 1934) p. 8 WAAA Files, Box 2 Birmingham University.
84. Robert J. Maughan (ed.) *The Encyclopaedia of Sports Medicine: An IOC Medical Commission Publication* (Chichester: Wiley-Blackwell Publishing, 2009) p. 26.
85. Florence Carpentier and Pierre Lefèvre 'The Modern Olympic Movement, Women's Sport and the Social Order During the Inter-war Period' *The International Journal of the History of Sport* 23:7 2006 pp.1112–1127.
86. Clothilde Rowell '"Our Ludy" Comes Home' *The Winthrop College News* 10:5 20 October 1922 cover Women and Sport File IOC archive, Lausanne.
87. Anon. 'The American Girls At The First Women's Olympiad' *New York World* 10 September 1922 unpaginated press cutting Women and Sport File IOC archive, Lausanne.
88. Mel Watman 'Women Athletes between the World Wars: Hilda May Hatt [married names Bryant, Barrow] (1903–1975)' *Oxford Dictionary of National Biography* Oxford University Press http://www.oxforddnb.com/view/article/103699 accessed 15 August 2012.
89. Mel Watman 'Women Athletes between The World Wars: Vera Maud Palmer [married name Searle] (1901–1998) and Eileen Winifred Edwards (1903–1988)' *Oxford Dictionary of National Biography* Oxford University Press http://www.oxforddnb.com/view/article/103699 accessed 15 August 2012.
90. Neil Carter *Medicine, Sport and the Body: A Historical Perspective* (London and New York: Bloomsbury Academic, 2012) p. 150.
91. Joe Palmer; Major W. B Marchant; Mr E. H. Knowles; Mrs F. Millichip (née Birchenough) and Mrs V. Searle (née Palmer) 'Resumee of the main WAAA events 1921–1927' *WAAA Minutes 1921–1991* WAAA Files, Box 1 Birmingham University.
92. Sophie Elliott-Lynn *Athletics for Women and Girls: How To Be An Athlete and Why* (London: Robert Scott, 1925); F. A. M. Webster *Athletics of To-day for Women: History Development and Training* (London: Frederick Warne, 1930).
93. Vera Searle 'Early Days of the WAAA' pp. 26–27.
94. ibid..

95. Alice Milliat *Letter to Count Baillet Latour President of IOC, 14 Rue Guimard Brusselles 4 January 1927;* Alice Milliat *Letter to Hirschmann Secretary General of the Olympic Committee of the Netherlands 20 January 1927;* Alice Milliat *Letter to Count Baillet Latour President of IOC 27 April 1927* Women and Sport File IOC archives, Lausanne.

96. Lynne Emery 'An Examination of the 1928 Olympic 800m race for women' *NASSH Proocedings 1985* p. 30 http://www.la84foundation.org accessed 10 July 2012.

97. From Our Geneva Correspondent 'Olympic Games and Women: Ban Likely' *Manchester Guardian* 12 April 1929 p. 5 Women and Sport File IOC archives, Lausanne.

98. Ian Buchanan 'Kinuye Hitomi: Asia's First Female Olympian' *Journal of Olympic History* 8:3 2000 pp. 22–23.

99. Fédération Sportive Féminine Internationale *Jeux Féminins Mondiaux Londres 1934* p. 8 WAAA files, Box 2 Birmingham University.

100. Wray Vamplew 'Muriel Amy Cornell (1906–1996)' *Oxford Dictionary of National Biography* Oxford University Press http://www.oxforddnb.com/view/article/62157 accessed 17 August 2012.

101. Miho Koishihara 'The Emergence of the 'Sporting Girls' in Japanese Girls' Magazines: Descriptions and Visual Images of the Female Athlete in Japanese Culture of the 1920s and 1930s' *Fourth Meeting of the Transnational Scholars for the Study of Gender and Sport* Pädagogische Hochscule Ludwigsburg 27–30 November 2008.

102. Miho Koishihara 'Description of Themes in Japanese Girls' Magazines: Handout' *Fourth Meeting of the Transnational Scholars for the Study of Gender and Sport* Pädagogische Hochscule Ludwigsburg 27–30 November 2008 pp. 1–2.

103. Mel Watman 'Women Athletes between the World Wars: Gladys Anne [Sally] Lunn (1908–1988)' http://www.oxforddnb.com/view/article/103699 accessed 15 August 2012.

104. Barbara Keys *Globalising Sport: National Rivalry and International Community in the 1930s* (Cambridge, Massachusetts and London: Harvard University Press, 2006) p. 5.

105. Mel Watman Women Athletes between the World Wars: Ethel Edburga Clementina Scott (1907–1984)' http://www.oxforddnb.com/view/article/103699 accessed 15 August 2012.

106. Avery Brundage *American Olympic Committee Letter to Count Henri Baillet-Latour 23 June 1936* p. 1 Women and Sport File IOC Archives Lausanne.

107. Fédération Sportive Féminine Internationale *Jeux Féminins Mondiaux Londres 1934: Fourth Womens World Games Official Programme Thursday-Saturday 9–11 August 1934* White City Stadium London p. 7 (London: Fleetway, 1934) WAAA files, Box 2 Birmingham University.

108. Vanessa Heggie *A History of British Sports Medicine* (Manchester and New York: Manchester University Press, 2011) pp. 110–111.

109. British Pathé Newsreel 'French Ladies Football Team 1922 Cardiff' film number 262.04 http://www.britishpathe.com/video/french-ladies-football-team accessed 3 August 2012.

110. Liselott Diem 'Woman [sic] and Olympism: Retrospection on Former Publications of the Olympic Academy' Paper presented at the Olympic Academy Conference 1978 pp. 7–8 Women and Sport File IOC archives, Lausanne.

111. M. Ann Hall *The Grads Are Playing Tonight* p. 60–61.

112. Fédération Sportive Féminine Internationale *Fourth Womens World Games Official Programme* p. 8.

113. Ian Buchanan *British Olympians: A Hundred Years of Gold Medallists* (London: Guinness Publishing, 1991) p. 181.
114. International Olympic Committee *Official Source: Olympic Records, World Records, Olympic Medalists* http://www.olympic.org/medallists accessed 28 July 2012.
115. Benedict Anderson *Imagined Communities* (New York: Verso, 1991).
116. Richard Holt 'Audrey Kathleen Court [née Brown] (1913–2005)' *Oxford Dictionary of National Biography* Oxford University Press http://www.oxforddnb.com/view/article/96973 accessed 17 August 2012.
117. A. Hector *Secretary General of the Fédération Équestre Internationale Letter to Count Henri Baillet-Latour 13 April 1934*; Albert Demaurex *Secretary General of the Fédération Internationale De Hockey Fédération Letter to Count Henri Baillet*-Latour 8 January 1934; Kaarina Kari *Finnish Federation of Physical Education for Women Letter to Count Henri Baillet-Latour 8 June 1936* Women and Sport File IOC archives, Lausanne.
118. Laurence Prudhomme Poncet *Histoire du Football Feminine* p. 168.
119. Raymond Ruffin *La Diablesse: La Véritable Histoire de Violette Morris* (Paris: Pygmalion, 1989); Raymond Ruffin *Violette Morris: La Hyène de la Gestap* (Paris: Le Cherche Midi, 2004).
120. Obituaries 'Micheline Ostermeyer 1922–2001' *The Telegraph* http://www.telegraph.co.uk/news/obituaries/1360539/Micheline-Ostermeyer accessed 3 August 2012.
121. Kevin Wamsley 'Womanizing Olympic Athletes: Policy and Practice during the Avery Brundage Era' in Stephen R. Wenn, Gerald P. Schaus (eds.) *Onward to the Olympics: Historical Perspectives on the Olympic Games* (Ontario: Wilfred Laurier University Press and the Canadian Institute in Greece, 2007) pp. 273–282.
122. Art Gravure Picture Section 'American Girl Athletes' *The Cincinnati Enquirer* 20 August 1922 unpaginated Women and Sport File IOC archives, Lausanne.
123. Photogravure Section 'Olympic girls' *Chicago Tribune* 16 July 1922 pp. 6–7 Women and Sport File IOC archives, Lausanne.
124. Mark Dyreson 'Icons of Liberty or Objects of Desire? American Women Olympians and the Politics of Consumption' *Journal of Contemporary History* 38:3 2003 pp. 435–460.
125. Clothilde Rowell '"Our Ludy" Comes Home' *The Winthrop College News* (South Carolina: Winthrop: 1922) p. 4 Women and Sport File IOC archives, Lausanne.
126. Anon. 'Profile: Ludy Godbold' *Columbia College Staff Development Magazine* May 1976 p. 16 Women and Sport File IOC archives, Lausanne.
127. Nancy Struna 'The Recreational Experiences of Early American Women' in D. Margaret Costa and Sharon R Guthrie (eds.) *Women and Sport: Interdisciplinary Perspectives* (Champaign, Illinois: Human Kinetics, 1994) p. 57.
128. Women's Division N.A.A.F. *A Team for Every Girl and Every Girl On the Team: Will You Help Make Real This Ideal?* December 1927 (New York: Women's Division NAAF, 1927) Women and Sport File IOC archives, Lausanne.
129. Michael Oriard *King Football; Sport and Spectacle in the Golden Age of Radio and Newsreels, Movies and Magazines, The Weekly and Daily Press* (Chapel Hill and London: University of North Carolina Press, 2001).
130. Mary Van Horn *Women's Division, National Amateur Athletic Federation Newsletter 2 1 March 1929* (New York: Women's Division NAAF, 1 March 1929) pp. 1–2 Women and Sport File IOC archives, Lausanne.

131. Joan S. Hult 'The Story of Women's Athletics: Manipulating a Dream 1890–1985' in D. Margaret Costa and Sharon R Guthrie (eds.) *Women and Sport: Interdisciplinary Perspectives* (Champaign, Illinois: Human Kinetics, 1994) pp. 88–92.

132. Agnes Wayman *Vice Chair of NAAF Executive Committee Competition: A Statement by the Women's Division, National Amateur Athletic Federation 1 June 1929 (New York: Women's Division, NAAF, 1 June 1929)* Women and Sport File IOC archives, Lausanne.

133. Peter N. Lewis 'Joyce Wethered [married name Joyce Heathcoat-Amory, Lady Heathcoat-Amory] (1901–1997)' *Oxford Dictionary of National Biography* Oxford University Press http://www.oxforddnb.com/view/article/68365 accessed 15 January 2013.

134. M. S. Millar 'Charlotte Cecilia Pitcairn [Cecil] Leitch (1891–1977)' *Oxford Dictionary of National Biography* Oxford University Press http://www.oxforddnb.com/view/article/31347 accessed 15 January 2013.

135. Alan Bairner *Sport, Nationalism, and Globalization: European and North American Perspectives* (Albany: State University of New York Press, 2001).

136. Jeff Hill 'Rite of Spring: Cup Finals and Community in the North of England' in Jeff Hill and Jack Williams (eds.) *Sport and Identity in the North of England* 1996 p. 90 See also Nick Hayes and Jeff Hill *'Millions like Us'? British Culture during the Second World War* (Liverpool: Liverpool University Press 1999) p. 51.

137. Jeff Hill 'The Day was an Ugly One' in Paul Darby, Martin Johnes, Gavin Mellor (eds.) *Soccer and Disaster: International Perspectives* (London: Routledge, 2005) p. 34.

138. Kevin Jeffreys 'The Heyday of Amateurism in Modern Lawn Tennis' *International Journal of the History of Sport* 26: 15 2009 pp. 2241–2242.

139. Alan Little *Suzanne Lenglen* (London: Wimbledon Lawn Tennis Museum, 2007).

140. John Barrett and Alan Little *Wimbledon: Ladies' Singles Champions 1884–2004* (London: Wimbledon Lawn Tennis Museum, 2005).

141. Patricia Henry Yeomans 'Hazel Wightman and Helen Wills: Tennis At the 1924 Paris Olympic Games' *Journal of Olympic History* 11:2 2003 pp. 19–24.

142. Time Magazine Cover *Helen Newington Wills* 1 July 1929 http://www.time.com/time/covers/ accessed 20 August 2012.

143. Helen Wills *Self Portrait* (Los Angeles: Olympic Arts Competition and Exhibition, 1932) featured in Graham Budd (ed.) *Olympic Memorabilia* (London: Graham Budd Auctions and Sotheby's, 24–26 July 2012) p. 70.

144. Helen Wills *Tennis* (New York and London: Charles Scribner and Son, 1928); Helen Wills *Fifteen, Thirty: The Story of a Tennis Player* (New York and London: Charles Scribner and Son, 1938) and Helen Wills and Robert William Murphy *Death Serves an Ace* (New York: Charles Scribner and Son, 1939).

145. Charlie Lee Potter *Sportswear in Vogue since 1910* (New York: Abbeville Publishers, 1984 p. 21.

146. Anne Pimlott Baker 'Cuthbert Collingwood [Teddy] Tinling (1910–1990)' *Oxford Dictionary of National Biography* Oxford University Press http://www.oxforddnb.com/view/article/40669 accessed 15 January 2013.

147. The Daily Express *These Tremendous Years* p. 142.

148. Fred Perry *Fred Perry: An Autobiography* (London: Hutchinson, 1984); Jon Henderson *The Last Champion: A Life of Fred Perry* (London: Yellow Jersey, 2010).

149. Roy Mc Kelvie 'Table Tennis' in James Rivers (ed.) *The Sports Book* (London: Macdonald and Company, 1946) p. 280.

150. International Table Tennis Federation *World Championships Women's Singles 1927–2011* International Table Tennis Federation Museum www.ittf. com/museum/WorldChWSingles.pdf accessed 21 August 2012.

151. Mary Louise Adams 'From Mixed-Sex Sport To Sport for Girls: The Feminization of Figure Skating' in Carol Osborne and Fiona Skillen (eds.) *Women and Sport: Special Edition of Sport in History* 30:2 2010 pp. 218–241.

152. Mary H. Leigh 'The Enigma of Avery Brundage and Women Athletes' *Arena Review* 4:2 May 1980 pp. 11–21.

153. Howard Cox and Simon Mowatt 'Vogue in Britain: Authenticity and the Creation of Competitive Advantage in the UK Magazine Industry' *Business History* 54:1 2012 pp. 67–87.

154. Kevin Jeffreys 'The Heyday of Amateurism' p. 2243.

155. Stephen Gundle *Glamour: A History* (Oxford: Oxford University Press, 2008) p. 164.

156. Win Hayes, 'Lucy Morton (1898–1980)' *Oxford Dictionary of National Biography* Oxford University Press http://www.oxforddnb.com/view/article/92814 accessed 21 August 2012.

157. I am grateful to Gladys Carson's son, David Hewitt, for sharing his mother's scrapbook and collection of memorabilia with me including the undated CD of the local radio interview, Grimsby 10 July 2011.

158. Jean Williams 'Gladys Carson in Paris 1924: Half-Told Olympic Stories' *Sporting Biography 1993–2013: Approaches, Problems and Debates* International Centre for Sports History and Culture in conjunction with the Oxford Dictionary of National Biography De Montfort University Leicester 30 March 2012.

159. Lisa Bier *Fighting the Current: The Rise of American Women's Swimming 1870–1930* (Jefferson, North Carolina and London: McFarland & Company, 2011) p. 135.

160. Patricia Vertinsky and Christiane Job 'Celebrating Gertrudes: Women of Influence' in Annette R. Hofmann and Else Trangbaek (eds.) *International Perspectives on Sporting Women in Past and Present* (Denmark: Institute of Exercise and Social Sciences University of Copenhagen, 2005) p. 252.

161. The Daily Express *These Tremendous Years* p. 122.

162. Peter Lovesey 'Violet Piercy (b. 1889?)' *Oxford Dictionary of National Biography* Oxford University Press http://www.oxforddnb.com/view/article/103698 accessed 17 August 2012.

163. Cindy Himes Gissendanner 'African American Women and Competitive Sport' in Susan Birrell and Cheryl Cole (eds.) *Women Sport and Culture* (Champaign, Illinois: Human Kinetics, 1994) pp. 81–92.

164. Barbara Keys *Globalising Sport* p. 11.

165. Juliet Gardiner *The Thirties: An Intimate History* (London: Harper Press, 2010) p. 116.

166. Jill Julius Matthews 'Mary Meta Bagot Stack (1883–1935)' *Oxford Dictionary of National Biography* Oxford University Press http://www.oxforddnb. com/view/article/45797 accessed 5 September 2012.

NOTES TO CHAPTER 5

1. All England Women's Hockey Association (AEWHA) *Minutes of All England Women's Hockey Association 1927–29* p. 76. All England Women's Hockey Association file A/1/1, University of Bath. Hereafter, AEWHA Files, University of Bath.

2. Anon. 'Miss Edith Thompson: An English Visitor' *The Sydney Morning Herald* 5 July 1933 p. 3.

3. Marion Stell 'Marie Montgomerie Hamilton (1891–1955)' *Australian Dictionary of Biography* National Centre of Biography, Australian National University http://adb.anu.edu.au/biography/hamilton-marie-montgomerie-10404/text18437 accessed 2 September 2012.

4. Douglas Booth *The Field: Truth and Fiction in Sport History* (London: Routledge, 2005).

5. Mark Dyreson 'Sport History and the History of Sport in North America' *Journal of Sport History* 34:3 Fall 2007 pp. 405–414.

6. Jeffrey Hill *Sport In History: An Introduction* (Hampshire and New York: Palgrave Macmillan, 2011) pp. 22–23.

7. Barbara J. Keys *Globalizing Sport: National Rivalry and International Community in the 1930s* (Cambridge, Massachusetts and London: Harvard University Press, 2006) p. 12.

8. Richard Holt and Tony Mason *Sport in Britain 1945–2000* (Oxford: Blackwell, 2000) p. 170.

9. Marjorie Pollard *Fifty Years of Women's Hockey: The Story of the Foundation and Development of the All England Women's Hockey Association 1894–1945* (Letchworth, Hertfordshire: St Christopher Press, 1945) p. 33.

10. Edith Thompson *Hockey as a Game for Women* (London: E. Arnold, 1905).

11. Edith Thompson 'Hockey–The National Game for Women' *The Times* 14 January 1933 p. 15.

12. Marjorie Pollard *Fifty Years of Women's Hockey* p. 40.

13. Obituary 'Miss E. M. Thompson: Services to Many Good Causes' *The Times* 26 Aug 1961 p. 12; Margot, Lady Davison 'Miss Edith Thompson' *The Times* 1 September 1961 p. 12.

14. Martin Pugh 'Gladys Sydney Pott (1867–1961)' *Oxford Dictionary of National Biography* Oxford University Press http://www.oxforddnb.com/view/article/41259 accessed 19 January 2013.

15. Jean Williams 'Hilda Mary Light (1890–1969)' *Oxford Dictionary of National Biography* Oxford University Press http://www.oxforddnb.com/view/article/103422 accessed 31 August 2012.

16. Marjorie Pollard *Hilda M. Light: Her Life and Times* (London: All England Women's Hockey Association, 1972) p. 24.

17. All England Women's Hockey Association *All England Women's Hockey Association England v The Rest Programme 24 January 1931* p. 2. AEWHA file D/1/20, University of Bath.

18. Marjorie Pollard *Fifty Years of Women's Hockey* p. 45.

19. Marjorie Pollard *Cricket for Women and Girls* (London: Hutchinson, 1934) p. 19.

20. Marjorie Pollard *Australian Women's Cricket Team in England 1937: A Diary* (Letchworth: Pollard Publications, 1937).

21. Jean Williams 'Edith Marie Thompson (1877–1961)' *Oxford Dictionary of National Biography* Oxford University Press http://www.oxforddnb.com/view/article/103423 accessed 31 August 2012.

22. Fernanda Helen Perrone 'Constance Mary Katherine Applebee (1873–1981)' *Oxford Dictionary of National Biography* Oxford University Press http://www.oxforddnb.com/view/article/102441 accessed 11 July 2012.

23. The United States Field Hockey Association (USFHA) 'British Guiana Touring Team' *The Eagle* 3:1 September 1939 cover International Federation of Women's Hockey Associations (IFWHA) file B/1/ 1, University of Bath.

24. Mike Huggins and Jack Williams *Sport and the English, 1918–1939 Between the Wars* (Oxon: Routledge, 2006) pp. 63–64 has one paragraph on car racing and aviation.

25. Juliet Gardiner *The Thirties: An Intimate History* (London: Harper Collins, 2010) pp. 52–67.
26. Ambrose McEvoy *Sir John William Alcock* (London: National Portrait Gallery, 1919) NPG reference 1894 http://www.npg.org.uk/collections/search/person/mp00062/sir-john-william-alcock accessed 1 October 2012.
27. Robin Higham 'Christopher Birdwood, Baron Thomson (1875–1930)' *Oxford Dictionary of National Biography* Oxford University Press http://www.oxforddnb.com/view/article/36500 accessed 28 September 2012.
28. Mark Pottle 'Mildred Mary Bruce (1895–1990)' *Oxford Dictionary of National Biography* Oxford University Press http://www.oxforddnb.com/view/article/63962 accessed 19 January 2013.
29. The Hon. Mrs Victor Bruce *Nine Lives Plus, Record Breaking on Land Sea And In the Air: An Autobiographical Account* (London: Pelham Books, 1974) pp. 20–23
30. The Hon. Mrs Victor Bruce *Nine Lives Plus* pp. 42–47.
31. Brian Laban *Motor Racing: The Early Years* (Königswinter, Germany: Tandem Verlag, 2001) pp. 16–23.
32. Martin Pugh *'Hurrah for the Blackshirts!: Fascists and Fascism Between the Wars* (London: Jonathan Cape, 2005) p. 142.
33. Robert Skidelsky 'Sir Oswald Ernald Mosley (1896–1980)' *Oxford Dictionary of National Biography* Oxford University Press http://www.oxforddnb.com/view/article/31477 accessed 28 September 2012.
34. Brian Belton *Fay Taylour: Queen of Speedway* (High Wycombe, Buckinghamshire: Panther Publishing, 2006) p. 5.
35. William Boddy *The History of Brooklands Motor Course: Complied from the Official Records of the Brooklands Automobile Racing Club* (London: Grenville Publishing, 1957) p. 238.
36. William Boddy 'Fay Taylour' *Brooklands Society Gazette* April 1983 p. 37.
37. Brian Belton *Fay Taylour* pp. 30–31.
38. Bruce Jones *Grand Prix Yesterday and Today: 100 Years of Motor Racing* (Singapore: Carlton Books, 2006) p. 96.
39. The Daily Express *These Tremendous Years 1919–1938: A History In Photographs of Life And Events, Big And Little, In Britain and the World since the War* (London: Daily Express Publications, 1938) p. 139.
40. Mike Cronin 'Arthur Elvin and the Dogs of Wembley' *Sports Historian* 22:1 2002 pp. 100–114.
41. The Royal Society of Arts http://www.thersa.org/ accessed 7 September 2012.
42. Royal Society of Arts *Annual Competition of Industrial Design: Scheme for the Improvement of Industrial Designs and the Particulars of Each Annual Competition from 1924 to 1933* file reference: RSA/PR/DE/100/13/16 Royal Society of Arts archive, London.
43. Fred Taylor *The Empire Shop* (London: Empire Marketing Board, c.1926–1939) reference CO 956/426 National Archives, London http://www.nationalarchives.gov.uk/education/empire accessed 7 July 2012.
44. Leo Villa *Life with the Speed King: World Record Breaking with Malcolm Campbell* (London: Marshall Harris & Baldwin, 1979).
45. Peter Swinger *Motor Racing Circuits in England: Then and Now* (Surrey: Dial House, 2001) pp. 34–40.
46. MacDonald Gill *Highways of Empire: Buy Empire Goods from Home and Overseas* (London: Empire Marketing Board, c. 1927) reference CO 956/537A National Archives, London http://www.nationalarchives.gov.uk/education/empire/g2/cs1/g2cs1s3.htm accessed 7 September 2012.
47. Bassano *Doreen Evans* (London: Bassano & Vandyk Studios, 1935) National Portrait Galley photographs collection NPG x34498; Bassano *Doreen Evans*

(and dog) (London: Bassano & Vandyk Studios, 1935) National Portrait Galley photographs collection NPG x34499 and Bassano *Doreen Evans* (London: Bassano & Vandyk Studios, 1935) National Portrait Galley photographs collection NPG x34500 http://www.npg.org.uk/collections/search/portrait/mw69298/Doreen-Evans accessed 11 October 2012.

48. Anon. 'The Scottish Rally: Yet Another Success, Riley, Singer and Ford Divide Principal Honours' *The Motor World and Industrial Vehicle Review (Incorporating the Motor Cyclist and the Scottish Cyclist)* 30: 1531 1 June 1934 pp. 321–327. I am grateful to Tony Beadle for this reference.
49. Anon. 'The Scottish Rally: Yet Another Success' pp. 328–331.
50. Anon. 'The Scottish Rally: Yet another success' pp. 332.
51. William Boddy *Montléry: The Story of the Paris Autodrome 1924–1960* (London: Cassell, 1961).
52. Karl Ludvigsen *Classic Grand Prix Cars: The Front Engined Formula 1 Era 1906–1960* (Stroud, Gloucestershire, 2000) pp. 8–9.
53. Kay Petre 'My Motor Racing' in The Publication Committee *The British Racing Drivers' Club Silver Jubilee Book* (London: The British Racing Drivers' Club, 1952) p. 139.
54. The Hon. Mrs Victor Bruce *Nine Lives Plus* p. 150.
55. A. G. Spalding and Brothers 'We've Gone Almost Completely English' *International Federation of Women's Hockey Associations (IFWHA) Hockey Programme 10 October 1936* (Philadephia & New York: A. G Spalding and Brothers, 1936) p. 4 IFWHA file B/1/1, University of Bath.
56. All England Women's Hockey Association *Minutes of All England Women's Hockey Association 1927–29: Education Sub-Committee* p. 74 AEWHA file A/1/1, University of Bath.
57. All England Women's Hockey Association *Garnet Valentine Spooner 1911–1930* AEWHA file D/1/11, University of Bath.
58. Nancy Tomkins and Pat Ward *The Century Makers: A History of the All England Women's Hockey Association 1895–1995* (Shrewsbury: All England Women's Hockey Assocation, 1995) p. 113.
59. Nancy Tomkins and Pat Ward *The Century Makers* p. 104.
60. Judith Wilson 'Marjorie Anne Pollard (1899–1982)' *Oxford Dictionary of National Biography* Oxford University Press http://www.oxforddnb.com/view/article/65061 accessed 31 August 2012.
61. All England Women's Lacrosse Association *All England Women's Lacrosse Association 1912–1993* files NA1312 The Women's Library, London Metropolitan University.
62. Joan L. Hawes *Women's Test Cricket: The Golden Triangle 1934–1984* (London: The Book Guild, 1987).
63. Jean Williams, 'Hilda Mary Light (1890–1969)'.
64. Christina M. Dony *9 Station Road Luton Bedfordshire*, signed undated letter in first scrapbook AEWHA file D/1/20, University of Bath.
65. Marjorie Pollard *Fifty Years of Women's Hockey* p. 19.
66. Hilda Light 'Women's Hockey' *Manchester Guardian* 12 Oct 1938 p. 23.
67. Rebecca Arnold *The American Look: Sportswear, Fashion and the Image of Women In 1930s and 1940s New York* (London and New York: I. B.Tauris, 2009).
68. Florence A. Somers *Principles of Women's Athletics* (New York: A. S. Barnes and Company, 1930) pp. 56–57.
69. Lynn E Couturier 'Considering The Sportswoman, 1924 to 1936: A Content Analysis' *Sport History Review* 41 2010 pp. 111–131.
70. Major A. U. Udal *Introductory Hints To Help Those Who Have Never Yet 'Crossed the Line' Aboard Ship* unpublished letter Battersea and Chelsea

Polytechnic Athletic Ground, Prince's Road Merton Abbey SW 19 17 June-22 August 1932 AEWHA file D/1/ 14, University of Bath.

71. All England Women's Hockey Association *All England Women's Hockey Association England v The Rest* Programme 24 January 1931 p. 3 AEWHA file D/1/20, University of Bath.

72. All England Women's Hockey Association *Minutes of All England Women's Hockey Association 1912–1920* p. 19 AEWHA file A/1/1, University of Bath.

73. Joyce Whitehead *Tour Diaries/ scrapbook 1925–1936* AEWHA file D/1/16–19 University of Bath.

74. International Federation of Women's Hockey Associations *Minutes of International Federation of Women's Hockey Associations (IFWHA) 12 July 1930* pp. 4–5 IFWHA file B/1/ 1, University of Bath.

75. All England Women's Hockey Association *Women's Hockey Association of Australia Tour of England Programme 18th October 1930* p. 3 AEWHA file D/1/20, University of Bath.

76. David Mitchell *Women on the Warpath* (London: Jonathan Cape, 1966) p. 35.

77. Eric Beeston 'Winsome Winnie' *LifeTimesLink: Sharing Salford's Fantastic Story* 26 (Salford: Salford Museums and Art Gallery, 2009) p. 4.

78. All England Women's Hockey Association *Magdeburg versus Northants Programme 3 January 1931* pp. 2–3 AEWHA file D/1/20, University of Bath.

79. All England Women's Hockey Association *Minutes of All England Women's Hockey Association 1927–29* p. 76 AEWHA file A/1/1, University of Bath.

80. International Federation of Women's Hockey Associations *Minutes of International Federation of Women's Hockey Associations (IFWHA) 25 July 1933* pp. 2–3 IFWHA file B/1/1, University of Bath.

81. Patricia Campbell *When the Girls Came Out to Play* (Amerhurst and Boston: University of Massachusetts Press, 2006) p. 90.

82. Marjorie Pollard *Fifty Years of Women's Hockey* p. 30.

83. Juliet Gardiner *The Thirties* pp. 615–616.

84. Joyce Whitehead *Tour Diaries/ scrapbook 1925–1936* AEWHA file D/1/16–19, University of Bath.

85. Undated, anonymous programme notes Joyce Whitehead *Tour Diaries/ scrapbook 1925–1936* AEWHA file Section D/1/16–19, University of Bath.

86. D. M. C. Prichard *The History of Croquet* (London: Cassell, 1981) pp. 92–94.

87. Mark Pottle 'Dorothy Dyne Steel (1884–1965)' *Oxford Dictionary of National Biography* Oxford University Press http://www.oxforddnb.com/view/article/63683 accessed 4 September 2012.

88. D. M. C. Prichard *The History of Croquet* p. 204.

89. V. Cox 'Going to Australia?' *Women's Cricket* 5:1 1934 (Welwyn, Hertfordshire: J. H. Lawrence and Sons, 1934) p. 6.

90. Dorothy Snell 'Australian Tour Accounts' *Women's Cricket Association Annual Report 1937* p. 3 (Maidstone: Women's Cricket Association, 1937) pp. 27–30.

91. All England Women's Hockey Association *AEWHA Balance Sheet and Accounts Year Ended 13 April 1946* AEWHA file D/1/26, University of Bath.

92. The Daily Mirror *These Tremendous Years* p. 114.

93. Eileen F. Lebow *Before Amelia: Women Pilots In the Early Days of Aviation* (Virginia: Brassey's Incorporated, 2002) p. 24.

94. Mary S. Lovell *Amelia Aerhart: The Sound of Wings* (London: Hutchinson, 1989) p. 55.

95. Judy Lomax *Women of the Air* (London: John Murray, 1986) p. 35.
96. Juliet Gardiner *The Thirties* p. 694.
97. Constance Babington Smith *Amy Johnson* (Bury St Edmunds: St Edmundsbury Press, 1967) p. 10.
98. Charles Dixon *Amy Johnson: Lone Girl Flyer* (London: Sampson, Low, Marston and Company Ltd, c1930) p. 22.
99. Robin Higham 'Amy Johnson (1903–1941)' *Oxford Dictionary of National Biography* Oxford University Press http://www.oxforddnb.com/view/article/34200 accessed 5 September 2012.
100. Oliver Stewart and M. C Curthoys, 'James Allan Mollison (1905–1959)' *Oxford Dictionary of National Biography* Oxford University Press http://www.oxforddnb.com/view/article/35055 accessed 5 September 2012.
101. Squadron Leader Beryl E. Escott *Women in Air Force Blue: The Story of Women In The Royal Air Force from 1918 To the Present Day* (Northants: Patrick Stephens, 1989) p. 104.
102. Midge Gilles *Amy Johnson: Queen of the Air* (London: Butler and Tanner Ltd, 2003) p. 210.
103. David Luff *Amy Johnson: Enigma of the Sky* (Shrewsbury: Air Life Publishing, 2002).
104. Anon. 'Aeronautics: Two Women' *Time Magazine* 26 March 1928 http://www.time.com/time/magazine/article/0,9171,787033,00.html accessed 21 August 2012.
105. Jayne Baldwin *West Over the Waves: The Final Flight of Elsie Mackay* (Dumfries & Galloway: Wigtown Publishers, 2008).
106. Janet Aitken Kidd *The Beaverbrook Girl* (London: Collins, 1987) pp. 130–131.
107. William Courtenay 'Speed on the Empire Flying Boats' *Speed: Land, Sea, Air* July 1937 p. 1462 Women Drivers file Brooklands archive, Weybridge.
108. Beryl Markham *West with the Night: The Classic of African Exploration* (London: Virago second edition 1984; originally published 1942).
109. Scott A. G. M. Crawford 'Sir Malcolm Campbell (1885–1948)' *Oxford Dictionary of National Biography* Oxford University Press http://www.oxforddnb.com/view/article/32271 accessed 5 September 2012.
110. Sir Malcolm Campbell *Speed On Wheels* (London: Sampson Low, Marston and Company Ltd, 1949).
111. G. E. T. Eyston *Flat Out* (Spalding, Lincolnshire: Vincent Publishing Company, second edition 1973; originally published 1933).
112. Lady Dorothy Campbell *Malcolm Campbell: The Man As I Knew Him* (London: Hutchinson & Co. Ltd, 1951).
113. Juliet Gardiner *The Thirties* p. 690–691.
114. G. E. T. Eyston *Safety Last* (Spalding, Lincolnshire: Vincent Publishing Company, 1975) p. 93.
115. William Boddy '"Les Girls" at Le Mans' *Motor Sport* November 1988 pp. 1174–1175 Women Drivers file, Brooklands archive.
116. Anon. 'The British Women's Motor-Racing Team' *The Daily Telegraph* 12 April 1935 unpaginated Women Drivers file, Brooklands archive.
117. Brooklands Museum and Archive 'Violet Cordery' *Alpahbetical Card Index of Races at Brooklands* Brooklands archive.
118. Gregor Grant 'Eric-Campbell' *British Sports Cars* (London: G. T. Foulis and Co. Ltd, 1947) p. 72.
119. Gregor Grant 'Silver Hawk' *British Sports Cars* (London: G. T. Foulis and Co. Ltd, 1947) pp. 144–145.
120. William Boddy *The History of Brooklands Motor Course: Compiled from the Official Records of the Brooklands Automobile Racing Club* (London: Grenville Publishing, 1957) p. 575.

121. Roger Munting '(Charles Ernest) Leonard Lyle, First Baron Lyle of West-bourne (1882–1954)'*Oxford Dictionary of National Biography* Oxford University Press http://www.oxforddnb.com/view/article/34644 accessed 17 October 2012.

122. Brooklands Museum and Archive 'Violet Cordery' *Alpahbetical Card Index of Races at Brooklands* Brooklands archive.

123. Ronald B. Weir 'Thomas Robert Dewar, Baron Dewar (1864–1930)' *Oxford Dictionary of National Biography* Oxford University Press http://www.oxforddnb.com/view/article/50411 accessed 21 January 2013.

124. William 'Bill' Boddy *Montlhéry* p. 27.

125. Royal Automobile Club '1926 Past Dewar Trophy Winner: Violet Cordery' http://www.royalautomobileclub.co.uk/Motoring/dewar-trophy accessed 14 October 2012.

126. British Pathé *Woman Drivers' Daring Trip. Miss Violet Cordery* British Pathé 1927 film number: 668.35 http://www.britishpathe.com/video/woman-drivers-daring-trip accessed 14 October 2012.

127. British Pathé *Miss Violet Cordery, travels through India* British Pathé 1927 film number: 755635 http://www.britishpathe.com/video/woman-drivers-daring-trip accessed 14 October 2012.

128. Royal Automobile Club 'Dewar Trophy Winners: Violet Cordery 1929' http://www.royalautomobileclub.co.uk/Motoring/dewar-trophy accessed 14 October 2012.

129. Brooklands Museum and Archive 'Violet Cordery' *Alpahbetical Card Index of Races at Brooklands* Brooklands archive.

130. Anon. 'Racing Motorist Miss Cordery Engaged' *The West Australian* Monday 7 September 1931 p. 9 Women Drivers file, Brooklands archive.

131. Jean and Simon Williams 'Violet Cordery (1903–1983) and John Hind-marsh (1907–1938)' *Oxford Dictionary of National Biography* May 2013 forthcoming.

132. R. J. Overy 'William Richard Morris, Viscount Nuffield (1877–1963)' *Oxford Dictionary of National Biography* Oxford University Press http://www.oxforddnb.com/view/article/35119 accessed 22 August 2012.

133. Andrea Green 'Woman in a Wolseley' *Brooklands Society Gazette* 18:4 1993 p. 9., Women Drivers file, Brooklands archive.

134. Ruth Urquhart Dykes 'The 12-Hours Record at Brooklands' *Brooklands Society Gazette* 18:4 1993 pp. 3–7 Women Drivers file, Brooklands archive.

135. Mark Curthoys 'Ruth and Bill Urquhart Dykes: personal communication' Oxford Dictionary of National Biography Research Editor 15 October 2012.

136. William Boddy *The History of Brooklands Motor Course* p. 241.

137. 'Sorting Out the Sunbeams' *Motor Sport: Incorporating Speed and the Brooklands Gazette* 49:2 (London: Teesdale, February 1973) p. 132 Women Drivers file, Brooklands archive.

138. Anon. 'Motor Racing Mishap: Man Killed, Miss Cunliffe Injured' *The Argus* Melbourne 25 June 1928 p. 17 http://trove.nla.gov.au/ndp/del/article/3935678 accessed 22 August 2012.

139. The Hon. Mrs Victor Bruce *Nine Thousand Miles in Eight Weeks: Being an Account of an Epic Journey by Motor-Car through Eleven Countries and Two Continents* (London: Heath Cranston Limited, 1927).

140. The Hon. Mrs Victor Bruce *The Woman Owner-Driver: A Collection of Fourteen Essays On Motoring for Women* (Dorset House, London: Iliffe and Sons, 1928); 'Where Evening Joins the Dawn' in Shirley Grey (ed.) *The Oxford Annual for Girls, Tenth Year* (London: Humphrey Milford and Oxford University Press, 1928) pp. 9–18; *The Peregrinations of Penelope* (with 40 drawings by Joyce Dennys) (London: Heath Cranston Limited, 1930); *The Bluebird's Flight* (London: Chapman & Hall, Ltd., 1931).

338 *Notes*

141. William 'Bill' Boddy *Montlhéry* p. 25.
142. The Hon. Mrs Victor Bruce *Nine Lives Plus* p. 92.
143. Michael Fahie 'Dorothy Norman Spicer (1908–1946)' *Oxford Dictionary of National Biography* Oxford University Press http://www.oxforddnb.com/view/article/67672 accessed 21 January 2013.
144. The Hon. Mrs Victor Bruce *Nine Lives Plus* p. 169.
145. M. L. T. 'Lady Competition Drivers' *Motor Sport incorporating Speed and the Brooklands Gazette* Teesdale: London 37:7 July 1961 p. 558 Women Drivers file, Brooklands archive.
146. Professor Edward E. Schweizer 'Letter to John Granger concerning Sheila Scott' 19 January 2000 Jill Scott file, Brooklands archive.
147. Professor Edward E. Schweizer 'Notes on Eileen 'Jill' May or Mary Fountain born 21 May 1902' Brooklands Archive, Jill Scott file, Brooklands archive.
148. Peter Roddis 'Letter to John Granger concerning Sheila Scott' undated Jill Scott file, Brooklands archive.
149. Jean Williams 'Gwenda Mary Hawkes (1894–1990)' *Oxford Dictionary of National Biography* Oxford University Press http://www.oxforddnb.com/view/article/92722 accessed 30 May 2013..
150. William 'Bill' Boddy *Montlhery* p. 64.
151. Anon 'Douglas-Pennant Inquiry' *The Daily Mirror* 1 November 1919 p. 6.
152. Elsie Wisdom 'Tete a Tete: What Do Women Motorists Think of the 1934 Models?' *The Autocar* 6 October 1933 Elsie 'Bill' Wisdom file, Brooklands Archive.
153. Dennis May '130 mph Plus' *The Motor* 9 November 1960 pp. 598–600 Gwenda Glubb/ Jansen/ Stewart/ Hawkes file, Brooklands archive.
154. Dennis May '1938: Mrs Hawkes looks back' *Speed* July 1938 pp. 2110–2112 Gwenda Glubb/ Jansen/ Stewart/ Hawkes file, Brooklands archive.
155. J. D. Alderson 'Gwenda Hawkes' *Brooklands Society Gazette* 1:4. 1976 p. 8 Gwenda Glubb/ Jansen/ Stewart/ Hawkes Drivers file, Brooklands archive.
156. S. C. H. Davis 'Gwenda Hawkes' *Atalanta: Women as Racing Drivers* (London: Foulis, 1957) pp. 98–99.
157. Jean Williams 'Elsie Mary Wisdom (1904–1972)' *Oxford Dictionary of National Biography* Oxford University Press http://www.oxforddnb.com/view/article/104422 accessed 30 May 2013..
158. Elsie Wisdom 'Woman on the Track: Mrs Wisdom talks to Sam Sloan' *The Auto Motor Journal* 3 March 1931 p. 33 Elsie 'Bill' Wisdom file, Brooklands archive.
159. Elsie Wisdom 'Tête à Tête: A Well-Known Woman Motorist Gives a Woman's View of the 1934 Models' *The Autocar* 6 October 1934 pp. 622–623 Elsie 'Bill' Wisdom file, Brooklands archive.
160. Elsie Wisdom 'Woman on the Track' p. 33.
161. William Boddy *The History of Brooklands Motor Course* p. 236.
162. David Price 'Joan Margaret Richmond' *Competition Special* http://www.joanrichmond.com/ accessed 2 October 2012.
163. John Reaburn 'Joan Margaret Richmond 1905–1999' Women Drivers file, Brooklands archive.
164. S. C. H. Davis 'Elsie Wisdom' *Atalanta: Women as Racing Drivers* (London: Foulis, 1957) pp. 109–110.
165. S. C. H. Davis 'Elsie Wisdom' *Atalanta* pp. 115–116.
166. Sammy Davis '"Bill" Wisdom: A Tribute' *The Motor* 20 April 1972 p. 2 Elsie 'Bill' Wisdom file, Brooklands archive.
167. Anon. 'Like Mother, Like Daughter' *Motor* 30 June 1936 p. 26 Elsie 'Bill' Wisdom file, Brooklands archive.
168. Joyce Kay 'Patricia Ann Moss (1934–2008)' *Oxford Dictionary of National Biography* Oxford University Press http://www.oxforddnb.com/view/article/100590 accessed 20 June 2012.

169. William Boddy *The History of Brooklands Motor Course* p. 217.
170. Kay Petre 'My Motor Racing' in The British Racing Drivers' Club (eds.) *Silver Jubilee Book* (London: The British Racing Drivers' Club, 1952) p. 139.
171. S. C. H. Davis 'Kay Petre' *Atalanta: Women as Racing Drivers* (London: Foulis, 1957) pp. 45–77. John Bullock *Fast Women* p. 137 tells much the same story.
172. Dennis May '130 mph Plus' *The Motor* 9 November 1960 pp. 599–600.
173. Malcolm Campbell Chair 'New members: Kay Petre' 26 July 1934 *BRDC Committee Minutes July 1931–Dec 1934* BRDC file, Brooklands archive.
174. Key Petre 'My Motor Racing' in *Silver Jubilee Book* p. 143.
175. Elly Beinhorn Rosemeyer and Chris Nixon *Rosemeyer! A New Biography* (Isleworth Middlesex: Transport Bookman Publications, 1986) p. 110–111.
176. HRH Prince Chula Chakrabonse of Thailand *Dick Seaman* (London and Edinburgh: Morisson and Gibbs Ltd, 1941) p. 130.
177. Graham Gauld *Reg Parnell: The Quiet Man Who Helped to Engineer Britain's Post-War Racing Revolution* (Yeovil, Somerset: Patrick Stephen Ltd, 1996) p. 26.
178. Rupert Prior (ed.) *Motoring the Golden Years: A Pictorial Anthology* (London: Tiger Books, 1994) p. 40 shows the photograph.
179. Elly Beinhorn Rosemeyer 'Memoir' in Chris Nixon *Racing the Silver Arrows: Mercedes Benz versus Auto Union 1934–1939* (London: Osprey Publishing Limited, 1986) p. 117
180. Alfread Neubauer *Speed Was My Life* (London: Barrif and Rockliff, 1960) p. 105.
181. Graham Gauld *Reg Parnell* p. 33.
182. Michael D. Kandiah 'Frederick James, First Earl of Woolton (1883–1964)' *Oxford Dictionary of National Biography* Oxford University Press http://www.oxforddnb.com/view/article/34885 accessed 21 January 2013.
183. Anon. 'Kay Petre' *The Bulletin of the Vintage Sports Car Club* 220 Autumn 1998 p. 2 Kay Petre file, Brooklands archive.
184. Neil Eason-Gibson 'Kay Petre' *The Bulletin of the Vintage Sports Car Club* 220 Autumn 1998 Cover photograph Kay Petre file, Brooklands archive.
185. William Boddy 'Kay Petre notes' Kay Petre file, Brooklands archive.
186. Kay Petre 'A Note From Mrs Petre' *The Radiator* November 1939 p. 3 Kay Petre file, Brooklands archive.
187. Constance Maynard *Green Book Diaries 1866–1935* and *Autobiography 1849–1927* http://www.library.qmul.ac.uk/archives/digital/constance_maynard accessed 2 September 2012.
188. F. I. Bryan *Tour Diary to Australia 28 May-23 July 1927* AEWHA file D/1/ 28 University of Bath.
189. Margaret Peggy Lodge *Tour Diaries 1929–1950* AEWHA file D/1/29–36, University of Bath.
190. Audrey Cattrell *Tour Diaries 1930–1936* AEWHA file D/1/ 38, University of Bath.
191. Phyllis Carlbach *Scrapbooks 1935 and 1936* AEWHA file D/1/ 40–41, University of Bath.
192. Barbara West *Scrapbooks 1935–56* AEWHA file D/1/ 42, University of Bath.
193. Mary Russell Vick (née de Putron) *Scrapbooks and Tour Diaries 1946–1953* AEWHA file D/1/ 44–46, University of Bath.
194. International Federation of Women's Hockey Associations *Executive Council 1950 Annotated Photograph* IFWHA file D/1/15, University of Bath.
195. Hilda Light 'The Development of Women's Hockey' in Patrick Rowley (ed.) *The Book of Hockey* (London: Macdonald, 1964) p. 114.

196. Barbara Cartland *The Isthmus Years: An Autobiographical Study Of the Years between the Two World Wars* (London: Hutchinson, 1942) p. 101–102.
197. Anon. 'Barbara Cartland notes' Barbara Cartland file, Brooklands archive.
198. British Racing Driver's Club *BRDC Committee Minutes April 1928- June 1931* and *BRDC Committee Minutes July 1931—Dec 1934* Silverstone Library and Archive, Northamtonshire.
199. S.C.H. Davis *Atalanta* p. 168.
200. Jean Batten *My Life* (London: George G. Harrap and Company Ltd, 1938) p. 15.
201. Jean Batten *Solo Flight* (Sydney: Jackson and O'Sullivan: 1934).
202. Ian Mackersey *Jean Batten the Garbo of the Skies* (London: Macdonald, 1990).
203. Count Giovanni Lurani (translated John Eason-Gibson) *Racing Round the World 1920–1935* (London: G. T. Foulis & Co. Ltd, 1936).
204. Simon Martin *Sport Italia: The Italian Love Affair with Sport* (London: I. B Tauris, 2011) pp. 88–89.
205. Rupert Prior (ed.) *Motoring* p. 54.
206. George C. Monkhouse *Mercedes-Benz Grand Prix Racing 1934–1955* (London: White Mouse Publishing, 1984); Erik Jensen *Body By Weimar: Athletes Gender and German Modernity* (New York: Oxford University Press, 2010) p. 119.
207. Elly Beinhorn Rosemeyer *Rosemeyer!* p. 70–78.
208. Barré Lyndon *Combat: A Motor Racing History* (London: Heinemann Ltd, 1933) p. 124.
209. The Daily Express *These Tremendous Years* p. 139.
210. Daily Express *These Tremendous Years 1919–1938* p. 139.
211. Joyce Kay 'Marjorie Elaine Foster (1893–1974)' *Oxford Dictionary of National Biography* Oxford University Press http://www.oxforddnb.com/view/article/65174 accessed 30 August 2012.
212. Richard Bowen 'Koizumi, Gunji (1885–1965)' *Oxford Dictionary of National Biography* Oxford University Press http://www.oxforddnb.com/view/article/75932 accessed 4 September 2012.
213. Sarah Mayer *Letters to G. Koizumi February 1934-January 1935* Richard Bowen files C.64, University of Bath
214. Jonathan Bradbury 'Dame Enid Mary Russell-Smith (1903–1989)' *Oxford Dictionary of National Biography* Oxford University Press http://www.oxforddnb.com/view/article/65870 accessed 4 September 2012.
215. Mark Bence Jones *Twilight of the Ascendancy* (London: Constable, 1987) p. 145.
216. Gillian Newsum *Women and Horses* (London: The Sportsman's Press, 1988) pp. 50–1.
217. Susanna Forrest 'Women, The Horse and World War One' http://susannaforrest.wordpress.com/2012/03/31 accessed 28 August 2012.
218. Betty and Nancy Debenham 'Diana Awheel: Motor Cycling Hints and Tips' *Brooklands Society Gazette* 18:4 1993 pp. 12–13 Women Drivers file, Brooklands archive.
219. Wolf Motorcycles *Wolf Motorcycle Postcard circa 1932* The Robert Opie Collection Museum of Advertising and Packaging Gloucester.
220. Lines Brother's Limited 'The Largest Exhibit in the Fair' *British Industries Fair Pamphlet February 1931* p. 4 Lines Brothers Limited file, V & A Museum of Childhood.
221. Lines Brother's Limited 'Record Breaking: Lines Bros' motors Move Rapidly' *Games and Toys September 1931* p. 42 Lines Brothers Limited file, V & A Museum of Childhood.

222. J. Tunis 'Changing Trends in Sport' *Harper's Monthly Magazine* 170 December 1934 to May 1935 p.86.
223. Anon. *The Sportswoman*, April 1936 7:8 back cover Women Drivers file, Brooklands archive.
224. Luo Lv and Zhang Huigang *Sneakers* (London: Southbank, 2007) pp. 12–13.
225. Charlie Lee-Potter *Sportswear in Vogue since 1910* (London: Condé Nast Publications, 1984) p. 35.
226. A.W. Gamage Ltd *Gamages Xmas Bazaar 1924: From Wembley to Gamages* (London: Gamages, 1924 pp. 56 Gamages Limited file, V & A Museum of Childhood.
227. H. and H. Motor Car Auctions 'Lot Number 68: 1933 Lagonda 2 Litre Tourer' *H. and H .Motor Car Auctions Sale Catalogue* 20 July 2011 http://www. classic-auctions.com/Auctions/20–07–2011 accessed 14 October 2012.

NOTES TO CHAPTER 6

1. Bevil Rudd 'Athletics' in James Rivers (ed.) *The Sports Book* (London: Macdonald and Company, 1946) pp. 18–19.
2. Roger T. Stearn 'Charles Dunell Rudd (1844–1916)' *Oxford Dictionary of National Biography* Oxford University Press http://www.oxforddnb.com/view/article/65577 accessed 22 October 2012.
3. M. A. Bryant 'Albert George Hill (1889–1969)' *Oxford Dictionary of National Biography* Oxford University Press http://www.oxforddnb.com/view/article/65170 accessed 22 October 2012.
4. James Huntington-Whiteley and Richard Holt *The Book of British Sporting Heroes* (London: National Portrait Galley Publications, 1998) p. 128.
5. Ian Buchanan *British Olympians: A Hundred Years of Gold Medalists* (Enfield, Middlesex: Guinness Publishing, 1992) p. 92.
6. Mel Watman *The Official History of the AAA 1880–2010: The Story of the World's Oldest Athletic Association* (Cheltenham: Sports Books Limited, 2011) p. 30.
7. Cecil Bear 'Happy and Glorious' *World Sports: The International Sports Magazine* 19:5 May 1953 (London: Country and Sporting Publications, 1953) p. 5.
8. David Maraniss *Rome 1960: The Olympics that Changed the World* (New York, London, Toronto and Sydney: Simon & Schuster, 2008) p. xiii.
9. Organising Committee for the XIV Olympiad *The Official Report of the Organising Committee for the XIV Olympiad* Part One and Part Two (London: Organising Committee for the XIV Olympiad, 1948); Janie Hampton *London Olympics, 1908 and 1948* (London: Shire, 2011); Janie Hampton *The Austerity Olympics: When the Games Came to London in 1948* (London: Aurum Press, 2012); Bob Phillips *The 1948 Olympics: How London Rescued the Games* (London: Sports Pages, 2007); Martin Polley *The British Olympics: Britain's Olympic Heritage 1612–2012* (London: English Heritage, 2011); Martin Polley *Britain, Britons and the Olympic Games: Sport in History Special Edition* 32:2 June 2012.
10. Tim O' Sullivan 'Television and The Austerity Games: London 1948' in Jeffrey Hill, Kevin Moore and Jason Wood (eds.) *Sport, History and Heritage: Studies in Public Representation* (Woodbridge, Suffolk and Rochester New York: Boydell and Brewer Ltd, 2012) pp. 79–80.
11. David Kynaston *Austerity Britain 1945–1951* (London: Bloomsbury, 2007) pp. 292–293.

12. Janie Hampton *The Austerity Olympics* p. 84.
13. Robert Edelman *Serious Fun: A History of Spectator Sport in the USSR* (New York: Oxford University Press, 1993) p. 25.
14. John Hughson 'An Invitation to "Modern" Melbourne: The Historical Significance of Richard Beck's Olympic Poster Design' *Journal of Design History* 25:3 2012 pp. 268–285.
15. Arnd Krüger 'What's the Difference Between Propaganda for Tourism or for A Political Regime?: Was the 1936 Olympics the First Postmodern Spectacle?' in John Bale and Mette Krogh Christensen *Post-Olympism? Questioning Sport in the Twenty-First Century* (Oxford and New York: Berg, 2004) pp. 33–49.
16. Peter J. Beck 'Britain and the Olympic Games: London 1908, 1948, 2012' *Journal of Sport and History* 39:1 2012 p. 37.
17. Lorna Chessum *From Immigrants to Ethnic Minority: Making Black Community in Britain* (Aldershot: Ashgate, 2000).
18. C. L. R. James *Beyond a Boundary* (London: Stanley Paul, 1963); Anna Grimshaw (ed.) *The C. L. R. James Reader* (Oxford: Blackwell, 1992).
19. Obituary 'Dr Arthur Wint' *Olympic Review* 303 January to February 1993 p. 12.
20. Roy Plomley and Arthur Wint *Desert Island Discs: Olympian Arthur Wint* BBC Radio 4 Friday 22 May 1953 http://www.bbc.co.uk/radio4/features/desert-island-discs/castaway/e344f893 accessed 10 November 2012.
21. Jenifer Parks 'Verbal Gymnastics: Sports, Bureaucracy, and The Soviet Unions' Entrance Into the Olympic Games 1946–1952' in Stephen Wagg and David L. Andrews (eds.) *East Plays West: Sport and the Cold War* (London and New York: Routledge, 2007) pp. 27–44.
22. Jack Crump 'The Real Result of the London Olympic Games' *Bulletin Du Comité International Olympique* 19 January 1950 pp. 18–19.
23. Janie Hampton *The Austerity Olympics* p. 144.
24. Ian Buchanan *British Olympians* p. 139.
25. Robert K. Barney 'The Genesis of Sacred Fire in Olympic Ceremony: A New Interpretation' in Hai Ren, Lamartine Da Costa, Ana Miragaya and Niu Jing (eds.) *Olympic Studies Reader 1* (Beijing, China and Rio De Janeiro, Brazil: Beijing Sport University and Universidade Gama Filho, 2009) pp. 249–278.
26. Anon. 'What Else is on Besides the Olympics?' *Radio Times: Journal of the BBC, Television Edition* 25–31 July 1948 http://www.bbc.co.uk/archive/olympics_1948/12122.shtml accessed 6 November 2012.
27. Picture Post *Picture Post: Hulton's National Weekly Olympic Games Special 14 August 1948* 40:7 (London; Hulton Press, 1948).
28. Martin Polley '"The Amateur Rules": Post-War British Athletics' in Adrian Smith and Dilwyn Porter (eds.) *Amateurs and Professionals in Post-War British Sport* (London and Portland Oregon: Frank Cass, 2000) p. 84.
29. William John Hicks 'What Games Do Girls Like Best?' in Carolyn Dingle (ed.) *News Chronicle Sport for Girls* (London: News Chronicle Publications Department, 1951) p. 20.
30. Clare Hanson 'Save the Mothers/Representations of Pregnancy in the 1930s' *Re-visiting the 1930s: A Special Edition of Literature and History* 12:2 2003 pp. 51–61.
31. Kevin B. Walmsley 'Laying Olympism to Rest' in John Bale and Mette Krogh Christensen *Post-Olympism? Questioning Sport in the Twenty-First Century* (Oxford and New York: Berg, 2004) pp. 231–50.
32. Susan Noel 'Women in Sport' *World Sports: The International Sports Magazine* July 1949 (London: County and Sporting Publications, 1949) p. 14.

33. Marjorie Brutnell 'ABC to the Origins of Games' in Carolyn Dingle (ed.) *News Chronicle Sport for Girls* (London: News Chronicle Publications Department, 1951) pp. 139–140.
34. Melanie Tebbutt (ed.) *Growing Up in the North West 1850s-1950s* (Exeter: Short Run Press for Manchester Centre for Regional History, 2011).
35. Karl Lennartz 'The IOC During World War Two' *Journal of Olympic History* 20:1 2012 pp. 52–55.
36. Chris Wrigley, 'Ernest Bevin (1881–1951)' *Oxford Dictionary of National Biography* Oxford University Press http://www.oxforddnb.com/view/article/31872 accessed 6 November 2012.
37. David Edgerley 'How about Volunteering at the 1948 Oympics?' *Journal of Olympic History* 20:1 2012 pp. 16–17.
38. Organising Committee for the XIV Olympiad *The Official Report of the Organising Committee for the XIV Olympiad* Part One p. 29.
39. Organising Committee for the XIV Olympiad *The Official Report of the Organising Committee for the XIV Olympiad* Part One pp. 191–193.
40. Ina Buchanan and Wolf Lyberg 'The Biographies of all IOC Members Part XI' *Journal of Olympic History* 20:2 2012 p. 69.
41. Bob Phillips *The 1948 Olympics* p. 41.
42. Owen Williams, rev. Anita McConnell 'Sir Arthur James Elvin (1899–1957)' *Oxford Dictionary of National Biography* Oxford University Press http://www.oxforddnb.com/view/article/33017 accessed 6 November 2012.
43. Organising Committee for the XIV Olympiad *The Official Report of the Organising Committee for the XIV Olympiad* Part One p. 29.
44. Jean Williams 'Frisky and Bitchy: Unlikely British Olympic Heroes?' in Carol Osborne and Fiona Skillen (eds.) *Women and Sport: A Special Edition of Sport in History* 30:2 2010 pp. 242–267; Jean Williams 'A Life less Written: The Bridge Career of Fritzi Gordon' *Historical Perspectives on Jews and British Sport* De Montfort University, Leicester 8 September 2011.
45. Wray Vamplew 'Sir Arthur Abraham Gold (1917–2002)' *Oxford Dictionary of National Biography* Oxford University Press http://www.oxforddnb.com/view/article/76890 accessed 6 November 2012.
46. Martin Polley *The British Olympics* cover.
47. Bob Phillips *The 1948 Olympics* p. 44.
48. Mel Whatman *The Official History of the AAA* pp. 58–59.
49. John Rodda 'Sydney Wooderson: Obituary' *The Guardian* Wednesday 3 January 2007 http://www.guardian.co.uk/news/2007/jan/03/guardianobituaries.athletics accessed 5 November 2012.
50. Bob Phillips *The 1948 Olympics* pp. 24–25.
51. International Olympic Committee 'Helsinki 1952: Searchable Database of Medalists' International Olympic Committee http://www.olympic.org/content/results-and-medalists/ accessed 7 November 2012.
52. Janie Hampton *The Austerity Olympics* pp. 146–147.
53. Anon. 'Women Win Athletic Fame' *Picture Post* p. 19.
54. International Olympic Committee 'London 1948: Searchable Database of Medalists' International Olympic Committee http://www.olympic.org/content/results-and-medalists/ accessed 7 November 2012.
55. International Olympic Committee 'Audrey Mickey Patterson 29 July 1948' *London 1948* http://www.olympic.org/news/audrey-mickey-patterson-athletics/179793 accessed 7 November 2012.
56. M. C. Curthoys 'Maureen Angela Jane Gardner (1928–1974)' *Oxford Dictionary of National Biography* Oxford University Press http://www.oxforddnb.com/view/article/104312 accessed 6 November 2012.

57. Tony Mason 'Geoffrey Harry George Dyson (1914–1981)' *Oxford Dictionary of National Biography* Oxford University Press http://www.oxforddnb.com/view/article/100477 accessed 6 November 2012.
58. Maureen Dyson 'We are winning!' in Carolyn Dingle (ed.) *News Chronicle: Sport for Girls* (London: News Chronicle Publications Department, 1951) p. 10.
59. William John Hicks 'What Games Do Girls Like Best?' p. 20.
60. Organising Committee for the XIV Olympiad *The Official Report of the Organising Committee for the XIV Olympiad* Part Two p. 235.
61. Anthony Bijkerk 'Xenia Stad-De Jong (1922–2012): Obituary' *Journal of Olympic History* 20:2 2012 p. 76.
62. Dr F. M. Messerli *La Participation Fèminine Aux Jeux Olympiques Modernes* (Édité par le Comité International Olympique Lausanne: An 1 de la XVme Olympide, 1952) unpaginated Women and Sport file IOC archive, Lausanne.
63. Amanda Schweinbenz and Alexandria Cronk 'Femininity Control at the Olympic Games' *Thirdspace: A Journal of Feminist Theory & Culture: Special Edition Gender, Sport and the Olympics* 9:2 2010 pp. 1–12.
64. Graham Gardner Limited 'Maureen Gardner Shorts' *World Sports: The International Sports Magazine* 19:5 May 1953 (London: Country and Sporting Publications, May 1953) p. 2.
65. Geraldine Biddle-Perry 'Fair Play and Fascism: The Development of British Olympic Team Uniforms' in Martin Polley (ed.) *Britain, Britons and the Olympic Games: A Special Edition of Sport in History* 32:2 2012 pp. 231–256.
66. Anon. 'Pong Sik Pak: The Competitor From Korea' *Picture Post* p. 20.
67. Sarah Kramer 'Alice Coachman 88' *The New York Times* http://www.nytimes.com/interactive/2012/07/22/sports/olympics/olympians-1948-london-photos accessed 7 November 2012.
68. Mrs Francina Blankers-Koen 'Foreword' in George Pallet *Women's Athletics* (London: The Normal Press, 1955).
69. International Olympic Committee 'Berlin 1936: Searchable Database of Medalists' International Olympic Committee http://www.olympic.org/content/results-and-medalists/gamesandsportsummary/ accessed 7 November 2012.
70. Janie Hampton *The Austerity Olympics* pp. 196–197.
71. International Olympic Committee 'London 1948: Searchable Database of Medalists' International Olympic Committee http://www.olympic.org/content/results-and-medalists/gamesandsportsummary/ accessed 7 November 2012.
72. Edgar Joubert 'Top Notch Athlete: Top Note Pianist' *World Sports: The International Sports Magazine* July 1949 (London: Country and Sporting Publications, 1949) p. 35.
73. Kathleen Green '1948 Olympians: Dorothy Parlett and Dorothy Tyler (Athletics)' *London, Oral History and Publication* http://www.katherinegreen.co.uk/1948-olympians/ accessed 7 November 2012.
74. Organising Committee for the XIV Olympiad *The Official Report of the Organising Committee for the XIV Olympiad* Part Two p. 226–236.
75. Ian Buchanan *British Olympians* pp. 176–177.
76. Jack Crump 'Women's Athletics' in Carolyn Dingle (ed.) *News Chronicle: Sport for Girls* (London: News Chronicle Publications Department, 1951) pp. 137–138.
77. Mary Rand *Mary Mary: Autobiography of an Olympic Champion* (London: Hodder and Stoughton, 1969) pp. 39–44.

78. Michael Dawson 'Acting Global, Thinking Local: "Liquid Imperialism" and the Multiple Meanings of the 1954 British Empire & Commonwealth Games' *The International Journal of the History of Sport* 23: 1 February 2006 pp. 3–27; Robert Bartlett 'Failed Bids and Losing Cities: Adelaide's Failure to Secure the 1962 British Empire and Commonwealth Games' *Sporting Traditions* 15:2 May 1999 pp. 37–53.
79. M. B Davies B.Sc. *Physical Training: Games and Athletics in Schools: A Textbook for College Students* (London: George Allen and Unwin Ltd, seventh edition 1949; first published in 1927) pp. 264–265.
80. W. J. Howcroft 'Swimming' in James Rivers (ed.) *The Sports Book 2* (London: Macdonald and Company, 1948) p. 76.
81. Organising Committee for the XIV Olympiad 'Swimming' *The Official Report of the Organising Committee for the XIV Olympiad* Part Two pp. 444–447.
82. The Amateur Swimming Association *ASA Swimming Instruction* (London: The Amateur Swimming Association and Educational Productions Ltd, revised edition 1963; first published in 1919) p. 100.
83. Graham Walker 'Nancy Riach and the Motherwell Swimming Phenomenon' in Grant Jarvie and Graham Walker (eds.) *Scottish Sport In the Making of the Nation: Ninety-Minute Patriots?* (London: Leicester University Press, 1994), 142–153.
84. Angus Calder 'Nancy Anderson Long Riach (1927–1947)' *Oxford Dictionary of National Biography* Oxford University Press http://www.oxforddnb.com/view/article/65073 accessed 17 November 2012.
85. Scottish Swimming Hall of Fame 'Nancy Riach' *Scottish Swimming Hall of Fame* http://www.scottishswimminghalloffame.co.uk/inductees/nancy-riach.html accessed 12 November 2012.
86. W. J. Howcroft 'Swimming' p. 270.
87. Angus Calder, 'Nancy Anderson Long Riach (1927–1947)'.
88. Graham Walker 'Nancy Riach' p. 150.
89. British Pathé *Nancy Riach Funeral, 1947* film number 2168.10 http://www.britishpathe.com/video/stills/nancy-riach-funeral accessed 12 November 2012.
90. Margaret Wellington 'Swimming to be a Champion-7 Days a Week' in Carolyn Dingle (ed.) *News Chronicle: Sport for Girls* (London: News Chronicle Publications Department, 1951) p. 29.
91. British Pathé *Margaret Wellington: Mermaid in the City 1946* film number 1388.02 http://www.britishpathe.com/video/mermaid-in-the-city accessed 12 November 2012.
92. Ian Buchanan *British Olympians* pp. 162–167.
93. Margaret Wellington 'Swimming to be a Champion 7 Days a Week' pp. 31–32.
94. International Olympic Committee *Swimming Medalists 1948* http://www.olympic.org/content/results-and-medalists/gamesandsportsummary/ accessed 12 November 2012.
95. Anon. 'Cathie Gibson Scotland's Backstroke Prodigy 1946' *Daily Herald* archive at the National Media Museum, Bradford http://www.scienceandsociety.co.uk/ accessed 12 November 2012.
96. Graham Walker 'Nancy Riach' p. 152.
97. Organising Committee for the XIV Olympiad 'Swimming' *The Official Report of the Organising Committee for the XIV Olympiad* Part Two p. 447.
98. W. J. Howcroft 'Swimming' p. 263.
99. Graham Budd 'Lots 399 to 406: Helen Orr Gordon 1948–1956' *Graham Budd Auction Catalogue GB21* (London: Graham Budd Auctions, 2012) pp.105–107.

100. International Olympic Committee *Swimming Medalists Melbourne/ Stockholm 1956* http://www.olympic.org/content/results-and-medalists/ gamesandsportsummary/ accessed 12 November 2012.
101. Graham Budd 'Lot 417: Helen Orr Gordon 1948–1956' *Graham Budd Auction Catalogue GB22* (London: Graham Budd Auctions, 2012) p. 119.
102. W. J. Howcroft 'Swimming' p. 272.
103. W. J. Howcroft 'Swimming' in James Rivers (ed.) *The Sports Book 2* p. 87.
104. Margaret Wellington 'Swimming to be a Champion' p. 30.
105. Ian Buchanan *British Olympians* pp. 143–144.
106. Ian Buchanan *British Olympians* p. 36.
107. International Olympic Committee *Swimming Medalists Melbourne/ Stockholm 1956* http://www.olympic.org/content/results-and-medalists/gamesandsportsummary/ accessed 12 November 2012.
108. Aileen Harding 'There's Fun In Fencing' in Carolyn Dingle (ed.) *News Chronicle: Sport for Girls* (London: News Chronicle Publications Department, 1951) pp. 15–16.
109. Anon. 'Asthma Sufferer Is a Good Swimmer' *The Montreal Gazette* 4 August 1954 p. 10.
110. Aileen Harding 'There's Fun in Fencing' p. 16.
111. H. R. H. Prince Phillip *Handwritten Note, undated* Dame Mary Glen Haig file IOC archive, Lausanne.
112. Ian Buchanan *British Olympians* p. 147.
113. Carol Dyhouse *Students: A Gendered History* (London and New York: Routledge, 2006) pp. 181–182.
114. Sue Lopez *Women On The Ball: A Guide To Women's Football* (London: Scarlet Press, 1997) p. 57.
115. Organising Committee for the XIV Olympiad 'Swimming' *The Official Report of the Organising Committee for the XIV Olympiad* Part Two p. 261; Ian Buchanan *British Olympians* pp. 149–150.
116. Organising Committee for the XIV Olympiad *The Official Report of the Organising Committee for the XIV Olympiad* Part Two p. 547.
117. Organising Committee for the XIV Olympiad 'Arts Competitions' *The Official Report of the Organising Committee for the XIV Olympiad* Part Two pp. 533–534.
118. Sten Svenson '15,000 Gymnasts in Swedish Festival' *World Sports: The International Sports Magazine* July 1949 (London: County and Sporting Publications, 1949) pp. 10–11.
119. Organising Committee for the XIV Olympiad 'Arts Competitions' *The Official Report of the Organising Committee for the XIV Olympiad* Part Two pp. 719–722.
120. John R. Gold and Margaret M. Gold 'Future Indefinite? London 2012, The Spectre of Retrenchment and The Challenge of Olympic Sports Legacy' *The London Journal* 34:2 July 2009 pp. 179–196.
121. Bob Phillips *The 1948 Olympics* p. xi.
122. William John Hicks 'What Games Do Girls Like Best?' p. 20.
123. Mollie Hide 'Girl Cricketers' in John St John (ed.) *The Young Cricketer: Approved By The MCC* (London: Naldrett Press, 1950) pp. 153–158.
124. Ross McKibben *Classes and Cultures: England 1918–1951* (Oxford: Oxford University Press, 1998) p. 367.
125. Margaret Jones and Rodney Lowe (eds.) *From Beveridge to Blair: The First Fifty Years of the Welfare State 1948–98* (Manchester: Manchester University Press, 2002) p. 6.
126. Margaret Jones and Rodney Lowe (eds.) 'Chronology of Events' in *From Beveridge to Blair* p. x.

127. Rodney Lowe *The Welfare State in Britain since 1945* (Basingstoke: Macmillan-Palgrave, 1993) pp. 35–45.
128. Robert M. Page *Revisiting the Welfare State* (Berkshire: Open University Press, 2007) p. 40.
129. The Mass-Observation Archive is housed in the Special Collections section of the library at the University of Sussex, Brighton UK www.massobs,org.uk. Books based on the collection include Peter Hennessy *Never Again: Britain 1945–1951* (London: Jonathan Cape, 1992) and Simon Garfield *Our Hidden Lives: The Remarkable Diaries of Post-War Britain* (London: Random House, 2005).
130. Steven Fielding (ed.) *The Labour Party: Socialism and Society since 1951* (Manchester: Manchester University Press, 1997) pp. 2–3.
131. Martin Johnes *Wales since 1939* (Manchester, Manchester University Press, 2012) p. 86.
132. Sally Tomlinson *Education in a Post-Welfare Society* (Buckingham and Philadelphia: Open University, 2001) p. 3.
133. Patricia Thane and Esther Breitenbach (eds.) *Women and Citizenship in Britain and Ireland in The Twentieth Century: What Difference Did the Vote Make?* (London: Continuum, 2009).
134. Maureen Dyson 'We are winning!' pp. 8–9.
135. Graeme Moir *A Social History of Bowling in the North of England 1945-present* unpublished PhD thesis De Montfort University, Leicester 2013.
136. Cynthia Abraham *Women's Bowls: Personal Communication 6 November 2012* www.bowlsengland.com accessed 6 November 2012.
137. Herbert Collings 'Bowling' in James Rivers (ed.) *The Sports Book* (London: Macdonald and Company, 1946) p. 52.
138. Collings 'Bowling' ibid.
139. Claire Langhamer *Women's Leisure in England, 1920–1960* (Manchester: Manchester University Press, 2000) pp. 25–27.
140. G. T. Burrows 'Bowls' in in James Rivers (ed.) *The Sports Book 2* (London: Macdonald and Company, 1948) pp. 123–126.
141. E. J. Linney *A History of the Game of Bowls* (London: T. Werner Laurie Ltd, 1933) p. 53.
142. Surrey County Women's Bowling Association http://www.ladiesbowlssurrey.co.uk/history/ accessed 1 November 2012.
143. Godfrey R. Bolsover 'Mrs Ethel S. Tigg (Tiggie)' *Who's Who and Encyclopedia of Bowls* (Nottingham: Rowland Publishers Ltd, 1959) p. 364.
144. George Burrows *All About Bowls: A Manual for Novice and Expert Players* (London: Hutchinson's Library of Sports and Pastimes, second edition 1949; first published in 1915) p. 34.
145. Ruth House *Bowls England personal communication 21 November 2012* I am grateful to Ruth House for her help with career details of Ethel Tigg and the number of clubs affiliated to the EWBA Yearbook 1951.
146. Angela Davies 'A Critical Perspective On British Social Surveys and Community Studies and Their Accounts of Married Life c.1945–70' *Cultural and Social History* 6:1 2009 pp. 47–64.
147. Jane Hamlett 'The British Domestic Interior and Social and Cultural History' *Cultural and Social History* 6:1 2009 pp. 97–107.
148. Frank Bilson 'Drawing A Bow At Venture' *World Sports: International Sports Magazine* August 1949 (London: Country and Sporting Publications, 1949) p. 21–22.
149. Frances Mountford *Reigate Surrey Bowmen* (Dorking, Surrey: self-published by Frances Mountford, 1983) p. 6.
150. William John Hicks 'What Games Do Girls Like Best?: How the Voting Went in Detail' pp. 23–25.

151. Marjorie Pollard 'This Year of Fulfilment' in Carolyn Dingle (ed.) *News Chronicle: Sport for Girls* (London: News Chronicle Publications Department, 1951) pp. 87–90.
152. I am grateful to Rowena Edlin-White for all family details and for the loan of her aunt's cricket memorabilia, referred to hereafter as the Eileen White Collection, Nottingham.
153. Marjorie Pollard 'Round-up' *Women's Cricket* 5:4 August 1934 pp. 63 Eileen White Collection, Nottingham.
154. Eileen White 'Curriculum Vitae' *Australia Tour 1951 File* Eileen White Collection, Nottingham.
155. Martin Pugh *Women and the Women's Movement in Britain 1914–1959* (London: Macmillan, 1992) p. 149; Valerie Wood *Women and Work in Nottingham 1945–1955* (unpublished MA thesis University of Nottingham, 2007) p. 11.
156. Women's Cricket Association *List of Members April 1931* p. 4; *Women's Cricket Association Report 1937* p. 8; *Women's Cricket Association Report 1957* p. 6 Eileen White Collection, Nottingham.
157. Joan L. Hawes *Women's Test Cricket: The Golden Triangle 1934–1984* (Lewes: The Book Guild Ltd, 1984).
158. Nevile Cardus 'Eve of the Test' *World Sports: The International Sports Magazine* August 1951 (London: Country and Sporting Publications, 1951) pp. 6–7.
159. Eileen White 'Autographed Scorecard: Warwickshire and Nottingham versus Australia 13 June 1951' *Australia Tour 1951 File* Eileen White Collection, Nottingham.
160. Eileen White 'Report to Women's Cricket Executive Committee September 1953' *New Zealand Tour 1954 File* Eileen White Collection, Nottingham.
161. Nevile Cardus 'Eve of the Test' p. 7.
162. Peter Wynne-Thomas *Trent Bridge 1838–1988: A History of the Ground to Commemorate the 150th Anniversary* (Nottingham: Nottinghamshire County Cricket Club, 1988) p. 177.
163. Martin Polley 'Sport and National Identity in England' in Adrian Smith and Dilwyn Porter (eds.) *Sport and National Identity In the Post-War World* (London and New York: Routledge, 2004) p. 23.
164. Carol Salmon *World Cup 1993: Official Brochure for the Fifth International Women's Cricket Tournament* (Maidstone, Kent: Modern Press Ltd, 1993) p. 6.
165. W. J. Mills 'Queen of the Road' *World Sports: The International Sports Magazine* May 1953 (London: Country and sporting Publications, 1953) p. 46.
166. Eileen Sheridan *Wonder Wheels: The Autobiography of Eileen Sheridan* (London: Nicholas Kaye, 1956).
167. Eileen Sheridan 'The Greatest Woman Cyclist Britain Has Produced' *World Sports: Official Magazine of the British Olympic Association* June 1956 (London: Country and Sporting Publications, 1956) p. 41.
168. Eileen Newman 'Never A Dull Moment' and Valerie Tomlinson 'Continental Tour for Two' in Carolyn Dingle (ed.) *News Chronicle: Sport for Girls* (London: News Chronicle Publications Department, 1951) pp. 43–45 and pp. 61–64.
169. Anon. 'Eileen Sheridan, Famous Woman Cyclist' *The Isle of Man Daily Times* 30 January 1957 p. 5; Anon. 'Scooter Queen of Europe' *The Isle of Man Daily Times* 11 June 1957 p. 3 and Anon. 'Millie Wins Her Race' *The Isle of Man Daily Times* 18 June 1957 p. 8.
170. Adrian Smith *The City of Coventry: A Twentieth Century Icon* (London and New York: I. B. Tauris, 2006).

171. Beryl Burton with Colin Kirby *Personal Best: The Autobiography of Beryl Burton* (Huddersfield: Springfield Books, 1986) p. 55.
172. Hylton Cleaver 'Up the Spurs!' *World Sports: Official Magazine of the British Olympic Association* October 1956 (London: Country and Sporting Publications, 1956) p. 15.
173. Captain Tony Collings 'High Spot of Horseman's Year' *World Sports: The International Sports Magazine* July 1951 (London: Country and Sporting Publications, 1951) p. 15.
174. Jeffrey Hill 'Patricia Rosemary Smythe (1928–1996)' *Oxford Dictionary of National Biography* Oxford University Press http://www.oxforddnb.com/view/article/62144 accessed 1 December 2012.
175. Wray Vamplew 'Sir Henry Morton Llewellyn (1911–1999)' *Oxford Dictionary of National Biography* Oxford University Press http://www.oxforddnb.com/view/article/73227 accessed 1 December 2012.
176. Lucozade 'Pat Smythe . . . Another Lucozade Enthusiast' *World Sports* September 1955 (London: Country and Sporting Publications, 1955) p. 10.
177. Jean Williams 'The Immediate Legacy of Pat Smythe: The Pony-Mad Teenager In 1950s and 1960s Britain' in Dave Day (ed.) *Sporting Lives* (Manchester: MMU Institute for Performance Research, 2011) pp. 16–29.
178. Dawn Palethorpe *My Horses and I* (London: Country Life, 1956); Hylton Cleaver 'Books' *World Sports: Official Magazine of the British Olympic Association* June 1956 (London: Country and Sporting Publications, 1956) p. 40.
179. The Pony Club http://www.pcuk.org/About-Us/History accessed 27 January 2011.
180. http://www.riding-for-disabled.org.uk/about-us/ accessed 27 January 2010.
181. Caroline Ramsden *Ladies in Racing: Sixteenth Century to the Present Day* (London: Paul, 1973); Joyce Kay 'Women' in Wray Vamplew and Joyce Kay (eds.) *Encyclopedia of British Horseracing* (London and New York: Routledge, 2005) pp. 341–344; Roger Munting 'Ladies on Horseback: Women in Eventing and Racing' *British Society of Sports History Members' Bulletin* May 2012 pp. 2–4.
182. Wray Vamplew 'Florence Nagle (1894–1988)' *Oxford Dictionary of National Biography* Oxford University Press http://www.oxforddnb.com/view/article/62668 accessed 1 December 2012.
183. Marcus Armytage 'Diary: Helen Johnson-Houghton, First Lady To Train A Classic Winner Approaches Her 100th Birthday' *The Telegraph* http://www.telegraph.co.uk/sport/horseracing/ accessed 1 December 2012.
184. British Pathé *Woman Wins Training Rights 1966* film number 1799.14 http://www.britishpathe.com/video/woman-wins-training-rights accessed 1 December 2012.
185. J. Miller *How Does the Labour Process Impact On Employment Relations In the Small Firm? A Study of Racehorse Training Stables In The United Kingdom* unpublished PhD, London Metropolitan University, 2010 p. 28.
186. James Lambie *The Story of Your Life: A History of The Sporting Life Newspaper, 1859–1998* (Leicester: Matador, 2010) pp. 481–483.
187. Anon. 'Meriel Tufnell, Obituary' *The Telegraph* 17 October 2002 http://www.telegraph.co.uk/news/obituaries/1410396/Meriel-Tufnell.html accessed 1 December 2012.
188. Joyce Kay 'Meriel Patricia Tufnell (1948–2002)' *Oxford Dictionary of National Biography* Oxford University Press http://www.oxforddnb.com/view/article/77356 accessed 1 December 2012.
189. Roger Munting 'Ladies on Horseback' p. 4.
190. 'Babe' Didrikson Zaharias *This Life I've Led: The Autobiography of 'Babe' Didrikson Zaharias* (London: Robert Hale, 1956).

350 *Notes*

191. Willy Meisl '"The Babe": A Genius With An Infinite Capacity for Taking Pains' *World Sports: Official Magazine of the British Olympic Association* November 1956 (London: Country and Sporting Publications, 1956) pp. 34–35.
192. Geoffrey Cousins 'Golf' in James Rivers (ed.) *The Sports Book 2* (London: Macdonald and Company) 1948 p.191.
193. ibid. p. 200.
194. Susan Noel 'Women in Sport' *World Sports: Official Magazine of the British Olympic Association* August 1956 (London: Country and Sporting Publications, 1956) p. 27.
195. Susan Noel 'Veronica-Story of A Girl Who Was Started on the Road To Golf Fame By Illness' *World Sports: Official Magazine of the British Olympic Association* April 1956 (London: Country and Sporting Publications, 1956) p. 40.
196. Susan Noel 'Women in Sport' *World Sports: International Sports Magazine* January 1950 (London: Country and Sporting Publications, 1950) p. 34.
197. Peter Wynn *Women and Golf in Suburban London: A Study of Fulwell Golf Club* unpublished MA thesis De Montfort University, Leicester 2009 p. 12.
198. Wynn *Women and Golf in Suburban London* p. 14.
199. Roy Mc Kelvie 'Table Tennis' in James Rivers (ed.) *The Sports Book* (London: Macdonald and Co 1946) p. 277.
200. Fred Perry *An Autobiography* (London: Arrow Books Ltd, 1984) p. 10; Jon Henderson *The Last Champion: The Life of Fred Perry* (London: Yellow Jersey, 2010) p. 23.
201. Stanley Doust 'Lawn Tennis' in James Rivers (ed.) *The Sports Book* (London: Macdonald and Company, 1946) p. 195.
202. Stanley Doust 'Lawn Tennis' p. 201.
203. John Olliff 'What's Wrong With British Tennis?' *World Sports Magazine* May 1951(London: Country and Sporting Publications, 1951) p. 21.
204. Stanley Doust 'Lawn Tennis' pp. 223–225.
205. James Huntington-Whiteley and Richard Holt *The Book of British Sporting Heroes* p. 174.
206. Susan Noel 'Women in Sport' *World Sport: International Sports Magazine* September 1955 (London: Country and Sporting Publications, 1955) p. 46.
207. James Huntington-Whiteley and Richard Holt *The Book of British Sporting Heroes* p. 143.
208. Susan Noel 'Women in Sport: One Day She Should Be Really Smashing!' *World Sports Magazine: Official Magazine if the British Olympic Association* May 1956 (London: Country and Sporting Publications, 1956) p. 40.
209. Stanley Doust 'Lawn Tennis' p. 200.
210. Susan Noel 'Women in Sport' *World Sports Magazine: The International Sports Magazine* September 1949 (London: Country and Sporting Publications, 1949) p. 30.
211. Gussy Moran 'Making A Job of It' in Carolyn Dingle (ed.) *News Chronicle: Sport for Girls* (London: News Chronicle Publications Department, 1951) pp. 17–18.
212. Richard Evans 'Gussie Moran: Obituary' *The Guardian* 20 January 2013 http://www.guardian.co.uk/sport/2013/jan/20/gussie-moran/ accessed 20 January 2013. I am grateful to Neil Carter for this reference.
213. Stanley Doust 'Lawn Tennis' p. 228.
214. Susan Noel 'Women in Sport' *World Sports: Official Magazine of the British Olympic Association* September 1956 (London: Country and Sporting Publications, 1956) p. 17; Bruce Schoenfeld *The Match: Althea Gibson & Angela Buxton* (New York: Harper Collins, 2004) p. 5.

215. Flic Everett and Angela Buxton 'Woman's Hour' *BBC Radio 4* 22 July 2004 http://www.bbc.co.uk/radio4/womanshour/2004_29_thu_02.shtml accessed 24 November 2012.

216. Wimbledon Lawn Tennis Museum 'Timeline' http://www.wimbledon.com/en_GB/history/ accessed 21 November 2012.

217. Susan Noel 'The Gibson Girl' *World Sports Magazine: The International Sports Magazine* November 1950 (London: Country and Sporting Publications, 1956) p. 35.

218. Cecil Bear 'Althea Gibson: Is this Her Year?' *World Sports Magazine* June 1957 (Country and Sporting Publications, 1957) cover.

219. Frances Clayton Gray and Yannick Rice Lamb *Born to Win: The Authorized Biography of Althea Gibson* (New Jersey: John Wiley and Sons Ltd., 2004) p. 58.

220. Althea Gibson with Ed Fitzgerald *I Always Wanted to be Somebody* (New York: Harper and Row, 1958) Althea Gibson and Richard Curtis *So Much To Live for* (New York: G. P. Putnam & Sons, 1968).

221. Althea Gibson Foundation http://www.altheagibson.com/ accessed 24 November 2012.

222. John Barrett and Alan Little *Wimbledon: Ladies Singles Champions 1884–2004* (London: Wimbledon Lawn Tennis Museum, 2005) pp. 68–69.

223. Roy Mc Kelvie 'Table Tennis' p. 280.

224. Britain's Ltd *Greyhound Races* (London: Glevum Series, 1937); Simpson's Department Store *Simpson's Christmas Catalogue 1951* (Toronto, Canada: Simpson's, 1951) pp. 31–35; Whiteley's Department Store *Christmas at Whiteley's 1960* (London: William Whiteley, 1960) p. 5 Retailer files, V & A Museum of Childhoood, Bethnal Green London.

225. Roly Larson 'The Great Amateur Sham' *Lilliput: A Man's Magazine* (London: Hulton 1956) p. 25.

226. Roly Larson 'The Great Amateur Sham' p. 27.

227. Diane and Rosalind Rowe 'Table Tennis Twins' in Carolyn Dingle (ed.) *News Chronicle: Sport for Girls* (London: News Chronicle Publications Department, 1951) pp. 27–28.

228. Victor Barna 'The World at Wembley' *World Sports: The International Sports Magazine* April 1954 (London: Country and Sporting Publications, 1954) p. 15.

229. Susan Noel 'Women in Sport' *World Sports: The International Sports Magazine* November 1954 (London: Country and Sporting Publications, 1954) p. 17.

230. Susan Noel 'Women in Sport' *World Sports: The International Sports Magazine* October 1949 (London: Country and Sporting Publications, 1949) p. 28.

231. Fred Brundle 'Can Heather Bring Us Luck?' *World Sports: The International Sports Magazine* March 1957 (London: Country and Sporting Publications, 1957) pp. 22–23.

232. Tom Stenner 'Speedway Racing' in James Rivers (ed.) *The Sports Book* (London: Macdonald and Company, 1946) p. 241.

233. Tom Stenner 'Speedway Racing' p. 248.

234. M. L. T. 'Lady Competition Drivers' *Motor Sport incorporating Speed and The Brooklands Gazette* 37:9 September 1961 (London: Teesdale, 1961) p. 729.

235. Anon. 'Patsy Burt Obituary' *The Telegraph* 9 October 2001 http://www.telegraph.co.uk/news/obituaries/1358856/Patsy-Burt.html accessed 30 November 2012.

236. Anon. 'The Rootes Group and Competition Motoring' *Motor Sport Incorporating Speed and The Brooklands Gazette* 31: 7 July 1955 (London: Teesdale, 1955) p. 380.

237. M. L. T. 'Lady Competition Drivers' *Motor Sport Incorporating Speed and The Brooklands Gazette* 37:8 August 1961 (London: Teesdale, 1961) p. 558.

238. M. L. T. 'Lady Competition Drivers' *Motor Sport Incorporating Speed and The Brooklands Gazette* 37:7 July 1961 (Teesdale: London, 1961) pp. 558–559.

239. Alan Henry 'Pat Moss: Obituary' *The Guradian* 27 October 2008 http://www.guardian.co.uk/sport/2008/oct/27/pat-moss-carlsson-obituary accessed 30 November 2012.

240. Paul Parker 'On Days Like These' *Motor Sport incorporating Speed and The Brooklands Gazette* March 2001 77: 3 (London: Haymarket Publications, 2001) pp. 61–65.

241. Anon. 'Pat Moss: Obituary' *The Telegraph* 17 October 2008 http://www.telegraph.co.uk/news/obituaries/3219388/Pat-Moss.html accessed 30 November 2012.

242. Graham Robson 'Liege Healey' *Historic Race and Rally* 1:1 (Dorset: Pegasus, 2000) pp. 48–51.

243. Will Carling and Robert Heller *The Way to Win: Strategies for Success in Business and Sport* (London: Little Brown and Company, 1995) pp. 168–170.

244. Women's Amateur Athletics Association *Fifteenth Annual Coronation Championships Programme, White City Stadium Shepherds Bush 7 August 1937* Women's Amateur Athletics Association files Box 3, Birmingham University.

245. Mel Watman *The Official History of the AAA* p. 70.

246. Women's Cross Country and Road Walking Association *The Grange Farm, Winton Worsley Womens' Senior Cross County Championship Programme 5 March 1949* Women's Amateur Athletics Association files Box 3, Birmingham University.

247. Women's Amateur Athletics Association *International Athletic Match Programme White City Stadium London 20 August 1949* pp. 1–3 Women's Amateur Athletics Association files Box 3, Birmingham University.

248. Women's Amateur Athletics Association *Junior and Intermediate Track and Field Championships Programme The Alexander Sports Ground Perry Barr Birmingham 9 July 1955* pp. 3–4 Women's Amateur Athletics Association files Box 3 Birmingham University.

249. Women's Amateur Athletics Association *Junior and Intermediate Track and Field Championships Programme The Alexander Sports Ground Perry Barr Birmingham 9 July 1955* Cover Women's Amateur Athletics Association files Box 3 Birmingham University.

250. Lynne Duval 'The Development of Women's Track and Field in England: The Role of the Athletic Club, 1920s-1950s' *The Sports Historian* 21:1 2001 p. 9.

251. Graham Budd 'Lot 372: Connie Mason Silver Plated Goblet' *Graham Budd Auction Catalogue GB22* (London: Graham Budd Auctions, 2012) p. 105.

252. C. Mary Bickley, 'There Are Definite Benefits in Cross Country Running' *Modern Athletics*, January 1958 2:1 pp. 20–21. Bickley was the honorary secretary of the Women's Cross Country and Road Walking Association.

253. Women's Amateur Atheitcs Association *WAAA and Women's National Cross County Championship (under WAA rules) Programme Parliament Hill Secondary School Hampstead 4 March 1950* pp. 2–4 Women's Amateur Athletics Association files Box 3, Birmingham University.

254. Roger Bannister *The First Four Minutes* (Stroud, Gloucestershire: Putnam, 1955 reprinted 2004); John Bale *Roger Bannister and the Four-Minute*

Mile: Sports Myth and Sports History (New York and London: Routledge, 2004).

255. Diane Charles 'The First Female Runner To complete A Mile In Less Than fFive Minutes' *BBC Radio 4 Woman's Hour* 6 May 2004 http://www.bbc. co.uk/radio4/womanshour/2004 accessed 9 November 2012.

256. British Pathé *Moscow Athletes Versus Northern Selected: White City Manchester, Diane Leather and Gordon Pirie* film number 2632.16 accessed 9 November 2012.

257. Joe McGhee and Jean Scrivens 'Two More Athletes Disclose "Our Plans for Melbourne"': *World Sports: Official Magazine of the British Olympic Association* May 1956 (London: Country and Sporting Publications, 1956) p. 42.

258. George Pallett *Women's Athletics* (Dulwich. London: The Normal Press Ltd, 1955).

259. George Pallett *Women's Athletics* p. ii Dedication.

260. Norris McWhirter '"Ballerina" Nina' *World Sports: International Sports Magazine* September 1955 (London: Country and Sporting Publications, 1955) pp. 30–31.

261. Neil Carter *Medicine Sport and the Body: A Historical Perspective* (London: Bloomsbury, 2012) p. 210.

262. Geoffrey Dyson 'A Tribute from the Chief National Coach' in H. Palfreman and A. Grant *Pole Vaulting for Beginners* (Hull, London and Northampton: English Schools Athletic Association with A Brown and Sons, 1953) p. 2.

263. Nottinghamshire Education Committee *Rural Schools Course for Twelve Year Olds November 1953* (Nottingham: Nottinghamshire Education Committee, 1953) pp. 1–8.

264. Paul Gallico 'This Man's World: To Hell With Boxing, Turtles and Tonicates: Bully for the Bassoon Players' *Esquire: The Magazine for Men* September 1955 (London: Strato Publications, 1955) p. 43.

265. Michael Dillon *Self: A Study of Ethics and Endocrinology* (London: William Heinemann, 1946).

266. Roberta Cowell *Roberta Cowell, Her Story by Herself* (Melbourne, London and Toronto: Heinemann, 1954).

267. Economic and Social Research Council *Women in Britain in the 1950s: Impact Report Details* http://www.esrc.ac.uk/my-esrc/grants/RES-451-26-0682/ accessed 21 November 2012.

268. Harold M. Abrahams 'Athletics' in James Rivers (ed.) *The Sports Book 2* (London: Macdonald and Company, 1948) pp. 13–14.

269. Harold Abrahams 'Athletics' p. 29.

270. George Pallet *Women's Athletics* p. 2.

271. International Olympic Committee 'Helsinki 1952: Searchable Database of Medalists' International Olympic Committee http://www.olympic.org/content/results-and-medalists/ accessed 7 November 2012.

272. Mrs Francina Blankers-Koen 'Foreword' in George Pallet *Athletics for Women*.

273. Ian Buchanan *British Olympians* pp. 176–177.

274. Malcolm Brodie 'Her Supreme Highness' *World Sports: Official Magazine of the British Olympic Association* June 1956 (London: Country and Sporting Publications, 1956) pp. 26–27.

275. Eric L. Cowe *Early Women's Athletics: Statistics and History, Volume One* (Bingley, Eric Cowe Publications, 1999) p. 76.

276. Stephen Wagg '"If You Want the Girl Next Door . . .": Olympic Sport and the Popular Press In Early Cold War Britain' in Stephen Wagg and David L. Andrews (eds.) *East Plays West: Sport and the Cold War* (London and New York: Routledge, 2007) p. 101.

277. Debbie Johnsey *Sport Horses* http://www.johnseysporthorses.com/index. html accessed 1 December 2012.
278. Gilliam Newsum (Foreword by Pat Koechlin-Smythe) *Women and Horses* (Hampshire: The Sportsman's Press, 1988) pp. 18.
279. International Olympic Committee *Jeanette Altwegg: Olympic Athlete 1948 St Moritz, Oslo 1952* http://www.olympic.org/jeannette-altwegg accessed 8 November 2012.
280. Susan Noel 'Women in Sport' *World Sports: The International Sports Magazine* December 1949 (London: Country and Sporting Publications, 1949) p. 22.
281. Mary Louise Adams *Artistic Impressions: Figure Skating, Masculinity and the Limits of Sport* (Toronto, Buffalo and London: University of Toronto Press, 2011) pp. 158–159.
282. Ian Buchanan *British Olympians* p. 186–187.
283. Daphné Bolz 'Olympic Heritage-An International Legacy: The Invention of the Modern Olympic Stadium from Coubertin to 1948' in Jeffrey Hill, Kevin Moore and Jason Wood *Sport, History and Heritage: Studies in Public Representation* (Woodbridge, Suffolk and Rochester, New York:Boydell and Brewer Ltd, 2012) p. 235.
284. P. G. Piley 'The Silent Games' *World Sports: Official Magazine of the British Olympic Association* December 1956 (London: Country and Sporting Publications, 1956) p. 37.
285. J. R. Silver *The Role of Sport in the Rehabilitation of Patients with Spinal Injuries* (Stoke Mandeville: National Spine Injuries Centre, 2004) pp. 237–243.
286. Vanessa Heggie *A History of British Sports Medicine* (Manchester: Manchester University Press, 2011) pp. 84–86.
287. Conchita Cintron *Torera!: Memoirs of a Bullfighter* (London, Melbourne: Macmillan & Company Ltd, 1968); Patricia McCormick *Lady Bullfighter: The Autobiography of the North American Matador* (London: Robert Hale Ltd, 1956); Ed Douglas 'Eileen Healey: Obituary 1921–2010' *The Guardian* 22 November 2010 http://www.guardian.co.uk/world/2010/nov/22/eileen-healey-obituary accessed 28 November 2012.
288. Mike Cronin 'Arthur Elvin And the Dogs of Wembley' *The Sports Historian* 22:1 2002 pp. 100–114.
289. Mike Huggins and Jack Williams *Sport and the English 1918–1939* (London and New York: Routledge, 2006) p. 65.
290. Aubrey London 'Greyhound Racing' in James Rivers (ed.) *The Sports Book* (London: Macdonald and Company, 1946) p. 75.
291. Jim Pike 'Darts' in James Rivers (ed.) *The Sports Book* (London: Macdonald and Co., 1946) pp. 94–102.
292. Hazel Freestone 'They Are Real Enthusiasts' in Carolyn Dingle (ed.) *News Chronicle:Sport for Girls* (London: News Chronicle Publications Department, 1951) p. 96; Villers Butler *Amy Gentry OBE* Elmbridge Museum, 1952 http://www.bbc.co.uk/arts/yourpaintings/paintings/amy-gentry-obe-founder-of-womens-rowing-13644 accessed 21 November 2012.
293. Victoria Bennett *Invisible Women/Hidden Voices:Women Writing On Sport In the Twentieth Century* unpublished PhD thesis De Montfort University, Leicester 2003 p. 25.
294. Joyce Kay 'A Window of Opportunity? Preliminary Thoughts on Women's Sport in Post-war Britain' in Carol Osborne and Fiona Skillen (eds.) *Women in Sports History* (London and New York: Routledge, 2012) pp. 19–20.
295. Anon. 'for the Coming Autumn' *Country Life* 4 August 1955 (London: Country Life and George Newnes, 1955) pp. 264–266.

296. Rufflette 'Rufflette curtain track' *House Beautiful: Furniture Exhibition Number* February 1959 (London: House Beautiful and Samuel Stephens, 1959) p. 75
297. Londonus Super Sportswear *Vanity Fair* May 1955 (London: The National Magazine Co. Ltd, 1955) p. 47; ICI 'Terylene: The Clothes that Give You Tennis Terylinity' *Vanity Fair* April 1956 (London: The National Magazine Co. Ltd, 1956) p. 5.
298. Sarah Banks Coates Viyella Brand Licensing Archivist *Personal Communication to Noreen Marshall Bethanl Green Museum of Childhood 19 March 1998* Viyella File V& A Museum of Childhood, Bethnal Green London.
299. Epco Ltd: Leeds 'The Epco Minor, Just the Jack for Jill: For Speed Safety and Simplicity' *Motor Sport* 32 October 1956 (London: Motor Sport Ltd, 1956) p. 671.
300. Volkswagen 'Your Car Madam' *Motor Sport incorporating Speed and The Brooklands Gazette* 37:7 July 1961 (Teesdale: London, 1961) p. 581.
301. BSA *Bantam125/150* poster number BB664 1955 BSA archive Birmingham.
302. BSA Sunbeam *The Scintillating BSA Sunbeam scooter* poster number BB655 1956 BSA archive Birmingham.
303. Lambretta *Innocenti* poster number 698 1957 London: George Harvey Collection.
304. Vespa *Vespa* poster 1956.Robert Opie Collection, Museum of Advertising and Packaging, Gloucester.
305. Odhams *John Bull and Illustrated* 18 October 1958 cover Robert Opie Collection, Museum of Advertising and Packaging, Gloucester.

NOTES TO THE CONCLUSION

1. Dr Willy Meisl 'Happy Birthday Wimbledon: The Crowning Glory' *World Sports* June 1957 (London: Country and Sporting Publications, 1957) p. 11.
2. Anon. 'Quick Guide To: The World Netball Series' in *Skysports Magazine* October 2009 (Middlesex: BSkyB Publications Ltd, 2009) p. 9.
3. Anon. 'Men Versus Woman' in *Skysports Magazine* October 2009 (Middlesex: BSkyB Publications Ltd, 2009) p. 17.
4. Ronnie O' Sullivan 'Reader's Q and A with 'Rocket Ronnie O' Sullivan' in *SkySports Magazine* October 2009 (Middlesex: BSkyB Publications Ltd, 2009) p. 27.
5. Virgin London Marathon 'London Marathon Race History' http://www.virginlondonmarathon.com/history-race-report-1981 accessed 3 February 2012.
6. Mark Hughes 'Racing On A Shoestring' *Historic Race and Rally* 4:1 March 1993 (London: Bookman Press, 1993) p. 79.
7. Eleanor Goodman 'A Breath Of Fresh Air: A Page For The Woman Motorist' *Modern Motoring and Travel* February 1962 (London: Country and Sporting Publications, 1962) p. 24.
8. Mary Johns 'Nomads in the Alps' *Modern Motoring and Travel* London, February 1962 p. 37.
9. Richard Coopey, Sean O'Connell and Dilwyn Porter *Mail Order Retailing in Britain: a Business and Social History* (Oxford: Oxford University Press 2005).
10. Simon Garfield *Our Hidden Lives: The Remarkable Diaries of Post War Britain* (London: Ebury Press, 2005) p. 498.
11. Wendy Owen *Kicking Against Tradition* (Gloucester: Tempus, 2005).

12. *Evening Standard* 20 October 1964.
13. *Daily Express* 20 October 1964.
14. Christina Boxer Olympic Athlete *The Sunday Times* Sport 16 August 2009 p. 19.
15. N. Blain and R. Boyle 'Battling along the Boundaries: Marking of Scottish Identity in Sports Journalism' in Grant Jarvie and Graham Walker (eds.) *Scottish Sport In the Making Of the Nation: Ninety-Minute Patriots?* (London: Leicester University Press, 1994) p. 137.
16. Jeane Hoffman '47—and She Still Won 100 Events Last Year' *World Sports: The International Magazine* June 1988 (London: Country and Sporting Publications, 1958) pp. 24–25.
17. Anon. Eunice Shriver: Obituary *The Sunday Times* News Review 16 August 2009 p. 12.
18. Michael Cockayne *Modern sport in Altrincham* p. 92.
19. W. Arthur Deakin *The Story of Loughborough 1888–1914* (Loughborough: Echo Press, 1979) p. 122.
20. Patricia Vertinsky 'Women Sport and Exercise in the 19th Century' in D. Margaret Costa and Sharon R Guthrie (eds.) *Women and Sport: Interdisciplinary Perspectives* (Champaign, Illinois: Human Kinetics 1994) pp. 70–72.
21. The Radcliffe College Archives at the Schlesinger Library, Harvard File RAD.SCHL: 302276 Abastenia St. Leger Eberle photograph with a sculpture of a girl roller skating taken by Jessie Tarbox Beals circa 1905–08, accession number PC60–106–6; Female telegraph office worker on roller skates taken by the Western Union Telegraph Company in 1936, accession number olvwork277461; the Catherine Filene Shouse Papers, German Youth Activities Program: GYA Centre photograph albums 1950, accession number olvwork20029690 http://via.lib.harvard.edu: accessed 10 October 2009.
22. Lou LV and Zhang Huiguang *Sneakers* (London: Southbank, 2007) pp. 186–188.

Bibliography

A. PRIMARY SOURCES

1. Archival Sources:

Amateur Swimming Association Musem and Archive, British Swimming Loughborough
Amateur Swimming Association Handbooks 1902–1914; contemporary publications; Olympic memorabilia.

Birmingham University Special Collections
Fédération Sportive Féminine Internationale artifacts; Harold Abrahams Collection: Women's Amateur Athletics Association Files 1922–1960.

British Olympic Association Museum and Archive, Wandsworth London
Minutes of British Olympic Council Meetings 20 December 1904–1948; National Olympic Committee Correspondence Files 1900–1983; British Olympic Association Yearbooks 1906–1956; Desborough Press Clippings File; Official Reports 1908–1948; Women and Sport Files 1900–1976.

Brooklands Museum and Archive, Weybridge, Surrey
Alpahbetical Card Index of Drivers and Races at Brooklands; Brooklands Automobile Racing Club (BARC) Minutes 1906–1939; Brooklands Society Gazette 1955–1998; contemporary publications; Kay Petre File; Gwenda Glubb/Jansen/Stewart/Hawkes File; Elsie 'Bill' Wisdom File; Women Drivers File.

Fédération Internationale de Football Associations(FIFA) Archive, Zurich
Women's football artifacts and documentation 1880–1991.

International Olympic Committee (IOC) Museum and Archive, Lausanne
Correspondence of the National Olympic Committee of Great Britain Files 1900–1983; Fédération Sportive Féminine Internationale and IOC correspondence; Mary Glen Haig File; Publications of the NOC of Great Britain 1906–1960; Women and Sport Files 1900–1976, including Women's World Games and Ludy Godbold material.

Leicestershire County Record Office, Wigston
Kelly's Directory of Leicestershire and Rutland 1896–1914; contemporary local history publications.

Leicester County Museum Store, Barrow Upon Soar
Corah's of Leicester Files; Jantzen license plans; swimsuits and labels 1890–1920.

London Metropolitan University: The Women's Library
Autograph Letter Collection: Female Educationalists File 1850–1951; All England Women's Lacrosse Association Files 1912–1993.

Royal Society of Arts Library and Archive, London
Files and photographs for Royal Society of Arts Annual Competition of Industrial Design from 1924 to 1933.

Silverstone Library and Archive, Northamptonshire
British Racing Driver's Club (BRDC) Committee Minutes 1927–1948; contemporary publications; Women Drivers File.

Sudbury Hall National Trust Museum of Childhood Sudbury, Derbyshire
Betty Cadbury Collection and Toy Collection 1850–1960.

The Museum at the Fashion Institute of Technology, New York
Women's sporting garments, shoes and accessories from 1850–1940.

The National Football Museum, Preston
Preston North End Board Minute Books 1900–1920; Dick, Kerr Ladies FC memorabilia; women's football artifacts 1895–1960 including the FIFA collection.

The National Sporting Library, Middleburg Virginia
Equestrian manuals, personal collections and literature 1676–1960.

Union des Associations Européennes de Football (UEFA) Archive, Nyon
Minutes of meetings on women's football and other artifacts 1880–1973.

University of Bath Archives and Special Collections
All England Women's Hockey Association (AEWHA) Files 1895–1998; International Federation of Women's Hockey Associations (IFWHA) Files 1930–1983; individual player files and tour diaries.

University of Leicester, Special Collections
Corah's of Leicester 1815–1965 File; local history publications.

V & A Museum of Childhood, Bethnal Green London
Retailer Files: Gamage's; Hamley Brothers Ltd; Simpson's Department Store; Whiteley's Department Store. Manufacturer Files: Lines Brothers Ltd; Coates-Viyella.

Wimbledon Lawn Tennis Museum and Archive, Wimbledon
Collections of the All England Tennis Club, artifacts, library and literature 1850–1960.

A. 2. Printed Works:

Newspapers and Periodicals

The Badminton Magazine of Sports and Pastimes (1895–1910)
Bailey's Magazine (1860–1922)
Country Life (1897–1959)
The Field (1869–1918)
World Sports: Official Magazine of the British Olympic Association/The International Sports Magazine (1949–1959)

A. 3. Contemporary Parliamentary Papers, Books, Articles and Artifacts

Abrahams, Harold M. 'Athletics' in James Rivers (ed.) *The Sports Book 2* (London: MacDonald and Company, 1948).

Abrahams, Harold *Fifty Years of the Amateur Athletic Association Championships* (London: Carborundum, 1961.

Aitken-Kidd, Janet *The Beaverbrook Girl* (London: Collins, 1987).

Alderson, J. D. 'Gwenda Hawkes' *Brooklands Society Gazette* 1:4. 1976.

Alken, Henry Thomas *Going to Epsom Races: A Ludicrous Amusement Consisting of Modern Costume, Characters, Dandies, Equipages and Horsemanship* (London: S & H Fuller, 1819).

Allen, David and Sons *The Original English Lady Cricketers* circa 1895 poster number TN.2008.297 MCC Museum Lord's, London.

Allen, John *Principles of Modern Riding for Ladies, In Which All Late Improvements Are Applied to Practice On the Promenade & the Road* (London: Tegg, 1825).

All England Women's Hockey Association *Women's Hockey Association of Australia Tour of England Programme* 18 October 1930.

All England Women's Hockey Association *Magdeburg versus Northants Programme* 3 January 1931.

All England Women's Hockey Association *All England Women's Hockey Association England V The Rest* Programme 24 January 1931.

Amateur Swimming Association *ASA Swimming Instruction* (London: The Amateur Swimming Association and Educational Productions Ltd, revised edition 1963; first published in 1919).

American Association for Health, Physical Education, and Recreation (previously the National Section on Women's Athletics) *Official Basketball Guide for Women and Girls: Revised Rules, 1939–1940* (Offical Sports Library for Women, New York: A. S. Barnes and Company, 1938).

Anon. 'Aeronautics: Two Women' *Time Magazine* 26 March 1928.

Anon. 'An Autocar Wedding: The First Event of the Kind in England' *The Autocar* 1 May 1897.

Anon. 'An Old English Garden' *The New Monthly Magazine and Literary Journal* 3 1822 (Philadelphia and New York: E. Litterell and R. N. Henry, 1822).

Anon. 'Another Win for Dick, Kerr's' *The Lancashire Daily Post* 15 August 1921.

Anon. 'Asthma Sufferer Is A Good Swimmer' *The Montreal Gazette* 4 August 1954.

Anon. 'Can Girls Play Football? Of Course They Can' *The Football Favourite* 32 9 April 1921 (London: Amalgamated Press, 1921).

Anon. 'Carriage Builders Messrs. Thomas Whittingham and Wilkin, London' *The Autocar* 15 April 1899.

Anon. 'College Oratory' *Princetonian* 1:13 22 February 1877.

Anon. 'Court Circular' *The Times* 25 April 1898.

Anon. 'Dick, Kerr's Still Winning' *The Lancashire Daily Post* 2 March 1921.

Anon. 'Dick, Kerr's Ladies' Success' *The Lancashire Daily Post* 21 March 1921.

Anon 'Dick, Kerr's Most Successful Season' *The Lancashire Daily Post* 6 June 1921.

Anon. 'Double '"Double 12"': When A 250cc Motorcycle and A 5.7 litre Car Shared Brooklands for a Unique Record' *Brooklands Society Gazette* 8:1 1983.

Anon 'Douglas-Pennant Inquiry' *The Daily Mirror* 1 November 1919.

Anon. 'Eileen Sheridan, Famous Woman Cyclist' *The Isle of Man Daily Times* 30 January 1957.

Anon. 'Eunice Shriver: Obituary' *The Sunday Times* News Review 16 August 2009.

Anon. 'For the Coming Autumn' *Country Life* 4 August 1955 (London: Country Life and George Newnes, 1955).

Anon. 'Health Giving Kicks–Girl Footballer Who Scored 368 Goals Saw Doctor Only Once' *The Daily Mirror* 9 December 1921.

Anon. 'History's Most Wonderful Derby' *Daily Sketch* 5 June 1913.

Anon. 'Kay Petre' *The Bulletin of the Vintage Sports Car Club* 220 Autumn 1998.

Anon. 'Ladies at football' *Lancashire Daily Post* 27 December 1917.

Anon. 'Ladies International Match: Scotland Versus England' *The Glasgow Herald* 9 May 1881.

Anon 'Ladies Football-Banned by the Football Association' *The Lancashire Daily Post* 6 December 1921.

Anon 'Lady Footballers' Tour' *The Isle of Man Daily Times* 8 August 1921.

Anon. 'Lady Footballers' *The Isle of Man Daily Times* 15 August 1921.

Anon. 'Like Mother, Like Daughter' *Motor* 30 June 1936.

Anon. 'Look Out for the Girl Athletes' *Collier's: The National Weekly* 21 February 1925.

Anon. *Lords and Ladies Who Deal in the Sport: The Pleasures of 1722* (London: Songs: 1722).

Anon. 'Mary Callinack (Kelynack), eighty-four years of age, walked from Penzance to the Great Exhibition' *London Times* 24 September 1851.

Anon. 'Men Versus Woman' *Skysports Magazine* October 2009 (Middlesex: BSkyB Publications Ltd, 2009).

Anon. 'Millie Wins Her Race' *The Isle of Man Daily Times* 18 June 1957.

Anon. 'Miss Agnes Beckwith' *The Pall Mall Gazette* 2 September 1875.

Anon. 'Miss Edith Thompson: An English Visitor' *The Sydney Morning Herald* 5 July 1933.

Anon. 'Miss Lines' *Daily News* 28 April 1921.

Anon. 'Miss Quimby Dies in Airship Fall' *The New York Times* 2 July 2 1912.

Anon. 'Motor Racing Mishap: Man Killed, Miss Cunliffe Injured' *The Melbourne Argus* 25 June 1928.

Anon. 'Neo-Amazonian' *Louisville Herald* 7 July 1912.

Anon. 'New and Notes: Gala Meeting of the Essex Motor Club' *The Motor* 20 August 1912.

Anon. 'New Rivals to Dick, Kerr's Eleven' *The Daily Mirror* 23 March 1921.

Anon. 'Obituary: Miss E. M. Thompson, Services to Many Good Causes' *The Times* 26 August 1961.

Anon. 'Pong Sik Pak: The Competitor from Korea' *Picture Post: Special Olympic Souvenir Issue July 1948* (London: Picture Post, 1948).

Anon. 'Prof. Beckwith's Amphibious Family' no place, publisher or date given shelfmark Evan.814 The British Library, London.

Anon. 'Quick Guide to the World Netball Series' *Skysports Magazine* October 2009 (Middlesex: BSkyB Publications Ltd, 2009).

Anon. 'Racing Motorist Miss Cordery Engaged' *The West Australian* Monday 7 September 1931.

Anon. 'Rational Dress for Cyclists' *The Pall Mall Gazette* 26 February 1894.

Anon. 'Rowing Exercise for Ladies' *Routledge's the Art of Rowing for Beginners* (London: Henry Lea, 1863).

Anon. 'Rugby is the secret of 106-year-olds longevity!' *Penarth Times* 23 January 2006.

Anon. 'Scooter Queen of Europe' *The Isle of Man Daily Times* 11 June 1957.

Anon. 'Sir John Shelley-Rolls: Obituary' *The Times* 21 February 1951.

Anon. *Swimming: A Bibliographical List of Works on Swimming* (London: John Russell Smith, 1868).

Anon. 'The American Girls At The First Women's Olympiad' *New York World* 10 September 1922.

Anon. 'The Baths, Bournemouth, August 1892' *The Era* 27 August 1892.

Anon. 'The British Motor League' *The Motor* 21 January 1919.

Anon. 'The British Women's Motor-Racing Team' *The Daily Telegraph* 12 April 1935.

Anon. 'The Brookland's Nut' *Car* 4 October 1911.

Anon. 'The Diving Belle' *The Pall Mall Gazette* 17 March 1894.

Anon. 'The Doctor's Car' *The Motor* 21 January 1919.

Anon. 'The Ladies Archery Match in the Royal Toxophilite Society's Grounds, Regent's Park' *The Graphic* 9 July 1870.

Anon. 'The Rootes Group and Competition Motoring' *Motor Sport Incorporating Speed and The Brooklands Gazette* 31:7 July 1955 (London: Teesdale, 1955).

Anon. 'The Scottish Rally: Yet Another Success, Riley, Singer and Ford Divide Principal Honours' *The Motor World and Industrial Vehicle Review (incorporating The Motor Cyclist and The Scottish Cyclist)* 30:1531 1 June 1934.

Anon. 'What Else is on Besides the Olympics?' *Radio Times: Journal of the BBC, Television Edition* 25–31 July 1948 http://www.bbc.co.uk/archive/olympics_1948/12122.shtml accessed 6 November 2012.

Anon.'Women Footballers' Fine Record' *The Daily* Mirror 7 June 1921.

Anon. 'Women's "International" Dick, Kerr's, The Women's "Soccer" Side, Defeated The French Women's Team 5–1 (Exclusive)' *The Daily Mirror* 18 May 1921.

Anon. 'Workless Women' *The Lancashire Daily Post* 9 February 1921.

Art Gravure Picture Section 'American Girl Athletes' *The Cincinnati Enquirer* 20 August 1922.

Babington-Smith, Constance *Amy Johnson* (Bury St Edmunds: St Edmundsbury Press, 1967).

Barna, Victor 'The World at Wembley' *World Sports: The International Sports Magazine* April 1954 (London: Country and Sporting Publications, 1954.

Batten, Jean *Solo Flight* (Sydney: Jackson and O'Sullivan: 1934).

Batten, Jean *My Life* (London: George G. Harrap and Company Ltd, 1938).

Beach, Belle *Riding and Driving for Women* (New York: C. Scribner's Sons, 1912).

Bear, Cecil 'Happy and Glorious' *World Sports: The International Sports Magazine* 19:5 May 1953 (London: Country and Sporting Publications, 1953).

Bear, Cecil 'Althea Gibson: Is this Her Year?' *World Sports Magazine* June 1957 (Country and Sporting Publications, 1957).

Beaufort, His Grace, the Duke K.G. (ed.) *Driving* (London: Longman, Greens and Company, 1889).

Beckwith, Mrs Professor 'Swimming for Ladies' *The Oracle* 11 October 1890.

Beinhorn-Rosemeyer, Elly and Chris Nixon *Rosemeyer! A New Biography* (Isleworth Middlesex: Transport Bookman Publications, 1986).

Beinhorn-Rosemeyer, Elly 'Memoir' in Chris Nixon *Racing The Silver Arrows: Mercedes Benz versus Auto Union 1934–1939* (London: Osprey Publishing Limited, 1986).

Bennett, James A. *The Art of Swimming for Beginners: Exemplified by Diagrams from Which Both Sexes May Learn to Swim and Float on Water* (London: H. Lea, 1858).

Bergvall, Eric (translated by Edward Adams-Ray) *The Fifth Olympiad: The Official Report of The Olympic Games of Stockholm 1912* (Stockholm: Wahlström & Widstrand, 1912).

Bickley, C. Mary 'There Are Definite Benefits in Cross Country Running' *Modern Athletics*, January 1958.

Bilson, Frank 'Drawing A Bow At Venture' *World Sports: International Sports Magazine* August 1949 (London: Country and Sporting Publications, 1949).

Bisland, Elizabeth *A Flying Trip around the World in Seven Stages* (New York: Harper Brothers, 1891).

Blankers-Koen, Mrs Francina 'Foreword' in George Pallet *Women's Athletics* (London: The Normal Press, 1955).

Bly, Nellie *Nellie Bly's Book: Around the World in Seventy-Two Days* (New York City: Pictorial Weeklies Company, 1890).

Boddy, William *The History of Brooklands Motor Course: Complied from the Official Records of the Brooklands Automobile Racing Club* (London: Grenville Publishing, 1957).

Boddy, William *The Story of Brooklands: The World's First Motor Course: Complied from the Official Records of the Brooklands Automobile Racing Club* Volume 2 (London: Grenville Publishing, 1959).

Boddy, William *Montléry: The Story of the Paris Autodrome 1924–1960* (London: Cassell, 1961).

Boddy, William 'Fay Taylour' *Brooklands Society Gazette* April 1983.

Boddy, William '"Les Girls" at Le Mans' *Motor Sport* November 1988.

Bolsover, Godfrey R. 'Mrs Ethel S. Tigg (Tiggie)' *Who's Who and Encyclopedia of Bowls* (Nottingham: Rowland Publishers Ltd, 1959).

Boxer, Christina 'Olympic Athlete' *The Sunday Times* 16 August 2009.

Brodie, Malcolm 'Her Supreme Highness' *World Sports: Official Magazine of the British Olympic Association* June 1956 London: Country and Sporting Publications, 1956).

Brown, Paul *Aintree: Grand National Past and Present* (New York: The Derrydale Press, 1930).

Brooklands Automobile Racing Club 'On the Track' *The Autocar* 3 August 1912.

Bruce, The Hon. Mrs Victor *Nine Thousand Miles in Eight Weeks: Being an Account of an Epic Journey by Motor-Car Through Eleven Countries and Two Continents* (London: Heath Cranston Limited, 1927).

Bruce, The Hon. Mrs Victor *The Woman Owner-Driver: A Collection of Fourteen Essays On Motoring for Women* (Dorset House, London: Iliffe and Sons, 1928).

Bruce, The Hon. Mrs Victor 'Where Evening Joins the Dawn' in Shirley Grey (ed.) *The Oxford Annual for Girls, Tenth Year* (London: Humphrey Milford and Oxford University Press, 1928).

Bruce, The Hon. Mrs Victor (with 40 drawings by Joyce Dennys) *The Peregrinations of Penelope* (London: Heath Cranston Limited, 1930).

Bruce, The Hon. Mrs Victor *The Bluebird's Flight* (London: Chapman & Hall Ltd, 1931).

Bruce, The Hon. Mrs Victor *Nine Lives Plus, Record Breaking on Land Sea and In the Air: An Autobiographical Account* (London: Pelham Books, 1974).

Brundle, Fred 'Can Heather Bring Us Luck?' *World Sports: The International Sports Magazine* March 1957 (London: Country and Sporting Publications, 1957).

Brutnell, Marjorie 'ABC to The Origins of Games' in Carolyn Dingle (ed.) *News Chronicle: Sport for Girls* (London: News Chronicle Publications Department, 1951).

BSA *Bantam125/150* poster number BB664 BSA archive Birmingham 1955.

BSA *The Scintillating BSA Sunbeam Scooter* poster number BB655 BSA archive Birmingham 1956.

Burns, Eugene *Fishing for Women* (New York: A.S. Barnes, 1953).

Burrows, G. T. 'Bowls' in James Rivers (ed.) *The Sports Book 2* (London: MacDonald and Company, 1948).

Burrows, George *All about Bowls: A Manual for Novice and Expert Players* (London: Hutchinson's Library of Sports and Pastimes, second edition 1949; first published in 1915).

Burton, Beryl with Colin Kirby *Personal Best: The Autobiography of Beryl Burton* (Huddersfield: Springfield Books, 1986).

Buxton, Meriel *Ladies of the Chase* (London: Sportsman's Press, 1987).

Cade, Lawrence 'T. T. Racing' in James Rivers (ed.) *The Sports Book* (London: MacDonald and Company, 1946).

Campbell, Sir Malcolm *Speed On Wheels* (London: Sampson Low, Marston and Company Ltd, 1949).

Campbell, Lady Dorothy *Malcolm Campbell: The Man As I Knew Him* (London: Hutchinson & Co. Ltd, 1951).

Cardus, Neville 'Eve of the Test' *World Sports: The International Sports Magazine* August 1951 (London: Country and Sporting Publications, 1951).

Carpenter, Shirley 'The Lady Autocarist Prepares for the Hazards of a Motor Drive (sic)' *The Autocar* 9 December 1955.

Cartland, Barbara *The Isthmus Years: An Autobiographical Study of the Years between the Two World Wars* (London: Hutchinson, 1942).

Chakrabonse, HRH Prince Chula of Thailand *Dick Seaman* (London and Edinburgh: Morisson and Gibbs Ltd, 1941).

Chalmers, Patrick *Forty Fine Ladies* (London: Eyre and Spottiswoode; New York: Scribner, 1929).

Chaplin, Charles (with David Robinson) *My Autobiography* (London: Penguin Modern Classics 1966, first published by Bodely Head 1964).

Cheney, Leo for Raleigh *Raleigh, the Gold Motorcycle: Takes Everything in Its Stride* (Nottingham: Raleigh Industries, 1924).

Children's Employment Commission *Appendix to the Report of the Commissioners Trades and Manufactures Part II Reports and Evidence from Sub Commissioners* (London: British Parliamentary Papers, 1842).

Cholmondeley-Pennell, Henry (ed.) *Fishing: Salmon and Trout* (London: Longmans, Green and Company, 1885)

Cholmonedley-Tapper, T. P. *Amateur Racing Driver* (London: G. T. Foulis & Co. Ltd, 1953).

Cintron, Conchita *Torera!: Memoirs of a Bullfighter* (London, Melbourne: Macmillan & Company Ltd, 1968).

Clarke, J. Stirling *The Ladies' Equestrian Guide; or The Habit and the Horse* (London: Day & Son, 1857)

Claxton, Edgar 'Register of Death: Dorothy Elizabeth Levi, 22 May 1922 reference number DYD 047027 *General Register Office, Crown Copyright* (North Marylebone, London, 22 May 1922).

Cleaver, Hylton 'Up the Spurs!' *World Sports: Official Magazine of the British Olympic Association* October 1956 (London: Country and Sporting Publications, 1956).

Clymer, Floyd *Indianapolis 500 Mile Race History* (Los Angeles: Floyd Clymer Publishing, 1946).

Collings, Herbert 'Bowling' in James Rivers (ed.) *The Sports Book* (London: MacDonald and Company, 1946).

Collings, Captain Tony 'High Spot of Horseman's Year' *World Sports: The International Sports Magazine* July 1951 (London: Country and Sporting Publications, 1951).

Cotteral, Bonnie and Donnie (Department of Physical Education, St Joseph's High School, Missouri) *Tumbling, Pyramid Building and Stunts for Girls and Women* (New York: Barnes and Noble, 1926).

Courtenay, William 'Speed on the Empire Flying Boats' *Speed: Land, Sea, Air* July 1937.

Cousins, Geoffrey 'Golf' in James Rivers (ed.) *The Sports Book 2* (London: Mac-Donald and Company, 1948).

Cowell, Roberta *Roberta Cowell, Her Story by Herself* (Melbourne, London and Toronto: Heinemann, 1954).

Cox, V. 'Going to Australia?' *Women's Cricket* 5:1 1934 (Welwyn, Hertfordshire: J. H. Lawrence and Sons, 1934).

Crump, Jack 'The Real Result of The London Olympic Games' *Bulletin Du Comité International Olympique* 19 January 1950.

Crump, Jack 'Women's Athletics' in Carolyn Dingle (ed.) *News Chronicle: Sport for Girls* (London: News Chronicle Publications Department, 1951).

Curzon, Lady Georgiana 'Tandem Driving' in His Grace The Duke of Beaufort K. G. (ed.) *Driving* (London: Longman, Greens and Company, 1889).

Davies, M. B. B.Sc. *Physical Training: Games and Athletics in Schools: A Textbook for College Students* (London: George Allen and Unwin Ltd, seventh edition 1949; first published in 1927).

Davis, S. C. H. *A Racing Motorist: His Adventures at the Wheel in Peace and War* (London: Iliffe and Sons Ltd, 1949).

Davis, S. C. H. *Atalanta: Women as Racing Drivers* (London: G. T. Foulis & Co. Ltd, 1957).

Davis, Sammy '"Bill" Wisdom: A Tribute' *The Motor* 20 April 1972.

Deakin, W. Arthur *The Story of Loughborough 1888–1914* (Loughborough: Echo Press, 1979).

Dean, Basil *No Limit* (London: Associated Talking Pictures, 1935).

Debenham, Betty and Nancy 'Diana Awheel: Motor Cycling Hints and Tips' *Brooklands Society Gazette* 18:4 1993.

De Grineau, Bryan 'The Mannin Beg . . . An Artists Impressions' *The Light Car* 8 June 1934.

De Hurst, C. *How Women Should Ride* (New York: Harper & Brothers, 1892)

Diana Up-to-Date 'Sportswoman's Page' *The Illustrated Sporting and Dramatic News* 1 June 1901.

Dillon, Michael *Self: A Study of Ethics and Endocrinology* (London: William Heinemann, 1946).

Division for Girls and Women's Sports of the American Association for Health, Physical Education, and Recreation (previously the National Section on Women's Athletics) *Official Individual Sports Guide: Archery-Fencing-Golf-Riding-Tennis* (New York: A. S. Barnes and Company, 1942/43).

Dixon, Charles *Amy Johnson: Lone Girl Flyer* (London: Sampson, Low, Marston and Company Ltd, c1930).

Dod, Lottie 'Lawn Tennis for Ladies' in J. M. Heathcote (eds.) *Tennis, Lawn Tennis, Badminton, Fives: The Badminton Library of Sports and Pastimes* (London: Longmans, Green and Company, 1890).

Doust, Stanely 'Lawn Tennis' in James Rivers (ed.) *The Sports Book* (London: MacDonald and Company, 1946).

Drummond, Maud F. 'Croquet, with hints and tips for Players' *The Girl's Own Paper* 303: 2 April 1905.

Dyson, Geoffrey 'A Tribute from the Chief National Coach' in H. Palfreman and A. Grant *Pole Vaulting for Beginners* (Hull, London and Northampton: English Schools Athletic Association with A Brown and Sons, 1953).

Dyson, Maureen 'We are winning!' in Carolyn Dingle (ed.) *News Chronicle: Sport for Girls* (London: News Chronicle Publications Department, 1951).

Egan, Pierce *Tom & Jerry: Life in London, or, The Day and Night Scenes of Jerry Hawthorn, esq. and His Elegant Friend Corinthian Tom, in Their Rambles and Sprees Through the Metropolis* (London: Thomas Tegg, 1821).

Eliott-Lynn, Sophie C. *Athletics for Women and Girls: How To Be An Athlete and Why* (London: Robert Scott, 1925).

Epco Ltd: Leeds 'The Epco Minor, Just the Jack for Jill: for Speed Safety and Simplicity' *Motor Sport* 32 October 1956 (London: Motor Sport Ltd, 1956).

Eyston, George *Safety Last* (Spalding: Vincent Publishing, 1975).

Eyston, George *Flat Out* (Spalding: Vincent Publishing Company, 1976; first published in 1933).

Faithfull, Lilian M. *In the House of My Pilgrimage* (London: Chatto & Windus, 1924).

Fédération Sportive Féminine Internationale *Jeux Féminins Mondiaux Londres 1934* (Paris: 3 Rue De Varenne, 1934).

Fédération Sportive Féminine Internationale *Jeux Féminins Mondiaux Londres 1934: Fourth Womens World Games Official Programme Thursday-Saturday 9–11 August 1934* White City Stadium London p. 7 (London: Fleetway, 1934).

Fermata School *Fermata Spur* 10:2 (Aiken, SC: Fermata School, May 1938).

Forrest, George *Routledge's Sixpenny Handbooks: A Handbook of Swimming and Skating* (London: Routledge, Warne and Routledge, 1860).

Fraichard, Georges (translated by Louis Klemantaski) *The Le Mans Story* (London: The Bodley Head, 1954).

Freestone, Hazel 'They Are Real Enthusiasts' in Carolyn Dingle (ed.) *News Chronicle: Sport for Girls* (London: News Chronicle Publications Department, 1951).

From Our Geneva Correspondent 'Olympic Games and women: Ban likely' *Manchester Guardian* 12 April 1929.

Frost, H. and H. Cubberley *Field Hockey and Soccer for Women* (New York: Charles Scribner and Sons, 1923).

Furbor, Professor *The Lady's Equestrian Companion; or, Golden Key to Equitation* (London: Saunders and Otley, 1847).

Gallagher, Linda M. '1st Female Olympic Medallist is SC Native' *The State* unpaginated c. 1922.

Gallico, Paul 'This Man's World: To Hell With Boxing, Turtles and Tornicates: Bully for the Bassoon Players' *Esquire: The Magazine for Men* September 1955 (London: Strato Publications, 1955).

Gamages Ltd, A. W. 'The Sports House of the West' *Golf, Programme and Regulations: Olympic Games of London 1908* (London: British Olympic Council, 1908).

Gamages Ltd, A.W. *Gamages Xmas Bazaar 1924: From Wembley to Gamages* (London: Gamages, 1924).

Gardner, Graham Limited 'Maureen Gardner Shorts' *World Sports: The International Sports Magazine* 19:5 May 1953.

Garrett, Millicent, Dame Fawcett *Women's Suffrage: A Short History of a Great Movement* (London and Edinburgh, T. C. and E. C. Jack, c. 1912).

Garrud, Edith 'The World We Live In: Self Defence' *Votes for Women* 4 March 1910.

Garrud, Edith 'Ju-Jitsu as a Husband-Tamer: A Suffragette Play with a Moral' *Health and Strength* 8 April 1911.

Gibson, Althea with Ed Fitzgerald *I Always Wanted to Be Somebody* (New York: Harper and Row, 1958).

Gibson, Althea and Richard Curtis *So Much to Live For* (New York: G. P. Putnam & Sons, 1968).

Gill, MacDonald *Highways of Empire: Buy Empire Goods from Home and Overseas* (London: Empire Marketing Board, c. 1927).

Goodman, Eleanor 'A Breath of Fresh Air: A Page for the Woman Motorist' *Modern Motoring and Travel* February 1962 (London: Country and Sporting Publications, 1962).

Grant, Gregor *British Sports Cars* (London: G. T. Foulis & Co. Ltd, 1947).

Green, Andrea 'Woman in a Wolseley' *Brooklands Society Gazette* 18:4 1993.

Greville, Beatrice Violet, Lady (ed.) *The Gentlewoman's Book of Sports* (London: Henry, 1892).

Greville, Beatrice Violet, Lady (ed.) *The Gentlewoman in Society* (London: Henry, 1892).

Greville, Beatrice Violet, Lady (ed.) *Ladies in the Field: Sketches of Sport* (London: Ward and Downey Ltd, 1894).

Groves, Mrs Lilly FRGS (ed.) Illustrated by Percy Macquoid *Dance* (London: Longmans, Green and Company, 1895).

Grozier, J. A. *Round the World With Nelly Bly: A Novel and Fascinating Game with Plenty of Excitement on Land and Sea* (New York: McLoughlin Bros. 1890).

Gurr, Henry *The Champion Handbooks: Swimming* (London: Darton and Hodge, 1866).

Gwyn Jeffreys, Dorothy, Winifred Gwyn Jeffreys and E. M. Thompson *Hockey Jottings* (unpublished, c. 1898).

Gwyn-Jeffreys, Winifred *A Victorian Nursery* (Cheltenham: Hayman and Son Ltd, 1970).

Harding, Aileen 'There's Fun In Fencing' in Carolyn Dingle (ed.) *News Chronicle: Sport for Girls* (London: News Chronicle Publications Department, 1951).

Harmsworth, Alfred C. (ed.) *Motors and Motor Driving* (London and Bombay: Longmans, Green and Company, 1902).

Hastings Swimming Baths 'The Beckwith's Farewell' Hastings Swimming Baths 3 September 1888, shelfmark Evan.1667 The British Library, London.

Hawes, Joan *Women's Test Cricket: The Golden Triangle 1934–1984* (London: The Book Guild, 1987).

Henry, Alan 'Pat Moss: Obituary' *The Guardian* 27 October 2008.

Heyhoe-Flint, Rachael and Netta Rheinberg *Fair Play: The Story of Women's Cricket* (London: Angus and Robertson, 1976).

Hicks, William John 'What Games Do Girls Like Best?' in Carolyn Dingle (ed.) *News Chronicle: Sport for Girls* (London: News Chronicle Publications Department, 1951).

Hide, Mollie 'Girl Cricketers' in John St John (ed.) *The Young Cricketer: Approved By The MCC* (London: Naldrett Press, 1950).

Hoffman, Jeane 'Stella Walsh, 47—And She Still Won 100 Events Last Year' *World Sports: The International Magazine* June 1958 (London: Country and Sporting Publications, 1958).

Hoggan, Mrs MD *Swimming and Its Relation to the Health of Women: Read Before the Women's Union Swimming Club at 36 Great Queen Street WC 21 April 1879* (London: The Women's Printing Society Ltd, 1879).

Hopkins, Mary Sergent (ed.) *The Wheelwoman* July 1896.

Howcroft, W. J. 'Swimming' in James Rivers (ed.) *The Sports Book 2* (London: MacDonald and Company, 1948).

Hughes, Mark 'Racing On A Shoestring' *Historic Race and Rally* 4:1 March 1993 (London: Bookman Press, 1993).

Hughes, Thomas *The Whole Art of Swimming* (London: W. Lewis, 1820).

ICI 'Terylene: The Clothes that Give You Tennis Terylinity' *Vanity Fair* April 1956 (London: The National Magazine Co. Ltd, 1956).

Jarvis, John Arthur *The Art of Swimming: With Notes on Polo and Aids to Life Saving* (London: Hutchinson and Co, 1902).

Jeune, Lady and Baron Zuylen de Nyvelt 'Dress for Motoring' in Alfred C. Harmsworth (ed.) *Motors and Motor Driving* (London and Bombay: Longmans, Green and Company, 1902).

Johns, Mary 'Nomads in the Alps' *Modern Motoring and Travel* February 1962 (London: Sporting Handbooks, 1962).

Joubert, Edgar 'Madame Ostermeyer: Top Notch Athlete, Top Note Pianist' *World Sports: The International Sports Magazine* July 1949 (London: Country and Sporting Publications, 1949).

Joy, Nancy *Maiden Over* (London: Sporting Handbooks, 1950).

Kellermann, Annette *How to Swim* (London: George H. Doran Company, 1918).

Knighton, M. 'Development of Soccer for Girls' *The American Physical Education Review* 34 1929.

Lafitte, Pierre & Company *La Vie Au Grande Air* No 649 25 February (Paris: Pierre Lafitte & Company, 1911).

Lafitte, Pierre & Company *La Vie Au Grande Air* No. 665 17 June (Paris: Pierre Lafitte & Company, 1911).

Lambert-Chambers, Dorothea (Lady Champion 1903, 1904, 1906) *Lawn Tennis for Ladies* (London: Methuen & Co. Ltd, 1910).

Lambretta *Innocenti* poster number 698 (London: George Harvey Collection, 1957).

Larson, Roly 'The Great Amateur Sham' *Lilliput: A Man's Magazine* (London: Hulton 1956).

Leahy, 'Seargeant' (sic) and Mrs Oliphant *The Art of Swimming in the Eton Style* (London: Macmillan & Company, 1875).

Lebeaud *The Principles of the Art of Modern Horsemanship for Ladies and Gentlemen: In Which All Late Improvements Are Applied to Practice* (Philadelphia: E. L. Carey & A. Hart, 1833).

Legh, Alice 'Ladies' Archery' in C. J. Longman and H. Walrond (eds.) *Archery: The Badminton Library of Sports and Pastimes* (London: Longmans, Green and Company, 1894.

Levit, John 'Islington: Highbury household schedule number: 233 piece: 196 folio: 22' *1901 England Census:* 'Islington: Highbury p. 36 http://ancestry.co.uk accessed 29 June 2012.

Levitt, Dorothy *The Woman and the Car: A Chatty Little Handbook for All Women Who Motor Or Who Want to Motor* (Hugh Evelyn: London, 1909).

Light, Hilda 'Women's Hockey' *Manchester Guardian* 12 Oct 1938.

Light, Hilda 'The Development of Women's Hockey' in Patrick Rowley (ed.) *The Book of Hockey* (London: MacDonald, 1964).

Lines Brother's Limited 'The Largest Exhibit in the Fair' *British Industries Fair Pamphlet February 1931* (London: British Industries Fair, 1931).

Lines Brother's Limited 'Record Breaking: Lines Brothers Motors Move Rapidly' *Games and Toys September 1931* (London: Games and Toys Industry Assocation, 1931).

Linney, E. J. *A History of the Game of Bowls* (London: T. Werner Laurie Ltd, 1933).

London, Aubrey 'Greyhound Racing' in James Rivers (ed.) *The Sports Book* (London: MacDonald and Company, 1946).

Londonus 'Super Sportswear' *Vanity Fair* May 1955 (London: The National Magazine Co. Ltd, 1955).

Lowther, Toupie 'Ladies' Play' in Reginald Frank and Hugh Lawrence Doherty *Lawn Tennis* (New York: The Baker and Taylor Company, 1903).

Lucozade 'Pat Smythe . . . Another Lucozade Enthusiast' *World Sports* September 1955 (London: Country and Sporting Publications, 1955).

Lurani, Count Giovanni (translated John Eason-Gibson) *Racing Round the World 1920–1935* (London: G. T. Foulis & Co. Ltd, 1936).

Lyndon, Barré *Combat: A Motor Racing History* (London: Heinemann Ltd, 1933).

McCormick, Patricia *Lady Bullfighter: The Autobiography of the North American Matador* (London: Robert Hale Ltd, 1956).

McGhee, Joe and Jean Scrivens 'Two More Athletes Disclose "Our Plans for Melbourne"' *World Sports: Official Magazine of the British Olympic Association* May 1956 (London: Country and Sporting Publications, 1956).

McKelvie, Roy 'Table Tennis' in James Rivers (ed.) *The Sports Book* (London: MacDonald and Company, 1946).

McWhirter, Norris '"Ballerina" Nina' *World Sports: International Sports Magazine* September 1955 (London: Country and Sporting Publications, 1955).

Margot, Lady Davison 'Miss Edith Thompson Remembered' *The Times* 1 September 1961.

Markham, Beryl *West With the Night: The Classic of African Exploration* (London: Virago second edition 1984; originally published 1942).

Marriott, Alice Lee *Hell On Horses and Women* (Norman: University of Oklahoma Press, 1953).

May, C. A. N. *Shelsley Walsh: England's International Speed Hill-Climb* (London: G. T. Foulis & Company Ltd, 1946).

May, Dennis '1938: Mrs Hawkes looks back' *Speed* July 1938.

May, Dennis '130 mph Plus' *The Motor* 9 November 1960.

Mayer, Sarah *Letters to G. Koizumi February 1934-January 1935* Richard Bowen files, University of Bath.

Mead, Theodore *Horsemanship for Women* (New York: Harper & Brothers, 1887).

Meisl, Willy '"The Babe": A Genius With An Infinite Capacity for Taking Pains' *World Sports: Official Magazine of the British Olympic Association* November 1956 (London: Country and Sporting Publications, 1956).

Meisl, Dr Willy 'Happy Birthday Wimbledon: The Crowning Glory' *World Sports* June 1957 (London: Country and Sporting Publications, 1957).

Melville, Whyte; Kate Coventry Surtee and the Honourable Crasher *The Art of Teaching in Sport: Designed as a Prelude to a Set of Toys for Enabling Ladies to Instil the Rudiments of Spelling, Reading, Gramma, and Arithmetic under the idea of Amusements* (John Marshall: London, 1770).

Mérillon, M. D. (ed.) *Expostition Universelle Internationale de 1900 À Paris: Concours Internationaux D'Exercises Physiques et de Sports* (Paris: Ministére Du Commerce, De L'Industrie Des Postes et Des Télégraphes, 1901).

Messerli, Dr F. M. *La Participation Fèminine Aux Jeux Olympiques Modernes* (Édité par le Comité International Olympique Lausanne: An 1 de la XVme Olympide, 1952).

Mitchell, David *Women On the Warpath* (London: Jonathan Cape, 1966).

M. L. T. 'Lady Competition Drivers' *Motor Sport incorporating Speed and The Brooklands Gazette* Teesdale: London 37:7 July 1961.

Montagu, Lord (ed.) 'Mrs Maurice Helwett, the First Englishwoman to Gain an Aviator's Certificate' *The Car: A Journal of Travel by Land, Sea and Air (Illustrated)* 497:29 November 1911 (London: Countryside Publishing, 1911).

Moran, Gussy 'Making A Job of It' in Carolyn Dingle (ed.) *News Chronicle: Sport for Girls* (London: News Chronicle Publications Department, 1951).

Neubauer, Alfred *Speed Was My Life* (London: Barrif and Rockliff, 1960).

Noel, Susan 'Women in Sport' *World Sports: The International Sports Magazine* July 1949 (London: County and Sporting Publications, 1949).

Noel, Susan 'Veronica-Story of A Girl Who Was Started On the Road To Golf Fame By Illness' *World Sports: Official Magazine of the British Olympic Association* April 1956 (London: Country and Sporting Publications, 1956).

Noel, Susan 'The Gibson Girl' *World Sports Magazine: The International Sports Magazine* November 1957 (London: Country and Sporting Publications, 1957).

Nomad 'My Notebook' *Yorkshire Sports* 8 January 1921.

Nomad 'My Notebook' *Yorkshire Sports* 11 June 1921.

Nomad 'My Notebook' *Yorkshire Sports* 10 December 1921.

Nottinghamshire Education Committee *Rural Schools Course for Twelve Year Olds November 1953* (Nottingham: Nottinghamshire Education Committee, 1953).

Obituaries 'Dr Arthur Wint' *Olympic Review* 303 January to February 1993.

Odhams *John Bull and Illustrated* 18 October 1958 (London: Odhams, 1958).

O'Donoghue, Nannie Power *Ladies On Horseback: Learning, Park-Riding and Hunting* (London: W. H. Allen & Company, 1881).

O'Donoghue, Nannie Power *Riding for Ladies: With Hints On the Stable* (London: W. Thacker, 1887).

Olliff, John 'What's Wrong With British Tennis?' *World Sports Magazine* May 1951 (London: Country and Sporting Publications, 1951).

Organising Committee for the XIV Olympiad *The Official Report of the Organising Committee for the XIV Olympiad* Part One and Part Two (London: Organising Committee for the XIV Olympiad, 1948).

O' Sullivan, Ronnie 'Reader's Q and A with "Rocket" Ronnie O' Sullivan' in *SkySports Magazine* October 2009 (Middlesex: BSkyB Publications Ltd, 2009).

Owen, Wendy *Kicking against Tradition* (Gloucester: Tempus, 2005).

Paige, Marian G. 'Maxwell: Votes for Women' *The Motor* 27 July 1915.

Paige, Marian G. '£20, 000 to be invested in Light Cars' *The Light Car* 6 December 1916.

Palethorpe, Dawn *My Horses and I* (London: Country Life, 1956).

Pallett, George *Women's Athletics* (Dulwich. London: The Normal Press Ltd, 1955).

Pearce, Paulin Huggett *The Warriors' Swimming Book and Ladies' Guide: Including the Poem on Waterloo; Queen Victoria's Reign; Death and Funeral of the Duke of Wellington etc in Two Parts* (London: T. H. Roberts, 1869).

Pennell Mrs Elizabeth Robins 'Cycling' in Beatrice Violet, Baroness Greville (ed.) *Ladies in the Field: Sketches of Sport* (London: Ward and Downey Ltd, 1894).

Perry, Fred *Fred Perry: An Autobiography* (London: Hutchinson, 1984).

Petre, Kay 'A Note from Mrs Petre' *The Radiator* November 1939.

Petre, Kay 'My Motor Racing' in The Publication Committee (eds.) *The British Racing Drivers' Club Silver Jubilee Book* (London: The British Racing Drivers' Club, 1952).

Photogravure Section 'Olympic girls' *Chicago Tribune* 16 July 1922.

Picture Post *Picture Post: Hulton's National Weekly Olympic Games Souvenir Special 14 August 1948* 40:7 (London; Hulton Press, 1948).

Pike, Jim 'Darts' in James Rivers (ed.) *The Sports Book* (London: MacDonald and Co., 1946).

Piley, P. G. 'The Silent Games' *World Sports: Official Magazine of the British Olympic Association* December 1956 (London: Country and Sporting Publications, 1956).

Plomley, Roy and Arthur Wint *Desert Island Discs: Olympian Arthur Wint* BBC Radio 4 Friday 22 May 1953 http://www.bbc.co.uk/radio4/features/desert-island-discs/castaway/e344f893 accessed 10 November 2012.

Plowden, William *The Motor Car and Politics 1896–1970* (London: The Bodley Head, 1971).

Pollard, Marjorie *Cricket for Women and Girls* (London: Hutchinson, 1934).

Pollard 'Round-up' *Women's Cricket* 5:4 August 1934.

Pollard, Marjorie *Australian Women's Cricket Team in England 1937: A Diary* (Letchworth: Pollard Publications, 1937).

Pollard, Marjorie *Fifty Years of Women's Hockey: The Story ff the Foundation and Development ff the All England Women's Hockey Association 1895–1945* (Letchworth: St. Christopher Press, 1945).

Pollard, Marjorie 'This Year of Fulfilment' in Carolyn Dingle (ed.) *News Chronicle: Sport for Girls* (London: News Chronicle Publications Department, 1951).

Pollard, Marjorie *Hilda M. Light: Her Life and Times* (London: All England Women's Hockey Association, 1972).

Powers, S. R. *Why Do Women Not Swim? Voices from Many Waters: Ladies' National Association for the Diffusion of Sanitary Knowledge* (London: Groombridge and Sons, 1859).

Rand, Mary *Mary Mary: Autobiography of an Olympic Champion* (London: Hodder and Stoughton, 1969).

Reynal, Eugene *Thoughts Upon Hunting Kit In a Series ff Nine Letters to a Friend* (Millbrook, New York : Privately printed for the author, 1934).

Richardson, Mervyn *Horsemanship, or, The Art of Riding and Managing A Horse* (London: Longman, Brown, Green and Longmans, 1853).

Rowe, Diane and Rosalind 'Table Tennis Twins' in Carolyn Dingle (ed.) *News Chronicle: Sport for Girls* (London: News Chronicle Publications Department, 1951).

Rowell, Clothilde '"Our Ludy" Comes Home' *The Winthrop College News* 10:5 20 October 1922.

Royal Aquarium Westminster *Agnes Beckwith, the Greatest Lady Swimmer in the World Patronized by Their Royal Highnesses the Prince and Princess of Wales* c. 1885, shelfmark Evan.339 The British Library, London.

Rudd, Bevil 'Athletics' in James Rivers (ed.) *The Sports Book* (London: MacDonald and Company, 1946).

Rufflette 'Rufflette Curtain Track' *House Beautiful: Furniture Exhibition Number* February 1959 (London: House Beautiful and Samuel Stephens, 1959).

Sabretache *Stand To Your Horses; Being the Whole Art and Mystery of Horse-Back Riding* (London: Ocean Publshing Company, 1932).

Scott, Audrey *I Was a Hollywood Stunt Girl* (Philadelphia: Dorrance, 1969).

Sheddon, Lady Diana Maud Nina (FitzRey) *'To whom the goddess . . . ':Hunting and Riding for Women* (London: Hutchinson & Company, 1932).

Sheridan, Eileen *Wonder Wheels: The Autobiography of Eileen Sheridan* (London: Nicholas Kaye, 1956).

Sheridan, Eileen 'The Greatest Woman Cyclist Britain Has Produced' *World Sports: Official Magazine of the British Olympic Association* June 1956 (London: Country and Sporting Publications, 1956).

Somers, Florence A. *Principles of Women's Athletics* (New York: A. S. Barnes and Company, 1930).

Somerville, E. *Through Connemara In a Governess Cart* (London: W. H. Allen & Company, 1893).

Spalding, A. G. and Brothers 'We've Gone Almost Completely English' *International Federation of Women's Hockey Associations (IFWHA) Hockey Programme 10 October 1936* (Philadephia & New York: A. G Spalding and Brothers, 1936).

Stanley, Edward *The Young Horsewoman's Compendium of the Modern Art of Riding* (London: James Ridgway, 1827).

Steed, Charles (several years champion swimmer of England and Victoria) *Manual Swimming* (London: Lockwood and Company, 1867).

Stenner, Tom 'Speedway Racing' in James Rivers (ed.) *The Sports Book* (London: MacDonald and Company, 1946).

Sterry, Mrs Charlotte 'My Most Memorable Match' in Mrs Lambert Chambers *Lawn Tennis for Ladies* (London: Methuen & Company Ltd, 1910).

Strutt, Joseph and William Hone (eds.) *The Sports and Pastimes of the People of England; Including the Rural and Domestic Recreations, May Games, Mummeries, Shows, Processions, Pageants and Pompous Spectacles from the Earliest Period to the Present Time* (London: Thomas Tegg, 1845).

Stuart-Menzies, Mrs *Women In the Hunting Field* (London: Vinton, 1913).

Svenson, Sten '15,000 Gymnasts in Swedish Festival' *World Sports: The International Sports Magazine* July 1949 (London: Country and Sporting Publications, 1949).

The Sporting Life *Olympic Games of London 1908: A Complete Record with Photographs of Winners of the Olympic Games held at the Stadium, Shepherd's Bush London July 13–25* (London: The Sporting Life, 1908).

Tan-Sad *Tan-Sad: Pillion Riding Comfort and Safety Motor Cycle Series A* (Gloucester: Robert Opie Collection, Museum of Advertising and Packaging, undated).

Taylor, Fred *The Empire Shop* (London: Empire Marketing Board, c. 1926–1939).

The Daily Express *These Tremendous Years 1919–1938: A History in Photographs of Life and Events, Big and Little, in Britain and the World since the War* (London: Daily Express Publications, 1938).

The United States Field Hockey Association (USFHA) 'British Guiana Touring Team' *The Eagle* 3:1 September (Philadelphia: USFHA, 1939).

Thompson, Edith *Hockey as a Game for Women* (London: E. Arnold, 1905).

Thompson, Edith 'Hockey-The National Game for Women' *The Times* 14 January 1933.

Time Magazine 'Helen Newington Wills' *Time Magazine* 1 July 1929 http://www.time.com/time/covers/ accessed 20 August 2012.

Tompkins, E. S. *Speed Camera: The Amateur Photography of Motor Racing* (London: G. T. Foulis & Co. Ltd, 1946).

Tomkins, Nancy and Pat Ward *The Century Makers: A History of the All England Women's Hockey Association 1895–1995* (Shrewsbury: All England Women's Hockey Assocation, 1995).

Triumph *The Triumph Girl: Motor Cycle Series B* (Gloucester: Robert Opie Collection, Museum of Advertising and Packaging, undated).

Urquhart-Dykes, Ruth 'The 12-Hours Record at Brooklands' *Brooklands Society Gazette* 18:4 1993.

Vallet, L. *Seven Tinted Prints of Ladies In Riding Attire* (n.p., 1890).

Verne, Jules *Around the World in Eighty Days* (Philadelphia: Porter & Coates, 1873 originally published in France in 1872.

Vespa *Vespa* poster circa 1956 Robert Opie Collection, Museum of Advertising and Packaging, Gloucester 1956.

Villa, Leo *Life With the Speed King: World Record Breaking With Malcolm Campbell* (London: Marshall Harris & Baldwin, 1979).

Volkswagen 'Your Car Madam' *Motor Sport Incorporating Speed and The Brooklands Gazette* 37:7 July 1961 (Teesdale: London, 1961).

Walrond, Colonel H. 'Archery: The Royal Toxophilite Society' *British Olympic Association Yearbook 1914* (London: British Olympic Association, 1914).

Webb, Captain Matthew *Swimmers' Companion* (London: R. March and Company, circa 1877).

Webb, C. W. *An Historical Record of Nathaniel Corah & Sons Ltd. Manufacturers of Hosiery, Underwear and Outerwear* (St. Margaret's Works Leicester: N. Corah & Sons Ltd, 1948).

Webster, F. A. M. *Athletics of To-day for Women: History Development and Training* (London: Frederick Warne, 1930).

Wellington, Margaret 'Swimming to be a Champion-7 Days a Week' in Carolyn Dingle (ed.) *News Chronicle: Sport for Girls* (London: News Chronicle Publications Department, 1951).

White Heather Club *Menu Card for the 40th Anniversary Dinner of the White Heather Club 1927* object number TN.2008.411 MCC Museum Lord's, London.

Wisdom, Elsie 'Woman on the Track: Mrs Wisdom Talks to Sam Sloan' *The Auto Motor Journal 3* March 1931.

Wisdom, Elsie 'Tete a Tete: What Do Women Motorists Think of the 1934 Models?' *The Autocar* 6 October 1933.

Willard, Francis E. *A Wheel Within A Wheel: How I Learned to Ride the Bicycle* (London: Hutchinson and Company, 1895).

Wills, Helen *Self Portrait* (Los Angeles: Olympic Arts Competition and Exhibition, 1932) featured in Graham Budd (ed.) *Olympic Memorabilia* (London: Graham Budd Auctions and Sotheby's, 24–26 July 2012).

Wills, Helen *Tennis* (New York and London: Charles Scribner and Son, 1928).

Wills, Helen *Fifteen, Thirty: The Story of a Tennis Player* (New York and London: Charles Scribner and Son, 1938).

Wills, Helen and Robert William Murphy *Death Serves an Ace* (New York: Charles Scribner and Son, 1939).

Wilson, Helen *My First Eighty Years* (Hamilton: Paul's Book Arcade, 1951).

Wolf Motorcycles *Wolf Motorcycle Postcard circa 1932* The Robert Opie Collection Museum of Advertising and Packaging Gloucester.

Wollstonecraft, Mary *A Vindication of the Rights of Woman* 1792 available to download at Project Gutenberg Literary Archive Foundation http://www.gutenberg.org/etext/3420 accessed 14 August 2009.

Women's Amateur Athletics Association *Fifteenth Annual Coronation Championships Programme, White City Stadium Shepherds Bush 7 August 1937* (London: Women's Amateur Athletics Association, 1937).

Women's Cross Country and Road Walking Association *The Grange Farm, Winton Worsley Womens' Senior Cross County Championship Programme 5 March 1949* (Birmingham: Women's Cross Country and Road Walking Association, 1949).

Women's Amateur Athletics Association *International Athletic Match Programme White City Stadium London 20 August 1949* (London: Women's Amateur Athletics Association, 1949).

Women's Amateur Athletics Association *WAAA and Women's National Cross County Championship (under WAA rules) Programme Parliament Hill Secondary School Hampstead 4 March 1950* London: Women's Amateur Athletics Association, 1950).

Women's Amateur Athletics Association *Junior and Intermediate Track and Field Championships Programme The Alexander Sports Ground Perry Barr Birmingham 9 July 1955* (London: Women's Amateur Athletics Association, 1955).

Zaharias, 'Babe' Didrikson *This Life I've Led: The Autobiography of 'Babe' Didrikson Zaharias* (London: Robert Hale, 1956).

B SECONDARY SOURCES

Adams, Carly 'Fighting for Acceptance: Sigfrid Edström and Avery Brundage: Their Efforts to Shape and Control Women's Participation in the Olympic Games' in Kevin B. Wamsley, Robert K. Barney and Scott G. Martyn (eds.) *Global Nexus Engaged: Sixth International Symposium for Olympic Research 2002* (International Centre for Olympic Studies: University of Western Ontario Canada, 2002).

Adams, Mary Louise 'From Mixed-Sex Sport to Sport for Girls: The Feminization of Figure Skating' in Carol Osborne and Fiona Skillen (eds.) *Women and Sport: Special Edition of Sport in History* 30:2 2010.

Adams, Mary Louise *Artistic Impressions: Figure Skating, Masculinity and the Limits of Sport* (Toronto, Buffalo and London: University of Toronto Press, 2011).

Allison, Lincoln *Amateurism in Sport: An Analysis and a Defence* (London: Frank Cass, 2001).

Anderson, Benedict *Imagined Communities: Reflections on the Origin and Spread of Nationalism* (London; New York: Verso, 1983, revised edition 2006).

Archetti, Eduardo P. *Masculinities: Football, Polo and the Tango in Argentina* (London: Berg, 1999).

Armytage, Marcus 'Diary: Helen Johnson-Houghton, First Lady to Train a Classic Winner Approaches Her 100th Birthday' *The Telegraph* http://www.telegraph.co.uk/sport/horseracing/ accessed 1 December 2012.

Armstrong, Madie *Breaking the Shackles of Convention: Elizabeth Le Blond in the Mountains (1880–1920)* unpublished PhD, Leicester: De Montfort University 2013.

Arnold, Rebecca *The American Look: Sportswear, Fashion and the Image of Women In 1930s and 1940s New York* (London & New York: I. B.Tauris, 2009).

Arrowsmith, Rupert *Modernism and the Museum: Asian, African, and Pacific Art and the London Avant-Garde* (Oxford: Oxford University Press, 2011).

Ashton, Rosemary 'Marian Evans [George Eliot] (1819–1880)' *Oxford Dictionary of National Biography* Oxford University Press http://www.oxforddnb.com/view/article/6794 accessed 12 December 2012.

Bailey, Peter *Leisure and Class in Victorian England* (London: Routledge, 1978).

Bailey, Paul and Wray Vamplew *100 Years of Physical Education* (London: Physical Education Association Centenary Publication, 1999).

Baines, Paul 'William Shenstone (1714–1763)'*Oxford Dictionary of National Biography* Oxford University Press http://www.oxforddnb.com/view/article/25321 accessed 29 December 2012.

Bairner, Alan *Sport, Nationalism, and Globalization: European and North American Perspectives* (Albany: State University of New York Press, 2001).

Baker, Anne Pimlott 'Cuthbert Collingwood [Teddy] Tinling (1910–1990)' *Oxford Dictionary of National Biography* Oxford University Press http://www.oxforddnb.com/view/article/40669 accessed 15 January 2013.

Baldwin, Jayne *West Over the Waves: The Final Flight of Elsie Mackay* (Dumfries & Galloway: Wigtown Publishers, 2008).

Bale, John *Roger Bannister and the Four-Minute Mile: Sports Myth and Sports History* (New York and London: Routledge, 2004).

Bale, John Mette K. Christensen and Gertrude Pfister (eds.) *Writing Lives in Sport: Biographies, Life-Histories and Methods* (Langelandsgade: Aarhus, 2004).

Bancroft, James 'Sybil Fenton 'Queenie' Newall 1854–1929' *Oxford Dictionary of National Biography* Oxford University Press www.oxforddnb.com accessed 24 April 2012.

Bandy, Susan and Anne Darden *Crossing Boundaries: An International Anthology Women Experiences In Sport* (Champaign, Il: Human Kinetics, 1999).

Bandy, Susan 'Shared Femininities and Shared Feminisms: Women's Sporting Magazines of the Late 19th and Early 20th Centuries' in Annette R. Hofmann and Else Trangbaek (eds.) *International Perspectives on Sporting Women in Past and Present* (Denmark: Institute of Exercise and Social Sciences University of Copenhagen, 2005).

Bannister, Roger *The First Four Minutes* (Stroud, Gloucestershire: Putnam, 1955 reprinted 2004).

Barney, Robert K. 'The Olympic Games in Modern Times: An Overview' in Gerald P. Schaus and Stephen R. Wenn (eds) *Onward to the Olympics: Historical Perspectives on The Olympic Games* (Waterloo, Ontario: Wilfred Laurier University Press, 2007).

Barney, Robert K. 'The Genesis of Sacred Fire in Olympic Ceremony: A New Inter-pretation' in Hai Ren, Lamartine Da Costa, Ana Miragaya and Niu Jing (eds.) *Olympic Studies Reader 1* (Beijing, China and Rio De Janeiro, Brazil: Beijing Sport University and Universidade Gama Filho, 2009).

Barrett, John and Alan Little *Wimbledon: Ladies' Singles Champions 1884–2004* (London: Wimbledon Lawn Tennis Museum, 2005).

Bartlett, Robert 'Failed Bids and Losing Cities: Adelaide's Failure to Secure the 1962 British Empire and Commonwealth Games' *Sporting Traditions* 15:2 May 1999.

Beamish, Rob 'Totalitarian Regimes and Cold War Sport' in Stephen Wagg and David L. Andrews (eds.) *East Plays West: Sport and the Cold War* (London and New York: Routledge, 2006).

Beardwood, Lynette 'Muriel Annie Thompson (1875–1939)' *Oxford Dictionary of National Biography* Oxford University Press http://www.oxforddnb.com/view/article/68164 accessed 12 January 2013.

Beaumont, Jacqueline 'Dorothea Beale (1831–1906)' *Oxford Dictionary of National Biography* Oxford University Press http://www.oxforddnb.com/view/article/30655 accessed 10 March 2012.

Beck, Peter J. 'Britain and The Olympic Games: London 1908, 1948, 2012' *Journal of Sport and History* 39:1 2012.

Beckett, Ian F. W. 'William Henry Grenfell, Baron Desborough (1855–1945)' *Oxford Dictionary of National Biography* Oxford University Press http://www.oxforddnb.com/view/article/33566 accessed 4 January 2013.

Beeston, Eric 'Winsome Winnie' *LifeTimesLink: Sharing Salford's Fantastic Story* 26 (Salford: Salford Museums and Art Gallery, 2009).

Belton, Brian *Fay Taylour: Queen of Speedway* (High Wycombe, Buckingham-shire: Panther Publishing, 2006).

Bence Jones, Mark *Twilight of the Ascendancy* (London: Constable, 1987).

Benn, Tansin and Ida Webb 'Rhoda Anstey (1865–1936)' *Connecting Histories Project* and *Birmingham Stories*: The School of Education at Birmingham University http://www.connectinghistories.org.uk/ accessed 10 August 2009.

Bennett, Daphne *Emily Davies and The Liberation of Women* (London: André Deutsch, 1990).

Bennett, Victoria *Invisible Women/Hidden Voices: Women Writing On Sport In the Twentieth Century* unpublished PhD thesis De Montfort University, Leic-ester 2003.

Biddle-Perry, Geraldine 'Fair Play and Fascism: The Development of British Olym-pic Team Uniforms' in Martin Polley (ed.) *Britain, Britons and the Olympic Games: A Special Edition of Sport in History* 32:2 2012.

Bier, Lisa *Fighting the Current: The Rise of American Women's Swimming 1870–1926* (New York: McFarland and Company, 2011).

Bijkerk, Anthony 'Xenia Stad-De Jong (1922–2012): Obituary' *Journal of Olym-pic History* 20: 2 2012.

Billig, Michael *Banal Nationalism* (London: Sage, 1995).

Bilsborough, Peter 'John Arthur Jarvis (1872–1933)' *Oxford Dictionary of National Biography* www.oxforddnb.com/view/article/65070 accessed 15 October 2011.

Blain, N. and R. Boyle 'Battling along the Boundaries: Marking of Scottish Identity in Sports Journalism' in Grant Jarvie and Graham Walker (eds.) *Scottish Sport In the Making of the Nation: Ninety-Minute Patriots?* (London: Leicester Uni-versity Press, 1994).

Boas, G. C. rev. H. C. G. Matthew 'Peter John Locke King (1811–1885) *Oxford Dic-tionary of National Biography* Oxford University Press http://www.oxforddnb.com/view/article/64231 accessed 20 June 2012.

Boddy, Kasia *Boxing: A Cultural History* (London: Reaktion Books, 2008).

Bolz, Daphné 'Olympic Heritage–An International Legacy: The Invention of the Modern Olympic Stadium from Coubertin to 1948' in Jeffrey Hill, Kevin Moore and Jason Wood *Sport, History and Heritage: Studies in Public Representation* (Woodbridge, Suffolk and Rochester, New York: Boydell and Brewer Ltd, 2012).

Booth, Doug *The Field: Truth and Fiction in Sport History* (London and New York: Routledge, 2005).

Borish, Linda J. 'Women Sport and the American Jewish Identity in the Late Nineteenth and Early Twentieth Centuries' in Timothy Chandler and Tara Magdalinski (eds.) *With God on Their Side: Sport in the Service of Religion* (London: Routledge, 2002).

Boutle, Ian 'Speed Lies in the Lap of the English': Motor Records, Masculinity and the Nation, 1907–1914 *Twentieth Century British History* published online January 28 2012 doi:10.1093/tcbh/hwr068 accessed 31 January 2012.

Bouzanquet, Jean-François *Fast Ladies: Female Racing Drivers 1888–1970* (Dorchester: Veloce, 2009).

Bowen, Richard 'Koizumi, Gunji (1885–1965)' *Oxford Dictionary of National Biography* Oxford University Press http://www.oxforddnb.com/view/article/75932 accessed 4 September 2012.

Boyce, D. George 'Alfred Charles William Harmsworth, Viscount Northcliffe (1865–1922)' *Oxford Dictionary of National Biography* Oxford University Press http://www.oxforddnb.com/view/article/33717 accessed 9 January 2013.

Brace, Reginald 'Slazenger's Centenary' in John Barrett and Lance Tinjay (eds.) *Slazenger's World of Tennis 1981: The Official Yearbook of the International Tennis Federation* (London: Slazenger's/ Queen Anne Press, 1981).

Bradbury, Jonathan 'Dame Enid Mary Russell-Smith (1903–1989)' *Oxford Dictionary of National Biography* Oxford University Press http://www.oxforddnb.com/view/article/65870 accessed 4 September 2012.

Braithwaite, Brian *Women's Magazines: The First 300 Years* (London: P. Owen, 1995).

Braybon, Gail *Women Workers in the First World War* (London: Croom Helm, 1981).

Braybon, Gail and Penny Summerfield *Out of the Cage: Women's Experiences in Two World Wars* (London: Pandora, 1987).

Breedon, Piers *The Motoring Century: The Story of the Royal Automobile Club* (London: Bloomsbury Publishing, 1997).

Brennan, Patrick *The Munitionettes: A History of Women's Football in North East England during the Great War* (Tyne and Wear: Donmouth Publishing, 2007).

British Olympic Association *Chasing Gold: Centenary of the British Olympic Association* (London: Getty Images, 2005).

Brooks Auctions 'Frederick Gordon Crosby *The MG Girl* advertisement, watercolour and charcoal-cover artwork for *The Autocar* 29 April 1932' *Brooks Auctions Motor Sport Catalogue 1990* (London: Brooks, 1990).

Brown Kenneth D. *The British Toy Business: A History since 1700* (London and Rio Grande: The Hambledon Press, 1996).

Bryant, M. A. 'Albert George Hill (1889–1969)' *Oxford Dictionary of National Biography* Oxford University Press http://www.oxforddnb.com/view/article/65170 accessed 22 October 2012.

Buchanan, Ian *British Olympians: A Hundred Years of Gold Medallists* (London: Guinness Publishing, 1991).

Buchanan, Ian 'Kinuye Hitomi: Asia's First Female Olympian' *Journal of Olympic History* 8:3 2000.

Buchanan, Ian and Wolf Lyberg 'The Biographies of All IOC Members Part XI' *Journal of Olympic History* 20:2 2012.

Budd, Graham 'Lots 399 to 417: Helen Orr Gordon 1948–1956' *Graham Budd Auction Catalogue GB21* (London: Graham Budd Auctions, 2012.

Bullock, John *Fast Women: The Drivers Who Changed the Face of Motor Racing* (London: Robson Books, 2002).

Burke, Peter *A Social History of Workplace Australian Football 1860–1939* unpublished PhD Royal Melbourne Institute of Technology University Melbourne, 2008.

Burman, Barbara 'Racing Bodies: Dress and Pioneer Women Aviators and Racing Drivers' *Women's History Review* 9:2 2000.

Burscough, Margaret *The Horrockses: Cotton Kings of Preston* (Preston: Carnegie Publishing, 2004).

Caine, Barbara 'Charlotte Maria Shaw Mason (1842–1923)' *Oxford Dictionary of National Biography* Oxford University Press http://www.oxforddnb.com/view/article/37743 accessed 4 January 2013.

Calder, Angus 'Nancy Anderson Long Riach (1927–1947)' *Oxford Dictionary of National Biography* Oxford University Press http://www.oxforddnb.com/view/article/65073 accessed 17 November 2012.

Campbell Warner, Patricia *When the Girls Came Out to Play* (Amerhurst and Boston: University of Massachusetts Press, 2006).

Carling, Will and Robert Heller *The Way to Win: Strategies for Success in Business and Sport* (London: Little Brown and Company, 1995).

Carpentier, Florence and Pierre Lefèvre 'The Modern Olympic Movement, Women's Sport and the Social Order During the Inter-war Period' *The International Journal of the History of Sport* 23:7 2006.

Carter, Neil *Medicine, Sport and the Body: A Historical Perspective* (London and New York: Bloomsbury Academic, 2012).

Cashman, Richard and Amanda Weaver *Wicket Women: Cricket and Women in Australia* (Kensington: New South Wales University Press, 1991).

Chessum, Lorna *From Immigrants to Ethnic Minority: Making Black Community in Britain* (Aldershot: Ashgate, 2000).

Clarsen, Georgine *Eat My Dust: Early Women Motorists* (Baltimore, Maryland: Johns Hopkins University Press, 2008.

Clayton-Gray, Frances and Yannick Rice Lamb *Born to Win: The Authorized Biography of Althea Gibson* (New York: John Wiley and Sons Ltd., 2004).

Cockayne, Michael *The Evolution and Development of Modern Sport in Altrincham and Its Immediate Surrounds circa 1850–1914* (unpublished MA thesis, Leicester: De Montfort University, 2008).

Colley, Ann C. *Victorians in the Mountains: Sinking the Sublime* (Burlington and Surrey: Ashgate, 2010).

Colley, Linda *Britons—Forging the Nation 1707–1837* (London: Pimlico, 2003).

Collins, Tony and Wray Vamplew *Mud, Sweat and Beers: A Cultural History of Sport and Alcohol* (Oxford and New York: Berg, 2002).

Collins, Tony *Rugby's Great Split: Class, Culture and the Origins of Rugby League Football* (London: Cass, 1998; new and expanded edition London: Routledge, 2006).

Collins, Tony *Rugby League in Twentieth Century Britain* (London: Routledge, 2006).

Collins, Tony *A Social History of English Rugby Union* (London: Routledge, 2009).

Corley, T. A. B. 'Thomas Holloway (1800–1883)' *Oxford Dictionary of National Biography* Oxford University Press http://www.oxforddnb.com/view/article/13577 accessed 12 December 2012.

Coopey, Richard Sean O'Connell and Dilwyn Porter *Mail Order Retailing in Britain: A Business and Social History* (Oxford: Oxford University Press, 2005).

Coutts, Elizabeth 'Frances Mary Buss (1827–1894)' *Oxford Dictionary of National Biography* Oxford University Press http://www.oxforddnb.com/view/article/37249 accessed 10 March 2012.

Couturier 'Considering the Sportswoman, 1924 to 1936: A Content Analysis' *Sport History Review* 41 2010.

Couturier, Lynn E. 'Dissenting Voices: The Discourse of Competition in *The Sportswoman*' *Journal of Sport History* 39:2 Summer 2012.

Cowe, Eric *Early Women's Athletics: Statistics and History, Volume One* (Bingley, Eric Cowe Publications, 1999).

Cox, Howard and Simon Mowatt 'Vogue in Britain: Authenticity and the Creation of Competitive Advantage in the UK Magazine Industry' *Business History* 54:1 2012.

Crawford, Elizabeth *The Women's Suffrage Movement: A Reference Guide 1866–1928* (London and New York: Routledge, 2001).

Crawford, Elizabeth and Jill Liddington 'If Women Do Not Count, Neither Shall They Be Counted': Suffrage, Citizenship and the Battle for the 1911 Census' *History Workshop Journal* http://hwj.oxfordjournals.org/hwj.dbq064 accessed 29 June 2012.

Crawford, Scott A.G.M. 'Sir Malcolm Campbell (1885–1948)' *Oxford Dictionary of National Biography* Oxford University Press http://www.oxforddnb.com/view/article/32271 accessed 5 September 2012.

Creedon, Pamela 'Women in Toyland: A Look in American Newspaper Sports Journalism' in Pamela J. Creedon (ed.) *Women Sport and Media: Challenging Gender Values* (London: Sage, 1994).

Creese, Mary 'Dame Helen Charlotte Isabella Gwynne-Vaughan (1879–1967)' *Oxford Dictionary of National Biography* Oxford University Press http://www.oxforddnb.com/view/article/33623 accessed 29 December 2012.

Crewe, Steve '*With Comradeship and Good Temper': A Cross-Sector Analysis of Company Welfare* unpublished PhD thesis, De Montfort University Leicester, 2013.

Cronin, Mike 'Arthur Elvin and the Dogs of Wembley' *The Sports Historian* 22:1 2002.

Cronin, Mike and Richard Holt 'The Globalisation of Sport' *History Today* 53: 7 July 2003.

Cronin, Mike and Mark Duncan, Paul Rouse *The GAA: A People's History* (Cork: The Collins Press, 2009).

Crouthamel, James *Bennett's New York Herald and the Rise of the Popular Press* (Syracuse, New York: Syracuse University Press, 1989).

Cunningham, Hugh *The Children of the Poor: Representations of Childhood since the Seventeenth Century* (Oxford: Blackwell, 1991).

Curthoys, Mark C. 'Maureen Angela Jane Gardner (1928–1974)' *Oxford Dictionary of National Biography* Oxford University Press http://www.oxforddnb.com/view/article/104312 accessed 6 November 2012.

Dahl, Roald *Matilda* (London: Puffin, 2007 originally published by Jonathan Cape 1988).

Daly, John 'A New Britannia in the Antipodes: Sport Class and Community in Colonial South Australia' in J.A Mangan (ed.) *Pleasure, Profit and Proselytism: British Culture and Sport at Home and Abroad 1700–1914* (London: Frank Cass, 1988).

Daniels, Stephanie and Anita Tedder '*A Proper Spectacle': Women Olympians 1900–1936* (Bedford: Zee Na Na Press, 2000).

Davenport, Joanna 'Monique Berlioux: Her Association with Three IOC Presidents' *Citius, Altius, Fortius* (became *Journal of Olympic History* in 1997) 4:3 1996.

Davies, Angela 'A Critical Perspective On British Social Surveys and Community Studies and Their Accounts of Married Life c. 1945–70' *Cultural and Social History* 6:1 2009.

Davies, Hunter *Boots, Balls and Haircuts* (London: Cassell Illustrated, 2003).

Dawson, Michael 'Acting Global, Thinking Local: "Liquid Imperialism" and the Multiple Meanings of the 1954 British Empire & Commonwealth Games' *The International Journal of the History of Sport* 23:1 February 2006.

Day, Dave '"A Modern Naiad": Nineteenth Century Female Professional Natationists' *Women's History Network Women and Leisure Conference* University of Staffordshire 8 November 2008.

Day, Dave *Coaching Practices and Coaching Lives In Nineteenth and Early Twentieth Century England* unpublished PhD thesis De Montfort University Leicester, 2008.

Day, Dave 'London Swimming Professors: Victorian Craftsmen and Aquatic Entrepreneurs' in Neil Carter (ed.) *Sport in History: Special Edition Coaching Cultures* 30:1 2010.

Day, Dave 'Frederick Edward Beckwith, (1821–1898)' *Oxford Dictionary of National Biography* Oxford University Press http://www.oxforddnb.com/view/article/102444 accessed 12 December 2012.

Day, Dave 'Walter Septimus Brickett (1865–1933)' *Oxford Dictionary of National Biography* Oxford University Press http://www.oxforddnb.com/view/article/102445 accessed 8 January 2013.

De Aragues, Richard *TT3D: Closer to the Edge* (London: Entertainment One, 2011).

De Coubertin, Pierre *Olympic Memoirs* (Lausanne: International Olympic Committee, 1997).

Dee, David '"Nothing Specifically Jewish in Athletics?": Sport, Physical Recreation and the Jewish Youth Movement in London 1895–1914' *The London Journal* 34:2 2010.

De Frantz, Anita 'Women's Participation in the Olympic Games: Lessons and Challenges for the Future' in International Olympic Committee *Final Report of the International Olympic Committee's 2nd IOC Conference on Women and Sport: New Perspectives for the XXI Century* (Paris: International Olympic Committee, 2000).

Dietschy, Paul *Histoire du Football* (Paris: Librairie Académique Perrin, 2010).

Doughan, David 'Muriel Lilah Matters-Porter (1877–1969)' *Oxford Dictionary of National Biography* Oxford University Press http://www.oxforddnb.com/view/article/63878 accessed 9 January 2013.

Douglas, Ed 'Eileen Healey: Obituary 1921–2010' *The Guardian* 22 November 2010.

Drazin, David *Croquet: A Bibliography of Specialist Books and Pamphlets Complete to 1997* (New Castle, Delaware and Winchester: Oak Knoll Press and St Paul's Bibliographies, 1999).

Drevon, André *Alice Milliat: La Pasionaria du Sport Feminine* (Paris: Vuibert, 2005).

Duval, Lynne 'The Development of Women's Track and Field in England: The Role of the Athletic Club, 1920s-1950s' *The Sports Historian* 21:1 2001.

Dyhouse, Carol *Students: A Gendered History* (London: Routledge, 2006).

Dyreson, Mark 'Icons of Liberty or Objects of Desire? American Women Olympians and the Politics of Consumption' *Journal of Contemporary History* 38:3 2003.

Dyreson, Mark 'Sport History and the History of Sport in North America' *Journal of Sport History* 34:3 Fall 2007.

Economic and Social Research Council *Women in Britain in the 1950s: Impact Report Details* http://www.esrc.ac.uk/my-esrc/grants/RES-451-26-0682/ accessed 21 November 2012.

Edelman, Robert *Serious Fun: A History of Spectator Sport in the USSR* (New York: Oxford University Press, 1993).

Edgerley, David 'How About Volunteering At the 1948 Oympics?' *Journal of Olympic History* 20:1 2012.

Edlin-White, Rowena *A Hundred Years Ago: The Beginnings of Girl Guiding in Nottinghamshire* (Nottingham: Smallprint, 2009).

Edwards, Owen Dudley 'Sir Arthur Ignatius Conan Doyle (1859–1930)' *Oxford Dictionary of National Biography* Oxford University Press http://www.oxforddnb.com/view/article/32887 accessed 9 January 2013.

Elias, Norbert et al. *The Civilizing Process: Sociogenetic and Psychogenetic Investigations* (Oxford: Blackwell, 2000).

Emery, Lynne 'An Examination of the 1928 Olympic 800m Race for Women' *NASSH Proocedings 1985* p. 30 http://www.la84foundation.org accessed 10 July 2012.

Emery, Lynne 'From Lowell Mills to the Halls of Fame: Industrial League Sport for Women' in D. Margaret Costa and Sharon R. Guthrie (eds.) *Women and Sport: Interdisciplinary Perspectives* (Champaign, Illinois: Human Kinetics, 1994).

Escott, Squadron Leader Beryl E. *Women In Air Force Blue: The Story of Women In the Royal Air Force from 1918 to The Present Day* (Northants: Patrick Stephens, 1989).

Evans, Richard 'Gussie Moran: Obituary' *The Guardian* 20 January 2013.

Fahie, Michael 'Dorothy Norman Spicer (1908–1946)' *Oxford Dictionary of National Biography* Oxford University Press http://www.oxforddnb.com/view/article/67672 accessed 21 January 2013.

Fielding, Steven (ed.) *The Labour Party: Socialism and Society since 1951* (Manchester: Manchester University Press, 1997).

Fletcher, Sheila *Women First: The Female Tradition in English Physical Education 1880–1980* (London: Frank Cass, 1984).

Fletcher, Sheila 'Martina Sofia Helena Bergman Österberg (1849–1915)' *Oxford Dictionary of National Biography* Oxford University Press http://www.oxforddnb.com/view/article/47656 accessed 13 December 2012.

Freer, Wendy *Women and Children of the Cut* (Derby: The Railway and Canal Historical Society, 1995).

Galvin, Robert and Mark Bushell *Football's Greatest Heroes: The National Football Museum Hall of Fame* (London: Robson Books, 2005).

Gardiner, Juliet *The Thirties: An Intimate History* (London: Harper Press, 2010).

Garfield, Simon *Our Hidden Lives: The Remarkable Diaries of Post War Britain* (London: Ebury Press, 2005).

Gauld, Graham *Reg Parnell: The Quiet Man Who Helped to Engineer Britain's Post-War Racing Revolution* (Yeovil, Somerset: Patrick Stephen Ltd, 1996).

Gilbert, David 'The Vicar's Daughter and the Goddess of Tennis: Cultural Geographies of Sporting Femininity and Bodily Practice in Edwardian Suburbia' *Cultural Geographies* 18:2 2011.

Gilles, Midge *Amy Johnson: Queen of the Air* (London: Butler and Tanner Ltd, 2003).

Gissendanner, Cindy Himes 'African American Women and Competitive Sport' in Susan Birrell and Cheryl Cole (eds.) *Women Sport and Culture* (Champaign, Illinois: Human Kinetics, 1994).

Godfrey, Emelyne 'Edward William Barton Wright (1860–1951)' *Oxford Dictionary of National Biography* Oxford University Press http://www.oxforddnb.com/view/article/103464 accessed 15 May 2012.

Gold, John and Margaret M. Gold 'Future Indefinite? London 2012, The Spectre of Retrenchment and the Challenge of Olympic Sports Legacy' *The London Journal* 34:2 July 2009.

Goodall, M. H. *Flying Start: Flying Schools and Clubs at Brooklands, 1910–1939* (Weybridge: Brooklands Museum Trust, 1995).

Gordon, Ian and Simon Inglis *Great Lengths: The Historic Indoor Swimming Pools of Britain* (London: English Heritage, 2009).

Graydon, Jan '"But It's More Than a Game, It's An Institution": Feminist Perspectives on Sport' *Feminist Review* 13 February 1983.

Griffin, Emma *Blood Sport, Hunting in Britain since 1066* (New Haven and London: Yale University Press, 2007).

Grimshaw, Anna (ed.) *The C. L. R. James Reader* (Oxford: Blackwell, 1992).

Gundle, Stephen *Glamour: A History* (Oxford: Oxford University Press, 2008).

Guttmann, Allen *Women's Sports: A History* (New York: Columbia University Press, 1991).

Guttmann, Allen *From Ritual to Record: The Nature of Modern Sports* (New York: Columbia University Press, 2004, originally published 1978).

Guttmann, Allen 'Historical Vicissitudes' in Annette R. Hofmann and Else Trangbaek (eds.) *International Perspectives on Sporting Women in Past and Present* (Denmark: Institute of Exercise and Social Sciences University of Copenhagen, 2005).

Halberstam, Judith *Female Masculinity* (Durham, North Carolina: Duke University Press, 1998).

Hall, M. Ann *The Grads Are Playing Tonight: The Story of the Edmonton Commercial Graduates Basketball Club* (Edmonton: The University of Alberta Press, 2011).

Hall, Radclyffe *The Well of Loneliness* (London: Jonathan Cape, 1928).

Hamlett, Jane 'The British Domestic Interior and Social and Cultural History' *Cultural and Social History* 6:1 2009.

Hammal, Rowena 'How Long Before the Sunset? British Attitudes To War 1871–1914' *History Review* 2010 http://www.historytoday.com accessed 21 April 2012.

Hampton, Janie *London Olympics, 1908 and 1948* (London: Shire, 2011).

Hampton, Janie *The Austerity Olympics: When the Games Came to London in 1948* (London: Aurum Press, 2012).

Hansen, Peter H. 'Elizabeth Alice Frances Le Blond (1860–1934)' *Oxford Dictionary of National Biography* Oxford University Press http://www.oxforddnb.com/view/article/52565 accessed 7 December 2012.

Hanson, Clare 'Save the Mothers/Representations of Pregnancy in the 1930s' *Revisiting the 1930s: A Special Edition of Literature and History* 12:2 2003.

Hardy, Stephen 'Entrepreneurs, Organizations and the Sports Marketplace: Subjects in Search of Historians' *Journal of Sport History* 13:1 Spring 1986.

Hardy, Stephen 'Entrepreneurs, Organizations and the Sports Marketplace' in S. W. Pope (ed.) *The New American Sport History: Recent Approaches and Perspectives* (Urbana and Chicago: University of Illinois Press, 1997).

Hargreaves, Jennifer 'Women and the Olympic Phenomenon' in Alan Tomlinson and Gary Whannel (eds.) *Five Ring Circus: Money, Power and Politics at the Olympic Games* (London: Pluto Press, 1984).

Hargreaves, Jennifer *Sporting Females: Critical Issues in the History and Sociology of Women's Sport* (London: Routledge, 1994).

Hargreaves, Jennifer *Heroines of Sport: The Politics of Difference and Identity* (London: Routledge, 2000).

Hargreaves, Roger and Bill Deedes *Daily Encounters: Photographs from Fleet Street* (London: National Portrait Gallery, 2007).

Harvey, Adrian *Football: The First Hundred Years, the Untold Story* (London: Routledge, 2005).

Hayes, Nick and Jeff Hill *'Millions like Us'? British Culture during the Second World War* (Liverpool: Liverpool University Press, 1999).

Hayes, Win 'Lucy Morton [married name Heaton] (1898–1980)' *Oxford Dictionary of National Biography* http://www.oxforddnb.com/view/article/92814 accessed 14 July 2011.

Heggie, Vanessa *A History of British Sports Medicine* (Manchester: Manchester University Press, 2011).

Henderson, Jon *The Last Champion: A Life of Fred Perry* (London: Yellow Jersey, 2010).

Hess, Rob and Nikki Wedgewood (eds.) *Women, Football and History* (Hawthorn, Victoria: Maribyrnong Press, 2011).

Hewitt-Soar, Hugh D. 'Alice Blanche Legh (1856–1948)' *Oxford Dictionary of National Biography* Oxford University Press www.oxforddnb.com accessed 24 May 2012.

Higham, Robin 'Amy Johnson (1903–1941)' *Oxford Dictionary of National Biography* Oxford University Press http://www.oxforddnb.com/view/article/34200 accessed 5 September 2012.

Higham, Robin 'Christopher Birdwood, Baron Thomson (1875–1930)' *Oxford Dictionary of National Biography* Oxford University Press http://www.oxforddnb.com/view/article/36500 accessed 28 September 2012.

Hill, Jeffrey 'Rite of Spring: Cup Finals and Community in the North of England' in Jeff Hill and Jack Williams (eds.) *Sport and Identity in the North of England* (Keele: Keele University Press, 1996).

Hill, Jeffrey *Sport, Leisure and Culture in Twentieth Century Britain* (Basingstoke: Palgrave Macmillan, 2002).

Hill, Jeffrey 'The Day Was an Ugly One' in Paul Darby, Martin Johnes, Gavin Mellor (eds.) *Soccer and Disaster: International Perspectives* (London: Routledge, 2005).

Hill, Jeffrey *Sport in History: An Introduction* (Basingstoke: Palgrave Macmillan, 2011).

Hill, Jeffrey 'Patricia Rosemary Smythe (1928–1996)' *Oxford Dictionary of National Biography* Oxford University Press http://www.oxforddnb.com/view/article/62144 accessed 1 December 2012.

Hillier, Kenneth *Ashby De La Zouch: The Spa Town* (Ashby: C. J. Lewis, 1983).

Hindley, Deborah *In the Outer—Not on the Outer: Women and Australian Rules Football* unpublished PhD thesis, Perth: Murdoch University, 2006.

Hirsch, Pam 'Barbara Leigh Smith Bodichon (1827–1891)' *Oxford Dictionary of National Biography* Oxford University Press http://www.oxforddnb.com/view/article/2755 accessed 12 December 2012.

Hirshman, Linda and Jane Larson *Hard Bargains: The Politics of Sex* (Oxford and New York: Oxford University Press, 1998).

Hobsbawm, E. J. *Nations and Nationalism since 1780: Programme, Myth, Reality* (Cambridge: Cambridge University Press, 1990).

Hobsbawm, Eric and Terence Ranger *The Invention of Tradition* (Cambridge: Cambridge University Press, 1992).

Holloway, Gerry *Women and Work in Britain since 1840* (London and New York: Routledge, 2005).

Holt, Richard *Sport and the British* (Oxford: Clarendon Press, 1991).

Holt, Richard and Tony Mason *Sport in Britain 1945–2000* (Oxford: Blackwell, 2000).

Holt 'Audrey Kathleen Court [née Brown] (1913–2005)' *Oxford Dictionary of National Biography* Oxford University Press http://www.oxforddnb.com/view/article/96973 accessed 17 August 2012.

Honeyman, Katrina *Women, Gender and Industrialization in England 1700–1870* (Basingstoke: Macmillan, 2000).

Horn, Pamela *Women in the 1920s* (Stroud: Amberley, 2010 first published 1995).

Horrall, Andrew *Popular Culture in London, c. 1890–1918* (Manchester: Manchester University Press, 2001).

Howarth, Janet 'Dame Millicent Garrett Fawcett (1847–1929)' *Oxford Dictionary of National Biography* Oxford University Press http://www.oxforddnb.com/view/article/33096 accessed 13 December 2012.

Huggins, Mike *Flat Racing and British Society* (London and New York: Routledge, 2001).

Huggins, Mike and J. A. Mangan (eds.) *Disreputable Pleasures: Less Virtuous Victorians at Play* (London and New York: Frank Cass, 2004).

Huggins, Mike *The Victorians and Sport* (Hambledon: Continuum, 2004).

Huggins, Mike and Jack Williams *Sport and the English 1918–1939 Between the Wars* (London: Routledge, 2006).

Hughson, John 'An Invitation to "Modern" Melbourne the Historical Significance of Richard Beck's Olympic Poster Design' *Journal of Design History* 25:3 2012.

Hult, Joan S. 'The Story of Women's Athletics: Manipulating a Dream 1890–1985' in D. Margaret Costa and Sharon R Guthrie (eds.) *Women and Sport: Interdisciplinary Perspectives* (Champaign, Illinois: Human Kinetics, 1994).

Hunt, Peter 'Kenneth Grahame (1859–1932)' *Oxford Dictionary of National Biography* Oxford University Press http://www.oxforddnb.com/view/article/33511 accessed 18 May 2012.

Huntingdon-Whitely, James and Richard Holt *The Book of British Sporting Heroes* (London: National Portrait Gallery, 1999).

Huws-Jones, Enid 'Madeleine Septimia Shaw-Lefevre (1835–1914)' *Oxford Dictionary of National Biography* Oxford University Press http://www.oxforddnb.com/view/article/48463 accessed 12 December 2012.

Jacobs, Barbara *The Dick, Kerr's Ladies* (London: Constable and Robinson, 2004).

James, C. L. R. *Beyond a Boundary* (London: Stanley Paul, 1963).

Jeffreys, Kevin 'The Heyday of Amateurism in Modern Lawn Tennis' *International Journal of the History of Sport* 26:15 2009.

Jenkins, Rebecca *The First London Olympics 1908* (London: Piaktus, 2008).

Jensen, Erik *Body By Weimar: Athletes, Gender, and German Modernity* (New York: Oxford University Press, 2010).

Jeremy, David J. 'Sir (Frederick) Henry Royce, baronet (1863–1933)' *Oxford Dictionary of National Biography* Oxford University Press http://www.oxforddnb.com/view/article/35860 accessed 18 May 2012.

Johnes, Martin *Wales since 1939* (Manchester, Manchester University Press, 2012).

Johnsey, Debbie *Sport Horses* http://www.johnseysporthorses.com/index.html accessed 1 December 2012.

Jones, Bronwen 'Helen Mary Wilson 1869–1957' *The Dictionary of New Zealand Biography: Te Ara—the Encyclopedia of New Zealand* http://www.teara.govt.nz/en/biographies/3w24/1 accessed 12 December 2012.

Jones, Bruce *Grand Prix Yesterday and Today: 100 Years of Motor Racing* (Singapore: Carlton Books, 2006).

Jones, Helen 'Employer's Welfare Schemes and Industrial Relations in Inter War Britain' *Business History* 25:1 1983.

Jones, Margaret and Rodney Lowe (eds.) *From Beveridge to Blair: The First Fifty Years of the Welfare State 1948–98* (Manchester: Manchester University Press, 2002).

Jones, Stephen 'Sport, Politics and The Labour Movement: The British Workers' Sports Federation, 1923–1935' *The International Journal of the History of Sport* 2:2 1985.

Jones, Stephen 'The British Workers' Sports Federation: 1923–1935' in Arnd Krüger and James Riordan (eds.) *The Story of Worker Sport* (Champaign, Illinois: Human Kinetics, 1996).

Kandiah, Michael D. 'Frederick James, First Earl of Woolton (1883–1964)' *Oxford Dictionary of National Biography* Oxford University Press http://www.oxforddnb.com/view/article/34885 accessed 21 January 2013.

Kay, Joyce '"No Time for Recreations till the Vote is Won?" Suffrage Activists and Leisure in Edwardian Britain' *Women's History Review* 16:4 2007.

Kay, Joyce 'It Wasn't Just Emily Davison! Sport, Suffrage and Society in Edwardian Britain' *International Journal of the History of Sport* 25:10 2008.

Kay, Joyce 'A Window of Opportunity? Preliminary Thoughts on Women's Sport in Post-war Britain' in Carol Osborne and Fiona Skillen (eds.) *Women in Sports History* (London and New York: Routledge, 2012).

Kay, Joyce 'Marjorie Elaine Foster (1893–1974)' *Oxford Dictionary of National Biography* Oxford University Press http://www.oxforddnb.com/view/article/65174 accessed 30 August 2012.

Kay, Joyce 'Meriel Patricia Tufnell (1948–2002)' *Oxford Dictionary of National Biography* Oxford University Press http://www.oxforddnb.com/view/article/77356 accessed 1 December 2012.

Keil, Ian and Don Wix *In the Swim: The History of the Amateur Swimming Association from 1869 to 1994* (Loughborough: Swimming Times Publications Ltd, 1996).

Kelly, Thomas *A History of Adult Education in Great Britain from the Middle Ages to the Twentieth Century* (Liverpool: Liverpool University Press, 1992).

Kennedy, Sarah *The Swimsuit: A Fashion History from 1920s Biarritz and the Birth of the Bikini to Sportswear Styles and Catwalk Trends* (London: Carlton Books, 2007).

Keys, Barbara *Globalising Sport: National Rivalry and International Community in the 1930s* (Cambridge, Massachusetts and London: Harvard University Press, 2006).

Kidd, Bruce 'Missing: Women from Sports Halls of Fame' *CAAWS Action Bulletin* Winter, 1995 http://www.caaws.ca/e/milestones/women_history/missing accessed 3 January 2012.

Koishihara, Miho 'The Emergence of the 'Sporting Girls' in Japanese Girls' Magazines: Descriptions and Visual Images of the Female Athlete in Japanese Culture of the 1920s and 1930s' *Fourth Meeting of the Transnational Scholars for the Study of Gender and Sport* Pädagogische Hochscule Ludwigsburg 27–30 November 2008.

Korr, Charles P. *West Ham United the Making of a Football Club* (Michigan: University of Illinois Press, 1986.

Kramer, Ann *Sussex Women: A Sussex Guide* (Alfriston, Sussex: Snake River Press, 2007).

Krüger, Arnd and John Marshall Carter *Ritual and Record: Sports Records and Quantification in Pre Modern Societies* (Westport, Connecticut: Greenwod Press, 1990).

Krüger, Arnd 'What's the Difference Between Propaganda for Tourism or for A Political Regime?: Was the 1936 Olympics the First Postmodern Spectacle?' in John Bale and Mette Krogh Christensen *Post-Olympism? Questioning Sport in the Twenty-First Century* (Oxford and New York: Berg, 2004).

Kushner, Tony *Anglo-Jewry since 1066: Place Locality and Memory* (Manchester: Manchester University Press, 2009).

Kynaston, David *Austerity Britain 1945–1951* (London: Bloomsbury, 2007).

Kynaston, David *W.G.'s Birthday Party* (London: Bloomsbury, 2010).

Laban, Brian *Motor Racing: The Early Years* (Königswinter, Germany: Tandem Verlag, 2001).

Lambie, James *The Story of Your Life: A History of The Sporting Life Newspaper, 1859–1998* (Leicester: Matador, 2010).

Langhamer, Claire *Women's Leisure in England* 1920–1960 (Manchester: Manchester University Press, 2000).

Lebow, Eileen *Before Amelia: Women Pilots In the Early Days of Aviation* (Virginia: Brassey's Incorporated, 2002).

Lee Potter, Charlie *Sportswear in Vogue since 1910* (New York: Abbeville Press, 1984).

Leigh, Mary H. and Thérèse M. Bonin 'The Pioneering Role of Madame Alice Milliat and the FSFI in Establishing International Track and Field Competition for Women' *Journal of Sport History* 4:1 1977.

Leigh, Mary H. 'The Enigma of Avery Brundage and Women Athletes' *Arena Review* 4: 2 May 1980.

Lennartz, Karl 'The IOC During World War Two' *Journal of Olympic History* 20:1 2012.

Lewis, Peter N. 'Joyce Wethered [married name Joyce Heathcoat-Amory, Lady Heathcoat-Amory] (1901–1997)' *Oxford Dictionary of National Biography* Oxford University Press http://www.oxforddnb.com/view/article/68365 accessed 15 January 2013.

Lewis, R. M. 'American Croquet in the 1860s: Playing the Game and Winning' *Journal of Sport History* 18:3 December 1991.

Little, Alan *Suzanne Lenglen: Tennis Idol of the Twenties* (London: Wimbledon Lawn Tennis Museum, 2005).

Lomax, Judy *Women of the Air* (London: John Murray, 1986).

Lopez, Sue *Women on the Ball* (London: Scarlet, 1997).

Love, Christopher 'Social Class and the Swimming World: Amateurs and Professionals' *International Journal of the History of Sport* 24:5 2007.

Love, Christopher *A Social History of Swimming in England, 1800–1918* (London: Routledge, 2007).

Lovell, Mary S. *Amelia Aerhart: The Sound of Wings* (London: Hutchinson, 1989).

Lovesey, Peter 'Conan Doyle and The Olympics' *Journal of Olympic History* 10 December 2001.

Lovesey, Peter 'Violet Piercy (b. 1889?)' *Oxford Dictionary of National Biography* Oxford University Press http://www.oxforddnb.com/view/article/103698 accessed 17 August 2012.

Lowe, Rodney *The Welfare State in Britain since 1945* (Basingstoke: Macmillan-Palgrave, 1993).

Lowerson, J. R. 'Ralph Slazenger (1845–1910)' *Oxford Dictionary of National Biography* Oxford University Press http://www.oxforddnb.com/view/article/39048 accessed 28 June 2012.

Lucas, Shelley 'Women's Cycle Racing: Enduring Meanings' *Journal of Sport History* 39:2 Summer 2012.

Ludvigsen, Karl *Classic Grand Prix Cars: The Front Engined Formula 1 Era 1906–1960* (Stroud, Gloucestershire, 2000).

Luff, David *Amy Johnson: Enigma of the Sky* (Shrewsbury: Air Life Publishing, 2002).

Lunt, James 'Sir John Bagot Glubb (1897–1986)' *Oxford Dictionary of National Biography* Oxford University Press http://www.oxforddnb.com/view/article/40128 accessed 12 January 2013.

Lv, Luo and Zhang Huigang *Sneakers* (London: Southbank, 2007).

Lykke Poulson. Anne 'Women's Gymnastics and Citizenship in Denmark in the Early Twentieth Century' *Women's History Magazine* 59 2008 (Oxford: Women's History Network. 2008).

MacAloon, John J. *This Great Symbol: Pierre de Coubertin and the Origins of the Modern Olympic Games* (Chicago: University of Chicago Press, 1981).

MacAloon, John J. *Brides of Victory: Nationalism and Gender in Olympic Ritual* (London: Berg, 1997).

Mackersey, Ian *Jean Batten—The Garbo of the Skies* (London: Macdonald, 1990).

McKibben, Ross *Classes and Cultures: England 1918–1951* (Oxford: Oxford University Press, 1998).

Maclure, J. S. *Educational Documents: England and Wales: 1816 to the Present Day* (London: Methuen, 1979).

Mair, Lewine *One Hundred Years of Women's Golf* (Edinburgh: Mainstream Publishing in conjunction with the Ladies Golf Union, 1993).

Malcolmson, Robert *Popular Recreations in English Society 1700–1850* (Cambridge: Cambridge University Press, 1973).

Malies, Jeremy 'Charlotte [Lottie] Dod (1871–1960)' *Oxford Dictionary of National Biography* Oxford University Press http://www.oxforddnb.com/view/article/37363 accessed 7 January 2013.

Mallon, Bill 'The First Two Women Olympians' *Citius, Altius, Fortius* (became *Journal of Olympic History* in 1997) 3:3 1995.

Mallon, Bill *The 1900 Olympic Games: Results for All Competitors in All Events, with commentary* (Jefferson, North Carolina: McFarland and Company, 1998).

Mallon, Bill *The 1904 Olympic Games: Results for All Competitors in All Events, with commentary* (Jefferson, North Carolina: McFarland & Co. 1999).

Mallon, Bill & Ian Buchanan *The 1908 Olympic Games: Results for All Competitors in All Events, with Commentary* (McFarland, 2000).

Mangan, J. A. and Roberta J. Park (eds.) *From 'Fair Sex' to Feminism: Sport and the Socialization of Women in the Industrial and Post- Industrial Eras* (London: Frank Cass, 1987).

Mangan, J. A. (ed.) *Pleasure, Profit and Proselytism: British Culture and Sport at Home and Abroad 1700–1914* (London: Frank Cass, 1988).

McCrone, Kathleen 'The "Lady Blue": Sport at the Oxbridge Women's Colleges from their foundation to 1914' *British Journal of Sports History* 3 September 1986.

McCrone, Kathleen *Playing the Game: Sport and the Physical Emancipation of English Women 1870–1914* (Lexington: University Press of Kentucky, 1988).

McCrone, Kathleen 'Emancipation or Recreation? The Development of Women's Sport at the University of London' *The International Journal of the History of Sport* 7:2 1990.

McCrone, Kathleen 'Class, Gender and English Women's Sport 1890–1914' *Journal of Sport History* 18:1 Spring 1991.

McCrone, Kathleen 'Lady Margaret Rachel Scott (1874–1938)' *Oxford Dictionary of National Biography* Oxford University Press http://www.oxforddnb.com/view/article/50305 accessed 7 December 2012.

McDermott, Alice 'In Florence Nightingale's Footsteps: A Biography of Mary O'Connell Bianconi with Particular Reference to her Nursing Career' (Waterford: Waterford Institute of Technology) www.wit.ie/MaryOConnellBianconiBiographyfull. pdf accessed 29 June 2012.

Maragaya, Ana Maria *The Process of Inclusion of Women in the Olympic Games* unpublished PhD thesis Universidade Gama Filho, Rio De Janeiro 2006.

Maraniss, David *Rome 1960: The Olympics that Changed the World* (New York, London, Toronto, Sydney: Simon & Schuster, 2008).

Martin, Simon *Sport Italia: The Italian Love Affair with Sport* (London: I. B Tauris, 2011).

Maughan, Robert J. (ed.) *The Encyclopaedia of Sports Medicine: An IOC Medical Commission Publication* (Chichester: Wiley-Blackwell Publishing, 2009).

Marwick, Arthur 'The Fundamentals of History: What is History?' *Institute of Historical Research: Focus* http://www.history.ac.uk/ihr/Focus/Whatishistory/marwick1.html accessed 13 March 2012.

Mason, Tony *Association Football and English Society 1863–1915* (Brighton: Harvester, 1980).

Mason, Tony *Sport in Britain* (London: Faber and Faber, 1988).

Mason, Tony 'All the Winners and the Half Times . . . ' *The Sports Historian* 13:2 May 1993.

Mason, Tony and Eliza Riedi *Sport and the Military: The British Armed Forces 1880–1960* (Cambridge, Cambridge University Press, 2010).

Mason, Tony 'Geoffrey Harry George Dyson (1914–1981)' *Oxford Dictionary of National Biography* Oxford University Press http://www.oxforddnb.com/view/article/100477 accessed 6 November 2012.

Matless, David *Landscape and Englishness* (London, 1988).

Matthews 'Mary Meta Bagot Stack (1883–1935)' *Oxford Dictionary of National Biography* Oxford University Press http://www.oxforddnb.com/view/article/45797 accessed 5 September 2012.

Melling, Alethea '"Ray of the Rovers" The Working Class Heroine in Popular Football Fiction 1915–25' *The International Journal of The History of Sport* 16:1 April 1998.

Melling, Alethea 'Cultural Differentiation, Shared Aspiration: The Entente Cordirale of International Ladies' Football 1920–45' *The European Sports History Review* 1 April 1999.

Michallat, Wendy 'Droit au But: Violette Morris and Women's Football in "Les Années Folles"' *French Studies Bulletin* 26:1 2005.

Middleton, Dorothy 'Lady Florence Caroline Dixie [née Douglas] (1855–1905)' *Oxford Dictionary of National Biography* Oxford University Press www.oxforddnb.com/view/article/32836 accessed 22 May 2012.

Millar, M. S. 'Charlotte Cecilia Pitcairn [Cecil] Leitch (1891–1977)' *Oxford Dictionary of National Biography* Oxford University Press http://www.oxforddnb.com/view/article/31347 accessed 15 January 2013.

Miller, J. *How Does the Labour Process Impact On Employment Relations In the Small Firm? A Study of Racehorse Training Stables In The United Kingdom* unpublished PhD, London Metropolitan University, 2010.

Mitchell, Sally *The New Girls: Girls' Culture in England 1880–1915* (New York: Columbia University Press, 1995).

Monkhouse, George C. *Mercedes-Benz Grand Prix Racing 1934–1955* (London: White Mouse Publishing, 1984).

Moir, Graeme *A Social History of Bowling in the North of England 1945-Present* unpublished PhD thesis De Montfort University, Leicester 2013.

Moore, Katharine 'The Pan-Britannic Festival: A Tangible but Forlorn Expression of Imperial Unity' in J.A Mangan (ed.) *Pleasure, Profit and Proselytism:*

British Culture and Sport at Home and Abroad 1700–1914 (London: Frank Cass, 1988).

Moore, Kevin *Museums and Popular Culture: Contemporary Issues in Museum Culture* (Leicester: Leicester University Press, 1996).

Moore, Tina *Bobby Moore: By the Person Who Knew Him Best* (London: HarperSport, 2006).

Morgan, Carol E. *Women Workers and Gender Identities 1835–1913: The Cotton and Metal Industries in England* (London: Routledge, 2001).

Morse, Elizabeth 'Dame Louisa Innes Lumsden (1840–1935)' *Oxford Dictionary of National Biography* Oxford University Press http://www.oxforddnb.com/view/article/48571 accessed 10 March 2012.

Mosley, Charles (ed.) *Burke's Peerage, Baronetage & Knightage Volume 1* (Wilmington: Burke's Peerage Genealogical Books Ltd, 2003).

Munting, Roger 'Dick Seaman-Was He a Hero or a Villain?' *Bulletin of the British Society of Sports History* December 2010.

Munting, Roger 'Ladies on Horseback: Women in Eventing and Racing' *British Society of Sports History Members' Bulletin* May 2012.

Munting, Roger '(Charles Ernest) Leonard Lyle, first Baron Lyle of Westbourne (1882–1954)'*Oxford Dictionary of National Biography* Oxford University Press http://www.oxforddnb.com/view/article/34644 accessed 17 October 2012.

Murphy, Ann B. and Deirdre Raftery (eds.) *Emily Davies: Collected Letters 1861–1875* (Charlottesville: University of Virginia Press, 2003).

Myerscough, Keith *Blackpool's Triplets: Health, Pleasure and Recreation 1875–1904* unpublished MA Sport History and Culture thesis De Montfort University Leicester, 2009.

Myerscough, Keith 'Nymphs, Naiads and Natation' *Seventh Annual Conference of Sports History Ireland*, Hunt Museum Limerick 10 September 2011.

Nead, Lynda *The Haunted Gallery: Painting, Photography and Film c1900* (New Haven and London: Yale University Press, 2007)

Nielsen, Neils Kayser 'The Stadium in the City—A Modern Story' in John Bale and Olaf Moen (eds.) *The Stadium and the City* (Keele University Press: Keele, 1995).

Nelson, Carolyn (ed.) *A New Woman Reader: Fiction, Articles, and Drama of the 1890s* (London: Broadview Press, 2000).

Newsham, Gail *In a League of Their Own! Dick, Kerr Ladies' Football Club* (Chorley, Lancashire: Pride of Place, 1994).

Newsum, Gillian *Women and Horses* (London: The Sportsman's Press, 1988).

O'Connell, Sean *The Car and British Society: Class, Gender and Motoring 1896–1939* (Manchester: Manchester University Press, 1998).

Odendaal, André 'South Africa's Black Victorians: Sport and Society in South Africa in the Nineteenth Century' in J. A. Mangan (ed.) *Pleasure, Profit and Proselytism: British Culture and Sport at Home and Abroad 1700–1914* (London: Frank Cass, 1988).

O'Kane, Peter 'A History of the "Triple Crown" of Motor Racing: The Indianapolis 500, the Le Mans 10 Hours and the Monaco Grand Prix' *International Journal of the History of Sport* 28:2 2011.

Oriard, Michael *Dreaming of Heroes: American Sports Fiction, 1868–1980* (Chicago: Nelson- Hall, 1982).

Oriard, Michael *Reading Football: How the Popular Press Created an American Spectacle* (Chapel Hill and London: University of North Carolina Press, 1993).

Oriard, Michael *King Football: Sport and Spectacle in the Golden Age of Radio, Newsreels, Movies & Magazines, The Weekly & The Daily Press* (Chapel Hill and London: University of North Carolina Press, 2001).

Osborne, Carol and Fiona Skillen (eds.) *Women and Sport A Special Edition of Sport in History* 2:2 June 2010.

Osbourne, John 'To Keep the Life of the Nation on the Old Lines': The *Athletic News* and the First World War *Journal of Sport History* 14:2 Summer, 1987.

O' Sullivan, Tim 'Television and The Austerity Games: London 1948' in Jeffrey Hill, Kevin Moore and Jason Wood (eds.) *Sport, History and Heritage: Studies in Public Representation* (Woodbridge, Suffolk and Rochester New York: Boydell and Brewer Ltd, 2012).

Overy, R. J. 'William Richard Morris, Viscount Nuffield (1877–1963)' *Oxford Dictionary of National Biography* Oxford University Press http://www.oxforddnb.com/view/article/35119 accessed 22 August 2012.

Page, Robert M. *Revisiting the Welfare State* (Berkshire: Open University Press, 2007).

Paisley, Jessie 'In Her Own Words' *Liverpool Football Club* http://www.liverpoolfc.tv/news/latest-news/jessie-paisley-in-her-own-words accessed 8 February 2012.

Parker, Claire 'The Rise of Competitive Swimming 1840–1878' *The Sports Historian* 21:2 2001.

Parker, Paul 'On Days Like These' *Motor Sport incorporating Speed and The Brooklands Gazette* March 2001 77:3 (London: Haymarket Publications, 2001).

Parks, Jennifer 'Verbal Gymnastics: Sports, Bureaucracy, and The Soviet Unions' Entrance into the Olympic Games 1946–1952' in Stephen Wagg and David L. Andrews (eds.) *East Plays West: Sport and the Cold War* (London and New York: Routledge, 2007) pp. 27–44.

Parr, Susie *The Story of Swimming* (Stockport: Dewi Lewis Media, 2011).

Parry, Colin 'Dame Ethel Locke King [née Gore-Browne] (1864–1956)' *Oxford Dictionary of National Biography* Oxford University Press http://www.oxforddnb.com/view/article/52021 accessed 20 June 2012.

Parratt, Catriona M. 'From the History of Women in Sport to Women's Sport History: A Research Agenda' in D. Margaret Costa and Sharon R Guthrie (eds.) *Women and Sport: Interdisciplinary Perspectives* (Champaign, Illinois: Human Kinetics, 1994).

Parratt, Catriona M. '"The Making of the Healthy and the Happy Home": Education, Recreation, and the Production of Working-Class Womanhood at the Rowntree Cocoa Works, York, c. 1889–1914' in Jack Williams and Jeff Hill (eds.) *Sport and Identity in the North of England* (Keele: University of Keele Press, 1996).

Parratt, Catriona M. *'More than Mere Amusement': Working Class Women's Leisure in England 1750–1914* (Boston: Northeastern University Press, 2002).

Pearson, Jeffrey *Lottie Dod: Champion of Champions, The Story of an Athlete* (Wirral, Meryseside: Countyvise, 1988).

Peiss, Kathy *Cheap Amusements: Working Women and Leisure in Turn of the Century New York* (Philadelphia: Temple University Press, 1986).

Perrone, Fernanda Helen 'Constance Mary Katherine Applebee (1873–1981)' *Oxford Dictionary of National Biography* Oxford University Press http://www.oxforddnb.com/view/article/102441 accessed 11 July 2012.

Phillips, Bob *The 1948 Olympics: How London Rescued the Games* (London: Sports Pages, 2007).

Polley, Martin '"The Amateur Rules": Post-War British Athletics' in Adrian Smith and Dilwyn Porter (eds.) *Amateurs and Professionals in Post-War British Sport* (London and Portland Oregon: Frank Cass, 2000).

Polley, Martin 'Sport and National Identity in England' in Adrian Smith and Dilwyn Porter (eds.) *Sport and National Identity In the Post-War World* (London and New York: Routledge, 2004).

Polley, Martin *The British Olympics: Britain's Olympic Heritage 1612–2012* (Swindon: Played in Britain, 2011).

Polley, Martin *Britain, Britons and the Olympic Games: Sport in History Special Edition* 32:2 June 2012.

Porter, Dilwyn and Jean Williams 'Kit: Selling Sports Clothing in Britain, c. 1870–1950' *British Society for Sports History Annual Conference* 18 July 2009 University of Stirling.

Pottle, Mark 'Dorothea Katharine Lambert Chambers [née Douglass] (1878–1960)' *Oxford Dictionary of National Biography* Oxford University Press http://www.oxforddnb.com/view/article/32353 accessed 23 April 2012.

Pottle, Mark 'Sophie Catherine Theresa Mary Heath, Lady Heath (1896–1939) *Oxford Dictionary of National Biography* Oxford University Press http://www.oxforddnb.com/view/article/67141 accessed 10 August 2012.

Pottle, Mark 'Dorothy Dyne Steel (1884–1965)' *Oxford Dictionary of National Biography* Oxford University Press http://www.oxforddnb.com/view/article/63683 accessed 4 September 2012.

Pottle, Mark 'Mabel Emily Stringer (1868–1958)' *Oxford Dictionary of National Biography* Oxford University Press http://www.oxforddnb.com/view/article/63388 accessed 7 December 2012.

Pottle, Mark 'Mildred Mary Bruce (1895–1990)' *Oxford Dictionary of National Biography* Oxford University Press http://www.oxforddnb.com/view/article/63962 accessed 19 January 2013.

Pugh, Martin *Women and The Women's Movement in Britain 1914–1999* (London: Macmillan, 2000).

Pugh, Martin *'Hurrah for the Blackshirts!: Fascists and Fascism Between the Wars* (London: Jonathan Cape, 2005).

Pugh, Martin 'Nancy Witcher Astor, Viscountess Astor (1879–1964)' *Oxford Dictionary of National Biography* Oxford University Press http://www.oxforddnb.com/view/article/30489 accessed 11 July 2012.

Pugh, Martin 'Gwendolen Florence Mary Guiness, Countess of Iveagh (1881–1966)' *Oxford Dictionary of National Biography* Oxford University Press http://www.oxforddnb.com/view/article/33602 accessed 11 July 2012.

Pugh 'Gladys Sydney Pott (1867–1961)' *Oxford Dictionary of National Biography* Oxford University Press http://www.oxforddnb.com/view/article/41259 accessed 19 January 2013.

Pulford, John 'Hugh Fortescue Locke King (1848–1926)' *Oxford Dictionary of National Biography* Oxford University Press http://www.oxforddnb.com/view/article/66280 accessed 20 June 2012.

Purvis, June and Margaret Hales, *Achievement and Inequality in Education* (London: Routledge and Kegan Paul, 1983).

Pritchard, D. M. C. *The History of Croquet* (London: Cassell Ltd, 1981).

Prudhomme-Poncet, Laurence *Histoire du Football Feminine au XXème Siècle: Espaces et Temps du Sport* (Paris: L'Harmattann, 2003).

Quintillan, Ghislane 'Alice Milliat and the Women's Games' *Olympic Review* 36:31 2000 pp. 27–28 (Lausanne: International Olympic Committee, 2000) http://www.la84foundation.org/OlympicInformationCenter/OlympicReview/2000 accessed 12 August 2012.

Radford, Peter 'Women's Foot-Races in the 18th and 19th Centuries: A Popular and Widespread Practice' *Canadian Journal of History of Sport* 25:1 May 1994.

Radford, Peter *The Celebrated Captain Barclay: Sport, Money and Fame in Regency Britain* (London: Headline, 2001).

Ramsden, Caroline *Ladies In Racing; Sixteenth Century To the Present Day* (London: Paul, 1973).

Redhead, Steve *Post-Fandom and the Millennial Blues* (London and New York: Routledge, 1997).

390 *Bibliography*

Reid, Deborah 'Scotland: Women Gardeners' Memories Wanted' *Royal Horticultural Society* http://www.rhs.org.uk/News/Scotland accessed 6 March 2012.

Rendell, Jane *The Pursuit of Pleasure: Gender, Space & Architecture in Regency London* (London: Continuum, 2002).

Ridley, Jane and Clayre Percy 'Ethel Anne Priscilla Grenfell, Lady Desborough (1867–1952)' *Oxford Dictionary of National Biography* Oxford University Press http://www.oxforddnb.com/view/article/40733 accessed 4 January 2013.

Ritchie, Andrew *Quest for Speed: A History of Early Bicycle Racing 1868–1903* (San Francisco: Cycle Publishing/Van der Plas Publications, 2011).

Robinson, Lynne *Tripping Daintily Into the Arena: A Social History of English Women's Athletics 1921–1960* unpublished PhD thesis, Warwick University, 1997.

Robson, Graham 'Liege Healey' *Historic Race and Rally* 1:1 (Dorset: Pegasus, 2000).

Roche, Maurice *Mega-Events and Modernity: Olympics and Expos in the Growth of Global Culture* (London: Routledge, 2000).

Rodda, John 'Sydney Wooderson: Obituary' *The Guardian* Wednesday 3 January 2007 http://www.guardian.co.uk/news/2007/jan/03/guardianobituaries.athletics accessed 5 November 2012.

Rouxel, Claude and Laurent Friry *Gotha de L'Automobile Francaise* (Paris: Editions ETAI, 2010).

Rowbotham, Sheila *Hidden from History: Three Hundred Years of Women's Oppression* (London: Pluto, 1973).

Royal Aeronautical Society 'From Pioneers to Presidents: Celebrating a Century of Flight' *Royal Aeronautical Society Women in Aviation and Aerospace Conference* Hamilton Place, London 14 October 2011.

Royal Automobile Club 'Past Dewar Trophy Winners: Violet Cordery, 1926' http://www.royalautomobileclub.co.uk/Motoring/dewar-trophy accessed 14 October 2012.

Royal Automobile Club 'Past Dewar Trophy Winners: Violet Cordery, 1929' http://www.royalautomobileclub.co.uk/Motoring/dewar-trophy accessed 14 October 2012.

Ruffin, Raymond *La Diablesse: La Véritable Histoire de Violette Morris* (Paris: Pygmalion, 1989).

Ruffin, Raymond *Violette Morris: La Hyène de la Gestap* (Paris: Le Cherche Midi, 2004).

Russell, Dave *Popular Music in England 1840–1914: A Social History* (Manchester and New York: Manchester University Press, 1987, revised edition 1997).

Ryan, Mark 'The Langrishe Sisters and the Early Years of the Irish Championships' *Tennis Forum.com* http://www.tennisforum.com accessed 16 March 2012.

Ryan, Mark 'Muriel Robb (1878–1907): A Little-Known Wimbledon Singles Champion' *Tennis Forum* http://www.tennisforum.com accessed 24 April 2012.

Ryan, Mark 'Ethel Warneford Larcombe [née Thomson] (1879–1965)' *Oxford Dictionary of National Biography* Oxford University Press http://www.oxforddnb.com accessed 15 May 2012.

Sabor, Peter (ed.) John Cleland *Memoirs of a Woman of Pleasure* (Oxford: Oxford University Press, 1999 originally published in two parts in 1748 and 1749).

Sanderson, Michael *Education and Economic Decline in Britain 1870 to the 1990s* (Cambridge: Cambridge University Press, 1998).

Schoenfeld, Bruce *The Match: Althea Gibson & Angela Buxton* (New York: Harper Collins, 2004).

Schott, Ben *Schott's Sporting, Gaming and Idling Miscellany* (London: Bloomsbury, 2004).

Schweinbenz, Amanda and Alexandria Cronk 'Femininity Control at the Olympic Games' *Thirdspace: A Journal of Feminist Theory & Culture: Special Edition Gender, Sport and the Olympics* 9:2 2010.

Searle, G. R. *The Quest for National Efficiency 1899–1914* (Oxford: Basil Blackwell, 1971).

Sidhe, Wren 'H. V. Morton's Pilgrimages to Englishness' *Literature and History* 12:1 Spring 2003.

Silver, J. R. *The Role of Sport in the Rehabilitation of Patients with Spinal Injuries* (Stoke Mandeville: National Spine Injuries Centre, 2004).

Simonton, Deborah *A History of European Women's Work, 1700 to the Present* (London: Routledge, 1998).

Simonton, Deborah *Women in European Culture and Society: Gender, Skill and Identity from 1700* (London and New York: Routledge, 2011).

Simri, Uriel *A Concise History of Women's Sports* (Netanya: Wingate Institute, 1983).

Skidelsky, Robert 'Sir Oswald Ernald Mosley (1896–1980)' *Oxford Dictionary of National Biography* Oxford University Press http://www.oxforddnb.com/view/article/31477 accessed 28 September 2012.

Smith, Adrian *The City of Coventry: A Twentieth Century Icon* (London and New York: I. B. Tauris, 2006).

Smith, Adrian 'Sport, Speed and the Technological Imperative: Dealing With the Declinists' *Historians on Sport Symposium* De Montfort University, Leicester 30 October 2007.

Smyth, J. G. 'Charlotte Renaigle Sterry (née Cooper) 1870–1966' *Oxford Dictionary of National Biography* Oxford University Press www.oxforddnb.com accessed 30 October 2011.

Sontag, Susan *On Photography* (London: Penguin, 1979).

Souhami, Diana *The Trial of Radclyffe Hall* (New York: Doubleday, 1999).

Sports Council *Women and Sport: A Consultation Document* (London: Sports Council 1992).

Sports Council *Women and Sport: Policy and Frameworks for Action* (London: Sports Council, 1993).

Stearn, Roger T. 'Charles Dunell Rudd (1844–1916)' *Oxford Dictionary of National Biography* Oxford University Press http://www.oxforddnb.com/view/article/65577 accessed 22 October 2012.

Stearns, Peter *Childhood in World History* (London and New York: Routledge, 2011 second edition).

Stell, Marion 'Marie Montgomerie Hamilton (1891–1955)' *Australian Dictionary of Biography* National Centre of Biography, Australian National University http://adb.anu.edu.au/biography/hamilton-marie-montgomerie-10404/text18437 accessed 2 September 2012.

Stewart, Oliver and M. C. Curthoys, 'James Allan Mollison (1905–1959)' *Oxford Dictionary of National Biography* Oxford University Press http://www.oxforddnb.com/view/article/35055 accessed 5 September 2012.

Storey, Richard A. 'Frederick Richard Simms (1863–1944)' *Oxford Dictionary of National Biography* Oxford University Press http://www.oxforddnb.com/view/article/40814 accessed 11 January 2013.

Struna, Nancy '"Good Wives" and "Gardeners", Spinners and "Fearless Riders": Middle and Upper Rank Women in Early American Sporting Culture' in J. A. Mangan and Roberta J. Park (eds.) *From 'Fair Sex' to Feminism: Sport and the Socialization of Women in the Industrial and Post- Industrial Eras* (London: Frank Cass, 1987).

Struna, Nancy 'The Recreational Experiences of Early American Women' in D. Margaret Costa and Sharon R Guthrie (eds.) *Women and Sport: Interdisciplinary Perspectives* (Champaign, Illinois: Human Kinetics, 1994).

Struna, Nancy *People of Prowess: Sport, Leisure and Labor in Early Anglo-America* (Urbana: University of Illinois Press, 1996).

Struna, Nancy 'Reframing the Direction of Change in the History of Sport' *International Journal of the History of Sport* 18:4 December 2001.

Sutherland, Duncan 'Katharine Marjory Stewart-Murray, Duchess of Atholl (1874–1960)' *Oxford Dictionary of National Biography* Oxford University Press http://www.oxforddnb.com/view/article/36301 accessed 11 July 2012.

Sutherland, Duncan '(Frances) Elaine Burton, Baroness Burton of Coventry 1904–1991' *Oxford Dictionary of National Biography* Oxford University Press http://www.oxforddnb.com/view/article/49597 accessed 18 December 2012.

Sutherland, Gillian *Faith, Duty and Power of Mind: The Cloughs and Their Circle, 1829–1960* (Cambridge, Cambridge University Press, 2006).

Sutherland, Gillian 'Anne Jemima Clough (1820–1892)' *Oxford Dictionary of National Biography* Oxford University Press http://www.oxforddnb.com/view/article/5710 accessed 7 March 2012.

Swain, Peter 'Pedestrianism, the Public House and Gambling in Nineteenth-Century South-East Lancashire' *Sport in History* 32:3 September 2012.

Swinger, Peter *Motor Racing Circuits in England: Then and Now* (Surrey: Dial House, 2001).

Taylor, Matthew *The Leaguers: The Making of Professional Football in England, 1900–1939* (Liverpool: Liverpool University Press, 2005).

Tebbutt, Melanie (ed.) *Growing Up in the North West 1850s–1950s* (Exeter: Short Run Press for Manchester Centre for Regional History, 2011).

Tennant, John *Motor Racing: The Golden Age* (London: Cassell Illustrated, 2004).

Terret, Thierry 'From Alice Milliat to Marie-Thérèse Eyquem: Revisiting Women's Sport in France (1920s–1960s)' *The International Journal of the History of Sport* 27:7 2010.

Thane, Patricia and Esther Breitenbach (eds.) *Women and Citizenship in Britain and Ireland in the Twentieth Century: What Difference Did the Vote Make?* (London: Continuum, 2009).

Thoms, David 'Selwyn Francis Edge (1868–1940)' *Oxford Dictionary of National Biography* Oxford University Press http://www.oxforddnb.com/view/article/32970 accessed 29 June 2012.

Tomlinson, Alan 'Olympic Survivals: The Olympic Games As a Global Phenomenon' in Lincoln Allison (ed.) *The Global Politics of Sport: The Role of Global Institutions in Sport* (Oxon: Routledge, 2005) pp. 46–62.

Tomlinson, Sally *Education in a Post-Welfare Society* (Buckingham and Philadelphia: Open University, 2001).

Tosh, John *A Man's Place: Masculinity and the Middle-Class Home in Victorian England* (New Haven and London: Yale University Press, 2007).

Traikovski, Louie 'The Importance of Sport to Students and Headmistresses at Four Private Melbourne Schools from 1900 to 1914' *Australian Society for Sports History Bulletin* 28 June 1998.

Tranter, Neil *Sport, Economy and Society in Britain 1750–1914* (Cambridge: Cambridge University Press, 1998).

Vamplew, Wray *The Turf* (London: Penguin, 1976).

Vamplew, Wray and Joyce Kay (eds.) *Encyclopaedia of British Horseracing* (London and New York: Routledge, 2005).

Vamplew, Wray 'Muriel Amy Cornell (1906–1996)' *Oxford Dictionary of National Biography* Oxford University Press http://www.oxforddnb.com/view/article/62157 accessed 17 August 2012.

Vamplew, Wray 'Sir Arthur Abraham Gold (1917–2002)' *Oxford Dictionary of National Biography* Oxford University Press http://www.oxforddnb.com/view/article/76890 accessed 6 November 2012.

Vamplew, Wray 'Sir Henry Morton Llewellyn (1911–1999)' *Oxford Dictionary of National Biography* Oxford University Press http://www.oxforddnb.com/view/article/73227 accessed 1 December 2012.

Vamplew 'Florence Nagle (1894–1988)' *Oxford Dictionary of National Biography* Oxford University Press http://www.oxforddnb.com/view/article/62668 accessed 1 December 2012,

Van Someren, Janine *Women's Sporting Lives: A Biographical Study of Elite Amateur Tennis Players at Wimbledon* unpublished PhD thesis, University of Southampton, 2012.

Vaukins, Simon *The Isle of Man Tourist Trophy Motorcycle Races 1907 to the 1960s: Politics, Economics and National Identity* (unpublished PhD thesis, University of Lancaster, 2008).

Vertinsky, Patricia *The Eternally Wounded Woman: Women, Doctors and Exercise in the Late Nineteenth Century* (Manchester and New York: Manchester University Press, 1990).

Vertinsky, Patricia and Christiane Job 'Celebrating Gertrudes: Women of Influence' in Annette R. Hofmann and Else Trangbaek (eds.) *International Perspectives on Sporting Women in Past and Present* (Denmark: Institute of Exercise and Social Sciences University of Copenhagen, 2005).

Wagg, Stephen '"If You Want the Girl Next Door . . .": Olympic Sport and the Popular Press In Early Cold War Britain' in Stephen Wagg and David L. Andrews (eds.) *East Plays West: Sport and The Cold War* (London and New York: Routledge, 2007).

Walker, Graham 'Nancy Riach and the Motherwell Swimming Phenomenon' in Grant Jarvie and Graham Walker (eds.) *Scottish Sport In the Making of the Nation: Ninety-Minute Patriots?* (Leicester: Leicester University Press, 1994).

Walmsley Kevin B. 'Laying Olympism to Rest' in John Bale and Mette Krogh Christensen *Post-Olympism? Questioning Sport in the Twenty-First Century* (Oxford and New York: Berg, 2004).

Walmsley, Kevin 'Womanizing Olympic Athletes: Policy and Practice during the Avery Brundage Era' in Stephen R. Wenn, Gerald P. Schaus (eds.) *Onward to the Olympics: Historical Perspectives on the Olympic Games* (Ontario: Wilfred Laurier University Press and the Canadian Institute in Greece, 2007).

Walmsley, Sarah (ed.) *Pell Mell and Woodcote: The Magazine of the Royal Automobile Club* 134 April 2011 (London: Royal Automobile Club, 2011).

Walton, John *The English Seaside Resort: A Social History 1750–1914* (Leicester: Leicester University Press, 1983).

Walton, John *The British Seaside: Holidays and Resorts in the Twentieth Century* (Manchester: Manchester University Press, 2000).

Ward, Margaret *Female Occupations: Women's Employment 1850–1950* (Berkshire: Countryside Books, 2008).

Warren, Allen 'Robert Stephenson Smyth Baden-Powell, first Baron Baden-Powell (1857–1941)' *Oxford Dictionary of National Biography* Oxford University Press http://www.oxforddnb.com/view/article/30520 accessed 4 January 2013.

Warren, Allen 'Olave St Clair Baden-Powell, Lady Baden-Powell (1889–1977)' *Oxford Dictionary of National Biography* Oxford University Press http://www.oxforddnb.com/view/article/30779 accessed 4 January 2013.

Watman, Mel *The Official History of the AAA: The Story of the World's Oldest Athletic Association* (London: Sportsbooks, 2011).

Watman, Mel 'Women athletes between the world wars 1919–1939' *Oxford Dictionary of National Biography* Oxford University Press http://www.oxforddnb.com/view/article/103699 accessed 18 December 2012.

Weir, Ronald B. 'Thomas Robert Dewar, Baron Dewar (1864–1930)' *Oxford Dictionary of National Biography* Oxford University Press http://www.oxforddnb.com/view/article/50411 accessed 21 January 2013.

Whitelaw, Nancy *Joseph Pulitzer and The New York World: Makers of the Media* (Greensboro, North Carolina: Morgan Reynolds, 2000).

Whorlow, Rosie '"The Latest Scare": British Leisure Magazines and the Cause of the Feminine Motorcycle Rider' *Women and Leisure 1890–1939: Women's History Network Conference Midlands Region* University of Staffordshire 8 November 2008.

Williams, Elizabeth 'Walter Whitmore Jones 1831–1872' *Oxford Dictionary of National Biography* Oxford University Press http://www.oxforddnb.com/view/article/100464 accessed 15 May 2012.

Williams, Jack and Jeff Hill (eds.) *Sport and Identity in the North of England* (Keele: University of Keele Press, 1996).

Williams, Jack '"A Wild Orgy of Speed": Responses to Speedway in Britain before the Second World War' *The Sports Historian* 19:1 May 1999.

Williams, Jean *A Game for Rough Girls: A History of Women's Football in England* (London: Routledge, 2003).

Williams, Jean *A Beautiful Game: International Perspectives on Women's Football* (London: Berg 2007).

Williams, Jean 'The Curious Mystery of the "Olimpick Games": Did Shakespeare Know Dover . . . and Does It Matter?' in Jeff Hill and Jean Williams (eds.) *Sport and Literature: A Special Edition of Sport in History* 29:2 June 2009.

Williams, Jean 'The Immediate Legacy of Pat Smythe: The Pony-Mad Teenager In 1950s and 1960s Britain' in Dave Day (ed.) *Sporting Lives* (Manchester: MMU Institute for Performance Research, 2011).

Williams Jean 'Aquadynamics and the Athletocracy: Jennie Fletcher and the British Women's 4 x 100 metre Freestyle Relay Team at the 1912 Stockholm Olympic Games' in John Hughson (ed.) *Costume* 46: 2 Summer 2012.

Williams Jean 'The Most Important Photograph in the History of Women's Olympic Participation: Jennie Fletcher and the British 4×100 Freestyle Relay Team at the Stockholm 1912 Games' in Martin Polley (ed.) *Sport in History, Special Issue: Britain, Britons and the Olympic Games* 32:2 Summer 2012.

Williams, Jean 'Making the Pilgrimage to the Yard of Brick: The Indianapolis 500' in Jeffrey Hill, Kevin Moore and Jason Wood (eds.) *Sport, History and Heritage: An Investigation into the Public Representation of Sport* (Rochester, New York and Woodbridge, Suffolk: Boydell and Brewer, 2012).

Williams, Jean 'Lilian Parr (1905–1978)' *Oxford Dictionary of National Biography* Oxford University Press http://www.oxforddnb.com/view/article/102447 accessed 18 December 2012.

Williams, Jean 'Edith Marie Thompson (1877–1961)' *Oxford Dictionary of National Biography* Oxford University Press http://www.oxforddnb.com/view/article/103423 accessed 18 December 2012.

Williams, Jean 'Jane 'Jennie' Fletcher (1890–1968)' *Oxford Dictionary of National Biography* Oxford University Press http://www.oxforddnb.com/view/article/102443 accessed 8 January 2013.

Williams, Jean 'Gwenda Glubb, Janson, Stewart, Hawkes (1894–1990)' *Oxford Dictionary of National Biography* Oxford University Press http://www.oxforddnb.com/view/article/92722 accessed 30 May 2013.

Williams, Jean and Simon 'Violet Cordery (1903–1983) and John Hindmarsh (1907–1938)' *Oxford Dictionary of National Biography* http://www.oxforddnb.com/view/article/101214 accessed 30 May 2013.

Williams, Linda 'Sportswomen in Black and White: Sports History from an Afro American Perspective' in Pamela J. Creedon *Women Media and Sport: Challenging Gender Values* (London: Sage, 1994).

Williams, Owen rev. Anita McConnell 'Sir Arthur James Elvin (1899–1957)' *Oxford Dictionary of National Biography* Oxford University Press http://www.oxforddnb.com/view/article/33017 accessed 6 November 2012.

Williamson. David J. *Belles of the Ball: A History of Women's Football* (Devon: R&D Associates, 1991.

Wilson, Judith 'Florence Madeline 'Madge' Syers [née Cave] 1881–1917' *Oxford Dictionary of National Biography* Oxford University Press www.oxforddnb. com accessed 24 April 2012.

Wilson, Judith 'Marjorie Anne Pollard (1899–1982)' *Oxford Dictionary of National Biography* Oxford University Press http://www.oxforddnb.com/view/article/65061 accessed 31 August 2012.

Wojtczak, Helena *Railway Women: Exploitation, Betrayal and Triumph in the Workplace* (Sussex: Hastings Press, 2005).

Wong, Edlie 'Around the World and Across the Board: Nellie Bly and the Geography of Games' *American Studies Department Symposium* (New Brunswick, New Jersey: Rutgers University, 4 February 2005) available at www.lateledipenelope.it/public/EdlieWongSymposiumPaperSp05.pdf accessed 12 December 2012.

Wood, Valerie *Women and Work in Nottingham 1945–1955* (unpublished MA thesis University of Nottingham, 2007).

Wosk, Julie *Women and the Machine: Representations from the Spinning Wheel to the Electronic Age* (Baltimore, Maryland: The Johns Hopkins University Press, 2001).

Wrigley, Chris 'Ernest Bevin (1881–1951)' *Oxford Dictionary of National Biography* Oxford University Press http://www.oxforddnb.com/view/article/31872 accessed 6 November 2012.

Wynn, Peter *Women and Golf in Suburban London: A Study of Fulwell Golf Club* unpublished MA thesis De Montfort University, Leicester 2009.

Wynne-Thomas, Peter *Trent Bridge 1838–1988: A History of the Ground to Commemorate the 150th Anniversary* (Nottingham: Nottinghamshire County Cricket Club, 1988).

Yeomans, Patricia Henry 'Hazel Wightman and Helen Wills: Tennis At the 1924 Paris Olympic Games' *Journal of Olympic History* 11:2 2003.

C. Websites:

Amateur Athletic Association http://www.aaa-athletics.org/history.htm accessed 11 July 2009.

Aquascutum http://www.aquascutum.com/timeline accessed 1 November 2011.

Ashby De La Zouch Museums http://www.ashbydelazouchmuseum.org.uk accessed 6 April 2012.

Beaulieu Motor Museum *Flying Lady Centennial Exhibition 5 May-30 October 2011* http://www.beaulieu.co.uk/news/flying-lady accessed 5 January 2012.

Big Lottery Fund; West Yorkshire Archive Service; the University of Huddersfield; The Bronte Society; Hull Local Studies Library, and Leeds City Council Libraries *History to Herstory: Yorkshire Women's lives online, 1100 to the Present* http://www.historytoherstory.org.uk/ accessed 5 March 2012.

Brennan, Patrick 'Women's Football' http://www.donmouth.co.uk/womens_football/ accessed 12 December 2012.

British Broadcasting Company 'BBC Sports Personality of The Year' http://www.bbc.co.uk/pressoffice/keyfacts/stories/spoty.shtml accessed 19 October 2009.

British Pathé moving images http://www.britishpathe.com accessed 29 June 2012.

Burberry 'Company History' http://www.burberryplc.com/bbry/corporateprofile/history accessed 1 November 2011.

Central Park Conservancy http://www.centralparknyc.org/history-of-ice-skating.html accessed 2 December 2011.

David Simkin 'William Pankhurst Marsh' *Sussex Photo History Society* http://www.photohistory-sussex.co.uk/MarshGallery.htm accessed 11 April 2012.

Davies, Emily collections at *Orlando: Women's Writing in the British Isles from the beginnings to the Present* Cambridge University Press http://orlando.cambridge.org accessed 7 March 2012.

Davies, Emily collections 1847–1919 at http://www-lib.girton.cam.ac.uk/archive/davies.htm accessed 12 March 2012.

English Heritage 'Musical Gymnastics at North London Collegiate School' *Visible in Stone: Women's History Through Buildings 1850–1950* http://www.english-heritage.org.uk/discover/people-and-places/womens-history/visible-in-stone accessed 12 March 2012.

'Fashion V Sport' Victoria and Albert Museum, London http://www.vam.ac.uk/microsites/fashion-v-sport accessed 2 November 2011.

General Post Office 'Transmission of press telegrams between the United Kingdom and Sweden, Denmark and Norway: transmission of telegrams respecting the Olympic Games, Stockholm 11 April 1913' record T 1/11533, The National Archives, Kew http://www.nationalarchives.gov.uk accessed 16 May 2012.

H. and H .Motor Car Auctions 'Lot Number 68: 1933 Lagonda 2 Litre Tourer' *H. and H. Motor Car Auctions Sale Catalogue* 20 July 2011 http://www.classic-auctions.com/Auctions/20–07–2011 accessed 14 October 2012.

International Olympic Committee *Olympic.Org: Official Website of the Olympic Movement* http://www.olympic.org/medallists accessed 23 April 2012.

International Swimming Hall of Fame http://www.ishof.org/honorees/ accessed 15 October 2011.

ITN Source collections at http://www.itnsource.com accessed 29 June 2012.

International Table Tennis Federation Museum *World Championships Women's Singles 1927–2011* www.ittf.com/museum/WorldChWSingles.pdf accessed 21 August 2012.

Jaques of London 'Traditional Games from Jaques of London' http://www.jaqueslondon.co.uk/ accessed 18 December 2012.

Lyons, J. & Company online archive http://www.kzwp.com/lyons/index.htm accessed 10 August 2012.

Mann, Ida '*The Chase*': *First Part of her Draft Autobiography [1974]* Catalogue of papers of Ida Mann, 1921–2007 Bodleian Library, University of Oxford http://www.bodleian.ox.ac.uk/bodley/library accessed 11 January 2012.

Manning, Jo 'First champ "would be thrilled"' *BBC News* 11 August 2008 http://news.bbc.co.uk/1/hi/wales/7554196.stm accessed 8 December 2012.

Matters, Muriel 'Scrapbook for 1909: Muriel Matters' BBC Archive National Programme 9 February 1939 http://www.bbc.co.uk/archive/suffragettes/8315.shtml accessed 16 May 2012.

Moving Dangerously: A Conference on Women and Travel 1850–1950 Newcastle University, 13–14 April 2012 http://movingdangerously.wordpress.com accessed 11 April 2012.

National Portrait Gallery, collections http://www.npg.org.uk accessed 15 September 2012.

Radcliffe College Archives at the Schlesinger Library http://via.lib.harvard.edu: accessed 10 October 2009.

Riding for the Disabled http://www.riding-for-disabled.org.uk/about-us/ accessed 27 January 2010.

Royal Humane Society 'History of the Society' Royal Humane Society' http://www.royalhumanesociety.org.uk accessed 12 March 2012.

'Sally Fox Collection' Schlesinger Library, Harvard University, Cambridge, Massachusetts http://www.radcliffe.edu/schles accessed 2 November 2011.

'Sporting Life' The Museum at the Fashion Institute of Technology, New York City http://fitnyc.edu accessed 2 November 2011.

Sport Scotland 'Isabella 'Belle' Mary Moore (1894–1975)' *Scottish Sports Hall of Fame* Sport Scotland http://www.sportscotland.org.uk/sshf/Isabella_Mary_ Moore accessed 8 December 2012.

The British Library *Nineteenth Century British Library Newspapers Database* http://newspapers.bl.uk/blcs/ accessed 19 June 2009.

The Children's Society *Hidden Lives Revealed: A Virtual Archive of Children's Lives in Care 1881–1981* http://www.hiddenlives.org.uk accessed 5 March 2012.

The Pony Club http://www.pcuk.org/About-Us/History accessed 27 January 2011.

The Wellingborough Museum at William Dulley's Baths run by the Winifred Wharton Trust http://www.wellingboroughmuseum.co.uk accessed 29 February 2012.

Wimbledon Lawn Tennis Museum *Roll of Honour* http://aeltc2011.wimbledon. com/players/rolls-of-honour/ladies-singles accessed 14 June 2011.

Index